Understanding Russian Politics

A fresh and compelling interpretation of Russian politics by a leading authority, this textbook focuses on political developments in the world's largest country under Putin and Medvedev. Using a wealth of primary sources, it covers economic, social and foreign policy, and the 'system' of politics that has developed in recent years. Opposing arguments are presented and students are encouraged to reach their own judgements on key events and issues such as privatisation and corruption. This textbook tackles timely topics such as gender and inequality issues; organised religion; the economic *krizis*; and Russia's place in the international community. It uses numerous examples to place this powerful and richly endowed country in context, with a focus on the place of ordinary people which shows how policy is translated to Russians' everyday lives.

Stephen White is James Bryce Professor of Politics at the University of Glasgow and a Senior Associate Member of its School of Central and East European Studies. He is also Adjunct Professor of European Studies at the Johns Hopkins University Bologna Center and Visiting Professor at the Institute of Applied Politics in Moscow. His most recent books include the edited collections *Developments in Russian Politics 7* (2010), *Media, Culture and Society in Putin's Russia* (2008) and *Politics and the Ruling Group in Putin's Russia* (2008). He was elected a fellow of the British Academy in 2010.

Understanding Russian Politics

Stephen White

CAMBRIDGE
UNIVERSITY PRESS

CAMBRIDGE UNIVERSITY PRESS
Cambridge, New York, Melbourne, Madrid, Cape Town,
Singapore, São Paulo, Delhi, Tokyo, Mexico City

Cambridge University Press
The Edinburgh Building, Cambridge CB2 8RU, UK

Published in the United States of America by Cambridge University Press, New York

www.cambridge.org
Information on this title: www.cambridge.org/9780521688611

First published 2011

Printed in the United Kingdom at the University Press, Cambridge

A catalogue record for this publication is available from the British Library

ISBN 978-0-521-86857-0 Hardback
ISBN 978-0-521-68861-1 Paperback

Contents

Figures

Tables

Preface

Russia is no longer the Soviet Union. But it still accounts for a seventh of the world's land surface, stretching across two continents and eleven different time zones. It was a founding member of the United Nations and holds one of the permanent seats on its Security Council. It has one of the world's largest and most technically advanced concentrations of military might. It is also one of the world's biggest economies, with accumulations of natural resources that are among the largest in the world and a vital component of the energy balance of many European and more distant countries. How Russia is governed is accordingly a matter of direct concern to the whole world, and not just to Russians themselves.

An earlier version of this study focused on 'Russia's new politics' at a time when it was still conventional to speak of a more general 'transition to democracy'. The focus of this new and very different book is the Putinist system that came into existence in the early years of the new century, amid a widespread acceptance that early and more optimistic forecasts of Russia's political direction had been mistaken or at least premature. But it is, I hope, much more than a study of the institutions of government that became established during these years: because the process of government can scarcely be understood without an examination of the changes that have been taking place in a much more divided society, in an economy that has been moving from state ownership to a more complex hybrid, and in Russia's relations with the rest of the world community.

This is a book that draws on many years' experience of teaching graduates and undergraduates at my own institution in Scotland, in Italy (at the Orientale in Naples and more recently the Johns Hopkins Bologna Center) and in the United States. It draws very heavily on the printed press, much of it read in the periodicals room of the Historical Library in Moscow. It draws only when I am unable to avoid it on electronic sources: not, I hope, because of any obscurantism, but because sources of this kind do not contain page references or (usually) graphics, may disappear or otherwise become unavailable, and in a small but disturbing number of cases may differ from the printed original. I have also made extensive use of a series of national representative surveys, conducted not just in Russia but in some other post-Soviet republics as well, between 1993 and 2010 (details are provided in a separate appendix), and of archives, interviews and (obviously) printed books of all kinds, many of them collected on frequent visits to the larger Russian cities.

It is a book that draws at least as much on a close working relationship over many years with other scholars in several countries. My collaboration with Ol'ga Kryshtanovskaya of the Institute of Sociology of the Russian Academy of Sciences goes back to the late Soviet years, with a particular focus on the political elite. I have worked closely for many years with Ian McAllister of the Australian National University, and before that with Richard Rose of Strathclyde and Aberdeen, on the analysis of survey data. At Glasgow I owe a particular debt to Bill Miller, who helped to introduce me to the quantitative analysis of post-Soviet politics, and to Sarah Oates, with whom I have shared much more than a scholarly interest in political communications. My work would have been inconceivable without the expert assistance of Tania Konn-Roberts and her colleagues, and the world-class resources of Glasgow University Library. I am indebted to the Leverhulme Trust for a Major Research Fellowship that provided me with the time I have needed to bring this study to a conclusion, and to the Economic and Social Research Council for their continuing support under grants RES 000-22-2532 (a joint award with the Australian Research Council), RES 062-23-1378 (Crafting Electoral Authoritarianism) and RES 062-23-1542 (The Putin Succession). It was two of these ESRC awards that allowed me to appoint Tania Biletskaya and Valentina Feklyunina as research assistants, and this is my opportunity to thank them for their wisdom and good humour as well as practical assistance.

Several of those I have already mentioned are part of a larger 'family' that has built up over the past ten years or so, many of them organised in a 'transformation group' that operates under the joint leadership of myself and another Glasgow colleague, Jane Duckett. It includes Sarah, Tania and Valentina as well as Derek Hutcheson, Elena Korosteleva, Yulia Korosteleva, Sam Robertshaw, Anke Schmidt-Felzmann and Vikki Turbine. Derek and Valentina are part of a still larger extended family of former research students, many of whom are making their own contribution to academic or public life around the world. It is a pleasure to list them here: Aadne Aasland, Ayse Artun, Mervyn Bain, Youcef Bouandel, Janet Campbell, James Cant, Laura Cleary, Peter Duncan, Katsuto Furusawa, Åse Grødeland, Mohammed Ishaq, Peter Lentini, Eero Mikenberg, Atsushi Ogushi, Clelia Rontoyanni, Alison Swain, Reza Taghizade and John Watts, and a separate Korean 'family', including Taikang Choi, Younhee Kang, Seongjin Kim, Ik Joong Yun and Yeongmi Yun.

There are many others to whom I am indebted for advice on specific matters, or for their comradeship over the years: Archie Brown, Tim Colton, Graeme Gill, Bob Grey, Henry Hale, Ron Hill, Grigorii Ioffe, David Lane, Ellen Mickiewicz, Stefanie Ortman, Tom Remington, Richard Rose, Richard Sakwa, Mike Urban and David Wedgwood Benn, and the Slavic Reference Service at the University of Illinois. I should also take this opportunity to thank my publisher, Cambridge University Press, especially John Haslam, for their patience and understanding as I moved towards completion. I am equally grateful to the Political Science Program at the Australian National University for appointing me a Visitor in early 2010, which allowed me to complete the manuscript in the idyllic environment of their Canberra campus, and to Grinnell College in Iowa, where I was able to make the final corrections.

I have sometimes been asked if this is a study that offers a particular interpretation. I hope all its readers will feel the evidence has been presented fairly, and that they have been left free to draw their own conclusions. But it will not escape many of them, particularly those who consult the final chapter, that I believe Russia has been poorly served by the concentration of power in its central institutions that developed over the years of the Putin presidency, a concentration that appears to have prejudiced many of the leadership's own objectives (in terms of social and economic development) quite apart from its baneful effects on the quality of its public life. In this respect, the Russian system offers us a fully developed example of the typical strengths and weaknesses of authoritarian government: above all its lack of an effective rule of law, which leaves individual liberties vulnerable to abuse by the authorities and discourages foreign and domestic investment. It is perhaps some consolation that, unlike in the Soviet years, Russian scholars can now debate these issues for themselves, and in dialogue with scholars in other countries, even if it may often be easier for them to do so in academic journals and conferences than in the mainstream media.

Finally, a note on conventions. For the transliteration of Russian I have relied on the scheme favoured by the journal *Europe-Asia Studies*, departing from it where other forms have become widely accepted in English (accordingly Yeltsin rather than Yel'tsin, Igor rather than Igor', Archangel rather than Arkhangel'sk, and place names more generally without hard or soft signs, although I have transliterated strictly in the footnotes). References are given in full on their first occurrence in each chapter, and thereafter in shortened form. The notes are not limited to source references, but include some additional and (I think) important detail; each chapter ends with suggestions for further reading, limited to a small number of works in English. Place names are generally rendered in their contemporary form, rather than ones adopted at a later period (accordingly it is Leningrad up to 1990, and St Petersburg thereafter, although there is still a Leningrad region).

All translations are my own, unless otherwise stated.

Russia: administrative units under the 1993 Constitution

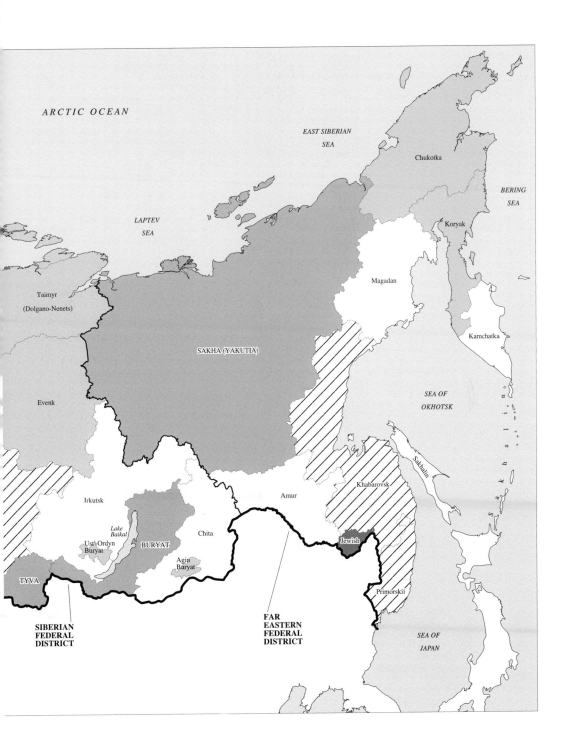

1 From communist to postcommunist rule

Mikhail and Raisa Gorbachev on an official visit to India, 1986 (Novosti)

The Union of Soviet Socialist Republics was still growing economically in the Brezhnev years, and expanding its international influence. But growth rates were falling, and social problems were deepening. The Gorbachev leadership, from 1985 onwards, set out a rather different agenda: of *glasnost'* (openness) and *perestroika* (or restructuring) 'We can't go on like this', the new party leader told his wife as he assumed his responsibilities. In the end, for reasons that are still debated, the reform agenda failed to achieve its objectives and the state itself collapsed as its fifteen constituent republics became independent states after the collapse of an attempted coup in August 1991 that had been intended to preserve a viable union. Gorbachev resigned as Soviet president on Christmas Day and the Russian president, Boris Yeltsin, took over the Kremlin as the head of what was now an independent Russian Federation and by far the largest of the post-Soviet republics.

In early 1982 Leonid Brezhnev was apparently at the height of his powers. General Secretary of the ruling Communist Party since October 1964 and, since 1977, Chairman of the Presidium of the Supreme Soviet of the USSR or head of state, he had presided over a steady rise in living standards at home and an expansion of Soviet influence throughout the wider world. Under Brezhnev's leadership national income had doubled between 1960 and 1970 and more than trebled by 1980. Industrial output had more than quadrupled. Agricultural performance was less impressive (in 1981 and 1982 the harvests were so poor the figures were simply suppressed), but the real incomes of ordinary citizens had more than doubled over the two decades and the wages paid to collective farmers had increased more than four times. Nor was this simply statistics. By the end of Brezhnev's administration, three times as many Soviet citizens had acquired a higher education; there were more hospital beds, more cars and many more colour televisions. And despite the disappointments in agriculture, for which climatic conditions were at least partly responsible, there had been considerable improvements in the Soviet diet. The consumption of meat, fish and fruit per head of population was up by about half, while the consumption of potatoes and bread, the staples of earlier years, had fallen back considerably.[1]

By the early 1980s, in parallel with these domestic changes, the USSR had begun to acquire an international influence that accorded rather more closely with the country's enormous territory, population and natural resources. Forced to back down in humiliating circumstances in the Cuban missile crisis of 1962, the USSR had since acquired a strategic capability that gave it an approximate parity with the United States by the end of the decade. The Soviet Union had one of the world's largest armies and one of its largest navies, and it dominated the Warsaw Treaty Organisation, which was one of the world's most powerful military alliances. It was the centre of one of the world's largest trading blocs, the Council for Mutual Economic Assistance (or Comecon), and a founding member of the United Nations (UN), where it had a permanent seat on the Security Council. The USSR's status as a superpower had been confirmed by a series of agreements with its capitalist rival, the United States, particularly the Strategic Arms Limitation Treaty (SALT I) in 1972 and its unratified successor, SALT II, in 1979. And it was represented much more widely in international affairs: the USSR had diplomatic relations with 144 foreign states by the early 1970s, twice as many as in the early 1960s; it took part in the work of over 400 international organisations and was a signatory to more than 7,000 international treaties or conventions.[2] The Soviet Union was 'one of the greatest world powers', the official history of Soviet foreign policy could boast by the early 1980s, 'without whose participation not a single international problem can be resolved'.[3] If this was an exaggeration, it was a pardonable one.

Leonid Brezhnev, the symbol of this developing military and politico-economic might, had increasingly become the central element in the political system that underpinned it. Originally, in 1964, a 'collective leadership', it had become a leadership 'headed by comrade L. I. Brezhnev' by the early 1970s. In 1973, in a further sign of his increasing dominance, Brezhnev's name was listed first among the members of the Politburo even though the KGB chairman, Yuri Andropov, had joined at this point and should, on alphabetical principles, have displaced him. The General Secretary made his own contribution to these developments, complaining whenever he thought he was being neglected by the newspapers (it was 'as if I don't exist', he told *Pravda* in 1975),[4] and taking 'organisational measures' to ensure that his public addresses were greeted with sufficient enthusiasm.[5] By 1976, at its 25th Congress, Brezhnev had become the party's 'universally acclaimed leader' and *vozhd'* (chief), a term previously used to describe Stalin; there was 'stormy, prolonged applause' when it was announced that he had been re-elected to the Central Committee, and a standing ovation when Brezhnev himself announced that he had once again been elected General Secretary.[6] He became a Marshal of the Soviet Union later the same year, and a bronze bust was unveiled in his birthplace;[7] an official biography, published in December, declared the General Secretary an 'inspiring example of selfless service to the socialist motherland [and] to the ideals of scientific communism'.[8]

In 1977 Brezhnev consolidated his position by adding the largely ceremonial chairmanship of the Presidium of the Supreme Soviet of the USSR, or collective presidency, at the same time as the dominant position of the Communist Party was itself being acknowledged in Article 6 of the new constitution. He took receipt of the Gold Medal of Karl Marx, the highest award of the Academy of Sciences, for his 'outstanding contribution to the development of Marxist-Leninist theory';[9] in 1978 he received the Order of Victory for his 'great contribution' to the success of the Soviet people and their armed forces in the Great Patriotic War,[10] and then in 1979 the Lenin Prize for Literature for memoirs that had been written for him by an assistant who himself received the Order of Lenin a few days later.[11] At the 26th Party Congress in 1981, Brezhnev was hailed as an 'outstanding political leader and statesman', a 'true continuer of Lenin's great cause' and an 'ardent fighter for peace and communism';[12] his speech was punctuated seventy-eight times by 'applause', forty times by 'prolonged applause' and eight times by 'stormy, prolonged applause',[13] and there were shouts of 'hurrah' when it was announced that he had unanimously been re-elected to the Central Committee.[14] Unprecedentedly, the whole Politburo and Secretariat, Brezhnev included, were re-elected without change; Brezhnev's son Yuri, a first deputy minister of foreign trade, became a candidate member of the Central Committee at the same time, and so too did his son-in-law Yuri Churbanov, a first deputy minister of internal affairs.

Brezhnev's seventy-fifth birthday, in December 1981, brought these tributes to a new pitch of intensity. Seven of *Pravda*'s eight pages on 19 December were wholly or partly devoted to the event, and tributes continued to appear in the central press throughout the following week. Brezhnev himself attended a ceremony in the Kremlin where he was invested with a series of distinctions by the leaders of the East European communist states, who had come to Moscow for the occasion. The Soviet awards, which he had himself to authorise as head of state, included a seventh Order of Lenin and a fourth Hero of the Soviet Union citation, Mikhail Suslov, a few years his senior, remarking at the conferment that 75 was regarded in the Soviet Union as no more than 'middle age'.[15] Brezhnev's life was turned into a film, *Story of a Communist*; his wartime exploits in the Caucasus, little noted at the time, were presented as all but the decisive turning-point in the struggle against the Nazis; his memoirs became the subject of a play, a popular song and a full-scale oratorio. He had already accumulated more state awards than all previous Soviet leaders taken together, and more military distinctions than Marshal Zhukov, who had saved Leningrad and liberated Berlin, and so many foreign awards that he entered the Guinness Book of Records;[16] when he died more than 200 decorations followed his coffin to the grave.[17] Even a modest poem, 'To the German Komsomol', written when he was seventeen, attracted national attention when it was republished in *Pravda* in May 1982.[18]

Brezhnev's personal and political powers, nonetheless, were clearly failing. According to subsequent accounts, he began to suffer serious ill health at the end of the 1960s, and in January 1976 was clinically dead for a short time following a stroke.[19] For two months he was unable to work, as his speech and writing had been impaired, and thereafter he was constantly surrounded by doctors, with a fully equipped ambulance following his car on trips abroad. His speech became slurred, his breathing laboured, his concentration limited; visiting Baku in one of his last public appearances, he startled his audience by referring repeatedly to 'Afghanistan' instead of 'Azerbaijan' (he had been reading the wrong speech); visiting Prague, he read out some pages twice and asked for a translation when the Czech party leader ended his welcoming address with a passage in Russian (there was a 'deathly silence in the hall').[20] Newspapers did what they could to conceal Brezhnev's physical decline by using a much earlier photograph, adding new medals as they were awarded.[21] But there was no disguising his condition from immediate colleagues, to whom, indeed, he had twice suggested resignation;[22] Politburo meetings, which used to take several hours, dwindled to fifteen or twenty minutes,[23] and public occasions, however formal, left a 'pitiful impression'.[24] Among the wider public, unkind anecdotes were already circulating: his eyebrows, in one of these, were 'Stalin's moustache at a higher level'; in yet another, he was to have an operation to enlarge his chest to accommodate the medals he had been awarded (even his son-in-law had to concede that this was one of the General Secretary's weaknesses[25]).

Perhaps most serious of all, Brezhnev's grip on affairs of state became increasingly infirm. The death of Suslov, in January 1982, seems in retrospect to have been crucial. One of the Politburo's oldest and longest-serving members, with acknowledged authority in both ideology and foreign affairs, Suslov had served as kingmaker in 1964, declining the general secretaryship for himself and backing Brezhnev for the position, and then becoming the 'second person in the party' towards the end of his period of rule.[26] With Suslov gone, the Brezhnev leadership began to disintegrate rapidly. At the end of the same month, the death was reported of Semyon Tsvigun, first deputy chairman of the KGB and the husband of the younger sister of Brezhnev's wife; rumour suggested it was a case of suicide precipitated by his impending arrest on corruption charges.[27] At the beginning of March 1982 came the arrest of 'Boris the gypsy' and other figures from the world of circus entertainment on charges of bribery and currency speculation; all were close friends of Brezhnev's daughter Galina and their arrest showed that the General Secretary's authority was no longer sufficient to protect them.[28] Later the same month the head of the trade union organisation, Aleksei Shibaev, was replaced amid reports that he had diverted union funds to build dachas for his relatives and friends, and led a disreputable private life; in April the Procurator General announced that a former fisheries minister had been executed for his part in a caviare fraud.[29]

Still more significantly, in May 1982 a plenary session of the Central Committee of the CPSU (Communist Party of the Soviet Union) took place at which Brezhnev was unable to secure the election of his 'faithful Sancho Panza',[30] Konstantin Chernenko, to the powerful position of Central Committee Secretary with responsibility for ideology that had become vacant with the death of Suslov. In a development widely seen as significant both at home and abroad, it was the head of the KGB, Yuri Andropov, who was successful, apparently with the support of the armed forces lobby. Another Brezhnev associate lost his position when in July 1982 the Krasnodar first secretary, Sergei Medunov, was summarily dismissed (he had extracted bribes on a massive scale but deflected all criticism by entertaining investigators to a variety of forms of hospitality including a 'rest home' where they were provided with sexual favours); later still came the arrest of the manager of Moscow's most famous food store and his wife, both of whom were close associates of Brezhnev's daughter.[31] All of this suggested that Brezhnev's political authority as well as physical health were in decline, and reports circulating in the West suggested that it had already been decided he would retain the largely ceremonial presidency, allowing another figure to be elected to the more demanding post of party leader. Brezhnev, in the event, anticipated any changes of this kind by dying suddenly on the morning of 10 November 1982, his health undermined by a two-hour stint in the reviewing box at the anniversary parade in Red Square three days earlier. *Pravda*'s obituary mourned the passing of a 'continuer of the cause of Lenin, a fervent patriot, an outstanding revolutionary and protagonist of peace and communism, [and] an outstanding political and government leader of the contemporary era'.[32]

It had widely been expected that a decent interval would elapse before a successor was named as General Secretary, and indeed that a prolonged succession struggle might ensue. On 11 November, however, it was announced that Andropov was to chair the committee making arrangements for Brezhnev's funeral, and the following day, as was now expected, it was announced that an emergency meeting of the Central Committee had elected him to the vacant general secretaryship. Andropov's main rival for the succession, Konstantin Chernenko, had the task of proposing his candidacy to the Central Committee, where it was accepted unanimously. Brezhnev was buried on 15 November, Andropov making the funeral oration, and a week later the new General Secretary made his first speech as party leader to the Central Committee, a brief but effective review of Soviet foreign and domestic policy.[33] In May 1983 it became known that Andropov had succeeded Brezhnev as chairman of the Defence Council, which had ultimate authority in military and security matters, and in June he was elected to the chairmanship of the Presidium of the Supreme Soviet, thus concentrating in his hands after only seven months the same combination of posts that Brezhnev had taken almost thirteen years to accumulate. A series of changes in the membership of the Politburo and Secretariat, and at lower levels of the party and state, had meanwhile begun to put into place a coalition of reform-minded technocrats who might be expected to support both the new General Secretary and the policies he intended to promote.

Andropov's own health, however, was far from certain. An elderly man (already 68 when he assumed the party leadership) with a history of heart trouble, there were rumours of incapacity from almost the outset of his period of office. The 'Brezhnev mafia' continued to lose influence, but Andropov's rival for the general secretaryship, Konstantin Chernenko, remained prominent, making the opening speech at the June 1983 Central Committee plenum and chairing the Politburo in his absence. Andropov's effective authority in fact lasted for only a few months: he was last seen in public in August 1983, and then failed to attend the anniversary parade in Red Square on 7 November and the Central Committee and Supreme Soviet meetings that took place a few weeks later. It became known that he was receiving kidney dialysis treatment at the Central Committee hospital near Moscow and that Mikhail Gorbachev, the youngest member of the Politburo and apparently the one most closely attuned to the General Secretary's own thinking, was maintaining links between him and other members of the leadership.[34] A series of 'interviews', and an address that was circulated to the Central Committee plenum he was unable to attend, suggested that Andropov's intellectual powers were largely unimpaired; and further changes in the Politburo and Secretariat at the December 1983 plenum indicated that his control over the most important of all the powers of a party leader, that of appointment, was scarcely diminished. Nonetheless, explanations in terms of 'colds' began to wear thin, and it was not entirely unexpected when on 11 February 1984 the central press reported that the General Secretary had died two days earlier after a 'long illness'.[35] Once again the party leadership was plunged into the search for a successor.

As before, there were two principal contenders: Chernenko, whose political fortunes had revived with Andropov's illness, and Gorbachev, who was the youngest member of the leadership at the time but evidently Andropov's own favoured candidate for the succession.[36] Chernenko was named on 10 February to head the funeral committee, which appeared to suggest he was all but certain to secure the nomination; the formal choice took rather longer to arrange because of the divisions within the leadership that it reflected, with a 'Brezhnevite' faction supporting Chernenko and composed for the most part of long-serving members of the leadership like Prime Minister Nikolai Tikhonov, Kazakh party leader Dinmukhamed Kunaev and Moscow party secretary Viktor Grishin, and an 'Andropovite' faction consisting of the younger, more reform-minded members who had joined or advanced within the leadership under the late General Secretary, including Vitalii Vorotnikov, who headed the government of the largest of the republics, as well as Gorbachev himself.[37] The choice fell finally on Chernenko, partly, it appears, because of his seniority and experience, and partly because a Gorbachev leadership would have been likely to last rather a long time: Gorbachev was just 52 and had been a full member of the Politburo for less than four years.

At all events, on 13 February 1984, four days after Andropov had died, another extra-ordinary meeting of the Central Committee took place at which Chernenko, proposed by Tikhonov, was elected unanimously to the vacant general secretaryship.[38] It emerged subsequently that Gorbachev had also addressed the plenum,[39] and unofficial reports suggested that he had been installed as a de facto second secretary with the power of veto, on behalf of the younger 'Andropovite' faction, over leadership decisions.[40] Gorbachev's greater prominence was apparent in, for example, his more advanced placing in the line-up of leaders beside Andropov's coffin, and in the ranking he received in pre-election speeches and other formal party and state occasions. In turn it indicated that the Chernenko leadership was a relatively evenly balanced coalition, containing both supporters of the late party leader's reforming policies and those who believed they had been pressed too far. These internal divisions were sufficient in themselves to slow down the momentum of reform, quite apart from what the new General Secretary might have wished, and they persisted throughout his period of office as neither side could allow the other to gain a decisive advantage by adding to the number of their supporters in the Politburo or Secretariat.

The chairmanship of the Presidium of the Supreme Soviet and of the Defence Council, as well as the party leadership, had become vacant on Andropov's death. It became known later in February 1984 that Chernenko had also assumed the chairmanship of the Defence Council, and in April 1984, on Gorbachev's nomination, the first session of the newly elected Supreme Soviet elected him to the chairmanship of its Presidium, which made him de facto head of state.[41] Chernenko was nevertheless, at 72, the oldest General Secretary ever to have assumed office, and he had a history of lung disease that caused difficulty in breathing. Perhaps inevitably, it was regarded as a transitional general secretaryship from the outset. Two regular Central Committee plenums were held during Chernenko's period of office: the first, in April 1984, was devoted to the work of the elected soviets and educational reform, the second dealt with land improvement. Neither made any change in the membership of the Politburo or Secretariat or even in the membership of the Central Committee itself, and neither could be said to have initiated any major departure in public policy (the educational reforms, which were of some importance, had been launched the previous year). There was equally little success when efforts were made to develop the significance of Chernenko's service in the border guards in the early 1930s ('there could be no personality cult', it was pointed out, 'in the absence of a personality'); nor could much be made of his undistinguished war record.[42] A series of missed engagements suggested that Chernenko's health was already deteri-orating, and official spokesmen had to admit that the recently elected General Secretary was suffering from a serious cold, or perhaps worse.

Chernenko was last seen in public at the end of December 1984. He failed to meet Prime Minister Papandreou of Greece on his visit to Moscow in February 1985 and failed to deliver the customary eve-of-poll address to the Soviet people in the republican and local elections later the same month. Although he was shown voting on television on 24 February and was pictured in the central press receiving his deputy's credentials a week later,[43] rumours of the General Secretary's physical incapacity were strengthened rather than dispelled by his evident infirmity. Finally, on the evening of 10 March 1985, he died, the medical bulletin recording that he had expired as a result of heart failure following a deterioration in the working of his lungs and liver.[44] The following day, with unprecedented speed, an extraordinary session of the Central Committee elected Mikhail Gorbachev as its third General Secretary in three and a half years, Gromyko proposing him in an eloquent speech that had the support of the Andropovite faction within the leadership and of the regional first secretaries, who were 'increasingly determined not to let the Politburo manoeuvre another old, sick or weak person into the top position again'.[45] Gorbachev, who had just celebrated his fifty-fourth birthday, was still the youngest member of the Politburo and apparently in robust good health, which was in itself a considerable change. As one of the earliest jokes put it: 'What support does Gorbachev have in the Kremlin?' Answer: 'None – he walks unaided.'[46]

A changing policy agenda

Gorbachev began his acceptance speech by paying tribute to Chernenko as a 'true Leninist and outstanding figure of the CPSU and the Soviet state'.[47] Although he was later concerned to emphasise the decisive break that had occurred with his election and still more so with the April 1985 Central Committee plenum at which his programme had first been set out, there was in fact a good deal of continuity between the policy agenda that had been established by Andropov and Chernenko and the agenda that Gorbachev came to promote over the years that followed. The decisive break had arguably taken place under Andropov, whose security background tended to obscure his earlier exposure to the East European reform experience while Soviet ambassador to Hungary in the mid-1950s and a penetrating, somewhat puritanical intellect that was completely at odds with the complacency and corruption of the later Brezhnev era.[48] Even Chernenko, despite his background in propaganda and party administration and his career links with Brezhnev, had a number of special priorities that associated him with broadly 'liberal' opinion in the leadership context of the time, among them an interest in letters from the public, an emphasis on the consumer sector of the economy and a commitment to détente.[49] There were, in fact, a number of elements in common throughout the reorientation of policy that took place between the death of Andropov and the accession of Gorbachev, although the reformist impetus undoubtedly slackened under Chernenko and acquired a new scope and urgency under Gorbachev.

One element in that reorientation of policy was leadership renewal, which had already begun in the last months of Brezhnev's term of office but which was now pursued with especial urgency. At the November 1982 meeting of the Central Committee, just ten days after Andropov's election as General Secretary, Nikolai Ryzhkov, an experienced manager who had been working in the state planning office, joined the leadership as a member of the Secretariat.[50] Further changes took place in June 1983 when the Leningrad party leader, Grigorii Romanov, moved to Moscow to become another new member of the Secretariat and Vitalii Vorotnikov, who had been banished to Cuba as Soviet ambassador by Brezhnev, became a candidate member of the Politburo (and shortly afterwards prime minister of the Russian Republic).[51] The December 1983 Central Committee plenum, the last under Andropov's leadership, saw Vorotnikov consolidate his rapid advance by becoming a full member of the Politburo, and Yegor Ligachev, who had been first secretary in Tomsk, became a Central Committee secretary with responsibility for appointments and the supervision of lower-level party bodies.[52] There was no further movement in the party's leading bodies under Chernenko's rather shorter general secretaryship, apart from the loss that unavoidably occurred with the death of Defence Minister Ustinov;[53] the change that had taken place since the death of Brezhnev, however, was already a far-reaching one. In the Politburo that had been elected in March 1981, all but three of its fourteen full members had been born before the revolution, and the average age was over 70; Arvid Pel'she, born in 1899, had taken part himself in the October revolution. In the Politburo that Gorbachev inherited in March 1985, by contrast, just five of its ten full members were of prerevolutionary origin, and four (including Gorbachev himself) were in their fifties or early sixties, alarmingly young by recent Soviet standards. At least as notable, it had become a leadership of much greater technical and managerial competence. Vorotnikov, for instance, was a qualified aviation engineer who had spent the early part of his career in a Kuibyshev factory; Ryzhkov, before coming to Gosplan, had been the successful director of a massive engineering works in Sverdlovsk; Ligachev was an engineering graduate; and the new head of the Committee of State Security (KGB), Viktor Chebrikov, also an engineer, had a background in industrial management as well as party work in the Ukraine.[54]

A further priority, associated particularly with Andropov, was social discipline. In part this meant a firm and sustained campaign against the bribery and corruption that had increasingly disfigured the later Brezhnev years. The late General Secretary's family and friends were among the first to feel the effects of the new policy. In December 1982, just a month after Andropov's accession, Interior Minister Nikolai Shchelokov was dismissed from his position[55]– a close associate of Brezhnev's from Dnepropetrovsk days, he had enjoyed considerable opportunities for enrichment as head of Soviet law enforcement, acquiring a fleet of foreign cars, a photographer, a cook and a 'masseuse', as well as rare books from public library collections.[56] Shchelokov was replaced as interior minister by Vitalii Fedorchuk, an experienced KGB career officer and trusted Andropov associate, and in June he and another Brezhnev crony, the former Krasnodar first secretary,

Medunov, were dismissed from the Central Committee for 'mistakes in their work'.[57] Although his family reportedly celebrated Chernenko's election with an all-night party, Shchelokov continued to lose favour, suffering the humiliation of expulsion from the party and losing his military rank in November 1984 for 'abuse of position for personal gain and conduct discrediting the military title of General of the Soviet Union';[58] his wife had already committed suicide, his son – who had speculated in foreign cars – was dismissed from the bureau of the Komsomol (Young Communist League), and the disgraced interior minister took his own life early the following year.[59]

Brezhnev's immediate family was also affected. His daughter Galina and her husband Churbanov were banished to Murmansk; Churbanov lost his post as first deputy interior minister in December 1984 and then his position on the Central Committee,[60] and in December 1988 he was given twelve years' imprisonment for massive bribe-taking and stripped of his state honours.[61] Brezhnev's son Yuri lost his ministerial post and Central Committee membership, and his secretary was sentenced to nine years' imprisonment for abuse of his position;[62] Brezhnev's books – in nearly 3 million copies – were withdrawn from public sale,[63] and his widow was forced to return his decorations to public custody (his Order of Victory had meanwhile been rescinded).[64] The city of Brezhnev, formerly Naberezhnye Chelny, reverted to its original name in 1988; so too did Brezhnev Square in Moscow, and the Brezhnev – formerly Cherry Tree – district in the capital (humorists unkindly suggested that the Brezhnevs themselves might soon become the 'Cherry Tree family').[65] Brezhnev, according to opinion polls, was already more unpopular than Stalin; the very name, his grandson told a Moscow weekly, had 'become a curse'.[66] The campaign against corruption may have owed something to Andropov's own asceticism: he lived modestly and refrained from any attempts to promote the careers of his own children, although his son Igor became a prominent member of the diplomatic service. More important, perhaps, was the concern of both Andropov and his successor that corruption, if allowed to go unchecked, might reduce the effectiveness of party control and ultimately compromise the regime itself, as had clearly happened in Poland in the late 1970s and early 1980s.

The other side of the post-Brezhnev leadership's campaign of social discipline, which also continued under Chernenko, was an attempt to strengthen discipline in the workplace and law and order in the wider society. One of the first clear signs of this new direction in official policy was the series of raids that the police began to make in early 1983 on shops, public baths and even underground stations in order to find out which of those present had taken time off their work without permission. There was certainly some room for improvement. An official report in late 1982 found that of every 100 workers surveyed, an average of 30 were absent 'for personal reasons' at any given moment, in most cases to go shopping or visit the doctor. Another investigation in 800 Moscow enterprises found that in some cases no more than 10 per cent of the workforce were still at their places during the last hour of the shift.[67] A further series of decrees on 'socialist labour discipline' sought to reduce poor-quality workmanship, alcoholism and absenteeism at the workplace,[68] and the positive example of Aleksei Stakhanov was again held up for emulation, nearly fifty years after his record-breaking exploits in the Donbass coalmines (rather later, in 1988, it was revealed that the champion miner had been transferred to office work, turned to drink and died a lonely and disillusioned man).[69]

In terms of politics the Andropov period saw no liberalisation, despite early and perhaps inspired reports that the new General Secretary spoke English, liked jazz and modern Western literature. There was an open attack, for instance, upon 'alien' and 'decadent' trends in the arts, particularly at the Central Committee meeting in June 1983 that was devoted to this subject, and there were sharply worded attacks upon the Soviet film industry (which had begun to explore some contemporary social issues) and the independent-minded literary journal *Novyi mir*.[70] Direct-dialling facilities with the outside world were ended, apparently at Andropov's behest, in September 1982; postal and customs regulations became more stringent;[71] and the law on 'anti-Soviet agitation and propaganda' became more restrictive.[72] Steps were also taken against a number of prominent dissidents. The writer Georgii Vladimov, author of *Faithful Ruslan*, a novel about a guard-dog at a prison camp, was obliged to emigrate in early 1983 and stripped of his Soviet citizenship, and the historian Roy Medvedev, untouched for many years, was called to the Procurator General's office and warned that if he did not give up his 'anti-Soviet activities' he would face criminal proceedings.[73] The theatre director Yuri Lyubimov and the historian Mikhail Geller, both resident abroad, also lost their citizenship (so did others),[74] and the number of Jews allowed to emigrate, another normally reliable barometer of liberalism, fell sharply from up to 50,000 a year in the late 1970s to 2,700 in 1982, 1,300 in 1983 and only 896 in 1984.[75]

The immediate post-Brezhnev period, however, saw no reversion to hardline Stalinism. Dissidents and oppositionists, certainly, were harshly treated, but for those who were content to advance their objectives within the system, there was a greater emphasis than before on consultation and accountability. For the first time in modern Soviet history, for instance, reports began to appear in *Pravda* of the subjects that had been discussed at the weekly meetings of the Politburo.[76] Attempts were also made to revive the Khrushchevian practice of meeting members of the public face to face at home or in their workplace. Andropov made a symbolic gesture of some importance by visiting the Ordzhonikidze machine tool factory at the end of January 1983 for an extended and frankly worded exchange with its workforce; Chernenko made a less remarkable visit to the 'Hammer and Sickle' metallurgical plant in April 1984.[77] The rights of ordinary workers at their workplace were also strengthened, at least on paper, by a law on labour collectives, adopted in June 1983 after an extended public discussion, which gave workforce meetings greater rights in relation to management and the appointment of leading personnel, but which also required them to take more responsibility for poor workmanship and shirking.[78] The annual plan and budget, for the first time ever, were submitted to the All-Union Council of Trade Unions for its consideration in late 1984.[79]

In public life more generally, there was a greater emphasis upon openness and publicity, or what soon became widely known as *glasnost'*. One indication of this rather different approach was the decision, at the June 1983 Central Committee plenum, to establish a national public opinion centre;[80] another was the revival of the Khrushchevian practice of publishing the full proceedings of Central Committee meetings, at least in this instance.[81] And there was a continuing emphasis, throughout the period, upon the need to take account of the concerns of ordinary citizens, particularly in the form of letters to party and state bodies and to the press. The harsher penalties that were imposed upon bribery and corruption were reported to have been prompted by communications of this kind, and the strengthening of law and order was similarly presented as a response to pressure from citizens in Gorky, who had complained that they were afraid to walk the city streets at night.[82] Difficult though it was to assess such matters precisely, these new emphases in public policy appeared to have been well received by the Soviet public: according to an unpublished opinion poll that was reported in the Western press, fully 87 per cent of those who were asked took a 'positive' view of the first three months of the new regime and by implication of post-Brezhnev changes more generally.[83]

Still more fundamentally, there was a reconsideration in the Andropov and Chernenko periods of the official ideology from which the regime still claimed to derive its right to rule. One of the most important contributions was Andropov's article 'The Teaching of Karl Marx and Some Questions of Socialist Construction in the USSR', which appeared in the party theoretical journal *Kommunist*. Its sober and realistic tone marked off the post-Brezhnev era from the optimism of Khrushchev, and equally from Brezhnev's somewhat complacent notion of 'developed socialism'; it was, in effect, the 'first public criticism by a ruling leader of the party's general line'.[84] There was a need, Andropov insisted, to understand the stage of development that had been reached in the USSR, and to avoid setting targets that would be impossible to achieve. The Soviet Union, he emphasised, was only at the beginning of the long historical stage of developed socialism; there should be no exaggeration of their closeness to the ultimate goal of full communism, and an honest acknowledgement of the difficulties that still awaited.[85] Andropov's speech at the June 1983 Central Committee plenum, which dealt extensively with the revisions that would be required in the Party Programme, noted similarly that there were elements of 'isolation from reality' in the existing text, adopted in 1961, and which had notoriously promised that a communist society would 'in the main' be established by 1980. It was vital, Andropov had already insisted, to take proper account of the situation that actually existed, and to avoid 'ready-made solutions'.[86]

Chernenko, who became chairman of the commission preparing a new programme at the same time as he became party leader, took the same practical and unheroic approach. Addressing the commission in April 1984, he reminded the participants that developed socialism would be an 'historically protracted' period and urged them to concentrate their attention on the complicated tasks that still remained rather than what Lenin had called the 'distant, beautiful and rosy future'.[87] These emphases in turn became the basis for a developing specialist literature which acknowledged, more openly than ever before, that socialism had not necessarily resolved complex issues such as environmental conservation, inter-nationality relations or gender inequalities. Still more provocatively, it was suggested that Soviet-type societies contained 'contradictions' based on the different interests of the various groups of which they were composed, and that these could lead to 'serious collisions' of the kind that had occurred in Poland in the early 1980s unless far-reaching democratic reforms were instituted.[88] The debate was suspended in 1984, but two years later it was one of those to which Gorbachev devoted particular attention in his report to the 27th Party Congress.[89]

The Gorbachev leadership

The advent of a new General Secretary had normally meant a significant change in the direction of Soviet public policy, although any change took some time to establish itself as the new leader gradually marginalised his opponents and co-opted his supporters onto the Politburo and Secretariat. At the outset of his administration, Gorbachev's objectives, and indeed his personal background, were still fairly obscure even at leading levels of the party. Unlike his two main rivals, Grigorii Romanov and Viktor Grishin, he had never addressed a party congress; he had no published collection of writings to his name; and he had made only a couple of official visits abroad, to Canada in 1983 and the United Kingdom in late 1984, on both occasions as the head of a delegation of Soviet parliamentarians. Andrei Gromyko, proposing his candidacy to the Central Committee, explained what had convinced him personally that Gorbachev would be a suitable General Secretary: Gorbachev, he told them, had chaired meetings of the Politburo in Chernenko's absence, and had done so 'brilliantly, without any exaggeration'.[90] Gorbachev himself told the Politburo that agreed to nominate him that there was 'no need to change their policies',[91] and in his acceptance speech he paid tribute to the late General Secretary and promised to continue the policy of his two predecessors, which he defined as 'acceleration of socioeconomic development and the perfection of all aspects of social life'.[92] At the same time there were some elements in the new General Secretary's biography which suggested that this new administration would be more than a continuation of the ones that had immediately preceded it.

One of those elements was Gorbachev's own background, particularly his education and age-group, which placed him among the reform-minded '1960ers' who had been inspired by 20th Party Congress in 1956 and by the process of de-Stalinisation that followed it rather than the Brezhnev generation, whose formative experience had been their military service during the Second World War and who had in turn been led to believe that the Soviet system rested on popular support and that it was capable of supreme achievement.[93] Gorbachev himself, born on 2 March 1931 to a peasant family in the north Caucasus, was too young to have taken a direct part in the hostilities, although he had vivid memories of the German occupation of his native village and of the destruction that had taken place in other parts of the country.[94] His father was wounded in the conflict, and he was brought up mainly by his maternal grandparents, who were poor peasants of Ukrainian origin.[95] He worked first as a mechanic at a machine-tractor station and then in 1950, with the help of his local party organisation, enrolled in the Law Faculty at Moscow State University. Gorbachev was a Komsomol activist while at university and joined the CPSU itself in 1952. He graduated in 1955, the first Soviet leader since Lenin to receive a legal training and the first to graduate from the country's premier university, although it was an institution in which the Stalinist *Short Course* still held pride of place and in which the 'slightest deviation from the official line ... was fraught with consequences'.[96]

The Czech communist and later dissident Zdeněk Mlynář, who was Gorbachev's friend and classmate at this time, recalled him as an open-minded student who had particularly liked Hegel's dictum that the truth was 'always concrete' and who was prepared, even before the death of Stalin, to take issue with the purges (Lenin, he pointed out, had at least allowed his Menshevik opponents to emigrate).[97] Gorbachev himself remembered object-ing when one of his instructors insisted on reading out Stalin's newly published *Economic Problems of Socialism in the USSR* page by page (there was an immediate investigation); one of his fellow students, indeed, recalled him as 'all but a "dissident" at this time'.[98] But he graduated without incident and returned to Stavropol, where he worked in the Komsomol and party apparatus and later completed a correspondence course at the local agricultural institute. In 1966 he became first secretary of the city party committee, in 1970 he was appointed to head the territorial party organisation and the following year he joined the Central Committee as a full member. In 1978 Gorbachev replaced his mentor Fedor Kulakov in the Central Committee Secretariat, taking responsibility for agriculture. In 1979, in addition, he became a candidate and then in 1980 a full member of the ruling Politburo; this made him, in his late forties, one of the very few 'super Secretaries' who were represented on both of the party's leading bodies and who formed the most obvious pool of candidates for the succession.[99]

Gorbachev met his wife Raisa, a philosophy graduate, while they were both at Moscow University (they met, apparently, at a class in ballroom dancing[100]). Born in the town of Rubtsovsk in Siberia in 1932, Raisa Maksimovna was the eldest daughter of a Ukrainian railway engineer. Her family, like Gorbachev's, had suffered during the Stalin years: Gorbachev's grandfather had been released after torture had failed to extract a confes-sion; Raisa's own father had been arrested, and her grandfather had been shot for 'counter-revolutionary agitation' (it was not until 1988 that the family received a formal certificate of rehabilitation).[101] The Gorbachevs married in 1953 and then moved to Stavropol two years later, after their graduation; Raisa was able to pursue research into the nature of social relations in the nearby countryside and was awarded a candidate of science degree (roughly equivalent to a Western doctorate) in 1967. In the 1970s she lectured for some years at Moscow University.[102] Previous party leaders' wives had played a very discreet role in Soviet public life: it was not even known that Andropov's widow was still alive until she appeared at his funeral in 1984. Mrs Gorbachev, however, swiftly assumed a prominent position in domestic and international affairs, acting as a Soviet 'First Lady' when the General Secretary travelled abroad on official occasions. Her views, equally, had a strong influence upon him: they discussed 'everything' at home in the evenings, Gorbachev told an NBC interviewer in late 1987 in remarks that were censored for Soviet domestic consumption; others, including his bodyguard, thought he was even 'subordinate' to her.[103]

It was not customary for a Soviet leader to discuss his personal affairs with the mass media, but Gorbachev did venture some information on this subject when he was interviewed by the Italian communist paper *L'Unità* in May 1987. His main weakness, Gorbachev believed, was that he had too many interests. He had enrolled in the law faculty at university, but had originally intended to study physics. He liked mathematics, but also history and literature. In later years he had turned more and more to the study of economics, while remaining interested in philosophy (this was not, to put it mildly, the intellectual background of his immediate predecessor).[104] Curiosity about the General Secretary's private life was hardly satisfied by such revelations, and there were further queries in the spring of 1989. Did Mikhail Sergeevich, for instance, like fishing? And why did *glasnost'* not apply to the person who had invented it?[105] Gorbachev was a little more forthcoming when he gave an interview to a Central Committee journal later the same year. He earned 1,200 roubles a month, he explained, the same as other members of the Politburo. He had additional earnings from royalties and other sources (his book *Perestroika* alone had appeared in more than a hundred countries), but he had donated any earnings of this kind to the party budget and charitable causes. Literature, theatre, music and cinema remained his hobbies, although he had less and less time to devote to them.[106] The General Secretary, it also emerged, had been baptised; though not himself a believer, he supported the constitutional provision by which citizens were free to practise their faith if they wished to do so, and his mother was known to be an active worshipper.[107]

As well as his personal characteristics, there were also clues in Gorbachev's speeches before his assumption of the general secretaryship as to the direction of policy he was likely to pursue. Perhaps the clearest indication of this kind was a speech he delivered to an all-union conference on ideology in December 1984. The speech contained positive references to self-management, which Lenin had 'never counterposed to Soviet state power', and drew attention to the various interests of different social groups and to the need for a greater measure of social justice (which had become a coded form of attack on the Brezhnev legacy). There was enormous scope, Gorbachev went on, for the further development of the Soviet political system, and of socialist democracy. This was partly a matter of developing all aspects of the work of the elected soviets, and of involving workers more fully in the affairs of their own workplace. It was also a matter of securing a greater degree of *glasnost'* or openness in party and state life. As well as tributes to Chernenko, there were clear and positive allusions to Andropov in his remarks about the 'two previous years' and the need to avoid 'ready-made solutions'.[108] Gorbachev's electoral address in February 1985, made at a time when Chernenko's serious illness was widely known, repeated many of these themes, combining almost populist references to Soviet power as a form of rule 'of the toilers and for the toilers' with more abrasive remarks about the need for self-sufficiency in enterprise management and better discipline on the shop floor.[109]

The direction of reform became still clearer at the April 1985 Central Committee plenum, the first that Gorbachev addressed as party leader and the one from which it became conventional to date the start of *perestroika*. There had been significant achievements in all spheres of Soviet life, Gorbachev told the plenum. The USSR had a powerful, developed economy, a highly skilled workforce and an advanced scientific base. Everyone had the right to work, to social security, to cultural resources of all kinds and to participation in the administration of state affairs. But further changes were needed in order to achieve a 'qualitatively new state of society', including modernisation of the economy and the extension of popular self-government. The key issue was the acceleration of economic growth. This was quite feasible if the 'human factor' was called more fully into play, and if the reserves that existed throughout the economy were properly utilised. This in turn required a greater degree of decentralisation of economic management, including cost accounting at enterprise level and a closer connection between the work people did and the rewards that they received.[110] The months and years that followed saw the gradual assembly of a leadership team to direct these changes and the further extension of what was already a challenging reform agenda.

The formation of a new leadership was the easier of these tasks and the one that advanced more rapidly. The April 1985 Central Committee plenum itself made a start with the appointment of Yegor Ligachev and Nikolai Ryzhkov, both Andropov appointees, to full membership of the Politburo without passing through the customary candidate or non-voting stage. There had been no promotions of this kind for at least twenty years, and it was an early demonstration of Gorbachev's control over the vital power of appointment.[111] There were further changes in July 1985: Grigorii Romanov, Gorbachev's principal rival for the leadership, retired from both Politburo and Secretariat 'on grounds of ill health' (just over 60, his rumoured weakness for women and alcohol hardly suggested infirmity), and two new Central Committee secretaries were elected, one of them Boris Yeltsin, who had been party first secretary in Sverdlovsk.[112] At the Supreme Soviet session that took place the following day, Foreign Minister Andrei Gromyko, rather than Gorbachev himself, was elected to the vacant chairmanship of the Presidium, and the Georgian party leader, Eduard Shevardnadze, became foreign minister in his place (he had no diplomatic experience but was committed, like Gorbachev, to a change in Soviet relations with the outside world);[113] and then in September, Ryzhkov replaced the veteran Brezhnevite, Nikolai Tikhonov, as prime minister.[114] A still more extensive restructuring took place at the 27th Party Congress in March 1986, including the appointment of five new Central Committee secretaries. One of them was Alexander Yakovlev, a close Gorbachev associate who had previously served as ambassador to Canada and as director of one of the institutes of the Academy of Sciences, another was Alexandra Biryukova, a former Secretary of the All-Union Council of Trade Unions and the first woman member of the leadership since the early 1960s. Remarkably, nearly half the members of this newly elected Politburo and Secretariat were people who had not served in either body before Gorbachev's election to the general secretaryship the previous year.[115]

There were further changes in the leadership in the months that followed, all of which tended to strengthen Gorbachev's position still further. The Central Committee plenum that took place in January 1987 brought Alexander Yakovlev into the Politburo as a candidate member, and Anatolii Luk'yanov, a leading jurist and head of the general department in the Central Committee apparatus, and the Belarusian party leader, Nikolai Slyun'kov, became Central Committee secretaries (Luk'yanov, it later emerged, had been a member of the Komsomol committee at the same time as Gorbachev when both of them were at Moscow University in the early 1950s[116]). Two Brezhnev appointees, Dinmukhamed Kunaev and Mikhail Zimyanin, left the Politburo and Secretariat respectively at the same time; Kunaev, whose resignation was ostensibly 'in connection with his retirement on a pension', was expelled from the Central Committee itself the following June for 'serious shortcomings' in his tenure of the Kazakh first secretaryship.[117] At the same meeting Yakovlev moved up from candidate to full Politburo membership, and Dmitri Yazov, the new defence minister, became a candidate member, replacing Marshal Sokolov who had been discredited by the ability of a young West German, Matthias Rust, to land a small plane in Red Square (which began to be called 'Moscow's fourth international airport').[118] Changes in the party leadership were only a part of a much wider-ranging replacement of leading officials at all levels. All the fourteen republican first secretaries had been replaced by 1989, some more than once, and there was an equally far-reaching turnover in the Central Committee, an overwhelming 84 per cent of whom when elected in 1990 had never previously held party office of any kind.[119] Two-thirds of the leading officials of lower-level party organisations had been replaced by late 1988,[120] and 88 per cent of the deputies elected in March 1989 to the Congress of People's Deputies were entirely new to representative duties.[121] In the economy, Gorbachev himself reported, more than two-thirds of the country's industrial managers and farm directors had been replaced by early 1989.[122]

Of all the policies that were promoted by the Gorbachev leadership, *glasnost'* was perhaps the most distinctive and the one that had been pressed furthest by the end of communist rule.[123] *Glasnost'*, usually translated as openness or transparency, was not the same as freedom of the press or the right to information; nor was it original to Gorbachev (it figured, for instance, in the Constitution that had been adopted in 1977 under Leonid Brezhnev). It did, however, reflect the new General Secretary's belief that without a greater awareness of the real state of affairs and of the considerations that had led to particular decisions, there would be no willingness on the part of the Soviet people to commit themselves to his programme of *perestroika* ('the better the people are informed', he told the Central Committee that elected him, 'the more consciously they act, the more actively they support the party, its plans and programmatic objectives').[124] Existing policies were in any case ineffectual and often counterproductive. The newspaper *Sovetskaya Rossiya* reported the case of Mr Polyakov of Kaluga, a well-read man who followed the press closely and never missed the evening television news. He knew a lot about what was happening in various African countries, Polyakov complained, but had 'only a very rough idea what was happening in his home town'.[125] In late 1985, another reader complained, there had been a major earthquake in Tajikistan, but all they were told was that 'lives had been lost'. At about the same time, there had been an earthquake in Mexico and a volcanic eruption in Colombia, both covered in full with on-the-spot reports and details of the casualties. Was Tajikistan really further from Moscow than Latin America?[126]

Influenced by considerations such as these, the Gorbachev leadership made steady and sometimes dramatic progress in broadening the scope of public debate and exposing the Soviet past as well as the Soviet present to critical scrutiny. The Brezhnev era was one of the earliest targets. It had been a time, Gorbachev told the 27th Party Congress in 1986, when a 'curious psychology – how to change things without really changing anything' – had been dominant.[127] There had been real achievements in the early years of Brezhnev's rule, with the development of new branches of industry, an improvement in living standards and an increase in the Soviet Union's international influence. But the promise of these achievements had been dissipated by a failure to carry the reforms through to their logical conclusion, or to make the changes that had become necessary in social policy and in the leadership itself; the result had been a period of 'stagnation', with the economy slipping into crisis and party and government leaders lagging increasingly behind the needs of the time.[128] The Stalin question was a still more fundamental one, for all Soviet reformers. Gorbachev, to begin with, was reluctant even to concede there was even a question. Stalinism, he told the French press in 1986, was a 'notion made up by enemies of communism' which was 'widely used to discredit the Soviet Union and socialism as a whole'; Stalin himself, he insisted elsewhere, had made an 'indisputable contribution to the struggle for socialism [and] to the defence of its achievements'.[129] By early 1987, however, Gorbachev was insisting there must be 'no forgotten names, no blank spots' in Soviet literature and history,[130] and by November of that year, when he came to give his address on the seventieth anniversary of the revolution, he was ready to condemn the 'wanton repressive measures' of the 1930s, 'real crimes' in which 'many thousands of people inside and outside the party' had suffered.[131]

In the course of his speech, Gorbachev announced that a Politburo commission had been set up to investigate the repression of the Stalinist years, and this led to the rehabilitation of many prominent figures from the party's past (and thousands of others) from 1988 onwards. The most important figure to be restored to public respectability in this way was the former *Pravda* editor Nikolai Bukharin, whose sentence was posthumously quashed in February 1988 (his expulsions from the party and the Academy of Sciences were also rescinded).[132] Trotsky had not been sentenced by a Soviet court and there was therefore no judgement to be reconsidered; but his personal qualities began to receive some recognition in the Soviet press, and from 1989 onwards his writings began to appear in mass-circulation as well as scholarly journals.[133] An extended discussion took place about the numbers that Stalin had condemned to death: for some it was about a million by the end of the 1930s, but for others (including the historian Roy Medvedev, whose own father had perished) it was at least 12 million, with a further 38 million repressed in other ways.[134] Some of the mass graves of the Stalin period began to be uncovered at the same time, the most extensive of which were in the Kuropaty forest near Minsk. The victims, as many as 40,000, had been shot between 1937 and 1941;[135] this, and the other graves that were still being discovered in the early 1990s, was an indictment of Stalinism more powerful than anything the historians could hope to muster.[136]

Glasnost' led to further changes in the quality of Soviet public life, from literature and the arts to statistics and a wide-ranging discussion about the future of socialism itself. There was new information about infant mortality and life expectancy, the figures for which had been suppressed since the early 1970s, and there was information on abortions and suicides, which had not been reported since the 1920s.[137] Subjects that had been unmentionable in the Brezhnev years, such as violent crime, drugs and prostitution, began to receive extensive and even sensational treatment. Many events of the past, such as the devastating earthquake in Ashkhabad in 1948 and the nuclear accident in the Urals in 1957, were belatedly acknowledged. The first meaningful figures for defence spending and foreign debt were revealed to the newly elected Congress of People's Deputies when it met in 1989; figures for capital punishment followed in 1991. Virtually all the books by banned writers had been published by the same date, including Pasternak's *Doctor Zhivago*, Zamyatin's futuristic *We* and Grossman's *Life and Fate* (all in 1988); Solzhenitsyn's *Gulag Archipelago* and Nabokov's *Lolita* both appeared in 1989 (so did Orwell's *1984*), and by 1990 Hitler's *Mein Kampf* was being serialised in the leading journal of military history. Libraries opened up their closed stacks; museums brought out their Chagalls and Kandinskys; archives introduced a thirty-year rule, in line with international practice. The new press law, adopted in June 1990, went even further by abolishing censorship entirely.[138] Opinion polls suggested that *glasnost'*, for all its limitations, was the change in Soviet life that was most apparent to ordinary people, and the one they were most likely to think had done more good than harm.[139]

The 'democratisation' of Soviet political life was an associated change, and one that was intended to unlock the human energies that, for Gorbachev, had been choked off by the bureaucratic centralism of the Stalin and Brezhnev years. The Soviet Union, he told the 19th Party Conference in the summer of 1988, had pioneered the idea of workers' control and the right to work, and equality for women and national minorities. The political system established by the October revolution, however, had undergone 'serious deformations', leading to the development of a 'command-administrative system' that had made possible the 'omnipotence of Stalin and his entourage' and then a 'wave of repressive measures and lawlessness'. The role of party and state officialdom had increased out of all proportion, and a 'bloated administrative apparatus' had begun to impose its own priorities in political and economic matters. Nearly a third of the adult population were regularly elected to the soviets, or to the commissions that advised them, but few had any real influence over the decisions that were taken by their executives. Social life as a whole had become 'straitjacketed' by controls of various kinds, and ordinary working people had become 'alienated' from the system that was supposed to represent their interests. It was this 'ossified system of government, with its command-and-pressure mechanism', that had become the main obstacle to *perestroika*.[140]

The Party Conference agreed to undertake a 'radical reform' of the political system, and this led to a series of constitutional and other changes from 1988 onwards that – for the reformers – had as their ultimate objective the development of a model of socialism that would recover the democratic gains that had been won in the early postrevolutionary years while still retaining a framework of public ownership and comprehensive welfare. An entirely new election law, approved in December 1988, broke new ground by providing for – though not specifically requiring – a choice of candidate, and giving ordinary citizens the right to make nominations (see Chapter 2).[141] A new state structure was established, incorporating a smaller working parliament for the first time in modern Soviet history and – from 1990 – a powerful executive presidency (see Chapter 3). A reform of the political system would not be enough, however, unless it was accompanied by a strengthening of the rule of law; this led to a series of related changes, including a constitutional supervision committee that had the right to consider the legality of government decisions, and reforms in court procedures that strengthened the independence of judges. Ultimately, it was hoped, these and other reforms would help to establish a 'law-based state', first mentioned in 1988 and the subject of a resolution at the Party Conference in the summer of that year.[142] The CPSU itself was meanwhile 'democratised', although the changes took some time to come into effect. Leading officials, it was agreed, should be elected by competitive ballot for a maximum of two consecutive terms; members of the Central Committee should be involved much more directly in the formulation of party policy; and there should be much more information about its activities, from income and expenditure (members complained they knew more about the financial affairs of the American presidency and the British royal family) to the composition of its mass membership (including such details as the presence of 125 Eskimos, 7 Englishmen, 3 Americans, 2 'negroes' and one Bolivian).[143]

There was a still larger objective, discussed by academics and commentators as well as the political leadership: the elaboration of a 'humane and democratic socialism' that would build on Soviet achievements but combine them with the experience of other nations and schools of thought into a body of social thought that could serve as the basis of a global civilisation in the new century. Khrushchev had promised that the USSR would construct a communist society 'in the main' by 1980 in the party programme that had been adopted under his leadership in 1961. His successors dropped that commitment and began to describe the USSR, from the early 1970s, as a 'developed socialist society', whose evolution into a fully communist society was a matter for the distant future. Gorbachev, for his part, avoided the term 'developed socialism'[144] and opted initially for 'developing socialism', in effect a postponement into the still more distant future of the attainment of a fully communist society.[145] In 1990, in a Programmatic Declaration that was approved at the 28th Party Congress, the objective became 'humane, democratic socialism' (did this mean, some asked ironically, that there could be a socialism that was inhumane and undemocratic?);[146] later still, in a revised version of the Party Programme that was approved by the Central Committee in the summer of 1991, the slogan had changed to 'Socialism, Democracy, Progress', with communism mentioned only as the 'epitaph on a tombstone'.[147] The new programme committed the party to 'all-human values', democracy, 'freedom in all its forms', social justice and a 'new world civilisation'; it was also, in Gorbachev's words, an acknowledgement that the communist ideal was unrealisable in the foreseeable future.[148]

It remained unclear, these generalities apart, how a 'humane and democratic' socialist society of this rather different kind was to be constructed. Gorbachev resisted calls to set out the way ahead in any detail: did they really want a new *Short Course*, he asked the Party Congress in 1990, referring to the discredited Marxist primer that had been produced under Stalin's auspices in 1938? And what was the point of programmes like railway timetables, with objectives that had to be achieved by certain dates: wasn't an authentic socialism the achievement of working people themselves, not something they were directed towards by others?[149] Gorbachev's objectives emerged as a set of fairly abstract propositions; they were set out, for instance, in the 'seven postulates of *perestroika*' that were formulated in his address to the Central Committee meeting that took place in January 1987. These included a 'resolute overcoming of the processes of stagnation' as well as a greater reliance on the 'creative endeavour of the masses', including socialist self-management. There would be a greater emphasis on intensive factors of growth, including what Gorbachev described as 'socialist entrepreneurship'; there would also be a 'constant concern for the spiritual wealth and culture of every person and of society as a whole', and the elimination of 'any deviation from socialist morality'. The ultimate aim, as Gorbachev explained it, was to achieve the 'fullest disclosure of the humanistic character of our social order in all its decisive aspects'.[150] However adequate this might have been as a statement of the leadership's overall philosophy, it offered little guidance to party officials in their practical activity, nor did it carry conviction for a wider public at a time of economic difficulty, more assertive nationalism and an increasingly open acknowledgement of mistakes in policy for which a party that had monopolised political power for seventy years could scarcely avoid responsibility.

It was one of Gorbachev's central assumptions that it had been 'subjective' factors, and in particular the quality of its leadership, that had led to the degeneration of Soviet socialism over the whole postrevolutionary period. What was the reason for their difficulties, he asked the Central Committee in April 1985? Natural and external factors were certainly important; but the main reason was that the necessary changes had not taken place in the management of a changing society.[151] For years, Gorbachev explained to the 27th Party Congress in 1986, party and government leaders had failed to challenge the bureaucratic 'command-administrative system' that had developed in the Stalinist years; it was a failure that was 'above all of a subjective character', and one that would only be remedied when leaders brought their methods of government into line with changing circumstances.[152] Speaking in July 1990, Gorbachev acknowledged that the replacement of leading officials was 'not a panacea'; but people mattered more than institutions, and the right appointments were of 'decisive' significance.[153] The 'root cause' of their difficulties, he told the Central Committee the following October, was the 'inertia of old thinking'.[154] And in a speech in November 1990, he declared that the 'most important revolution' was the 'revolution in minds, in our heads, in us our-selves'.[155] There could be little doubt, as the Gorbachev leadership drew to a close, that the Soviet leadership had been renewed more extensively than at any time in post-war history; it was much less obvious that the replacement of leading officials and their 'conservative thinking' was decisive to the success of *perestroika* and that deeper, more systemic choices could be avoided.

The August coup and the end of party rule

The attempted coup of August 1991, which led directly to the end of communist rule, was itself a demonstration of the limits of a leadership style that placed its main emphasis on personal rather than institutional factors. Many of the conspirators had been Gorbachev's own appointees, even friends, and he was affected more profoundly by this than by any other aspect of the short-lived emergency (the whole family had been particularly close to Gorbachev's head of staff, Valerii Boldin, and had 'told him everything, even the most personal things').[156] The coup, in fact, had not come without warning. Foreign Minister Shevardnadze, tendering his resignation in December 1990, had told the Soviet parliament that a 'dictatorship' was approaching, although no one yet knew what form it would take.[157] Speaking in early August 1991, he again thought it possible there would be an attempt to resolve the country's difficulties by resorting to a 'strong hand'.[158] An 'Appeal to the People', published in the newspaper *Sovetskaya Rossiya* in July, called for national and patriotic unity and was signed by two of the organisers of the coup as well as other prominent hardliners.[159] Alexander Yakovlev, in a television interview on 12 August, warned that 'conservative and reactionary forces' had been mobilising and that they would be only too glad to 'turn back the clock'. Speaking a few days later, just before the conspiracy was launched, he warned again that a 'Stalinist grouping' had become dominant in the party leadership and that it was preparing a 'party and state coup'.[160]

These warnings notwithstanding, the attempted coup of August 1991 was a shock as well as a surprise to the Soviet leader and to the outside world.[161] August, by a coincidence, was the month in which General Kornilov had attempted to overthrow the Provisional Government in 1917, and it was the month in which the Soviet President took his family holidays in the Crimea. In 1987, he spent the time writing his bestselling *Perestroika*. On 18 August 1991, he was working on the text of a speech when four emissaries arrived unexpectedly from Moscow. All his telephones had been disconnected, so this was clearly no courtesy visit. Gorbachev refused either to resign or to sign a decree instituting a state of emergency and was thereupon placed under house arrest and isolated from the outside world.[162] In the early hours of 19 August, a self-styled State Emergency Committee informed a startled world that Gorbachev was 'unwell', and that his responsibilities would be assumed in these circumstances by Vice-President Gennadii Yanaev. The Emergency Committee, it later emerged, had eight members. Apart from Yanaev himself, there was the KGB chairman, Vladimir Kryuchkov, Defence Minister Dmitri Yazov, Interior Minister Boris Pugo, Prime Minister Valentin Pavlov; and three other members of less prominence, Oleg Baklanov, Vasilii Starodubtsev and Alexander Tizyakov.[163] Yanaev and four other members of the Committee addressed a hastily convened press conference later the same day. The Vice-President, they explained, had assumed power on the basis of Article 127 of the Soviet Constitution, which allowed him to do so if the President was 'for whatever reason' unable to carry out his responsibilities; Gorbachev, they added, was 'very tired', but it was hoped that 'once he had recovered' he would return to his official duties.[164]

The Committee, in a series of decrees, meanwhile suspended the activities of all parties (other than those that had supported the emergency), banned the publication of all but a small number of newspapers (including *Pravda*), ordered the surrender of firearms and prohibited meetings, strikes and demonstrations. The Committee's message was not simply a coercive one; it also promised to cut prices and increase wages, and to place food supplies under strict control with priority being given to schools, hospitals, pensioners and the disabled.[165] In a 'message to the Soviet people', broadcast on the morning of 19 August, the Committee offered a more extended justification of its action. The Soviet people, it explained, were in 'mortal danger'. *Perestroika* had reached an 'impasse'. The country had become 'ungovernable', and 'extremist forces' were seeking to break up the Soviet state and seize power for themselves. Meanwhile the economy was in crisis, with the breakdown of central planning, a 'chaotic, ungoverned slide towards a market' and famine a real possibility; and crime and immorality were rampant. The Committee, it promised, would reverse these trends, strengthen public order, arrest the fall in living standards and restore the Soviet Union's international standing; it appealed, in turn, for the support of 'all true patriots and people of goodwill', but made no reference of any kind to socialism.[166]

The coup, it soon became clear, had been poorly planned – two of its principal members, Yanaev and Pavlov, were drunk for most of its duration[167] – and it was opposed from the outset by Boris Yeltsin, who had been elected Russian president two months earlier and who made a dramatic call for resistance on 19 August, standing on one of the tanks outside the Russian parliament building. Yeltsin denounced the Committee's action as a 'right-wing, reactionary, unconstitutional coup' and declared all its decisions illegal. Gorbachev, he insisted, must be restored immediately to his position, and he called for an indefinite strike until the Soviet parliament had met and constitutional propriety had been restored.[168] Huge demonstrations in front of the Russian parliament the following day were addressed by Shevardnadze, Yakovlev, Andrei Sakharov's widow Elena Bonner and other democrats. The critical moment was the evening of 20 August when about 70,000 Muscovites defied the curfew and assembled in front of the 'White House' (as the parliamentary building was known) to defend it against an expected attack by pro-coup forces. That night, three men were killed – one shot and two crushed by tanks – but the attack on the parliament itself did not materialise.[169] It later emerged that substantial sections of the armed forces had declared against the coup, and that the elite KGB 'Alpha' anti-terrorist group had rejected the order they had been given to storm the building.[170]

On Wednesday 21 August the coup began to collapse. The Russian parliament met in emergency session and gave Yeltsin their unqualified support; media restrictions were lifted, and the Ministry of Defence ordered troops to return to their barracks. The Presidium of the Supreme Soviet of the USSR declared the action of the Emergency Committee illegal, and the Procurator General's office announced that criminal proceedings for high treason had been instigated against its members. One of the coup leaders, Boris Pugo, committed suicide; several others went to the Crimea to seek Gorbachev's forgiveness (the Russian parliament sent its own representatives to bring the Soviet President back safely); and others still, such as Foreign Minister Alexander Bessmertnykh, tried to explain why they had – in his case – suffered a sudden 'cold' while the emergency was in force (he was dismissed two days later). The most ambiguous figure of all was the Chairman of the Supreme Soviet, Anatolii Luk'yanov, who had refused to denounce the coup at the time and was accused of being its 'chief ideologist' (by the end of the month he was one of the fourteen people involved in the coup who had been arrested and charged with high treason).[171]

Gorbachev was flown back to Moscow in the early hours of 22 August, where he later addressed a crowded press conference. He thanked Yeltsin as well as the Russian parliament for securing his release, and then described the difficult circumstances under which he had been held. He had refused to accept the conditions his captors had tried to dictate to him or the food they had provided, but had rigged up a makeshift radio on which he had been able to listen to Western radio broadcasts; he had even recorded four copies of a video message to the Soviet people explaining the real nature of the emergency. There was some surprise that the Soviet leader continued to defend the Communist Party, whose role in the attempted coup had been obscure.[172] Later, however, when the complicity of the party leadership became clear, Gorbachev resigned the general secretaryship and called upon the Central Committee to take the 'difficult but honourable decision to dissolve itself'.[173] Yeltsin had signed a decree suspending the activity of the Communist Party throughout the Russian Federation on 23 August, at a meeting of the Russian parliament that Gorbachev attended.[174] Another decree on 25 August transferred all the assets of the party into the hands of elected bodies of government and froze its bank accounts;[175] and then in November 1991 the party was suppressed entirely.[176]

The Soviet Union itself was a still greater casualty of the coup. Seeking to block the signature of a new union treaty that would have established a loose confederation, the conspirators – in the event – accelerated the collapse of the state they had sought to preserve. Lithuania had already declared its independence, in the spring of 1990; the other Baltic republics followed immediately; and by the end of 1991 all of the republics – apart from Russia – had adopted declarations of a similar kind. Ukraine's decision, backed by the support of over 90 per cent of its voting population in a referendum on 1 December, appears to have convinced Yeltsin that there was no future in a reconstituted USSR of which the second largest republic was not a member, and on 8 December he met the Ukrainian President and the Belorussian parliamentary chairman at a country house near Minsk and concluded an agreement establishing a Commonwealth of Independent States. The new Commonwealth was not a state, it had no common parliament and in particular it had no presidency; but with its establishment, according to the agreement, the USSR as a subject of international law and a geopolitical reality had 'ceased its existence'.[177] On 12 December the Russian Supreme Soviet approved the agreement and withdrew from the treaty of union that had been concluded in 1922 (the Constitution left little doubt that the full Congress of People's Deputies should have considered the matter and that a further referendum should have been conducted);[178] a further agreement on 21 December in Alma-Ata brought all the remaining republics outside the Baltic into the new association.[179] With the disappearance of the USSR, the position of its president had obviously become untenable, and Gorbachev resigned his last remaining public office on 25 December. As *Pravda* pointed out, the exchange rate had slid from 0.6 to more than 90 roubles to the dollar during his incumbency and the gold reserves were almost exhausted, but there were twelve registered political parties instead of one and the annual sale of Big Macs had increased from zero to 15 million.[180]

Further reading

The origins of the collapse of the USSR, what had 'collapsed' and whether any of it had been 'inevitable' are still vigorously debated inside Russia as well as outside it. Cohen (2004, more fully in his 2009 book) provides a spirited 'revisionist' account; Shlapentokh (1999, at greater length in his 2001 book) also cautions against determinism, at least in the short term; Strayer (1998) includes a range of views in a student-friendly collection of extracts. On Gorbachev himself the fundamental study is Brown (1996), supplemented by Brown (2007); see also Sakwa (1990), Dunlop (1993) and White (1994), which expands on the material presented in this chapter. Gorbachev's own *Perestroika*, in effect a 'mission statement' for his leadership as a whole, appeared in 1987; an abbreviated translation of his *Memoirs* appeared in 1996. The USSR's final day, 25 December 1991, is freshly illuminated in O'Clery (2011).

Brown, Archie, *The Gorbachev Factor* (Oxford and New York: Oxford University Press, 1996).
  Seven Years that Changed the World (Oxford and New York: Oxford University Press, 2007).
Cohen, Stephen F., 'Was the Soviet system reformable?', *Slavic Review*, vol. 63, no. 3 (Autumn 2004), pp. 459–88, with commentaries and a rejoinder, pp. 489–554.
  Soviet Fates and Lost Alternatives (New York and Chichester: Columbia University Press, 2009).
Dunlop, John, *The Rise of Russia and the Fall of the Soviet Empire* (Princeton, NJ: Princeton University Press, 1993).
Gorbachev, Mikhail, *Perestroika: New Thinking for Our Country and the World* (London: Collins and New York: Harper and Row, 1987); an expanded edition was published the following year (New York: Perennial Library and London: Fontana, 1988).
  Memoirs, trans. Georges Peronansky and Tatjana Varshavsky (New York and London: Doubleday, 1996).
O'Clery, Conor, *Moscow, December 25, 1991: The Last Day of the Soviet Union* (New York: Public Affairs / London: Transworld, 2011).
Sakwa, Richard, *Gorbachev and His Reforms* (New York and London: Philip Allen, 1990).
Shlapentokh, Vladimir, 'The Soviet Union: a normal totalitarian society', *Journal of Communist Studies and Transition Politics*, vol. 14, no. 4 (December 1999), pp. 1–16.
  A Normal Totalitarian Society: How the Soviet Union Functioned and How It Collapsed (Armonk, NY, and London: M. E. Sharpe, 2001).
Strayer, Robert W., ed., *Why Did the Soviet Union Collapse? Understanding Historical Change* (Armonk, NY, and London: Sharpe, 1998).
White, Stephen, *After Gorbachev*, 4th edn (Cambridge and New York: Cambridge University Press, 1994).

2 Voters, parties and parliament

Voting in the 2008 presidential election in a village in the Novgorod region (Novosti)

The new Russian Federation, under the Constitution it adopted in December 1993, was to be a 'democratic federal law-based state with a republican form of government'. What kind of form of government this might be took some time to establish, but from the outset it was a state in which the right to rule was based on regular elections to a new parliament, whose lower house was called the State Duma.

Parties, however, remained very weak, elections were increasingly controlled by the authorities themselves, and under Vladimir Putin, from 2000 onwards, the Kremlin itself became the dominant player, acting through a 'party of power' that it had itself established and subordinating the country as a whole to a top-down 'executive vertical'. Law-making authority, formally speaking, was still in the hands of the State Duma, but the Kremlin controlled the party that held two-thirds of its seats, and the more political power was centralised, the more the parliament became a marginal participant in the policy process.

Voting was still quite new in early postcommunist Russia.[1] Voting, that was, in the sense of choosing. Under the Soviet system there had been elections at regular intervals but no opportunity to select, not just among candidates and parties but (in practice) whether to vote at all. In a variation on Brecht's suggestion that the government 'elect a new people', it was the leadership that determined the composition of each new parliament and the constituencies in which they would themselves be nominated. Voters had only to drop the ballot paper, unmarked and possibly unread, into the box; if they wished to vote against they had to go to the screened-off booth at the side of the polling station, where 'everyone could guess their intentions'.[2] In 1987, in the first departure from this tradition, a small number of constituencies in local elections were allowed to nominate more candidates than seats available;[3] then in 1988, as 'democratisation' developed further, a new electoral law was adopted that allowed any number of candidates to be nominated, by ordinary citizens as well as approved organisations, with the result determined by a vote that had to be cast inside a polling booth.[4] The outcome, in the election that took place to a new Congress of People's Deputies in March 1989, was described as 'political shock therapy' by the party's leading conservative, Yegor Ligachev; there were, in fact, more party members among the successful candidates than ever before, but thirty-eight leading officials, including a member of the Politburo, were rejected by a newly enfranchised electorate, and Boris Yeltsin won nearly 90 per cent of the vote in Moscow in a result that was the clearest possible rebuff to the party leadership's attempt to marginalise his challenge to their authority.[5]

A Russian parliament was elected on the same partly competitive basis, in March 1990; and it was this parliament, a Congress of People's Deputies with a smaller working Supreme Soviet, that took Russia into the postcommunist era. Tensions were always likely to develop between a parliament and a president that could both claim a mandate from the electorate; they were still more likely between a parliament that was overwhelmingly Communist at the time of its election and a president who had resigned from the CPSU, banned it after the August coup, and then dissolved the state it had created. Those tensions, in the end, were resolved by another coup when President Yeltsin, emboldened by the results of a referendum in April 1993 at which the policies of his government had been given majority support, dissolved the parliament the following September and then ordered the army to shell the parliament building in early October when a popular demonstration broke through the blockade and encouraged the parliamentary leaders to seek control of the state itself. According to official sources, 145 lost their lives in the bloodiest street fighting since the October revolution – a confrontation that for Yeltsin's first deputy premier, Yegor Gaidar, had been nothing less than a 'short civil war'.[6] The suppression of parliament was an acknowledged violation of the Constitution, which explicitly prohibited any attempt by the president to dissolve the Duma or suspend its operation; it was a constitution, moreover, that Yeltsin had pledged himself to uphold when he was inaugurated as Russia's first elected president in July 1991. But he had made up his mind some time before this that the country could 'no longer have such a parliament',[7] and he did not regard himself as bound by a constitution that had been amended many times since he had sworn to uphold it.[8]

The suppression of the parliament allowed Yeltsin to introduce and then secure approval for an entirely new and postcommunist constitution within which the powers of the presidency were still further enhanced. The new constitution, ratified in December 1993, abolished the Congress of People's Deputies and established a two-chamber Federal Assembly in its place. The upper house, the Council of the Federation, was a 'Senate' that represented Russia's eighty-nine republics and regions, and drew two of its members from each of them. The lower house, the State Duma, was a 'House of Representatives', half of whose 450 members were drawn from individual constituencies with the result determined by simple majority, the other half from a nationwide competition among parties and electoral alliances with the seats distributed proportionally among all that reached a 5 per cent threshold (the single-district members disappeared and there were other changes from 2007 onwards). The president, under the relevant legislation, had no authority to call a referendum, and what took place on 12 December was accordingly a 'national vote' of doubtful constitutionality in which 54.8 per cent of the electorate were reported to have taken part (at least 50 per cent was required for the vote to be valid and there were persistent reports that the total had been artificially inflated); of those who voted, 58.4 per cent supported the presidential text, and it entered into force when it was published in the central press on 25 December.[9] The new constitution, whatever the circumstances of its adoption, established a framework for what was now a postcommunist system; it was unclear, at the same time, how a directly elected parliament would interact with a directly elected president, and whether Russians could be persuaded to express their political preferences through the forms of multiparty politics – or indeed if they would bother to vote at all.

From Soviet to Russian elections

Under the Soviet system only a single party had enjoyed a legal existence ('two parties?', asked local humorists, 'isn't one bad enough?'). Mentioned in passing in earlier versions, the constitution that was adopted under the guidance of Leonid Brezhnev in 1977 had converted the effective dominance of the Communist Party into a formal political monopoly. The CPSU, according to an entirely new Article 6, was the 'leading and guiding force of Soviet society and the nucleus of its political system, of all state organisations and public organisations', and it imparted a 'planned, systematic and theoretically substantiated character to their struggle for the victory of communism'. In 1990, however, the party agreed to relinquish its monopoly; Article 6 was amended to include 'other political parties as well as trade union, youth, and other public organisations and mass movements', and Article 51 added the right of all citizens to 'unite in political parties and public organisations and to participate in mass movements contributing to their greater political activity and to the satisfaction of their diverse interests'.[10] The party, Gorbachev told a meeting of the Central Committee in February, was not so much abandoning its political monopoly as acknowledging that the USSR had already become a multiparty society, although the parties and movements that had come into existence in the late 1980s had not yet acquired a legal basis; it would certainly make every effort to retain the leadership of a changing society, but it could do so only 'within the framework of the democratic process', without any kind of 'political or legal privileges'.[11]

A formal framework for multiparty politics was established the following October when a new law on public associations was adopted, covering political parties as well as trade unions, women's and veterans' associations, and sport clubs. At least ten citizens were needed to establish an association under the law, and they were required to hold a founding congress at which their statutes could be adopted and their office-holders elected. The statutes, as adopted, had then to be registered with the Ministry of Justice or its counterparts at other levels of government, which could refuse registration if (for instance) the objectives of the association appeared to conflict with the Constitution. Political parties, in particular, should have the basic goal of participation in elected institutions and in government; they were expected to have a programme, which had to be made publicly available, and they had the right to nominate candidates for election, to campaign on their behalf and to form organised groups in the bodies to which their candidates were elected.[12] The registration of new and existing parties, including the CPSU, began on this basis in 1991; twenty-five parties had been registered by the summer of 1992, though many claimed no more than a few hundred members and there were no more than 30,000 active members of all political parties put together.[13] The new constitution nonetheless made clear that postcommunist Russia was firmly committed to 'political diversity and a multiparty system', subject only to the requirement that parties and associations refrain from the use of force and from incitement to social, ethnic or religious strife; the same principles were affirmed in a new law on public organisations, approved by the Duma in April 1995, pending the adoption of a special law on parties themselves.[14]

The first test of this emerging but still weakly formed party system was the election of December 1993 and particularly the election to the State Duma, which was to be based on a national competition among party lists with a parallel series of contests in single-member constituencies all over the country (see Table 2.1). The suspension and then bombardment of the parliament had created an inhospitable environment for the conduct of these first postcommunist elections. Yeltsin's main rivals, parliamentary speaker Ruslan Khasbulatov and his vice-president, Alexander Rutskoi, had come out of the parliament building with their hands in the air and were in prison facing serious charges. There was a brief period of censorship; fifteen newspapers were banned on the grounds that they had contributed to the 'mass disorder in Moscow'; a state of emergency, incorporating a ban on demonstrations and a curfew, lasted until mid-October. The

Table 2.1 **Russian Duma elections, 1993–2007**

Date	PL seats[a]	SMC seats	% PL threshold	PL contenders	PL winners	Turnout (%)[b] 'voted'	'took part'
12 Dec 1993	225	225	5	13	8	n.d.	54.81[c]
17 Dec 1995	225	225	5	43	4	64.38	64.73
19 Dec 1999	225	225	5	26	6	61.69	61.85
7 Dec 2003	225	225	5	23	4	55.67	55.75
2 Dec 2007	450	–	7	11	4	63.71	63.78

Source: official communiqués of the Central Electoral Commission, including subsequent revisions.
Note: PL=party list; SMC=single-member constituency.
a: Although conventionally described as 'parties', successive election laws in fact defined those eligible to nominate national lists of candidates as 'electoral associations' (including but not limited to parties) or 'electoral blocs' (1993), 'associations' or 'blocs' but without any explicit reference to parties (1995), 'electoral associations' including but not limited to parties (1999), and 'electoral blocs' as well as 'political parties' (2003). The election law that applied in 2007 was the first that gave the exclusive right to nominate to 'political parties' and this was accordingly the first strictly defined 'party-list' election.
b: Shows respectively those who 'took part in the voting' by casting a valid or invalid ballot, and the slightly larger number who 'took part in the election' by receiving a ballot paper but not necessary using it (which was the formal criterion for establishing the validity of an election until the law was amended in April 2007 and the turnout requirement was removed). In both cases, until 2007, slightly different numbers took part in the single-member constituency and party-list elections (in 2003, for instance, 55.3 per cent of the registered electorate cast ballots in the single-member constituencies, but 55.7 per cent in the party-list contest); the totals reported are for the party-list contest in every case. In 2007 voting was exclusively by party list, so there was no divergence.
c: *Vybory deputatov Gosudarstvennoi Dumy. 1995. Elektoral'naya statistika* (Moscow: Ves' mir, 1996), p. 52. The official election communiqué reported the number who had cast valid ballots in the party-list election, but not the number who had cast invalid ballots or 'taken part in the election' by receiving a ballot paper. The turnout figure that was made public was for the number who had 'taken part' in the vote on the draft constitution and is the basis of the figure reported above, which must accordingly be regarded as an approximation to the number who had 'taken part' in the Duma election. The official communiqué omitted the Communist Party from the list of the electoral associations or blocs that had won seats but was later corrected: see *Byulleten' Tsentral'noi izbiratel'noi komissii Rossiiskoi Federatsii*, no. 1(12), 1994, pp. 27–33, at p. 32, and *ibid.*, no. 10, 1994, p. 24 (correction).

Constitutional Court, which had ruled that there were grounds for Yeltsin's impeachment, was prevented from meeting and its chairman forced to resign. Sixteen parties or organisations were suspended on the grounds that they had been involved in the 'events' of 3–4 October; the Communist Party of the Russian Federation (CPRF), whose leader had urged both sides to 'refrain from provocations', was eventually legalised, but most of the others remained subject to a ban that deprived them of any opportunity to take part. In the end, thirty-five parties or alliances began a campaign to collect the 100,000 signatures that were required to put forward a list of candidates; twenty-one claimed to have

Table 2.2 Elections to the Russian State Duma, 1993–2003

	1993				1995				1999				2003			
	List %	List seats	SMC seats	Total seats	List %	List seats	SMC seats	Total seats	List %	List seats	SMC seats	Total seats	List %	List seats	SMC seats	Total seats
LDPR	22.9	59	5	64	11.2	50	1	51	6.0	17	0	17	11.5	36	0	36
RC	15.5	40	27	67	3.9	0	9	9	–	–	–	–	–	–	–	–
CPRF	12.4	32	16	48	22.3	99	58	157	24.3	67	46	113	12.6	40	12	52
WR	8.1	21	2	23	4.6	0	3	3	2.0	0	0	0	–	–	–	–
AP	8.0	21	11	33	3.8	0	20	20	–	–	–	–	3.6	0	2	2
Yabloko	7.9	20	6	26	6.9	31	14	45	5.9	16	4	20	4.3	0	4	4
PRUC	6.7	18	1	19	0.4	0	1	1	–	–	–	–	–	–	–	–
DPR	5.5	14	1	15	–	–	–	–	–	–	–	–	0.2	0	0	0
OHR	–	–	–	–	10.1	45	10	55	1.2	0	7	7	–	–	–	–
Unity	–	–	–	–	–	–	–	–	23.3	64	9	73	–	–	–	–
FAR	–	–	–	–	–	–	–	–	13.3	37	31	68	–	–	–	–
URF	–	–	–	–	–	–	–	–	8.5	24	5	29	4.0	0	3	3
UR	–	–	–	–	–	–	–	–	–	–	–	–	37.6	120	103	223
Rodina	–	–	–	–	–	–	–	–	–	–	–	–	9.0	29	8	37
Others	8.7	0	8	8	34.0	0	32	32	12.2	0	9	9	12.5	0	23	23
Indepts	–	–	141	141	–	–	77	77	–	–	105	105	–	–	67	67
Agst all	4.2	–	–	–	2.8	–	–	–	3.3	–	–	–	4.7	–	–	–

Source: Central Electoral Commission, incorporating subsequent corrections. Figures show share of party-list vote, party-list seats, single-member constituency (SMC) seats, and total seats won by parties that in any election exceeded the 5 per cent party-list threshold. In 1993, 1999 and 2003. there were no valid results in six, nine and three single-member constituencies respectively; these were filled in subsequent ballots. Party abbreviations are: LDPR: Liberal Democratic Party of Russia (competing, in 1999, as the Zhirinovsky Bloc); RC: Russia's Choice (in 1995, Russia's Democratic Choice); CPRF: Communist Party of the Russian Federation; WR: Women of Russia; AP: Agrarian Party; PRUC: Party of Russian Unity and Concord; DPR: Democratic Party of Russia; OHR: Our Home is Russia; FAR: Fatherland–All Russia; URF: Union of Right Forces; UR: United Russia.

collected the number that was needed, and of these, thirteen were included on the ballot paper after their documentation had been verified.[15]

Western governments had supported Yeltsin's moves against the parliament on the grounds that he had promised to submit himself for re-election in the summer of 1994 (an undertaking that was later withdrawn), and in the expectation that a new election would allow Russians to rid themselves of a 'communist parliament' that had represented an obstacle to reform. The result was a considerable shock, not just in Russia but also to the wider international community (see Table 2.2). Most successful of all were the independents, who won 141 of the 225 single-member constituencies; this gave them nearly a third of all the seats in the new assembly. The most successful of the parties was Russia's Choice, led by the former acting prime minister, Gaidar, and fully committed to the policies of the Yeltsin administration. But there was a sensational result in the party-list contest, which was won by the right-wing nationalist Liberal Democratic Party led by Vladimir Zhirinovsky with the Communists in third place; and there was some disappointment that barely half of the electorate had voted, continuing a steady decline from the heady days of the first competitive elections in the last years of Soviet rule. The result was a 'fiasco' for Russian pollsters, who had predicted a win for Russia's Choice with Liberal Democrats in the 'zone of defeat';[16] it was still more serious for the regime itself. Television coverage was suddenly suspended in the early morning because of 'technical difficulties', and US Vice-President Al Gore, who had been invited to welcome the birth of Russia's new democracy, had to leave in some embarrassment. Gaidar acknowledged that the reformers had suffered a 'bitter defeat'; the Moscow evening paper put it even more dramatically, warning that Russians had 'woken up in a new state' after the 'Communo-Fascists' success'.[17] The new Duma, however, was an extraordinary one, elected for just two years; its successor would define the shape of parliamentary politics for a normal four-year term, and perhaps for rather longer.

According to the Central Electoral Commission, 273 parties or other organisations had the right to nominate candidates in the more conventional Duma election that took place in December 1995, and there were fears that Russia might set a 'world record for the number of electoral associations per head of population'.[18] Nominations in the 225 single-member constituencies, under a newly adopted election law, required the written support of at least 1 per cent of the local electorate; 2,627 candidates were successfully nominated on this basis, 1,055 of whom had been put forward by electors rather than the political parties.[19] Parties or 'electoral associations' that wished to put forward candidates in the national competition for the other half of the Duma had this time to collect the signatures of at least 200,000 electors, not more than 7 per cent of whom could be drawn from any single republic or region; forty-three parties and movements eventually satisfied these requirements, with a total of 5,746 candidates on their lists (it was an exceptionally large ballot paper).[20] The election law made it illegal to offer inducements to potential supporters, and it was also illegal to contribute to the nomination of more than a single list of candidates. Press reports made clear that many of the parties, in fact, took little notice of these restrictions: a week before nominations closed, prospective signatories in the Belgorod region were being offered two kilograms of flour, and in Krasnodar a bottle of beer; the average price of a signature had already reached 2,000 roubles (about 50 cents at the prevailing rate of exchange), and it increased still further as the deadline approached.[21]

An anguished appeal by President Yeltsin on the eve of the poll warned that 'certain parties' wanted to 'return the country to the past'. Surely the experience of the last seventy years had allowed them to 'draw some conclusions'?[22] In the event, the Communist Party was the biggest single winner of the 1995 election, with by far the largest share of the party-list vote and of the single-member constituency seats; it was apparently surprised by the extent of its own success.[23] The Liberal Democratic Party of Russia came second, well down on the share it had obtained in 1993 but still ahead of the Kremlin-sponsored grouping Our Home Is Russia, which was headed by Prime Minister Viktor Chernomyrdin. As before, the largest share of seats in the single-member constituencies went to independents who had been nominated directly by electors, and they had the second-largest share of seats in the entire assembly. Yeltsin insisted that there was 'no reason' to regard the result as a tragedy,[24] and Prime Minister Chernomyrdin made clear there would be no change in government policy or personnel as a direct consequence of an election in which his own party had won barely 10 per cent of the party-list vote and an even smaller share in the single-member constituencies.[25] It was true that the Duma had little direct influence on the conduct and composition of the Russian government; but this was hardly an endorsement of the policies they had been pursuing, nor was it a propitious environment for a presidential contest that would have to take place, under the Constitution, within the following six months.

The election of 1995 had a further consequence, in that only four of the forty-three parties and movements on the ballot paper had won representation, with a combined vote that was just 50.5 per cent of the entire party-list total. This meant that nearly half of all those who voted had been denied the opportunity to be represented in the Duma by a party of their choice. It also meant that the four parties that had reached the threshold could share out all the seats among them, giving them almost twice as many party-list seats as their share of the vote would otherwise have warranted. Another new election law, approved in June 1999, introduced a number of changes that were designed to eliminate these deficiencies. One of them allowed parties that had secured less than the 5 per cent threshold to be added to the allocation of seats if the parties or movements that had been more successful had less than half the party-list vote among them; similarly, if a single party took more than 50 per cent of the entire party-list vote and none of the others reached 5 per cent, the party with the second-largest total would be included. Candidates and parties, for the first time, were allowed to register by paying a deposit as well as by collecting signatures; and all candidates were obliged to declare any court sentence they had not discharged, as well as their income and property, in an attempt to frustrate the increasing penetration of elected bodies by criminals who were attracted by the opportunities for money-making and the immunity that deputies enjoyed from prose-cution.[26] There was a modest sensation when two of the Liberal Democrats' top three candidates failed to declare some of their assets and the party was disqualified (Zhirinovsky himself had 'forgotten' his Volga and Mercedes), but a 'Zhirinovsky Bloc' was quickly established that was its functional equivalent.

The 1999 election took place against a background that might ordinarily have been expected to give an even greater advantage to parties and candidates that were opposed to Boris Yeltsin and the government he appointed. National income had been steadily declining since 1990; there had been a slight improvement in 1997, but it was followed by a spectacular crash in August 1998 when Russia defaulted on its international obligations and the rouble dropped sharply on foreign exchanges. Over the year, according to official estimates, more than two-thirds of the population suffered a fall in their living standards, and about a third were left below subsistence.[27] Russians, according to the surveys that were carried out at this time, were worried more than anything else by the rapid increase in prices they had been experiencing, but unemployment and unpaid wages were also widespread concerns.[28] Nor was there much confidence that the Russian government would be able to resolve these difficulties. It was a very unstable government, for a start: there had been five different prime ministers between March 1998 (when Viktor Chernomyrdin, the long-serving premier, had been dropped) and August 1999 (when Yeltsin's choice fell unexpectedly on Vladimir Putin, who had been appointed the year before to head state security). Putin, Yeltsin told Russians in a television broadcast, would be able to 'consolidate society' and 'ensure the continuation of reform'. The real reason for the appointment, suggested the outgoing premier, Sergei Stepashin, was rather different: to protect Yeltsin and his closest associates – widely known, in its Sicilian sense, as 'the Family' – from a criminal investigation that was beginning to threaten their positions, their privatised wealth and ultimately their liberty (see pp. 81–2).[29]

Altogether, thirty-five parties or electoral blocs sought to register their candidates for the December 1999 election; twenty-six of them were able to satisfy the various requirements of the election law, with more than 3,700 candidates on their lists. The other half of the Duma, as before, was composed of deputies elected by the 225 single-member constitu-encies, for which a further 2,300 independent or party-sponsored candidates had been nominated.[30] The final results took some time to emerge, but from early on election night it was apparent that pro-Kremlin parties – and particularly a newly formed grouping called Unity – had performed much better than in all previous elections. The winner, as in 1995, was the Communist Party, and with a larger share of the vote. But Unity, which defined itself by its unqualified support for Vladimir Putin, took almost as many votes and a substantial share of the single-member constituencies, and another new party that was more oppositional in character, Fatherland–All Russia, was forced into third place, with a smaller share of the vote than the polls had predicted. At least a large part of the explanation was the influence of the mass media, particularly state television, which gave far more coverage to the parties and candidates that were seen as Kremlin-friendly.[31]

Another was the launching of a vigorous military offensive in Chechnya in the late summer after explosions in Moscow and Dagestan, apparently precipitated by terrorists, had claimed almost three hundred lives (see pp. 83–5). The six parties that reached the threshold accounted, among them, for more than 80 per cent of the party-list vote, a result that gave few grounds for challenging the representative nature of the exercise. Still more important, it was a result that for the first time gave the Kremlin a substantial level of support in the Duma and in practice a working majority.[32]

The elections that followed, in 2003 and 2007, saw the Kremlin consolidate its growing ascendancy. Unity itself merged with Fatherland–All Russia in December 2001 to form a new party, United Russia, that was similarly defined by its unqualified support of what was now a Putin presidency, and it soon established a strong position at all levels of the electoral system. In the Duma election of December 2003, it took more than a third of the party-list vote and almost half the single-member constituencies, campaigning as 'Putin's party'; but by the time the new Duma held its first meeting, at the end of the same month, enough independents or deputies elected under the auspices of other parties had been persuaded to transfer their loyalties to bring the United Russia total up to 300[33] – a majority that was sufficient to allow it to vote through constitutional and not simply general legislation. Not only this, but its main competitor, the Communist Party, lost about half its previous support, although it was still able to finish second in the party-list ballot and third (after United Russia and independents) in the overall distribution of seats. One reason for the fall in the Communist vote was the appearance of a new party, Rodina (Motherland), formed earlier the same year with the support of the Kremlin and its 'political technologists'. Part of its vote appeared also to have gone to the Liberal Democrats, who took an unexpectedly large share of the party-list total, although they once again failed to win any of the single-member constituencies. The biggest shock of all was the failure of the 'democratic' parties, Yabloko and the Union of Right Forces (URF), to reach the threshold, and it was unclear that either of them had any serious future in Russian national politics.

Up to this point, Duma elections shared a number of important and distinctive characteristics. Among them were the following:

- nominations could be made not only by political parties but also by 'blocs' of parties (the four groupings that won party-list seats in December 2003, for instance, included three registered political parties as well as Rodina, which was a bloc of three individual parties). Earlier elections, up to 1999, had allowed a wider range of 'associations' to take part, provided their statutes made a corresponding provision; in the 1995 election the contenders had included bodies as varied as an Association of Advocates and a Union of Workers of the Housing and Communal Economy as well as a number of 'blocs' grouped around individual leaders.
- candidates in single-member constituencies could be nominated directly by electors as well as by parties, blocs or associations. In December 2003, for instance, more than a

third (38 per cent) of candidates in the single-member constituencies were nominated on this basis, and they accounted for 67 of the 222 single-member seats that were filled on polling day.[34]

Moreover,

- parties, blocs or associations did not necessarily sponsor candidates in all the single-member constituencies as well as in the national party-list contest: in 2003, in fact, none of them did so (the most active was the Communist Party, which put forward candidates in 175 of the 225 seats available).[35] Nor did parties that nominated candidates in single-member constituencies necessarily put forward a national party list (in 2003, six decided not do so).[36]

In addition to this,

- candidates did not have to be members of the parties or electoral blocs that put them forward, in either the single-member constituencies or the federal lists;
- they did not have to take their seat in the new Duma with the other deputies that had been sponsored by the same party or electoral association (in 2003, as we have seen, United Russia nominated 223 successful candidates but had 300 in its party fraction by the time the new Duma held its first meeting; deputies could also change their allegiance in the course of a new parliament or form entirely new fractions).

Still more important,

- the party leaders who headed their respective lists in the nationwide contest did not necessarily take their seats at all (in 2003, for instance, as many as thirty-seven candidates on the United Russia list, mostly ministers and regional chief executives, declined to do so; this included the first four names on the list, the 'locomotives' who had led the campaigning and helped to establish the party's electoral identity).[37]

All of this meant that there was a very loose association between the popular vote and the composition of each new Duma; the composition of the Duma, in any case, had no obvious implications for the Russian government, which was nominated or appointed by the president and surrendered its powers to a newly elected head of state rather than a newly elected parliament.

A series of important changes took place from 2005 onwards, the effect of which was to extend the Kremlin's control over the electoral process still further and convert the Duma into an entirely subordinate instrument of executive authority. They followed a hostage-taking crisis at Beslan in the northern Caucasus at the start of September 2004, which allowed Putin to insist that government structures would have to be 'fundamentally restructured for the purpose of bolstering the country's unity and preventing crises'; in particular, that there should be a 'single system of authority', with governors nominated by the president, and a fully proportional system of elections to the lower house.[38] A new election law was duly adopted in May 2005 that departed in fundamental respects from the election laws that had preceded it.[39] The previous law, adopted in 2002, had already provided that the threshold for party-list representation would be raised from 5 to 7 per cent. The 2005 law went much further, in particular by eliminating the single-member constituencies and providing for the election of all the Duma's 450 deputies through the national party-list ballot; this took the electoral process out of the hands of local elites who might have had their own agenda and placed it under the direct control of the Presidential Administration and the national party leaderships, who could be more easily manipulated. An amendment to the law in 2006 removed the opportunity that had previously existed to vote 'against all' the candidates and party lists (it had been an increasingly popular option and in 2003 even 'won' three of the single-seat constituencies[40]); another amendment in 2007 removed the minimum turnout requirement, which had previously been 25 per cent.[41] The effect of these and other changes was to provide the Kremlin with a set of mechanisms that might be expected to ensure that no future legislature could present even a potential challenge to its authority.

Given such circumstances, there was little doubt that the Kremlin's favoured party, United Russia, would take the largest share of the vote and of the seats available in the Duma election that was due to take place in December 2007. But it was still more important to the Kremlin that turnout should be at such a level that the outcome could not seriously be questioned, and that the outcome itself should be of a kind that ensured that its chosen candidate for the presidential election the following year – as it turned out, Dmitri Medvedev – would start as the overwhelming favourite. It was also important that United Russia should win at least two-thirds of the parliamentary seats so that it had the kind of majority that was necessary to adopt constitutional as well as ordinary legislation on the basis of its own deputies. The strategy it chose to do so was once again to associate itself as closely as possible with the Russian President, describing itself as 'Putin's party' and the election as a 'national referendum in support of Vladimir Putin'.[42] For his part, the Russian President agreed to head the United Russia list of candidates, although he was not (and did not become) a party member, adding that he might consider becoming prime minister if United Russia itself was successful in the election and if there was a president who was a 'decent, capable, effective and modern-thinking person with whom it would be possible to work'.[43] United Russia's ratings improved immediately, and the only questions that remained open on polling day were the size of its majority and the number of parties that would also be able to reach a new and more demanding threshold.

Under the terms of the 2005 election law, parties that were represented in the outgoing Duma had the right to nominate a list of candidates without further formalities. Other parties had either to collect the signatures of at least 200,000 electors or to pay an electoral deposit of 60 million roubles (about $2.5 million). If more than 5 per cent of the signatures were declared invalid, or if the number of signatures fell below the minimum once invalid signatures had been excluded, the party was refused registration (although any decision of this kind could be challenged in the Supreme Court). The Central Electoral Commission completed its deliberations at the end of October. Of the fourteen parties that had sought registration, three were already entitled to nominate a list of candidates as they were represented in the outgoing Duma: United Russia, the Communist Party and the Liberal Democrats. Of the remaining parties, the Union of Right Forces, Yabloko, Patriots of Russia and A Just Russia registered by paying the electoral deposit, and the others sought to do so by gathering the support of individual electors. Three were found to have included an excessive number of invalid signatures in their nomination papers (the Greens, the People's Union and the Peace and Unity Party) and were accordingly disqualified, but the Agrarian Party, Civic Force, the Democratic Party of Russia and the Party of Social Justice were able to satisfy the various requirements of the law and were duly included among the eleven parties that eventually appeared on the ballot paper, with a total of 4,684 candidates on their federal and regional lists.[44]

As the single candidate at the head of the United Russia list, Putin's own addresses set the tone of the entire campaign. A rally for his supporters at Luzhniki stadium in Moscow was especially notable. It was the first speech in which the Russian President called directly for a vote for United Russia, emphasising the need to continue the kind of policies that had so far ensured the country's 'stable development'. But the speech also contained a sharp attack on the integrity of his political opponents, accusing them of wanting to 'restore the oligarchic regime based on corruption and lies' that had 'brought Russia to mass poverty and rampant bribery', and of 'slinking around foreign embassies' in search of support instead of relying on their own people.[45] Here and in other speeches, including an address to the diplomatic corps shortly before the vote, Putin repeatedly insisted that Russia would not allow its political choices to be 'corrected from outside',[46] and official spokesmen made clear they had in mind the way in which (in their view) the electoral process in other post-Soviet republics had been used to set off a series of spurious 'coloured revolutions' that had actually been intended to convert them into Western dependencies.[47] Putin reiterated these messages in an eve-of-poll address, calling on Russian voters to reject those who wanted to return them to a time of 'humiliation, dependence and collapse' and warning against the 'dangerous illusion' that current policies would simply continue without the 'active support' of the President and the entire electorate.[48]

The exit polls that were reported by national television as soon as the last polling stations had closed were, in the event, very close to the final results, and both of them were close to the forecasts that had been made throughout the campaign by the main survey agencies.[49] So the results themselves were hardly a surprise (Table 2.3). From the official point of view, there was evident satisfaction that the outcome had been so similar to the final predictions, which suggested that falsification of whatever kind had been minimal, and that the turnout had been relatively high – higher, at least, than the 55.8 per cent that had been recorded four years earlier.[50] 'Thank God the election campaign is over', declared the Russian President as he appeared to cast his vote at the Academy of Sciences building on Leninskii prospekt in Moscow, accompanied by his wife and a retinue of newspaper and television journalists. 'We're so happy', an elderly women

Table 2.3 **The Russian Duma election, 2 December 2007**

Name of party	Votes cast	Share of vote (%)	Seats
United Russia	44,714,241	64.30	315
Communist Party of the Russian Federation	8,046,886	11.57	57
Liberal Democratic Party of Russia	5,660,823	8.14	40
A Just Russia: Rodina/Pensioners/Life	5,383,639	7.74	38
[7 per cent threshold]			
Agrarian Party of Russia	1,600,234	2.30	–
Yabloko	1,108,985	1.59	–
Civic Force	733,604	1.05	–
Union of Right Forces	669,444	0.96	–
Patriots of Russia	615,417	0.89	–
Party of Social Justice	154,083	0.22	–
Democratic Party of Russia	89,780	0.13	–
Invalid votes	759,929	1.09	–

Source: based on the Central Electoral Commission communiqué published in *Vestnik Tsentral'noi izbiratel'noi komissii Rossiiskoi Federatsii* no. 19(222), 2007, pp. 5–22. The registered electorate was 109,145,517, and 69,537,065 (63.71 per cent) cast a valid or invalid ballot.

told him as he waited for his wife to cast her ballot, 'We'll never forget what you've done for us.'[51] Commenting on the results the following day, Putin was understandably gratified by the confidence that had been placed in the list of candidates of which he was himself the head but also by the way in which the four parties that reached the threshold had among them secured 90 per cent of the vote, rather than the 70 per cent that had been represented in the outgoing Duma. This, he thought, would help to improve its public standing.[52]

Western governments did not generally question the legitimacy of the election, or call into doubt the overwhelmingly large majority that had been won by United Russia. But both foreign and domestic observers were increasingly insistent that elections of this kind were some distance short of 'free and fair' and raised questions about the nature of Russia's postcommunist politics. There was no doubt that Putin and the party he represented enjoyed a high level of public support, commented an observer mission that represented the parliamentary assemblies of the Council of Europe and the Organization for Security and Co-operation in Europe (OSCE). The manner in which they had achieved their victory, however, was deeply flawed. The merging of party and state was an 'abuse of political power and a clear violation of international commitments and standards'; the media had been heavily biased in favour of Putin and United Russia; the new election law made it extremely difficult for smaller parties to compete; and there had been widespread harassment of opposition candidates and movements.[53] There was no mission from the OSCE's Office for Democratic Institutions and Human Rights, as in previous elections, because it was unable to accept the terms on which it had been invited to operate.[54] Local monitors nonetheless reported a series of violations of various kinds,[55] and a member of the Central Electoral Commission itself recorded a dissenting opinion when the final results were declared, insisting that the entire exercise had been a 'violation of the principle of free elections' with pro-Kremlin parties in a 'privileged position' in terms of media coverage and the resources of the state itself employed to ensure a high level of turnout.[56]

Press reports gave details of some of the ways in which the state itself had been directly involved in the campaign, advantaging United Russia and disadvantaging its various opponents. In Nizhnii Novgorod, for instance, foremen went round the workforce at the city's massive vehicle factory telling them to vote for Putin's party, and to phone in after they had left the polling station. 'Names would be taken, defiance punished.' Some, leaving nothing to chance, were told to obtain absentee certificates and fill them out in front of their immediate superiors. The factory director, a senior United Russia official, was able to report that nearly 80 per cent of the workforce had voted; indeed, one of the factory workers became a deputy himself. Elsewhere in the city, teachers handed out leaflets promoting 'Putin's Plan' and told children to lobby their parents. A number were 'threatened with bad grades if they failed to attend "children's referendums"'; at other schools, parents were simply 'ordered to attend mandatory meetings with representatives of United Russia'. At university level, students were told that unless they voted for the ruling party they would be evicted from their dormitories. Evidently very concerned, they went out and 'voted "like a line of soldiers"'. By contrast, canvassers for the Union of Right Forces 'received hundreds of calls at all hours, warning them to stop working for their candidates. Otherwise [they] would be hurt'; and leaflets were distributed suggesting that the party supported gay rights and employed canvassers with AIDS (neither was true).[57]

There were similar difficulties when the openly oppositional 'Other Russia' coalition sought to communicate its views or organise in public. The former world chess champion Gary Kasparov, who was one of its leaders, was among the dozens who were arrested by riot police when he took part in an anti-Kremlin protest rally in Moscow on 24 November, his speech interrupted by a 'screeching noise from loudspeakers on top of a nearby building';[58] the chess player himself was sentenced to five days in prison for leading the protest and resisting arrest.[59] In St Petersburg the following day, 'scores of demonstrators were detained and some beaten … as riot police broke up a protest over the Kremlin's lurch towards authoritarianism'; nearly 200 were arrested, among them the Union of Right Forces leader Boris Nemtsov.[60] Opposition leaders were repeatedly harassed by pro-Kremlin youth in the run-up to the poll – stalked by activists, their news conferences disrupted and recordings of 'loud, maniacal laughter' played at their public meetings. One pro-Kremlin activist handcuffed himself three times to Kasparov's car; another tried to put a butterfly net over Nemtsov's head with a sign saying 'political insect'; others still pelted him with condoms.[61] Kasparov spoiled his ballot paper on polling day and urged supporters to do likewise; the election, he complained, if that was what it could be called, had been the 'most unfair and dirtiest in the whole history of modern Russia'.[62] But it had, at least, delivered a decisive verdict.

The contemporary party spectrum

The Russian party spectrum in the early years of the new century hardly conformed to a 'classic' left–right formation. The parties themselves avoided such terms, and barely a quarter of the electorate were able to locate themselves at any point on this kind of scale, a level much lower than in the established democracies.[63] Several other classifications have been suggested: parties, for instance, might be 'bureaucratic' or 'charismatic' (following Max Weber); alternatively, they could be 'parties of power' or 'parties of the elite'.[64] Another, more elaborate classification distinguished between 'parties of the leader' (such as the Liberal Democrats, who have been all but indistinguishable from their long-standing chairman, Vladimir Zhirinovsky, or Yabloko, headed until 2008 by co-founder Grigorii Yavlinsky); 'parties of values' (such as the Communist Party, or the Union of Right Forces); and 'parties of power', such as United Russia, which has been virtually defined by its support of the president, or before it the pro-Kremlin party Our Home is Russia.[65] The 'party of power' was a particularly helpful concept; it denoted a party that had been organised by the authorities themselves in their own support, similar in many ways to the 'parties of the state' that existed in some of the countries of Latin America.[66] But as long as they could do so, in the single-member constituencies from 1993 up to 2003 (with the exception of United Russia in that single year), ordinary Russians were more likely to support independents than any of the party-sponsored lists of candidates.

Political parties are regulated by a law of 2001, with subsequent modifications.[67] In order to register in the first place, under the amended version of the law that was approved in December 2004, a party must have at least 50,000 members with sections in at least half of Russia's republics and regions, each of which must have at least 500 members. A political party is defined in the law as a 'public association established to facilitate the participation of citizens of the Russian Federation in the political life of society by means of the formation and expression of their political will, their participation in public and social actions, in elections and referendums, and also in order to represent the interests of citizens in organs of state power and local self-government'. As in many other countries, parties are not allowed to engage in 'extremist activity', nor may they be formed on an occupational, racial, national or religious basis, or consist of members of a single profession. Parties are registered by the state on presentation of the appropriate documentation, including a statute and a programme. Members must be Russian citizens who are at least 18 years old, and they are allowed to belong to no more than a single party. Parties, under the law, have the right to take part in elections and referendums, hold meetings and otherwise propagate their views. Parties, in fact, are the only bodies that are allowed to put forward their own candidates at elections, and (following the introduction of the new election law in 2005) they must do so individually, rather than in a bloc with another party or organisation. If they make no nominations over a five-year period to elected bodies at any level, or to the presidency, they are dissolved on the advice of the Supreme Court.

The 2001 law also defines the sources from which a party may draw its financial support, which include membership dues, donations and income from commercial and other activities.[68] Donations may not be accepted from foreign states, companies or citizens, or from Russian companies with more than 30 per cent of foreign ownership, or from international organisations or government bodies, military or police units, charities or religious organisations; in addition, the value of donations from individuals and companies may not exceed a specified amount. As originally formulated, the total value of donations in a single year from a single person could not exceed 10,000 roubles, or from a single company 100,000, or from all sources 10 million minimum salaries (in the values that prevailed at the time, about $28.6 million). These sums were adjusted by subsequent legislation, and from January 2009 the maximum annual contribution from a single individual was 4.33 million roubles (about $185,000), from a single company 43.3 million roubles (about $1.85 million), or from all sources 4.33 billion roubles (about $185 million).[69] The new law, at the same time, introduced provisions for the state support of political parties, initially on a modest scale. The total sum available was to be not less than .005 of a minimum salary for every member of the registered electorate at a Duma or presidential election (this was increased to 5 roubles in 2005 and then to 20 roubles ($0.87) in 2008),[70] and individual parties were to receive the same level of support for each of the votes they received at either of these elections, provided they obtained at least 3 per cent of the total ballot. Payments are annual, in the case of Duma elections, or once only, in the case of presidential elections; the parties, in their turn, are required to report annually on their income and expenditure to the Central Electoral Commission, which displays their accounts on its website.[71]

As of the start of 2008, fifteen parties had completed all the necessary formalities and were on the register of the Central Electoral Commission (see Table 2.4); most, but not all, had taken part in the Duma election at the end of the previous year. The entire system was dominated by the 'party of power', *United Russia*, the 'political force [he had] relied on throughout these four years' and which had 'consistently supported [him]', as President Putin told interviewers in November 2003.[72] Putin was not a member of this or any other party, but he lost no opportunity to advertise his personal commitment to United Russia, indeed his 'most direct contribution' to its establishment;[73] the party in turn defined itself by its support of the Russian President and of the policies with which he was associated. United Russia had officially been founded in 2001, but its origins lay in the 'Unity' party that had been formed with Kremlin support a few months before the Duma election of December 1999 and which had come a close second to the Communists, campaigning as the 'party of Putin'. After the election it began to move towards the third-placed party,

Table 2.4 Russia's political parties, 2007–2010

Name of party	Leader	Members	2007 PL vote (%)
Communist			
Communist Party	Gennadii Zyuganov	184,181	11.57
Agrarian Party[a]	Vladimir Plotnikov	164,089	2.30
Party of Peace and Unity	Sazhi Umalatova	71,232	–
Centrist			
United Russia	Boris Gryzlov	1,256,578	64.30
Democratic Party	Andrei Bogdanov	82,183	0.13
Party of Social Justice	Aleksei Podberezkin	60,446	0.22
Party of Russian Renewal	Gennadii Seleznev	53,279	–
A Just Russia	Sergei Mironov	244,286	7.74
Greens	Anatolii Panfilov	60,989	–
Liberal-democratic			
Union of Right Forces[b]	Nikita Belykh[b]	57,410	0.96
Yabloko	Sergei Mitrokhin[c]	60,440	1.59
Civic Force[b]	Mikhail Barshchevsky	59,842	1.05
National-patriotic			
Liberal Democrats	Vladimir Zhirinovsky	146,235	8.14
Patriots of Russia	Gennadii Semigin	81,414	0.89
People's Union	Sergei Baburin	70,842	–

Source: derived from the official list of registered parties displayed on the CEC website (www.cikrf.ru/politparty, accessed 24 June 2008), which also lists the parties' own websites. Party membership figures are those provided by the Federal Registration Service as reported in 'Politicheskie partii i izbiratel'noe zakonodatel'stvo Rossiiskoi Federatsii', special issue of the *Zhurnal o vyborakh*, 2007, various pages. The classification is based on the official election handbook *Vybory deputatov Gosudarstvennoi Dumy Federal'nogo Sobraniya Rossiiskoi Federatsii. 2003. Elektoral'naya statistika* (Moscow: Ves' mir, 2004), p. 235.

a: The Agrarian Party, originally a rural ally of the Communists, announced its intention to merge with United Russia in September 2008; the merger was formalised at United Russia's congress later in the year (*Izvestiya*, 21 November 2008, p. 2).

b: The Union of Right Forces (URF) and Civic Force, together with the still smaller Democratic Party, merged in November 2008 into a new party, 'Right Cause', which was formally registered in early 2009 with a claimed 56,000 members (*Izvestiya*, 19 February 2009, p. 2); Belykh stood down as URF party leader in September 2008 and the following December was elected governor of Kirov region.

c: Until the party's 15th Congress in June 2008, Grigorii Yavlinsky.

Fatherland–All Russia, which up to this point had been mildly oppositional, and in December 2001 the two merged their identities into a new 'All-Russian Party of Unity and Fatherland', known more simply as United Russia (this became the party's official name at its 4th Congress in December 2003).[74] Putin, as we have seen, headed its list of candidates at the 2007 Duma election, and in April 2008 he took on the symbolic position of chairman of the party while formally remaining outside its ranks.[75] The daily conduct of party business was in the hands of Boris Gryzlov, who was chair of the party's Supreme Council and of its Duma fraction.

It was less clear what the new party stood for, other than support for the President and whatever policies he put forward. The party made an initial attempt to define its position with the adoption of a programmatic document, 'The Path of National Success', at its second congress in March 2003, prepared with the assistance of the Presidential Administration.[76] The new programme called for a 'nationwide recovery' based on an 'ideology of success' and urged the 'responsible political forces of the country' to unite around such purposes, leading to a 'new level of internal unity' across the entire society. The programme envisaged a mixed economy that combined state regulation and market freedoms, with the benefits of further growth allocated for the most part to the less fortunate. The party itself rejected the 'utopias' of left and right in favour of a 'political centrism' that would similarly unite all sections of the society and which was expressed in the policies of President Putin, whose reforms were 'vital for Russia'.[77] Party leader Boris Gryzlov called in similar terms for a 'political centrism' that focused on the 'real problems' society currently confronted, and disparaged the 'abstract schemes cut off from life' that were being offered by their political opponents.[78] The party's ideology was simply 'common sense', Gryzlov explained later in the year, and its only purpose was to 'do what [wa]s good for the majority of our citizens'.[79] The same concerns were apparent in the party's 2003 election manifesto, which committed it to whatever policies would improve the living standards of ordinary people, and to the policies of the Russian President in particular.[80]

The party manifesto at the following election, in December 2007, was simply called 'Putin's Plan: A Worthy Future for a Great Country', although interviewers found that a majority of those they spoke to were unable to say what the plan actually was[81] and Putin himself insisted that it was really the creation of a 'large collective', which made it more of a 'plan of Russian society'.[82] Russia, the manifesto claimed, had been following a strategy that ensured it would once again become one of the 'world centres of political and economic influence, cultural and moral attraction', a strategy that guaranteed a 'new quality of life for all the country's citizens'. This was 'Putin's Plan', and over the following four years it would mean the 'further development of Russia as a unique civilisation', a more competitive economy, and full implementation of the 'national projects' in health, education, housing and agriculture that Putin had set out in a speech to the Russian government in September 2005 (see pp. 147–8). There would also be 'significant increases' in pay and pensions, support for the institutions of civil society, and a further strengthening of sovereignty and defensive capacity so that Russia once again took a 'worthy place in a multipolar world'. Putin himself was described as Russia's 'national leader', and the party as his 'political support'.[83] In the end, United Russia was something of a demonstration of the truth of one of Chernomyrdin's celebrated aphorisms, that 'whatever party we establish, all the same we end up with the CPSU' – a party dominated by officials, with a more or less nominal membership, and no clear ideology other than support for the regime itself.

Of the other parties, *A Just Russia* was also something of a Kremlin creation. It had been formally established in early 2007 on the basis of the Party of Life led by Sergei Mironov, speaker of the Federation Council and a close Putin associate, together with the Pensioners' Party and Rodina (a left-patriotic party that had been formed with Kremlin support as a means of taking votes away from the Communists in the 2003 election).[84] The new party, Mironov promised, would offer voters a 'third version of socialism appropriate to our country', one that was neither Soviet nor West European;[85] his intention, it appeared, was to establish a moderately left-wing grouping that would balance United Russia as a second 'party of power', or even a second 'Putin party' (the Kremlin, in the end, decided it had no need of such arrangements, which left it in some difficulty).[86] A socialist perspective for Russia, explained the party's manifesto for the December 2007 election, involved a socially oriented economy, a strong state that was under democratic control and a dynamically developing society. It also meant policies that reflected the interests of the majority of the population, an equitable distribution of incomes, protection from poverty and official arbitrariness, and accessible health and educational systems. Taxation should be more progressive, with special duties on luxuries, and there should be higher salaries for all who worked in the state sector. Not surprisingly, given the party's origins, there was a strong emphasis on pensions, which should represent at least 65 per cent of previous rates of pay; there was no reference at all to the institutions of government themselves, or to defence and foreign affairs.[87]

On the 'left' of the political spectrum was the *Communist Party of the Russian Federation*, which was the successor to the party originally formed in 1898 that had taken power in the October revolution and then dominated Soviet public life until the end of the 1980s. Formally speaking, the CPRF had been founded in 1990 as the Russian section of the Communist Party of the Soviet Union, and then re-established in early 1993 after the ban on its activity imposed in late 1991 had been pronounced unconstitutional.[88] The newly re-established party inherited a great deal from its Soviet predecessor, including a mass membership, a well-established press and a functioning national organisation. It also inherited a leadership in the person of Gennadii Zyuganov, a party official from the late Soviet period whose booming voice and homely features ensured his nationwide recognition. Originally a rural schoolteacher, Zyuganov completed his military service in the mid-1960s and had then begun work as a Komsomol official, moving to the ideological department of the Central Committee itself in the late 1980s. Zyuganov, explained biographers, was 'no monster' and had problems of his own reconciling the various elements within his increasingly fractious party, leaning himself towards the 'national-patriotic' end of the spectrum.[89] Zyuganov was the party's standard-bearer in the 1996 presidential election, when he took Boris Yeltsin to a second round, but was less successful in 2000 (when Putin won on the first round) and did not compete in 2004; he stood again in the 2008 presidential election, winning a distant but respectable second place.

The party programme, as reformulated in 1995 and again in 2008, reflected nationalist as well as socialist concerns. Russia, it warned, stood at an 'historic crossroads'. The current ruling group was making every effort to return to a 'barbaric and primitive capitalism', a path of 'political reaction and social regression' that would lead to 'national catastrophe'. But resistance was steadily increasing, based on the 'forces of social and national liberation'. The party saw its own purpose as the merging of these two elements into a 'single mass movement of resistance', giving it a 'more conscious and focused character'. This implied a series of more specific objectives, including 'people's power', based on the elected soviets and other forms of democratic self-management; social justice, including guaranteed employment, free education and healthcare; equality, based on the elimination of exploitation and the primacy of public forms of ownership; patriotism and the friendship of nations; a renewed form of socialism, set out in a future constitution; and communism as the 'historic destiny of mankind'. The larger conflict between social systems, in the party's view, had not in the least been resolved by the changes that had taken place at the end of the 1980s. Capitalism was still a system based on the exploitation of working people and of natural resources of all kinds, and it had led to a divided world that was ruled by a small number of rich countries in their own interests. The party stood for a rather different pattern of global development, one in which more emphasis was placed on the stable and equitable development of all of the members of the international community on the basis of their own circumstances and experience.[90]

Communists, in spite of these ambitious objectives, were losing ground in the early years of the new century. Part of the problem was an ageing and dwindling membership;[91] another part of the problem was their ambiguous attitude towards Vladimir Putin (and his successor) – they supported the Russian President insofar as he was a 'patriot' who defended Russia's interests against the Western powers, but could hardly approve of his moves towards the private ownership of land and the reduction or elimination of state subsidies for housing, transport and other public services. A more immediate problem was fragmentation, as leading members found themselves tempted to retain their influential positions on Duma committees even if the party instructed them to withdraw, or as entire parties were created by the Kremlin to compete for a share of the vote that might otherwise have gone to their most serious opponents, such as Rodina in 2003 or A Just Russia in 2007. The Kremlin had enormous resources to commit to such purposes, including its ability to offer well-paid public employment as well as access to state television, and it drew on the advice of its own pollsters and 'political technologists' in elaborating an appropriate strategy. The Kremlin was able to marginalise the CPRF in other ways as well: in particular, its increasing control over local as well as national elections reduced the party's presence in legislative bodies all over the country and deprived it of the regional governorships that had provided many of its earlier opportunities for attracting income and dispensing patronage.

The CPRF's 2007 election manifesto, 'Power for the Working People!', took a gloomy view of the position in which Russia now found itself. But it insisted that a 'breakthrough to the future [was] possible', and that other countries – including 'socialist China', India,

Brazil, 'fraternal Belarus', Cuba and Vietnam, Venezuela and Bolivia – had shown the way. The crucial element was an independent politics, and a 'refusal to live under the dictate of the imperialists'. The party's 'seven steps to a worthy future' included the nationalisation of natural resources and strategic industries, increases in pay and pensions, and state-led modernisation of industry, agriculture and transport. There would be moves towards 'people's power', including more honest elections and reductions in the state bureaucracy, and all officials and deputies would be required to make annual declarations of their income and property; in due course, a new constitution would be put to a popular vote that would restore power to the soviets of people's deputies. There would be a new emphasis on domestic security, including restoration of the death penalty for especially serious crimes, and a return to free, high-quality education and healthcare. And in foreign affairs, a new priority would be given to the improvement of relations with the other former Soviet republics, including Ukraine, Belarus 'and possibly Kazakhstan'.[92] As well as Zyuganov, the party's list of candidates was headed by Nobel laureate Zhores Alferov and its contender in the 2004 presidential election, deputy and former state farm director Nikolai Kharitonov.

Two small parties occupied the 'liberal democratic' position on the party spectrum, Yabloko and the Union of Right Forces. *Yabloko* (Apple), originally formed as an electoral bloc in late 1993, was one of the oldest of the new Russian parties, although its support dwindled steadily from election to election; it fell below the party-list threshold in 2003 and 2007, and put forward no candidate at all in the 2004 and 2008 presidential elections.[93] The party was led from the outset until the summer of 2008 by Grigorii Yavlinsky, an academic economist who had served briefly in government at the end of the Soviet period, and it incorporated the first letter of his surname as well as of the other liberal politicians who had taken part in its establishment, Yuri Boldyrev and Vladimir Lukin. Yabloko, according to the updated version of the party's 'Democratic Manifesto' that was approved at its congress in June 2006, was committed to a 'law-based social state, the formation of an effective market economy and the establishment of a civil society'. The party was equally opposed to the 'authoritarian-bureaucratic regime' that was being established under the Putin leadership, and to the misconceived reforms of the 1990s that had given rise to it. Only stable democracy, in the party's view, would allow the country to develop its full potential, more specifically a 'European path of development' that was itself an expression of Russia's own history, culture and geographical location. This meant that, in the first instance, Russia should bring its legislation into line with the norms of the Council of Europe; in the long run it meant full membership of the European Union itself, as the 'only way' in which they could 'both survive the global challenges of the 21st century'.[94]

Yabloko's manifesto for the 2007 Duma election reflected the same concerns but laid particular emphasis on the need for political reform, including 'genuinely free elections', a 'real separation of powers' and 'independent courts'. Governors should once again be directly elected, and there should be no more 'political censorship' in the mass media. In the economy, priority should be given to the development of small and medium business, and to the wider diffusion of ownership; there should be a one-off tax on the superprofits that had arisen from the privatisation of the 1990s, workers' rights in their places of employment should be strengthened, income inequalities should be reduced, and there should be a 'scrupulous and independent audit of all national monopolies, beginning with [the state gas company] Gazprom'. Apart from this there should be better support for health and education, which must remain 'completely free', and Yabloko was the only one of the major parties to attach a clear priority to the protection of the environment: it called for penalties to be introduced on the basis of the principle that 'the polluter pays', and a ministry of the environment should be re-established that would have the right to close down particularly noxious enterprises.[95] The list of candidates was headed, as usual, by party leader Yavlinsky, but its poor showing – with the lowest share of the vote it had ever recorded – was assumed to be one of the reasons for his decision to stand down at the party congress that took place in the summer of 2008 in favour of the head of its Moscow organisation, the sociologist and former Duma deputy Sergei Mitrokhin.[96]

Yabloko's counterpart on the 'democratic' wing of the political spectrum was the *Union of Right Forces*, formed in August 1999 shortly before the Duma election of that year, and more directly oriented towards younger voters and those who had done well out of the reforms of the 1990s than towards those who remained in the state sector or belonged to the traditional intelligentsia. Its original leaders were the former Prime Minister Sergei Kirienko, businesswoman Irina Khakamada and former Deputy Prime Minister Boris Nemtsov, who became party leader and chair of its Duma fraction in May 2000 after Kirienko had resigned to take up the position of presidential representative in the Volga federal district. The party programme, as approved in December 2001, was broadly 'conservative' as compared with Yabloko's more 'social democratic' orientation, and this was one of the reasons for the failure of the two parties to reach more than tactical and short-term accommodations. Under the terms of its programme, the URF was committed to 'liberal values', including freedom of speech and association, the separation of powers, decentralisation, the rule of law, democratic control of society over the state, equality of rights and opportunities for all citizens, and tolerance of diversity. Only a free market economy, in the party's view, would be able to generate an increase in the national wealth and ensure it was properly allocated; there was less emphasis than in the case of Yabloko on redistribution, and rather more on the 'sacred and inviolable' rights of private property.[97] The URF had won a substantial share of the vote, with what appeared to be the Kremlin's tacit support, in the December 1999 election,[98] but it fell below the party-list threshold in December 2003 and its three successful candidates in the single-member constituencies joined the United Russia fraction in the new Duma.

The URF did so badly at the December 2003 election, indeed, that Nemtsov felt obliged to resign as party leader, and although Khakamada contested the 2004 presidential election, she did so without the party's official support and later withdrew entirely to establish an independent party of her own (and then left politics entirely).[99] A new leader was finally elected in May 2005: Nikita Belykh, a businessman from Perm just short of his fortieth birthday who had up to this point been the region's deputy governor. The URF, he promised, would 'never be the party of the Kremlin, it [would] never be the party of specific interest groups, it [would] never be the party of a specific individual'.[100] The party's manifesto for the 2007 Duma election called for a 'liberal breakthrough' in various directions: strengthening the rights of private property, protecting small and medium business, and restoring a genuine federalism ('Russia isn't just Moscow'). It added a series of other commitments: to the support of private farmers and pensioners and to the rights of employees at their place of work, the formation of a professional army, a 'free press' and political reforms including restoration of the direct election of governors. Unlike others, the URF saw the demise of the USSR as a 'positive development', and it defended the reforms of the 1990s. But it was very critical of the idea of a 'special path' – Russia, whatever its particularities, should have 'the same political and economic institutions and the same system of social security as in the West', and it should at all costs avoid an isolation that would lead inevitably to the 'third world'.[101] In the event its vote fell even further, and at the end of 2008 it agreed to merge with two other parties, Civic Force and the Democratic Party, in a pro-business grouping that would be known as 'Right Cause' and which was expected to play the role of a 'constructive opposition' in future parliaments (Belykh, who favoured a more uncompromising position, had already stood down).[102]

The oldest of the new parties was the *Liberal Democratic Party of Russia* (LDPR), led by its outspoken chairman, Vladimir Zhirinovsky. The party's founding congress was in March 1990, shortly after the existence of multiparty politics had been formally legalised, and it appeared to owe something to the CPSU's wish to set up a client opposition of its own before a more authentic alternative had been able to establish itself.[103] Despite its name, the party was usually seen as right-wing nationalist or even fascist, and it had openly supported the attempted coup of 1991; it also opposed the break-up of the USSR at the end of the year. The LDPR was the surprise winner of the party-list competition in 1993 and took party-list seats again in 1995, 1999, 2003 and 2007 – the only party, apart from the Communists, to do so, although it was less successful in the single-member constituencies. The Liberal Democrats were very closely identified with their leader, a madcap but compelling media performer who was sometimes compared with Charlie Chaplin's Hitler in *The Great Dictator* and had stood with some success in all but one of the Russian presidential elections.[104] Zhirinovsky was noted for his extravagant but eye-catching proposals: such as re-establishing the Russian state within its nineteenth-century boundaries, which would have meant incorporating Finland, Poland and Alaska;[105] or dealing with crime by allowing the police to shoot gang leaders 'on the spot';[106] or bringing the Lithuanians into line by threatening to blow radioactive dust at them across the border.[107] In spite of the party's oppositional rhetoric it was broadly pro-government in its voting behaviour in the Duma, and the Kremlin appeared to offer the party its covert support so as to ensure that it regularly reached the party-list threshold.

The LDPR programme, in the revised version that was approved at its 17th congress in December 2005, aimed squarely at the 'revival of Russia as a great power'. As a nationalist party, the LDPR supported the 'great Russian people, the Orthodox faith, the restoration of the country's territory [and] the defence of fellow nationals abroad'. It called for the restoration of a unitary Russian state and for a simplification of the federal system into a smaller number of 'territories', each of which would be headed by an appointed governor. Russians themselves should be recognised as the country's 'consolidating people', with a unique culture that should be specially protected. The LDPR favoured a 'multi-level economy' with equal rights for different forms of property, led by a state that should itself take responsibility for longer-term and more capital-intensive programmes. It would seek to restore a level of social security that was no less than had been achieved in the Soviet period, based on traditional Russian values of community and social justice. Healthcare and a 'thoroughly reformed' system of education should be available to all, without charge. And there should be a professional army and a unified security service with a much larger budget. In foreign affairs the Liberal Democrats were strongly opposed to the domination of 'Western Christian civilisation', proposing instead a 'Slavic solidarity'; they opposed the United States' 'hegemony', the expansion of NATO to the east and the Western-led occupation of Iraq, and called instead for a closer association among the former Soviet republics and a 'strategic union' with China.[108]

The LDPR manifesto for the 2007 Duma election represented the party as Russia's 'oldest and most experienced', and as the only one that offered 'constructive opposition' to government policies. So far, it claimed, only officials and oligarchs had gained from sixteen years of economic reform. The LDPR called for a 'new, progressive scenario' that would ensure the benefits of economic growth went instead to the society as a whole. Oil and gas resources would be taken back from the oligarchs and used to raise the living standards of ordinary people. There would be a progressive income tax, with the rich paying more. The revenue this generated would be invested in pensions and housing, and all salaries would be 'significantly increased'. Extra help would be given to small businesses, to the armed forces and to the health service. There would be a seven-hour working day, with an additional day off on Wednesdays. The federation itself would be simplified, with just fifty 'territories' instead of more than eighty republics and regions. The president would be elected by parliament itself, for a period of five years; and there would be an 'active multivector foreign policy', with its primary emphasis on Russia's southern neighbours while also seeking to reunite the former Soviet republics within a new 'Russian Empire'.[109] The party's list of candidates included Zhirinovsky and his son and also the controversial figure of Andrei Lugovoi, who was wanted for questioning in the United Kingdom in connection with the murder of former KGB agent Alexander Litvinenko (see p. 279); it finished third, behind United Russia and the Communists but ahead of A Just Russia and above the all-important 7 per cent threshold.

Political parties and the Russian public

So far, there has been little evidence that Russia's parties have engaged the loyalties of its long-suffering electorate; some, indeed, have called it a 'non-party' political system.[110] In part, this simply reflected the fact that there had been a high level of turnover in the parties themselves. In all, more than eighty parties or blocs took part in at least one of the Duma elections between 1993 and 2007, but only three (the Communists, Liberal Democrats and Yabloko) contested all five, only two (the Communists and Liberal Democrats) won list seats in all of them, and only the Communist Party won single-member (until they were abolished in 2005) as well as list seats in all of them. To put this another way, all the parties or movements that contested the 1993 party-list election, taken together, won no more than 24 per cent of the list vote in 2007 (only five of the original thirteen appeared on the ballot paper). Conversely, four of the eleven parties on the ballot paper in December 2007 had never previously contested a parliamentary election, including one of the four (A Just Russia) that reached the electoral threshold. It was all but impossible to construct formal measures of 'volatility' in such circumstances;[111] nor was it clear that the concept had a great deal of meaning, as it assumed a shift in the 'demand' for parties on the part of voters when what had taken place was a change in the 'supply' of parties made available by the regime itself that had obvious consequences for the ability of voters to express whatever preferences they might otherwise have had.[112]

Not only were they in constant flux, Russia's parties had also to operate in a context of public suspicion or even hostility. One of the most direct measures of the way in which political parties were perceived was the regular question about 'trust' in civic institutions that has been asked by the national opinion research centre since the early 1990s (see Table 2.5). Consistently, the church and the armed forces enjoyed the highest levels of public confidence, although neither could count on the support of a majority of the society and what support they had earlier enjoyed was tending to diminish. The presidency, after a bad patch in the later Yeltsin years, exceeded them both in the early years of the new century and continued to do so under Putin's successor Dmitri Medvedev.[113] Local and regional government was normally more widely respected than central government, and the media more than the agencies of law enforcement, which were more often associated with corruption and maltreatment than with the administration of justice.[114] Levels of trust in civic institutions had admittedly been falling all over the world, not just in Russia. But Russian levels were exceptionally low, perhaps even 'the lowest in the world', in the early years of the new century;[115] and political parties, in turn, were consistently at the bottom of this list of exceptionally low ratings, below the parliament in which they were represented and below all the institutions of executive authority.[116]

Membership was another way in which ordinary Russians could relate to their political parties. But although the totals had been increasing, they were difficult to take at face

Table 2.5 **Trust in civic institutions, 1998–2010**

	1998	2000	2002	2004	2006	2008	2010
President	2	45	61	62	56	71	63
Church	32	39	40	41	38	40	54
Army	28	35	28	28	20	37	36
Security organs	18	21	23	20	23	32	29
Government	4	20	24	12	14	30	35
Media	24	26	23	26	22	28	29
Regional government	15	20	19	19	19	28	18
Local government	18	19	21	18	16	28	15
Parliament	7	10	11	9	11	23	21
Courts	12	12	16	13	14	15	16
Police	–	14	12	11	11	15	14
Trade unions	11	11	13	10	9	12	14
Political parties	4	7	7	5	4	10	10

Source: derived from All-Russian Public Opinion Research Centre (VTsIOM) and (from 2004) Levada Centre data as reported in *Monitoring obshchestvennogo mneniya*, various issues.
Note: 'Courts' in 1998 refers to law enforcement generally (courts, police and procuracy); references to 'parliament' from 2002 onwards are to the State Duma specifically. Figures show rounded percentages who 'completely trusted' a given institution.

value and rather low in comparative terms.[117] According to the survey evidence, just under 2 per cent of Russians were members of a political party in 2010; this was slightly more than those who were engaged in charity work (just over 1 per cent) but less than the numbers that were engaged in a residential association or a literary society, and well below the proportion that were members of a sports club (8 per cent) or a trade union (9 per cent).[118] On top of this, there were considerable variations over time in their individual membership. The Communist Party, in the early years of the new century, was usually considered the country's largest, with about half a million members, but by the time its records had been scrutinised at the start of 2006, it was down to 184,000.[119] United Russia, conversely, claimed a membership of about 300,000 at the start of 2003, but by the end of 2008 it had reached more than 2 million and party leaders were beginning to contemplate a deliberate reduction so as to ensure it was more ideologically coherent.[120] A rapid increase in membership of this kind was unlikely to have been entirely spontaneous, and press reports made clear that many had been recruited in a somewhat 'Soviet' fashion, on the basis of quotas handed down from above by government officials. In a shopping complex in the Moscow region, for instance, each retail unit had been told it would have to provide two members;[121] in a Tula arms factory, compulsory enrolments began to be carried out after the director had met the presidential envoy;[122] in a town in the Pskov region, local employees were being fired or had their wages withheld until they had completed the necessary formalities.[123]

Some of these matters were clarified in late 2006 when the Federal Registration Service completed an examination of the records of all the parties that sought official status, in order to bring the revised law on political parties into full effect. In the end, just nineteen of the thirty-five that had existed at the beginning of the year satisfied the Service; the others were obliged to dissolve or become public associations. The number fell further when three of the newly registered parties – Rodina, the Russian Party of Life and the Russian Party of Pensioners – merged into the new pro-Kremlin grouping, A Just Russia. In the view of experts, not all of the parties that had been registered were likely, in reality, to have a minimum of 50,000 members; equally, some of those that had not been registered were likely to have been treated less indulgently because of their openly anti-Kremlin orientation. This was certainly the case with the Republican Party, led by an outspoken and independent-minded deputy, Vladimir Ryzhkov, and which had itself claimed 60,000 members. Ryzhkov regarded the whole exercise as a 'purge of genuinely oppositional parties' in advance of the Duma and presidential elections;[124] and the Republican Party leader was kept out of the new Duma altogether when Kremlin officials, according to representatives of Yabloko and the Union of Right Forces who were 'speaking on condition of anonymity', made clear that they had been 'obliged to give up many candidates', among them Ryzhkov, who might otherwise have joined the electoral list of the Union of Right Forces and had some chance of retaining a seat.[125]

If the electoral show was closely regulated by the Kremlin and regarded with some scepticism by the wider public, there were all the same some regularities in the ways in which voters engaged with the choices that were available to them. Broadly speaking, electoral preferences could be organised under four headings, corresponding to 'party families' rather than a much more fluid list of individual organisations.[126] First of all, there were 'communist' parties, including not just the Communist Party of the Russian Federation but also the Agrarian Party (which reflected the interests of collective farm rather than private agriculture, at least until it merged with United Russia at the end of 2008) and the left-wing Party of Peace and Unity. A rather different grouping could be classified as 'national-patriotic', based around Zhirinovsky's Liberal Democratic Party of Russia but also including a variety of smaller and mostly short-lived electoral formations such as 'For a Holy Russia', the Popular-Republican Party, Patriots of Russia and Rodina. From 1999 onwards, broadly pro-Kremlin 'centrists' were the largest grouping: they included United Russia, the 'Greens', the People's Party, the Democratic Party, the Russian Party of Pensioners, the Party of Social Justice, the Party of Russian Renewal and the Russian Party of Life (which later became the main constituent of A Just Russia). The 'liberal-democratic' parties, finally, included at various times the Union of Right Forces, Yabloko, Civic Force, the Russian Constitutional-Democratic Party, SLON (a 'Union of People for Education and Science') and 'New Course–Automobile Russia'.

Based on this fourfold division, Table 2.6 sets out the distribution of the party-list vote at successive parliamentary elections from 1993 to 2007. Several trends are immediately apparent. 'Communist' support, for instance, rose initially, then declined, but remained

Table 2.6 **Voting support by 'party family', 1993–2007**			
	Communist	National-patriotic	Centrist	Liberal-democratic
December 1993	21	24	26	29
December 1995	33	21	23	21
December 1999	28	7	44	15
December 2003	17	22	46	10
December 2007	14	9	72	4

Source: adapted from the party-list vote totals as classified in *Vybory deputatov Gosudarstvennoi Dumy Federal'nogo Sobraniya Rossiiskoi Federatsii. 2003. Elektoral'naya statistika* (Moscow: Ves' mir, 2004), p. 235, and 2007 results as classified in Table 2.4, in rounded percentages.

substantial. 'Liberal-democratic' support fell much more sharply and consistently, and had almost disappeared by the time of the 2007 Duma election. 'National-patriotic' support was the most variable, reflecting not only the fluctuating fortunes of the Liberal Democratic Party itself but also the occasional appearance of left-patriotic groupings such as Rodina, which took an unexpected 9 per cent of the party-list ballot in 2003 and then collapsed into A Just Russia, which could be regarded as 'centrist'. The clearest trend of all was indeed the steady rise in support for 'centrist' parties of all kinds, based around 'Unity' or (after 2001) United Russia, and accounting for almost three-quarters of the entire vote in 2007. The same patterns were apparent in successive presidential elections, with the two 'centrist' candidates taking nearly 73 per cent of the ballot in March 2008 (see Chapter 3); this left just 18 per cent for the 'communist' Zyuganov and 9 per cent for the 'national-patriotic' Zhirinovsky, with no candidate at all that could be classified as a 'liberal democrat' (these totals, up to and including the 2003 Duma election, did not take account of the single-member constituencies, in which 'independents' were more successful than any of the political parties or – in that year – any of the other parties except United Russia).

A substantial literature has sought to identify the determinants of these patterns of electoral choice. In the most elaborate exercise of its kind to date, Rose, Mishler and Munro have isolated the separate effects of social, political, economic and time-related factors on Russian political behaviour over the entire postcommunist period. Social characteristics, they found, such as age and education, had relatively little effect on the propensity of Russians to support their current form of government once other factors had been taken into account, although respondents who assigned themselves to a higher socioeconomic status were more likely to be supportive and older respondents were more likely to be hostile. Political values, including evaluations of regime performance, were rather more important. Not surprisingly, those who supported democracy as a political ideal had a more positive view of the prevailing regime, all other things being equal, and so did those who thought it had enlarged their individual liberties. But the more positive the view of the Soviet past, the less support there was for the regime that actually existed;

and the prevailing regime was also likely to lose support the more it was thought to be corrupt, a view that was taken by increasing numbers of respondents. Overall, most Russians thought there had been great gains in freedom under the new regime, but a majority were also likely to take a positive view of its communist predecessor. Taken together, political performance influenced both regime support and the rejection of alternatives, and the decisive factor was the way in which ordinary Russians evaluated the performance of the regime they had experienced in the past and of the one that had succeeded it at the start of the 1990s.[127]

Traditionally, it was economic factors that were given primacy in explanations of political behaviour. But these themselves were a complex of different elements, including individual or household ('egocentric') judgements and 'sociotropic' judgements that related to the country as a whole. Judgements about the past and present had also to be balanced against future expectations; and the most important of the individual variables – such as inflation, growth and employment – might often be moving in different directions at different times in an economy that was itself undergoing far-reaching change. Economic factors of this kind, according to the same investigation, made a further and substantial contribution to evaluations of the current regime, but they did so in quite specific ways. There was general agreement that the economic system of the Soviet past was to be preferred to the postcommunist economy of the present, and relatively few said they were satisfied with their own economic position in spite of the fact that many more of them had expensive consumer durables (the overwhelming majority had a colour television, about half had a home entertainment system and more than a quarter had a car). But the influence of these factors on support for the regime itself was not a simple one. What voters said about their own economic position, for instance, had little direct effect on their evaluation of the regime under which they currently lived. And although evaluations of the national economic situation had an 'exceptionally strong influence on support for the current regime', their influence on the rejection of alternatives was of 'secondary importance'; in this case it was political values that made the greatest difference.[128]

The 2007 Duma election suggested very similar conclusions (Table 2.7). United Russia clearly enjoyed some advantage among women, as did the liberal-democratic parties. The most remarkable gender disparity, however, was the overwhelmingly male nature of the LDPR electorate, a disparity that had been characteristic of earlier elections[129] and one that was reflected in evaluations of the party leaders individually. It was for reasons of this kind that the Liberal Democrats had rarely been successful in the single-member constituencies, where the outcome was determined by simple majority; the party was not surprisingly one of the most determined advocates of party-list rather than constituency-based representation, and pressed for its wider adoption. Communists had by far the oldest electorate, on the same evidence, with relatively few in their early adult years and more than half of pensionable age. In this sense the Communist electorate was indeed 'dying out', but it was still a substantial constituency, with more than 30 million of the

Table 2.7 Patterns of voting support, 2007 Duma election

	Gender		Age		Residence		Education		Living standard	
	Male	Fem.	< 30	60+	Urb.	Rur.	2nd	3rd	Poor	Rich
Communist Party (CP)	47	53	8	51	78	22	49	18	46	10
A Just Russia	45	55	15	25	80	20	38	26	30	8
Liberal Democrats	73	27	23	6	75	25	40	11	32	9
Union of Right Forces	38	62	14	10	91	9	24	29	14	24
United Russia	40	60	25	19	74	26	38	16	18	18
Yabloko	24	76	6	18	82	18	12	41	47	12
All	*46*	*54*	*24*	*21*	*75*	*25*	*41*	*11*	*25*	*14*

Source: 2008 survey, rounded percentages. In terms of education, 2nd = up to and including a complete secondary education; 3rd = a completed third-level education or higher. Living standards are as self-assessed, 'poor' or 'very poor' and 'rich' or 'very rich' combined. Ns are respectively CP = 167, Just Russia = 89, LDPR = 106, URF = 21, UR = 944, Yabloko = 17.

population (or about a third of the entire electorate) over working age, and it was a constituency whose individual members were more likely than others to exercise their democratic rights.[130] The Communists were evidently much more successful in mobilising this substantial segment of the electorate than A Just Russia, even though A Just Russia had incorporated the well-established Pensioners' Party and appealed directly for the support of those who had voted for them in previous contests.

All of the parties, except the Liberal Democrats, had more highly educated supporters than the society as a whole, particularly Yabloko, which was traditionally the favoured party of professionals and the mainstream party that appealed most directly for the support of those who favoured liberal causes such as education, the environment and civilian control of the armed forces. Communist and United Russia supporters were rather more representative of the wider society in this respect; indeed, what was most striking about United Russia supporters was the extent to which they represented a cross-section, usually no more than a few percentage points above or below the sample as a whole. This was very similar to the way in which Putin's own support drew almost without differentiation on all social categories and reflected the way in which both the President and his party had sought to develop a programme that was more or less the same as a national development plan, appealing in a plebiscitary way for the backing of the entire society for what it regarded as their collective best interests.[131] United Russia supporters were also representative of the wider society in terms of their self-perceived living standards, although slightly more prosperous than the average; Communist supporters were much more likely to regard themselves as 'poor' or 'very poor' (so were the much smaller numbers of Yabloko supporters, who were often employed in the state sector), and Union of Right Forces supporters were – predictably – the most likely to regard themselves as 'rich' or 'very rich'.

What made a difference among these various variables? Was it, for instance, that those who lived in the country had lower incomes, such that location itself had little to do with their voting choices? Or that those who lived in the cities were more highly educated, which was the difference that made a difference? Multivariate analysis of voting patterns in the December 2007 election indicates that the various structural factors we have considered did have some explanatory power, but that they were generally less important than attitudinal differences. In particular, assessments of the national economic situation were a powerful determinant. Among United Russia voters, for instance, 60 per cent said they believed the country's economy had improved over the previous twelve months; Communist supporters were much less positive. United Russia voters were also more likely to have a positive view of Putin's leadership than the electorate as a whole when other factors were held constant. But this was less because they had a positive view of Putin himself, and much more because of his apparently successful stewardship of the national economy. By contrast, and in line with the comparative literature, what respondents thought about their own economic situation made relatively little differ-ence.[132] Putin's popular support, in other words, was 'substantially based on strong economic performance', and it was this that had 'underpinned the widespread popular support for the party with which he [was] identified'.[133]

The scholarly literature has taken a rather different view of the related issue of party identification, often reflecting differences in question wording.[134] Differences on matters of this kind have also been a consequence of the date on which questionnaires are fielded: questions about 'party support' that are asked at around the time of parliamentary elections have typically been almost interchangeable with questions about voting behav-iour, and questions about the salience of parties in general have been heavily contami-nated by being asked at such times (which are of course the times at which research funding for such purposes is most readily available). Asked a month or two after the December 2007 Duma election – in other words, at a time of heightened awareness of such matters – no more than a third of our respondents thought of themselves as 'supporters' of a political party; asked a similar question, about 90 per cent of British or US electors see themselves in such terms.[135] Equally, fewer than half the electorate thought of themselves as 'close' to any of the parties at this time, and of these, fewer than half were strong identifiers. In Russia, it has been argued, party identification is 'simply another way of describing the party a person has voted for – but may not vote for four years hence, even if it is still on the ballot'; overall, perhaps '[o]nly a sixth of Russians, those feeling close to the Communist Party, fit the model of party identification developed in party systems in equilibrium'.[136]

At least two explanations could be offered for the relatively weak attachment of ordinary Russians to the political parties that sought to represent their views: 'cultural' and 'structural'. One part of the explanation, certainly, was the long experience of Soviet rule, and of a single monopolistic party that had discredited the word itself. As a teacher from Vitebsk wrote to *Izvestiya* shortly after the change of regime, 'wouldn't it be better without parties altogether?' What was a party but 'always and everywhere a struggle for posts and positions', fed by a lust for power that was 'more powerful than any narcotic'?[137] Even in 2008, according to the survey evidence, only a quarter (26 per cent) supported the party system that actually existed; rather more thought there should be fewer parties (33 per cent), or only one (19 per cent), and some (9 per cent) thought there should be none at all.[138] Behind this lay a lengthy history in which a single party had, on its own admission, monopolised political power and then abused it; behind this again was a pattern of political development that had not allowed parties to exist legally until the early years of the twentieth century, and then only under a variety of restrictions.[139] Other countries, of course, had experienced authoritarian rule; but even in comparison with them, let alone the established democracies, levels of party membership, and of associations of all kind, were *particularly* low in the former Soviet republics.[140] This suggested that there were *particular* factors that were relevant in the former Soviet republics, but not elsewhere.

At the same time, ordinary Russians were reacting to the political parties that actually existed. Not only surveys but also more qualitative studies found that they were often perceived as remote, bureaucratic and corrupt. Focus groups conducted after the 2003–4 elections and again in 2008–10 in a variety of locations found a wide range of attitudes, but an underlying disenchantment.[141] Even United Russia was scarcely seen as a party at all, but as an opportunity to vote for a popular president. In Tula, for instance, 'almost everybody voted for United Russia precisely because it was the President's party. Russians love their President and don't want to go against him.' It was the 'presidential party', others explained, and so it was 'bound to win'. Nelya, a local student, explained that 'I like Putin myself, in principle, so I voted for United Russia, not because it reflects my interests, but simply because of Putin.' El'vira, a housewife in her early twenties in the town of Odintsovo in the Moscow region, had voted for United Russia just 'because my husband told me to – it was all the same to me'. Nikolai in Ryazan, a 40-year-old industrial worker, openly admitted that he had little idea what the party stood for – he simply 'voted that way, because Putin asked us to'. These remarks were corroborated by the survey evidence, which showed that United Russia voters were a remarkably representative cross-section of the entire population, and that there was little about their views that was particularly distinctive.[142]

Supporters of the CPRF, according to the survey evidence, stood somewhat apart: they reached their voting decisions earlier, maintained their loyalties more consistently from election to election and claimed to be influenced by the party programme as much as by its leadership.[143] There was some evidence of this, certainly, in focus group responses. Lyudmila Ivanovna, for instance, a pensioner with a higher education in Odintsovo, was a straightforward Communist supporter – 'there are honest people there, they want a fair society. They're against robbery, and for equality.' Pavel, in the Komi capital Syktyvkar, was another Communist supporter and thought his was the only one that could really be called a party: 'the other ones aren't parties, just supporters' clubs'. But others were disappointed in the Communists as well, and particularly by the decision to include some representatives of big business in their list of candidates (two Yukos representatives had taken a prominent place on the party's central list in the 2003 election).[144] Mikhail, a Syktyvkar pensioner in his sixties, had been a member of the CPSU but had no time for its postcommunist successor. 'Zyuganov should have been replaced ages ago. And now we hear that at the Duma elections, the Communists included oligarchs in their party list – what can you make of that? I'd say that such a party no longer has the right to call itself communist.' Gennadii, in Ryazan, took the same view; he would normally have voted Communist but just couldn't bring himself to do so with so many oligarchs and their nominees on the party list.

It was not necessarily any prior antipathy towards parties that influenced ordinary Russians, so much as their own disillusioning experience. Some, for instance, had been enthusiastic about the left-nationalist party Rodina but were dismayed by the way in which it had collapsed so soon after entering the Duma in December 2003. Liliya, a Biisk pensioner, was another who had been disappointed by Rodina, after a good campaign; the party leader, economist Sergei Glaz'ev, had been very appealing, 'young and clever', but then there had been a disagreement, apparently about money, and 'now I just don't know'. Those who had supported the liberal-democratic parties were even more despairing. 'Not long ago we had such a powerful democratic movement', lamented Yelena, an activist in her early thirties from the middle Russian town of Voronezh. 'And then in one day of elections the democrats were destroyed. I don't believe they lost the elections. It was just decided to destroy them and they were destroyed.' Alevtina in Syktyvkar, a librarian in her early fifties, was another disappointed democrat. Her local branch of Yabloko had asked the party headquarters for advice, but what had they been told? 'What are you, children? Are we supposed to lead you all by the hand? Do something yourselves!' So nothing at all had happened. As for the Yabloko leader of the time, Grigorii Yavlinsky, he 'talks a lot, and very persuasively, but never actually does anything', complained Lena, a 19-year-old Tula student teacher; people had 'just got fed up of listening to him'.

Nor was it easy to contact a party if they wished to do so. 'Here in Odintsovo there's no sign of any parties', complained Lyudmila Ivanovna, 'they're all somewhere in Moscow'. Alexander, a Voronezh businessman, had supported the Union of Right Forces in the 2003 election but had no idea if it would continue to exist after its comprehensive defeat. The branch in Voronezh was still in existence, but inactive: 'It waits for instructions from Moscow, but there aren't any instructions at all. And no money either.' There was a similar view at Odintsovo in the Moscow region. Mariya Sergeevna had wanted to join Yabloko,

but it wasn't clear how I could do so. Our parties in this respect leave a lot to be desired. People are ready to join, but they don't know how. The parties are scarcely engaged with ordinary people. They shut themselves off in their Duma work, forgetting that people would like to join them. They could learn a lot from the CPSU in terms of recruiting a membership.

She had helped Yabloko collect signatures at one of the previous elections and started to make contact with them, 'but after the elections they all disappeared'. She would have been glad to help the URF co-founder, Irina Khakamada, gather signatures for her 2004 presidential bid – 'but they don't get in touch with you. And I've no idea how to find their headquarters.' The parties were all busy doing deals in the Duma, but where did they exist on the ground, asked Svetlana, a Kolomna lawyer in her early twenties. 'In my opinion, on another planet.'

Most generally of all, there was simply a lack of belief that political parties would implement their promises, or that deputies would do anything for the electorate as distinct from advancing their personal agenda. They could choose anyone they liked, explained Valentin from the Komi republic, an unemployed worker in his late forties,

but once they're in power, they change. They forget everything they promised. They begin to steal, to put everything in their own pockets, without any thought for ordinary people . . . So at the moment of election we seem to choose, but after the election we have no influence at all.

Sergei, a scientist in his mid-fifties, thought each of the parties had enough good intentions, 'but experience shows that when parties come to power, they forget their own programme. A programme and good intentions are one thing – objective reality and party funds are quite another.' Understandably, there were many who disengaged entirely. 'I don't trust any of them', declared Igor, an entrepreneur in his thirties who lived in the Komi capital Syktyvkar. 'They're all just clans of their leaders. They don't think about ordinary people.' The parties that did win representation were 'happy enough just sitting in the Duma', and had 'no intention of working with ordinary people'. 'I can say one thing for sure', a Tula salesgirl told one of our groups. 'I don't believe in anything they say. Not Nemtsov, not Yavlinsky, not Zyuganov, nor anyone else.' The main thing, a Bryansk accountant concluded, was trust. There were parties that reflected her interests, but she had no confidence in their activities. 'We have no trust in anyone: either in government, or in the parties.'

But as well as 'cultural' factors, there were features of Russia's institutional design that undermined the position of political parties. One was certainly the constitutional framework. Government was accountable not to parliament (in normal circumstances), but to the president: which meant that Russian parties were unable to 'win power' at a parliamentary election and were in no position to compel the formation of a government that reflected the composition of a new Duma or the preferences of the electorate. As we have seen, when Prime Minister Chernomyrdin's party, Our Home is Russia, won just over 10 per cent of the party-list vote in the 1995 parliamentary election, he did not resign and made it clear that the election result would make not the slightest difference to the composition of the government or the policies it would be pursuing.[145] When Boris Yeltsin dismissed the entire government four times in 1998–9, equally, it had nothing to do with a change in the party balance in the Duma, still less a national election; and when Vladimir Putin dismissed his two prime ministers, in February 2004 and September

2007, it was before a parliamentary election not after it. Under the terms of the law on state service that applied until 2003, indeed, ministers were not allowed to have a party affiliation, and under the law on the government until it was amended in 2004, they were not allowed to hold a paid position in a public organisation of any kind.[146] This reflected the Soviet view that the business of government was to implement the directives of the Kremlin leadership, not set national priorities of their own.

There were occasional indications that the balance between executive and legislature might be reconsidered, perhaps even that the Constitution might eventually be modified. Putin, at least, spoke of the formation of a 'professional, effective government relying on a parliamentary majority' in his address to the Federal Assembly in the spring of 2003.[147] A number of Russian jurists had for some time been arguing that the Russian parliament needed more powers – perhaps approving appointments to key ministries as well as to the prime ministership; or being required to give its approval if a prime minister was dismissed, not simply when he was nominated.[148] The logic of these changes was a semi-presidential system, along the lines of the French system in which the president appoints the government, but the government in its turn requires the support of a parliamentary majority.[149] At first sight, Putin's appointment as prime minister after he had stood down from the presidency in 2008 at the same time as he was leader of the dominant party in the Duma appeared to represent a move in this direction. But the parties, in France, are autonomous, the electoral process is fully competitive and the prime minister may represent a parliamentary majority that is opposed to the president and presidential policies – the arrangement known as 'cohabitation'. In Russia, up to the present, the entire process has been dominated by the Kremlin, and the distribution of leading members of the ruling group across the various executive offices has been of little political significance (Putin, in any case, had spoken of a government that commanded the support of the legislature, not of party government as such, and later made clear he would oppose any move in this direction for the foreseeable future).[150] As long as these circumstances obtained, Russians would have few obvious reasons to join a political party and the parties themselves would have more to do with the regulation of society from above than the conquest of power from below.

Making laws

Just as its elections lacked any element of choice until the late Gorbachev years, so too the Soviet system had lacked any element of parliamentarianism. The soviets or councils on which the system was based were meant to be very different. There was no separation of powers, for a start, as working people were assumed to have a common interest that was based upon their ownership of the means of production, and it was that common interest that was reflected in a single slate of candidates in local and national elections. Why, it was asked, should working people need different parties to reflect social interests that were in fundamental agreement? The USSR Supreme Soviet, for these reasons, met very rarely, for no more than a week of the year, and its votes were normally unanimous.[151] Nor was it surprising that speakers were in agreement, as the texts of their contributions had often been prepared beforehand by party officials, leaving them with barely enough time to read through 'their' speech before delivering it.[152] Parliamentary journalists, for their part, could file their story before the session they were reporting had taken place.[153] Much of the work of the Supreme Soviet was in fact conducted through a committee system, and the budget was given quite detailed consideration; but all the deputies were part-timers, deliberately so as they were meant to combine parliamentary duties with their ordinary employment and not become a separate, 'parasitic' class. There was a high rate of turnover, which gave the largest possible number of working people the opportunity to run their 'own' state, and deputies at all levels were chosen so that they reflected the society they represented: about a third were women, and more than half were workers or collective farmers.[154]

All of this was changing in the late Soviet period. A part-time parliament, certainly, was unlikely to offer a direct challenge to the dominance of the CPSU; but it was also a parliament that was unlikely to expose the Soviet government to effective scrutiny, or to criticise any of its members who were guilty of incompetence or corruption. Ministers, as a consequence, held their position for long periods of time, in some cases for decades. Equally, the lack of effective scrutiny meant that policies were poorly considered, and more likely to lead to serious and costly mistakes. It was not until 1986 that a costly and ambitious plan to divert the Siberian rivers, with enormous implications for the global environment, was formally abandoned;[155] the same ministry had reportedly made plans to irrigate the Sahara desert.[156] All of this, as Gorbachev pointed out in his speech to the 19th Party Conference in 1988, had led to the formation of a massive governmental apparatus that had begun to 'dictate its will' in political and economic matters, and to a caste of state officials who had become indifferent to the responsibilities with which they had been entrusted and were sometimes inclined to use their position for private gain.[157] Responding to this lead, an entirely new representative system was established at the end of that year as part of a deliberate move towards a 'Soviet parliamentarianism'. In future, there would be a large, 2,250-member Congress of People's Deputies and a smaller working body, the Supreme Soviet, which would be in session for six to eight months of the year; ministers, too, would be elected by direct competitive ballot and hold their positions for a maximum of two five-year terms. This was the parliament that was elected in March 1989, with responsibility for the whole of the USSR; there was also a Russian Congress of Deputies, elected in March 1990, and it was this parliament that took Russia into the postcommunist era.

The constitution that was approved in December 1993 established another new representative system: an upper house, the Federation Council, which was to draw its membership from each of Russia's (originally eighty-nine) republics and regions, and a lower house, the State Duma, which was to be elected by a combination of single-member constituencies and a national party list. The Federation Council, as in other systems of this kind, considered all the questions that were of relevance to the federation as a whole. It was the Federation Council, for instance, that approved boundary changes and the introduction of martial law or a state of emergency. It appointed judges to the Supreme Court on the nomination of the president and authorised the use of Russian armed forces outside the national territory; it also considered legislation emanating from the Duma on the budget, taxes and currency matters, international treaties and war and peace (all of these matters were specified in Article 102 of the Russian Constitution). Initially, in 1993, the Federation Council had been directly elected, two from each region; but it was formed thereafter in a variety of other ways, representing the executive and the legislature respectively. This did not prove an entirely satisfactory arrangement, and there were periodic calls to restore the principle of direct election so that the 'senators' had a more obviously democratic mandate.[158] President Medvedev, in his first parliamentary address in November 2008, called for them to be selected in future from among citizens who had themselves been elected to legislative bodies within the relevant region, which was at least a step in this direction, and the corresponding legislative changes were approved in early 2009.[159]

The lower house, the State Duma, has a range of more conventional parliamentary prerogatives. It is the Duma, first of all, that approves nominations to the prime minister-ship on the nomination of the president (art. 103). If it fails to do so three times in a row, the president is obliged to appoint a candidate, dissolve the Duma and call fresh elections (art. 111). The Duma, equally, may express its lack of confidence in the government as a whole; but if it does so twice within three months, the president is bound to announce the resignation of the government or the dissolution of the Duma itself (art. 117). The Duma has other powers of appointment: it confirms and dismisses the chairman of the State Bank, the chairman of the Accounting Chamber and the Commissioner on Human Rights or ombudsman, and it has the exclusive right to declare an amnesty (art. 103) – as it did, controversially, when it pardoned all who had been implicated in the attempted coup of 1991 and the confrontation of September–October 1993. The Duma, in addition, adopts federal legislation; its decisions have to be confirmed by the Federation Council, but the Duma can override the upper house if it votes in favour a second time by a two-thirds majority of its entire membership (art. 105). The president, equally, can refuse to sign a law that has passed the Duma and the Federation Council, but any decision of this kind can be overridden by a two-thirds majority of the entire membership of both chambers (art. 107). In practice, once United Russia had established a dominant position, there was little basis for conflict among the various branches of government, and it became increasingly uncommon for legislation to be contested in this way or any other.

The Duma is organised in fractions, which since 2007 have corresponded exactly to the seats won in the preceding parliamentary election by the various political parties. Up to this point, deputies were not obliged to belong to the fraction of the party that had nominated them, or to any fraction at all; indeed they could join the fraction of an

Table 2.8 The composition of the Duma, 2000–2011

Fraction or group	2000–2003	2004–2007	2008–2011
Communist Party	89	52	57
Unity	82	–	–
Fatherland–All Russia	44	–	–
Union of Right Forces	31	0	0
Yabloko	20	0	0
Liberal Democrats	17	36	40
United Russia	–	306	315
A Just Russia	–	–	38
Rodina	–	38	–
[Groups:]			
People's Deputy	56	–	–
Agroindustrial Group	41	–	–
Regions of Russia	40	–	–
Unaffiliated	19	15	–
Totals	439	447	450

Sources: adapted from *Rossiiskii statisticheskii yezhegodnik 2000*, p. 24 (as of 21 February 2000), *2004*, p. 48 (as of 2 February 2004; the Rodina total has been corrected), and *2008*, p. 55 (as of 1 January 2008). These figures show the distribution of seats at the start of each new legislature; in the first two legislatures there were minor changes over the legislative term as vacancies were filled and deputies changed their factional allegiance.

entirely different party if it agreed to admit them. All of this led to a considerable element of volatility over the course of each Duma (see Table 2.8), particularly during the weeks after each election when the newly elected deputies negotiated their future allegiance; it was in the course of these discussions that United Russia moved from the 223 seats it had won in the 2003 Duma election to the 300 that had agreed to join its fraction by the time the new parliament held its first meeting at the end of the same month.[160] Gradually, however, these arrangements became more prescriptive. The minimum size of a deputies' fraction was raised to fifty-five in December 2003,[161] which deprived some of the smaller groupings of the right to form an association of this kind and to enjoy the rights it conferred. The decision to end single-member constituencies under the 2005 election law removed the only way in which 'independents' could secure representation, and the same law introduced the 'imperative mandate', by which elected deputies were obliged to belong to the fraction of the party that had nominated them. Further changes established that deputies who chose to leave the fraction through which they had been elected would lose their Duma membership entirely.[162] All of this involved a substantial transfer of power from individual deputies and the parliament itself to the heads of the various fractions, and beyond that to the Kremlin.

As with the Federation Council, much of the work of the Duma takes place through its network of committees and commissions. Committees, according to the Duma's standing orders, give preliminary consideration to the legislative proposals that are submitted to the parliament by those who have the right to do so, suggesting amendments where they think it appropriate.[163] They handle the Duma's relations with the Constitutional Court, and organise parliamentary hearings; and not least, they make recommendations about the various provisions of the annual state budget. Committees and commissions, 'as a rule', reflect the internal composition of the Duma itself in terms of its deputy fractions; unless otherwise provided, they may have not fewer than twelve and not more than thirty-five members (art. 21 of the standing orders). Chairmen and other officers of the committees and commissions are elected by the chamber as a whole, and replaced on the same basis (art. 22). As with the Federation Council, all deputies, apart from those who hold official positions, must be a member of one or other of the Duma's committees, and of not more than one (art. 23). Meetings are convened 'as necessary, but not less often than twice a month' (art. 24). There were thirty-two committees in the Duma that met from 2008 onwards, with remits that covered all areas of government business; commissions dealt with other more specific matters, including the Duma's own affairs and particular issues of public policy such as anti-corruption legislation or (in previous convocations) the Beslan hostage-taking crisis of 2004 and the ongoing Chechen conflict.

A wide range of actors have the right to place draft legislation before the Duma, including the president, the Federation Council and its individual members, the government and the legislatures of the various subjects of the federation, as well as Duma deputies themselves. Legislation that relates to taxation or state loans, or whose adoption would lead to a charge on the federal budget, however, may only be introduced with the approval of the Russian government (art. 104 of the Constitution). Draft legislation passes through five distinct stages before it becomes law (see Figure 2.1). In the first instance, it must be approved at three separate readings in the Duma (or in the case of the federal budget, four readings).[164] According to the Duma's standing orders, the first reading is intended to establish whether or not there is support for the basic principles of a law. Laws are introduced at this stage by those who propose them, who also reply to the debate; a decision is taken at this point, and proposals that are rejected receive no further consideration. The relevant Duma committee then prepares a revised draft, listing proposed amendments and with its own recommendation whether or not to accept them, which is considered in a second reading. The draft law is introduced at this stage by the chair of the Duma committee that has been responsible for its consideration. The amendments that have been recommended by the committee are accepted if there are no objections, or otherwise put to a vote. The draft law is then approved or rejected. If approved, it goes to a third reading at which a final decision is made; no amendments, or objections to the legislation as a whole, can be considered at this stage.

Draft legislation that has been approved by the Duma is then passed to the Federation Council, which may adopt or reject (but not amend) it, or decide not to consider it at all, in

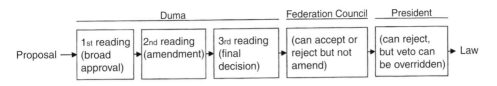

Figure 2.1 The legislative process (simplified)

which case after fourteen days it is automatically adopted. The Federation Council must, however, give formal consideration to any proposed legislation that relates to the budget, taxation, financial and currency issues, international treaties, the state border, or war and peace (art. 106 of the Constitution). In the event of disagreement between the two chambers, a 'conciliation commission' will typically be formed by representatives of both sides, following which the law may be returned to the Duma for further consideration. The Duma, as we have seen, can override the objections of the Federation Council in the last resort if a two-thirds majority of its entire membership decide accordingly (art. 105:5). A law that has satisfied these procedures is sent to the president for signature, which must take place within fourteen days of receiving it (art. 107). The president can veto legislation at this stage, but any such decision can in turn be overridden by a two-thirds majority of the entire membership of both houses (art. 107). Federal constitutional laws that have been approved by both houses may not be vetoed, but have to be signed and published within fourteen days of their receipt (art. 108).

The Duma has generally been a marginal presence in Russian political life, and for various reasons. One, certainly, is the manner in which the deputies have conducted themselves. For a start, there were periodic affrays on the floor of the house itself, often involving the mercurial leader of the Liberal Democratic Party, Vladimir Zhirinovsky. In 2005, for instance, he was walking out of the chamber after complaining that a set of regional election results that had just been announced had been falsified. Why, asked a Rodina deputy, Andrei Savel'ev, hadn't he protested when the results had been more favourable to his own party? The LDPR leader, 'shouting and spraying saliva', turned towards the deputy, promised to 'smash his ugly mug' and spat at him; but the deputy dodged the spit and slapped the LDPR leader on the face, at which Zhirinovsky jumped over the seats and threw himself on the offending deputy from above. Savel'ev, 'who knows karate', intercepted the Liberal Democratic leader in mid-air and pinned him to the floor; he ended up himself with a broken nose, and Zhirinovsky was banned from the chamber for a week.[165] Other failings were perhaps more serious: poor attendance, for instance, although attempts were made to conceal it by deputies running round the chamber casting votes for their colleagues, and an unfortunate tendency to appropriate items of property that belonged to the Duma itself, including soap, towels, telephones, light bulbs and mirrors.[166] The Duma had a commission that attempted to regulate the ethics of its members in such matters, but with limited success.

More serious again was the evidence that the support of deputies and indeed of whole fractions was available for purchase. The first serious incident of this kind occurred in May 1994, when money or other inducements had apparently been used to persuade Zhirinovsky and his Liberal Democratic Party to support the draft budget, leading eventually to a 'firm business relationship'. Other deputies got the point, and soon 'many laws adopted or rejected by the Duma ha[d] a concrete price, customers, clients and executors'.[167] According to a former member of the Communist fraction, members were 'bought for a variety of reasons: to pass amendments to a law or approve a certain wording of a law'; a vote in favour of Chernomyrdin's nomination as prime minister in 1998, for instance, had been worth an immediate $10,000, and the budgetary vote was a 'time to reap a harvest'.[168] A popular Moscow paper even published a 'price list' of the services that a deputy might be willing to provide for an appropriate consideration: a three-month pass that allowed entry into the Duma building would cost $50–100 (in 1997 prices), the promotion of an item of legislation 'to order' could run to millions of dollars.[169] Becoming a deputy in the first place was often a commercial transaction; the price that was paid was directly related to the opportunities for enrichment it provided, and sometimes to the immunity from criminal prosecution that all deputies enjoyed. Payments were made, for instance, for a place on the list of a party that was standing at a Duma election; the better the party's prospects and the higher the position on the list, the larger the payment that would be required. Generally, 'guaranteed' seats cost from half a million dollars upwards; but there was a legendary case, spoken about in Duma corridors, in which a seat on a party list had been sold for $10 million to a businessman with a particularly unsavoury reputation.[170]

Beyond this, there were still larger issues of institutional design. In particular, once United Russia had secured a dominant position as a result of the changes that had taken place in the electoral system, there was little reason for them to take any notice of the views of other deputies. And they had no more reason to take account of the opinion of deputies within their own fraction, once the legislation had been approved that obliged every deputy to sit with the fraction of the party that had sponsored their election or lose their seat. The dominant party, United Russia, was itself a Kremlin creation, wholly committed to the realisation of 'Putin's Plan', and there was accordingly no reason in the first place to expect a divergence of opinion between the parliamentary majority and the preferences of an all-powerful executive. In practice, the decisive meetings took place before draft legislation even reached the chamber, in 'zero readings' that brought together the leader of the United Russia fraction – and sometimes other fraction leaders and committee chairs – and the Kremlin administration.[171] If the Kremlin chose accordingly, all three readings of a draft piece of legislation could take place on the same day, which left little room for scrutiny, let alone a discussion of first principles.[172] The Kremlin itself made clear that it saw the Duma in a subordinate capacity, as a means of processing its legislative preferences rather than contesting them. The Duma was 'not a place for staging political battles but a place for constructively and effectively doing the work of government', its speaker, Boris Gryzlov, had made clear in December 2003 as the new parliament assembled.[173] Putin insisted similarly during the 2007 campaign that the Duma should 'not be a gathering of populists' but a 'responsible parliament, working in the interests of all citizens'.[174]

The largest issues of all were constitutional. Government ministers were appointed by the president (or in the case of the prime minister, nominated by him) and did not necessarily reflect the outcome of an election or the views of the public at large. There was some discussion, during the Putin years, of the possibility of a 'government of the parliamentary majority' that would reflect the composition of a new Duma. But this was a meaningless concession as long as the executive was able to ensure that each successive Duma was overwhelmingly pro-Kremlin; there was certainly no basis for the 'cohabitation' that periodically took place in France under a semi-presidential system in which president and parliament could represent different and perhaps opposing parties. Parties, accordingly, did not 'win power' when they secured a majority of seats in a new Duma, at elections that from 2011 onwards would take place at five-year rather than four-year intervals;[175] it was closer to a Soviet arrangement, in which (broadly speaking) the Kremlin determined the composition of each new legislature in advance and local officials competed to satisfy its various requirements, much as they would have competed in earlier times to bring in a good harvest. There was no alternative to an elected assembly if Russians were to express their views and advance them through a legislative process; but they were almost as far from representative and accountable government by the early years of a new century as they had been at the end of the Soviet period when the first steps had been taken away from a single-party monopoly towards a form of rule that rested on the freely expressed consent of the electorate.

Further reading

There is a thorough study of the 'democratisation' of the Gorbachev period in Urban, Igrunov and Mitrokhin (1997). Elections and voting behaviour in the early postcommunist years are considered in White, Rose and McAllister (1997) and Colton (2000). On the Putin years and later, see Rose and Munro (2002), Rose, Mishler and Munro (2006) and Rose, Mishler and Munro (2011). There is a statistically rigorous but absorbing study of the way in which the electoral system has become subject to Kremlin manipulation in Myagkov, Ordeshook and Shakin (2009); a collective study of 'Russia's authoritarian elections' appears in White *et al.* (2011). The most comprehensive collection of published data is White (2010); see also 'Russia' in Rose and Munro (2009). An archive of election and referendum statistics since 1993 as well as a collection of legislation in English as well as Russian is available at the website of the Central Electoral Committee www.cikrf.ru. On political parties, see Hale (2006), Gel'man (2008) and White (2009).

Colton, Timothy J., *Transitional Citizens: Voters and What Influences Them in the New Russia* (Cambridge, MA, and London: Harvard University Press, 2000).

Gel'man, Vladimir, 'Party politics in Russia: from competition to hierarchy', *Europe-Asia Studies*, vol. **60**, no. 6 (August 2008), pp. 913–30.

Hale, Henry E., *Why Not Parties in Russia? Democracy, Federalism, and the State* (Cambridge and New York: Cambridge University Press, 2006).

Myagkov, Mikhail, Peter C. Ordeshook and Dimitri Shakin, *The Forensics of Election Fraud: Russia and Ukraine* (Cambridge and New York: Cambridge University Press, 2009).

Rose, Richard, William Mishler and Neil Munro, *Russia Transformed: Developing Popular Support for a New Regime* (Cambridge and New York: Cambridge University Press, 2006).

  Popular Support for an Undemocratic Regime: The Changing Views of Russians (Cambridge and New York: Cambridge University Press, 2011).

Rose, Richard, and Neil Munro, *Elections without Order: Russia's Challenge to Vladimir Putin* (Cambridge and New York: Cambridge University Press, 2002).

  Parties and Elections in New European Democracies (Colchester: ECPR Press, 2009).

Urban, Michael E., with Vyacheslav Igrunov and Sergei Mitrokhin, *The Rebirth of Politics in Russia* (Cambridge and New York: Cambridge University Press, 1997).

White, Stephen, 'Russia's client party system', in Paul Webb and Stephen White, eds., *Party Politics in New Democracies*, rev. edn (Oxford and New York: Oxford University Press, 2009), pp. 21–52.

  'Russia/USSR', in Dieter Nohlen and Philip Stöver, eds., *Elections in Europe: A Data Handbook* (Baden-Baden: Nomos, 2010), 1623–68.

White, Stephen, Richard Rose and Ian McAllister, *How Russia Votes* (Chatham House, NJ: Chatham House, 1997).

White, Stephen *et al.*, 'Russia's authoritarian elections', special issue of *Europe-Asia Studies*, forthcoming.

3 Presidential government

'We'll win together!': Putin and Medvedev on an election hoarding in central Moscow, February 2008 (Stephen White)

Russia had already established a directly elected presidency during the final year of Soviet rule. But it had also elected a new parliament, and it was not until the adoption of the 1993 Constitution, after parliamentary resistance had been violently suppressed, that it became what some called a 'superpresidency', with the government headed by the prime minister as its executive agency. Yeltsin was succeeded in 2000 by Vladimir Putin, and then Putin, after the end of his second four-year term, by Dmitri Medvedev, with Putin remaining as prime minister. Russians themselves called this new arrangement a 'tandem'. It did not, all the same, appear to represent a real and enduring redistribution of authority, Putin continued to be seen as the dominant figure, and it was widely expected that he would return to the presidency in 2012, when Medvedev's first term expired. Whoever held the leading positions, this was clearly a political system dominated by a powerful executive. It was less clear that there were mechanisms that would help to ensure that this dominant power was not abused by those who exercised it, and perhaps in their own interests.

The end of the Soviet period saw the establishment of an executive presidency in Russia as well as the USSR itself, although the dominance of a single leader was of much older origin. Brezhnev, when he became chairman of the Presidium of the Supreme Soviet in 1977, was already being referred to in foreign capitals as 'president', or at least the 'first person' in Soviet public life. The move to a formally constituted presidency came some years later, as a part of the reform of political institutions that was being undertaken throughout the Gorbachev years. Gorbachev himself became the first (and, as it turned out, last) Soviet president in March 1990, when he was elected to the newly established office by the Congress of People's Deputies; Russia gained its first president a year later, in June 1991, when Boris Yeltsin defeated five other candidates in a nationwide contest; and by the end of the Soviet period a presidential system had been adopted much more widely throughout the republics and regions.[1] The presidency, it was agreed, should normally be elective, and a position of executive authority: neither Gorbachev nor Yeltsin, as former Prime Minister Nikolai Ryzhkov remarked, liked the idea of 'reigning like the Queen of England'.[2] After December 1993, indeed, it was the presidency that defined the entire political system, as Yeltsin used the advantage he had obtained after the parliament had been forcibly dissolved to secure the adoption of a constitution that extended his already impressive powers. 'I don't deny that the powers of the president in the draft constitution are considerable', he told *Izvestiya*, 'but what do you expect in a country that is used to tsars and strong leaders?'[3]

A strongly personalist leadership, as Yeltsin suggested, was indeed a long-standing Russian tradition, extended into the Soviet period by the dominance of the General Secretary within a Communist Party whose dominant position within the system as a whole had been given a legal basis in Article 6 of the 1977 Constitution. At the time he secured this position for himself, Gorbachev recalled, 'not a single world leader had more power than the General Secretary of the Central Committee of the CPSU'.[4] The party itself appeared to be in a position of permanent government, beyond the reach of ballot box, the media or courts of law; within the party the leadership was effectively beyond the reach of ordinary members, still less the public at large. And yet, even in the Soviet period, there were countervailing forces. Leadership, after Stalin, was increasingly collective. The general secretaryship had been separated from the position of prime minister after 1964 to avoid an excessive concentration of power in the hands of a single person. The state system itself was strengthened, through the reform of local government and an expanded committee system within the Soviet parliament, and ministries began to acquire more autonomy in their day-to-day activities.[5] Indeed effective authority was already migrating from party to state in the late communist years as Gorbachev was elected first to the chairmanship of the Presidium of the Supreme Soviet in 1988, then to a newly established chairmanship of the Supreme Soviet in 1989, and to the presidency itself in 1990.

All of this was part of a wider trend towards executive presidencies, not only in the former Soviet republics but throughout the postcommunist world. Turkmenistan had been the first of the republics to institute a presidency of this kind, in October 1990. Georgia followed in May 1991, Russia in June and most of the others had done so by the end of the year; by 1994, when Belarus adopted a new constitution with a directly elected presidency, all the former Soviet republics outside the Baltic had moved in the same direction. A few, indeed, had moved even further, towards what was virtually the restoration of 'emirates',[6] with presidents – often their former communist first secretaries – who were able to use the considerable powers of the office to extend their mandate almost indefinitely.[7] Most of Eastern Europe had moved towards an executive presidency by the same time, with the Czech Republic, Hungary and Slovakia, where a more ceremonial figure was elected by parliament, the main exceptions.[8] The late 1980s, however, had also seen the development of a body of scholarship that 'took institutions seriously', and there were many indications, in this literature, that an executive presidency was unlikely to contribute towards the formation of a party system or political stability more generally.[9] Did the Russian experience, after the Putin as well as Yeltsin presidencies, bear out these gloomy forecasts? Had a working balance been found between an elected president, the government he appointed and a parliament that was also directly elected? And how did the institution of presidential government relate to a society that was familiar not only with strong leadership, but also with its tendency to abuse the powers with which it had been entrusted?

The emergence of presidential government

The decision to establish a directly elected Russian presidency was made in March 1991, as the wider population took part in a referendum on the future of the USSR itself. The decision to create the office of president within what was still one of the Soviet republics had not originally been controversial.[10] At the first Russian Congress of People's Deputies, in May–June 1990, the proposal had the support of all the parliamentary factions; Yeltsin himself was elected chairman of the Supreme Soviet after several inconclusive ballots, and on 12 June the Congress adopted a 'declaration of sovereignty' in terms of which Russian laws were to have precedence over those of the USSR within its own territory.[11] But once Yeltsin had resigned from the CPSU and become, in effect, the leader of the extraparliamentary opposition, the issue of the presidency became more partisan and the question of who might fill the position much more contentious. At the second Russian Congress, in December 1990, all that was agreed was that the Supreme Soviet would consider amendments to the Constitution and submit them to the full Congress.[12] As an amendment of this kind would require a two-thirds majority, Yeltsin's hardline opponents seemed well placed to resist any change that might be to their disadvantage. The decision to call a referendum on the future of the USSR, however, altered the situation once again. In January 1991 the Presidium of the Supreme Soviet proposed an additional question on the establishment of a directly elected presidency, the proposal was approved by the Supreme Soviet itself, and then in March Russia's voters were asked to express their views. A resounding 70 per cent approved the change.[13]

The Congress of People's Deputies had originally been elected in March 1990, with a substantial representation of Communists. Led by its speaker, economics professor Ruslan Khasbulatov, it took an increasingly hostile attitude towards the market-oriented reforms that were being promoted by the President and his government. The outcome of the referendum and the evidence it provided of public support for constitutional change influenced the Congress in a different direction, and on 5 April it was agreed that a presidential election would be held on 12 June 1991. The Supreme Soviet was meanwhile asked to prepare a law on the presidency as well as any amendments that might be necessary to the Russian Constitution.[14] A new law was approved by the Supreme Soviet on 24 April,[15] and a month later the full Congress of People's Deputies amended the Constitution to incorporate its various provisions. The president was described as the 'highest official of the Russian Federation and the head of executive power'; whoever held that office had the right of legislative initiative and could veto the legislation that went through the Supreme Soviet, reporting to the full Congress of Deputies once a year and appointing the prime minister 'with the consent of the Supreme Soviet'. There was also a Vice-President, elected at the same time; Yeltsin's choice was Alexander Rutskoi, a moustachioed fighter pilot who had been a hero of the war in Afghanistan and then went on to head a moderate Communist grouping within the Russian parliament. The Supreme Soviet, for its part, could overrule a presidential veto by a simple majority in both houses, and the Congress of Deputies could impeach the president or vice-president if they violated the Constitution or laws, or if the president violated his inaugural oath.[16]

Yeltsin owed much of his authority to the fact that he had been directly elected, unlike Gorbachev, who had been chosen by Soviet parliamentarians. He had also won respect when he faced down the attempted coup of August 1991, at some risk to his own life. At the same time, he had to govern through a Congress of People's Deputies that had also been chosen by popular ballot, and which was able to claim the same right to represent the will of the electorate. The Congress had initially been supportive, electing Yeltsin its chairman and then, in the aftermath of the coup, granting him additional powers.[17] Yeltsin, however, used his position to launch a programme of far-reaching change under the guidance of Yegor Gaidar, a formerly orthodox but now fervently pro-market economist who had become deputy premier in November 1991, and parliamentary resistance strengthened as its consequences became apparent. In April 1992, at the first Congress after the abandonment of most forms of price control, an attempt to debate a motion of no confidence in the government was narrowly defeated and a resolution was adopted that called for 'major changes' in the reform programme, including a substantial increase in public spending.[18] Gaidar, who had been appointed acting prime minister in June, was obliged to stand down at the 7th Congress in December 1992 at the same time as the economic performance of the government was pronounced 'unsatisfactory';[19] and at the 8th Congress, in March 1993, the President was stripped of his emergency powers and ordered to act in accordance with the Constitution, in terms of which the Congress was itself the 'supreme body of state power'.[20] Yeltsin's supporters had already spoken of the need for extraordinary measures in response to what they regarded as parliamentary sabotage of their programme, and on 20 March, in a television address, the President called for a 'special form of administration' under which the Congress would continue to meet but would be unable to challenge his decisions.[21] The Congress, hurriedly convened for an emergency session, voted to impeach him but not by the necessary two-thirds majority; the outcome was an agreement that a referendum, originally approved the previous December, would be held on 25 April 1993 to decide 'who rules Russia'.[22]

The referendum, in the event, did little to resolve a continuing impasse. Voters were asked if they 'had confidence' in Yeltsin as Russian president, and if they supported the policies that the President and government had been pursuing; they were also asked if they favoured early presidential or parliamentary elections. Of those who voted, 58.7 per cent supported the President and 53.1 per cent approved his policies; 49.5 per cent favoured early presidential elections and a more substantial 67.2 per cent early parliamentary elections, but in both cases this fell short of the majority of the electorate – and not just of voters – that would have been necessary for the decisions to have constitutional effect. These were better results than the polls had forecast, although there were substantial regional variations: eighteen of the republics and regions declared a lack of confidence in the President, there was no voting at all in the Chechen republic, and in Tatarstan the turnout was so low the whole exercise was invalid.[23] For Yeltsin and his supporters, this was nonetheless a verdict that justified pressing ahead with a constitution that provided for a presidential republic, and by the end of the year they had attained their objective. Yeltsin had already made clear, in an uncompromising address in December 1992, that the Congress was creating 'intolerable working conditions for the government and the President', and claimed that it was aiming in the last resort at the 'restoration of a total-itarian Soviet-communist system'. It had 'become impossible to go on working with such a Congress', he warned deputies, and he called for a referendum to resolve the tension between 'two irreconcilable positions'.[24]

For parliamentarians and their speaker, the issue was a rather different one: whether government should be accountable to elected representatives, and whether a broadly representative parliament should be allowed to act as a check on what would otherwise be a disproportionately powerful executive. For Khasbulatov, the Russian state had for centuries been identified with the power of an autocratic ruler. Marxism–Leninism had not only continued this tradition but taken it to 'absurd lengths', with a Communist Party General Secretary who had 'practically become a tsar'. It was vital, in these circum-stances, to establish a secure division of powers, which was the basis of democratic politics in other countries. Not only did it guarantee the effective operation of the state machine, it had a 'deeper humanistic significance' in that it helped to defend individual liberties based on the rule of law. A parliament, in this context, was the 'institutionalisa-tion of democracy'; it represented the entire society and helped to reconcile its various elements; it acted as a 'counterbalance' to the executive, encouraged the formation of political parties and helped to stabilise the system as a whole.[25] Opening the Russian parliament in March 1992, Khasbulatov accused the government of an 'attack on democracy' and complained that individual ministers had a dismissive attitude towards the representative institutions through which it was expressed.[26] He insisted that government should be accountable to the Congress and Supreme Soviet rather than to the 'collective Rasputin' that surrounded the President.[27] And he argued more generally that a presidential republic was not appropriate to the particular circumstances of postcommunist Russia, with its need to maximise consensus and public understanding.[28]

These differences, in the end, were resolved by force when parliament was dissolved by presidential decree on 21 September 1993 and then stormed by the Russian army on 4 October following an attempt by parliamentary supporters to occupy the Kremlin and establish their ascendancy (see pp. 28–31). Yeltsin had produced his own draft of a new constitution in April 1993, in the immediate aftermath of the referendum, and a constitutional conference that met in June and July with a number of deputies in attendance produced another version that was in his opinion 'neither presidential nor parliamentary'.[29] But the Russian President had also predicted a 'decisive battle' between the supporters and opponents of his programme of reforms, and in the different circumstances that obtained after the suppression of what he described as a parliamentary insurrection, it was a rather more centralist draft that was published in November 1993 and then approved at a 'national vote' the following month.[30] Most of the changes in the draft were minor, but several were significant, particularly those that concerned the relationship between the central government and the regions. The Constitution as it stood incorporated the Federation Treaty, concluded in the spring of 1992, which defined relations between the federal authorities and lower levels of government; the November draft left it out, undermining the position of what were now to be known as 'subjects of the federation'. And the position of the government in relation to the president was further weakened: under a new article it would be required to resign on the election of a new president, who could dismiss it without reference to parliament.[31] The outcome was what *Izvestiya* described as a 'superpresidential republic'; others thought it 'monarchical'.[32]

The newly defined presidency was certainly a formidable one. Some called him (it has always, so far, been a male) a 'president-tsar'; Gorbachev, indeed, claimed the Russian president was *more* powerful than the Tsar had been before the revolution.[33] The president was head of state and guarantor of the Constitution itself, to which he swore allegiance. It was the President who represented the Russian Federation at home and abroad and who defined the 'basic directions of the domestic and foreign policy of the state' (art. 80), particularly in an 'annual address on the situation in the country' that he delivered to both houses of parliament (art. 84). The president was directly elected for four – from 2012, six – years by universal, direct and equal ballot, and could not be elected for more than two consecutive terms (art. 81). A Russian president had to be a citizen who was at least 35 years old and had lived in the country for at least the previous ten years (*ibid.*); this ruled out the 'wild card' émigré candidacies that had enjoyed considerable success in some of the other postcommunist countries. The president, moreover, had extensive powers of appointment. He appointed the prime minister 'with the consent of the State Duma' and could preside at meetings of the government. He nominated candidates to head the State Bank, appointed and dismissed deputy premiers and ministers, and nominated candidates to the Constitutional Court, the Supreme Court and the Procuracy. It was the president who formed and headed the Security Council and appointed his representatives in the Russian regions as well as the high command of the armed forces and diplomatic representatives (art. 83). In addition, he could initiate legislation and dissolve the Duma in specified circumstances (art. 84) and issue his own decrees, which had the force of law throughout the Federation (art. 90).[34]

There were in fact few limits on the powers of a Russian president. He could still be impeached, but less easily than before: the Duma had first of all to vote in favour of proceedings by a two-thirds majority of its entire membership on the initiative of at least a third of the deputies, after a special commission of deputies had decided he was guilty of an act of treason or a crime of similar magnitude. The Supreme Court had to rule that there were grounds for an action of this kind, and the Constitutional Court had to confirm that the proper procedures had been followed; the Federation Council had then to vote in favour by a two-thirds majority of its entire membership, not more than three months after the original charges had been presented (art. 93). There was no upper age limit, as there had been in the document it replaced, presumably because Yeltsin would just have passed his sixty-fifth birthday when his first term came to an end. And there was no provision, as there had been in the Constitution that was valid at the time of Yeltsin's September decree, that the president could not dissolve the Congress of Deputies or Supreme Soviet, or suspend their operation. It was for the president to approve the 'military doctrine of the Russian Federation' (art. 83), and it was for the president, not the parliament, to call a referendum once the necessary procedures had been completed.[35] Nor was there any provision for a vice-president, who could deputise for the president and perhaps – as Rutskoi had done – offer a political alternative as well as a mechanism that could be invoked if the president were to become incapable of exercising the functions of his office at some point in the future.[36]

The president, indeed, had additional powers that were not fully specified by the Constitution. The Constitution, for instance, made provision for an 'Administration of the President of the Russian Federation' (art. 83) but gave no indication of the role it was expected to perform. It was, in fact, a kind of super-government, with a staff of nearly 2,000 that was in many ways reminiscent of the central bureaucracy of the CPSU, housed in the same buildings and headed by presidential counsellors whose influence could eclipse that of the corresponding ministers.[37] The head of the Presidential Administration was a figure of considerable influence in his own right. Up to the end of 1998, it had been Valentin Yumashev, a journalist who had identified with Yeltsin at the outset of his career and who (more important) was a trusted member of the President's 'inner circle' – indeed shortly after leaving office he became a part of the President's own family when he married Yeltsin's younger daughter Tat'yana (their children from earlier marriages were already attending the same school in England).[38] Yumashev was succeeded by Alexander Voloshin, a railway engineer who had previously been an adviser on economic policy, and then by future president Dmitri Medvedev (2003–5) and Sergei Sobyanin (2005–8), who had been governor of oil-rich Tyumen. After Medvedev himself became president in 2008 the position went to Sergei Naryshkin, another Leningrader with a higher education in engineering and economics who had formerly been head of the government apparatus.

Prime minister and government

The prime minister had a distinct but subordinate position within this structure of executive authority (at least he did until May 2008, when Putin moved from the presidency to the premiership without apparently ceasing to be the dominant partner in the relationship). A Russian prime minister, as we have seen, was appointed by the president 'with the consent of the State Duma' (art. 111); the entire government submitted its resignation to a new President, and the President had in turn to submit his prime ministerial nomination within two weeks of taking office (arts. 116 and 111). But unlike parliamentary systems, there was no question of the prime minister submitting his resignation to a newly elected Duma and securing the support of deputies in order to continue. Equally, the dismissal of the prime minister and government had nothing to do with the balance of power in the Duma, still less the outcome of a parliamentary election; it was a presidential prerogative, under Article 83 of the Constitution, and it could be exercised whenever the president chose to do so. The Duma, for its part, did have some influence over the choice of prime minister, but it was a power of last resort. It had a week to vote on any nomination; if it rejected three nominations in a row, the president was required and not merely empowered to dissolve it and call a new election (art. 111). The Duma had another power of last resort, which was its right to call a vote of no confidence in the government as a whole. If it voted accordingly twice in three months, the president had either to announce the resignation of the government or else dissolve the Duma (the government could also offer its own resignation, which the president could accept or reject (art. 117)). But neither of these powers was likely to be used in normal circumstances, as they would precipitate a constitutional crisis and almost certainly the dissolution of the Duma itself.

It was the prime minister, in turn, who took responsibility for the ordinary business of government. It was the prime minister, under the Constitution, who made proposals to the president on the structure of the government as a whole, and on the appointment of deputy premiers and ministers (art. 112), and who was responsible for identifying the 'basic guidelines' of government activity and 'organis[ing] its work' (art. 113). The government as a whole was responsible for submitting an annual budget to the Duma and reporting on its fulfilment; ministers, under the Law on the Government of 1997,[39] could also be required to respond to the questions that were addressed to them by members of the Duma or Federation Council. The government, similarly, took responsibility for finance, credit and currency matters, and it conducted a 'uniform state policy' in culture, science, education, health, social security and the environment. The government was also responsible for state property, public order and foreign policy (art. 114 of the Constitution), and it could issue resolutions in order to carry its decisions into effect (art. 115). Under the terms of the 1997 law, it was the president who directed the ministries and other government bodies that had responsibility for defence, security, internal affairs, foreign affairs and emergencies (justice was added in 2004),[40] although the government as a whole was supposed to 'coordinate their activity' and the relevant ministers took part in its regular meetings, which took place 'at least once a month' (a smaller working Presidium met 'whenever necessary').[41] The full list of ministries, organised in accordance with these principles, is shown in Table 3.1.

Viktor Chernomyrdin had been elected prime minister in December 1992 after the Congress of Deputies refused to accept Yeltsin's nomination of Yegor Gaidar, and he was confirmed in his position after the 1996 presidential election. Yeltsin, however, was apparently jealous of the prominent role that Chernomyrdin had been playing in domestic and international affairs – newspapers suggested he had made the President 'almost redundant'[42] – and in March 1998 he unexpectedly dismissed the entire government and appointed Sergei Kirienko acting prime minister, explaining at the same time that there would be 'no change in policy'.[43] Kirienko, a boyish 35-year-old who had served as energy minister since the previous November, was virtually unknown to the wider public ('Sergei who?', asked *Moscow News*[44]); but he was formally nominated as prime minister four days later, Yeltsin introducing him as a 'technocrat' who was 'open to a dialogue with all who [we]re ready to hear a variety of opinions'.[45] Kirienko, it emerged, was a former Komsomol official from Nizhnii Novgorod with a degree in shipbuilding who had moved into factory management and banking, and there was general agreement that he had a 'disarming and easygoing manner'.[46] He was nonetheless rejected in a first vote on 10 April and by a larger majority on 17 April; he was finally approved a week later, with deputies aware that if they rejected his nomination a third time not simply would the Duma itself be dissolved but the President would also be able to impose his own choice until a new parliament had been convened.[47]

Political life was thrown into disarray once more in August 1998 when the President made another unexpected change of prime minister and government. Yeltsin, who was on holiday at the time, had told journalists a few days earlier that he was 'quite satisfied' with his youthful premier, and Kirienko himself had been giving interviews to mark his 'first hundred days' in office.[48] But on 23 August, in a country already reeling from a sudden collapse in the rouble (p. 142), the Russian President dismissed the entire

Table 3.1 The Russian government, 2010 (simplified)

Prime Minister* (from May 2008, Vladimir Putin)
2 First Deputy Prime Ministers* (Igor Shuvalov and Viktor Zubkov)
7 Deputy Prime Ministers* (one of whom, Sergei Sobyanin, was also head of the government apparatus; another, Aleksei Kudrin, was also Finance Minister)

Federal ministries subordinated to the president
Ministry of Internal Affairs*
Ministry of Civil Defence, Emergencies and the Liquidation of the Consequences of Natural Disasters
Ministry of Foreign Affairs*
Ministry of Defence*
Ministry of Justice
State Courier Service
Foreign Intelligence Service
Federal Security Service
Federal Service for Narcotics Control
Federal Guard Service
Main Administration of Presidential Special Programmes
Presidential Business Office

Federal ministries subordinated to the government
Ministry of Health and Social Development*
Ministry of Culture
Ministry of Education and Science
Ministry of Natural Resources and Ecology
Ministry of Industry and Trade
Ministry of Regional Development*
Ministry of Information Technologies and Communication
Ministry of Agriculture*
Ministry of Sport, Tourism and Youth Policy
Ministry of Transport
Ministry of Finances*
Ministry of Economic Development*
Ministry of Energetics

Source: adapted from *Sobranie zakonodatel'stva Rossiiskoi Federatsii*, no. 20, 2008, item 2290, 12 May 2008, and press reports; federal services and agencies subordinate to federal ministries are not shown. Members of the Presidium are as listed in *ibid.*, item 2370, 16 May 2008. The current individual membership of the government may be found at www.government.ru.
*= member of the Presidium.

government once again and nominated Viktor Chernomyrdin to the premiership, just five months after he had dispensed with his services.[49] In a 'difficult' economic situation, Yeltsin explained in a television address, they needed a 'heavyweight' with the kind of 'experience and authority' the former Prime Minister could provide; and they also needed someone who could ensure 'continuity of government', which suggested that Chernomyrdin would be his favoured candidate at a future presidential election.[50]

Chernomyrdin, however, had still to secure the endorsement of the Duma, which showed no willingness to accept a candidate whose policies had so manifestly failed; he was rejected on 31 August by a large majority, and then on 7 September by an equally decisive margin.[51] Yeltsin told interviewers he would 'insist' on Chernomyrdin in the third and decisive vote, dissolving the Duma if necessary;[52] but he had no wish to face an even more hostile parliament, which polls suggested was the most likely outcome, and in negotiations with the party leaders a different and more widely supported candidate emerged, Foreign Minister Yevgenii Primakov. He was nominated on 10 September and endorsed by the Duma the following day by 317 votes to 63 with the support of the Communists and of Yabloko, who had first proposed his name earlier in the year.[53]

Primakov, explained Yabloko leader Grigorii Yavlinsky, was not an ideal candidate, but he was an 'adaptable politician without personal ambitions whose main goal [would] be to maintain stability'.[54] Yeltsin himself, in another television address, emphasised that Primakov was a 'consensus candidate', and one who for the first time would be able to count on the support of the Federal Assembly as well as the President.[55] This was nonetheless the first time Yeltsin had been obliged to yield ground to his political opponents, and it marked what appeared to be at least a temporary shift towards a more balanced relationship between President, government and parliament. Indeed there were moves against the President himself: the Duma had voted in favour of his resignation in the immediate aftermath of the collapse of the rouble in late August, and most Russians, according to the survey evidence, thought he should step down immediately.[56] Yeltsin himself rejected such demands, insisting he would remain until the end of his second term,[57] but spokesmen made clear that he would be withdrawing to a more 'strategic' role in which he would no longer be 'distracted by day-to-day issues', although he was still reluctant to consider any formal transfer of his considerable powers or – still more so – any modification of the Constitution that might diminish them.[58] The new government, reflecting the broadly based nature of its support, was in effect a coalition: its economics minister was a Communist, its finance minister had belonged to Yabloko, it included the first minister from Zhirinovsky's Liberal Democrats, and there were eight representatives of the Russian regions. Opinion polls suggested it was also a government that rested on the support of a substantial majority of Russia's long-suffering citizens.[59]

The Primakov government lasted until May 1999, helping to stabilise the Russian economy after the collapse of the currency and establishing a better working relationship with the Duma. But Primakov had also authorised an anti-corruption campaign against the rich 'oligarchs' that were associated with the Yeltsin leadership and who claimed to have played a 'decisive role' in helping the Russian President win re-election in 1996, following which they had been allowed to acquire state assets at a fraction of their market value in a notorious 'loans for shares' privatisation exercise.[60] Not only this, but an investigation into the lavish redecoration of the Kremlin palaces by a Swiss firm called Mabetex had established that the cost had run into hundreds of millions of dollars and that the same firm had underwritten the credit card transactions of dozens of highly placed Russian officials, including Yeltsin and his two daughters. All of this evidence was placed at the disposal of the Russian Prosecutor General, Yuri Skuratov, by his counterpart in Switzerland, where the investigation had originated. In early 1999 Skuratov was preparing to take matters further but was compromised when a naked man 'resembling' the Prosecutor General was secretly photographed in a sauna with two female companions in an operation that had evidently been set up by state security. Skuratov offered to resign, but the Federation Council, which was the only body that had the power to remove him, steadfastly refused to accept his offer to do so even after the compromising videotape had been shown on national television.[61] To make matters worse, Skuratov's protector, Prime Minister Primakov, came himself to be seen as an increasingly plausible candidate for the presidency in the election that was due to take place the following year, when Yeltsin would be obliged to stand down at the end of his second presidential term.

Yeltsin, who was already in a difficult position because of impeachment charges that were about to be considered by the Duma, once again responded pre-emptively by sacking the entire government. He had no criticism of Primakov's 'personal qualities', the President explained in another television broadcast, but there was a need for more 'dynamism and energy'.[62] Yeltsin's chosen replacement was Sergei Stepashin, a former first deputy prime minister and, perhaps more important, a former head of state security of whose loyalty he could be entirely confident. Stepashin was approved by an overwhelming majority, but in August 1999 he too was dismissed and replaced by Vladimir Putin, who was at this time head of the Federal Security Service (which was the successor to the KGB of the Soviet period) and the recently appointed Secretary of the Security Council. It had been Putin, as head of state security, who appeared to have arranged the compromising of Skuratov, and it was Putin who had made a public appearance after the videotape had been shown on television to confirm its authenticity.[63] When he became not just prime minister but acting president at the end of the year, Putin's first substantive decree was one that granted immunity from prosecution to the former President together with the inviolability of his private and business premises, transport and communications, personal bodyguards for his entire family, free medical care, a government dacha for his lifetime use and a substantial salary.[64] This was an act of doubtful constitutionality and almost certainly an abuse of the powers with which the president had been entrusted, which allowed him to grant pardons but not to exempt selected individuals from the rule of law itself. If this was a pay-off, both sides had certainly kept their part of the bargain.

He had chosen Putin, Yeltsin explained in a television address, because he believed he would be able to draw together the wide range of political forces that were united in their wish to 'renew Great Russia in the new, 21st century'.[65] Writing later in his memoirs, Yeltsin explained that he had become convinced that Stepashin would be unable to mount an effective campaign in the parliamentary election that was due by the end of the year, or in the presidential election that would follow it. But he had formed a very different impression of Putin, who had come to his attention a couple of years earlier when the future President had been a member of the Kremlin administration. Putin's reports had been a 'model of clarity', he had responded coherently even to unexpected questions, and his reform of the security service had been well considered. They met early one morning in the presidential office. He had decided, Yeltsin told Putin, to offer him the premiership; the situation in the country was very difficult, and much would depend on his decisions. Putin, initially, was overwhelmed: 'I don't know, Boris Nikolaevich. I don't think I'm ready for it', he eventually replied; but Yeltsin asked him to think it over, and the nomination was announced in a national television broadcast on 9 August.[66] Putin claimed in his own version of the conversation that he had not been directly asked if he would be willing to take the place of the outgoing prime minister, nor had there been any talk of a 'successor'. Yeltsin, however, had spoken of him as a 'prime minister with a future',[67] and in his television address he went further, making clear that he saw the FSB head not just as a premier but as his favoured candidate for the presidency in the election that was due to take place the following year.

Speaking to deputies before the nomination was put to a vote, Putin laid particular emphasis on stability and promised that most of the outgoing administration would remain in their posts. The economic policies of the new government would also continue largely unchanged. Every effort would be made to bring pension payments up to date, and then to increase them. Those who worked in the state sector should also receive their wages on time. It would be a 'basic task' to restore the country's defensive might, improving the material conditions of the armed forces and recovering the positive image they had previously enjoyed. But an effective economy also meant one that had largely eliminated economic crime, and one that had restored the effectiveness of government itself. He had 'deep respect' for the rights of the various regions and republics, Putin told the deputies, but there could be no special privileges for any of them that were not justified by their economic circumstances. The situation in the North Caucasus, in particular, had clearly been deteriorating. A new state commission would carry out a more detailed examination, including all the political and socio-economic issues that were associated with it. But Russia's territorial integrity could not be a matter for discussion, and he would 'deal severely' with any attempt to encroach upon it. In foreign policy too there would be a greater emphasis on the promotion of Russian interests, and on the protection of Russian nationals in other countries.[68] The nomination was approved by 233 in favour and 84 against (17 abstained), which was the necessary majority of the entire membership;[69] the flow of elections, appointments, resignations and dismissals over the entire post-Soviet period is shown in Table 3.2.

Chechen fundamentalists had crossed into neighbouring Dagestan at the start of August 1999, holding several villages until they were forced to retreat. Their leader, Shamil Basaev, had warned that they would switch to 'military-political' methods, understood as a reference to terrorism, and at the very end of the month there was some indication of what was to come when a bomb went off in a Moscow shopping mall, killing one person and wounding more than sixty.[70] Then on 4 September a car bomb demolished a five-storey army barracks in Buinaksk, in Dagestan; sixty-four were killed

Table 3.2 **Russian presidents and prime ministers since 1991**

Presidents	Elected	Inaugurated	Re-elected	Left office
Boris Yeltsin	12 June 1991	10 July 1991	3 July 1996	31 Dec 1999[a]
Vladimir Putin	26 Mar 2000	7 May 2000	14 Mar 2004	7 May 2008
Dmitri Medvedev	2 Mar 2008	7 May 2008		
Prime ministers	Nominated	Approved	Re-appointed	Left office
Yegor Gaidar	8 Dec 1992	–	–	9 Dec 1992[b]
Viktor Chernomyrdin	14 Dec 1992	14 Dec 1992	10 Aug 1996	23 Mar 1998
Sergei Kirienko	23 Mar 1998	24 Apr 1998	–	23 Aug 1998
Yevgenii Primakov	10 Sep 1998	11 Sep 1998	–	12 May 1999
Sergei Stepashin	12 May 1999	19 May 1999	–	9 Aug 1999
Vladimir Putin	9 Aug 1999	16 Aug 1999	–	7 May 2000
Mikhail Kas'yanov	7 May 2000	17 May 2000	–	24 Feb 2004
Mikhail Fradkov	1 Mar 2004	5 Mar 2004	12 May 2004	12 Sep 2007
Viktor Zubkov	12 Sep 2007	14 Sep 2007	–	7 May 2008
Vladimir Putin	7 May 2008	8 May 2008		

Notes: [a] Yeltsin's premature resignation took effect at midnight, and Putin became acting president from this point up to his inauguration the following May; [b] Gaidar became acting premier on 15 June 1992, but his formal nomination on 8 December 1992 was rejected the following day by the Congress of People's Deputies.

and twice as many were injured.[71] There was still greater loss of life over the following weeks when two apartment buildings in Moscow were blown up, one on Guryanov Street on 9 September (92 were killed and 264 injured) and the other on Kashkir Highway on 13 September (121 were killed and 9 injured).[72] Terrorism, Yeltsin declared in a national television address, had 'declared war on the people of Russia'; they would respond 'harshly, quickly and decisively' to this new challenge.[73] Putin, speaking to deputies, described the bombings as acts of 'international terrorism' and Chechnya itself as a 'huge terrorist camp'.[74] Two days later another bomb went off, this time outside an apartment building in the southern city of Volgodonsk; 18 were killed and 66 injured.[75] On 23 September the Russian media reported that a further explosion had been pre-empted, in the provincial city of Ryazan, which was later and somewhat mysteriously explained as an FSB training exercise.[76] The same evening Putin publicly praised the vigilance of the security forces and ordered the air-strikes that marked the onset of another war; the first bombs fell on the Chechen capital the following day.[77]

There was considerable public support for the resumption of hostilities against the breakaway republic, defined by the Chechens themselves as a struggle for independence and by the Russian authorities as a terrorist campaign that was a challenge to Western civilisation as a whole.[78] Putin, speaking at a press conference in the Kazakh capital, Astana, made a crudely worded promise that later became notorious, to 'wipe out the terrorists even if they [were] on the john',[79] and he soon became, in effect, the main repository of the hopes of millions of ordinary Russians who had been persuaded to believe they were under attack from a fanatical and externally funded adversary and that only the state and its armed forces could protect them. Indeed for at least some well-placed observers, the terrorist atrocities had been organised by the federal authorities themselves precisely to generate the kind of public hysteria they would need if they were to have a hope of prevailing at the coming parliamentary and (more important) presidential elections.[80] The increase in Putin's own popularity was certainly remarkable – just 2 per cent were prepared to back him for the presidency in August 1999, but half of those asked were prepared to do so by December and by mid-January his support had reached 62 per cent.[81] Putin had assumed the powers of acting president by this time, in addition to the premiership, after Yeltsin unexpectedly resigned on the last day of December with six months of his second term remaining. As voting took place in the parliamentary election on 19 December, federal troops were tightening their grip on Grozny; the Russian flag was flying again in the Chechen capital early in the new year after very heavy civilian and military losses had taken place and the city itself had been reduced to rubble.

Yeltsin and the Russian presidency

The man who exercised the far-reaching powers of the Russian presidency for almost the entire decade had been born in the village of Butko in the Sverdlovsk region of western Siberia in 1931, the son of peasant parents. According to his autobiography, Yeltsin was lucky to be alive at all: the priest nearly drowned him when he was being baptised, remarking calmly that if he could survive such an ordeal he must be a 'good tough lad'.[82] Both his father and his uncle were persecuted in 1934 when they fell foul of the campaign against the kulaks, who were rich or simply more efficient farmers. They were accused of conducting anti-Soviet agitation and, although they protested their innocence, given three months' hard labour; Yeltsin himself, though only three, professed to remember the 'horror and fear' years later.[83] The future president grew up during the years of famine that had followed the brutal collectivisation of agriculture: there were always shortages of food, and the family might not have survived the war but for the milk and sometimes the warmth of their nanny-goat. He lost two fingers in an accident, broke his nose and contracted typhoid fever; his father, a harsh disciplinarian, beat him regularly. Later, he lost almost all hearing in his right ear – not an unmitigated loss for a Russian politician, as his bodyguard pointed out in his memoirs.[84] But he did well at school and graduated as an engineer at the Urals Polytechnical Institute, where he perfected his volleyball technique and met his future wife (they had fallen in love during the second year, she told journalists).[85]

After completing his studies, Yeltsin worked as a construction engineer, managing a large state enterprise that specialised in prefabricated housing. In 1961 he joined the

CPSU, becoming a full-time party functionary in 1968 and in 1976 first secretary of the entire Sverdlovsk region. He joined the Central Committee at the following party congress in 1981, as a full member from the outset. One of his early decisions was to order the destruction of the Ipat'ev house in which Tsar Nicholas II's family had been shot in 1918, and which had become a place of pilgrimage. The decision, he explained later, had been taken secretly by the Politburo and there was no alternative but to carry it out, although he knew that 'sooner or later' they would all be ashamed of what they had done (much later again, in 1998, he was able to make atonement in a dignified speech when the remains of the royal family, as verified by scientific analysis, were buried in the Cathedral of St Peter and Paul in St Petersburg).[86] Yeltsin's managerial qualities – he had, on his own admission, become 'steeped in command-administrative methods' by this time[87] – caught the attention of the party leadership, and early in 1985 he was invited to Moscow to take up a position in the central party administration as head of its construction department. In December 1985, after Gorbachev had taken office, he was transferred to the position of first secretary of the Moscow party organisation in succession to a disgraced Brezhnevite;[88] two months later he moved into the Politburo itself.

Yeltsin's outspoken comments soon began to attract attention. His speech at the 27th Party Congress in early 1986 began with the usual commonplaces about the 'Leninist optimism' that prevailed at their deliberations, but went on to ask why over so many years the party had failed to eliminate social injustice and the abuse of official position while at the same time tolerating a group of 'infallible' leaders who had openly practised a 'dual morality'.[89] Then in October 1987 – according to those who were present, almost by accident[90] – he was called to speak to the Central Committee plenum that was considering Gorbachev's draft report on the seventieth anniversary of the revolution. Yeltsin wanted, he wrote later, to 'screw up [his] courage and say what [he] had to say'; his speech was no more than a few headings on a sheet of paper. It was nonetheless the decisive moment in his political career. There had been no changes in the way the party Secretariat operated, Yeltsin told the delegates, nor in the conduct of its head, Yegor Ligachev. More and more instructions were being issued, but they were attracting less and less attention. Meanwhile in the Politburo, there had been a 'noticeable increase' in what he 'could only describe as adulation of the General Secretary'. In seventy years, he declared in another version of the speech that circulated unofficially, they had failed to feed and clothe the people they claimed to represent, while providing for themselves abundantly. And there were criticisms of the General Secretary's wife, who had been acquiring her own 'cult of personality'.[91]

Yeltsin knew what would happen next: he would be 'slaughtered, in an organised, methodical manner', and 'with pleasure and enjoyment'.[92] The plenum itself described his speech as 'politically mistaken' and called for his dismissal as Moscow party secretary; Gorbachev, 'almost hysterical', denounced him at the Politburo and complained that everything in the Soviet capital was 'going badly'.[93] The Moscow party organisation, when it met in November, dragged a 'barely conscious' Yeltsin out of a hospital bed to listen to a series of charges of incompetence and even 'Bonapartism' in what was the political equivalent of a Stalinist show trial, and then voted to remove him from his post.[94] Yeltsin himself, after an 'almost fatal' dose of painkiller, spoke briefly and like a 'hypnotised lunatic'; the plenum itself affected his health and left him in a 'very low mood, confined to bed, and if anyone visited him he shook the hand that was extended with two cold fingers'.[95] He was dropped from the Party Politburo in February 1988 and urged to retire, but in the end moved to a junior ministerial position at the State Construction Committee that was a logical continuation of his earlier responsibilities. A 'political outcast, surrounded by a vacuum',[96] Yeltsin's political career seemed at an end; even his membership of the CPSU was in doubt as the Central Committee, in a decision without post-war precedent, voted to investigate his increasingly outspoken views to determine if they were compatible with party policy.[97]

But the more Yeltsin was attacked by the party leadership, the more he came to be seen as a champion of ordinary citizens against an overpowerful, often corrupt establishment; and the introduction of competitive elections at the same time as his disgrace allowed him to turn this popular following to his political advantage. In March 1989, standing for the Moscow national-territorial constituency, he won over 89 per cent of the vote against a party-approved competitor;[98] his winning margin, over 5 million votes, was so large it entered the *Guinness Book of Records*, and it contrasted sharply with Gorbachev's decision to take one of the hundred seats that had been reserved for the CPSU and for which exactly a hundred candidates had been nominated, avoiding a direct appeal to the electorate and still more so a confrontation with his leading opponent. A year later, in elections to the Russian parliament, Yeltsin secured another popular mandate when he took over 80 per cent of the vote in his native Sverdlovsk in elections to the Russian Congress of Deputies,[99] and he began to use his position, once he had become parliamentary chairman at the end of May 1990, to advance the claims of the republics and especially of Russia itself against the federal government and the party leadership. Yeltsin's best-known formulation, expressed several times during a visit to the Volga republics in August 1990, was that they should 'take as much power as they [could] swallow':[100] in effect, that they should all combine against the federal authorities, or what Yeltsin himself had begun to call 'the Centre'.

Yeltsin's appeal was based in the first instance on his uncompromising opposition to the party-state bureaucracy, but he also advanced more specific proposals. Speaking to the Central Committee in February 1990, he called for the private ownership of land, independence for the republics, financial autonomy for factories and farms, freedom of political association, and freedom of conscience.[101] His address to the 28th Congress in July 1990 argued that the CPSU could still reform itself, but only if it agreed to a 'fundamental restructuring' and became a parliamentary party with a different name, drawing on the energies of its ordinary members and leading a 'broad social base for the renewal of society'. Speaking at a later session, he announced his own resignation so that he could properly represent all the deputies who had elected him to the chairmanship of the Russian Supreme Soviet and not just those who were members of the same political organisation.[102] Asked in the summer of 1990 if he was still a socialist, Yeltsin turned the question on its head: what, he asked in reply, was meant by 'socialism'? It could mean the 'developed socialism' that the USSR itself was supposed to have established under Brezhnev, or the repressive 'socialism' of Pol Pot's Cambodia. In Hitler's Germany there had been national socialism; and there were many different kinds of capitalism too. What was the point of arguing about definitions?[103] His models, he told interviewers, were Peter the Great and Yaroslav the Wise, grand duke of Kievan Rus' in the early eleventh century;[104] but in general, he confessed, he was happy to rely on his intuition.[105] A study of his speeches by three academics found that the Russian President was 'predictable in only one respect – his unpredictability'.[106]

Yeltsin admitted in the memoirs he published in 1994 that he depended first of all on the self-image he and his associates had created, as a 'wilful, decisive, uncompromising politician'. But he also acknowledged that he was greatly influenced by the opinion of people he respected, and sometimes his train of thought could be changed entirely by 'a word said in passing or a line in a lengthy newspaper article'. There was, it seems, a decisive moment in this intellectual trajectory, in late 1989, when Yeltsin visited a Moscow bathhouse on the insistence of his staff so that he could relieve himself of some of the pressure under which he had been operating. He found himself surrounded by a crowd of about forty naked men, all urging him to maintain his challenge. It was (he hardly needed to add) 'quite a sight'. And it was at this moment in the *banya*, with everything reduced – so to speak – to its essentials, that he had 'changed [his] world-view, realised [he] was a communist by Soviet tradition, by inertia, by education, but not by conviction'.[107] Yeltsin was also influenced by a visit to the United States in September 1989, his first to a capitalist country. Amazed by the array of foodstuffs that was readily available in a Houston supermarket, he commented that this disproved the 'fairytales' that were being peddled in the USSR itself about the superiority of socialism. In the view of Lev Sukhanov, one of his closest aides, it was at this time the future president decided to leave the ranks of the CPSU;[108] it could in fact have seen the end of his career entirely as he took his staff swimming late at night in shark-infested waters, paying no attention to the warning notices or to the 'little wave' that appeared beside him.[109]

In a newly established and weakly institutionalised system of the Russian kind, formal position mattered rather less than the shifting patterns of influence that revolved around the President himself. A great deal of importance attached, for instance, to relations with the President's younger daughter, who had become responsible for his 'image' in 1997 and who wielded a great deal of influence over other matters, including appointments and larger questions of strategy.[110] A common regional background was also important (a 'Sverdlovsk mafia' provided many of the President's earliest and most senior appointees), and so were services to his re-election campaign in 1996, or even his choice of tennis partner – including the national coach, with whom he played four or five times a week.[111] The head of presidential security up to 1996, for instance, Alexander Korzhakov, held a position of no constitutional significance. But he saw the President daily, played tennis with him regularly (making sure to lose more often than he won), and began to offer views on current politics that appeared to carry considerable weight at the very centre of the administration.[112] Korzhakov himself concluded that Yeltsin was influenced more than anything else by the 'interests of his family clan, not of the state', and in particular by his daughter Tanya and her 'chosen circle'.[113] One of these was the financier Boris Berezovsky, who was the main owner of the international carrier Aeroflot (whose chief executive was the husband of Yeltsin's elder daughter) and of the most important national television channel; one of the 'seven bankers' whose support had (in their view) been crucial to Yeltsin's re-election in 1996, he shortly afterwards became deputy secretary of the Security Council (1996–7) and then executive secretary of the Commonwealth of Independent States (1998–9).[114]

The result was what the liberal politician Grigorii Yavlinsky described as a 'Byzantine court', with members who were constantly engaged in 'palace intrigues';[115] a system of 'checks and balances', as others put it, but one in which, in the President's absence, 'the "checks" immediately declare[d] war on the "balances"'.[116] There was constant competition among the President's 'close associates' to become the 'closest of all', just as Politburo members had jostled for the central positions above the Lenin Mausoleum for the parade on the anniversary of the revolution.[117] And there was a pervasive atmosphere of suspicion, in which telephones were tapped and presidential aides exchanged their views in the form of notes that were later destroyed.[118] It was also a male environment, in which there could be physical threats, off-colour anecdotes that were 'reminiscent of the mores of the time of Ivan the Terrible', drinking bouts and buffoonery.[119] Annoyed by his press secretary, Vyacheslav Kostikov, during a boat trip on the Yenisei, for instance, Yeltsin brusquely demanded that he be 'thrown overboard'; Korzhakov, admiring the Siberian countryside from the lower deck, thought at first it was an 'enormous bird' as the offending staff member sailed past him, flailing the air with his arms and legs.[120] Kostikov himself 'mainly invited members of the sexual minorities' to join his staff, and one of its members who regularly staged homosexual orgies was found under the window of his flat with most of his bones broken after he had been ritually beaten for his 'complete sexual satisfaction' and then thrown from the third floor (this did not improve the press secretary's own reputation).[121] The President himself had more conventional tastes and simply 'love[d] a good time', according to the testimony of his bodyguard. He was fond of drinking songs and was a skilful instrumentalist with a good sense of rhythm; even on official trips he would demand 'bring spoons!' His 'favourite trick', Korzhakov recalled, 'was to play knick-knack-paddy-whack' on the head of his chief of staff. At first he would beat on his own leg,

and then he would beat loudly on the head of his subordinate. The latter did not dare to take offence, and just smiled affectedly. The audience burst out laughing. On one occasion, Yeltsin took aside the president of one of the former Soviet states, Askar Akayev of

Kyrgyzstan, and played the spoons on his head. He could torture one to death with this musical instrument.[122]

Several other members of the President's staff offered their own evaluations in memoirs and interviews. Yekaterina Lakhova, for instance, a qualified doctor from the same part of Russia who had worked in his administration as well as a party politician, found the President a contradictory character: 'by nature very stern, strong-willed, even dictatorial', a man who 'did not tolerate verbosity and vagueness', who always wanted the tasks before him to be set out 'clearly and precisely', and who set out tasks in this way before his subordinates. But at the same time, he was 'kind and responsive', even 'overly trustful', which meant that his relations with others were often based on his personal impressions rather than a balanced assessment of their performance.[123] Press secretary Kostikov also found him a creature of moods who rose to the occasion when it was necessary but fell into depression at other times, who liked to be the centre of attention and feel that 'all the applause belonged to him'. He had found it difficult to adapt to democratic politics, Kostikov believed, and was happier dealing with practical matters than with abstractions. He had no interest in culture and his musical tastes extended no further than folksong, but he could nevertheless reproduce an entire passage from Shostakovich's 'Leningrad Symphony'. He also found it difficult to establish a relationship with other Russian politicians and increasingly referred to himself in the third person, but liked to speak of 'my friend Bill [Clinton]' or 'my friend Helmut [Kohl]'; he had no particular philosophy, in Kostikov's view, other than the 'ideology of power itself'.[124]

The former acting prime minister, Yegor Gaidar, was another who had roots in the Sverdlovsk region and knew from his own sources that Yeltsin was well regarded locally. His speeches at the October 1987 plenum and at the 1988 Party Conference, thought Gaidar, had shown the President's 'strength and political potential, his ability to seize on problems that really mattered to people', but also 'complete uncertainty about where this political potential would be directed', especially in terms of economic policy. Equally, when he won the Moscow seat in the Congress of People's Deputies in 1989, it was clear that this was a 'real political leader', but there were few clues about the way he would use the support he had been able to mobilise. Yeltsin, for Gaidar as for others, was a 'complicated, contradictory character'. His strongest quality was his 'intuitive ability to feel the popular mood and take account of it before taking the most important decisions', and in questions of principle he trusted his instincts more than his advisers. He was able to listen, but could also be manipulated. And, like Kostikov, he noted that the President was capable of 'very long periods of passivity and depression'.[125] Closest of all was Yeltsin's former bodyguard Alexander Korzhakov, whose revealing memoir appeared in 1997. Yeltsin, he disclosed, had several times tried to kill himself, the first occasion in 1990 when he jumped off a bridge into the Moscow river in what had been thought at the time to be a drunken escapade, and on another occasion when Korzhakov had to break into a sauna to rescue him.[126] Others still consulted the stars: Yeltsin, they noted, was an

Aquarian, like three other heads of state in the CIS: this meant they were 'strong-willed, ambitious people, able to achieve what they wanted whatever the cost'.[127]

From Yeltsin to Putin/Medvedev

The struggle for influence within the presidency took place against a steady fall in the public standing of the President himself. Yeltsin had already overtaken Gorbachev in the opinion ratings before he became Russian president: in 1989 it was the Soviet President who was 'man of the year', and by a wide margin, but by 1990 Yeltsin (with 32 per cent) came first, ahead of Gorbachev with 19 per cent.[128] Another survey agency, in a less authoritative set of findings, suggested that Yeltsin could even be seen as the most outstanding Russian leader of the twentieth century, ahead of Lenin, Gorbachev and (by another wide margin) Nicholas II.[129] Yeltsin, in more qualitative terms, was seen as 'open and straightforward' (34 per cent), 'ambitious' (26 per cent), but also 'resolute' (24 per cent). Gorbachev, by contrast, was 'hypocritical' (28 per cent), 'weak and lacking in self-confidence' (20 per cent) and 'indifferent to human suffering' (19 per cent), although he was also 'flexible and capable of adapting to change' (18 per cent).[130] According to the All-Union Centre for the Study of Public Opinion, it was in the summer of 1990 that Yeltsin's popular support overtook that of the Soviet President. The peak of his popularity, with an approval rating of 80 per cent, was in July 1990, soon after he had been elected chairman of the Russian parliament; his support rose again, to 74 per cent, after he had faced down the attempted coup in August 1991.[131]

Once in office, however, Yeltsin's support declined rapidly (see Figure 3.1). It had slipped to about 45 per cent at the time of the collapse of the USSR at the end of 1991, and fell still further after the spring of 1992 as Gaidar's economic policies began to bite. The President's popularity recovered a little at the time of the April 1993 referendum and again during the conflict with the Russian parliament in September and October 1993, but then resumed its earlier decline, and by the end of 1994 his support was down to 34 per cent. Just 3 per cent of Russians, by this time, were ready to say they 'completely shared' his views and policies; 10 per cent supported him 'in the absence of other worthy political leaders', but 25 per cent were 'disappointed' in the Russian President and 26 per cent were his declared opponents.[132] It was at this point, in December 1994, that Yeltsin sent Russian forces into Chechnya to restore federal authority and perhaps to recover his public reputation in what was expected to be a 'short, victorious war'.[133] If this was the intention, it badly misfired. Chechen resistance proved unexpectedly stubborn; the Russian campaign was incompetently conducted, particularly in its early stages, and losses were heavy, up to 30,000 within the first year. Yeltsin's support, in the event, plunged still further, a majority holding him personally responsible for the war and just under 6 per cent prepared to support him in the event of an early presidential election.[134]

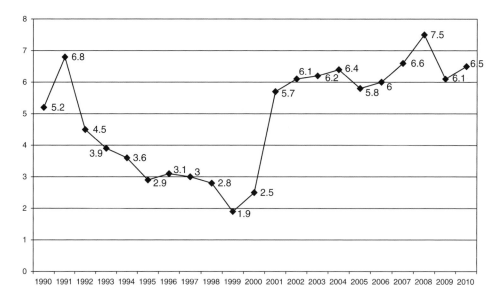

Figure 3.1 Presidential popularity, 1990–2010
Source: adapted from VTsIOM and Levada Centre data. Respondents were asked to evaluate presidential performance on a 10-point scale.

Yeltsin announced in February 1996 that he would nonetheless be seeking a second term, and then mounted a remarkable campaign that carried him to victory in the two rounds that took place in June and July.[135] It was a victory, in the end a decisive one, that owed a good deal to the prerogatives of the presidency itself. Yeltsin made full use of his influence over the state media, particularly television. He invited the head of Russia's newly established independent television service, which had been critical of his policies in Chechnya, to join his campaign staff. He committed public funds with increasing abandon: to small businesses and the Academy of Sciences, to pensioners and those who had lost their savings. An end was declared to the conscription in the armed forces, and the troops themselves were allowed to avoid compulsory duty in Chechnya and other hot spots.[136] Perhaps as much as $500 million was spent on his campaign, and certainly much more than the $3 million allowed by the electoral law.[137] But most important of all, Yeltsin campaigned with increasing confidence, travelling the country with an energy that belied his 65 years, and presenting himself as the only serious alternative to a return to communist rule. After one of his trips, at least four of the accompanying journalists had to be taken to hospital with pneumonia, and so had two of Yeltsin's own staff.[138] The changes in his behaviour were so extraordinary that ordinary Russians began to believe he had been connected to a battery, or perhaps that an impostor had taken his place; another view, put about by a financier involved in his campaign, was that 'At key points in his life, Yeltsin wakes up.'[139]

Table 3.3 **The Russian presidential election, 1996**

	First round, 16 June 1996		Second round, 3 July 1996	
	Votes	%	Votes	%
Boris Yeltsin	26,665,495	35.28	40,203,349	53.83
Gennadii Zyuganov	24,211,686	32.03	30,104,589	40.30
Alexander Lebed'	10,974,736	14.52		
Grigorii Yavlinsky	5,550,752	7.34		
Vladimir Zhirinovsky	4,311,479	5.70		
Svyatoslav Fedorov	699,158	0.92		
Mikhail Gorbachev	386,069	0.51		
Martin Shakkum	277,068	0.37		
Yuri Vlasov	151,282	0.20		
Vladimir Bryntsalov	123,065	0.16		
Others*	308	0.00		
Against all	1,163,921	1.54	3,604,462	4.83
Invalid votes	1,072,120	1.42	780,592	1.04

Source: adapted from *Vybory Prezidenta Rossiiskoi Federatsii. 1996. Elektoral'naya statistika* (Moscow: Ves' mir, 1996), pp. 127–30, incorporating subsequent amendments. In the first round the registered electorate was 108,495,023. Of these, 75,744,553 'took part in the elections' by receiving a ballot paper (69.81 per cent) and 75,587,139 cast a valid or invalid ballot (69.67 per cent). In the second round the registered electorate was 108,589,050. Of these, 74,800,449 'took part in the elections' (68.88 per cent) and 74,691,290 cast a valid or invalid ballot (68.78 per cent).
*Votes cast for Aman-Gel'dy Tuleev in the first round, before his withdrawal.

The outcome in the first presidential ballot, on 16 June 1996, was a narrow plurality (see Table 3.3). But within a few days, Yeltsin had arranged a meeting with the third-placed candidate, former general Alexander Lebed', and offered him a place in the administration as Secretary of the Security Council with particular responsibility for public order. Gennadii Zyuganov, the Communist candidate, found himself unable to extend his coalition of supporters between the two contests, and Yeltsin, in the second round, won a clear victory with most Lebed' supporters behind him as well as the overwhelming majority of the voters that had backed liberal reformers such as Grigorii Yavlinsky in the first round.[140] It was a striking success; yet it also made clear that Yeltsin's committed supporters were no more than a quarter of the electorate, fewer than non-voters, and a much smaller number than had been prepared to support him in June 1991 and again in the April 1993 referendum. The distribution of support for pro-Yeltsin reformers and for Communists and their allies, in fact, had scarcely changed between the December 1995 Duma election and the first round of the presidential election in June 1996: the broadly Communist electorate was about a third (32 per cent) in both contests, nationalist parties and candidates took just over a fifth (20 per cent), and centrists and reformers broadly loyal to the Kremlin were more numerous than either but still short of an overall majority (between 42 and 45 per cent).[141]

Yeltsin had first been elected president when Russia was still a constituent republic of the USSR. The Constitutional Court, however, ruled that this must be regarded as a first election to the post he now occupied,[142] and so he had no alternative but to stand down at the following election, which was due to take place in June 2000 at the end of his second presidential term. In the event he took the political world by surprise when he resigned at the end of December 1999, allowing Prime Minister Putin to take over as acting president until an early election could be held. He had agonised over his decision for a 'long time', Yeltsin told a national television audience. But in the end he concluded that he had 'accomplished [his] life's work', in that Russia would 'never go back to the past'. Now it was time to go forward into a new millennium with 'new politicians, with new faces, with new, intelligent, strong, energetic people'. Why, Yeltsin asked, should he hold on to power for another six months when the country already had a 'strong man worthy of being president' and when 'practically every Russian citizen today [had] pinned their hopes for the future on that man?' But he also wanted to apologise that so many of their earlier aspirations had not been realised. He himself had believed they could leap forward in a 'single bound' from the 'grey, stagnant, totalitarian past into a bright, rich, civilised future'. Perhaps he had been too naïve, or perhaps the problems had been too great; there had certainly been 'mistakes and failures'. But his only wish had been to make the lives of ordinary people 'at least a little bit easier and better'.[143]

With Yeltsin's early resignation the presidential election was brought forward to 26 March 2000, which gave Putin, now the incumbent, a substantial advantage. He refused to campaign directly or use the funds he had been allocated for such purposes, and did not issue a pre-election manifesto. He did, however, publish a thoughtful statement on 'Russia on the Eve of the Millennium' when he took over his new position at the end of the year (p. 101), and he issued an 'Open Letter to Russian Voters' as a kind of manifesto (he had used this unusual format, staff explained, to avoid having to make the kind of policy commitments that might have drawn him into a more detailed discussion).[144] The 'Open Letter' reiterated some of the themes he had addressed in his New Year message, and others that became more familiar over the course of his two-term presidency. The 'first and most important problem', Putin suggested, was Russia's loss of 'political will'. One example of this lack of resolution was crime – in Chechnya, where an 'entire republic' had been taken over by criminals, or on the streets. His own answer was a 'dictatorship of law', within a strong state, because it was only an effective, strong state that could guarantee freedom of enterprise, freedom for individuals and freedom for society as a whole. Within that context, there were several particular priorities: the elimination of poverty; the protection of business from bureaucrats and criminals; the revival of a greater sense of the 'personal dignity of citizens in the name of a higher national dignity'; and a foreign policy that was 'based on the national interests of our country'.[145]

Apart from this, a series of extended interviews with a group of newspaper journalists was published in early March 2000 under the title *First Person*, and then distributed as part of Putin's official campaign. A great deal was autobiographical, with evidence from family and friends as well as the acting President himself, but there was also a heavy emphasis on the need for a strong or, as Putin preferred to put it, 'effective state'. It was only a state of this kind, he argued, that could provide a framework of law that would protect the rights of private property and ensure that Russia did not become dependent on the 'strategic reserves' of other countries.[146] Equally, it was only a strong and effective state that could prevent a 'second Yugoslavia on the entire territory of the Russian Federation' if fundamentalist Islam was allowed to spread from Chechnya to the middle Volga, averting a 'global catastrophe'.[147] Putin's campaign was greatly assisted by the attention he automatically attracted as prime minister and, from January onwards, acting president. He made a further contribution by undertaking a series of energetic stunts, like piloting an air force jet between two of his engagements,[148] that underscored the difference between him and his ailing predecessor. It was also clear that he had made full use of the advantages of office, or what Russians had begun to describe as 'administrative resources': this meant, for instance, that an 'extraordinary number of senior officials' were on his campaign staff, although they were all supposed to have taken leave of their positions for as long as they were engaged in such activities.[149]

In the event, Putin won an overall majority on the first ballot (see Table 3.4). The runner-up, once again, was Communist leader Gennadii Zyuganov, with a more respectable vote than many had expected. The leader of the liberal Yabloko party, Grigorii Yavlinsky, came third, but with a smaller share of the support of the electorate than he had secured in 1996; and none of the other candidates took as much as 3 per cent, which meant that they would be obliged to return the state funds that had been made available for their campaign. This gave Putin a decisive victory, and one that took him well beyond a margin that could have been attributed to his manipulation of the airwaves. It was equally clear that it owed a great deal to the advantages of office, including the de facto support of the state machine and the disproportionate degree of attention he had received in the mass media (including nearly a third of the television coverage that was devoted to all the candidates and almost half of the entire news and current affairs output[150]). International observers concluded that the election had generally been conducted within a constitutional and legislative framework that was 'consistent with internationally recognised democratic standards', but they also drew attention to the 'renewed pressure' that had been exercised on the electronic and printed media, and to the ways in which the advantages of incumbency had been 'fully exploited'.[151] These had been identified as shortcomings of the previous presidential election, in 1996,[152] and they became increasingly familiar features of Russian electoral practice.

The 2004 presidential election was more of a coronation. It came just three months after a Duma election in which the pro-Kremlin United Russia party had emerged as by

Table 3.4 **The Russian presidential election, 26 March 2000**

Name	Nominated by	Vote	%
Vladimir Putin	Independent	39,740,467	52.94
Gennadii Zyuganov	Independent	21,928,468	29.21
Grigorii Yavlinsky	Independent	4,351,450	5.80
Aman-Gel'dy Tuleev	Independent	2,217,364	2.95
Vladimir Zhirinovsky	Liberal Democratic Party of Russia	2,026,509	2.70
Konstantin Titov	Independent	1,107,269	1.47
Ella Pamfilova	Electoral association 'For Civic Dignity'	758,967	1.01
Stanislav Govorukhin	Independent	328,723	0.44
Yuri Skuratov	Independent	319,189	0.43
Aleksei Podberezkin	Independent	98,177	0.10
Umar Dzhabrailov	Independent	78,498	0.10
Against all	–	1,414,673	1.88
Invalid votes	–	701,016	0.93

Source: adapted from *Vybory Prezidenta Rossiiskoi Federatsii. 2000. Elektoral'naya statistika* (Moscow: Ves' mir, 2000), pp. 189–91. The registered electorate was 109,372,043, of whom 75,181,073 'took part in the elections' by receiving a ballot paper (68.74 per cent), and 75,070,770 cast a valid or invalid ballot (68.64 per cent). 'Independents' were nominated by 'initiative groups' of at least 100 electors that were themselves required to collect at least a million signatures in support of the nomination.

far the largest (see Chapter 2), bringing into being a new parliament in which the authorities could expect the loyal support of at least two-thirds of the membership. Putin's own popularity rating was still at a very high level, and there could be no doubt he was going to win; indeed for some time after the Duma election, the only question was whether he would face any opposition and if not, whether he would have to arrange his own 'competition' to ensure there was at least the semblance of a contest. The Communist Party, which had provided the most serious opposition in the past, fielded a Duma deputy and state farm manager, Nikolai Kharitonov, rather than the party leader; the Liberal Democrats nominated a bodyguard, Oleg Malyshkin, rather than Zhirinovsky himself; and Yabloko, shaken by a poor showing in the Duma election, nominated no-one at all. Of the others, both Irina Khakamada (formerly of the Union of Right Forces) and Sergei Glaz'ev (one of the leaders of Rodina at the Duma election) stood as independents, without the support of their respective parties. None of the rival candidates expressed any expectation of defeating the incumbent president, and one of them, speaker of the upper house Sergei Mironov, openly campaigned in his favour. 'We've said more than once that we support the President's policies', Mironov explained; 'the President himself has to be supported'.[153]

In the end, seven candidates were successfully registered, two of them without the need to collect signatures in that their parties had won seats in the party-list contest to the Duma the previous December. Mironov, whose party had not contested the previous

Table 3.5 **The Russian presidential election, 14 March 2004**

Name	Nominated by	Vote	%
Vladimir Putin	Independent	49,558,328	71.31
Nikolai Kharitonov	Communist Party of the Russian Federation	9,514,554	13.69
Sergei Glaz'ev	Independent	2,850,610	4.10
Irina Khakamada	Independent	2,672,189	3.84
Oleg Malyshkin	Liberal Democratic Party of Russia	1,405,326	2.02
Sergei Mironov	Russian Party of Life	524,332	0.75
Against all	–	2,397,140	3.45
Invalid votes	–	578,847	0.83

Source: adapted from the corrected results as reported in *Vestnik Tsentral'noi izbiratel'noi komissii Rossiiskoi Federatsii* no. 5, 2006, pp. 19–20. The registered electorate was 108,064,281 (*Vybory Prezidenta Rossiiskoi Federatsii. 2004. Elektoral'naya statistika* (Moscow: Ves' mir, 2004), p. 106), of whom 69,572,177 'took part in the elections' by receiving a ballot paper (64.38 per cent) and 69,501,326 cast a valid or invalid ballot (64.31 per cent). 'Independents' nominated themselves but were required to have the support of an electors' group of at least 500 and were registered on the basis of the signatures of at least 2 million electors.

Duma election, collected the number of signatures that was required, and so did four other candidates, who were nominally independents. One of the independent candidates, Ivan Rybkin, a former parliamentary speaker and Secretary of the Security Council, attracted some controversy when he mysteriously 'disappeared' in early February, a few days after he had accused Putin of complicity in the bomb attacks in Moscow that had led to the second Chechen war,[154] but was then discovered in Kyiv five days later and offered 'no coherent explanation for his disappearance' when he returned to Moscow.[155] He later took refuge in London, but was not allowed to make use of the advertising to which he would otherwise have been entitled and withdrew from an election that had become a 'farce' on 5 March.[156] The campaign was otherwise unremarkable: Putin, once again, did not campaign at all, relying on the advantages of incumbency including a subservient media (a lengthy meeting with his supporters, carried in full on national television, was not regarded as a campaign event),[157] and his opponents had no incentive to spend money – if they had it – in what appeared to be a hopeless cause. Indeed, a major concern for the authorities was that turnout might fall so low that the result would be discredited or even invalid (which would happen if those 'taking part' were less than 50 per cent of the registered electorate), and a campaign was launched to maximise the turnout that sometimes involved direct administrative pressure.[158]

A provisional result was announced on 16 March, and a final result a week later. Turnout, at 64 per cent, was down on the 69 per cent that had been recorded in 2000, and the vote 'against all' had almost doubled (see Table 3.5). Putin's margin of victory, however, was very much greater – indeed it represented a majority of the popular vote in every one of the country's eighty-nine republics and regions. In four of the republics,

Dagestan, Ingushetia, Mordovia and war-torn Chechnya, both turnout and the vote in favour of Putin were over 90 per cent; in Bashkortostan, turnout was 89 per cent and the vote in favour of Putin was 92 per cent. All of this was reminiscent of Soviet elections of the recent past and suggestive of heavy pressure at the level of regional administrations.[159] Once again, media coverage was grossly unbalanced: on state-controlled television, in particular, Putin received a degree of attention that was 'far beyond what was reasonably proportionate to his role as Head of State', and the live coverage of his meeting with supporters on one of the state-owned television channels was a 'clear breach of the legal provision for equal treatment of candidates'.[160] There was no suggestion, in any of this, that Putin had stolen his victory. But it was also clear that a combination of mechanisms had been developed that allowed the Kremlin to secure the kind of result it wanted, acting in association with local leaders who had been left in no doubt that their future was likely to depend on the kind of vote they were able to mobilise in the region for which they were responsible in much the same way that Soviet regional first secretaries had been judged on their ability to fulfil their plan targets.

The Kremlin was in an even more dominant position at the 2008 presidential election, in which Putin was no longer able to compete as the Constitution did not allow the same person to serve more than two consecutive terms. There had been a lengthy discussion inside the country and outside it about the '2008 problem' that arose as a result, and there was continuing speculation about the possibility that the Constitution might be amended to allow him to run again. The Belarusian Constitution had been amended in this sense in 2004, and there was strong public support for a third term, some of it evidently orchestrated from above,[161] although Putin himself had repeatedly insisted he had no wish to change the rules of the game to his advantage and in his final news conference claimed he had never even considered the possibility of doing so.[162] Another idea that appeared to have found official sanction was that a new position of some kind might be found, a vaguely defined 'national leader' perhaps, or the presidency of a more fully developed union with Belarus that would have constitutional precedence over the presidential office in either of its member countries. Yet another possibility was that a close Putin associate might be found who could be relied on to continue Putin's policies without entertaining any ambitions of his own and who might indeed step down before the end of his four years, allowing new elections to take place in which Putin would be able to compete for another term and perhaps beyond it.[163]

In the event, the Kremlin chose a variant of this last scenario: the election of a new but absolutely loyal candidate to the presidency with Putin's explicit support, allowing Putin himself to be nominated to the premiership (which was the position he had occupied before he became president). Putin, as we have seen, had already indicated that he would be willing to become prime minister if there was a 'decent, capable, effective and modern-thinking person' in charge of the presidency, and on 10 December 2007, after the Duma election had delivered a new parliament with an overwhelming pro-Kremlin majority, he nominated his close associate, First Deputy Prime Minister Dmitri Medvedev, to the position, with the support of United Russia and three of the other parties.[164] Medvedev himself, the following day, announced that he would be nominating Putin to the premiership if he was successful in the election that would be taking place at the start of March.[165] In the end there were just four candidates: apart from Medvedev, the Communist leader Gennadii Zyuganov, the LDPR leader Vladimir Zhirinovsky, and the little-known leader of the Democratic Party who was formally campaigning as an independent and appeared to have been included so as to ensure that there would be at least the semblance of a competition if the other candidates withdrew. A potentially much more serious challenger, the former Prime Minister Mikhail Kas'yanov, was refused registration on 27 January (too many of the signatures on his nomination papers were deemed unacceptable; the decision, he believed, had been 'made by Vladimir Putin himself'[166]), and the following day Medvedev announced that because of 'pressures of work' he would not be taking part in any of the studio debates with other candidates.[167]

Medvedev, indeed, scarcely 'campaigned' at all, although his official duties and a series of tours around the country in this capacity were sufficient to ensure that he received the full attention of the print and electronic media. His first extended statement was a speech to a Civic Forum on 22 January 2008 in which he made clear he would be continuing the policies of his predecessor – Russia needed 'ten years of stable development' – but with a new emphasis on the dangers of 'legal nihilism' and on the larger issue of state-level corruption, which was on a 'huge scale'.[168] He set out a fuller agenda in a speech at an economic forum in Krasnoyarsk on 15 February, which closely followed a speech by Putin to the State Council that had set out a longer-term strategy for the period up to 2020.[169] The Krasnoyarsk speech was intended to suggest some of the ways in which this larger vision could be implemented, but it also renewed the emphasis on 'legal nihilism' and the related need for a reform of the judicial system so as to ensure that it was genuinely independent of the other branches of government; people should feel that courts were 'a place where fair decisions [were] taken [and] where they [could] be protected from those who violate the law, whether a hooligan on the street or an official'.[170] He took a single day's unpaid leave of absence in late February to campaign in the city of Nizhnii Novgorod; in a brief address, repeatedly broadcast on national television, he reiterated the need for 'political stability', for a 'plan for combating corruption', and for 'decades of stable development' on the basis of the 'course that had proved its effectiveness over the past eight years: the course of President Putin'.[171]

On the evening of 2 March, as the first results were announced, the two presidents emerged from the Kremlin to attend a celebratory concert on Red Square that had evidently been organised some time in advance. Putin congratulated Medvedev on the victory he had already secured and declared it a 'guarantee that the successful policies [they had] pursued these past eight years [would] continue'; Medvedev himself, in 'democratic jeans, a sweater and a jacket', thanked those who had voted for him and assured them in very similar terms that the outcome of the election had made it clear they would 'be able to continue along the path that Vladimir Putin [had] put forward'.[172]

Table 3.6 The Russian presidential election, 2 March 2008

Name	Nominated by	Vote	%
Dmitri Medvedev	United Russia	52,530,712	70.28
Gennadii Zyuganov	Communist Party of the Russian Federation	13,243,550	17.72
Vladimir Zhirinovsky	Liberal Democratic Party of Russia	6,988,510	9.35
Andrei Bogdanov	Independent	968,344	1.30
Invalid votes		1,105,533	1.36

Source: adapted from the Central Electoral Commission communiqué in *Vestnik Tsentral'noi izbiratel'noi komissii Rossiiskoi Federatsii*, no. 3, 2008, pp. 213–16. The registered electorate was 107,222,016, of whom 74,746,649 (69.71 per cent) cast a valid or invalid ballot (it was no longer possible to vote 'against all', and with the abolition of minimum turnout requirements the number who 'took part' had no legal significance and was not reported in the official announcement).

Speaking to journalists later the same evening, Medvedev repeated that his policies would be a 'direct continuation of the policies that [had] been conducted and [were] being conducted by President Putin'. They had 'a comradely partnership based on the fact that they [had] worked together for a rather long time and trust[ed] each other', he went on. Otherwise, it was clear that the President had certain constitutional prerogatives, and so had the prime minister, and 'nobody [was] proposing to change them'; this was a new but 'effective combination', and he was sure it would be a 'very positive factor' in the development of the Russian state.[173] Medvedev was formally inaugurated on 7 May; the following day Putin was elected prime minister by a record margin, 392 in favour and 56 against (one of the Communist deputies found himself unable to vote with his party colleagues and recorded the single abstention).[174] A new regime had begun – although the mandate it had received was to continue the same policies under more or less the same leadership.

Putin and Medvedev

There had been a more obvious change when Putin himself succeeded Boris Yeltsin at the end of the 1990s: much younger and a specialist in the martial arts, he started every day with a 45-minute workout[175] and had even co-authored a judo textbook (this did not prevent an embarrassing moment when he took on a 10-year-old schoolgirl on a visit to Japan soon after his inauguration and was 'promptly [thrown] ... over her shoulder to appreciative applause from the Japanese audience').[176] His priorities, however, remained somewhat opaque, apart from bringing the 'anti-terrorist operation' in breakaway Chechnya to a successful conclusion. Putin, born in Leningrad in 1952, had graduated from the university's law faculty in 1975 and worked thereafter for the KGB, first of all in

Leningrad itself and then in Dresden, where he perfected his knowledge of the language and drank (he thought) too much beer. He had, of course, been a party member, and did not resign: the CPSU simply 'ceased to exist', so he took his membership card and put it into a drawer.[177] He returned to Leningrad in 1990 to work as an assistant to the university rector and then as an adviser to the chairman of Leningrad city council who was by this time his former teacher, law professor Anatolii Sobchak. When Sobchak was elected the city's first mayor in June 1991 Putin joined his administration, taking charge of foreign relations. He moved to Moscow in 1996, after failing in his attempt to secure Sobchak's election as regional governor; he worked first of all in the Presidential Administration and then from July 1998 as director of the Federal Security Service, moving to the premiership itself in August 1999.

Some of Putin's objectives became a little clearer in the address he issued at the end of 1999, 'Russia at the Turn of the Millennium', as he took up the duties of acting president on Yeltsin's premature resignation. Putin rejected a return to the totalitarian past, while recognising its considerable achievements; at the same time he rejected the 'abstract models and schemes taken from foreign textbooks' that had been applied during the free-market experiments of the 1990s. He appeared to recognise the importance of universal values, such as freedom of expression and the freedom to travel abroad, but there was rather more emphasis on traditional Russian principles of government, such as patriotism and the special destiny of the nation itself. Russia, Putin insisted, was and would always remain a great power, in economic and cultural if not necessarily in military terms. 'Statism' was another traditional virtue: the institutions of government itself had always been strong in Russia, and there was no immediate or even long-term prospect that Russia would become a 'second edition of, say, the US or Britain in which liberal values have deep historic traditions'. Social solidarity was also important, with its emphasis on cooperation rather than individualism. This, clearly, was a view of the Russian future that would respect liberal freedoms, but one that would also reflect the need for a 'certain restoration of the guiding and regulating role of the state' in line with rather longer-standing national patterns – and indeed in line with what Putin himself described as a 'global trend'.[178]

Newspaper accounts meanwhile began to fill out the future president's early years, with some emphasis on the qualities that identified him as a combative, streetwise, somewhat unruly figure. An aunt in Ryazan, for instance, told *Komsomol'skaya pravda* about the time little Vova had climbed out onto the ledge of their fifth-floor apartment, and about the time he had fallen into the river during a fishing trip – fortunately he could already swim, but it had been a 'watery christening'.[179] Putin's school contemporaries were more inclined to recall his tendency to become involved in fights, although they also told the same paper how the future president had made all the arrangements after the unexpected death of a schoolfriend, and how he had bought his mother the biggest cake in the shop with his first paycheck.[180] His German teacher, in her 'recollections of a future president', remembered Putin as a student of modest attainment who was one of the last to be admitted into the Pioneers youth movement, but who turned out to have a 'sharp and lively mind, an excellent memory and exceptional curiosity'.[181] The first volume of an authorised biography appeared at the end of 2001, and another volume shortly afterwards (it was intended that there would eventually be three, or perhaps even more).[182] Putin, who had evidently given the project his entire support, told the author he had been educated on the street, which was 'just like living in the jungle', but that he had learned one important lesson, which was that in order to win he 'had to go to the end in any fight and strike out as if in the last, decisive combat'.[183]

A modest personality cult was meanwhile developing. Within a year of his accession, foundry workers in the Urals were casting him in bronze; not far away, weavers were making rugs with the President's face inside a golden oval. In Magnitogorsk, the overalls Putin had worn during a visit were on display in the city museum.[184] A factory in Chelyabinsk had begun to produce a watch with a presidential image on its dial, and a local confectioner was selling a cake with the same design; a 'Putin bar' had opened elsewhere in the town, selling 'Vertical power' kebabs and 'When Vova was little' milkshakes.[185] An all-female band had meanwhile 'taken the airwaves by storm' with its single 'Someone like Putin' (someone who, among other things, 'doesn't drink' and 'won't run away').[186] Putin's fiftieth birthday, in September 2002, brought these tributes to a new pitch of intensity: those who wrote in to the weekly paper *Argumenty i fakty* (Arguments and Facts) wanted to present the Russian leader with a samurai sword, an aeroplane on skis (so that he could combine his favourite hobbies), a portable toilet 'so that he can wipe out whoever he wants whenever he wants',[187] some genuine Siberian pancakes 'to sustain him in his future work', or even 'my love and perhaps a child as well'.[188] The most original was from a former deputy prime minister of Bashkortostan: a three-page ode that consisted exclusively of words beginning with the letter 'p' and concluded with the assurance that 'Po planete postavyat pamyatniki Pervomy Prezidentu Planety Putin' ('All around the planet they will put up monuments to the first president of the planet, Putin').[189]

Matters went even further in Izborsk, an unprepossessing town in the Pskov region where the presidential motorcade had made an unscheduled stop in August 2000. Visitors were offered a tour 'In Putin's footsteps' that included the places 'where Putin bought a cucumber', 'where Putin took off his jacket and tried water from a spring' and 'where Putin touched a tree and made a wish'.[190] The interior minister, the human rights ombudsman and the Latvian ambassador were among the state officials who made a pilgrimage to the town over the months that followed, all of them dutifully visiting the tree that Putin had touched and 'mak[ing] their secret wish just as Putin did'; a local paper meanwhile reproduced a recipe for the cucumbers, advising that they should be picked early in the morning and 'washed three times, preferably in holy water'.[191] In Irkutsk the chair on which Putin had sat during his visit was sold at public auction to the local veterinary inspector, who hoped the 'Putin spirit [would] infect us with its energy, decency and honesty'.[192] In St Petersburg a tree the future president had planted was decorated with a commemorative plaque; elsewhere, ski slopes and churches were being renamed in his honour.[193] And there were tours of the President's home town – not of its familiar tourist attractions but of the 'tiny communal flat' in which the future president's family had maintained a 'clean and orderly' single room, of the 'backstreets and alleys where the young son of an engineer [had grown] up' and of the nearby school where his 'penchant for political leadership [had] first emerged'.[194]

The President appeared to enjoy particularly high levels of support among women. *Pravda* reported a distressing case from Yaroslavl, where there was a 'new category of patients – women who are madly in love with President Vladimir Putin'. Lyudmila, who was in her late thirties, had started to collect newspaper articles about the President; she soon accumulated a thick file, which she kept in a bedside cabinet. She asked her husband to turn down the television when Putin was speaking on the radio, and made no move to feed him two weeks later when he came home from work, sitting 'bedazzled' in front of the television as Putin gave an interview (they had such a fight they stopped speaking to each other for three days). Finally she moved into the children's room, where she hung a portrait of the President above the bed, but her husband came in and threw everything on the floor. Lyudmila herself dissolved in tears, and the only way forward appeared to be a private psychiatrist. Lyudmila's case, he explained, was 'not unique'; women saw Putin as a 'superhusband, the ideal partner', someone who would 'never betray them, and never get drunk'.[195] There was an equally enthusiastic response from Russian gays when photographs of a bare-chested President appeared on the Kremlin website in the summer of 2007, and then in the daily papers; it was followed by a whole sequence of action-man displays as the President saved a film crew from a Siberian tiger, went swimming in a Tuvan river, explored Lake Baikal in a submarine, fired darts into a grey whale off the coast of Kamchatka, and co-piloted an amphibious aircraft over the wildfires that followed exceptionally high temperatures in the summer of 2010.[196]

The Putin name, it became clear, could be used for all kinds of purposes. An Astrakhan company began to produce a range of pickled aubergines under the 'PuTin' label, avoiding the restrictions that would have applied to the use of the presidential name by substituting a sword for the middle letter (it sold so well they decided to launch a parallel line of fish products).[197] Ordinary portraits could be picked up in bookshops, and chocolate ones from a variety of confectioners;[198] enthusiasts could buy a more elaborate version made of Swarovski crystal, or commission a painting from a professional artist for a thousand dollars upwards.[199] There was a popular vodka called Putinka (although it 'tasted like all the others'),[200] a 'Vladimir Putin collective farm',[201] a 'Putin Avenue' in Grozny,[202] and a computer game called 'The Four Oligarchs' in which the President recovered banks and oil companies from his opponents and installed his loyalists in parliament.[203] An exhibition in St Petersburg was meanwhile offering visitors 'Three Minutes with V.V. Putin', an opportunity to spend a little time with a model of the President in his study reading a book about the history of the Baltic fleet with his faithful Labrador by his side.[204] And there were Putin jokes, some of them taking their cue from the President's celebrated assurance that he would 'wipe out the terrorists even if they were on the john'. A Russian general, for instance, is asked: 'Why haven't you killed a single terrorist?' He replies: 'They don't use the john . . .' Or an announcement on the door of the toilet: 'Don't come in! Wiping out terrorists. Putin'. Or 'It's [oligarch Vladimir] Gusinsky's turn for the john'.[205]

Matters reached the point of a fully-fledged cult in the village of Bolshaya yelnya in Nizhnii Novgorod, home to the 'Rus' Resurrecting' sect, where a group of local residents had come to the conclusion that Putin had been the Apostle Paul in a previous life, not to mention Prince Vladimir of Kievan Rus' (who had embraced Christianity in the tenth century and made it the official faith) and the biblical King Solomon. It was a cult in the most literal sense: its members 'cross themselves, kiss a portrait of their saviour and beg him to save Russia from its impending apocalypse'; the congregation of a neighbouring church organised a formal procession in an attempt to cast out the heresy. 'We didn't choose Putin', the cult's leader told the Moscow evening newspaper, explaining how she had first set eyes on the 'holy one' at the same time as Yeltsin had been naming Putin as his successor. 'My soul exploded with joy!', she told the paper. 'A Superman! God himself ha[d] chosen him.' Yeltsin, Mother Photinya went on, 'was a destroyer, and God replaced him with a Creator'. The sect had a Putin icon that had appeared in mysterious circumstances; Photinya herself claimed to be related to the Russian President, although 'not in this century'. 'He has given us everything', she told reporters, pointing meaningfully upwards (the paper uncharitably added that Photinya's real name was Svetlana Frolova and that she had been convicted some years earlier on fraud charges; but there were more than five hundred active sects of this kind, one of them even celebrating a former provincial traffic policeman as the second coming of Christ).[206]

Putin's successor, Dmitri Medvedev, was also a Leningrader and had also graduated from the city's university with a law degree, going on to postgraduate studies. Like Putin, he was of modest stature, and like Putin, he had taken up physical exercise and lost a little weight; some even thought he had begun to ape the speech and behavioural mannerisms of his plain-speaking predecessor.[207] But he came from a rather different, more academic background (his father had been a professor at the Technological Institute, his mother a philology graduate), and he had worked himself at Leningrad University throughout the 1990s, teaching civil law. He was not particularly engaged in the political activism of the *perestroika* years (during the attempted coup of August 1991 he had been in hospital with a broken leg[208]), but being more than a decade younger than Putin – he was born in 1965 – his experience of the Soviet system was rather less, and he had never been a member of the Communist Party (or at any rate known to have been).[209] Medvedev met Putin while they were both working as assistants to the Leningrad mayor, Anatolii Sobchak, and later became a legal adviser to the committee on foreign relations that was a part of the city administration and which was headed at this time by Putin. He was also involved in private commercial activity, joining the board of several small companies and advising them on legal matters. Medvedev met his wife Svetlana while they were attending the same school; he was just 14 years old at the time.[210] According to insiders, she has always taken a close interest in his political career and in public life in general.[211]

Medvedev's career trajectory changed abruptly when Putin, who had already moved to Moscow to work in the Presidential Administration and then the FSB, became prime minister in the late summer of 1999. Just three months later, in November 1999, Medvedev himself moved to Moscow to become deputy head of the governmental apparatus; and when Putin became acting president at the end of the year Medvedev followed him to become the deputy and then from June 2000 the first deputy head of the Presidential Administration. He directed Putin's election campaign in the spring of 2000, and then in October 2003 moved up again to become head of the Presidential Administration, or in other words Putin's chief of staff. He became chairman of the board of the state gas monopoly Gazprom, in addition, in the summer of 2000, and also (from November 2003) a member of the Security Council. In November 2005 he moved into the Russian government as first deputy prime minister, taking particular responsibility for the ambitious 'national projects' in health, agriculture, education and housing.[212] It was a position that gave him first-hand knowledge of a wide range of public policy, and at the same time some media exposure as he took charge of meetings of the board that had been established to supervise the projects and travelled around the country to check on their fulfilment. He was widely seen, together with Defence Minister and fellow First Deputy Premier Sergei Ivanov, as a likely successor if Putin did indeed stand down at the end of his second term, although Putin himself was careful to avoid becoming a lame duck and publicly identified 'at least five' possible candidates.[213]

A series of interviews had meanwhile begun to provide a little more of the personal background of the new president (as he became in May 2008). His particular passion was the vinyl records of the 1970s and 1980s, and hard rock groups such as Deep Purple and Black Sabbath. But he had come to spend more time on sport, swimming twice a day and working out in the gym.[214] He was also a religious believer and had taken a personal decision to be christened when he was in his early twenties, with his friends, in one of the Leningrad cathedrals; from that time onwards he had begun 'another life'.[215] Perhaps the most distinctive of his personal interests was yoga, which he was mastering 'little by little', he told interviewers in the spring of 2007. It helped him to relax from managing the national projects, where the responsibility was 'huge'; he had even learned how to stand on his head.[216] Kremlin officials were convinced there would soon be more yoga schools than there were in India. 'This is how things work in Russia', they told interviewers. 'If the head of the state has a hobby, it will become the hobby of the nation.'[217] Colleagues in government insisted that the new president, in spite of his apparent diffidence, was 'not weak or lacking in resolve', he simply did not practise the 'soviet-management style of leadership, with its shouting and boorishness'. He also had a 'unique capacity for work' and was able to communicate it to others, although he was not always so effective in implementing his plans, as his management of the national projects had made clear.[218]

Medvedev's speech to the economic forum in Krasnoyarsk in February 2008 was perhaps the closest to a 'manifesto' of the new leadership.[219] As we have already noted, there was a heavy emphasis on the damage that was being done by 'legal nihilism', which remained a 'characteristic feature' of Russian society. One reason for this was the quality of the laws themselves. Now it was time to work on their improvement, making use of public opinion and expert evaluations. There was just as much of a problem with ensuring respect for the laws that already existed, so that no longer was it the case that Russia was a country where 'the severity of the laws [was] compensated by the non-obligatory nature of their observance' (a famous quotation from the nineteenth-century writer Saltykov-Shchedrin). This meant an improvement in the work of the courts. The 'key priority of [their] work over the following four years should be ensuring the genuine independence of the court system from the executive and legislative branches', he explained. They had to end the practice of taking decisions 'by telephone', or 'for money'. There had to be a system of compensation for individuals and businesses in the event of judicial mistakes. The legal system should be humanised and made less severe, including sentences and the conditions in which prisoners themselves were detained. And there should be a 'real war' on corruption, which was the 'most serious illness infecting our society'. In the first instance, this might mean the development of a 'national anti-corruption plan'.

The rule of law in turn had implications for the economy and its development. It must become easier to open and conduct a business. The larger state companies should be better managed, with directors who were more independent. And private ownership should be more widely respected, notwithstanding the long experience of Soviet rule in which it had been anathema and then the disappointment that had accompanied the policies that had been pursued by the Yeltsin leadership in the 1990s. With so much uncertainty, many owners kept their capital abroad and some of them had acquired foreign citizenship as an additional precaution. At the same time, they could not isolate themselves from the international economy, with its risks as well as its opportunities. Levels of taxation, for instance, would have to be competitive with those of other countries. And in the longer term, Russia should itself become one of the world's financial centres, with the rouble as one of its reserve currencies. But there would be no progress of this kind as long as social issues had not been addressed, and more people lifted out of poverty and alcoholism. In the immediate future, he suggested, there were seven key tasks: the 'elimination of legal nihilism'; a 'radical reduction in administrative barriers'; a 'reduction in the tax burden'; the 'construction of a powerful and independent financial system'; the 'modernisation of the transport and energy infrastructure'; the formulation of a 'national innovation system'; and the full implementation of their programme of social development.

The problem of the Russian presidency

Even before its establishment, there had been criticisms that the Russian presidency was disproportionately powerful. There were still more serious implications when so much authority was entrusted to a single person whose health and judgement were often erratic. Under the Constitution, for instance, the president relinquished office ahead of time in the event of his resignation, impeachment or 'inability to perform the duties of his office for reasons of health'. In these circumstances the powers of the president passed on a temporary basis to the prime minister, and new elections had to be called within three months. But who was to decide if the president was 'totally unable to exercise his powers? The patient himself, by signing a decree? Or the prime minister? Or a special conference of doctors? Including whom? Or, perhaps, a presidential assistant – but which one?'[220] Yeltsin was generally hostile towards the medical profession, and he resisted the idea of a health bulletin of the kind that was regularly issued in France and the United States, and which was demanded from time to time by the parliamentary opposition.[221] The issue came up with particular force during his heart surgery at the end of 1996. Did surgery, or a lengthy hospitalisation, represent a 'continuing inability to perform the duties of his office'? Did the transfer of his powers to the prime minister require a formal decree, or was it sufficient for the President to issue the appropriate instructions? Or should it require the approval of a state body? And if so, which one?[222]

There were particular concerns, during the Yeltsin years, about alcoholic excess. The President himself admitted, in an interview in 1993, that he 'sometimes' allowed himself a glass of cognac on a Sunday evening with his family, or a beer after visiting the bathhouse.[223] His parliamentary critics were less indulgent. 'It's time to stop the public drunkenness of our President', a Communist deputy demanded after an unsteady performance during the President's first visit to the United States. 'When he's shown on television, he can't stand up without support.'[224] There was more criticism in early 1993 when the President, defending himself against impeachment, spoke uncertainly before the Russian parliament and had to be assisted from the hall (deputies agreed he had 'created a strange impression').[225] And there was an even greater reaction when Yeltsin arrived in Berlin the following year to take part in the withdrawal of Russian troops from Germany. The President was already 'tired' on his arrival but suggested he 'relax a bit' before proceedings began; the German Chancellor had to support him at the official ceremony, and at the lunch that followed he became increasingly animated. The two leaders went afterwards to lay a wreath in a specially equipped bus; Yeltsin ordered coffee to help him sober up but poured it all over his shirt (his support staff, fortunately, always carried a spare set of clothing).[226] There followed a 'stirring rendition of "Kalinka"' by the Berlin police band under the President's impromptu conductorship,[227] and later in the evening a convivial reception in the Russian embassy.[228] A number of advisers who had expressed their concern were simply left behind on the President's next trip, which concluded with a controversial non-appearance at Shannon airport to take part in discussions with the Irish Prime Minister. Yeltsin, his staff explained, had simply over-slept; his political opponents took a less charitable view and accused him subsequently of being in a 'permanent state of visiting Ireland'.[229]

Yeltsin himself insisted that Russians were used to having a single person in charge and 'some kind of vertical power structure, a strong hand that can not only talk, but act'. Parliamentary government, on the other hand, 'cannot solve anything because no one is responsible'; a strong parliament would be subordinated to parties, and 'there would be no kind of democracy'.[230] He was rather more sympathetic, in some interviews, to the idea of restoring the monarchy, which could guarantee the stability of the state as it appeared to have done during the Spanish transition, although there was little public support for such a view and even less clarity about the Romanov descendant that could make the strongest claim to the succession.[231] But he resisted any suggestion that the Constitution itself should be amended; the potential of the current one had 'not yet been exhausted', and any attempt to change it would only 'destabilise' the situation. 'As long as I am the President', he declared, 'I will not allow any change in the constitution.'[232] Putin declared himself in similar terms in his millennium address (they had a 'good constitution', he thought, what mattered was to make sure it was implemented),[233] and he took the same view throughout his presidency. Speaking in December 2003 on the tenth anniversary of its adoption, he argued that it was the stability of the Constitution that ensured the stability of government itself, and regular elections to representative insti-tutions at national and regional levels. Like Yeltsin, he insisted that the potential of the existing constitution was 'by no means exhausted', and anyone who had been 'trying to speculate on the subject of possible amendments to the Basic Law' should bear this in mind.[234]

A rather different view came from some of the political parties, and from constitu-tional lawyers. A Moscow University professor, Suren Avak'yan, was one of those who called repeatedly for a series of amendments that would ensure a better balance across the branches of government – 'a balance that simply does not exist today'. It should be more difficult, for instance, for the president to dissolve the Duma; and members of the government should be required, not just requested, to report on their implementation of its decisions. There were particular problems with Article 80, under which the president 'determined the basic directions of domestic and foreign policy'. Properly speaking the president, as head of state, should not be allowed to do more than implement any priorities of this kind, which were for the president and parliament to determine jointly.[235] In a larger study, Avak'yan argued for a series of further changes. The Constitution, for instance, divided up the legislative, executive and judicial functions, and allocated the executive function to the government. Where did the presidency fit into a separation of powers of this kind? Equally, the Duma had too little influence on the formation and conduct of government; to redress the balance, Avak'yan sug-gested that appointments to deputy premierships and to the more important ministries should require its approval, not just appointments to the prime ministership. Rather than undertake the complicated task of detailed amendment, he favoured the adoption of an entirely new constitution in these circumstances, using the mechanism of a national referendum.[236]

Where, others asked, was the principle of accountability in the Russian Constitution? It was the government, for instance, that conducted the affairs of the nation; but it was responsible for its actions and its composition, in practice, 'only to the President', with parliament taken into account only when the annual budget was being negotiated. The president was responsible to the electorate as a whole, not to a representative institution, which meant that the president was accountable, at best, in no more than a 'moral-political' sense. Even the annual address, unlike the State of the Union address in the United States, was less a rendering of account than a statement of government objectives for the immediate future. For another constitutional lawyer, Mikhail Piskotin, the president should be required to present a report on his tenure of office over the previous year, and it should be discussed rather than simply presented to the two chambers for their approval. Deputies, equally, should have the right to interrogate any member of the government and to vote their lack of confidence in individual ministers as well as in the government as a whole. It should be less easy for the president to dissolve parliament in the event of a disagreement; and it should be easier for the Duma itself to initiate the process of impeachment. All of this would require amendment of the 1993 Constitution; but constitutions, he pointed out, were most likely to require amendment in the period immediately following their adoption, and even the American Constitution, which was widely praised as an example of stability, had been amended ten times in its first four years.[237]

Another jurist, Oleg Kutafin, went even further, claiming that a presidential system of the Russian kind not only made any separation of powers 'meaningless' – it was a 'real threat to democracy' that opened the way to a 'regime of personal power'.[238] But others still were less persuaded that legal changes of any kind were the main issue: there was a more fundamental problem, which was Russia's low level of legal and political culture. Once Russia had become a more developed society, they argued, even the defects of the existing constitution – which were certainly significant – would not impede the democratic process, any more than they did in France, where presidential powers were also excessive and the Constitution a long way short of perfection. If every president or parliament tried to introduce a new constitution that operated to their own advantage, there would be 'neither a legal state, nor democracy, nor anything good for the society as a whole or its individual members'.[239] It was equally clear that amendment of any kind would not be simple. The Russian Constitution was 'probably the most complicated in the world in its procedure for amendment and supplementation'; not only did two-thirds of the republics and regions have to agree on a change, there was also a problem in that chapters 1, 2 and 9 (which covered its basic principles) could not be altered by parliament but only by a full-scale constitutional convention. Not only was there no law to regulate the composition and powers of a convention of this kind, there was not even a 'clear idea' about the role it should perform.[240]

The changes that took place after the 2008 presidential election gave rise to a new round of speculation, in particular the emergence of a 'tandem' in which president and prime minister shared executive authority between them. For some, this meant that Russia had already become a 'semi-presidential' republic, in that the prime minister headed a party that had a majority in the parliament although he did not necessarily owe his position to the composition of the legislature.[241] But Russia had never before been ruled by 'two tsars'; throughout the prerevolutionary and Soviet periods and the early postcommunist years there had always been a single person who had dominated public life, whether that person was called a tsar, a general secretary or a president. The only exceptions appeared to be the short-lived periods in which Nicholas II had ceded much of the daily business of government to Petr Stolypin (until the Prime Minister's assassination in 1911), or in which Leonid Brezhnev and Aleksei Kosygin had shared a 'collective leadership' in the second half of the 1960s.[242] At the outset of the Medvedev–Putin leadership, indeed, it was the prime minister rather than the president who was the key figure (at any rate it was Putin who generally appeared at the top of the lists of those who were regarded as the most influential in Russian public life).[243] Had this indeed made Russia a kind of 'parliamentary system', in which the government was now the locus of political authority and the president a secondary, more ceremonial figure?

Not, it seemed, so far as the two leaders themselves were concerned, both of whom insisted that they would respect the existing constitution and laws. There would be 'no redistribution of responsibilities', Medvedev made clear in an extended series of interviews shortly before his accession. Russia would continue to be a 'country with a strongly presidential system and an effective government'; 'no changes were envisaged' in the competence of either. According to the Constitution, Russia was a 'fully-fledged presidential republic'; both Medvedev and Putin saw this as a 'condition of its stability for years to come'. Any kind of redistribution of powers in favour of the government would mean the 'partial conversion of Russia into a parliamentary democracy', which would be an 'even more dangerous option than a change in the Constitution that removed the right of the president to seek no more than two terms'. The only result (in Medvedev's view) would be 'governmental paralysis'.[244] Speaking shortly before his election, Medvedev insisted that a parliamentary system would simply 'destroy' Russia, which could 'only be governed on the basis of presidential power'. If Russia became a parliamentary republic, it would 'disappear'. Russia had 'always developed around a strong executive authority. These lands have been gathered over the centuries, and they can't be governed any other way.'[245] Speaking elsewhere, Medvedev argued similarly that a parliamentary republic was simply not appropriate for Russia, at present or in the future, although it was a matter that could perhaps be considered again in 'two or three hundred years' time'.[246]

Putin, for his part, had made clear from the outset that there could be changes in the powers of the president if they were thought to be excessive. Or there could be an extension in the presidential term from its existing four years – a rather short period in which to choose a government, set out a programme, achieve some results and then present them for endorsement at a further election. Any changes of this kind should be the subject of a 'broad discussion', and he contributed to the discussion himself in the course of his presidency. But Russia, he pointed out, had from its very beginning been a 'supercentralised state', and this, he thought, had become a part of its 'genetic code, its traditions, and the mentality of its people'.[247] Speaking to the foreign press after he had taken up the premiership again, he reiterated that there was no intention of changing the 'key role of the head of state in the country's political system', although he also noted that the prime minister was now the leader of a party that had an overall majority in the parliament and suggested that this was a sign that Russia was 'paying more attention to multiparty politics and the increased influence of parliament'. The 'final word', nonetheless, 'remain[ed] with the President'.[248] For some, the constitutional reforms that had been taking place in neighbouring Ukraine were instructive: the only result of handing similar powers to the prime minister as well as the president, it appeared, was that they spent all their time trying to establish who was really dominant instead of concentrating on the business of government.[249]

Either way, it seemed likely that the new arrangement would be a temporary one, rather than a stable and enduring reconfiguration of executive authority. Putin certainly remained the key figure, because of the power he had accumulated over his eight-year presidency and the number of senior officials who depended on his support to retain their position, and Medvedev appeared to have been selected as his successor on the grounds that he was the least likely of his closest associates to develop a personal agenda.[250] One obvious possibility was that Medvedev would stand down at the end of his four-year term, or even earlier, allowing Putin to resume his presidential duties. Putin himself had always rejected the idea of a constitutional amendment that would allow him to remain beyond the end of his second term, but had not denied that he might seek office again at some point in the future (he would be only fifty-nine in 2012, he pointed out, which was hardly too old to consider returning to his presidential responsibilities).[251] At the same time there were repeated suggestions, many of them emanating from Putin loyalists, that the presidential term should be extended to five, six or even seven years;[252] Medvedev himself proposed an extension to six years in his first presidential address, and a constitutional amendment to this effect was approved in December 2008.[253] If Putin returned in 2012 to a presidency whose term of office had been extended in this way, he could serve until 2024, when he would still be in his early seventies.[254] Discussions of Putin as a 'Franklin Roosevelt' were relevant to this perspective;[255] the author of the New Deal had won four presidential elections in a row, after which the American Constitution was amended to prevent a future president serving more than two terms of any kind.

None of this resolved the largest issue of all, which was whether a stable and enduring balance could be found between government and the wider society over which it ruled. Government had to have the authority to act, if necessary decisively, whoever occupied its highest offices. But unless it was to degenerate into tyranny, it had to be limited by an effective rule of law, and held in check by countervailing institutions – not just a parliament, but an independent media and autonomous associations such as churches and trade unions. Soviet government had at least been effective government, with a monopoly of political power in the hands of the Communist Party and, within the party, a concentration of decision-making authority in the hands of its top leadership. The partly reformed system that existed after 1988 was an uneasy combination of party direction 'from above' and popular control 'from below', a tension that was eventually resolved in favour of the mass electorate. The postcommunist system, however, introduced a new source of tension with the separate election of an executive president and a working parliament, a tension that was resolved by the imposition of a system of vertical subordination in the unusual circumstances that obtained after the Russian parliament had been suppressed and the Constitutional Court effectively dissolved. The Russian tradition was strong in its emphasis on centralised direction, but even Putin had to accept that it had been accompanied by a deepening cleavage between government and citizen.[256] Its future was likely to depend upon the extent to which it could incorporate other, more Western traditions of accountability and popular consent; the problem was that any move in this direction would have to be led by those who were themselves the beneficiaries of this system of centralised authority.

Further reading

Editions of the Russian Constitution are readily available in printed and electronic form and in a variety of languages, although not all incorporate recent amendments. Belyakov and Raymond (1994) use the official translation of the Novosti press agency; online sources include www.constitution.ru, where the text is presented in Russian, English, French and German. In a weakly institutionalised system, the characteristics of individual leaders matter at least as much as the powers of their office, and the study of the Russian presidency is accordingly to a large extent a study of individual presidents. On Yeltsin, Aron (2000) and Ellison (2006) are strongly sympathetic; Colton (2008) is particularly full on the early life; Reddaway and Glinski (2001) is a clinical examination of the Yeltsin leadership as a whole from a more critical perspective. On Putin, his own *First Person* (2000) is indispensable; an appendix reprints his address on acceding to the presidency, 'Russia at the Turn of the Millennium'. The leading biography is Sakwa (2008), and there are studies of his popular appeal in White and McAllister (2008), Colton and Hale (2009), and Cassiday and Johnson (2010). A mass of documentation in English as well as Russian may be found on the presidential (www.kremlin.ru) and government (www.government.ru) websites; the important constitutional issues raised in this chapter are unfortunately almost entirely confined to Russian-language sources, but see Medushevsky (2006).

Aron, Leon, *Yeltsin: A Revolutionary Life* (New York: St Martin's and London: HarperCollins, 2000).

Belyakov, Vladimir V., and Walter J. Raymond, eds., *Constitution of the Russian Federation: With Commentaries and Interpretation* (Lawrenceville, VA: Brunswick Publishing Company and Moscow: Novosti, 1994).

Cassiday, Julie A., and Emily D. Johnson, 'Putin, Putiniana and the question of a post-Soviet cult of personality', *Slavonic and East European Review*, vol. **88**, no. 4 (October 2010), pp. 681–707.

Colton, Timothy J., *Yeltsin: A Life* (New York: Basic Books, 2008).

Colton, Timothy J., and Henry E. Hale, 'The Putin vote: presidential electorates in a hybrid regime', *Slavic Review*, vol. **68**, no. 3 (Fall 2009), pp. 473–503.

Ellison, Herbert J., *Boris Yeltsin and Russia's Democratic Transformation* (Seattle, WA, and London: University of Washington Press, 2006).

First Person: An Astonishingly Frank Self-Portrait by Russia's President Vladimir Putin, with Nataliya Gevorkyan, Natalya Timakova, and Andrei Kolsenikov, trans. Catherine A. Fitzpatrick (London: Hutchinson and New York: Random House, 2000).

Medushevsky, Andrey N., Russian *Constitutionalism: Historical and Contemporary Development*, trans. Ekaterina Luneva and Tatiana Baeva (London and New York: Routledge, 2006).

Reddaway, Peter, and Dmitri Glinski, *The Tragedy of Russia's Reforms: Market Bolshevism against Democracy* (Washington, DC: United States Institute of Peace Press, 2001).

Sakwa Richard, *Putin: Russia's Choice*, 2nd edn (Abingdon and New York: Routledge, 2008).

White, Stephen, and Ian McAllister, 'The Putin phenomenon', *Journal of Communist Studies and Transition Politics*, vol. **24**, no. 4 (December 2008), pp. 604–28.

4   From plan to market

A 'privatisation cheque' or voucher, 1993 (Stephen White)

The Soviet economy had achieved unprecedented rates of growth, but performance steadily deteriorated, and by the Gorbachev years it was in what the leader himself described as a 'crisis situation'. Under his leadership, tentative steps were taken towards private ownership and the market; much more decisive steps were taken by Boris Yeltsin after 1991, especially through a far-reaching privatisation of state property. The economy, however, continued to contract, and the currency itself collapsed in a 'default' in 1998 that, for many Russians, discredited the strategy he had been pursuing. Putin placed a much greater emphasis on state ownership and management, and higher oil prices allowed the economy to grow rapidly throughout the years of his presidency; output fell again during the international financial crisis that began in late 2008, but soon recovered. It remained unclear how long a strategy could be sustained that depended so heavily on the export of raw materials, and there were deepening problems of corruption and the rule of law that prejudiced the strategy of 'modernisation' to which the Medvedev leadership was publicly committed.

Lenin, in one of his later writings, had insisted that socialism would prevail 'in the long run' because of the greater productivity that was inherent in a system whose only purpose was the satisfaction of human requirements.[1] In the end it was capitalism that prevailed, and it appeared to have done so, more than anything else, because of its ability to secure a greater return from the resources it commanded and, as a result, to provide a higher level of human welfare. Capitalism, it was accepted, led to social divisions and a reserve army of unemployed; and although it was also capable of generating higher levels of prosperity, for some time the Soviet authorities could claim their system was superior in that it provided in a more comprehensive way for the needs of all its citizens, whatever their nationality, gender or age-group. This was what Gorbachev called the 'protectedness' of the Soviet people, and something that was 'characteristic of a socialist society';[2] it included the right to work, cheap housing, free education up to university level and free medical care. Whatever their inadequacies, it was these 'social guarantees' that gave ordinary citizens their confidence in the future;[3] and in these terms, he told television interviewers in December 1987, the USSR was not a poorer but a more advanced society than its US counterpart.[4]

For many, during the Brezhnev years, it began to appear as if the USSR and its counterparts in Eastern Europe had found an enduring formula of government on this basis, sustained by what some described as a 'social contract' between the communist authorities and the societies over which they ruled. There was no suggestion that governments of this kind were freely elected, although they were usually willing to concede some forms of public consultation and expert advice; but equally, they maintained an acceptable standard of living for the mass of ordinary citizens, including heavily subsidised prices for basic foodstuffs, rents for housing that had remained unchanged for decades, free education and healthcare, and guaranteed employment. Gorbachev had already identified these 'social conquests of the Land of Soviets' as an 'important factor in [its] political stability',[5] and addressing his first Central Committee meeting as party leader in 1985, he described them as the 'basic source of political stability, social optimism and confidence in the future'.[6] Some Western scholars, indeed, spoke more broadly of a 'corporatist polity' that allowed a variety of organised interests to take a direct part in policy formation on the basis of this wide-ranging consensus, with the party no more than a coordinating agency that sought to 'bring other elements together in a cooperative effort to determine and implement public policy'.[7]

Once economic growth started to slow down in the 1970s, however, it became increasingly difficult for the regime to fulfil its part of this tacit 'bargain'. If output stagnated but incomes went up, there would obviously be shortages. And the more consumption increased at prices that were maintained by government, the heavier the burden of budgetary subsidy. Higher prices, however, could hardly be reconciled with an official commitment that living standards would continue to improve. Slower growth also meant that it was no longer possible to satisfy all important interests at the same time – consumers as well as generals, poor regions as well as rich ones, the elderly as well as schoolgoers. And as pressures increased for price rises, lower subsidies and even unemployment, the more difficult it became to sustain the claim that Soviet-type systems offered a degree of economic security that made up for lower living standards and a restricted range of political liberties. As Chingiz Aitmatov, a writer who was also a Communist member of the Congress of People's Deputies, pointed out in 1989, workers in countries like Sweden and the Netherlands earned four or five times as much as their Soviet counterparts; even if they were out of work, their social assistance and welfare rights were vastly superior.[8] Perhaps, others suggested, it was societies such as these that had actually come closest to a meaningful 'socialism' in the late twentieth century.[9] Did they really want to work for capitalists, Gorbachev had asked a mass meeting at the Izhorsk factory in Leningrad when he visited in July 1989? 'Yes, if they pay well', answered a small but vocal section of his audience.[10]

This, in the end, was a metaphor for the collapse of the regime itself, unable to sustain living standards with which its people could be satisfied and yet unwilling to offer them the alternative of a form of government through which they could hold the party and state leadership to account for any shortcomings in their performance. But it left many questions unanswered. Had the existing system, based on public ownership and planning, been incapable of reform, or was its collapse at least compounded by errors of judgement?[11] How was it that the Chinese, with fewer natural advantages, had managed to sustain a high level of growth without rejecting communist rule?[12] How important were exogenous factors, such as the Chernobyl nuclear explosion in 1986 or the world price of oil? Equally, if the existing system was incapable of reform, how was it to be replaced – quickly or gradually, in all sectors at once or in a few to begin with? And what was the alternative – a wholly privatised economy, or one in which (as in many other non-communist countries) the state played a substantial role in regulation, and even ownership? During the early 1990s, the answer seemed to be the fastest possible transfer of state property into private hands; by the start of the new century the emphasis had shifted back to public ownership and the economy (coincidentally or otherwise) had recovered its growth dynamic, but it remained heavily dependent on the export of natural resources and there was increasing evidence that the benefits were being disproportionately enjoyed by a small circle around the Kremlin in a way that deepened the underlying problems of the rule of law and social justice.

The crisis of Soviet planning

At the time, the historical record of Soviet economic management appeared to be one of impressive achievement. Russia in 1913 was a backward country by the standards of the time, 'the poorest of the civilised nations' in the words of a contemporary but still authoritative account.[13] There was an active manufacturing sector, and levels of production in some areas – such as oil and textiles – were comparatively high. But the

Russian share of world industrial output as a whole was very small: just 5 per cent, compared with 14 per cent for the United Kingdom, 16 per cent for Germany and 36 per cent for the United States.[14] The overwhelming mass of the population – 77 per cent in the 1897 census – were classified as peasants, and only a small minority – 21 per cent in the Empire as a whole, just 5 per cent in Central Asia – could read and write (this compared with nearly 90 per cent in the United States and almost universal literacy in the United Kingdom).[15] Russia's relative backwardness was reflected with particular clarity in the development of modern communications. By 1900 Russia had an extensive railway network, with the Trans-Siberian nearing completion; but the United Kingdom (a much smaller country) had twice the length of track, and the United States ten times as much. More than fourteen times as many letters were sent in those two countries as in Russia, per head of population, and more than a hundred times as many telegrams;[16] still more strikingly, there was no more than a single telephone subscriber for every thousand Russians compared with 13 in Britain, 15 in Germany and 76 in the United States.[17]

Just a couple of generations later, the contrast could hardly have been greater. The USSR had by this time become one of the world's economic superpowers, with a gross domestic product (GDP) that was second only to that of the United States. In many areas – including oil, gas, cast iron, steel and tractors – Soviet levels of production were the highest in the world. The USSR had pioneered the exploration of outer space and led the world in the number of its scientific staff. The Soviet natural gas distribution system was one of the largest in the world, and Soviet oil wells were the deepest. The USSR maintained one of the world's largest merchant marines and deployed one of its most formidable concentrations of military might. According to official sources, Soviet national income had increased 149 times between 1917 and 1987, and industrial production 330 times. National income, 58 per cent of that of the United States in 1960, had increased to 67 per cent by 1980, and industrial production had increased from 55 to more than 80 per cent of the US total. Soviet industrial production, about 3 per cent of the global total in 1917, had increased to 20 per cent by 1987; indeed, the USSR by this date produced more than the entire world had done in 1950. Other indicators of development, less dependent on methods of calculation, showed a broadly similar picture: letters and telephones still lagged behind, but in numbers of students, hospital beds, newspaper circulations, calorie consumption or scientific research, the USSR was clearly one of the world's major industrial powers.[18]

These achievements, moreover, had taken place in historical circumstances that could scarcely have been more difficult. As Gorbachev reminded interviewers from *Time* magazine in 1985, the USSR had inherited a 'grim legacy' from its tsarist predecessor: 'a backward economy, strong vestiges of feudalism, millions of illiterate people'. To this had to be added the effects of two world wars, which had ravaged a large part of the USSR and destroyed much that had been created by the Soviet people. There had also been 'irreparable losses' of population: more than 20 million Soviet citizens had perished during the Second World War (the numbers, in fact, were much larger),[19] and millions

Table 4.1 **Soviet economic performance, 1951–1991: various estimates**

	1951–5	1956–60	1961–5	1966–70	1971–5	1976–80	1981–5	1986	1987	1988	1989	1990	1991
USSR	11.4	9.2	6.5	7.8	5.7	4.3	3.6	2.3	1.6	4.4	2.5	−4.0	−15.0
CIA	4.9	5.5	4.8	4.9	3.0	1.9	1.8	4.0	1.3	2.1	1.5	−2.4	−8.5
OECD	5.3	3.8	4.0	5.2	4.1	0.9	1.6	4.1	1.3	2.1	1.5	−2.4	−6.3

Sources: for the USSR: Soviet official data, national income produced; figures for 1991 are for the CIS member countries as reported in *Ekonomika i zhizn'*, no. 6, 1992, p. 13. CIA figures are adapted from Laurie Kurtzweg, comp., *Measures of Soviet Gross National Product in 1982 Prices: A Study* (Washington, DC: US Government Publications Office, 1990), pp. 58, 62 (for 1986 and 1987), GNP in 1982 factor costs expressed in roubles, and Richard F. Kaufman and John P. Hardt, eds., *The Former Soviet Union in Transition* (Armonk, NY: Sharpe 1993), p. 14 (the figures for 1990 and 1991 are approximations and for 1991 relate to CIS member countries only). OECD figures are adapted from Angus Maddison, *The World Economy: Historical Statistics* (Paris: Development Centre of the Organisation for Economic Co-operation and Development, 2003), p. 99, GDP expressed in million Geary-Khamis international dollars.

more had been wounded (Gorbachev, too young to have fought in the war himself, saw the damage it had wrought during his railway trips from southern Russia to Moscow in the late 1940s).[20] It had been asserted by the West at the time, Gorbachev went on, that fifty to a hundred years would be needed to make good what had been destroyed by the Nazi invaders. By doing so in a much shorter period, the Soviet people had achieved what had been thought to be impossible. The fact remained that, since the revolution, something like two decades had been devoted to wars and reconstruction, leaving barely fifty years in which they had turned the USSR into a 'world economic power'[21] (although the calculations were controversial, most economists agreed that the Soviet economy had grown more rapidly than at any time in prerevolutionary Russia and at a more rapid rate than anything the capitalist world had achieved up to that point).[22]

Yet if the economic achievements of the USSR over the longer term were clear, particularly when external circumstances were taken into account, it was equally apparent by the late 1970s that there were systemic shortcomings in the planned economy itself that had yet to be successfully resolved. These shortcomings were most obviously apparent in the rate of economic growth, which fell consistently from the 1950s to the 1980s with only a slight reversal in the late 1960s (see Table 4.1). Levels of economic growth, by the late 1970s and early 1980s, were in fact the lowest ever recorded in Soviet peacetime history. In 1979 national income rose just 2.2 per cent, and labour productivity a bare 1.4 per cent; agricultural output actually fell, by 3.2 per cent, or more than this if a modest increase in population was taken into account.[23] The 11th Five-Year Plan, covering the first half of the 1980s, was in turn substantially underfulfilled: the 26th Party Congress, in 1981, had approved directives that provided for an 18–20 per cent increase in national income by 1985, but the actual increase was 16.5 per cent, and the figures for grain production were so bad they had to be suppressed entirely.[24] The target for industrial output, in fact, had not been met in any of the five-year plans that had been adopted after 1970, whereas only once before that date – in the very first five-year plan – had there been a shortfall. And each extra unit of output had been bought at the cost of an increasing consumption of energy and raw materials, at a time when the leading Western countries were finding new ways of using their resources more efficiently.[25]

Even these figures, moreover, tended to exaggerate the real level of Soviet achievement. In particular, they concealed a steady increase in over-reporting, amounting to 3 per cent of total production by the 1980s – as much as a third in sectors such as cotton or road transportation.[26] And they concealed high levels of waste (as much as 40 per cent of the potato crop, for instance, was lost before it reached the consumer).[27] Nor did they allow adequately for concealed inflation, as cheaper goods were withdrawn and replaced by more expensive and not necessarily superior alternatives.[28] According to a controversial reassessment of official figures by economists Vasilii Selyunin and Grigorii Khanin, taking such factors into account Soviet national income had increased six or seven times between 1928 (when the first five-year plan had been launched) and 1985 – a creditable performance, but some distance from the ninetyfold that was claimed by official statistics.[29] Much of Soviet industrial output, in any case, was hardly a contribution to real wealth. More tractors and combine harvesters were produced than workers were available to operate them, for instance, and the quality of farm machinery was so unsatisfactory that a million people were employed in repair workshops – more than were engaged in producing the machinery in the first place.[30] More than twice as many pairs of footwear were produced as in the United States, similarly, but their quality was so poor that many more had to be imported; twice as much steel was produced, but there was a smaller output of finished products.[31] And even on official figures, some alarming developments were beginning to occur. Soviet national income, 67 per cent of that of the United States in 1980, had slipped to 64 per cent by 1988, and labour productivity in agriculture had fallen from 'about 20 per cent' in the 1970s to 16 per cent in the late 1980s.[32]

Several factors were usually blamed for the Soviet economic slow-down, both in the West and in the USSR itself.[33] One reason, certainly, was that the increase in the size of the industrial labour force was levelling off. Throughout the 1950s and 1960s, large numbers of people were leaving the land to work in industry, allowing output to increase through additional inputs of labour rather than higher productivity. By the early 1980s, this outflow had diminished, leaving economic growth much more dependent on the efficiency with which existing resources were used – or in the language of economists, 'intensive' rather than 'extensive' growth. The population, as in the West, had also been ageing: this meant an increase in the 'dependency ratio', or the numbers of pensioners, schoolchildren and others who were unable to work that had to be supported by other people who were still in some form of employment. Just under 7 per cent of the Soviet population was aged 60 or more in 1939; by 1987 the proportion had doubled, to almost 14 per cent, and by the year 2000, according to Soviet demographers, the proportion would increase still further, to about 17–18 per cent.[34] At the same time there was a steady falling off in the rate of growth of the population that was of working age,[35] and there was expected to be an absolute decline in Ukraine in the first half of the 1990s and in Russia itself in the first decade of the new century.[36] Indeed in some parts of Russia, Ukraine, Belarus and the Baltic republics there was already an absolute and not simply a relative decline in the numbers that were economically active.[37]

A further contribution to the economic slow-down came from the fact that raw materials that were conveniently located and of high quality had gradually been used up, making it increasingly necessary to extract resources from more remote locations and poorer sources of supply. By the 1970s fuel and raw materials were already running out in the European part of the USSR, where most of the population was concentrated, and efforts had to be made to develop new sources of supply. Oil and gas production were increasingly located in western Siberia, and timber and precious metals came increasingly from the Far East; the world's largest nickel plant was developed at Norilsk, above the Arctic circle and beyond the reach of roads and railway lines.[38] Resources of this kind, inevitably, were costlier, as they were more difficult to extract and more expensive to process and transport elsewhere. In the 1960s, it has been calculated, one rouble of production in the extractive industries required two roubles of investment; by the early 1980s it needed seven. An example was the oilfield at Samotlar in western Siberia, which had provided two-thirds of the country's needs up to the 1980s but was rapidly becoming exhausted. The most obvious alternative source of supply was Noyabrskoe, 300 kilometres to the north; but it was far from roads and rivers, and the oil was deeper and more difficult to reach.[39] More attention had also to be paid to quality and design, if goods were to find buyers in an increasingly competitive marketplace, and to environmental conservation, which raised unit costs still further.

Whatever the explanation, it was clear that a steadily falling rate of economic growth could not be sustained much further without serious damage to the international standing of the USSR and to the 'social contract' between the governing authorities and the wider population. Even the political stability of the USSR could not be taken for granted, several speakers warned the 27th CPSU Congress in 1986, if popular expectations of this kind continued to be disappointed: Yegor Ligachev, one of the leadership's more orthodox members, emphasised that political stability was largely a function of the party's 'correct social policy', and Gorbachev, in his closing remarks, reminded the delegates of Lenin's warning at the Party Congress in 1922 that there were revolutionary parties that had 'perished' because they were 'afraid to talk about their weaknesses'.[40] As Gorbachev had put it in a speech in December 1984, only a highly developed economy would allow the USSR to enter the twenty-first century as a great and flourishing power; the fate of socialism as a whole, not just of the USSR itself, depended upon their success.[41] Others argued, in still more apocalyptic terms, that unless the USSR adopted more efficient forms of economic management it would 'cease to be a great power' and quickly become a 'backward, stagnating state and an example to the rest of the world how not to conduct its economic life' (in the words of economists Leonid Abalkin and Nikolai Shmelev respectively).[42]

The Gorbachev strategy

The broad framework of economic reform was set out in Gorbachev's address to the 27th Party Congress in 1986. The top priority, in his view, was to overcome the factors that had been holding back the country's socioeconomic development as quickly as possible and resume the growth trajectory of earlier decades.[43] Not only was it necessary to accelerate the rate of economic growth: it must be a new kind of growth, based on scientific progress and a more efficient use of resources. There had been 'impressive successes' over the previous quarter of a century, Gorbachev told the Congress; national income and living standards had risen rapidly, and there had been welcome advances in science, medicine and culture. But difficulties had built up during the 1970s; growth rates had fallen and plan targets had not been met. The main reason, Gorbachev suggested, was that they had failed to respond to the need for a shift from extensive growth, based on additional labour and raw materials, to intensive growth, based on higher levels of productivity.[44] In the light of these requirements, the new five-year plan set out as its central objective a doubling of national income by the year 2000. This would require a thorough modernisation of the economy on the basis of the most advanced technologies; economic management would at the same time be decentralised, with Gosplan (the USSR State Planning Committee) concentrating its efforts on long-term objectives, and enterprises guided to a much greater extent by their performance in the marketplace. The financial system would be reorganised; prices would be more 'flexible'; and cooperatives of all kinds would be encouraged to extend the scale of their operations.[45]

More detailed guidelines for economic reform were approved by a Central Committee meeting in June 1987, at which Gorbachev again delivered the main address. There had been outstanding successes in the years since the revolution, he argued, but the centralised form of economic management established at that time had outlived its usefulness. Attempts had been made to reform it from the 1950s onwards, but they had all proved ineffective. Now, in the 1980s, the Soviet economy was in not just a difficult but a 'precrisis' situation. The rate of economic growth had dropped to a level that 'virtually signified the onset of economic stagnation'. Resources were being wastefully used, technological levels lagged increasingly behind those of the rest of the developed world and there were diminishing returns from capital investment. Budgetary deficits were being covered by the sale of raw materials on world markets and duties on the sale of liquor, which had more than doubled over the previous fifteen years. Spending on wages had meanwhile exceeded plan targets, while increases in output had been less than predicted; this meant that there was more money in circulation than goods available for purchase. Shortages, inevitably, had become worse, of everything from metal, fuel and cement to equipment and consumer goods; there was a 'chronic deficit of man-power'; and perhaps most serious of all, they had begun to lag behind their Western competitors in scientific and technical development. Nothing less than a 'deep, genuinely revolutionary' transformation of the entire system of economic management was needed to reverse these alarming trends.[46]

The centrepiece of the Gorbachev reform strategy was the Law on the State Enterprise, which was adopted the same month and brought into effect in January 1988. The main aim of the Law, Gorbachev explained, was to bring 'real economic independence' to individual factories, freeing them from the dictates of their ministerial superiors. This was not the end of central planning, as some Western press reports suggested; but it was certainly intended to represent a significant change in the nature of the guidance that was provided, with the plan being drawn up by factories themselves upon the basis of 'control figures', which specified the desired level of production and other general objectives, and 'economic normatives', which covered the contributions that were due to the state budget for land, labour and capital. Within this framework individual factories would be expected to prepare their own plans, based on 'state orders' placed by the central authorities and on commercial orders placed by other enterprises. The income from these activities, in line with the principle of 'self-financing', was intended to cover all the costs that were incurred, including wages and investment in new technologies. Equally, the new law sought to bring the 'human factor' into play by democratising the workplace, allowing workers to elect their managers at all levels and 'as a rule' on a competitive basis. A new council, elected every two or three years, would exercise the powers of the workforce as a whole between its periodic conferences, and it would make final decisions on all the matters that fell within its competence.[47]

The scope for rapid improvement – and the alleviation of the shortages of most immediate concern to ordinary citizens – was probably greater in agriculture than in industry, and this became the object of a wide-ranging package of reforms that was approved by a Central Committee plenum in March 1989. The reality, Gorbachev explained in his opening address, was that the USSR still lagged behind the Western countries in its agricultural productivity, and the gap was widening rather than narrowing. Part of the problem was historical, including the 'human tragedy' of collectivisation in the 1930s. But new equipment, roads and buildings would not be enough by themselves to bring about the improvements they all wanted to see; what was needed was a much more far-reaching change in rural economic relations, giving individual farmers more opportunity to develop their own initiative. There should be a diversity of forms of economic management based on a diversity of forms of property, and family farms should be allowed to develop without the prejudice that they were a 'lower' form of economic activity. Above all, leaseholding, by which groups of farmers received land or livestock on a contract basis with the right to sell any surplus, should be encouraged, and farmers themselves should be persuaded to become collectives of leaseholders, paying their way on a profit-and-loss basis. All of this, in Gorbachev's view, represented a 'drastic revision of the CPSU's agrarian policy', to be carried forward by party and state authorities in the very different local conditions in which they operated.[48]

The strategy of reform was completed by a number of other measures, all of them designed to encourage a wide variety of forms of non-state economic activity. Under legislation approved in late 1986, for instance, several forms of 'individual labour activity' were officially approved, including car repairs, tutoring, photography, handicrafts and private car rental; more than 670,000 were employed on this basis by 1990.[49] A further, more significant, change was the adoption in May 1988 of a Law on Cooperatives that was widely seen as the most radical economic measure to be introduced in the early years of the Gorbachev administration.[50] No special permission was required to establish a cooperative, and they were to have the same legal status as enterprises within the state sector; they could hire outside labour, lease property, set their own prices except when they were fulfilling state orders and engage in foreign trade. By January 1991 there were 245,400 cooperatives of various kinds in operation, including a cooperative bank; most of them were small, with an average of just twenty-five employees, but they employed a total workforce of over 6 million and official sources suggested that they could account for 10–12 per cent of national income by the mid-1990s.[51] There were parallel reforms in foreign trade, designed to encourage more direct links between factories themselves and deepen Soviet participation in the international division of labour, and plans were made for the rouble to become an internationally convertible currency.[52]

A deepening crisis

Gorbachev, his official spokesman pointed out, had won the Nobel Prize for Peace, not for Economics, and there would certainly have been no basis for such an award in the results that were announced over the later years of his general secretaryship. The 12th Five-Year Plan, adopted in 1986, had specified an average growth rate of 4.2 per cent; the 'basic directives' adopted by the 27th Party Congress called for the rate of growth to rise still further, to 5 per cent a year by the end of the century, in order to double national income by the year 2000.[53] The average rate of growth recorded between 1986 and 1989 was in fact a modest 3.7 per cent,[54] which was below the 'stagnation' years of the late 1970s; in 1990 there was a fall, rather than an increase,[55] and then in 1991, as the state itself collapsed, a more dramatic contraction as the economy moved into an open and deepening recession (see Table 4.1). As the State Statistics Committee reported in February 1992, the last year of the USSR had been one of 'intensified decline in the economy and people's standard of living and an exacerbation of the social atmosphere'. Gross national product had slumped; soap, washing powder and many other goods were being rationed; the output of oil and coal was down 10 per cent on the previous year, for reasons that included a wave of strikes; and foreign trade turnover was down because of a fall in the export of fuel and raw materials, still the main source of hard currency. Control over the money supply had meanwhile been lost completely (the value of the currency that was in circulation had increased nearly five times over the previous year), and the consumer price index had nearly doubled.[56]

Giving greater autonomy to industrial enterprises, it became clear, had allowed them more freedom to choose their output mix so that they were able to meet their obligations in the easiest possible way. One common response was to reduce or discontinue the production of cheaper items that were no less burdensome to manufacture, such as children's clothing or spare parts. As enterprises became more independent, they also found it easier to raise their prices; and as up to 40 per cent of industrial output was produced by monopoly suppliers,[57] there was little consumers or other producers could do about it. Enterprises, at the same time, had begun to enjoy a greater freedom in the payment of their employees, whether or not there had been a corresponding change in productivity. As the Komi first secretary told the CPSU Central Committee in April 1989, wages were advancing ahead of productivity at such a rate that soon the whole economy would be printing banknotes;[58] roubles, others complained, were becoming a 'measure of weight' instead of a measure of value.[59] Government itself found it more difficult to sustain the cost of social programmes that had become increasingly expensive at the same time as public spending was being forced up by the growing burden of consumer subsidies (which had cost 90 billion roubles in 1990 and were expected to cost half as much again in 1991).[60] The budgetary deficit, as a result, widened rapidly: by the end of 1991 it was approaching 30 per cent of GDP[61] and the national debt, to which it contributed, was running at a level more than twice as high.[62]

Shortages, meanwhile, were becoming more acute as consumers did what they could to convert their roubles into something more useful than rapidly depreciating pieces of paper. In Tambov, by the late 1980s, there were 'huge queues', even for matches, and salt had practically disappeared from retail sale.[63] In Saratov there were shortages of soap, washing powder and toothpaste.[64] Elsewhere there were 'day and night' queues for sugar, queues 'like in the war' for bread, and a 'catastrophic' lack of medicines.[65] In Novosibirsk things were so desperate that local people began spending the night in shops to be sure of obtaining their sausage in the morning, and there were assaults on sales staff by irate customers.[66] The shortage of soap and household detergents was a source of particular and understandable concern. 'What kind of a regime is it if we can't even get washed?' asked an indignant group of workers in Vladimir.[67] A housewife in the Moscow region threatened to send her dirty linen directly to the ministries. 'If they can't provide us with soap', she reasoned, 'let them do the washing themselves.'[68] Others wrote to the Central Committee to ask for assistance; it had to explain that it was 'not a department store'.[69] Shortages, at the same time, encouraged a burgeoning black market; the authorities did what they could to counteract it by rationing meat and other basic commodities, but the coupons themselves became an item of illicit trade, and in any case they could have no direct influence on the level of output.[70]

Not all of these difficulties, admittedly, were the result of official policies. Their success was also prejudiced by external circumstances, including the Chernobyl nuclear explosion of April 1986 and the Armenian earthquake of December 1988. At Chernobyl, a nuclear power complex eighty miles north of Kyiv, one of the reactors blew up after a routine safety test went wrong and started a chain reaction that became uncontrollable, sending a plume of highly radioactive fall-out into the atmosphere in the most serious environmental disaster that had so far taken place anywhere in the world. Despite early and alarmist reports, just thirty-one deaths, not all of them from radiation, occurred in the immediate aftermath of the explosion, but 600,000 had received a 'significant exposure' and there was a heavy and continuing loss of life, with up to 10,000 deaths over the following decade and an increased rate of serious illness among the children of survivors as well as among survivors themselves.[71] In addition, about 200,000 of the local population had to be resettled, an area the size of Belgium had been contaminated and 250,000 hectares were so badly affected they had to be taken out of cultivation altogether.[72] The economic costs were estimated at about $200 billion, with continuing costs for Ukraine alone of $1 billion a year, and it placed in doubt an energy policy that had begun to lay an increasing emphasis on nuclear power as oil production fell off.[73] The Armenian earthquake in December 1988, another catastrophe, left 45,000 dead and half a million homeless; it was the most powerful in the Caucasus for more than eighty years, and at its epicentre 'virtually nothing was left standing'.[74]

There were additional problems in foreign trade as the price of raw materials on world markets began to fall. About 12 per cent of Soviet gas was sold abroad, and about 20 per cent of the country's oil; in turn, fuel and electricity accounted for over 40 per cent of the value of all Soviet exports, allowing the USSR to import large quantities of Western manufactures and, increasingly, foodstuffs as well. Unfortunately for Soviet planners, the high world prices for oil that had sustained them throughout the Brezhnev years began to fail in the late 1980s. Oil lost about a third of its value on export markets between 1985 and 1990, and levels of output themselves began to decline; more natural gas was extracted but its value on export markets fell even more sharply, by nearly half. Imports, on the other hand, continued to rise as enterprises used the independence they now enjoyed to bring in greater quantities of foodstuffs and consumer goods at the same time as a dislocated market made it more difficult for domestic producers to satisfy the growing requirements of their own consumers. The foreign trade balance, as a consequence, moved into deficit in 1989 and into a still deeper deficit in 1990; the biggest losses in absolute terms were in trade with West Germany, but there were relatively much heavier losses in Soviet trade with the United States, with imports running at about four times the value of exports.[75] External debt rose as a result, from $5 billion in 1985 to nearly $69 billion at the end of 1990, by which time there was a serious threat of 'international bankruptcy'; foreign bankers were refusing to lend any further without guarantees from their own governments, and the rouble was on its 'last gasp'.[76]

On top of natural disasters and adverse movements in the terms of trade, there were misconceived initiatives, such as the anti-alcoholism campaign that was launched at the start of the new administration, in May 1985. There was certainly no doubt that 'something had to be done'. Levels of alcohol consumption had more than doubled between 1960 and the mid-1980s, reaching a level of 15 or 16 litres a year for all adults or as much as a bottle a day in some industrial cities.[77] More women were drinking, and more young people; life expectancies were falling, and there were heavy costs for the whole society in terms of family breakdown, violent crime, medical care and loss of output. Gorbachev himself was a moderate on such questions and the strongest pressure for a radical approach came from other members of the leadership, particularly Yegor Ligachev, whose puritan nature inclined him towards 'severe and administrative' measures,[78] as well as the chairman of the Committee of Party Control, Mikhail Solomentsev, who knew all about the problem from his personal experience.[79] Solomentsev, reflecting later on the campaign, pointed to the 'thousands of heart-rending letters', mostly from wives and mothers, that had persuaded the leadership to take action;[80] Gorbachev was also convinced the 'whole society' had called for the campaign.[81] Popular support, however, melted away as the campaign overreached its original objectives: there was an enormous increase in home brewing, a criminal underground became established, and the loss of tax revenues was one of the main causes of a deepening crisis in the public finances.[82]

The collapse of the economy, in the event, was so quick and comprehensive that some members of the leadership were inclined to explain it in terms of conspiracy and not simply misjudgement.[83] Whether this was true or not, it was certainly relevant that reformers as well as conservatives had little first-hand experience of a market economy, still less of a successful transition to a 'socialist market economy' that would combine state ownership and guidance with private and even foreign initiative in a manner for which there was no obvious precedent. Indeed there were few, particularly among the reformers, who had practical experience of economic management of any kind. Ryzhkov, a moderate, had run one of the country's largest engineering factories, but Gorbachev had spent his entire career in Komsomol and party work, and his closest associates, like Yakovlev and Vadim Medvedev, had a background in full-time party administration with a particular specialisation in foreign affairs and ideology. A more fundamental difficulty was the contradictory nature of *perestroika* itself. Was there, in particular, a basis on which public ownership could be reconciled with the disciplines of the market? Gaidar, at least, had 'more and more the impression of a dangerous disjunction between [Gorbachev's] good intentions and his actual economic policy'. He was always keen to find a consensus, but this led to 'constant ambiguity'; convinced that his task was to remove a number of isolated faults in Soviet socialism, he had no conception of the difficulties he would face or of the resistance he would encounter when he began to do so. Confronted by powerful and incomprehensible processes, Gorbachev 'panicked and lost his bearings'; in the end it was clear he had no strategy at all.[84]

Dismantling the planned economy

The practical and theoretical failure of the 'socialist market' meant that there was little resistance to the process of more far-reaching reform with which the newly elected Russian president, Boris Yeltsin, was quick to associate himself. Many of the old orthodoxies, in fact, had collapsed even before his election in the summer of 1991 and before the USSR itself had been dissolved at the end of that year. In 1990 a new law on property had established equality of status for all forms of ownership, including foreign ownership, and opened the way to private or 'non-socialist' ownership of the means of production.[85] In August of that year, there were government measures to 'create and develop small enterprises' and to 'demonopolise the economy'.[86] In July 1991 the Soviet parliament went even further, adopting a law on the 'denationalisation and privatisation of enterprises' on the basis of which up to half the assets of state-owned industry were to pass into private or cooperative hands by the end of the following year.[87] A law on entrepreneurship, adopted in April 1991, sanctioned the use of hired labour,[88] and employment exchanges reappeared in the summer, sixty years after the last of them had closed in what was supposed to have been an historic victory over the inherent evils of capitalism.[89] Price reform had meanwhile been initiated by a reluctant Ryzhkov, in what he later recalled as the 'most traumatic, most difficult speech' of his life,[90] and by the middle of 1991 about 45 per cent of all output was being sold without restriction.[91]

The alternative offered by the Yeltsin government was what had become known in other countries as 'shock therapy'. It was foreshadowed in a wide-ranging speech by the Russian President in October 1991 in which he called for 'thoroughgoing reforms' including the liberalisation of prices, further privatisation and military conversion. 'We must', Yeltsin insisted, 'provide economic freedom, lift all barriers to the freedom of enterprises and of entrepreneurship and give people the opportunity to work and to receive as much as they can earn, casting off all bureaucratic constraints.' There would be a tough monetary policy, cuts in public spending and tax reform. Most difficult of all, price controls would be abandoned, which meant that living standards would fall for six months until the consumer market had recovered. Other efforts would be made to expand private business, and to create a 'fundamentally new situation in the agrarian sector'.[92] Yeltsin himself was given additional powers to rule by decree in economic matters, and in the month that followed there were presidential directives that abolished limits on earnings, liberalised foreign economic relations, and commercialised shops and services;[93] going still further, a decree on prices in December abolished controls on all but a 'limited range' of goods and services from 2 January 1992.[94] Prices were duly 'freed', not only in Russia but in most of the other post-Soviet republics; within a month they had risen by 350 per cent, within a year by 2,600 per cent.[95] Price reform, Yeltsin acknowledged in a parliamentary address, was a 'painful measure', but it was a path the 'whole civilised world' had been obliged to follow and the 'only way' they would be able to extricate the country from its crisis.[96]

A 'memorandum on economic policy' appeared in February 1992 that placed these changes within a broader context. Already, it noted, about 90 per cent of consumer goods were being sold without any form of administrative control; by the end of the following month, all remaining price controls would be removed, apart from rents, municipal services and public transportation. Energy prices would be allowed to reach world levels by the end of 1993. The most vulnerable sections of the population would be protected, as far as possible, in the form of cash benefits for those with the lowest income levels. A balanced budget would be achieved through a series of cuts in subsidies to enterprises and a reduction of up to 15 per cent in public sector employment. Exchange controls would be abandoned, and export licences would be abolished in all but a limited number of cases as a step towards Russia's full integration into the international economy.[97] A further, more elaborate measure for the development of cooperation in trade and economic areas, the 'Programme for the Deepening of Economic Reforms in Russia', was approved in July 1992; it dealt with the medium term, up to 1996, and set out the same kinds of goals – deregulation, financial stabilisation, privatisation and the development of entrepreneurship, an 'active social policy' that would protect the most vulnerable, structural change (including demilitarisation), and the creation of a 'competitive market environment'. All of these, it was confidently predicted, would halt the collapse of production and restore economic growth at 3 or 4 per cent a year.[98]

The main outlines of Russia's privatisation programme had been approved by the Supreme Soviet the previous year in a law on the privatisation of state and municipal enterprises that has been described as a 'watershed in the Russian privatisation process'.[99] Its aim, through the transfer of ownership from the state into private hands, was to establish an 'effective, socially oriented market economy', and a Committee for the Management of State Property, headed by a chairman of ministerial rank, was established to supervise its implementation.[100] A law on 'personal privatisation accounts' was approved the same day, establishing the principle that all citizens would be given a credit to the value of their notional share of public assets.[101] A more detailed programme was approved by the Presidium of the Supreme Soviet in December 1991;[102] under its provisions a whole range of economic activities would be privatised over the following year, including retail and wholesale trade, public catering, construction, the processing of agricultural produce, and road freight.[103] The programme was extended again in a parliamentary resolution of June 1992, which made it clear that the exercise would be conducted in the first instance by issuing 'privatisation cheques' to all citizens and then gradually extended.[104] A presidential decree of August 1992, accompanied by more detailed regulations, set out a timetable according to which the first tranche of cheques, with a nominal value of 10,000 roubles each (just over $30 at the prevailing rate of exchange), would be distributed from 1 October onwards.[105]

Under the terms of the legislation, privatisation cheques – or vouchers, as they were called in spite of Yeltsin's objections[106] – would be issued to all permanent residents of the Russian Federation who had been born before 2 September 1992, including children, and to others, like diplomats and journalists, who were resident abroad for reasons that were related to the nature of their employment. The vouchers could be used to buy shares in the enterprises in which the owners worked themselves, or to take part in an auction at which other firms and companies were being sold, or they could be placed in investment funds, which could use them to buy company shares. Vouchers, equally, could be sold, given away or bequeathed, but they could not be used for the purchase of commodities (which would have had enormous inflationary implications). All such transactions had to be completed by the end of 1993, a deadline that was later extended to 1 July 1994.[107] Privatisation vouchers, as the legislation had provided, began to be distributed on 1 October 1992; by the following January more than 140 million had been distributed, which meant that 95 per cent of the entire population had already received them.[108] 'Those who haven't managed to save up any roubles from the construction of socialism can from today feel richer', *Izvestiya* told its readers as the process began. 'How much? That will depend on a series of circumstances, but for the first time since 1917 something is being given to us, not taken away.'[109] In Yekaterinburg, which was Yeltsin's home region, a newborn baby was christened 'Voucher'; a popular song, 'Wow, wow, voucher', reached No. 5 in the Russian hit parade.[110]

Privatisation, according to the legislation, could take three basic forms.[111] Under option 1, the workforce were given 25 per cent of the share issue in the form of non-voting stock and were allowed to buy a further 10 per cent for vouchers or cash at a 30 per cent discount (this, it emerged, was the option most likely to be chosen when the enterprise was capital intensive, as was often the case in the energy sector, or when relations on the shop floor were so confrontational that managers were reluctant to allow the issue of shares that would place voting rights in the hands of their employees). Option 2, which was by far the most popular, allowed 51 per cent of the voting equity to be sold to managers and workers at extremely low prices with the remaining 49 per cent sold at auction or held by the state for sale at a later date (this was essentially an employee–management buy-out).[112] A more ambitious option 3 allowed larger numbers of workers – but not necessarily the entire workforce – to reorganise and develop their own enterprise, receiving up to 40 per cent of its share issue in exchange. The balance would be available for purchase by ordinary citizens, using their privatisation cheques, or by investment funds acting on their behalf; but it was not a popular option, in part because the regulations had been written in 'traditional Russian bureaucratese'.[113] 'We need millions of property owners, not just a handful of millionaires', as Yeltsin had explained in a nationwide television address. 'The voucher', he added, 'is a sort of ticket for each of us to a free economy. The more property owners and business people there are in Russia, for whom concrete action is more important than idle discussion, the sooner Russia will be prosperous and the sooner its future will be in safe hands.'[114]

The scheme, however, soon encountered difficulties. Despite an expensive advertising campaign, there was some uncertainty about who could receive the vouchers: they were intended for all citizens, whatever their age, but it was not until January 1993 that the status of refugees and members of the Merchant Marine was finally clarified.[115] In other cases, vouchers were quite improperly exchanged for services: in Tyumen they were used to cover the cost of dentistry, or sold for vodka or eau de cologne; in Yaroslavl they were being offered as advance payment for funerals.[116] Vouchers were also counterfeited and stolen; some fake certificates in Rostov-on-Don were intercepted simply because they had been too skilfully manufactured.[117] And there were regional imbalances: Moscow and St Petersburg had large populations and large numbers of vouchers, but relatively few enterprises that could be acquired in this way; Siberia and the Far East had much smaller populations with fewer vouchers at their disposal, but many more enterprises in which they could be invested.[118] There were larger questions as well. For instance, the value of the assets that were being distributed was itself somewhat notional: the last appraisal had taken place twenty years earlier, and there were no valuations of any kind that were based on Western accounting conventions.[119] In the end the face value of 10,000 roubles was chosen 'for reasons of simplicity'; it represented the book value of the country's productive resources, divided by the total population, and then rounded up from 8,476 to a more manageable figure.[120]

These were new and unfamiliar procedures, and not surprisingly they led to a series of controversies as newly established funds began to compete for the assets of an inexperienced public.[121] In St Petersburg, three companies set up to receive investments simply disappeared – as did the savings of about 400,000 of their depositors. The whole incident became known as the 'affair of the century'.[122] The management of NeftAlmazInvest, a fund that promised to place its resources in the oil and diamond industries, got away with about 900,000 vouchers; another fund, 'Russkii dom selenga', collected the savings of 1.5 million luckless investors and then relocated to the Bahamas.[123] The largest scandal of all involved a pyramid investment company, MMMInvest, run by a businessman called Sergei Mavrodi. MMM took over the top floor of the Lenin Museum; its slogan, advertised all over the Moscow underground, was 'We'll make your voucher golden'. The company collapsed in 1994 and its director was seized in a spectacular raid on his private apartment; but there were demands that the Russian government redeem the claims of disappointed investors and Mavrodi himself became something of a folk hero, winning a seat in the Duma in a by-election that in turn secured his early release (his immunity was subsequently lifted and he was eventually imprisoned on fraud charges).[124] Between 15 and 20 million had lost their investments, and some had suffered heart attacks or been driven to suicide; Mavrodi himself had meanwhile sent most of the money abroad.[125] The 'party of the swindled', indeed, was already a substantial electoral force, with an estimated 24 million voters among the victims of one or other of these investment frauds.[126]

Table 4.2 **The progress of privatisation, 1993–2000**

	1993	1994	1995	1996	1997	1998	1999	2000
No. of privatised enterprises	42,924	21,905	10,152	4,997	2,743	2,129	1,536	2,274
Of which: federal	7,063	5,685	1,875	928	374	264	104	170
regional	9,521	5,112	1,317	715	548	321	298	274
municipal	26,340	11,108	6,960	3,354	1,821	1,544	1,134	1,830
Forms of privatisation (%)								
Share issue	31	45	28	23	18	–	–	–
Sale at auctions	6	4	4	4	6	–	–	–
Commercial competition	30	24	16	9	10	–	–	–
Investment competition	1	1	1	1	1	–	–	–
Redemption of lease	30	21	30	32	15	–	–	–
Sale of real estate	–	–	15	23	39	–	–	–
Sale of state and municipal property at auction	–	–	–	–	–	76	75	73
Of which: sale of real estate	–	–	–	–	–	48	48	57
Redemption of leased state and municipal property	–	–	–	–	–	7	8	18
Sale of shares of privatised firms	–	–	–	–	–	10	12	4

Source: adapted from *Rossiiskii statisticheskii yezhegodnik: statisticheskii sbornik* (Moscow: Goskomstat Rossii, 2001), p. 327; other categories account for residuals.

By the time voucher privatisation came to an end, in June 1994, something like 100,000 enterprises had changed their form of ownership, and more than 40 million Russians had become property owners – 'a process unprecedented in its scale and speed', according to *Izvestiya*.[127] Indeed there were more private shareholders in Russia by this time than in Britain or the United States, and it seemed reasonable to claim that there had been a change of mentality and not simply of ownership, reasserting the rights of private property and 'sharply altering the "Soviet" mind-set'.[128] A second stage of privatisation began in 1994, involving the sale of large enterprises at auction; a third stage, involving smaller individual projects, began in 1997.[129] The pace of privatisation was slowing down, with more than 40,000 enterprises privatised in 1993 but just a couple of thousand annually by the end of the decade (see Table 4.2); nor did 'privatisation' necessarily mean the transfer of property to ordinary citizens, as the great majority of the new owners were enterprises or other bodies that had been set up by local authorities.[130] By the late 1990s, nonetheless, more than 80 per cent of all industrial enterprises had nominally become private, although they accounted for less than 30 per cent of the value of industrial output; more than twice as much came from enterprises that were partly private and partly public, including those that had an element of foreign ownership.[131] Yeltsin congratulated the State Property Committee on its selfless labour, and hailed the 'foundation of the new edifice of the reviving economy of great Russia';[132] for some Western advisers the whole exercise had been an 'extraordinary achievement', and there was excited talk of a 'coming Russian boom'.[133]

Other views of the privatisation process were less complimentary; some of them came from Russian economists who had a better understanding of the realities of their own society but had not been consulted about this leap into an unknown capitalist future. What had taken place was not privatisation at all, they argued, but a '*nomenklatura* collectivisation of enterprises' that was simply another stage in the 'economic civil war' between the Yeltsin administration and the rest of the society.[134] Sergei Glaz'ev, a leading economist who had been minister of foreign economic relations in the Chernomyrdin government and was later a presidential candidate, described it even more forthrightly as the 'illegal appropriation (theft) of the most substantial property that had ever in world history come into the hands of a criminal community', which had led to the 'criminalisation of the economy, the destruction of productive and technological cooperation, chaos in property, a sharp fall in the volume and effectiveness of production, [and] an increase in social tension'.[135] *Pravda* spoke in similar terms of an 'enormous swindle' in which '60 per cent of the national economy had fallen into the hands of banks close to government ... and groups of organised criminals', as a result of which 'industry [was] at a standstill, workers [had received] no pay for months, and the number of unemployed [had] gone over ten million' while a 'narrow stratum of "new Russians" feeding off the budget and raw material exports [had got] richer and richer'.[136] Privatisation, in this view, had been imposed on Russia by Western financial institutions in their own interests,[137] and it would lead to a 'colonisation' of Russia by international capital and its local accomplices that would have 'disastrous consequences' for the Russian people as a whole.[138]

What did ordinary Russians make of it all? The most common reaction, it appeared, was 'massive disillusion'.[139] Russians were actually quite positive about the economic system they had experienced before the start of *perestroika*, but very critical of the arrangements that had been introduced after the end of communist rule – which was hardly surprising, as living standards had fallen catastrophically.[140] There was a particularly sceptical view of the programme of privatisation (in Russian, *privatizatsiya*); some, indeed, preferred to call it *prikhvatizatsiya* or 'seizure'. Not many thought it would 'make the economy more productive', 'give people a material stake in the economy' or 'put more goods in the shops' (between 35 and 40 per cent agreed with these various propositions); it was more likely, in the popular view, to 'make a few people rich' (86 per cent), 'increase prices' (84 per cent) and 'create unemployment' (82 per cent).[141] The programme was no more popular in retrospect: 77 per cent of those who were asked more than a decade later thought the owners of most private assets had acquired them illegally, 81 per cent thought privatisation had led to a plundering of the nation's resources and 70 per cent took the view that they now lived under a 'clan-based, quasi-criminal, oligarchic capitalism'.[142] It was certainly consistent with such an interpretation that so much of the programme had been enacted from above, bypassing the parliamentary process and sometimes existing legislation. Indeed the chair of the privatisation committee, Anatolii Chubais, openly acknowledged that a 'significant proportion' of the programme had been legislated in this way to avoid the resistance it would otherwise have encountered at the hands of Russia's elected representatives.[143]

Summing up the results of privatisation in the mid-1990s, the sociologist and reformer Tat'yana Zaslavskaya acknowledged that there had been a substantial change in property relations, although few had yet obtained any kind of dividend from their new investments. The change that had taken place, however, was not the establishment of a property-owning democracy but an 'even greater concentration of wealth in the hands of a narrow group of people'.[144] The change of ownership had certainly had little effect on enterprise behaviour. There was a fall, not an increase, in labour productivity.[145] Output was even more highly concentrated in a small number of factories than it had been before the move to private ownership.[146] Energy consumption per unit of output had increased, instead of diminishing.[147] And the productive base became even more obsolescent as capital investment dropped far below the levels that had been achieved in the late Soviet years.[148] Nor was there much evidence of a revolution in managerial attitudes. Factory directors, on the contrary, were just as keen as their Soviet predecessors to retain state subsidies and protection from their foreign competitors. And although there was an investment crisis of 'astounding proportions', managers as well as workers were opposed to the sale of shares in their enterprise even if a new owner was likely to bring the resources that were needed to expand and modernise.[149] The entire process, researchers concluded, had 'failed to bring any significant change in the way Russian companies were managed' and had had 'very little (if any) effect on gross output and average output per employee'.[150]

Privatisation of agriculture had been taken less far by the late 1990s, even though the private ownership of land had been incorporated into the Russian Constitution in late 1990 and then formed part of the new constitution that was approved in December 1993. A presidential decree of March 1992, and a further decree the following June, had provided for the sale of private plots of land.[151] A more far-reaching decree of October 1993, hailed in the press as an 'historic step',[152] established that it was legal for those who owned it to buy, sell, lease, mortgage or exchange land; every owner of a plot of land was to receive a certificate that would be entered in a state registry, compulsory deliveries were phased out and the state itself guaranteed the 'inviolability and protection of the private ownership of land as well as the protection of the rights of landowners during land transactions'.[153] But there were problems about the physical separation of the land that individual farmers might claim: among other things it had to take account of the 'rational organisation of land areas and compact land use', which provided all kinds of opportunities for differences of opinion that might ultimately have to be resolved by litigation. Changes in ownership, for this and other reasons, advanced slowly: the number of commercial farms increased to about 280,000 in the mid-1990s but then fell back; by the end of the decade, they accounted for no more than 7 per cent of all agricultural land, and for an even smaller 2.5 per cent of the value of agricultural output (they were most important for their production of sunflower seeds).[154]

The privatisation of land encountered further difficulties because of the high proportion of collective and state farms that were unprofitable, which gave little incentive to take over their ownership (only 3 per cent of farms were running at a loss in 1990, but energy and other costs increased more rapidly than whatever farmers were able to earn from the sale of their produce, and by the late 1990s the great majority were losing money).[155] There was strong opposition to the 'voucherisation of land relations' in any case, given the danger that it might lead to 'speculation' and the 'creation of a class of latifundistas'.[156] The Russian parliament, particularly its Communist and Agrarian deputies, pressed in these circumstances for lifetime leasing rather than outright ownership; fourteen of the Federation's eighty-nine subjects took no steps to legalise private land-ownership within their own area, and one – the Karachai-Cherkess republic – went so far as to prohibit land sales, in spite of the provisions of the Constitution.[157] A presidential decree in March 1996 sought to make more of a reality of the constitutional right to land, and to complete the issue of certificates of ownership.[158] But with high interest rates and competition from cheaper imports, it was more likely that farmers would simply 'pool their brand-new deeds, conclude contracts with the chairman and work exactly as they had done before'.[159] The value of agricultural output as a whole, in the event, fell by almost half over the course of the decade; the output of meat fell by more than half, and other staples like eggs and milk were down by about a third.[160]

Western assistance

The other vital element in the reform strategy was Western economic assistance, including direct investment. The USSR had already begun to move closer to the international economy, joining the European Bank for Reconstruction and Development in March 1991 and becoming a 'special associate member' of the International Monetary Fund later in the year;[161] a more favourable legislative environment was created at the same time for foreign investment.[162] Gorbachev, in an historic gesture, was invited to attend a summit of the Group of Seven industrial nations in the summer of 1991 at which the other leaders agreed to 'assist the integration of the Soviet Union into the world economy'.[163] Russia, now an independent and postcommunist state, became a member of the International Monetary Fund in April 1992, and joined the World Bank the following July;[164] in June 1993 it applied for membership of the General Agreement on Tariffs and Trade (which later became the World Trade Organization), although it did not at this point become formally affiliated.[165] The Group of Seven (G7) eventually became a Group of Eight (G8), with Russia a full participant, and a series of agreements was concluded with international financial institutions, starting with a rouble stabilisation fund in 1992 that was worth $24 billion.[166] A further $43 billion was approved in 1993, although not all of it was new money;[167] and the repayment of Soviet foreign debt, an estimated $80 billion, was suspended for ten years.[168]

And yet foreign assistance was unlikely, by itself, to achieve the kind of transformation that domestic reforms had been unable to accomplish. Much of it, for a start, failed to materialise: only about $10 billion of the $24 billion agreed in 1992, for instance, and this was in the form of commercial credits that would have to be repaid with interest charges on top.[169] Foreign debt mounted at the same time, from $97 billion in 1992 to $152 billion in 1998;[170] and the cost of borrowing rose in parallel, from about 30 per cent of GDP in 1994 to 60 per cent in 1997, much of it short-term and at high rates of interest (which meant that more than a third of government revenue had to be spent on servicing the debt).[171] Russian money was meanwhile being exported at a much faster rate. By 1996 it was estimated that about $700 billion had already been sent abroad, of which about half had been invested in property, and that a further $50 billion was leaving every year. Much of it took the form of the illegal export of gold and other valuables on a scale that had not been seen since 1918; this was a loss of resources every year that was about ten times the value of inward investment.[172] Hard currency was another of Russia's 'staple exports', with up to 400 tonnes of dollars leaving every year in search of a more hospitable environment. Indeed, it emerged that the Central Bank itself had been moving its funds to 'an obscure fund management company based in the tax haven of Jersey' in order to protect them from foreign creditors; according to the Prosecutor General, who was investigating the matter, as much as $50 billion of the bank's reserves might have been moved offshore over the previous five years.[173]

Much of the capital that flowed abroad went into property, some of it advertised in the Russian press. *Izvestiya*, in the early months of 1997, was offering 'a marvellous hill-top VILLA with a sea view' in Marbella, retailing at $1.65 million, and in July it advertised a 'tax heaven' in the Bahamas, a castle near Munich, and a 'tsarist life in a villa palace in the Arabian style' in Palma de Mallorca. In August an 'incredibly beautiful villa on the sea front near Cannes' was on offer, with its own parkland and a swimming pool with a waterfall.[174] There were specialised agencies catering for Russians who wished to invest elsewhere: several advertised in the publication *Property Abroad*, whose front-page offers included a hotel near Prague and a house in a 'picturesque corner' of Spain, as well as a flat in Thailand 'with a view of the jungle'. For those who were worried by crime and instability and seeking a future for their children as well as themselves, a villa was available in Greek Orthodox Cyprus;[175] other agencies offered European Union (EU) passports for $15,000 ('100 per cent legality guaranteed'), or citizenship of one of the Caribbean islands (the Dominican Republic found that nearly half its clients were from the former Soviet Union).[176] In Nice alone at least fifty villas valued at $850,000 or more were being sold to Russians every year in the late 1990s;[177] in the spa town of Carlsbad, in the Czech Republic, a 'rouble mafia' had bought up most of the hotels, and locals described it as a 'zone of peace' for Russian godfathers seeking a break from life at home and a convenient place to launder their profits.[178]

Foreigners, however, were slow to take the same interest in the postcommunist Russian economy as Russians were taking in the savings and investment opportunities that were available in other countries. Foreign direct investment worldwide was estimated at $913 billion at the end of the 1990s; Russia's share was just 0.4 per cent – less than Finland's, and about a tenth of the foreign direct investment that was pouring into mainland China.[179] The total value of foreign investment increased rapidly in the early years of the decade but fell back in 1998 and 1999 as the collapse of the currency (discussed below) took its effect; of this no more than 12 per cent represented direct investment in productive resources, and most of the remainder was in the form of credits of various kinds. Foreign investment, in turn, accounted for only 3 per cent of all domestic investment by the end of the decade (another 7 per cent came from joint ventures with foreign partners), and it was concentrated in 'middleman' or natural resource operations that yielded a relatively quick return, such as services and the extractive industries, rather than manufacturing. It was also concentrated geographically, with a third or more in Moscow but none at all, in some years, in a number of the other regions.[180] Joint ventures with foreign participation accounted for no more than 1 per cent of all industrial enterprises by the end of the decade, well down on the levels that had been reached in the early 1990s, although because they were concentrated in relatively high-value sectors, they accounted for almost 5 per cent of employment and 10 per cent of output.[181]

Why were foreign investors so reluctant to entrust their resources to a newly democratic Russia, but very willing to do so in the case of communist-ruled China? Some of them confided their concerns to the weekly paper *Argumenty i fakty*. A French electronics entrepreneur found the new Russian businessmen simply too vulgar: they threw their money around in the casino, while he read Tolstoy and Dostoevsky and developed his firm so that he could provide new forms of employment. A British computer manager who was a regular visitor thought 'serious big business' would never come to a country with such a level of crime, with 'bankers and businessmen being killed on your city streets every day'. And an Israeli banker was worried about political instability, and who would win at the next elections – if there were any.[182] A related concern was the level of corruption with which domestic and particularly foreign businessmen had to contend. Russia was the most corrupt country in Europe in the late 1990s, according to the international rankings published by Transparency International, and the 49th most corrupt of the fifty-two for which they published information; a decade later it was still among the most corrupt of a much larger group of nations (we return to this issue below).[183] Most Western businessmen found that 'key ministries would usually demand that large fees be paid to shadowy "consultants" before necessary approvals and licenses were issued' and that if they failed to oblige, the contract would go elsewhere. 'How to make a million in the former Soviet Union?' asked one exasperated American investor. 'Bring two million and it will soon be down to one.'[184]

The Yeltsin reforms: a balance sheet

What, by the end of the decade, was the outcome of the reform programme? There had certainly been a far-reaching change in ownership, but had there been any sign of the enterpreneurial energies the old system was supposed to have held in check? What, for instance, about growth, for many years the most sensitive of the 'success indicators'? As Figure 4.1 makes clear, there had indeed been growth but nearly all of it had been negative, as the economy experienced a series of contractions rather than (as the Kremlin and its Western advisers had promised) a short-term fall in output accompanied by a restructuring that aligned resources with market demand and then a vigorous and sustained advance. The fall in national income went back to the late Soviet period, but several years of market reform had certainly not reversed it. Indeed, in cumulative terms, the fall in national income that had taken place over the early years of Yeltsin–Gaidar reform was unprecedented – greater than the Great Depression that had taken place in the West at the end of the 1920s and greater than Russia itself had experienced in the course of the First World War, the civil war or even the Second World War.[185] In 1997, according to official figures, the decline was at last arrested and even reversed (by just 0.4 per cent); but other calculations, based on physical indicators such as electricity consumption that

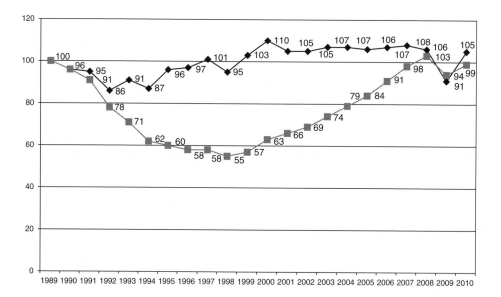

Figure 4.1 Economic performance, 1989–2010
Source: Rossiiskii statisticheskii yezhegodnik, various years. The upper line shows annual percentage changes in GDP, the lower line an index in which 1989=100. The values for 2010 are for January to June.

were less open to manipulation, suggested there had been a fall of 3–4 per cent,[186] and the following year, after the collapse of the currency (p. 142), there was a further contraction. By the end of the decade, GDP was not much more than half what it had been in the last years of communist rule.

Official statistics had never been entirely satisfactory (confidence was not improved when a group of senior officials at the statistical office were arrested in 1998 and charged with bribe-taking),[187] and although Russia conformed more closely to international reporting conventions as the decade advanced, they still tended to understate activity in the private and 'black' or informal sectors (the official series was revised in 1995 to take account of such factors, and earlier estimates of decline were somewhat moderated).[188] The size of the informal economy was nonetheless the subject of widely differing estimates: officially it was about 25 per cent of GDP, but the World Bank put it at 40 per cent and on other evidence it was as high as 60 or even 80 per cent.[189] It could also be argued that a fall in national income was an inevitable and indeed desirable development in that it reflected an economy in structural change, one that was no longer producing military hardware and other goods for which there was no demand. But in the event, the decline in the output of modern consumer goods was even sharper than that of the heavy industries of the Soviet past: between 1990 and the end of the decade coal, oil, steel and gas production all fell by about a third, but light industry was down by a massive 85 per cent and the output of products that embodied advanced technologies fell even more sharply – personal computers by 90 per cent, cameras by 96 per cent and video recorders by more than 99 per cent.[190] Capital investment had meanwhile collapsed to less than a quarter of its level at the start of the decade, and the manufacturing base had become even more obsolescent than it had been at the end of the Soviet period.[191]

These rates of decline had obvious implications for Russia's level of development in relation to other nations. In 1990, at its peak, Russian GDP had been about a third that of the United States; by the end of the decade it was less than a quarter.[192] Russia's share of world trade had meanwhile fallen by more than half, with imports and exports that were about the same in value as those of Hungary or Finland.[193] The Russian economy was still one the world's largest, ranked 16th overall by the World Bank, but by the end of the 1990s it had fallen behind Australia, Mexico and South Korea as well as the major Western democracies. If the comparison was expressed in terms of population, it ranked much lower – as low as 80th, if GDP per head was expressed in purchasing power parities (PPP) (which took account of local cost variations), or 98th, if it was calculated on the basis of current exchange rates. This made Russia a 'lower middle income country' in World Bank terms, well below the global average and behind countries like Malaysia, Gabon and South Africa.[194] Comparisons could be made with the developing countries more generally, and here again the results were unflattering. By the early 1990s, for instance, Russia had been overtaken in its per capita GDP by Peru, Jordan, Iraq and many others. If existing rates of growth continued, it was likely that several more countries, including Morocco and Swaziland, would overtake it by the end of the decade, and Vietnam and Mozambique were on course to do so by the end of the following decade.[195]

The Gorbachev leadership had insisted that the USSR would play a full part in the international division of labour; and for the postcommunist reformers, it was equally important that Russia should be an open economy, trading with the rest of the world on the basis of a fully convertible currency and drawing its growth dynamic from the pressure to compete successfully on price and quality with producers in other countries. The value of imports and exports both increased during the early postcommunist years, and there was a positive trade balance; exports and particularly imports fell sharply in the latter part of the decade following the collapse of the currency in 1998, but the trade balance remained positive and indeed exports to other countries, encouraged by a cheaper rouble, were running at about twice the level of Russian imports.[196] Imports, at the same time, accounted for an increasing proportion of the Russian diet: for about a third in the late 1990s, including half the cheese, tinned meat and pasta.[197] And exports, in spite of the intentions of the reformers, were even more likely to consist of raw materials than of manufactured goods. By the end of the decade, mineral products, including oil, accounted for almost half the value of Russian exports; metals and precious stones accounted for another quarter, which was even more than in 1990; and the biggest imports of all were of machinery and foodstuffs.[198] In effect, employment and living standards were being exported to other countries, because it was there rather than in Russia that value was being added.

The reformers had more success with inflation, which had been as high as 2,600 per cent in 1992 but was down to 22 per cent in 1996 and 11 per cent in 1997. The rouble devaluation of 1998, however, reversed the trend and consumer prices rose in that year by 84 per cent, and the following year by 37 per cent; in some regions this meant that consumer prices had increased by half or more in 1999 as compared with the previous year.[199] The slow-down in the growth of consumer prices had in any case owed much to unpaid wages or suppressed inflation. In 1998, according to the survey evidence, only 18 per cent of Russians were being paid regularly, 25 per cent were being paid less frequently and 57 per cent were not being paid at all; the main reason they continued working was the fear of losing their jobs.[200] Workers in a Krasnoyarsk factory, where no-one had been paid for a year, put up a gravestone in the form of a 500-rouble note to commemorate their last pay-day;[201] local utility workers held a 'wage funeral' to mark the period since they themselves had last received what they were due and threatened that if the deceased did not come back to life, they would 'deluge [their] beloved city with sewage'.[202] One worker, after a year without pay, committed suicide by jumping from the roof of the factory in which he had been working, leaving a message for the director that asked him at least to cover the cost of the burial.[203] Workers in Novosibirsk, in the late 1990s, were being paid 'almost two years late'; the record-holders were Eskimos in northerly Chukotka, who had not been paid their wages for five years.[204]

The state itself was in comparable difficulty because of a chronic failure to collect taxes. Of the 2.8 million enterprises and other bodies that were registered with the tax authorities in the late 1990s, nearly half were behind with their payments and 35 per cent presented no accounts at all; fewer than 17 per cent were up to date.[205] The state budget reflected these developments: it had been in surplus in 1990 but moved into a deepening deficit over the course of the decade.[206] This meant that all the activities that were funded by government itself were placed in some difficulty. Frontier posts, for instance, were understaffed, leading to a substantial loss of customs revenue.[207] The legal system broke down in the Komi republic, as courts in the capital city had no money for paper, pens or envelopes; in Karelia the police were not being paid and were responding only to emergencies.[208] The armed forces, although they continued to enjoy a large share of state spending, were in disarray, with unpaid salaries, serious shortages of housing and numerous reports of suicides, and commentators suggested they had become a 'danger to themselves'.[209] Science, meanwhile, was 'on the brink of death', with the budget of the Academy of Sciences just 5–7 per cent of what it had been at the end of communist rule.[210] The director of a Chelyabinsk research institute, many of whose staff had been subsisting on bread obtained by credit, was so distressed by the situation in his institution that he committed suicide; substantial numbers, anxious to continue their work as well as feed their families, emigrated to the West.[211]

Unemployment rose steadily throughout the postcommunist period, although it was often difficult to distinguish between the unemployed as they would have been defined in other countries, the rather smaller proportion that were registered with labour exchanges, the much larger proportion that were nominally employed but in fact required to take a period of unpaid leave or work a reduced week, and the still larger numbers that were not being paid on time or in full. So far as official figures were concerned, the unemployed had more than doubled over the course of the decade, from nearly 4 to more than 9 million, or from 5 to 13 per cent of the 'economically active population'. A relatively small proportion of the unemployed were actually registered with the authorities and receiving benefit (just under 12 per cent of the total), but nearly half of them had been looking for a job for a year or more.[212] There was, in fact, little incentive to register as unemployed because the benefits were so meagre, and enterprises had some incentive to keep surplus workers on their books to avoid the tax payments they would otherwise have been obliged to make. Taking these and other circumstances into account, the International Labour Organization estimated that the real level of unemployment by the late 1990s was closer to a third of the total workforce, which was twice the official figure.[213] Men were slightly more likely to be unemployed than women, although women were more than twice as likely to be receiving state benefit; equally, there were far higher levels of unemployment in some of the southern, often non-Russian regions than in Moscow – more than half the workforce in Ingushetia was out of work, for instance, and about a third in Dagestan and North Ossetia-Alania.[214]

The reformers' main achievement, as we have seen, had been a reduction in the rate of inflation; but even this became impossible to sustain in the late 1990s as the collapse of currencies in East Asia increased speculative pressure on the rouble and at the same time exposed the fundamental weakness of an economy that had been in almost continuous decline. There had already been several upsets on the money markets: on 'black Tuesday' in October 1994, on 'black Thursday' in October 1997 and then again in May 1998, when interest rates had to be increased substantially to protect the currency from speculative pressures. A much graver crisis developed later in the year when the Russian government announced that the exchange rate against the dollar was going to be less closely regulated (this was in effect a devaluation of up to 50 per cent, with major inflationary implications) and that foreign debts would be converted into longer-term obligations (which was in effect a default). Yeltsin, seeking to reassure an anxious public, had insisted there would be 'no devaluation' and that everything had been 'carefully worked out',[215] but journalists found he had some 'strange things to say' and concluded that he had 'little understanding of the kind of crisis the country was in'.[216] The official announcement, on 17 August, blamed 'world financial markets' and the 'latest drop in world oil prices' for an embarrassing volte-face,[217] and indeed for the collapse of the policies that had been followed since the end of communist rule. Prices rose sharply (food prices increased by 40 per cent in September alone);[218] real incomes fell by about a third;[219] and many individual Russians, particularly its embryonic middle class, found their savings had lost most of their value or disappeared entirely (even former President Gorbachev was left with nothing).[220]

Bringing the state back in

Several circumstances combined to bring about a change of course in the late 1990s. One of them was the shock of the currency collapse itself, which meant that there was widespread support for the restoration of economic stability even if it was achieved by methods that were sometimes reminiscent of the Soviet past. The devaluation of the currency had a more obviously beneficial effect, in that it made foreign goods more expensive on Russian markets but Russian goods more competitive abroad. Indeed the rouble lost more than half its value against the dollar in the single month of August 1998 and two-thirds of its value over the course of the year, with obvious consequences.[221] Imports fell sharply, as they began to cost a lot more; exports also declined, but less steeply.[222] The result was that foreign trade moved into increasing surplus, with exports growing more rapidly than imports; there was a substantial change in the course of 1998 itself, as the trade balance moved from approximate parity at the start of the year to a situation by the end of the year in which exports were running at twice the value of imports.[223] The positive effect of the devaluation was just as apparent in the economy as a whole. There was a further fall in GDP in 1998 as the shock of the adjustment was absorbed, but then a return to positive growth in 1999 (of more than 3 per cent), and in 2000 the rate of growth was a record-breaking 10 per cent. The economy continued to expand, at an average rate of about 7 per cent, throughout the two terms of the Putin presidency.[224]

There were more favourable external circumstances as well. In particular, the world price of oil began to rise. Russian export prices for oil had been relatively stable over the 1990s and actually fell (to $74 a tonne) in 1998. But they were up by almost a half the following year (to $111), and then increased again to $175 in 2000, $226 in 2004, $330 in 2005, $412 in 2006, $470 in 2007 and $663 in 2008.[225] The same was true of the other raw materials that accounted for the bulk of Russian exports. The price of natural gas, for instance, rose from $86 per thousand cubic metres in 2000 to $354 in 2008. The price of coal went up from $26 to nearly $80 a tonne, iron ore from $16 to $89, copper from $1,677 to $6,047 and nickel from $8,641 to a spectacular $33,855.[226] The result was that the trade balance improved even further, the rouble strengthened on foreign exchanges (which brought down the cost of imports), interest rates could be allowed to fall (which reduced the cost of borrowing), foreign debt could be paid off (by 2008 it was down to 3 per cent of GDP, which was one of the lowest levels in the world),[227] and at the same time gold and hard currency reserves could be accumulated that were the world's third largest (after China and Japan).[228] Indeed the improving state of the public finances was on such a scale that it allowed a 'stabilisation fund' to be established in 2004 that could be used when the price of oil fell below a certain level, or to absorb surplus liquidity.[229] It was no wonder that Russian leaders could speak at this time of the rouble as at least potentially an international reserve currency, and of the Russian economy itself as one of the world's most securely based.

In parallel, there was a wider reconsideration of the assumptions that had up to this point informed government policy. An alternative took some time to emerge, but it was clear from the outset that it would place a greater degree of emphasis on state regulation, the 'real economy' and the concerns of ordinary Russians, even if they departed from the prescriptions of the international financial community. This rather different approach was shaped, in part, by the advice of some of the Russian economists who had been prominent in the early Gorbachev years but then marginalised under Yeltsin and his Western advisers; they favoured the indexation of salaries, benefits and savings, the establishment of a national food reserve, closer regulation of foreign currency dealings, a 'controlled currency emission' that would allow salaries and pensions to continue to be paid, and a greater emphasis on reviving the domestic market as a means of stimulating growth and real incomes.[230] It had been the 'so-called reformers', insisted Prime Minister Primakov, who took office immediately after the devaluation of August 1998, that had been responsible for the financial collapse; they had pursued 'stabilisation for the sake of stabilisation', selling natural resources to buy manufactures and ignoring the 'social aspects of the economy'. Western economies had used the power of the state to pull themselves out of difficulties during the Great Depression, and in post-war Germany; it was only state regulation that could protect 'civilised' from 'primitive capitalism', and only the state that could launch an effective attack on a corruption problem that was already 'widespread'.[231]

The programme that was approved by the Russian government in October 1998 reflected these rather different priorities. The state itself would play an 'enhanced role', including direct government intervention to restructure larger enterprises, encourage small and medium businesses, and raise levels of technology. Privatisation would continue, but on a 'civilised basis', and only when it was justified by economic and social considerations. There would be immediate measures to distribute food and medicines in short supply, and to reduce duties on their import and transportation. Wages, pensions and other social benefits would be paid in full, and indexed; and the money supply would be sustained at a level that made it possible to do so. Measures would be taken to hold down the prices charged by local and national monopolies. The banking sector would be reorganised, and a new development bank established. Tax rates would gradually be brought down, but collection improved. In the longer term, there would be a shift from stabilisation towards 'socially oriented economic growth'.[232] One more specific measure had already been introduced, the restoration of a state vodka monopoly, which was intended to improve the flow of excise duties and at the same time protect the domestic market from low-quality and sometimes dangerous imports.[233] It remained unclear how far it would be possible to print more money and at the same time avoid hyperinflation; or to attract new loans and foreign investment while suspending repayment; or to protect the domestic producer without resorting to protectionism; or to reduce taxation but at the same time sustain higher levels of public spending.

The reorientation of Russian economic policy that took place at the end of the 1990s was in part a reaction to the disastrous legacy of Yeltsinite 'reform'. But it was also a reaction to the wider economic crisis that had begun with the collapse of several of the East Asian currencies at the end of the same decade. Capitalism, it began to be argued, was perfectly compatible with a strong or even interventionist state: indeed, this might be a condition of its success.[234] The need for a more interventionist state had already been suggested by economists who were considerably more eminent than those who had been advising the Russian and East European governments, including three Nobel prize-winners who were among the signatories of an open letter that appeared in the Russian press in the summer of 1996. Shock therapy, in their view, had been a failure, and they called for the state to be restored to the 'central, coordinating role' that it performed in the mixed economies of the West. In its absence, less desirable elements had filled the vacuum, and they had helped to bring about a transition 'not to a market, but to a criminalised economy'. There should be more emphasis on competition, rather than privatisation (this, if anything, was the 'secret' of the market economy). There should be a more sustained attempt to resume economic growth, and to mitigate the social consequences of existing policies. And more generally, there should be a gradual approach towards the process of reform, not a continuation of the radical measures that had led to a 'deep crisis'.[235]

Perhaps the most sustained critique of neoliberal orthodoxy came from another Nobel prize-winning economist, Joseph Stiglitz, who stood down as chief economist at the World Bank at the end of the 1990s. Stiglitz noted the sharp contrast between China, which had almost doubled its GDP after 1989 by following its own best judgement, and Russia, which had followed Western advice and experienced a slump of matching proportions. The reason, he thought, was an 'excessive reliance on textbook models of economics', combined with a refusal to consider the political acceptability and accordingly the realism of the prescriptions that Western governments and their neoliberal advisers had been putting forward. Privatisation as such was no particular achievement. It was 'easy to simply give away state assets – especially to one's friends and cronies'; the incentive to do so was 'especially strong if the politicians conducting the privatization can obtain kickbacks, either directly or indirectly, as campaign contributions'. The private property interests that were created in this way would in turn contribute to the 'weakening of the state and the undermining of the social order, through corruption and regulatory capture'. Not only this, but the newly rich oligarchs would make every effort to prevent an electoral outcome that could prejudice their acquisitions, buying political influence and taking their money out of the country just in case. The result was a kind of 'pseudo-capitalism' – institutions that had the 'superficial appearance of those of capitalism, but without the substance'.[236]

If reforms were to make sense, they would also have to take more account of the history and culture of the countries in which they were being conducted. Narrow economic criteria, as Stiglitz emphasised, were not enough – 'norms, social institutions, social capital, and trust' all played an important part, and it was this 'implicit social contract' that underpinned a successful market economy. Nor could it simply be 'legislated, decreed, or installed by a reform government'.[237] Russian commentators were particularly scathing in their condemnation of international consultants such as Jeffrey Sachs, then of Harvard University, who confessed to his own astonishment when the textbook knowledge he had brought to his task turned out to be a poor guide to the economy that actually existed.[238] The state could be a problem – when it resisted change, rented out monopolies and imposed excessive charges of its own. But it was also the state that built roads and railways, funded basic science, looked after the needs of young and old, and provided the kind of regulatory framework without which a functioning market could scarcely be contemplated. The World Bank itself began to argue, as the century drew to a close, that state and market were 'inextricably linked' and that the capacity for state action was 'central to providing a viable institutional framework for development'.[239] The insistence on private ownership had in any case been far from disinterested. Western governments wanted to transfer state property into private hands, not just because they thought it would make better use of resources, but so that the largest number possible would have a vested interest in the postcommunist order. Those who advised the East European governments had an interest of a more obvious kind in that they might gain directly from their knowledge of the way in which huge public assets were being transferred into private hands – what was known in Western countries as insider trading.[240]

There was a still larger question, which was the extent to which Russia would be free to determine its own destinies if its natural resources and leading industries were allowed to pass into foreign, not simply private ownership. Nationalists as well as Communists were concerned that the policies that were being urged by Western advisers were turning Russia into a 'dependent territory' that could be used as a 'source of industrial raw materials, a sparsely settled nature park and a place for disposing of dangerous waste'. Everything followed, for Sergei Glaz'ev, from the choice that had been made in 1991, at the behest of 'certain Western circles', in favour of the 'radical version of the extreme liberal approach to economic policy that is known in the specialist literature as the "Washington consensus"', and which had been developed for the 'underdeveloped countries of the third world'. It was a choice for which there was no objective basis, and it had been made against the advice of academic experts, in the face of the opposition of the elected Russian parliament and government. Its real aim, Glaz'ev argued, was not development at all, but the 'deconstruction of borrower countries in the interests of international capital', accompanied by the establishment of a 'client government' that would take decisions in the interests of their foreign pay-masters. Russia, in this analysis, had really been run, after the 'state coup' of October 1993, by the International Monetary Fund, working through a 'puppet government' staffed by the incompetent and corrupt, making decisions that had been dictated by the intelligence services of foreign states and then simply rubber-stamped by the Russian president.[241]

Not surprisingly, more or less conspiratorial views about the advice that had been offered from abroad were also popular in the Russian defence and security community, confronted by what they saw as a 'capitulation regime' that had lost control of its own destinies, with policies as well as key appointments that were being dictated by the US Treasury.[242] But they were more concerned, if Putin was any guide, by the danger that was represented by the collapse of the Russian state and a deepening demographic crisis that placed the future of the nation itself in question. Putin himself issued a stark warning in his address at the end of December 1999 when he took up the duties of acting president on Yeltsin's premature retirement. Russia's GDP had fallen by about half during the 1990s, he reminded his audience. By this stage it was no more than a tenth of its American counterpart, or a fifth of the G7 average. Labour productivity and real wages were very low. Capital investment had been falling, and science and technology had been neglected. Health and life expectancies had also been declining. The communist years had brought 'unquestionable achievements', although a heavy price had been paid and they offered no way forward. But neither did 'abstract models and schemes from foreign textbooks'. They could catch up with Spain and Portugal, in Putin's view, which were not the most advanced of the Western countries, if they achieved an annual rate of growth of 8 per cent over the following fifteen years; if they managed 10 per cent annually, they would be able to catch up with Britain and France. If not, there was a 'real danger of sliding into the second, or even the third echelon of world states'.[243]

The 'Putin Plan'

Once he had been elected president, Putin used his annual parliamentary addresses to set out a rather different agenda than the one his predecessor had favoured. The first addresses, perhaps understandably, gave most of their attention to the state itself – in 2000, a 'dictatorship of law'; in 2001, the restoration of a 'power vertical' from the Kremlin downwards; and in 2002, the 'modernisation of the system of executive power as a whole'.[244] There was a more direct emphasis on the economy in the fourth address, in May 2003. At last, Putin explained, they had restored the country's unity, strengthened the state and brought the regions into line. Russia's international credit rating had never been higher, and some firms had for the first time begun a 'serious expansion on world markets'. But the results they had achieved were still 'very modest'. For a start, as much as a quarter of the population was still living below the subsistence minimum. Not only this, but the rate of economic growth was unstable and had recently been falling. And the economic growth that had been achieved owed more than anything else to an exceptionally favourable conjuncture on foreign markets, which 'would and could not be eternal'. The main aim should be the 'return of Russia to the ranks of the rich, developed, powerful and respected countries of the world'. But this would be possible only when Russia was 'economically strong'; only then would Russia be independent of international financial organisations and of the unpredictability of world markets. All of this dictated the goal of 'at least doubling' GDP over the following ten years, and beyond that the construction of a state that was 'competitive in all respects'.[245]

The 2003 address identified a number of more specific 'priority socioeconomic tasks', although it was made clear that they were not to be understood in the same sense as the over-ambitious national programmes that had been favoured in the Brezhnev era.[246] Putin returned to the issue the following year, pointing out the opportunity that now existed to make forecasts not just for a few months, but for decades ahead.[247] The 2005 presidential address had relatively little to say about such 'long-term goals', choosing instead to develop some of the elements of Russia's distinctive understanding of 'democracy', but it suggested that the two addresses should be seen as a 'single programme of action' for the 'coming decade' and promised that it would be developed further in the near future.[248] It was indeed the centrepiece of a speech that Putin made the following September in which he set out a series of 'national priority projects' in public health, education, housing and agriculture.[249] Responsibility for implementing the projects was entrusted to a new 'council for the implementation of the priority national projects', established the following month.[250] Putin himself was chair of the council, with Dmitri Medvedev as first deputy chairman; Medvedev moved up to the chairmanship in mid-November,[251] giving him the kind of national prominence that was likely to place him in a strong position for the succession when Putin eventually stood down. Putin's presidential address in May 2006 renewed his earlier emphasis on the demographic problem, describing it as 'critical';[252] it became, in effect, a fifth 'national project', and the council was renamed accordingly.[253]

The 'national projects', in the event, were indeed all too reminiscent of the five-year plans of the Soviet period,[254] nor were they easy to reconcile with the responsibility for such matters that properly belonged to the Russian government (the prime minister himself was not even a member of the new council that directed them). How, it was asked, did the national projects differ from government programmes of a more conventional kind, or add to them? What did they contribute, other than to add a new bureaucratic structure? Was there not a danger that the new council would parallel and, in effect, undermine the work of government itself? Why, for that matter, have four and not five or six national projects, or even a couple of hundred?[255] And how had the national projects been elaborated – in particular, who had taken part? Unfortunately, commented economist Leonid Abalkin, they had been developed 'in private, without engaging scholars and specialists', and without taking into account the views of those who would be the ultimate judge of their success – 'that is, of Russian citizens'.[256] The principles of social and economic planning were certainly a well-established part of the practice of government in other modern societies, including the member countries of the EU. There remained a danger that Russian local circumstances were so varied that any central programme would be unworkable, and that the effect of national projects across an enormous territory would be so difficult to observe that 'hopes might be disappointed, with very unfortunate social consequences'.[257]

Putin looked even further forward in early 2008, setting out an ambitious strategy for the period up to 2020 in a speech to the State Council that took the 'plan' well into the new century. When he came to power, Putin recalled, 'a rich Russia had become a country of poor people'. It was at this point that the Putin plan had been put into effect – a 'plan for pulling Russia out of a systemic crisis', starting with the restoration of the constitutional order. With some difficulty they had arrested the process of disintegration and stopped the war in the North Caucasus. Chechnya had again become a full member of the federation, and relations between the central authorities and all the regions had been redefined. Foreign direct investment had meanwhile increased to seven times its previous level. Trade with foreign countries had increased more than five times in value. And more than 6 million Russians travelled abroad every year. All of this showed the 'qualitatively new condition of Russia as a modern state', one that was 'open to the outside world, among other things for business and honest competition'. If GDP was calculated in purchasing power parities, Russia had already reached the level of G8 countries such as Italy and France and become one of the world's seven largest economies. Real incomes had risen two and a half times since the start of his presidency, pensions by even more; unemployment and poverty had meanwhile been falling, and birth-rates had been higher than at any time in the previous fifteen years.

But less reassuringly, they had still not escaped from an energy-based scenario of development. Far too little effort was being made to modernise the economy, which would lead to a growing dependence on the import of goods and technology, and the status of a raw materials appendage. It could even lead, in the longer term, to a Russia whose very existence was in question. The only real alternative was a 'strategy of innovative development' that made use of one of Russia's main competitive advantages – its 'human potential'. This meant, for instance, that the educational system must be 'one of the best in the world', and that better results must be obtained from their expenditure on science, which was one of the highest. Levels of public health must also be improved, raising average life expectancies to 75 years, and further measures should be taken to strengthen the family, which would require a substantial improvement in housing conditions. Companies and ordinary people should meanwhile be encouraged to invest more heavily in their own education, health and pensions. By 2020, perhaps as many as 70 per cent of the population should be able to make provision for themselves in this kind of way, or in effect, belong to the middle class. Existing inequalities were entirely unacceptable and should be reduced; but at the same time it should be possible for as many people as possible to earn well and save up for their later years. All of this would lead to a 'society of real and equal opportunities, a society without poverty that guarantees the security of all its citizens'.

In economic terms the immediate priority was a radical improvement in levels of productivity, which were unacceptably low. In the main sectors they should be at least four times higher by 2020. That meant, in turn, that almost the entire stock of machinery and equipment would have to be renewed. New sectors would have to be developed that were internationally competitive, such as aviation, ship construction, energy generation, and informational, medical and other innovative technologies. And there would need to be further investment in the infrastructure: in new or reconstructed roads, railway stations, ports, airports and communication systems. With its enormous gold reserves, Russia should become one of the world's financial centres. Hundreds of thousands of new jobs would have to be created, which meant that it would have to become less difficult to open a new business, and less dependent on the payment of bribes. In all of this there were three key tasks: the establishment of a society of equal opportunities, the encouragement of innovation and a 'radical improvement in the effectiveness of the economy, based above all on a higher level of labour productivity'. There would have to be comparable changes in the state itself, which was still too bureaucratic and corrupt. Something like 25 million Russians – a third of the entire labour force – worked for the government in some capacity, and 'any, even the most elementary decisions, [took] months or even years to be determined'. They would also have to establish courts that were more independent and professional and that would protect businessmen from the arbitrariness of state officials; a more effective regional policy was also required that would allow them to achieve the 'harmonious development of the entire country'.[258]

A formal strategy was approved in November 2008 when the Russian government finally adopted a 'conception of the long-term socioeconomic development of the Russian Federation for the period up to 2020'. By this date Russia was expected to have become one of the world's five leading economic powers, based on a steady growth rate of 6–7 per cent a year, and the incomes of its individual citizens would have more than doubled (up to $30,000, and by 2030 up to $50,000 a year). Life expectancies, according to the new strategy, would rise to 75, and the population decline would be arrested and then reversed, helped by substantial new investment in housing. Additional provision would also be made for the support of health, education and the pension system.[259] As in the days of Soviet planning, additional and more specific arrangements were made for the various stages by which the strategy would be realised. A separate document dealt with the medium term, setting out the 'main directions of government activity for the period up to 2012' and the tasks of individual ministries for each of the intervening years, with specific quantitative targets, within an overall objective of increasing GDP to 'at least' 128 per cent of its 2008 level by the end of the planning period.[260] As newspapers commented, the world economic crisis that had already begun appeared to have had no influence on the form or content of either document; as Putin had told the United Russia congress, it was certainly no reason to withdraw from any of the developmental goals they had previously put forward.[261]

Crisis and challenge

On the face of it, the Putin years had brought about a remarkable improvement in Russian economic performance. Above all, this meant the resumption of economic growth, at levels that were high by international standards (although not always by comparison with those of other former Soviet republics). Almost all of the Yeltsin years had seen a further contraction in GDP; every one of the Putin years saw an improvement, generally at a level that would be sufficient to 'at least double GDP' within the ten years Putin had specified (see Figure 4.1). Over the eight years of the Putin presidency, *Izvestiya* concluded, there had been 'successes and failures' (Putin himself, at his final press conference, refused to admit even a single mistake[262]), but 'on the whole' the country had changed for the better. Gross domestic product was up 72 per cent; industrial output had increased by 56 per cent. Prices had increased by 178 per cent, but real incomes – in other words, allowing for inflation – were up 141 per cent; pensions had risen at a comparable rate (up 138 per cent), and there was less poverty (down 14 per cent).[263] Speaking in 2008 as he returned to the premiership, Putin could claim that Russia had already become the world's seventh largest economy and that it would overtake the United Kingdom later the same year[264] – although comparisons of this kind, expressed in purchasing power parities, tended to exaggerate the performance of less developed economies in which food and the basics of life were relatively cheap; comparisons based on exchange rate conversions were arguably a better guide to a country's place in the world economy, and they were considerably less flattering.[265]

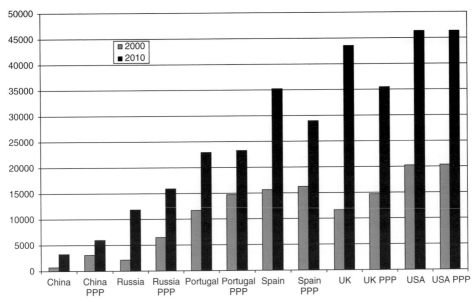

Figure 4.2 Comparative economic performance, 2000–2010
Source: *Human Development Report*, 2000 and 2010; values show GDP per head in US dollars expressed in current prices and adjusted to reflect purchasing power parities (PPP), and relate to 1998 and 2008 respectively.

It was a level of performance, moreover, that had to be set within an appropriate perspective. In the first place, the years of Putinist growth had hardly done more than return Russia to the level of development it had reached at the end of the communist period – it was only in 2008 that the collapse in output of the 1990s was finally overcome, and the contraction that took place in 2009 (of nearly 8 per cent) took it below again. Other countries – such as Portugal and Spain, which were the countries Putin had identified as targets in his 'millennium address' at the end of 1999 as he became acting president – had obviously not stood still in the meantime. At that time Russian GDP per head was just 16 per cent of Spain's and 21 per cent of Portugal's, or 38 and 42 per cent respectively in purchasing power parities; by the time he left office, Russian gross national income per head of population was 39 per cent of Portugal's or 70 per cent in purchasing power parities, but it was still less than half (48 per cent) of Spanish national income per head of population, expressed in the same terms, or as little as 26 per cent, if the comparison was expressed in dollars at current exchange rates (see Figure 4.2). This meant that Russia had moved, in World Bank terms, from being a 'lower middle income country' in 1999 to an 'upper middle income country' a decade later; but it was still a category below Spain and Portugal, which were among the world's 'high income' countries.[266] In other words, there had been a considerable advance – but in terms of the objectives Putin had originally put forward, there was still a great distance to be

Table 4.3 **Natural resource endowments, selected countries (per head of population)**

	Oil	Natural gas	Coal	Iron ore	Arable land	Fresh water	Forest
Russia	142	32	1,365	389	86	28	61
Europe	4	2	96	52	29	5	2
Asia	27	17	131	9	13	4	1
Africa	13	12	167	28	22	5	6
North America	34	28	1,725	94	65	15	13
Central and Southern America	27	13	50	42	118	41	30
Australia and Oceania	19	21	393	625	226	31	22
World	26	24	245	36	24	7	1
Russia as % of world	*542*	*137*	*558*	*1077*	*358*	*377*	*636*

Source: adapted from V.I. Zhukov, 'Rossiya v global'noi sisteme sotsial'nykh koordinat: sotsiologicheskii analiz i prognoz', *Sotsiologicheskie issledovaniya*, no. 12, 2008, p. 5.

Note: all figures are in tonnes per head of population except for arable land (hundredths of a hectare per person), fresh water (thousand cubic metres per person) and forest (tenths of a hectare per person), in rounded percentages.

made up; even more so if the comparison was not with the EU's poorest members but with the richest economies worldwide.

It was an economy, moreover, that relied as heavily as Brezhnev's Soviet Union had done on the export of oil and gas, sustained by steadily if erratically increasing prices for these commodities on world markets.[267] 'Mineral products' accounted for nearly two-thirds (65 per cent) of the value of all Russian exports in the last year of Putin's presidency, substantially more than in the years of Brezhnev and his successors, and 'metals and precious stones' accounted for another 16 per cent (at their peak, in 1984, 'fuel and energy' had accounted for just over half – 54 per cent – of Soviet exports).[268] Russia, indeed, was the world's largest exporter of natural gas, and its second largest exporter of oil and oil products;[269] in 2009 it overtook Saudi Arabia, at least temporarily, as the world's *largest* oil as well as gas exporter.[270] And although there were concerns, in the early years of the new century, that oil (particularly) and gas were approaching or had even passed their peak levels of output, the economy was unlikely to become less dependent on its natural resources as long as they remained so relatively abundant. With just 3 per cent of the world's population, Russia was estimated to have 5–6 per cent of the world's coal reserves, 10 per cent of its oil reserves, about 25 per cent of its iron ore and about a third of its natural gas reserves, as well as significant quantities of a whole range of other valuable minerals; and of all of these deposits, only about a third were in active exploitation in the early years of the new century.[271] Taking all minerals together, Russia had as much as half the extractable resources of the entire planet;[272] its relative advantage was even more striking when expressed in population terms (see Table 4.3).

A heavy dependence on natural resources was not just a Russian pattern – it was a familiar feature of the political economy of many other countries as they struggled to deal with a 'resource curse' that undermined the incentive to manufacture as long as whatever nature had provided could be exported more cheaply to whoever was willing to pay for it. This was sometimes called 'Dutch disease', after the discovery of natural gas in the North Sea in the 1960s had the apparent effect of weakening rather than strengthening the Dutch economy by encouraging a dependence on the export of natural resources that left manufacturers poorly placed to withstand international competition when the era of plenty came to an end. As export earnings rose, the national currency strengthened on the foreign exchanges; exports of manufactured goods were disadvantaged as they became increasingly uncompetitive abroad, while imports became increasingly affordable and domestic producers found themselves forced out of their own markets. The 'resource curse' had other consequences as well: typically, it led to a bloated public sector (as the usual constraints on spending could be relaxed), and to a generous programme of social benefits that became increasingly difficult to sustain when the supply of natural resources began to run out. Apart from this, it led to higher levels of unemployment (as natural resources required fewer people to engage directly in their production than the economic activity that had been displaced), and to a burgeoning problem of corruption (as powerful interests within and outside government made use of their ability to grant or withhold permission to develop new sources of supply).[273]

The 'resource curse' was certainly associated with corruption in the Russian case, still more so in that its judicial system was weak and heavily dependent on government itself. The most widely used measure of corruption in its various forms was the 'perceptions index', first produced by Transparency International of Berlin in 1993 and reported annually from 1995 onwards. Its inquiries originally focused on the liberal democracies, but they became increasingly comprehensive and from 1996 included Russia (from 1997 Ukraine as well). As Transparency International itself pointed out, these were reports on the extent to which corruption was perceived to exist among public officials and politicians, not necessarily on its 'objective' level; but every effort was made, by drawing on specialist opinion of various kinds, to ensure that perceptions were informed by an awareness of local circumstances. The index drew its primary data from the experience of businessmen in each of the countries concerned, averaged over two (formerly three) years so as to mitigate the effect of exceptional circumstances, and excluding countries in which there were insufficient observations in a given year to permit a calculation. In 1995 41 countries were included in the exercise; by 2010 there were 178.[274] Perceptions, it was acknowledged, were an imperfect measure of an ambiguous phenomenon; but they were found in practice to have a very high level of validity, and in any case they were typically combined with other indicators in a manner that helped to improve the reliability of any of these measures taken by itself (what was sometimes called 'triangulation').[275]

Traditionally, the Scandinavian countries were seen as the least affected by such problems, but New Zealand, Singapore and Hong Kong were also among the leaders in

Table 4.4 **Corruption: Russia in comparative perspective, 1996–2010**

	1996	1998	2000	2002	2004	2006	2008	2010
UK	12 (8.4)	11 (8.7)	10 (8.7)	10 (8.7)	11 (8.6)	11 (8.6)	16 (7.7)	20 (7.6)
USA	15 (7.7)	17 (7.5)	14 (7.6)	16 (7.7)	17 (7.5)	20 (7.3)	18 (7.3)	22 (7.1)
Japan	17 (7.1)	25 (5.8)	23 (6.4)	20 (7.1)	24 (6.9)	18 (7.3)	18 (7.3)	17 (7.8)
China	50 (2.4)	52 (3.5)	63 (3.1)	59 (3.5)	71 (3.4)	70 (3.3)	72 (3.6)	78 (3.5)
India	46 (2.6)	66 (2.9)	69 (2.8)	71 (2.7)	90 (2.8)	70 (3.3)	85 (3.4)	87 (3.3)
Ukraine	n.d.	69 (2.8)	87 (1.5)	85 (2.4)	122 (2.2)	99 (2.8)	134 (2.5)	134 (2.4)
Russia	*47 (2.6)*	*76 (2.4)*	*82 (2.1)*	*71 (2.7)*	*90 (2.8)*	*121 (2.5)*	*147 (2.1)*	*154 (2.1)*
N=	54	85	90	102	146	163	180	178

Source: compiled from www.transparency.org; shows rank as compared to other countries in each exercise, and score on a 1–10 scale (the lower the score, the greater the perceived corruption).

successive surveys (so honesty was not confined to Christian or European countries, nor was it simply a function of their level of development). Russia, by contrast, was almost always among the worst performers, below India and China (in most years) and – from 2005 onwards – below Ukraine as well (see Table 4.4). The Russian score was relatively constant, between 2 and 3 out of 10, but this was held to indicate 'rampant perceived corruption'. The 2008 score of 2.1 was as low as the lowest Russia had ever recorded; the 2010 score was the same but the ranking was even lower, placing Russian levels of corruption at the same point on the scale as those of Congo-Brazzaville and Kenya, and below those of Pakistan and Nigeria (according to Transparency International, the only country with a higher per capita income and more corruption was Equatorial Guinea).[276] Russia was poorly rated on other measures of the integrity of public and commercial life, such as the Bribe Payers Index, also sponsored by Transparency International, which was a measure of the propensity of firms headquartered in a particular country to offer improper inducements when operating abroad (in 2008 it was the worst of all the twenty-two countries included[277]). The Global Integrity Report, a measure of 'how well nations are fighting corruption', found similarly that Russia had made 'minimal progress in establishing and reinforcing effective anti-corruption mechanisms compared to other Soviet Union successor states' and that the 'consolidation of power and the crackdown on the media in Russia [had] negatively affected overall governance'.[278]

Dmitri Medvedev had called for a national anti-corruption programme in his speech at Krasnoyarsk in February 2008 as a part of his wider campaign against 'legal nihilism', and over the year that followed, a legislative and administrative framework was gradually assembled so that his objectives could be given practical effect. In May, a presidential decree, 'On Anti-Corruption Measures', established a national anti-corruption council, headed by the newly elected president.[279] A more elaborate legislative provision, the 'National Anti-Corruption Plan', was unveiled at the end of July. Corruption, it maintained, was holding back social change and economic reform; it was undermining trust in state institutions and creating a negative image of Russia in other countries; and it was a threat to national security. The plan set out a series of measures for dealing with the problem, including legislation and changes in the operation of government itself as well as improvements in legal training.[280] The anti-corruption council held its first meeting at the end of September. Medvedev, in his opening address, complained that corruption had 'not just acquired a mass scale' but become a 'familiar, everyday phenomenon that characterise[d] the very life of [their] society'. It was not just a matter of 'banal bribes', but of a 'serious illness' that ate up the economy and undermined the entire society, and cost anywhere between $20 billion and $40 billion a year.[281] By the end of the year, a more comprehensive piece of legislation, a federal law 'On Combating Corruption', had been adopted; the 'basic directions' of government policy on all matters of this kind would be defined by the President himself.[282]

An anti-corruption council, however, was not in itself particularly new (Putin had established one in 2003 that 'had little effect'[283]), and it made the heroic assumption that the state officials who were responsible for the problem were the most appropriate people to deal with it. Corruption, in any case, was part of a much wider environment that had little of the transparency and predictability that would be necessary if a market economy was to become securely established. Why should ordinary Russians, still more so foreign investors, put their money into investment opportunities if they risked being deprived of ownership at a later stage? Why, in particular, should they take any interest in investment opportunities of a kind that would take a long period to pay for themselves, rather than look for short-term speculative gains? Why should they regard the market as a reliable way of signalling the balance of advantage when so much depended, not just on a court system that could not be relied upon to be impartial, but on the Kremlin and its attitude towards particular individuals and the companies they represented? There were all kinds of cautionary examples. Perhaps the most compelling was Mikhail Khodorkovsky, the wealthiest of the oligarchs in the early years of the new century, who was arrested and sentenced to nine years of imprisonment in 2005 for reasons that appeared to have more to do with his political ambitions than the ostensible charges of fraud and tax avoidance (see p. 174). Another was Mikhail Gutseriev, who was obliged to sell his Russneft' oil refinery in 2007 after 'months of pressure by the tax authorities' and settle in the United Kingdom.[284] Yet another was Yevgenii Chichvarkin, a mobile phone billionaire, who also sold up and moved to the United Kingdom at the end of 2008 after he had been accused of involvement in the blackmail of a former employee; the real reason, it appeared, was his refusal to increase tax payments at a time of national economic difficulty.[285]

Foreign companies were still more likely to have difficulties, if the experience of British Petroleum was any guide. The company had signed up to a massive production-sharing agreement in 2003, which had been 'supposed to herald a new era in business relations with the former Soviet empire'.[286] But Putin became increasingly dissatisfied with arrangements of this kind, calling the agreement a 'colonial treaty' and publicly complaining that the Russian officials responsible for negotiating it had not been 'put in prison'. He was also critical of the number of foreign nationals that held senior positions in Russian companies, especially those that were involved in the energy sector; this, he thought, was why Russia imported so many foreign goods and gave so many jobs to foreign specialists.[287] The Federal Security Service raided BP's own offices as well as those of the joint company in March 2008, which was an obvious portent.[288] Its embattled chief executive, an American, left four months later after an 'organised campaign of harassment',[289] and its finance chief resigned suddenly in August 2008 after it had been made clear that he too would be unable to renew his visa; effective control within the company had meanwhile begun to shift towards the four Russian billionaires who owned half of the share capital (the company provided BP with a quarter of its global oil and gas production, but only a tenth of its profits).[290] These were reminiscent of the difficulties of another global giant, Shell, which had been obliged to hand over a large part of its Sakhalin gas field business to state-owned Gazprom after criticism from government regulators, and for much less than it would otherwise have been worth.[291] And reminiscent of the difficulties of many other firms that had lost money because of the collusion of officials and local financiers within a legal system that appeared to operate as an agency of government.[292]

Ostensibly, the takeover of foreign companies represented a return to state ownership, at least in 'strategic' industries such as energy and aviation. But it became increasingly apparent that what it actually meant was that resources of this kind had come into the hands of a small number of government officials, many of whom had become chairmen of the boards of the most important companies at the same time as they carried out their Kremlin responsibilities. Dmitri Medvedev had established a precedent of this kind when he joined the board of Gazprom in 2000; not just Russia's largest company, it became the third largest in the world later in the decade as measured by the value of its stock market capitalisation.[293] When Medvedev stepped down on becoming president in 2008 his position on the board was taken by Viktor Zubkov, former prime minister and later first deputy prime minister. Sergei Ivanov, a deputy or first deputy prime minister after 2005, chaired the board of United Aviation. Viktor Ivanov, deputy head of the Presidential Administration and then (from 2008) director of the federal drug control agency, was the chair of Aeroflot and of the diamond company Almaz-Antei. Sergei Naryshkin, head of the governmental and later of the Presidential Administration, was deputy chair of the oil company Rosneft'; Igor Sechin, deputy head of the Presidential Administration and then deputy prime minister, was chairman (see Table 4.5). And there were other examples.[294] It was notable that many of these key officials with a day job in the Presidential Administration or the government had a *silovik* (defence or security ministry) background; many of them, in addition, were from Putin's and Medvedev's home town of St Petersburg.

Although the process was hardly transparent, it also became clear that ways had been found to move substantial parts of these state-owned assets into private hands. It

---

Table 4.5 **The big two: Gazprom and Rosneft'**

The forced bankruptcy of Mikhail Khodorkovsky's Yukos oil company following the arrest of its chief executive in 2003 left two enormous state-owned corporations in a dominant position on the Russian market and underlined the extent to which the entire economy depended on natural resources.

Gazprom is one of the world's ten largest energy companies, accounting for about 17 per cent of the world's entire gas production. It owns the world's largest natural gas reserves and the world's largest gas transmission systems, and is itself just over 50 per cent owned by the state itself. Its origins lie in the USSR Ministry of the Gas Industry, which was transformed in 1989 into a state corporation. The chairman of the board of management in 2011 was Viktor Zubkov, a first deputy prime minister and former prime minister; his predecessor, until his election to the presidency, was Dmitri Medvedev. The board also included the Russian energy minister and the minister of economic development. Aleksei Miller, who had previously worked with Putin in St Petersburg and as a deputy energy minister, was chairman of the management board. Further details are available on the company's website, www.gazprom.com.

The Russian oil industry is similarly dominated by *Rosneft'*, which also emerged from the ministerial structures of the late Soviet period. It was established as a state enterprise in 1993 and became an open joint stock company in 1995, but the state currently holds more than 75 per cent of its assets. The company has expanded considerably since the 1990s, in large part by an aggressive programme of takeovers, and it absorbed most of the assets that had been held by Yukos until its forced dissolution. The Rosneft' board of directors is headed by Igor Sechin, a deputy prime minister who had been deputy head of the Presidential Administration; its chief executive is Eduard Khudainatov, who succeeded Sergei Bogdanchikov in September 2010. Further details are available on the company's website, www.rosneft.com.

---

was an intricate story, according to the version that appeared in a Western news magazine in late 2008. It started with the break-up of Yukos after the arrest of its chief executive Mikhail Khodorkovsky in 2003, and the transfer of most of its assets after an opaque auction to Rosneft', the state oil company chaired by Igor Sechin, at this time a leading official in the Presidential Administration. Rosneft' sold most of its oil to the outside world through a Dutch-registered trading firm called Guvnor, which had become the world's third largest oil trader with estimated revenues of $70 billion a year. One of Guvnor's founders was Gennadii Timchenko, who entered *Forbes'* list of Russian billion-aires in 2008. He was also the sponsor of a judo club of which Putin was honorary president and had worked in an oil company that had been given a large export quota as part of a controversial oil-for-food scheme set up by Putin while he was working in St Petersburg. Timchenko – like Putin, a former member of the KGB foreign directorate – insisted that he had not been involved in the deal, and that his success was not built on favours. But for others it was part of a larger pattern by which leading state officials had begun to take over entire businesses, instead of simply demanding a share of their profits; a firm might nominally be taken into state ownership, but then be 'quietly transferred into private bank accounts', and even if it was formally controlled by the state, 'the profits or proceeds from share sales [might] never reach its coffers'.[295]

It was ordinary Russians, in the end, who were the biggest losers of all – in the arbitrary and sometimes illegal appropriation of their savings, their houses, their jobs and indeed of their investment, if they tried to make one. A typical mechanism in the early years of the new century was 'raiding', or the illegal seizure of assets by gangs operating with the apparent complicity of the authorities. Aleksei Kurkov was one of their victims – he woke up one morning in 2004 to find himself locked out of the small Moscow fire-safety equipment factory at which he had worked for ten years. The new owner was a mysterious firm in the British Virgin Islands, which promptly sacked all the staff and sold off the company's valuable property. Kurkov applied to the courts but was told there was no evidence he had ever worked there. He was left with his meagre $200 a month pension, while the raiders made off with about $30m. Rather than taking over underperforming companies and then using their assets to better advantage, as in the West, Russian raiders targeted successful businesses, bankrupted them and then transferred the ownership to shell companies registered in other countries. The problem was most severe in Moscow, where land values were highest, but it existed all over the country – in river ports, nuclear science institutes, a factory making orthopaedic legs in Kazan, even a tank factory in Omsk; overall, there were something like 70,000 cases a year. The usual method was for the firm to be presented with a large but fabricated tax bill. Then the owner would be arrested; while he was in prison, the raiders would use false documents to sell on the business. 'It costs around $120,000–$170,000 to bankrupt an average company', Russian criminal sources told a Western newspaper. 'But [then] you can make $3–4m profit.' In extreme cases, the police not only failed to protect the original owners, but kept them in custody until they had signed over their property to the new owners. And only a very small number of cases reached the courts, suggesting that higher-level law enforcement officials and even the FSB – which had responsibility for economic crime as well as national security – were deeply implicated.[296]

Something of the vulnerability of the Russian economy became apparent in late 2008 when the effects began to be felt of the global financial crisis that had been triggered by the collapse of sub-prime mortgages in the United States.[297] At least initially, Putin and Medvedev were both inclined to see this as a foreign problem that had little to do with their own country. The turbulence that had been taking place on the Russian markets, Medvedev told Italian television in early September, could '80 per cent' be attributed to the 'negative processes' that were under way in the United States and the other countries that were the 'supporting pillars of the global economy', and 'only 20 per cent' to the consequences of the short war with Georgia that had just concluded – although the economy 'always suffer[ed]' in a conflict'.[298] Speaking to the French press later in the month, Putin insisted that Russia had escaped the crisis entirely. There had been some outflow of foreign capital, but this was because of the problems of the Western countries themselves. Russia, by contrast, had 'no liquidity crisis and no mortgage loan crisis . . . we did not have it, we have avoided it'.[299] For some, indeed, the crisis was all but a foreign conspiracy against a resurgent Russia that represented a much more serious global challenge than Boris Yeltsin's Russia had ever done.[300] There was certainly no cause for concern, Putin told foreign investors the same month at an international forum in Sochi; the Russian economy was more securely based than in the past, all the 'fundamental indicators' were sound, and the government and the Central Bank had more than enough reserves to protect the rouble and the financial system as a whole.[301]

But as the crisis deepened, it became increasingly clear that it had direct and unwelcome consequences for Russia itself. Russian banks, affected by the uncertainty on international markets, stopped lending to each other, and liquidity dried up; the biggest borrowers were soon in difficulties and (as in other countries) found they had to look for government support if they were to avoid collapse.[302] Loans began to be called in; credit became more difficult to obtain, and if it could be obtained at all, more expensive. This meant that individual companies were also in trouble, even in the protected defence sector, where 30 per cent of enterprises were reported to be on the verge of bankruptcy in the early months of 2009.[303] There were sharp falls in share values, of about 75 per cent over the course of the year,[304] and Moscow's stock markets had to suspend their activities.[305] The rouble was meanwhile losing ground on foreign exchanges as the price of oil dropped back from the record levels that had been attained in the summer of 2008; at that time it had been trading at 23.5 to the dollar, but it was down to 29.4 by the end of the year and by February 2009 it had reached a new low of 36.4,[306] even though about a third of the country's hard currency reserves had been exhausted in an attempt to moderate its sudden decline.[307] A fall in the exchange value of the rouble drove up the price of imports, fuelling inflation.[308] And huge sums left the country altogether – as much as $130 billion over the course of 2008, a new record that exceeded the 'most pessimistic estimates' and was six times the level that had been recorded during the economic crisis ten years earlier.[309]

As companies began to encounter difficulties, they responded as they did in other countries: among other things, by laying off staff. The official level of unemployment had reached just over a million by October 2008, but by March 2009 it was over 2 million and it was expected to reach nearly 3 million by the end of the year, or about 10 per cent of the workforce.[310] Government itself was affected as cuts began to be made in the numbers of public officials, especially at regional level.[311] And those who remained in work were also affected, as increasing numbers were shifted onto part-time contracts or found lengthening delays in the payment of their salaries at a time of accelerating inflation. There were particular difficulties in the 'monocities', where a very large proportion of the local population were employed by a single enterprise (or a very small number of enterprises). For instance, in the town of Pikalevo in Leningrad region, where the closure of a cement factory – the major employer – led hundreds of protestors to block the main road in the summer of 2009, chanting 'Work! Work!' Tanya, who had been on the factory payroll more than half of her life, told a reporter she had not eaten meat for months and could feed her child only because the factory canteen had been willing to extend credit. Pensioners, whose monthly benefit was not affected, became unexpectedly wealthy. Things were so bad that even utility bills were no longer being paid, which meant that the town's hot water supply was shut off until the governor found emergency funds to bail them out.[312]

Growth rate expectations, as a consequence, had to be revised sharply downwards. The World Bank had been predicting a 3 per cent increase in GDP as late as November 2008,[313] but by March 2009 it was taking a very different view, projecting a 4.5 per cent contraction over the year and warning that the financial crisis would push nearly 6 million Russians into poverty unless the government did more to support them. The Russian economy, explained the Bank, had 'deteriorated dramatically in early 2009'. The crisis was a global one, but it had been accentuated in Russia by its 'structural vulner-abilities: dependence on the oil and gas sector, a narrow industrial base and [a] limited small and medium-sized enterprise sector'. Nor could it be expected that there would be the same kind of rapid recovery that had taken place after the collapse of the currency in 1998 – one reason was that most of Russia's traditional trading partners were experiencing difficulties of their own and the market for Russian exports was inevitably contracting. Unemployment was expected to reach as much as 12 per cent by the end of 2009, more than domestic forecasters had been projecting, and greater numbers (up to 16 per cent) would be forced into poverty, raising the possibility of serious civil unrest.[314] By June the World Bank's forecast was even more gloomy, with a projected 8 per cent fall in GDP, unemployment up to 13 per cent and poverty levels of more than 17 per cent by the end of the year. There would be a return to modest growth in 2010, but not the same kind of a recovery (the Bank repeated) as in 1998, and GDP would not return to pre-crisis levels until at least 2012.[315]

The slide in the value of the rouble showed up the risks involved in a heavy dependence on the export of natural resources as the price of a barrel of Urals oil fell from an all-time high of \$147 in July 2008 to just \$34 the following December (although it subsequently recovered). The collapse of export earnings had serious implications for the public finances; a revised budget had to be introduced in March 2009 that took account of a sharp fall in revenues at the same time as the cost of social security was rising, and assumed a deficit of more than 7 per cent.[316] It also had implications for Russia's international creditworthiness, in that the price of oil underpinned the ability of the state to discharge its obligations. In December 2008 Standard and Poor's became the first ratings agency to downgrade Russia in a decade;[317] in February 2009 Fitch followed suit by reducing Russia's rating to BBB, just two points above 'junk', warning that a further downgrading was possible as a result of low commodity prices, high capital outflows, declining foreign currency reserves and corporate debt problems.[318] Putin, speaking to a meeting of the United Russia leadership in the spring of 2009, accepted that the economic situation was 'complicated' and that the coming year would be 'difficult', but insisted all the same that there would be 'no catastrophe'.[319] For some ministers the worst of their troubles were already behind them, with a rouble that had begun to stabilise and a price of oil that was once again increasing;[320] but other ministers warned that it would be no more than a 'temporary respite',[321] and others still, especially outside the country, were concerned that an increase in the price of oil would simply allow difficult but necessary choices to be postponed even further.[322]

'The people need potatoes', the writer Belinsky remarked in the middle of the nineteenth century, 'but they have not the slightest need of a constitution'.[323] The experience of postcommunist economic change and of the international financial crisis of the early years of the new century suggested almost the reverse. A rich natural resource endowment, and measures to support particular industries or sections of the society, would obviously buy time. But without a constitution, or more generally the rule of law, there would not be an environment in which property rights would be respected, contracts would be honoured and disputes would be resolved impartially. In the absence of an environment of this kind, agriculture would be unlikely to prosper and there would be fewer incentives to grow potatoes in the first place. Indeed, the question could be put more broadly, as it was not only the potato crop that was likely to suffer in the absence of a secure legal environment. The liberties of ordinary citizens were more likely to be at risk if they lacked the kind of ownership rights that could protect them, and so were their assets and employment, if they expressed any views or took part in any activities that were unpopular with the government of the day. The lack of securely protected ownership was of course a much older Russian, and not simply Soviet, problem; it had formed the basis of a patrimonial state in the prerevolutionary period, one that placed no limits on the exercise of state authority and accordingly provided no basis for the development of institutions that could make judgements about competing claims and in this way sustain the liberties of the individual.[324] In turn it suggested that the kind of economic changes the Kremlin had said it wanted would be unlikely to materialise until the inheritance of centuries, not simply of decades, had been overcome.

Further reading

On the final stages of the Soviet economy, see especially Nove (1992), Hanson (2003) and the interview-based study by Ellman and Kontorovich (1998). There are sharply observed studies of the political economy of the Putin years in Goldman (2008) and Pirani (2010); on Khodorkovsky and the 'Yukos affair', see Sakwa (2009) and Sixsmith (2010). The larger and still-continuing debate between neoliberals and Keynesian gradualists may be sampled in, for instance, Åslund (1995) and (2007), on the one hand, and the rather different views of Klein and Pomer (2001), Stiglitz (2002) and Goldman (2003). The Russian state statistics committee maintains a website that is available in English at www.gks.ru/eng/. Western sources of data and commentary include the Economist Intelligence Unit's monthly subscription-based *Country Reports: Russia* (see www.eiu.com), the European Bank for Reconstruction and Development's annual *Transition*

Report (www.ebrd.com) and the World Bank's quarterly *Russian Economic Reports* (www.worldbank.org.ru); all have something of a vested interest in 'reform'.

Åslund, Anders, *How Russia Became a Market Economy* (Washington, DC: Brookings, 1995).
   How Capitalism Was Built: The Transformation of Central and Eastern Europe, Russia, and Central Asia (Cambridge and New York: Cambridge University Press, 2007).
Ellman, Michael, and Vladimir Kontorovich, eds., *The Destruction of the Soviet Economic System: An Insiders' History* (Armonk, NY, and London: M. E. Sharpe, 1998).
Goldman, Marshall I., *The Piratization of Russia: Russian Reform Goes Awry* (New York and London: Routledge, 2003).
   Petrostate: Putin, Power, and the New Russia (New York and Oxford: Oxford University Press, 2008).
Hanson, Philip, *The Rise and Fall of the Soviet Economy: An Economic History of the USSR from 1945* (London and New York: Longman, 2003).
Klein, Lawrence R., and Marshall Pomer, eds., *The New Russia: Transition Goes Awry* (Stanford, CA: Stanford University Press, 2001).
Nove, Alec, *An Economic History of the USSR*, 3rd edn (Harmondsworth and New York: Penguin, 1992).
Pirani, Simon, *Change in Putin's Russia: Power, Money and People* (London: Pluto Press, 2010).
Sakwa, Richard, *The Quality of Freedom: Khodorkovsky, Putin, and the Yukos Affair* (Oxford and New York: Oxford University Press, 2009).
Sixsmith, Martin, *Putin's Oil: The Yukos Affair and the Struggle for Russia* (New York and London: Continuum, 2010).
Stiglitz, Joseph, *Democracy and its Discontents* (New York and London: Norton, 2002).

5 A divided society

'At a wedding, 1990s' (Stephen White)

A society that was more open to private ownership meant a society that was more divided: into rich and poor, young and old, donor and subsidised regions, heavy industry and the services. Income differences widened spectacularly, and a group of 'oligarchs' became among the richest people anywhere in the world, even beyond the international financial crisis that began to affect Russia towards the end of 2008. But millions were still living in poverty, and many of them were concentrated in poorer regions in the south of the country – some of them traditionally Muslim – where as many as a third of the adult population might be out of work. Glaring social inequalities, and a law enforcement system that was badly affected by corruption, meanwhile provided a basis for a high level of crime, including violent crime and contract killings. They also affected the position of women, who had lost the formal equality of the Soviet period but found themselves confronted by new or at least more intractable problems of prostitution, domestic violence and human trafficking.

The USSR was always a diverse society. It was European, but also Asian. It stretched over eleven time zones, bordering twelve other states and three oceans, with much of its northern territory permanently frozen but its southern republics largely desert. It was a mostly Christian society, but also the world's fifth-largest Muslim state, and there were substantial Jewish and Buddhist minorities. About half of its population was Russian, and three-quarters belonged to one of the Slavic nationalities; but there were more than a hundred recognised ethnic groups, and on other, more inclusive counts as many as eight hundred.[1] Its language was predominantly Russian, and 82 per cent of the population spoke it fluently or as a native language; but about 130 other languages were spoken somewhere on Soviet territory, using a variety of different alphabets.[2] Indeed, the state itself was based on diversity, as it was a 'voluntary union' of fifteen different republics within each of which a particular national group was supposedly predominant.[3]

But if the USSR was 'national in form', it was also 'socialist in content'. For a start, there was no private ownership of productive resources of a kind that could have led to a minority of owners and a majority of wage labourers. Private ownership was not illegal, and there was (for instance) a substantial private housing sector. But there were no private factories or farms, and it was illegal to live off the labour of others – this was what the Soviet authorities defined as 'exploitation'. In fact, it was illegal not to work at all: the Soviet Constitution, in a wording that appeared to have been drawn from St Paul's Second Epistle to the Thessalonians, insisted that those who 'did not work should not eat' (the words disappeared when a new constitution was adopted during the Brezhnev years, but the biblical principle remained).[4] It was illegal, equally, to own more than one house, or to own a house of more than a certain size, or to rent it out and live on the proceeds.[5] This was not a 'classless' society: official theory recognised the existence of workers and collective farmers, and of an additional 'stratum' of white-collar employees. But there was in principle no antagonism between these various groups because they collectively owned the society's resources, and there was accordingly no basis (it was suggested) for the conflicts that were characteristic of capitalism and other class-divided societies.

Official theory was admittedly an imperfect guide to the realities of daily life under the Soviet system, and even official theory began to change as the society itself underwent a far-reaching transformation. For Yuri Andropov, as late as 1982, a socialist society was a society without social antagonisms, and there was accordingly no basis for an 'organised opposition' of a kind that Western exponents of 'pluralism' were making every effort to encourage.[6] Under Gorbachev, just a few years later, it became possible to speak of 'socialist pluralism', and then of a 'pluralism of opinion' or even a 'pluralism of interests' that logically required the articulation of political alternatives through which they could be expressed and reconciled.[7] Changes in official thinking reflected a society that was itself evolving and becoming more difficult to classify. In 1985, when Gorbachev succeeded to the party leadership, more than 90 per cent were employed by the state itself. By 1990, as the Ryzhkov government began to introduce a 'regulated' market, more than 80 per cent were still working in the state sector, although private ownership was increasing and the first foreign-owned enterprises had made their appearance. By the end of the decade, after still more far-reaching changes under the Yeltsin leadership, public employment was down to 38 per cent and rather more (44 per cent) were working in the private sector, although substantial numbers – more than 9 million, 13 per cent of the total – had no work at all.[8] Formally at least, a monolithic USSR had been succeeded by a postcommunist Russia with a diversity of ownership and occupation that matched the diversity of opinion that was represented in its newly established political institutions.

Rich and poor in postcommunist Russia

One of the most obvious consequences of the transition to an economy based largely on private ownership was a rapidly widening gap in earnings, and accordingly in living standards. In 1991, the USSR's last year, the best-paid fifth of the population took 31 per cent of all money incomes, and the least well paid 12 per cent. By the end of the decade, the richest fifth took half as much again (among them, nearly half of all earned incomes), but the poorest fifth only two-thirds as much as they had received at the end of the Soviet period.[9] Differences of this kind are conveniently expressed in terms of the 'decile ratio', which relates the earnings of the most prosperous 10 per cent to those of the least prosperous 10 per cent. In 1990 it stood at 4.4; by the end of the decade it had jumped to 13.9.[10] The Gini coefficient, another internationally recognised measure of the concentration of incomes, moved over the same period from 0.260 to 0.394 – a substantial movement along a scale on which zero represents perfect equality and one perfect inequality.[11] No existing society, of course, is entirely equal or unequal; but these figures meant that by the end of the decade the richest 20 per cent of Russians were receiving a greater share of total income than in any other European country for which the World Bank reported figures, including all the former Soviet republics, and more than in all but a few countries in Africa and Latin America.[12] At the other extreme, nearly a third of the entire society (44 million people) were living below the subsistence minimum, and more than a third of them were in 'extreme poverty'.[13]

Money incomes are only one of the ways in which living standards are generated, and this was particularly true of early postcommunist Russia.[14] For a start, substantial numbers were not being paid all or even a part of their earnings, and official statistics distinguished accordingly between nominal incomes – the salaries and wages to which the working population were entitled – and the money incomes they actually received. Both of them, moreover, varied from year to year, falling sharply in 1992 as prices were allowed to find a new equilibrium, but recovering some ground the following year. Over the decade, this left real money incomes – in other words, after they had been adjusted for inflation – at a level that was not much more than half their value in the last full year of communist rule (see Table 5.1). Incomes could also be expressed in terms of the

	'90	'91	'92	'93	'94	'95	'96	'97	'98	'99	'00
Real money incomes			53	116	112	84	101	106	84	87	111
Index (1991=100)		100	53	61	69	59	59	62	52	45	49
Inequality: decile ratio	4	5	8	11	15	14	13	14	14	14	14
Gini coefficient		.260	.289	.398	.409	.387	.385	.390	.394	.400	.395
% below subsistence			34	32	22	25	22	21	23	28	29
Pensions (in real terms)			52	131	97	81	109	95	95	61	128
As % of subsistence	237	170	119	138	129	101	116	113	115	70	76

Table 5.1 Living standards in the 1990s (percentage changes, year on year)

Source: adapted from *Rossiiskii statisticheskii yezhegodnik 2001*, p. 171.

commodities for which they could be exchanged. A Russian on average earnings, for instance, could buy only two-thirds as many eggs at the end of the 1990s as at the start of the decade, no more than half as much meat, potatoes and milk, and about a third of the fish and cabbage.[15] Russians, as a result of these changes, were spending just over half their income on food by the later years of the decade,[16] while at the same time the quality of their diet was deteriorating. More alcohol was being sold by the end of the 1990s than at the start, and more tobacco, but meat, bread and vegetables were all down by about a third, and eggs were down by nearly half.[17] These, moreover, were averages: the biggest earners, as in other societies, ate the same quantities of bread and potatoes but twice as much fruit, vegetables, fish and meat as the least prosperous 10 per cent.[18]

There were differentials not only between social groups, but also between regions, and within regions, in their patterns of income distribution.[19] Across the entire country, at the end of the 1990s, money incomes were about 1.8 times higher than the subsistence minimum, which was considerably less than in previous years because of the collapse of the currency and a sharp rise in inflation. But in southerly Ingushetia they were less than half the subsistence minimum (44 per cent), while in the oil-rich regions of western Siberia they were three or four times as much, and in Moscow five and a half times as much.[20] Average incomes, once again, lumped together the poor and the very rich, and their relative proportions varied from region to region. At Magadan, in the Far East, the richest 20 per cent of the local population earned more than four times as much as the poorest 20 per cent; but in Moscow they earned nearly twenty-eight times as much.[21] This meant that there were large numbers of poor in the capital city, as well as most of the country's millionaires. In Moscow, similarly, 23 per cent of the population earned less than the subsistence minimum at the end of the decade, well below the national average of 30 per cent, but in Ingushetia more than 95 per cent were living below the subsistence minimum, and in easterly Chita, bordering Mongolia and China, more than 88 per cent were doing so.[22] There were related differences between occupations; rates of pay in agriculture dropped particularly sharply, from close to the national average in 1990 to just 41 per cent in 1999, and there were similar falls in healthcare and education, to about half their level at the start of the decade.[23]

Official statistics of this or any other kind could capture no more than a few of the changes that were taking place in patterns of social inequality. They could clearly take little account of illegal and undeclared earnings, or of the extent to which Russians were already living in an informal economy based on the exchange of services and the bartering of commodities, or of the contribution to living standards that was made by suburban allotments.[24] But official figures seemed likely, if anything, to understate the differences that were opening up between rich and poor. The subsistence minimum, for a start, had been set at an unreasonably low level (much lower than prison rations in tsarist times, which had contained twice as much meat).[25] And income differentials were almost certainly much wider than official figures suggested, as the rich had found ways of concealing their earnings and could protect their value by investing in real estate, while the poor included vagrants, beggars and alcoholics who often escaped the attention of official scrutineers entirely.[26] A number of Russians, similarly, had a second job; but only 11 per cent had an additional income of this kind on an occasional or more regular basis, their numbers were declining and they were likely in any case to be those who were already earning the most in their principal employment.[27] As a result, while government statistics identified about a third of the population as living in poverty in the early postcommunist years, calculations based on survey returns put the proportion as high as 80 per cent; and 20 per cent had an income so low that it covered no more than the physiological needs of family members with no provision for clothing, medical treatment or holidays, leaving them 'at risk of degradation'.[28]

Reliable statistics about the 'rich' were even more difficult to obtain – 'not because of the modesty of the new Russians, but because any study of this kind comes up against the question of the origins of their wealth'.[29] In the view of the most authoritative researchers, up to 5 per cent of Russians, by the mid-1990s, could be classified as 'rich' (with their families, they accounted for between 4 and 7 million of the population). Another 15 per cent were 'prosperous', with a monthly income of at least a thousand dollars for each family member. The 'middle' accounted for a very diverse 20 per cent, ranging from the staff of commercial firms, street traders and junior government officials to more prosperous businessmen and criminals, some of whom could hope to sustain a standard of living that was roughly equivalent to that of their middle-class counterparts in Western countries. Most of them were concentrated in Moscow, where they represented about a third of the population, and they were about 10 per cent of the population of most of the larger towns and cities. The 'relatively poor' accounted for another 20 per cent and the 'poor' for as much as 40 per cent, including a quarter who were destitute.[30] At this lowest level, public health issues that had earlier been forgotten were returning, and infectious diseases such as diphtheria and tuberculosis were becoming more widespread as malnutrition and poor housing had their effect on the most vulnerable. A differentiation of incomes of this kind had 'no counterpart in the East European countries' and was apparently 'unprecedented'.[31]

A more elaborate, still more sharply pointed classification was suggested by Tat'yana Zaslavskaya, perhaps the most eminent of the Russian sociologists. At the top, she suggested, was a 'renewed oligarchy' that accounted for just 1 per cent of the population, composed for the most part of former members of the *nomenklatura*, with 'no less power and a great deal more wealth' than their Soviet predecessors. Below it, accounting for another 4–5 per cent of the population, was an 'augmented and strengthened ruling bureaucracy', twice as large as in the Soviet period and based on the 'total corruption of the state apparatus and the law enforcement agencies'. The third group (about 14–17 per cent of the total) was a 'middle class in the Western sense', but a relatively narrow, heterogeneous and unstable one, without significant property, based for the most part in the towns, but 'because of their weakness not yet able to exercise a significant influence on social development'. The fourth and by far the largest group was what Zaslavskaya described as the 'base', accounting for 60–65 per cent of the population. As a result of the economic reforms, this was an even less prosperous group than it had been in the Soviet past; it had received no significant assets from the privatisation of state property, and at the same time it had lost its earlier social and economic security (it was affected, at the same time, by growing unemployment and the non-payment of wages and pensions). Below it came the 'honest poor', including the least qualified and those with the largest families (9–12 per cent of the total); and finally the 'underclass', a criminalised 7–9 per cent who had lost touch with most social institutions and lived by their own rules.[32]

The rich, as these accounts suggested, were a composite of several groups, including well-educated and hardworking businessmen who held high positions in commercial structures with links to the state, as well as a newer group of entrepreneurs who had close links to organised crime and a greater propensity to lead a flashy, free-spending lifestyle. The businessmen were more inclined to advance their interests by lobbying within government, and tended to invest their earnings in real estate; the entrepreneurs, by contrast, lived in less luxurious surroundings but indulged a taste for expensive cars and relaxed in nightclubs and striptease bars. The business elite were usually married, with a wife who had given up working; almost all had one or two children, whom they brought up as lawyers or economists; and their favourite cars were Volvos, Lincolns and Mercedes-Benzes, although they kept some Russian-made cars for their family members.[33] Very few had established their position independently, and there was little prospect of doing so without 'influential patrons'. In these circumstances, those who were most likely to get rich were those who were already rich, or in power, together with the members of criminal clans; it was least likely to be ordinary people, or the better educated.[34] The survey evidence suggested similarly that it was 'connections with important people' (49 per cent) that made the greatest difference in matters of this kind, although it was also possible to accumulate wealth because 'the economic system in our country allows the rich to profit from the poor' (45 per cent) or because of 'dishonesty' (39 per cent); 'ability and talents' or 'hard work', by contrast, counted for very little (14 and 11 per cent respectively).[35]

Who were the seriously rich? For the public at large, in the early postcommunist years, it was leading politicians like the Moscow mayor Gavriil Popov or his successor Yuri Luzhkov,[36] but for informed opinion the richest Russians at this time were almost invariably the country's leading bankers: figures such as Vladimir Potanin, a former official of the Ministry of Foreign Economic Relations who had founded an import–export bank at an advantageous moment and who later became, for a year, first deputy premier in the Chernomyrdin government; or Vladimir Gusinsky, an oil and gas engineer who was also a qualified theatre director and then went on to head Most Bank; or Mikhail Khodorkovsky, a Moscow engineer who had risen through the Communist Party's youth wing and then became (in the first instance) head of the banking and industrial group Menatep. Others owed their position to their control over the country's vast natural resources, including Rem Vyakhirev, an engineer who had risen from management of the gas industry in Tyumen to a deputy ministerial position and chairmanship of the state-owned giant Gazprom; he had been closely associated with former Prime Minister Chernomyrdin, another gasman, for more than thirty years.[37] The richest of all were often identified as the 'seven bankers' who had agreed to pool their resources at the Swiss resort of Davos in early 1996 in order to ensure a Yeltsin victory in the presidential election of that year, and then taken their reward in the form of state assets at bargain prices; according to a member of the group, Boris Berezovsky, they controlled about half the entire Russian economy among them at this time.[38]

Berezovsky himself, perhaps the most influential and certainly most prominent of the 'bankers', was a computer scientist with a doctorate in management who had gone on to become the head of an automobile dealership that became the centre of a group of companies. He was a close friend of the Yeltsin family, particularly of his younger daughter, and was also deputy chairman of the Security Council and later executive secretary of the Commonwealth of Independent States.[39] The influence of 'oligarchs' like Berezovsky was broadly based and often included a segment of the media. Berezovsky himself controlled Russian Public Television – the main national service – and TV6 as well as the business paper *Kommersant*, the weekly magazine *Ogonek* and the now ironically named *Nezavisimaya gazeta* (Independent Newspaper). Potanin's Oneksimbank owned the popular daily *Komsomol'skaya pravda* and shared ownership of *Izvestiya* with Lukoil; Gusinsky and his bank owned a series of newspapers including the daily *Segodnya* (Today) as well as the newly established television channel NTV and a radio station.[40] There was continuing controversy about the extent to which the oligarchs constituted the 'de facto government of Russia', as the *Financial Times* described them.[41] Surveys found that Berezovsky was perceived as the 'most influential person in Russian politics', but 63 per cent of those who were asked had difficulty in replying and 22 per cent thought there was no such person.[42] For the chairman of NTV, Igor Malashenko, on the contrary, 'all stories about the incredible power of the oligarchs' were 'complete nonsense', and often cultivated by the oligarchs themselves to exaggerate the political influence they could command.[43]

What did it mean to be rich in early postcommunist Russia? First of all, surveys suggested, it meant having no worries about the future. It also meant having a business of one's own (the most profitable were currency dealing, property, electronics and oil); and after that it meant having a car, a dacha or country house and a flat; earning enough to buy food in markets, drink cognac and spend time in restaurants; and being healthy.[44] The rich, surveys agreed, liked foreign cars (more Mercedes 500 and 600 saloons were being sold in the Moscow region than in the whole of Western Europe in the mid-1990s);[45] and they liked property abroad, particularly in Spain but also in the United States, Cyprus, Portugal, Greece and France (one British estate agent was 'dealing with so many Russians that he kept a bottle of Stolichnaya vodka permanently on ice in his Hampstead office').[46] The new rich had little time for holidays – on average just a week a year, nearly always in a foreign resort. More than half had a mistress, whom they visited two or three times a month, and they dined out in restaurants at least four times a week. As many as 40 per cent admitted they had been involved in illegal activities at an earlier stage in their career, and 25 per cent had current links with the criminal world.[47] Other studies found that the most important characteristic of a rich Russian was personal security, including a bodyguard (two-thirds of them 'lived and worked under the threat of terror'; Berezovsky himself had nearly been blown up in 1994 in a blast the police described as the 'most powerful in Moscow that year' and which decapitated his driver).[48] Another characteristic was property, including a second home in the country, a well-appointed flat and a car; and yet another was links with the criminal world and with government. Clothes and personal appearance, by comparison, were relatively unimportant.[49]

The new rich in the early postcommunist years, in fact, put most of their money back into their businesses, with just 15 per cent set aside for their own requirements (in some cases, where they felt their businesses had yet to establish themselves, they spent even less on any kind of private consumption). Beyond that, the easiest way of showing off new-found wealth was through the purchase of a prestigious motor car or a city-centre apartment[50] – although with rising levels of crime and popular hostility, it became increasingly common to move to well-protected residences in the nearby countryside (by the late 1990s the cost of residences of this kind in the Moscow region was running at up to $700,000 and competitions were being organised to identify the most luxurious).[51] The new rich worked out at 'fitness centres' where family membership cost more than four times the average annual income. There were special classes for the under-10s, where they could 'keep in shape before they join[ed] their parents on the stair master and treadmill', and fashion parades 'for the well-dressed 4- to 12-year-old' ('children', it was explained, 'need to be fashionable too', although kidnapping scares meant that all of this took place 'under the watchful eye of an armed bodyguard').[52] Descendants of the prerevolutionary nobility had another opportunity at their disposal, a newly opened school in which the twice-weekly etiquette class was the 'high point of their timetable'. By the time they graduated, they were 'little princes', able 'to waltz, and to dance the polka, to bow in front of a lady, and to eat a banana with cutlery at a dinner'.[53]

But many of the new rich just liked to have a good time. And there was a developing network of clubs that catered for their requirements, like the Golden Palace, which had a Perspex floor with 'fish swimming below your feet' but also 'evil-looking Vietnamese clients and shotgun-toting security'; or Hippopota M ('pricey; must check guns at the door'); or Voyazh Club ('heavy leathers and bikers' but a 'critical crowd; singer killed on stage last year by angry audience').[54] It was rarely difficult to identify the 'new Russians' on such occasions: they were dressed in 'raspberry-coloured jackets, green trousers, and unbelievably gaudy ties, inevitably bought in the most expensive shops of Paris and New York', or else 'like English gentlemen, although their sizes were not exactly the same'.[55] Their consumption, foreign journalists reported, was 'conspicuous even by Western standards'. They were protected by their bodyguards and the tinted windows of their Mercedes 600s; they bought villas in Europe, did their shopping in Paris and Milan, and thought nothing of spending hundreds of dollars for lunch at one of the five-star Western hotels in the Russian capital. When they held a public event, like Most-Bank's fifth birthday party, a 'parade of Mercedeses, BMWs and Cadillacs' wound their way round one of the city's most opulent hotels; security staff with walkie-talkies took up position outside the building; inside, 'men in Armani suits and women in diamonds, Versace cocktail dresses and Chanel suits checked their furs and joined the receiving line', the 'champagne was flowing' and the caviare was in 'buckets'. Later on, at somewhere like the Up and Down Club, they surrendered their pistols at the door and were frisked by armed guards before heading upstairs to watch young women in G-strings gyrate around a pole in the middle of the stage before taking it all off. 'We don't have any foreign customers', explained the bar manager, pouring another of the club's favourite drinks, a $100 Hennessy Paradis; 'they can't afford it'.[56]

The 'new Russians' were just as easy to identify on holiday, not least by their extravagant spending. During the winter they could be found at Alpine resorts, their suitcases full of foreign currency (one ski boutique had to close when a Russian lady, 'dollar bills fluttering from her bag', bought everything they had for sale).[57] During the summer they preferred the French Riviera, attracted by its 'snobbish reputation, high prices and anonymity';[58] they were welcomed in their turn because they spent five times as much as British or German tourists – not including hotel bills, which most of them insisted on paying in cash. Newspapers, indeed, reported that new Russians had 'over-taken oil sheikhs as the biggest and fastest spenders'; staff at the most expensive hotels 'watched goggle-eyed as families plonked down heaps of cash to cover bills that ran into thousands'. The new Russians had another, more familiar characteristic, and one Riviera hotel had to make changes in its catering arrangements when it was found that the small bottles of vodka in its minibars had 'usually been emptied by breakfast'; thereafter, it was supplied in litres.[59] Another had to change the bar regime, as its new Russian guests wanted to order vodka from ten o'clock in the morning. 'They choose all the dearest things on the menu', reported hotel staff in Cannes, 'like Arabs from the Persian Gulf twenty years ago', and 'usually ordered more than they could eat', including the most expensive wines, but rarely left any tips.[60] This was also the experience of local taxi-drivers: 'they never tip', one of them told journalists disgustedly, 'not like the British aristocracy'.[61]

There were more super-rich during the Putin years than ever before, but they had a rather different relationship with the state authorities. In particular, the new leadership was keen to establish that it would expect to be dominant in all relations of this kind, and that it would not tolerate any oligarchs who were too independent or (still more so) who expressed any political ambitions. Putin's 'Open Letter to Voters', published shortly before the 2000 presidential election, made clear that if he was elected, the 'so-called oligarchs' would be treated 'like everybody else. The same as the owner of a small bakery or a shoe-repair shop.'[62] Interviewed in his campaign headquarters two weeks later, Putin was even more insistent that there should be 'equal conditions for everyone who takes part in the political and economic life of Russia'; in particular, 'no clan, no oligarch should come close to regional or federal government – they should be kept equally distant from power'.[63] And in a radio interview on the eve of the poll, he appeared to call for the 'liquidation of the oligarchs as a class', which was what Stalin had said about rich peasants in the late 1920s. He avoided these precise words, according to the contemporary record, but the substance of his remarks was not very different. If oligarchs were simply the representatives of big business, there would be the same kind of cooperation with them as with anyone else. But if it meant the fusion of power and capital, he told Mayak on 18 March, 'there [would] be no oligarchs of this kind as a class . . . In this sense there [would] be no oligarchs.'[64] Or as a daily newspaper put it, 'power-hungry' oligarchs would 'cease to exist'.[65]

An early victim of the new dispensation was Vladimir Gusinsky, one of the 'seven bankers' whose NTV channel had annoyed the Kremlin by its critical coverage of the war in Chechnya that had begun in the late summer of 1999, and by its sympathetic coverage of the political opposition during the parliamentary and presidential elections that had followed later that year and in the spring of 2000. Two months after Putin's election, armed police raided the headquarters of Gusinsky's Media Most conglomerate in Moscow.[66] Then in a still more dramatic development, Gusinsky himself was arrested in mid-June and placed in Moscow's tuberculosis-ridden Butyrki prison on charges of the 'misappropriation of state property on an especially large scale' – the first time an action of this kind had taken place, even though he was quickly released.[67] In July the charges were dropped because of lack of evidence, but he left the country immediately afterwards for Spain, where his family was already established.[68] It later emerged that he had been pressured to agree to the sale of Media Most to the state gas monopoly Gazprom, to which it was heavily in debt, in order to secure his release in a deal that had been brokered directly by a member of the government.[69] A warrant for his arrest was issued in

November after he failed to return to answer questions, and an unsuccessful attempt was made to secure his extradition;[70] then in April 2001 NTV was taken over by armed security guards acting on behalf of Gazprom and the channel was placed under new and Kremlin-friendly management.[71] The staff of Gusinsky's news weekly, *Itogi*, were dismissed; the liberal daily *Segodnya* ceased publication;[72] and Most-Bank lost its licence to operate.[73] Gusinsky's elimination from Russian public life was completed the following October when he agreed to an out-of-court settlement in which his company's remaining assets were taken over to settle its debts to Gazprom.[74]

Another casualty was Boris Berezovsky, who soon found himself at odds with the new president but whose influence with the Yeltsin family had in any case been waning and whose commercial activities were beginning to attract the attention of the authorities.[75] Berezovsky had been elected to the Duma in December 1999, which gave him immunity from prosecution, but he became increasingly critical of the policies of the new president, in Chechnya and in relation to his reassertion of the authority of the central government throughout the national territory.[76] In July 2000 he surrendered his parliamentary seat, declaring that he 'did not wish to participate in Russia's collapse and the establishment of an authoritarian regime',[77] and in November 2000 he too decided 'not to return to Russia for questioning' when fraud charges were presented.[78] Instead he took up residence in the United Kingdom, where he quickly acquired an extensive property portfolio and then, in September 2003, political asylum; an attempt by the Russian authorities to secure his extradition was rejected by the British courts on the grounds that he would be unlikely to receive a fair trial in Russia itself.[79] Berezovsky became an increasingly outspoken critic of the Russian President in his British exile, calling in 2007 for a revolution that would overthrow him, if necessary by force ('it isn't possible to change this regime through democratic means', he told the *Guardian*).[80] He was also generous in his support of the 'coloured revolutions' that took place in many of the former Soviet republics in the middle years of the decade, although it appeared unlikely he would ever return to Russia itself, not least because of a six-year jail sentence that was passed on him *in absentia* on charges of embezzlement from the state airline Aeroflot.[81]

An even more spectacular casualty was Mikhail Khodorkovsky, another of the 'seven bankers' and at this time Russia's richest man and the world's 16th most wealthy. His arrest, in October 2003, appeared to owe more than anything else to his apparent presidential ambitions and his open support of opposition parties. It followed an officially sponsored investigation into the affairs of his oil company Yukos and its chief executives for a range of alleged crimes, including tax evasion, fraud and conspiracy to murder. The first signs of an approaching showdown appeared in the summer of that year with the arrest of a major shareholder, Platon Lebedev, on charges of defrauding the state over the privatisation of a fertilisation plant.[82] The crisis deepened dramatically when Khodorkovsky himself was arrested at gunpoint while his plane was refuelling at Novosibirsk airport and charged with tax evasion, fraud and falsification of official documents.[83] A large block of Yukos shares was seized as security, and a new management was appointed after Khodorkovsky himself had stood down to concentrate on his charitable work.[84] A lengthy hearing in the Moscow courts came to an end in May 2005 when he was sentenced to nine years' imprisonment for fraud and tax evasion, reduced to eight years on appeal.[85] He served out his sentence in a remote Siberian penal colony, thousands of miles from his family and legal advisers and in an area with a high level of background radiation; an application for parole was rejected,[86] and there was a short period of solitary confinement because of an interview he had given to a Western magazine.[87] At a further trial that concluded in December 2010 he was sentenced to an additional thirteen and a half years for embezzlement and money laundering, to be served concurrently, that would keep him in prison until 2017.[88]

But other oligarchs survived, and they were joined by increasing numbers of spectacularly rich associates. The most widely respected list was issued in the spring of every year by *Forbes* magazine, as part of a wider study of the world's super-rich. Russians made their first appearance on the eleventh list, which appeared in 1997; there were six of them, headed by Boris Berezovsky with an estimated wealth of $3 billion.[89] Just over a decade later, in March 2008, there were a staggering 87, up more than a third on the year before and more than anywhere else in the world apart from the United States, with 469 (Germany was in third place with 59). Their wealth was mostly in raw materials, but there were billionaires who had interests in property and finance (none, however, who had made their money by manufacturing anything that ordinary Russians or consumers in other countries might actually wish to buy on the basis of its quality, design or advanced technology). The richest Russian, Oleg Deripaska, was the ninth richest man in the world at this time; the second richest, Roman Abramovich, was the world's fifteenth wealthiest; and there were two more in the top twenty.[90] 'Nothing in Russia increases as quickly as the number of billionaires', commented *Izvestiya*.[91] The Moscow journal *Finans* published a similar list every year: on its figures the number of dollar billionaires was even greater – 101 – and it had also increased sharply.[92] *Forbes* published a separate Russian edition, from 2004 onwards, with its own list of Russia's 'golden hundred'; on its reckoning there were as many as 110 Russian billionaires in 2008, up from 60 the year before.[93]

The richest of the Russian super-rich had for some time been Roman Abramovich, although he dropped back to second place in 2008 following an expensive divorce. He spent much of his time in Britain, visiting his native country several times a year to perform his duties as governor of Chukotka, a small region in the Russian Far East.[94] He had been elected to the Duma in 1999 for the Chukotka constituency, and as governor in December 2000; he stood down in the summer of 2008[95] but was elected shortly afterwards to the local legislature and became its chairman.[96] Abramovich had made his billions during the 'loans for shares' deals of the mid-1990s, when he acquired most of his oil and aluminium holdings. He sold his Sibneft' oil company to Gazprom in 2005 for £7 billion, in what was at the time the biggest transaction in Russian corporate history, and had already ceased to be an 'oligarch' in the conventional sense when he bought Chelsea football club and became more of a London than a Moscow businessman (he had actually wanted to buy Manchester United).[97] An uncontested divorce from his second wife in 2007 was the occasion to enumerate his various assets: two Boeing airliners, two helicopters, a six-storey house in fashionable Knightsbridge, a country estate in West Sussex, a twelve-room penthouse in Kensington built with the marble that had been used for the Taj Mahal, a castle near Cap d'Antibes, a Georgian house in Belgravia, a house in San Tropez, a hotel in Cannes and a dacha in the Moscow region – on top of bank deposits ($15 billion), his football club, company shares and three yachts, one of them with a missile defence system and its own submarine.[98] His wife was believed to have agreed to a relatively modest $300 million divorce settlement, plus $100,000 a month for the costs of his five children.[99] The settlement, at all events, hardly cramped his style. In May 2008 he splashed out more than £60 million for two canvases by Lucian Freud and Francis Bacon;[100] German shipbuilders were meanwhile putting the final touches to the 12,000-tonne *Eclipse*, a yacht about two-thirds the size of the *Titanic* and the largest and most expensive of its kind anywhere in the world.[101]

At the top of the list, until he was himself overtaken in 2009, was the 'aluminium tsar' Oleg Deripaska. He came to prominence in the Putin years and, according to the Moscow magazine *Finans*, was the richest Russian of them all in 2008, with a fortune of £11 billion.[102] He operated from Russia but kept a £20 million house in London's wealthy Belgravia and entertained guests on a 238-foot yacht off Corfu, with its bathrooms finished in marble and gold (there was some controversy when an EU commissioner and a prominent British Conservative politician were among those who accepted his hospitality in the summer of 2008). Deripaska was born in the Nizhnii Novgorod region and studied physics at Moscow University, but came from an impoverished background and had to work on a building site to keep himself going. Soon afterwards he became a smelter, and then (in obscure circumstances) the co-owner of an aluminium plant in Siberia. He was widely described as 'ruthless', even a 'villain from a James Bond movie'. According to *Forbes*, 'when the smoke had cleared' in the aluminium business, 'dozens of executives, bankers, traders and mob bosses were dead'. His master company, Basic Element, owned RusAl, the world's largest aluminium producer, but he also had interests in minerals, airports, vehicle construction and banking. He was regarded as particularly close to the Kremlin and indeed had married the daughter of Yeltsin's former chief of staff, Valentin Yumashev. Like Abramovich, he spent a lot of his time in London, where his children were believed to be at school, but he was barred from the United States because of concerns about his 'criminal associations and relationships'.[103]

Not all the oligarchs (if the term was still appropriate) lived in conspicuous excess, and several of them took care to make occasional 'patriotic' gestures of a kind that might improve their standing with the Kremlin, particularly in the rather different climate that began to prevail after Putin had been elected to his first presidential term. Alisher Usmanov, one of the wealthiest members of the rich list and already a figure of international prominence as a major shareholder in London's Arsenal football club, bought the art collection that had been accumulated by cellist Mtsislav Rostropovich and his wife

Table 5.2 **The richest Russians, 2008–2010**

	Rank 2010	(*Forbes* 2010)	Rank 2009	Rank 2008	Assets (bn $)	Companies
Vladimir Lisin	1	32	3	3	18.8	NLMK Group
Mikhail Prokhorov	2	39	1	7	17.9	Onexim
Roman Abramovich	3	50	2	2	17.0	Millhouse Capital
Suleiman Kerimov	4	136	5	8	14.5	Politmetall, shares in Gazprom, Sberbank
Mikhail Fridman	5	42	6	4	14.3	Major shareholder in Al'fa Group
Oleg Deripaska	6	57	8	1	13.8	Basic Element
Alisher Usmanov	7	100	10	12	12.4	Metalloinvest
Vagit Alekperov	8	58	4	11	10.7	LUKoil
Alexei Mordashov	9	70	14	5	10.0	Severostal'
Vladimir Potanin	10	61	7	6	10.0	Noril'sk Nickel

Source: based on the listings produced by the Moscow-based journal *Finans*, 15 February 2010, various pages; the global listing in the second column is from 'The world's billionaires', *Forbes*, 10 March 2010, various pages. Various estimates of wealth appeared in different sources, and in different editions of the same journals; Prokhorov's wealth, for instance, was assessed at $9.5 billion and Abramovich's at $8.5 billion in *Forbes*' Russian edition (no. 5(62), May 2009, pp. 88–9).

Galina Vishnevskaya for $72 million in 2007 and presented it to the Konstantin Palace, the Russian president's St Petersburg residence.[104] Another of the super-rich, oil magnate Viktor Veksel'berg, spent 'more than $90 million' to buy the world's second-largest collection of Fabergé eggs in 2004 so that they could be returned to Russia and seen by 'as many people as possible';[105] he also paid $1 million to Harvard in 2008 for the return of a set of monastery bells that had been sold to an American industrialist in 1931 and then gifted to the university.[106] The banker Vladimir Potanin, who had devised the scheme in the mid-1990s by which the government sold off state enterprises very cheaply in return for loans, served for some months as a first deputy prime minister under Boris Yeltsin and later agreed to be nominated to the consultative Public Chamber that Putin had established in 2005, although it was unclear what 'public organisation' he represented; another of its members was Mikhail Fridman of the Al'fa Group, who like Potanin had been one of the original 'seven bankers'.[107]

The relative position of the super-rich was continually changing, and the entire list suffered a considerable shock at the end of 2008 as the world financial crisis began to deepen (see Table 5.2). Indeed, for *Izvestiya*, this was the end of the oligarch phenomenon itself: not only were they much less prosperous than the government, they were often dependent on it, and now it was the 'state itself' that was the biggest oligarch of all.[108] According to *Finans*, the main beneficiary of these changes – or at any rate the one who had suffered the least – was Russia's 'most eligible bachelor', Mikhail Prokhorov, who had sold off his banking and real estate interests while it was still advantageous to do so and held much of his wealth in cash. The most obvious loser was Oleg Deripaska, who had been obliged to sell off some of his assets to satisfy the banks from which he had borrowed heavily and slipped down to eighth place in the new ranking. Roman Abramovich was still in second place, but his assets had also diminished considerably, from an estimated $23 billion in 2008.[109] This, of course, was part of a much larger pattern, as the annual *Forbes* list made clear. In 2008 there had been 87 Russian billionaires on the list out of a global total of 1,125; a year later there were just 32 out of a smaller total of 793, two of whom (Boris Berezovsky and Mikhail Gutseriev) were resident abroad. *Forbes*, commented *Izvestiya*, had been 'obliged to act as a burial party'.[110] But another year later the number of Russian billionaires had recovered substantially, to 62 (which put Russia in third place globally, after the United States and China); the new head of the rich list was Vladimir Lisin, chairman of Novolipetsk Steel, a 'proletarian success story' who had spent his career in the metals industry and kept out of national politics.[111]

Given the lack of transparency of Russian business, there was considerable uncertainty about exactly who were the super-rich and still more so about exactly how wealthy they were. One of the most intriguing suggestions of all, in the later years of his second term, was that the then president himself might belong in the list – indeed at the very top of it. According, at least, to Russian journalist Stanislav Belkovsky, speaking to the Western press in December 2007 on the basis of information that had supposedly been obtained from within the Presidential Administration itself, Putin had secretly accumulated a 'personal fortune' of at least $40 billion – but it could be more, 'perhaps much more'. It was a sum sufficient to make him Europe's, not just Russia's, richest man. Putin, Belkovsky claimed, owned vast holdings in three Russian oil and gas companies, concealed behind a 'non-transparent network of offshore trusts' that was ultimately controlled from Switzerland or Liechtenstein. Most of these arrangements were supposedly in the hands of Guvnor, a mysterious Swiss-based oil trader founded by Gennadii Timchenko, a friend of the President's who had also worked in the KGB foreign directorate (see p. 157). Putin, it was alleged, owned 'at least 75 per cent' of Guvnor as well as a small share of Gazprom and controlled more than a third of the shares in Surgutneftegaz, an oil exploration company and Russia's third biggest oil producer.[112] Putin himself dismissed these suggestions as beneath contempt;[113] but such was the obscurity that surrounded such matters that it was just as difficult to disprove the charges as to gather the evidence to make them in the first place.

Whatever the origins of their wealth, it was certainly clear that rich Russians were among the biggest spenders anywhere in the world, and not just in their own country. They bought a great deal of housing, for instance, in the most desirable international locations. In London and the south-east of England, they had 'taken over from Arabs as the biggest buyers of multimillion-pound homes' in the early years of the new century – homes such as a £10 million period property in Chelsea with a copy of the Elgin Marbles on a frieze around its drawing room walls. Russian millionaires, apparently, saw London as a 'relatively safe and benign haven from a political and tax point of view'; and many were buying 'larger properties as homes for their families, so that their children [could] be educated in England'.[114] It was another Russian businessman who bought a luxury home on the Sandbanks peninsula in Poole Harbour, on the southern English coast, in 2008, the fourth most expensive address of its kind anywhere in the world. Not only this – dissatisfied with the layout, he decided to demolish it entirely and construct a modern glass-fronted property with six bedrooms, four bathrooms, a sun terrace and a lift. The anonymous owner, it was explained, had bought the house essentially for the land and the location; he 'also liked the fact that the property ha[d] its own rights to have a helicopter land there'.[115] It was Russia's richest man, Mikhail Prokhorov, who was reported to have bought 'the world's most expensive villa', in the south of France, for £400 million; the Villa Leopolda, between Nice and Monaco, had originally been constructed for King Leopold II of Belgium in 1902.[116] Another billionaire, restaurant-owner Arkadii Novikov, bought the spectacular Villa Fontanelle beside Lake Como from the fashion designer Giovanni Versace earlier the same year for a staggering $52 million.[117]

If they stayed in Russia itself, the rich liked increasingly to live in well-protected seclusion. For instance, on the housing estate that Aras Agalarov was completing near a village on the outskirts of Moscow, in a meadow 'dotted with fir trees and white camomile flowers'. Several of the residences had already been completed when Western journalists interviewed him in 2007: one was a 'vast neoclassical villa', another a 'Scottish baronial mansion'. A row of trees had been planted to 'hide the village over there', explained Agalarov, pointing to a row of dilapidated dachas. As well as houses, some that 'owe[d] a debt to the ancient Greeks' and others that had been 'done in doughty Gothic', there was an eighteen-hole golf course, an exclusive private school, fourteen artificial lakes, waterfalls, and a spa and beach resort with imported white sand. There were plans to build up to two hundred mansions on the estate, each of which would cost £10–15 million. Bodyguards – most families had five or six – would be banished to small houses on the edge of the community. The only remaining obstacle was a small hamlet adjoining the estate, where Agalarov had so far managed to buy up half of the houses with a view to demolishing them. One of the owners was still holding out, although he had been offered $1 million. 'He'll sell in the end', Agalarov insisted, telling journalists that what he had in mind was a 'kind of utopian social experiment – but without poor people'.[118] The owner himself, interviewed by *Izvestiya*, was in no mood to give way to the developers and was buying weapons. 'It was a lot better when the Germans were here', he told the paper, 'at least they allowed you to get water from the river.'[119]

The super-rich also had their own medical arrangements, including a 'clinic for millionaires' that opened in Moscow in the spring of 2008. It was a 'surgery without queues', *Izvestiya* discovered, and 'apparently without patients either', so 'empty and clean' was it in the 'elegant, beige and chocolate interiors'.[120] The entrance hall featured a 'light and water sculpture, armchairs of ivory leather and the latest issues of luxury magazines'; the clinic itself featured medical services that were 'currently available only in a select number of Western clinics'. An annual programme of treatment cost about 1.5 million roubles ($63,000); it included 'treatment from a personal physician, gynae-cologist, urologist, dietician, neurologist, physiotherapist and a programme of laboratory diagnostics'. A family programme cost 2.5 million roubles, and for 5 million roubles ($210,000) the entire clinic could be placed at the disposal of a client who needed exceptional levels of privacy. Every programme included a personal consultation with the director, who usually charged 250,000 roubles ($10,500) a session; he would also serve as a client's personal physician for 250 million roubles or $10.5 million a year (there were two or three on his list at any time). But even at these prices, the clinic had 'no problem finding clients' – there were more than 100,000 millionaires in Russia, and the clinic could accommodate no more than fifty of them; apart from this it was popular with Russians living abroad, who found it had a more sympathetic understanding of their particular difficulties. The main psychological problems with which the clinic had to deal were apparently marital infidelity, games and shopping addictions, depression, obesity, alcoholism – 'and, alas, impotence'.[121]

The children of the super-rich lived in their own kind of seclusion, behind a 'golden curtain'. One of their tutors told journalists about the ten-year-old's party she had recently attended in Rublevka, an exclusive residential area on the outskirts of the capital; every child had turned up with two armed bodyguards, a nanny and a driver. It was the same at Malakovka, in another outlying district, where the collapsing houses of locals stood next to 'giant mansions, with balustrades and towers and surrounded by high walls topped with CCTV'. One of the residents had tried to build a helipad on his roof to avoid the local traffic, until the authorities intervened. The result was a 'huge market in gated settlements around Moscow'. 'If you let all sorts of drunks and people in here they'd just spoil it', explained another resident, raising his voice to be heard over the noise of the construction of a five-metre earth barrier to screen the settlement and act as a walkway for guards. 'I want my grandchildren to be protected.' Inside, the children themselves were less satisfied. 'Why can't we be like other children?', one privileged 11-year-old asked her multimillionaire property-developer father, tugging at her Gucci T-shirt. 'Why can't I go out?' These, sociologists explained, were 'children from behind the fences' who could 'buy anything they want except freedom': they were in a kind of 'luxury prison', part of a widening gap between rich and poor that could generate social unrest and for the children themselves a limited upbringing that could lead to an unhappy, maladjusted adulthood.[122]

The super-rich certainly liked to spend their money, if they had it. The Bentley showroom in Moscow's Barvikha Luxury Village was always busy, even with prices that started at $320,000 for a budget model. Tinted glass was very popular – for Duma deputies, for instance, who had no wish to advertise the kind of money they were earning.[123] And there was a 'millionaires' fair', which went ahead again in November 2008 in spite of the crisis that was already raging on the international financial markets. Visitors to a giant exhibi-tion hall on the outskirts of Moscow could choose from a Gulfstream jet, a private island, a diamond-encrusted laptop, or a helicopter with Versace interior. There was 'always some kind of crisis', explained the Dutch organisers; the Russians they had spoken to were 'relaxed' about the latest one (indeed the first-ever summer millionaires' fair took place the following year).[124] Another option during the summer months was the Moscow Beach Club, with sand imported from the Maldives, unlimited lobster and champagne, and non-stop pole-dancing.[125] The super-rich also liked to stage parties with international stars. Abramovich invited the British singer Amy Winehouse to perform at the opening of his partner's new art gallery in 2008. The catering had been arranged in London, but the drinks were more traditional – vodka and fruit juice; the singer herself, a whisky and cola in her hand and 'somewhat unsteady on her feet', had reportedly been paid $2 million for her services.[126] Another singer, George Michael, collected a similar sum for his contribution to a New Year party that had been organised by Vladimir Potanin for 300 guests on his private estate twenty miles outside Moscow.[127] Nothing, apparently, was beyond reach. Even the Lenin Memorial Museum in Ul'yanovsk was turned into a 'wild party zone' with 'strippers and drunken businessmen'. The museum had to raise money somehow, explained its director, and Lenin would not have minded: he was 'very pragmatic and flexible'.[128]

Later on the super-rich could hang out at a night club, ideally one with strict *feis kontrol'*. For instance, at Rasputin's in Moscow, the second-oldest gentlemen's establishment in the city and supposedly the 'largest strip club in Europe', but not a 'place for people on social welfare or a shoestring budget'. One of its features was a 'hard room' where guests could spend the night in medieval conditions, 'complete with leg and neck chains that [were] bolted to the wall and stocks for the more adventurous'. On stage, 'girls wrestled with each other over a large vibrating machine (a coffee grinder? food processor? I really couldn't say), as a male midget ran around the room with a horse whip agitating the crowd'. Beyond this were separate Indian, Japanese, Tibetan and Turkish rooms where the pleasures of the respective countries could be sampled with several of their female representatives (although as the management warned one enterprising punter, 'Please don't treat any of the girls like she's your wife').[129] 'White Bear' was 'famous for its Russian folk dancing strip show', which had 'all your favourite characters from Russian folklore doing things you couldn't even dream about'. At 'Show Girls' there were 'erotic shows, lesbian shows and, perhaps best of all, a shower show where you're allowed to touch'; at 'Eclipse' there was a 'VIP fetish and bondage party' every Sunday night.[130] Russian clubs, guides explained, were 'unafraid of pushing the limits of entertainment and décor'. One club was 'famed for having live alligators roaming around under the glass dance floor'; another took its inspiration from Soviet-era prisons with staff dressed as police and prisoners, and sections that were 'zoned off with barbed wire and guarded by angry watchdogs'.[131]

The Russian super-rich could occasionally give rise to controversy when they took their pleasures in other countries. There was an 'enormous scandal' in Courchevel in the French Alps in early 2007 when one of the very richest, Mikhail Prokhorov, was arrested in his hotel room and taken away in handcuffs as part of a 'planned raid in connection with the struggle against prostitution'.[132] Police with dogs had burst into his hotel room and conducted themselves without the usual courtesies; several representatives of the Austrian travel company that had organised his visits were also detained, as well as twenty-six other Russians. Prokhorov was held on suspicion of procuring, a case the police had been pursuing for most of the previous year. The magnate's own explanation was that he 'liked to surround himself with pretty girls during his trips and [saw] nothing wrong in that' – indeed he held regular 'castings of young models from the provinces' for such purposes – and the girls themselves told reporters he was just a friend who was 'helping their careers'.[133] Local officials pointed out that there were 'many more prostitutes in Nice or in Paris than in Courchevel', and Prokhorov's press secretary thought the whole thing had been a 'big misunderstanding'; the billionaire himself was eventually released without charge, the mayor of Courchevel insisting that Russians were still 'welcome guests'. But there was already talk of a boycott, if the super-rich could no longer be sure they were beyond the reach of the authorities, and business subsequently declined, although this was for economic as well as other reasons.[134]

Courchevel itself had already been christened the 'winter capital of Russia' and become the setting for an 'annual phenomenon when Russia's super-rich and their entourages descend on the town in early January for two weeks of drinking, parties, extravagant spending and – if there is any time left over – a spot of skiing'.[135] Russians accounted for about 20 per cent of tourist numbers over the entire season, but they took up to 70 per cent of the hotel rooms in the first weeks of the New Year when they occupied 'all the restaurants and night clubs', paying up to $13,000 for a table and $650 for a bottle of Dom Pérignon; just a 'modest' dinner for two in a local restaurant could cost as much as $5,000. The trade had built up over the previous seven or eight years, *Izvestiya* reported. It had been a quiet, even provincial, resort until Potanin and Abramovich began to arrive with large groups of family, friends and partners, followed by show business stars, celebrities and high-class prostitutes, for whom it became part of a regular routine: in the summer to the 'Lazurka' (Cote d'Azur) and in the winter to 'Kurshevelovo', where restaurant and hotel managers 'welcomed them with open tills'.[136] Among the many attractions of Courchevel was that it was one of the few Alpine resorts with a private airfield for executive jets, and it was just a short trip across the border to the Swiss banks where many of the richest Russians deposited their millions. Locals came to call it 'Courchevelsky', and inevitably there were questions about the 'models' that accompanied the super-rich, who never skied, walked around the town in high heels, and in the evening were entertained to oysters, foie gras and lobster washed down with vodka and 'cripplingly expensive Château Pétrus 1972 – sometimes in the same glass'.[137]

So great was the presence and the spending power of the Russian super-rich at resorts of this kind that 'quotas' began to be introduced to restrict their numbers: a 10 per cent limit in the Austrian ski resort of Kitzbühel, for instance, as Russians were felt to lower the tone of the resort and put off other visitors. Russian guests were 'naturally welcome', local officials explained, but the resort wanted to avoid becoming a Russian 'stronghold'.

The number of Russian and Ukrainian tourists had been increasing every year since the millennium, and many establishments accepted payment in roubles and had menus in Cyrillic; the wife of the Moscow mayor, who had bought a golf course in the area and was apparently considering the construction of a hotel, was reported to have ordered 'kilos of caviare' in a single evening. But on top of their drinking and occasionally outrageous behaviour, Russians had been buying ski chalets and hotels, forcing up prices and leaving local people with no realistic opportunity to buy a property of their own. 'It's time to act before locals are pushed out', the mayor told journalists. 'You get a bit of a nationality imbalance when one nation gets the upper hand', added a local proprietor. 'It's more pleasant when there are not too many people from one country in the same hotel' (no-one had ever complained in this way about the Germans, who otherwise predominated).[138] There were similar concerns at the Kempinski Grand Hôtel des Bains in St Moritz, where a spokesman explained that 'sometimes our European guests do not feel so comfortable if the hotel is full of Russian guests'. Russians had 'developed a reputation for being rude and intolerant of other guests'; their lavish parties had 'become notorious' and their 'flashy show of wealth' annoyed other clients.[139]

There were objections of the same kind in other resorts during the summer months. 'The place was crawling with them', reported a British tourist just back from a week's stay at a five-star hotel in Turkey, 'men in hideously tight Speedo trunks, women who looked about 16 and dressed like prostitutes'.[140] Surveys found that Russians were the least popular nationality on such occasions; they were demanding, often drunk, and (if they were women) overly flirtatious. Dutch agencies were already offering 'tours without Russians'; in the Maldives some hotels had stopped accepting bookings altogether, and in Egypt a hotel was reported to have sent its Russian guests to another restaurant to have their meals – at the request of their West European clients.[141] A small Tuscan town, Forte dei Marmi, found itself overwhelmed after Russian opera singers discovered the nearby Lago di Torre, where Puccini had lived; house prices were now the highest in the country and a new hotel had opened up, with columns of translucent marble, fittings of solid gold and crystal chandeliers. It was a 'real problem for us', explained the mayor, elected in 2007 on a platform of returning the town to its traditional way of life.[142] It was the conspicuous, even aggressive, consumption of the new Russians that was most resented. This was certainly the case along the Riviera coast, where Russians were drawn by its associations with their own noble families during the years before the October revolution. One of the Russian clients on the books of a Riviera estate agent 'refuse[d] to look at anything costing less than 120 million euros as a matter of pride'. Others were impatient to make changes, even in older properties of historic importance. One was so annoyed by the noise of the train nearby, another Riviera estate agent explained, that he 'sent someone to the *mairie* to offer them 100 million euros to move the station'. In Saint-Jean Cap Ferrat, another oligarch was told he was not allowed to raise the height of his villa as no building in the area could be higher than the lighthouse built during the time of Napoleon III; he responded by offering 15 million euros to raise the lighthouse.[143]

Not only the rich were 'new Russians', in the early postcommunist years: so were the poor. The new poor were often those with large families, who were hit disproportionately hard by the rising cost of bringing up children.[144] And they included increasing numbers who had lost their employment entirely. Nina from St Petersburg, for instance, just 19 years old, had no job and no money and was offering herself as a surrogate mother to foreign clients; so was Zhenya, with two children already, but with no job and no other means of support.[145] The poor included whole towns like Yuzha, 200 miles west of Moscow in the depressed Ivanovo region, where four out of every five were living below the poverty line in the late 1990s and many of the unemployed, elderly and sick were too poor to have regular meals. No-one in the Lipatova family, for instance, had eaten for three days. 'The fridge still works', they told a Western journalist, 'but it's no use; it's empty.'[146] It was a town, *Izvestiya* reported, where school pupils fainted with hunger; where old people looked for food in rubbish tips but rarely found anything because nothing was thrown out; and where there were never any mouldy rolls or decomposing meat as it had all been eaten. Children visited graveyards to collect the sweets that were sometimes left there, and looked forward to Easter when offerings were particularly abundant. There were few cars, leaving locals to make their way about town in the snow on bicycles; there was a children's library, but not a single restaurant in a town of more than 30,000. In the local hospital a doctor who had worked there since 1953 told *Izvestiya* that there had never before been so many lice-ridden patients, a result of malnutrition and the cost of admission to the public bathhouse. The spinning mill, which had been the main source of local employment, was working at just 20 per cent capacity because the supply of Uzbek cotton had dried up, although the coffin workshop had plenty to do with four deaths in the area for every live birth. A committee had been set up to help the starving, as in the famine of the early 1920s. 'It was better during the war', commented locals.[147]

Another letter came from Svetlana T., who lived in Yartsevo, a town of 60,000 not far from Smolensk. The town, she told the newspaper, was 'dead'. Almost all its factories had stopped working in 1993. To feed themselves and their families, the men of the locality had to go to Moscow, about 200 miles away, and look for work. They had tried striking and stopped the Moscow to Minsk railway, but no-one took any notice. It was cold; the gas company wanted payment before it would resume supply, and there was nothing to pay them with – the town's gas debts were already more than its annual fuel bill. Salaries were being paid in margarine or flour, even in bicycles. The local textile factory had gone bankrupt and been taken over by the municipality; it used to have 14,000 employees, now it had 1,200.[148] In a mining town in Rostov region, according to another report, four of the five shafts had closed; there was an excavator factory, but it was usually closed as well, and so were the cotton and the knitwear factory. All this would have been bad enough if those who were still in work had been paid regularly, but as late as October they were still waiting for their wages from the previous year. 'My family has forgotten the taste of sausage', the wife of one of the miners who was still working told journalists.[149]

In Ivanovo and Murmansk locals were supplementing their porridge with animal feed;[150] in Khakasiya, in western Siberia, more than 500 children were unable to go to school throughout the winter months because they had no shoes.[151]

The new poor included many others who were continuing to work, but who had not been paid for – sometimes – a very long time. This, as we have seen (p. 140), was one of the ways that inflationary pressures were contained, at least in the late 1990s; but it led to intolerable difficulties for many families. The armed forces shared many of these deprivations. Not all of its problems were new – the bullying of recruits, for instance, was of long standing; but its housing problems became more acute as thousands of troops returned from Eastern Europe, and as pay levels fell steadily behind the rise in prices. There were deaths from malnutrition;[152] others were being fed with dogfood – so bad, apparently, that dogs themselves refused to eat it;[153] and at least 20 per cent became 'chronically ill' as a result of overcrowding, poor dietary and hygiene standards, and low levels of competence in the army medical corps.[154] Substantial numbers of servicemen, unable to endure the conditions in which they were living, committed suicide (between three and four hundred – almost an entire battalion – were taking their own lives annually in the early years of the new century).[155] Others turned to 'commerce', including the illegal sale of arms and equipment.[156] The poor also included the homeless, about 4 million throughout the country,[157] and street urchins; there were 'at least half a million' of them in the late 1990s, and up to 100,000 in Moscow alone.[158] They could be found 'outside mainline stations, queuing at voluntary soup kitchens or huddling in doorways or empty basements'; hundreds died of exposure during the winter months, and hundreds more had to be treated for frostbite. 'To be homeless in Russia', reporters commented, 'amounts to a death sentence.'[159]

Pensioners, as in other countries, were among the most likely to suffer. Old-age pensions kept their value for most of the 1990s but fell sharply when the currency collapsed in 1998, and by the end of the decade they were worth no more than 76 per cent of the subsistence minimum (or 31 per cent of average earnings). Expressed in terms of foodstuffs, an average pension by this time was worth no more than half the meat and eggs, and a quarter of the milk and bread, that it would have purchased at the end of the Soviet period. The number of pensioners, meanwhile, had been increasing, to just over a quarter of the total population, and there were fewer people of working age to support them.[160] For many, clearly, life was simply unbearable. Mrs Romanova from the Kemerovo region sent President Yeltsin a letter in which she explained that she had not received a pension for three months, and was cold and hungry with no prospect of an improvement; so she collected a burial certificate from her housing manager, took a tablet and lay down to sleep. 'By morning it will be all over.'[161] Many, however, were 'afraid of dying'. A funeral, with bottles of alcohol for gravediggers and the entertainment for the mourners, was likely to cost three times the minimum monthly wage. Not only this: local authorities, at least in Moscow, were refusing to make land available; graves were being reused with increasing frequency, which carried a threat of plague and cholera; and cemeteries had become breeding grounds for rats.[162] 'Refuseniks' were another problem – those who declined to take on the expense of burying members of their family. They filled out a form to this effect, and then it was 'just a matter of a truck and the crematorium'. The number of burials of this kind was 'growing steadily' in the early 1990s; there were husbands and wives who had both filled out a form 'and then live[d] out the rest of their days in unbearable torment because of what they ha[d] done and because the same fate [would] befall each of them'.[163]

Levels of poverty were at their highest in 1992, as prices were allowed to find a new equilibrium. A third of the population – nearly 50 million people – had incomes below subsistence at this time, a proportion that slowly diminished; but more than 40 million were still below subsistence at the end of the decade, more than 29 per cent of the entire society.[164] Other calculations, less dependent on official methodologies, suggested still higher figures. For the sociologist Natal'ya Rimashevskaya, for instance, the poor were about 40 per cent of the total population at this time and about two-thirds of all children, and they were an increasing rather than diminishing proportion of the entire society. Poverty, moreover, had become self-reproducing: poorer parents were less able to provide an adequate upbringing for their children, including diet, healthcare and education, and this made it much more likely that their children would also be poor. In addition, there was 'fluid' poverty, based on a 'new poor' whose living standards were held down by low levels of pay in state-owned enterprises, and by unemployment and delays in the payment of salaries and pensions. At the very bottom was a stable stratum of 'social paupers', including beggars, the homeless, orphans, alcoholics, drug addicts and prostitutes. There had been social groups of this kind in the Soviet period, but they had been much less numerous and the government had made every effort to keep the differences between them to a minimum. Studies suggested that 'marginals' of this kind accounted for as much as 10 per cent of the entire population, and their chances of resuming a normal existence were exceedingly remote.[165]

Living standards suffered a further fall after the collapse of the currency in August 1998. Prices went sharply upwards; wages remained the same, or even fell; and a few lost everything as their firms went into liquidation.[166] Real incomes, accordingly, dropped by about a third;[167] even in Moscow 'almost half' fell below the poverty line,[168] and in a number of regions people were 'simply starving', with a diet that included cats and dogs, crows, jackdaws and pigeons.[169] In provincial Penza things were so desperate that a policeman held up and robbed a pedestrian so that he could get a decent meal.[170] The crisis had particularly alarming implications for Russia's emerging but still fragile middle class of professionals and entrepreneurs. The seriously rich kept their money abroad and had withdrawn much of the rest before their accounts were frozen. State employees were protected by their benefits in kind, such as access to subsidised meals at their place of work. But those who depended on wages and pensions were affected much more seriously, and the middle strata most of all: many had lost their savings, others had been thrown out of work and almost all had been traumatised by the loss of so much that

Table 5.3 **Living standards in the 2000s**

	2001	2002	2003	2004	2005	2006	2007	2008
Real money incomes (% y-o-y)	109	111	115	110	112	114	112	102
Index (1990=100)	53	59	68	75	85	96	108	110
Inequality: decile ratio	13.9	14.0	14.5	15.2	15.2	16.0	16.8	16.9
Inequality: Gini coefficient	.397	.397	.403	.409	.409	.416	.423	.423
Per cent below subsistence	27.5	24.6	20.3	17.6	17.7	15.2	13.3	13.1
Pensions as % of subsistence	90	100	102	106	98	100	102	115
Real value of pensions (% y-o-y)	121	116	105	106	110	105	105	118

Source: adapted from *Rossiiskii statisticheskii yezhegodnik 2009*, various pages.

they had taken for granted.[171] In September 1997, 50 per cent of Russians had characterised their economic position as 'bad or very bad'; a year later 67 per cent did so, and the proportion who thought their position was 'intolerable' had risen from 36 to 61 per cent.[172] Even government statisticians recorded 44 million living in poverty by this time; the national living standards centre, using a different methodology, identified 79 million (which was more than half the entire population), and three times as many were living in poverty, on these calculations, as in the last years of Soviet rule.[173]

These, admittedly, were the worst of the postcommunist years, and a considerable improvement had begun even before Putin took over the presidency as the price of oil moved sharply upwards on world markets (see Table 5.3). Real incomes, in particular, increased rapidly: from less than twice as much as subsistence (189 per cent) in 2000 to more than three times as much (325 per cent) by 2008, which was more than the levels that had been attained at the end of the Soviet period.[174] Average rates of pay were going up at the same time, even when inflation had been taken into account, which meant that the purchasing power of wages and salaries had also been increasing. An average salary, for instance, could buy more than twice as much meat, eggs, fish and bread, nearly twice as much milk, and more than three times as much fruit by the end of Putin's second presidential term as at the start of the decade.[175] But Russians, in any case, were spending less on food and rather more on services and consumer goods. There were far more private motor cars by the end of the Putin presidency than there had been at the beginning, and eight times as many personal computers, but there were fewer sewing machines, as more Russians went shopping for what they wanted.[176] The value of retail trade as a whole increased by up to 16 per cent a year, and more than doubled over the course of Putin's two presidential terms.[177] There was far more foreign travel, and more of it was tourism, which had also doubled over the same period. And even the poor were gaining. Income differentials widened, but not dramatically; pensions more than kept up with prices; and the proportion who were living in officially defined poverty fell by more than half.[178]

But more than 18 million were still living in poverty, on the same figures, and levels were particularly high in some of the southern areas in which (perhaps not coincidentally) there had been the greatest incidence of civil unrest. Only 12 per cent were living below subsistence in Moscow in the early years of the new century, but 38 per cent in Kalmykia, 33 per cent in Tyva and more than a quarter of the population of three other republics or regions.[179] Many of the poor were unemployed, but an increasing number of those who were in full-time employment were also poor because they had jobs whose salary levels had fallen, perhaps below subsistence, and who might not have been paid in any case. Families with two wage-earners and a couple of children had been well off in Soviet times; now one in five lived in poverty. Below them came a substantial group of beggars, homeless, street urchins and street prostitutes, some of them children, who had often been obliged to take up this occupation for economic reasons. All of these were the 'socially excluded', who had more or less given up the struggle for survival and had almost disappeared from official statistics, which saw only the 'visible part of the iceberg'. The poorest of all were often relatively young; some even had a higher education. The main reason for their situation was loss of employment, which was a consequence of the economic reforms, but they were also heavy users of alcohol and narcotics, and many had been recruited by criminal fraternities. There were already 'two Russias', separated by their way of life as much as their incomes, and the gap between them appeared to be widening.[180]

The onset of the international financial crisis in the later months of 2008 sharpened these divisions still further, and even the rich began to feel the pinch. Oligarchs started selling their Bentleys, now they were no longer a way of demonstrating their wealth but a 'means of redistributing liquidity'.[181] There were 'more shop assistants than customers' in the expensive boutiques on Red Square, and 'visibly fewer 4×4s and limos' blocking the roads.[182] In fashionable Rublevka there were price reductions, most of all in the alcohol department (even the rich had to find a way of 'relieving their economic stress'). Japanese whisky was particularly popular, apparently because of the belief that it could restore the body's natural balance in the same way as 'Oriental' medicines. All the same, customers went straight on to the chemist, to buy valerian and other drugs, not convinced that alcohol alone could resolve their problems. The only shop where there had been no reductions was the Lamborghini salon: 'after all', sales staff explained, 'at a time of economic instability the winner is the one who travels the fastest!'[183] Indeed government itself had to make economies: prices went up in the Duma restaurant, there were fewer foreign trips (no more than a 'person-delegation' was sent to the official celebration of the sixtieth anniversary of the establishment of NATO), and a moratorium was placed on orders for new furniture. The Kremlin apparatus was slimmed down, and recruitment of new staff was suspended; in the regions (for instance, in St Petersburg) salaries were actually reduced.[184] And when it came to holidays, even highly placed officials were 'making do with Turkey and Egypt' instead of more exotic destinations.[185]

The 'middle class' were also economising. It became a bit easier to find a table in a fashionable restaurant, and there was less of a queue for presents on St Valentine's Day.[186] But there was an increasingly brisk demand for goods that had passed their sell-by date,[187] and for advice about making savings of whatever kind ('eat more pickled cabbage', suggested one government agency when *Izvestiya* rang up to ask). The papers had their own suggestions, of a kind that grandmothers had handed down over the generations: how to wash windows without using detergent, how to spread garlic on black bread so that it smelt like sausage, and how to boil tea-leaves seven times before discarding them.[188] Sales staff found that customers were reducing their daily spend by a third, or even a half, leaving nothing at all for clothes and footwear;[189] across the whole society more than 70 per cent were cutting down their expenditure on food and other essentials.[190] Efforts were also being made to explore new forms of employment: such as walking the dog (and then washing its paws) for 150 roubles, or cleaning windows for 300 roubles, or tidying up whole apartments for 800–1,000 roubles ($28) a time.[191] Women found additional, female-specific ways of increasing their income, such as posing *toples* for pornographic websites, or advertising themselves as personal assistants who might be prepared to offer 'additional services' in the home or take on the duties of an 'intimate secretary'. Straightforward domestics would make clear that 'intimacy was not to be suggested'; others would typically 'consider any proposal'.[192]

At the other end of the spectrum, the onset of the crisis meant increasing numbers of unemployed, and increasing numbers who had difficulty surviving at all. Many more, for instance, were standing in line at soup kitchens – more than had stood there at any time since the collapse of the currency in 1998. And more of them were homeless, with all they owned in a plastic bag. Some were out of work because they had lost their papers, including their residence permit, without which they could not be legally employed. One of them was so desperate he forced his way into the office of the government ombudsman, Vladimir Lukin, where he was told the ombudsman was out of town – although he had just been seen walking into the building.[193] Another new development was the return of adopted children to the orphanages from which they had originally been taken: they were being 'handed back in droves' as the crisis deepened, more than 6,000 in 2008 and more than 10,000 in the first half of 2009.[194] Some were so upset by the change in their circumstances that they took their own lives – among them a restaurateur in Yekaterinburg whose outlets had been closing down; the acting head of the personnel department in the Gorky automobile works, who hanged himself in the toilet rather than approve a list of the members of the workforce that were to be made redundant; and a bus driver in Nizhnii Novgorod who found it impossible to keep up his bank repayments and shot himself, leaving a wife and two children. Much larger numbers were simply demoralised by the 'endless reports of crisis and the indeterminate predictions of analysts'.[195]

There were additional difficulties for those who lived in the countryside, who were often an older generation that had more need of a satisfactory medical service and public transport. Things, certainly, had hardly improved for Sasha Ivanovich, a villager in his fifties who lived near Orel in central Russia. He showed a Western journalist the bucket of muddy potatoes, dug from a snow-encrusted garden, that stood in his fetid kitchen; this was his lunch, and his supper too, as he had nothing else to eat. Everything had become more expensive. Bread had gone up; so had cigarettes; his sister paid his gas bill; he couldn't afford vodka. Perhaps the journalist could advance him a spare hundred roubles (about $3)? All the young people had left the area, and most of the older men had died. 'It was much better during Soviet times', added another resident, in her late seventies. 'Pensions were small but equal. We lived well. Now our pensions are nothing.' She had spent three decades working in the police, but now survived on handouts from her son.[196] A young Moscow journalist, Liza Surnacheva, did her best to survive on the daily 'subsistence minimum' in the spring of 2008. Meat, poultry and fish were beyond her means; all she could afford was 'soup selection', which was the bones that were left over after the flesh had been removed, or 'stew selection', which was 'much the same, with added skin and fat'. Elderly and more experienced shoppers, she found, went for damaged fruit and vegetables, and for offal – liver, kidneys and bones. The daily funds at her disposal would not have been enough for a cup of coffee in central Moscow.[197]

Izvestiya made its own inquiries in the summer of 2008. They found a single female pensioner from the same central Russian town as Sasha Ivanovich, Orel. Their interviewee, Lyudmila Aleksandrovna, had been living for fourteen years on the minimum pension, at this time 3,383 roubles (about $150) a month, and 'demonstrating every day that you can't live on a pension. You can only survive.'[198] Never mind, the postman told her as he delivered her new passbook, the monthly payment would soon be going up. But inflation would consume all of the increase, and in any case that was hardly the point: it was just demoralising, after forty-two years of working life, to depend so abjectly on government handouts. A hundred roubles went immediately into her piggy-bank for unexpected emergencies. Utilities took another 850 – light, heating and the telephone. There was free public transport, but she preferred to walk for the good of her health. Another 1,800 roubles went on foodstuffs; then 350 roubles had to be set aside for household cleaning and 300 roubles for medicines. Much of the time she spent walking round shops looking for bargains; she was one of those who joined a two-hour queue for 'social' sausage that was well past its sell-by date, with everyone assuring everyone else it was perfectly safe to eat. She had her hair cut at the hairdressing school, which was cheaper than anywhere else but with the 'constant danger' that the youthful trainees would snip off a bit of ear as well. Or she could go into town and look around, but with some embarrassment because of her worn-out clothing and ridiculously unfashionable shoes.

Then the pipes burst in her flat. Fortunately, she lived on the first floor. But the cost of the repair took a big slice out of the savings she had accumulated over the years she had worked as a cloakroom attendant in a local surgery; she would never make good the loss and cried for three days in a row. A qualified engineer, widowed with no children, she had already lost all the savings she had accumulated for her old age with the collapse of the currency in 1998. And what about the subsistence minimum in the first place? What kind of a 'norm' was it for a great power if it assumed a new coat once every ten years, a pair of shoes every 3.6 years and a new outfit every five? Elsewhere in Europe the same calculations included items like mobile phones and digital radios; in Russia, it was 133.7 kilos of flour a year, 239 litres of milk and 92.6 kilos of potatoes. Serious periodicals, like *Novyi mir* or the weekly *Ogonek*, were beyond her reach; all that remained was the local paper, distributed without charge but eulogising the governor on every page. Protests, whenever there was any attempt to organise them, had simply been ignored or broken up. Visiting the chemist, she was asked if she wanted cheap tablets or ones that would really help with her blood pressure; she had to ask for the cheap ones. In the end, she made it to the end of the month – with two apples in reserve. Incomes had certainly been going up, the paper explained, and so had the minimum wage, but pensions still lagged behind subsistence and all that was promised was that they would catch up 'in the next few years'.[199]

Income inequalities were difficult to measure in postcommunist Russia – the largest incomes were typically concealed, many had an income in kind from their allotment, and regional differences made it almost meaningless to compute a national 'average'.[200] It was still more difficult to compare incomes across time and space. Western societies, clearly, were much 'richer'. But a higher level of GDP was not necessarily the same thing as a higher level of human welfare. What about the costs of economic growth, such as pollution and overcrowding? And what about the distribution of living standards across a huge and very diverse expanse of territory? An alternative approach was pioneered by the UN-sponsored Human Development Index (HDI), first published in 1990, and intended to provide a more discriminating measure of wellbeing than monetary income alone. The Index included three key variables: GDP per head expressed in purchasing power parities, life expectancy at birth, and education (which combined adult literacy and total enrolment).[201] On these calculations, Russia emerged as a society with a 'high' level of development in the 2010 exercise, but it ranked no better than 65 out of a global total of 169 and well behind Norway, Australia and New Zealand (at the top), the United States (4), the United Kingdom (26) and even post-Soviet Estonia (34), all of which were 'very high'. These, of course, were all wealthier and often much wealthier societies, which meant that they could more easily afford the educational and medical provision that was reflected in their impressive HDI ratings. How did Russia compare with other countries that had similar resources at their disposal?

The evidence (Table 5.4) was that Russia was less successful at raising living standards, life expectancies and educational provision than other societies even when comparisons were restricted to societies that had a relatively similar level of economic development. There were of course many other countries that had also been less successful in generating a level of welfare that corresponded to their level of development: among them India, China and the United Kingdom. But there were others again that had a higher HDI than their GDP rank, including Spain, Japan and Ukraine. Indeed *all* the former Soviet republics outperformed their level of development, apart from Russia itself, and many did so by substantial margins. Russian GDP levels had been pushed up by oil wealth; but life expectancies remained low and these were an important constituent of its HDI, leaving it

Table 5.4 **Comparing societies, c.2010**

	HDI rank 2010	GDP rank less HDI rank	Gini coefficient (x100)	Life exp'y (yrs) 2010	% adult literacy 2005-8	GNI per head in $/PPP 2008
United States	4	+5	40.8	79.6	n.d.	47,094
Japan	11	+11	24.9	83.2	n.d.	34,692
Spain	20	+6	34.7	81.3	97.6	29,661
United Kingdom	26	−6	36.0	79.8	n.d.	35,087
Portugal	40	0	38.5	79.1	94.6	22,105
Russia	*65*	*−15*	*43.7*	*67.2*	*99.5*	*15,258*
Ukraine	69	+20	27.6	68.6	99.7	6,535
China	89	−4	41.5	73.5	93.7	7,258
India	119	−6	36.8	64.4	62.8	3,337

Notes: A ranking of 1–42 was defined as 'very high', 43–85 as 'high', 86–127 as 'medium' and 128–169 as 'low'. Countries whose human development rankings are better or worse than their GDP ranking have positive or negative signs respectively. Gini coefficients are scaled from 0 (absolute equality) to 100 (absolute equality). GNI is Gross National Income, calculated for World Bank purposes in a manner that minimises the effect of exchange rate fluctuations.
Source: adapted from the *Human Development Report 2010*, various pages, at www.undr.org, last accessed 2 December 2010.

below the level of the Latin American countries and well behind the member countries of the OECD. It was issues of this kind that arguably represented the greatest challenge to Russian policy-makers as the Putin presidency came to an end and the economic growth that had sustained all sections of the society became more difficult to sustain. As Putin himself acknowledged at one of his later press conferences, they had succeeded in restoring the country's territorial integrity, strengthening the political system and re-viving the economy, all of which had allowed them to resolve the 'main social problems'. But they had not yet resolved the 'most basic social problem', which was the 'inequality of incomes between different categories of our citizens'.[202]

Crime and punishment

There had been relatively little crime in the Soviet system, for reasons that were con-nected with its lack of a full range of civil liberties. Hooliganism, robbery, violence and corruption all existed, as *Izvestiya* explained, and on a significant scale. But crime was unable to gain enough momentum to compete with law enforcement. Money was influential, but not all-powerful. There were millionaires, but they were underground; there were gangs, but they had to take enormous risks to equip themselves with weap-ons.[203] In any case, there were relatively few rich people with objects of value in their homes; it was less easy than in the postcommunist years to leave the country or to send stolen goods abroad; and it was almost impossible to conceal the movement of large sums of money when the only banking system was operated by the state itself. Crime statistics were not reported until the late 1980s, when the party leadership decided to make them available;[204] the 1988 statistical yearbook contained a new section with a wealth of detailed information drawn from the files of the Ministry of Internal Affairs, but it also showed that overall rates of crime had been falling since the start of *perestroika* and that the most serious crimes, including murder or attempted murder, had been falling in parallel.[205] The 1961 Party Programme, still valid when Gorbachev came to power, claimed that with rising prosperity and a higher level of consciousness it would eventually be possible to 'eliminate crime' entirely and replace sentencing with forms of moral persuasion.[206]

The political and economic changes that took place at the start of the 1990s, in the event, 'swept away the dams of repression that had held back the potential for crime' and led to what *Izvestiya* described as a 'criminal revolution'.[207] Rates of recorded crime were already increasing in the late 1980s, and over the years of *perestroika* the number of cases more than doubled. There had been an almost continuous increase over a much longer period, with particularly sharp upturns in 1983 (when Andropov was conducting an organised campaign and crimes were more likely to be reported), in 1989 and in 1992. By this time reported crime was running at three times the level of the late 1970s; the real incidence was considerably higher, as only half of all victims bothered to inform the police.[208] There were further increases in the years that followed and new forms of crime began to emerge on a significant scale, including kidnapping, drug-running, contract killings and the pirating of computer software. Other crimes were less novel, but their form had changed: the incidence of arson, for instance, was much the same, but there were far greater losses of life and property, and the cases that occurred were much more likely to stem from the struggle for dominance among criminal groupings.[209] About a fifth of the working population, by this time, were estimated to be engaged in various forms of criminal or 'precriminal' activity;[210] and levels of recorded crime were expected to rise still further as the economically marginal increased in number (more than half of those who were sentenced in the late 1990s had no regular employment),[211] and as even more Russians turned to drink (more than a third of all crimes were committed 'in a state of intoxication').[212]

There were changes among the criminals as well as in the crimes they committed (the pattern over the decade is set out in Table 5.5). They were still overwhelmingly male (over 80 per cent at the end of the decade),[213] but their origins reflected a rather different society. In 1990 more than half of all offenders were workers, and just 17 per cent had 'no constant source of income'. By 2000, those who had 'no constant source of income' were the largest single category, accounting for almost 55 per cent of all those detained; and of these, about a tenth were unemployed. More than a fifth of all offenders had previous convictions, a proportion that increased substantially over the decade; the proportion

Table 5.5 **Recorded crime, 1990–2000 (thousands)**

	1990	1992	1994	1996	1998	2000
Total cases	1,840	2,761	2,633	2,625	2,582	2,952
Murder or attempted murder	16	23	32	29	30	32
Grievous bodily harm	41	54	68	53	45	50
Rape or attempted rape	15	14	14	11	9	8
Robbery (*grabezh*)	83	165	149	121	122	132
Theft (*krazha*)	913	1,651	1,315	1,208	1,143	1,310
Robbery with violence (*razboi*)	17	30	38	35	39	39
Drug-related offences	16	30	75	97	196	244
No. of offenders	897	1,149	1,442	1,618	1,482	1,741
No. of sentences	538	661	725	1,111	1,071	1,184

Source: as Table 5.1, pp. 273–4.

that were juveniles fell by the same extent, although their absolute numbers almost doubled. But there was a very large increase in the number of offences that were committed by groups, and particularly by organised groups: from 3,500 in 1990 to 36,000 by the end of the decade.[214] The death penalty was clearly no disincentive: more sentences of this kind were carried out than anywhere else in the world apart from China and Ukraine until it was suspended in 1996 as part of the process by which Russia became a member of the Council of Europe, whose rules did not allow it.[215] As in many other countries, the death penalty had substantial public support: a few (11 per cent in a 2007 survey) wanted to abolish it entirely and 31 per cent thought the moratorium should continue, but 40 per cent wanted to return to earlier practices and another 8 per cent thought the penalty should be applied even more widely.[216]

There were significant regional differences in the forms and levels of reported crime. Moscow, for instance, favoured shootings as the ultimate means of resolving differences, St Petersburg preferred bombs.[217] The Far East, Urals and north Caucasus were the parts of the country most heavily involved in the undeclared or illegal economy, according to the interior ministry, with more than half of all economic activity controlled by criminal groups; these included the resource-rich regions of Tyumen and Tatarstan, and the major ports. In the Volga basin, which was more agrarian and likely (in the Yeltsin years) to have a Communist local administration, the corresponding figure was less than 20 per cent. Overall, black marketeers, criminals and corrupt officials were estimated to control more than two-thirds of the natural resources and industrial potential of the whole country.[218] In terms of the number of reported crimes, several regions in the Far East had levels that were up to twice the national average, and these were also the areas with the highest levels of crime against the person as well as against property. The lowest levels – perhaps because the continuing insurgency in Chechnya made it difficult to collect any statistics of this kind – were in the northern Caucasus, as well as in Moscow (but not St Petersburg).[219] Most violent of all was Tyva, with a rate of murder and of other crimes against the person that was nearly five times the national average;[220] perhaps not coincidentally it was also the region with the lowest life expectancy – for urban males, just 49 years.[221]

The Far East, as these figures suggested, was an area of particular difficulty in the early postcommunist years, and four of its towns headed the list of urban areas in which there was a particularly high level of organised crime (Vladivostok, Nakhodka, Ussuriisk and Khabarovsk).[222] Across the whole region there were further forms of specialisation in the kinds of crime in which its population typically engaged and in the ethnic groups with which they were most closely associated. A high level of crime was related to a number of circumstances, among them the region's relative openness to the outside world with border crossings into China, a free economic zone, and several busy trading and fishing ports. This encouraged a substantial 'market of intimate services' centred around restaurants, massage parlours and casinos, extending in some cases to the export of prostitutes to nearby countries. There was also a substantial trade in illegal weapons, many of them supplied by the armed forces that were based in the region (local police found 150 depth charges in the boot of a car whose driver had simply been presented with them after a particularly good-natured drinking session on board one of the ships of the Pacific Fleet). There was a narcotics trade, in which the region had specialised since prerevolutionary times; Vladivostok connected the 'golden triangle' in South-East Asia with lucrative markets in Europe and the United States, and levels of addiction were themselves higher than in the parts of Asia from which the drugs originated. Other forms of organised crime were more characteristic of the country as a whole, such as the improper operations that had taken place in the privatisation of the fish-processing industry and the illegal export of capital through fictitious joint enterprises which brought together the interests of former state directors, the new *nomenklatura* and the largest criminal groupings.[223]

Russia, of course, was not alone in reporting an increase in crime, and in violent crime particularly. But levels of reported crime were already very high by international standards – almost twice as high in relation to population as in any of the other post-Soviet states,[224] and very high as compared with the major Western nations. There were more murders in Moscow, for instance, than in New York.[225] Indeed there were more murders in Russia in relation to its population numbers than in any other country in the world, apart from South Africa; there were three times as many as in the United States, often considered a violent society, and more than thirty times as many as in the United Kingdom.[226] Russia was also distinctive in the extent to which organised crime – loosely described as 'the mafia' – had 'permeated every pore of entrepreneurship and trade' and was 'dominating both legitimate and illegitimate economic sectors simultaneously',[227] including half the banks and 80 per cent of joint ventures with foreign capital, and perhaps 40 per cent of the economy as a whole (there were even higher estimates).[228] A particularly alarmist report prepared for the US Congress in the late 1990s warned that criminals had already seized power and that the whole country was on the way to becoming a mafia-dominated nuclear superpower with a government that was no longer in control (the Russian authorities themselves complained the report was insulting as well as inaccurate).[229] A Sicilian mayor, visiting the country the same year, was reminded of 'Italy after the Second World War'.[230]

Women were much less likely to engage in crime than their male counterparts, and they accounted for no more than 15 per cent of all offenders in the early years of the new century.[231] Women were particularly associated with certain forms of crime, such as the theft of personal or state property, abuse of office for private gain, consumer fraud, profiteering and the illegal sale of alcohol; they also accounted for a significant proportion of other forms of criminal activity that were less easy to identify, such as bribery.[232] Women were less likely to find themselves in court, given that they could often plead the necessity of looking after young children and had the use of 'powerful emotional arguments such as tears, a confession, and a promise not to do it again'.[233] Women, nonetheless, made up an increasing share of all offenders in the early postcommunist years,[234] and they were involved in several new developments including an increasing number of cases in which they were used as 'bait' by gangs of criminals. There were even some instances of 'outright emancipation' in which a woman herself assumed the leadership. A gang that had been responsible for seventeen murders in Moscow, for instance, had been under the command of a 'godmother' with a 'long criminal record', who directed twelve heavily armed associates; and women were also prominent in the drugs business, which was 'held in high esteem both by semi-literate women with many prior convictions and by ladies with a higher, frequently medical education' who had formerly been 'law-abiding citizens'.[235]

Contract murders were another new development. Until the 1990s they were something that Russians 'used to know about only from films about the Italian mafia';[236] but 'these days', commented *Izvestiya*, 'reports that a banker's Mercedes has been blown up, that a general director has been shot down in the entranceway to his home or that the entire family of a chief administrator has been slaughtered dot newspaper pages and fill the airwaves'. To begin with, the criminals were settling scores among each other, and simply reducing their own numbers. But then the chairman of a Council of Entrepreneurs became the victim of a contract murder, and there was a series of attempts on the lives of enterprise executives as well attacks on those who were attempting to uphold the law. Weapons, at the same time, had become more widely available, many of them in the hands of private security forces.[237] Nor was it only the influential or prosperous that were being targeted: at least in Moscow there were increasing numbers of attacks on single people or the mentally ill, and on small shopkeepers and out-of-towners. The going rate was from $2,000 upwards, but for a really important figure more than a million was necessary.[238] A professional killing, by the late 1990s, could be as easily arranged as 'say, a restaurant dinner',[239] and hitmen were advertising their services in the local press, seeking 'any kind of one-off dangerous work'; they could also be hired to conduct 'conversations' with reluctant debtors (the standard fee was between 10 and 20 per cent of the sum outstanding).[240]

Crime was particularly pervasive in the sale of property. There were murders, for instance, of the owners of privatised housing; there were several Moscow 'firms' that specialised in the buying and selling of apartments on this basis.[241] Alcoholics could also be persuaded to sell their newly privatised flats, or even abandon their children.[242] Elderly people, particularly those who lived alone, were at particular risk from semi-legal firms that pressured them into signing over their property.[243] In 1993 more than 30,000 elderly Muscovites had been persuaded to sell their flats; enquiries later revealed that nearly 2,000 of them had come to a violent end.[244] A gang in Yaroslavl', less than 200 miles from Moscow, was found in 1998 to have established an entire system of this kind. They made friends with local people, many of them drifters or alcoholics, and offered them work outside the city. Once they had signed a contract, they were lured to a property in the countryside and suffocated. The bodies were disposed of and the gang then took control of the flats by transferring ownership through a chain of middlemen, forging signatures from the victims' contracts. To avoid arousing the suspicions of relatives, the gang sent telegrams home on behalf of the murdered owners and drew their pensions; they also killed one of the informers who had tipped them off about their fifteenth victim, a priest. The gang was finally caught as its members were covering the bodies of the last of their victims with concrete.[245] There were further conflicts over the control of graveyards, which had become a lucrative form of private business.[246]

The sale of property to the workforce required a more complex operation. First of all retired workers would be visited on the pretext of distributing 'humanitarian aid', and for a symbolic sum of money or after a brief discussion would be 'persuaded' to part with their shares in the enterprise in which they had worked. The head of the personnel department would then be bribed or forced to provide a list of the current workforce, who would be visited systematically in the same way. The plant's managers would typically be offered 'advantageous terms of surrender', or if they failed to cooperate, threatened with physical force. The public auction of the shares was turned into a 'stage play with extras in place and roles assigned in advance'; then the sale itself took place, with a representative of the interested criminals in a prominent position in the hall and an entourage of thugs to assist the meeting in its deliberations. As much as 70 per cent of the real estate put up for auction in St Petersburg, in the early stages of privatisation, ended up in the hands of purchasers who had been identified in advance, and who were often mafia kingpins laundering the money they had obtained through other activities.[247] More generally, the black economy already accounted for about 40 per cent of GDP, and 80 per cent of the voting shares in privatised enterprises had apparently passed by the late 1990s into the hands of domestic or foreign criminals;[248] the level of recorded economic crime was still increasing, by more than 12 per cent a year, and criminal businesses of various kinds had established a 'parallel monetary system' consisting of dollars and a variety of surrogates that allowed them to escape state control entirely.[249]

Crime had also become more inventive. There were 'ambulancemen', for instance, who called at the front door to tell unsuspecting parents that their children had been involved in an accident. This was often enough to allow them to gain entrance to the family home, and then to take whatever they wanted; there were 'dozens' of such cases in the late 1990s.[250] There were body-snatchers, who called distraught relatives and offered to relieve them of a corpse for the relatively modest charge of a million roubles (about $70 at the time) and more promptly than the state's free collection service, which might take three days to arrive. The body-snatchers were mostly off-duty or former health department workers who bought up old ambulances and who found their opportunities when they were tipped off, for a percentage, by the police or by a doctor or nurse involved in registering the death. The typical fee, for health service workers, was the equivalent of an average month's salary.[251] The repair of motor vehicles, particularly if they were Western and expensive, was another means of potential enrichment; in a spectacular case in the summer of 1998 the staff of a back-street and apparently innocuous Moscow garage were arrested after police exhumed the bodies of ten victims from their workshop floor.[252] Crops were seized from the fields, forcing farmers to organise patrols (a pensioner who found a thief on his potato field at midnight simply opened fire, and others handed out punishment on the spot – what else could they do when the competent authorities were unable to help them?);[253] there were even cases of the theft of therapeutic mud from lakeside health resorts.[254]

Most serious crime was carried out by organised gangs, of which there were an estimated 3,000 in the late 1990s with a total 'staff' of about 60,000 – the equivalent of three fronts during the Second World War, in other words a 'real army'.[255] They had divided up the country into their respective spheres of influence and often had a wider network of international contacts. Many were based on a particular nationality, often from the Caucasus, and these were distinguished by their particularly high level of commitment. In Moscow they were most often Azerbaijani or Chechen, each group with its own specialisation: drugs and gambling in the case of the Azerbaijanis, oil and banking in the case of the Chechens; Armenians, by contrast, specialised in car theft and swindling, Dagestanis in rape, Georgians in robbery and hostage-taking, the Ingusheti in gold mining, weapons and precious metals.[256] Around the country there was a further specialisation into 'zones of influence': there were three main criminal gangs in St Petersburg, for instance, who among them controlled the entire city; in Krasnodar territory a Kemerovo group dominated the city of Novorossiisk, Abkhazians were in charge of Krasnodar itself, and an Omsk group commanded the coastline.[257] Gangs of this kind, moreover, were 'virtually uncatchable', as they had good connections within the police and local government; figures with a criminal record, indeed, were elected mayors in a number of Russian towns and cities, including the third largest, Nizhnii Novgorod, as part of what *Izvestiya* called a 'criminalisation of power'.[258]

Russian crime, in the early postcommunist years, was often conducted on an extravagant scale (after eleven people had been slaughtered in a single incident in Saratov, newspapers remarked that even Al Capone had never eliminated more than seven at a time).[259] And the whole of public life was affected. Several Duma deputies, for instance, were murdered.[260] General Lev Rokhlin, chairman of the Duma armed forces committee and chairman of the oppositional Movement for the Support of the Army, the Defence Industry and Military Science, was shot dead in the summer of 1998 in what was apparently a domestic disagreement.[261] An attempt was made to blow up the leader of the Party of Economic Freedom, Konstantin Borovoi, but he 'survived by a miracle'.[262] The prominent liberal politician, Galina Starovoitova, was less fortunate when she was shot dead in November 1998 in what appeared to be a political assassination.[263] There was a still higher level of fatalities among deputies' assistants, who had increased rapidly in number. Positions of this kind conveyed a number of advantages, including easy access to the building, and some were prepared to offer them for sale, for between $4,000 and $5,000 each; deputies, for their part, found that assistants with a criminal background were well informed and often in a position to 'get things done' when more conventional methods had proved unavailing. For these and other reasons, there were as many as 15,000 parliamentary assistants by the late 1990s (one deputy alone had 132),[264] and one of them was being killed every month.[265]

There were equally heavy losses among government officials and ministers. A deputy minister of justice was found 'lying in a pool of blood' after being attacked with a kitchen knife, with his breakfast on the table and his tea still warm.[266] Another minister was killed in a drunken brawl.[267] Valentin Tsvetkov, governor of gold-rich Magadan region in the Far East, was gunned down in the street in October 2002 as he made his way to the region's Moscow office.[268] The governor of the southern republic of Ingushetia, Yunusbek Yevkurov, was gravely wounded by a suicide bomber in June 2009, and two of his bodyguards were killed.[269] City leaders were also at risk: the mayor of a town in the Murmansk region was stabbed to death in December 2008;[270] the mayor of Vladikavkaz, in the northern Caucasus, was shot by a sniper at his own front door.[271] And so were judges: the 'first attack on the chairman of the court of a subject of the federation in the history of modern Russia' took place in November 2008, when the chief justice of Samara region was seriously wounded on her way to work.[272] There were still more numerous casualties in the economy, a reflection of the extent to which business and crime had become interconnected. Bankers were particularly vulnerable: in just three years in the mid-1990s more than a hundred lost their lives, including several chief executives.[273] There were fewer deaths in the early years of the new century, but there was a particularly high-profile victim in 2006, the first deputy chairman of the Central Bank, Andrei Kozlov, who had alienated powerful interests by closing dozens of banks accused of money laundering and other crimes.[274]

Journalists reported these and similar developments at some risk to their own lives. According to the International Committee to Protect Journalists, fifty-two of their number had been killed in Russia between January 1992 and January 2010, which made Russia the world's third most dangerous country for journalists after Iraq and Algeria.[275] Other, more inclusive, counts suggested at least 300 deaths or 'disappearances' over the same period, although not all of them were directly connected with the practice of journalism.[276] Perhaps the most notable was the assassination of one of the Kremlin's leading critics, Anna Politkovskaya, which made headlines all round the world when it took place in October 2006.[277] Much of Politkovskaya's reporting had been concerned with Chechnya, which suggested an obvious motivation for the attack, and the report on which she had been working made the explosive claim that the Chechen authorities had been guilty of torturing their opponents.[278] But she had been just as much of a public critic of the abuse of power by the federal authorities, including the armed forces, and it was not the first attempt that had been made to impede or even terminate her journalistic career.[279] For her supporters, it was clear she had been 'murdered for telling the truth';[280] Putin, who was in Germany at the time, promised that those who were guilty would be 'exposed and punished', but added slightingly that Politkovskaya's influence on the country's political life had been 'negligible'.[281] Four men were eventually charged with an association with the crime, but not the murder itself; they were all acquitted in early 2009,[282] and two years later nobody had yet been brought before a court of law, still less convicted, on a charge of ordering the assassination or carrying it out.

Politkovskaya's paper, *Novaya gazeta*, was almost the only one in the Putin years that took a critical view of the Kremlin and its activities. It was a paper, explained the head of its investigations department, that 'focuse[d] on all aspects of the misappropriation of power by public officials, and on displays of protectionism and corruption – particularly within law enforcement agencies, the public prosecutor's office, the special services, and the army'; it also reported on 'human rights abuses (notably in the North Caucasus) and on the repression of opposition'. The death of Politkovskaya, unfortunately, was 'by no means the first'. In 1994 one of the paper's special correspondents had travelled to North Ossetia to look into the detention of an officer held in a solitary-confinement cell for interrogation. The officer was released and it was acknowledged that his arrest had been illegal, but the correspondent died later of poisoning. In 2000, one of *Novaya gazeta*'s columnists was murdered at the entrance to his home in Moscow; he had been reporting on corruption in Lipetsk region. The following year one of the paper's freelance correspondents was killed in Chechnya. Yuri Shchekochikhin, the paper's deputy editor and a member of the Russian parliamentary commission on corruption, died suddenly in 2003 after receiving a number of death threats; a preliminary diagnosis suggested poisoning, but there was no official investigation. Matters were considerably worse in the regions, where local officials reacted 'far more ruthlessly than the federal authorities', and were 'prepared to kill to maintain their status'.[283]

In early 2009 it was the turn of a human rights lawyer, Stanislav Markelov, who was shot dead in the middle of the afternoon on a busy street in Moscow's city centre. Markelov worked, as Politkovskaya had done, for *Novaya gazeta*; the killer also shot a trainee journalist, employed by the same paper, who had been walking him to the metro and had tried to give chase when the killer opened fire, using a pistol with a silencer. As well as working as a journalist, Markelov had represented the family of a young Chechen woman who had been raped and then murdered in 2000 by a drunken Russian army colonel, Yuri Budanov, in a case that became a cause célèbre. Budanov had been given a ten-year sentence in the face of fierce opposition from his fellow officers and nationalists but had been released early, just a few days before the killing; Markelov had announced that he would be appealing against the decision to the Russian Supreme Court.[284] It was one of several violent deaths that appeared to have a connection with the continuing conflict in Chechnya. One of the Chechen President's most bitter rivals, a former member of the Duma, had been shot dead outside the British Embassy in central Moscow in September 2008;[285] another, a former Chechen insurgent who had turned against the President and been granted asylum in Austria, was gunned down in Vienna in January 2009;[286] yet another, the brother of the former Duma deputy, was shot dead in a Dubai car park in March 2009.[287] And another human rights campaigner lost her life in July 2009 when Natal'ya Estemirova was abducted from her home in the Chechen capital and left for dead on the other side of the Ingusheti border.[288]

Most gruesome of all were the cases of serial murder and even cannibalism that were reported in the early postcommunist years and into the first decade of the new century. The most spectacular was the 'Russian Ripper', Andrei Chikatilo, who was pronounced sane and sentenced to death in a court in Rostov in 1992.[289] A graduate of the local university and a former Communist Party member, Chikatilo had been suspected of child abuse while a schoolteacher but was allowed to leave quietly so as to preserve the reputation of the institutions in which he had worked. He was brought to trial in 1991 and accused of fifty-three murders over a twelve-year period, and of mutilating and occasionally eating parts of his victims (the balance of his mind had apparently been disturbed when his younger brother had been cannibalised during the Ukrainian famine of the 1930s, and he had difficulty sustaining normal sexual relations; the crucial breakthrough was when a local professor identified the psychological mechanisms that had led him and others like him to commit their appalling crimes).[290] Few were aware that another serial killer had been on trial at the same time in an adjoining courtroom; or that there had been ten serial killings in the region in the previous three years, a Russian and (apparently) world record.[291] There was another serial killer in Taganrog, with a taste for girls in black stockings;[292] yet another, arrested in 1997, had kept five women in an underground dungeon where he tortured and sexually abused them before forcing some of them to take part in the ritual murder of some of the others.[293]

Human flesh, indeed, was 'back on the menu' more generally. In Saratov, a watchman was arrested in 1994 after he had broken into a hospital morgue, stolen human remains that had been removed during surgery and sold them as meat in the local market.[294] Others carried out the surgery themselves. In 1997, an elderly woman was arrested after the half-eaten body of her husband was found in her flat. Two unpaid soldiers in the Far East were reported to have eaten one of their colleagues. And a 'quiet street sweeper with a keen interest in cookery and pets' was picked up in St Petersburg after an inspection of his flat and particularly of his kitchen revealed various parts of three of his friends (he urged arresting officers to take the buckets of human bones for stock 'so they wouldn't go to waste').[295] In the city of Novokuznetsk in Siberia, a mother, her son and daughter had combined to murder thirty women and then turn them into meat pies which they sold as snacks at street corners, making cannibals out of their unsuspecting customers.[296] And in a city in the Urals, a man was arrested as he left a shop where he had gone to get mayonnaise and meat cubes to use in preparing dinner from the dismembered body of an unfortunate guest that he had suspected of trying to molest his girlfriend.[297] Another case was reported from Kamchatka in 2008, in which a homeless man had recruited two friends to help chop up the body of his victim and fry parts of it to eat.[298] In St Petersburg, the following year, two young men – one of them a butcher with a history of mental disorder – were arrested on suspicion of killing a 16-year-old girl and eating parts of her body; in Samara, another young man who had killed his mother and begun to consume her when his money ran out had his sentence reduced by a judge, who accepted that he had simply 'needed to eat'.[299]

Another serial killer, a 'Nizhnii Novgorod Chikatilo' called Vladimir Zhukov, came before the courts in the summer of 2008. He had a good job in a communications company and lived with a partner and her child; but he became increasingly interested in violent crime against children through the pornographic films he watched on the Internet, and began to drive around the town picking up children who were walking by themselves and driving them off to a place they would not be disturbed. Finding himself accurately described by one of the children he had violated, he decided that in future he would kill his victims; it was one of his other victims, who had suffered three days of torture and sexual violence but managed to survive, who in the end was able to identify him. He was eventually accused of twenty-one crimes against fourteen different children in several different locations, of some of which the police had been unaware, and sentenced to life imprisonment.[300] An even more spectacular case was the 'chessboard killer', Alexander Pichushkin, so called because he had been aiming to carry out sixty-four murders, one for each square. Pichushkin was finally arrested in October 2007 and charged with forty-eight murders and three attempted murders; he claimed to have carried out sixty-three, which would have made him an even bigger serial killer than Chikatilo. Most of his murders had taken place in Bitsa Park, in the south-west of Moscow; he usually promised his victims some vodka if they would join him in mourning the death of his dog, and then threw them into a sewage pit when they were drunk.[301]

Levels of recorded crime remained relatively steady throughout the early years of the new century; the number of offences began to move upwards towards the end of Putin's second presidential term, but the number of offenders was still below the levels of the mid-1990s and so were the figures for murders and grievous bodily harm (Table 5.6). This still meant that Russian crime levels were among the highest in the industrialised world (see Table 5.7). Comparisons of this kind are notoriously problematic: different countries have different definitions, levels of crime can vary over time and across countries because of the assiduousness with which the police carry out their investigations, and in some

Table 5.6 Recorded crime, 2001–2008 (thousands)

	2001	2002	2003	2004	2005	2006	2007	2008
Total cases	2,968	2,526	2,756	2,894	3,555	3,855	3,583	3,210
Murder or attempted murder	34	32	32	29	31	28	22	20
Grievous bodily harm	56	59	57	57	58	51	47	45
Rape or attempted rape	8	8	8	9	9	9	7	6
Robbery	149	167	198	251	344	357	295	244
Theft	1273	927	1,151	1,277	1,573	1,677	1,567	1,326
Robbery with violence	45	47	49	55	64	60	45	35
Drug-related offences	242	190	182	150	175	212	231	233
No. of offenders	1,644	1,258	1,237	1,223	1,297	1,361	1,318	1,256
No. of sentences	1,244	859	774	794	879	901	929	925

Source: adapted from *Rossiiskii statisticheskii yezhegodnik 2009*, pp. 297, 300.

Table 5.7 Comparative crime rates, *c.*2010

	Homicides per 100,000 (2003–8)	Prison population per 100,000 (2009)	Death penalty abolished?	Global Peace Index rating, 2010
Russia	19.9	629	1999 de facto	143
Ukraine	7.4	323	1999	97
United States	5.6	756	No	85
India	3.7	33	No	128
United Kingdom	2.1	153	1965/1998	31
China	2.1	119	No	80
Portugal	1.8	104	1976	13
Spain	1.2	160	1995	25
Japan	0.5	63	No	3

Source: adapted from the 2010 *Human Development Report* at www.hdr.undp.org, last accessed 2 December 2010; Roy Walmsley, ed., *World Prison Population List*, 8th edn (London: King's College London International Centre for Prison Studies, 2009; the UK figures are for England and Wales); and the *Global Peace Index 2010* (Sydney: Institute of Economics and Peace, 2010), pp. 10–11, ranked from 1 (most peaceful) to 149 (least peaceful). The United Kingdom retained but did not apply the death penalty for a small number of crimes until 1998.

cases there may be strong cultural biases against recording certain types of crime (such as suicides) in the same categories that are employed elsewhere. All the same, the evidence suggested that there were only thirteen countries with higher levels of homicide in the first decade of the new century than Russia, all of them in Africa or Latin America and most of them affected by drug-trafficking or civil war, or indeed both of them (highest of all was Honduras, with 60.9 per hundred thousand). Russian rates of incarceration were also among the highest in the world, behind only the United States and then Rwanda, still powerfully affected by the aftermath of its civil war in the 1990s.[302] A more general 'global peace index' that combined a variety of measures of this kind put Russia in 143rd place out of 149 in 2010, reflecting the effects of the short-lived Georgian war and the risk of violent demonstrations of a secessionist or social nature as well as continuing high levels of homicide, violent crime and numbers in detention.[303]

Nor was there much prospect of an early improvement, if public attitudes were any guide.[304] There was certainly little confidence in the police, with just a quarter prepared to trust them (nearly three-quarters regarded the service with at least some degree of apprehension). And the police came no higher than third place when ordinary Russians were asked to say how they would defend their personal security, after family or friends and central state institutions. The police, for their part, began to take an increasingly 'commercial approach' to the exercise of their responsibilities, extracting an income from their 'only asset, their power', just as pensioners made ends meet by collecting and returning empty bottles. Ordinary people were most concerned by what they saw as the venality of the police and law enforcement in general (41 per cent), followed by their inability to exercise any control over such activities (37 per cent) and the 'insults and humiliation' they were obliged to suffer (34 per cent). In the Soviet period, law enforcement had at least been predictable, based on a well-understood relationship between government, enforcement agencies and the wider society. But in the postcommunist years there were new and better-resourced participants, including private companies and criminal groups. All of this made the entire business of law enforcement more uncertain, and it was the reason large numbers of ordinary Russians had not only a general level of concern about their personal security but were likely to see themselves as potential victims of the arbitrary behaviour of the state itself.

And they were right to do so, if press reports were at all representative. In a case that attracted a great deal of public attention, a drunken police major, Denis Yevsyukov, ran amok in a Moscow supermarket in April 2009 after a disagreement with his wife, killing three and wounding six more with a stolen pistol. 'Considering the state of affairs in the police force', commented *Izvestiya*, 'something of the kind was bound to happen sooner or later'.[305] In May of the same year, another Moscow policeman beat a pregnant woman to death; in June, a police captain in a Moscow suburb shot dead a junior officer in what appeared to be a romantic rivalry and a drunken police officer in St Petersburg beat a young woman to death; in July, a drunken inspector in Yuzhno-Sakhalinsk beat two students to death and a drunken police captain in Podolsk ran down and killed a pedestrian on a zebra crossing and then concealed himself (there were many similar reports).[306] Surveys found that the police were regarded as the most criminal of all Russia's professions, ahead of terrorists and drug dealers; and they were certainly among the most corrupt, with the most lucrative police jobs in Moscow changing hands for anything up to $1 million; the problems were so serious, and so deeply rooted, that newspapers, and even a Duma deputy, called for the entire service to be disbanded.[307] Putin, in his December 2009 'direct line', refused to accept that more than a million servicemen could be 'painted black' but promised that there would be a 'rapid and harsh' response whenever the law had been violated.[308]

Gender, politics and society

Women, the Soviet Constitution stated, had 'equal rights'. They had equal rights to training and remuneration; they were expected to take an equal part in social and political life; and 'special conditions' would allow them to combine these duties with the responsibilities of motherhood, including paid maternity leave and a gradual reduction in working hours for women with young children. Nearly all women, in fact, had a job, and women represented just over half the workforce. They predominated in traditionally female occupations like book-keeping and librarianship, but they also accounted for 60 per cent of engineers and nearly two-thirds of all doctors (as compared with 12 per cent in the USA), and even in the chemical and petrochemical industries they were as numerous as their male counterparts.[309] Women could retire at 55 (men only at 60, even though women lived longer). Women, moreover, were excluded from particularly arduous forms of employment such as night shifts and mining; they had the right to be transferred to lighter work during the later stages of pregnancy; and they were guaranteed nearly four months of maternity leave at full pay – or a year's unpaid leave, if they preferred – without losing their position or seniority. Women made up half of all the deputies to the elected soviets, and about a third of the seats in the national parliament; there were signs, as Gorbachev told the 27th Party Congress in 1986, that they were also being 'more actively promoted to leadership positions' at all levels of the state and party.[310]

Despite these achievements, it was widely recognised that a real and not simply a formal measure of equality had yet to be established. Women, for a start, were concentrated in less well remunerated positions, so that their average earnings were only two-thirds of those of their male counterparts.[311] Within each occupation, women were concentrated in less senior positions – they were 75 per cent of all schoolteachers in 1990, for instance, but just 39 per cent of secondary school directors; and they were just 6 per cent of factory directors.[312] The same was true of political life. Women had secured the right to vote in 1917, well ahead of other countries, and they had more seats in the USSR Supreme Soviet (as the authorities proudly claimed) than in 'any capitalist parliament'; but only one or two ministers were women, about 1 per cent of the total (in the government that was formed after the parliamentary elections in 1984, there were none at all).[313] Women, similarly, accounted for about a third of the membership of the CPSU but they were no more than 7 per cent of the delegates who attended the 28th Party Congress in 1990, 'the lowest figure for the postwar years';[314] they were just 8 per cent of the Central Committee it elected, and almost non-existent within the party leadership (only three women out of a total of 157 had ever been elected to the party's ruling

Politburo, and only six out of a total of 103 had ever been a member of its Secretariat).[315] The outcome, the Central Committee's commission on women and the family concluded, was the 'effective removal of women from decision-making' and a more general neglect of the 'energies and potential' they could bring to public life .[316]

Some of the shortcomings in official policies had already been identified in the late Soviet period. Zoya Pukhova, chair of the Soviet women's committee, pointed out that the USSR lagged behind many of the developing, not to speak of developed, countries in its attention to women's rights and called for 'more profundity' in the speeches of Gorbachev and other leaders on such matters.[317] As she told the 19th Party Conference in the summer of 1988, nearly 3.5 million women worked in conditions that contravened the labour law and 4 million were employed, supposedly on a voluntary basis, on night shifts (this was twice the number of men that were employed at such times). Women in the countryside worked from dawn until dusk without days off or holidays, and without proper social or medical support; it was hardly surprising that they aged prematurely. Wage rates were formally equal, but women's pay was actually less than that of men because of their concentration in less well-paid occupations at lower levels of seniority. The economic reforms had added to their difficulties, as enterprises that had become self-accounting were less willing to take on women with small children or grant them the shorter working day and longer holidays to which they were entitled. If economies had to be made, they were always the first to be dismissed; and if they tried to advance themselves in their career, they would be systematically disadvantaged (only 7 per cent of women with a college or higher education, as compared with 48 per cent of men, were in managerial positions).[318]

Women were also disadvantaged in the home environment. According to a representative study that was published in the 1970s, women undertook three-quarters of all housework by themselves and shared the rest with other family members;[319] according to another, women spent more of their time cooking than anything else, followed by housework, while men were most likely to be watching television.[320] A deputy culture minister presented more up-to-date evidence in a newspaper article in early 1989. Women, she reported, spent forty hours a week on domestic duties at this time, men just six. An average woman brought home 2.5 tonnes of shopping a year, and walked about 12 kilometres about the house every day in carrying out her domestic duties. This left, on average, just 17 minutes a day for the upbringing of her children.[321] Women, as Pukhova had noted, were also more likely to suffer from the changes that were taking place as the central planning system gave way to a new and more commercial environment. Women, for instance, were the first to be sacked when there were economic difficulties. Many of them worked in the textile industry, which began to contract when supplies of cotton from Central Asia dried up; many more were single parents, for whom a salary was normally their only source of income. Kindergartens, meanwhile, were being sold off, and children's clothes had become much more expensive. Women were working longer hours to maintain their earnings, or just to keep their jobs.

Fewer were taking training courses, and fewer still were going on to management positions.[322]

Inequalities of this kind were not new; but what was novel was a developing discussion on women's social roles that reflected Western feminist influence, and which was also a response to Gorbachev's somewhat old-fashioned approach to such matters. Addressing the 27th Party Congress in 1986, he called in wholly conventional terms for a shorter working week and longer periods of maternity leave in order to allow women to combine motherhood with employment.[323] In his book *Perestroika*, published the following year, Gorbachev was equally concerned to encourage the active involvement of women in working life and in politics; at the same time he insisted that more attention should be paid to women's 'specific rights and needs arising from their role as mother and home-maker, and their indispensable educational function as regards children'. While they were out working, women no longer had enough time to devote to their 'everyday duties at home – housework, the upbringing of children and the creation of a good family atmosphere'. Many social problems had their origin in the weakening of such responsibilities; there was also the danger of women working in strenuous occupations that were a danger to their health. All of this, in Gorbachev's view, had led quite properly to a discussion of 'what we should do to make it possible for women to return to their purely womanly mission'.[324] His speech to the Party Conference in 1988 called similarly for 'questions that directly affected the interests of women' – but not, apparently, more general issues – to be resolved with their direct participation.[325]

These were not necessarily the views of Soviet women themselves, more than 80 per cent of whom wanted to work even if there was no economic necessity for them to do so,[326] and perhaps the most distinctive element in the debate on the 'woman question' in the Gorbachev period was the cautious articulation of a specifically feminist perspective. An Irkutsk professor, for instance, asked why women party officials were always given secondary and unimportant posts. Why, in their society of supposedly equal opportunities, had they no Indira Gandhi or Margaret Thatcher? And why were there no new women's organisations or movements, as in other countries?[327] Despite 'male *perestroika* eloquence', another writer pointed out, it was women who had to deal with long queues, runaway price increases, poorly stocked chemists' shops and illegal night work. Again, wasn't it time for a 'really serious women's movement, with its own programme, its own ideas, its left and right, even its hecklers?'[328] A still more far-reaching discussion on the whole question of gender roles began with an article by three feminist academics in the party theoretical journal *Kommunist*. Earlier Soviet writings on the subject, they suggested, had been biologically determinist. Zakharova and her colleagues argued by contrast that the division of labour was cultural in character, and that this allowed for a freer and more egalitarian choice of occupational and domestic roles. Equally, the emancipation of women made no sense without the emancipation of men, involving them, for instance, to a greater extent in the care of their children and endowing them with 'paternity rights' as in the Scandinavian countries.[329]

The fall in female representation in the first largely competitive elections of 1989 led to a still more energetic discussion of women's social roles. It was already clear from the nomination of candidates that the proportion of women in the newly elected parliament would be lower than ever before. This, complained a feminist academic, was 'manocracy' – at any rate it could hardly be called democracy if the views of the women and young people who made up a majority of the population were systematically ignored. Nor was the party setting a good example, with the occasional nomination of women to senior positions no more than an 'alibi for men'.[330] The letters that flowed up to the Central Committee – about a third of them from women, who made up more than half of those who visited the reception offices in party headquarters[331] – reflected very similar concerns. Why, for instance, were there no women in Gorbachev's Presidential Council, established in 1990, when there were plenty of 'well-prepared, talented women' who could be put forward for such positions? Why could they not adopt the practice of foreign countries, in which many women were ministers and some headed the government itself?[332] Why were there only five women speakers at the 19th Party Conference in the summer of 1988 when there were 1,258 women delegates? Why had only one of those speakers given women's issues a 'political dimension'? Why were Soviet contraceptives 'roughly on a par with personal computers: rock bottom'? Why, in decision-making areas, could women 'raise their hands, but not their voices?'[333]

Party leaders were slow to respond to the pressure for change, but in March 1991 the Secretariat adopted a resolution – the first of its kind since 1929 – that called for women to be recruited in greater numbers into party ranks, and to be represented in the party's elected bodies in proportion to their share of the total membership. Work with women and their particular concerns must become an 'organic part of the work of the party as a whole'; special courses should be organised for the business and political leaders of the future; and 'contemporary ideologists of the women's movement' should be published as well as the classics of earlier years. At the same time, there should be an 'active dialogue' with the women's organisations that were beginning to emerge in the wider society.[334] Women themselves had several other suggestions to make. One was to return to the quota-based representation that had prevailed in earlier years, by which women were guaranteed a certain proportion of seats in all elected bodies.[335] 'The parliaments of some developed countries and a great many ruling parties set aside a guaranteed number of seats for women', it was explained; 'that is where the feminisation of world politics begins'.[336] Another view was that a specifically women's political party should be established;[337] steps were already being taken to set up an organisation of this kind in Leningrad, Moscow and Perm'.[338] Yet another was that a woman should be nominated as a candidate at the next presidential elections, taking their cue from the election of a woman president in Ireland and a woman prime minister in Norway.[339]

There was, in fact, no return to quota-based representation in the postcommunist period, and the special provision for women and their concerns that had appeared in the Soviet Constitution was replaced by a more general statement that men and women had 'equal rights and freedoms and equal opportunities for their realisation' (art. 19.3), and

Table 5.8 **Women in the Soviet/Russian legislature, 1974–2007**

	1974 USSR	1979 USSR	1984 USSR	1989 USSR	1990 RSFSR	1993 RF	1995 RF	1999 RF	2003 RF	2007 RF
Number	457	487	492	352	56	58	46	34	44	63
%	31.3	32.5	32.8	15.7	5.3	12.9	10.2	7.7	9.8	14.0

Sources: compiled from the following: for the 1974–84 Supreme Soviet, V. V. Stolyarov and
T. P. Zakharova, comps., *Verkhovnyi Sovet SSSR odinadtsatogo sozyva: statisticheskii sbornik*
(Moscow: Izvestiya sovetov narodnykh deputatov SSSR, 1984), various pages, average of both houses;
for the 1989 Congress of People's Deputies, *Pervyi S"ezd narodnykh deputatov SSSR: stenograficheskii
otchet*, vol. I (Moscow: Izdanie Verkhovnogo Soveta SSSR, 1989), p. 44; for the 1990 Russian Congress
of People's Deputies, *Pervyi S"ezd narodnykh deputatov RSFSR: stenograficheskii otchet* (Moscow:
Izvestiya, 1992), vol. I, p. 5 (based on the deputies that had been elected by the opening of the first
meeting; the number is inferred from the percentage reported); for the State Duma in 1993,
Gosudarstvennaya Duma Federal'nogo Sobraniya Rossiiskoi Federatsii vtorogo sozyva (Moscow:
Izdanie Gosudarstvennoi Dumy, 1996), p. 12; in 1995, *Rossiiskii statisticheskii yezhegodnik* [*RSYe*]
1996, p. 12; in 1999, *RSYe 2000*, p. 24; in 2003, *RSYe 2004*, p. 48; and in 2007, *RSYe 2008*, p. 55.

that motherhood, childhood and the family were 'protected by the state' (art. 38.1). In
these circumstances, female political representation continued to decline (Table 5.8).
Women accounted for just 13 per cent of seats in the new State Duma that was elected
in December 1993, well down on Soviet levels, and for a single seat among the 178 that
were filled in the upper house, the Federation Council; at the following election, in
December 1995, female political representation fell still further, to 10 per cent, in part
because Women of Russia had failed to win seats in the party-list section of the Duma,
although three of the candidates it had sponsored were successful in single-member
constituencies. In parallel, there was a 'dramatic drop' in the proportion of women in local
government: in the Moscow region, for instance, they made up 48 per cent of the deputies
that had been elected in 1987, but by 1992, in what was now a genuinely competitive
exercise, the proportion had fallen to less than 10 per cent.[340] This, clearly, was a long way
from the practice in the Scandinavian countries, where women were represented equally
with men in all bodies of state power, and well behind the levels that had been achieved in
many other industrial societies.[341]

Women were no better represented in the Russian government, even after two of
them had taken over the health and social development and economic development
portfolios in 2007 and another took over the ministry of agriculture in 2009. This
brought the female share of the cabinet of ministers up to nearly 12 per cent. But
women were still no more than 3 per cent of the federal government as a whole
(including the heads of federal agencies and committees as well as ministries) and
just over 9 per cent of the leading officials within the Presidential Administration.
Women increased their representation to 14 per cent in the Duma that was elected in
December 2007, but they were disproportionately concentrated in the committees on

Table 5.9 **Female political representation: Russia in comparative perspective**

	Human Devt rank 2010	Gender-Related Devt Index	Gender Empowerment Measure	Gender Inequality Index	Earnings ratio (%)	% seats in parl	% in govt
USA	4	19	18	37	62	17	24
Spain	20	9	11	14	52	34	44
UK	26	17	15	32	67	20	23
Portugal	40	28	19	21	60	28	13
Russia	*65*	*59*	*60*	*41*	*64*	*11*	*10*
Ukraine	69	69	86	44	59	8	4
China	89	75	72	38	68	21	9
India	119	114	n.d.	122	32	9	10

Source: adapted from www.hdr.undp.org, various pages, rankings or rounded percentages (n=169). Parliamentary representation is as of February 2009 and where there is an upper house is a weighted average of both chambers; the figures for women in government are for January 2008 and do not include prime ministers unless they held departmental portfolios. The 'gender-related development index' measures male–female inequalities in the three dimensions that contribute to the Human Development Index: life expectancy, literacy combined with educational enrolments, and earned incomes in purchasing power parities. The 'gender empowerment measure' is based on political participation and decision-making as measured by women's and men's shares of parliamentary seats; economic participation and decision-making as measured by men's and women's shares of positions as legislators, senior officials and managers, and of professional and technical positions; and power over economic resources as measured by men's and women's estimated earned incomes in purchasing power parities. The 'gender inequality index', introduced in 2010, measures 'gender disparities in reproductive health, empowerment and labour market participation'. These measures have not been universally accepted; see for instance 'Revisiting the Gender-Related Development Index (GDI) and Gender Empowerment Measure (GEM)', a special issue of the *Journal of Human Development and Capabilities*, vol. 7, no. 2 (July 2006).

motherhood and childhood or social policy, rather than the most powerful – such as the committees on taxation, security and constitutional legislation. And they were just 4 per cent of the membership of the upper house, the Federation Council. They were, in other words, still 'on the periphery of the political process'.[342] The same was true at other levels of government: there was just a single woman, for instance, among the eighty-odd heads of republics and regions (Valentina Matvienko in St Petersburg), and they made up no more than 11 per cent of the deputies that were elected to regional legislatures in 2007 (itself an increase).[343] It was, of course, close to a universal that women were politically under-represented, and their share of the Russian legislature was not much less than in countries with a 'very high' level of development such as Japan (12 per cent) or Ireland (15 per cent); but their scores were very much lower on crossnational measures of 'development' and 'empowerment', which provided a fuller picture of their representation in business and public life as well as national politics (Table 5.9).

The proportion of women deputies in the Russian legislature in the early years of the new century was certainly much lower than it had been in the Soviet period; but some effort was made, among the deputies elected for the first time in December 2007, to ensure that they would at least attract more public attention. One of the new deputies was Svetlana Khorkina, a 'leggy blonde who was a seven-time Olympic medal-winning athlete' and who had appeared nude in *Playboy* magazine. 'It's very good to be sexy', she told journalists. Svetlana Zhurova, a former Olympic speed-skating champion, had also stripped for a men's magazine, although any impropriety was avoided by the careful positioning of a pair of skiing boots. Alina Kabaeva, a 'curvaceous rhythmic gymnast' and just 24 years old, had been pictured semi-naked in a fur rug; Natal'ya Karpovich, a boxer and bodyguard before she entered politics, had also appeared in a magazine wearing only her gloves. And there was Svetlana Zakharova, the elegant principal ballerina of the Bolshoi.[344] There was a short-lived sensation in the early months of 2008 when rumours began to circulate that Putin would be divorcing his wife to marry the rhythmic gymnast, apparently impressed by the ease with which President Nicolas Sarkozy of France had been able to make the same kind of change in his domestic arrangements;[345] but nothing came of the story, and the offending newspaper was forced out of business shortly afterwards.[346] Ordinary Russians, apparently, wanted nothing more than a Putin–Kabaeva union; but when the gymnast was reported to have given birth to a son in 2009, commentators were quick to note that it did not have steely-blue eyes.[347]

The fall in female political representation took place against a background of social and economic change that affected women even more directly than their male counter-parts. Women, for a start, were badly affected by the 'feminisation of poverty'. Families with young children were in the most difficult position of all, especially those that were headed by a single mother (there were about 6 million such families in the early postcommunist years). Among single-parent families with children under the age of 6, more than half had incomes below the poverty line, as did nearly half the single-parent families with children under 16.[348] Women were less likely to be unemployed than men (p. 141), but they were a majority of the rural unemployed, they were a still larger proportion (60 per cent) of those who were registered with the federal employment service and receiving benefit, and it took them slightly longer to find a new job.[349] Women were still concentrated in certain occupations: they were just under 50 per cent of the labour force as a whole in the early years of the new century but 80 per cent of those who worked in education and the health service, 79 per cent of those who worked in hotels and restaurants, and 70 per cent of those who worked in the social services.[350] Women were still less well represented in more senior positions, which was one of the main reasons that their average earnings remained well below those of men; on some estimates they had dropped from about two-thirds to 45–50 per cent of the male average by the end of the 1990s, although official statistics (as in Table 5.9) suggested that the differences were very similar to those that were characteristic of other industrial societies.[351]

With economic difficulty came a wider deterioration in family life. Kindergartens, for instance, closed down, or charged the kinds of fees that put them beyond the reach of ordinary parents. The number of such institutions and the number of children attending them both fell by almost a half between 1990 and 2008; there were fewer children in the first place because of the fall in the birth-rate, but even so the proportion of the relevant age-group attending kindergarten fell from 66 to 59 per cent over the same period.[352] There was a parallel decline in the number of children attending summer camps, and the number attending residential establishments of the traditional kind, located outside the main urban areas, was down by more than a half.[353] There were more orphans than ever before (the number nearly trebled over the 1990s, although it was more or less stable thereafter), but fewer places in institutions that could accommodate them.[354] More children were becoming homeless for other reasons as well, as their parents found it impossible to maintain them or indeed to sustain a family home; and there was a 'new category of homeless', children whose parents were alcoholics who had been persuaded to sell their apartments and then 'disappear who knows where', leaving the children to their fate[355] (the figures were contested, but there was general agreement that the problem was worse than it had been during the postrevolutionary or post-war years).[356] There was also more crime against children than ever before, more than half a million cases of various kinds by 2008; more than a quarter of them involved violence, and nearly two thousand children lost their lives as a result.[357]

Fewer Russians were getting married in the postcommunist years than in the late Soviet period, although the numbers were slightly higher in the early years of the new century than they had been in the 1990s; divorce rates were more stable, but still rather higher than they had been in the Brezhnev years.[358] The birth-rate was higher in the Putin years than it had been during the 1990s, but still much lower than it had been during the Soviet period, while the death-rate was much higher.[359] This meant a continuing decline in population numbers from 1992 onwards, compensated less than before by the resettlement of Russian-speakers from other former Soviet republics.[360] The abortion rate, originally one of the highest in the world, had been falling for some time, but it was still not much less than the birth-rate, and every year there were more than a million terminations.[361] The infant mortality rate was coming down as well, but at 8.5 for every thousand live births, it was well above the average in the developed countries of the West.[362] The steady fall in population that resulted from these various circumstances was a backdrop to the entire pattern of postcommunist policy-making, and the attempt to reverse it became one of the 'national projects' in the early years of the new century (pp. 147–8); an entirely new 'strategy' was developed in an attempt to reverse it.[363] The projections, certainly, were not encouraging: on United Nations estimates, Russia's population could be expected to fall from 148 million in 1990 to as little as 100 million by 2050 (the 'medium variant' was 116 million). On any of these estimates, this would mean a population by the middle of the century that was less than that of Egypt, Bangladesh, Ethiopia and the Democratic Republic of the Congo, as well as other countries that had always been more populous.[364]

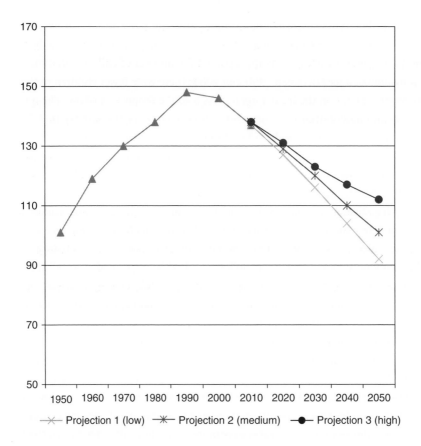

Figure 5.1 Russia's population projections, 1950–2050
Source: United Nations Population Division; millions.

Marriages themselves, moreover, were far from tranquil. In the early years of the new century, as many women lost their lives at the hand of a husband or partner every year as had lost their lives in the entire course of the Soviet war in Afghanistan (about 14,000), and levels of domestic violence were still higher: according to Amnesty International, one family in every four was affected.[365] The pop star Valeriya – 'Russia's Madonna' – attracted a great deal of attention when she wrote her own account of the years of brutality she had endured at the hands of her second husband, who beat her so regularly that 'bruises and cuts and broken fingers became a normal part of life'; he even tried to shoot her when she was pregnant with her second child. She was finally obliged to take her three children and seek refuge in her parents' one-bedroom flat hundreds of miles away, and only returned to the music scene when she met the man who became her third husband and manager.[366] There were many other accounts of this kind, some of them collected by foreign journalists. 'Irina', for instance, also had a husband who beat her regularly, but what could she do with three small children? She would never be able to remarry, and 'everyone around me told me it was competely normal' (she ended up in hospital with 'small tubes sticking out of [her] stomach and drips in [her] veins'). 'Lyudmila' was in hospital for about a month after a similar assault but found the police took no interest as they 'wouldn't get any bonuses for it'. 'Masha' from St Petersburg had a 'nice marriage', but her husband became increasingly violent, 'raped her like a piece of meat' in front of their two children and then forced her onto the streets until she became seriously ill and doctors referred her to a crisis centre.[367]

Sexual harassment was also increasing, as employers took advantage of their position. Lena, for instance, was delighted to get a job at a water plant in Murmansk until the division head started showing up at night to see if she was 'following instructions', and then to demand 'sexual services'. He was drunk, he stank and on every shift the same thing happened. In the end she had to go to the police. Women employees elsewhere were 'often forced to provide sexual services to a firm's clients and its bosses or [were] forced to have sex when they [came] to interview for a job'. In the 'kiosk business', where there were no laws and rarely any documents, sales staff were 'reduced to the status of concubines of medieval feudal lords'. Businesswomen had the same problems when it came to finalising a contract; 'sexual services' were sometimes demanded, in addition to payment, for the 'most ordinary commodities'.[368] There had always been problems of this kind; but with jobs hard to find and insecure, it had become much worse. One survey in the early years of the new century found that 71 per cent of those who were asked confirmed that sexual pestering took place at their own workplace.[369] And there was little prospect that any who sought to complain would be supported in the courts. One advertising executive who sued her boss for sexual harassment lost her case in 2008 after a judge ruled that employers were obliged to make overtures to female staff in order to ensure the survival of the species. 'If we had no sexual harassment we would have no children', he ruled. Only two women had ever won cases for sexual harassment since the demise of the Soviet Union, one in 1993 and the other in 1997.[370]

Another result of women's postcommunist 'emancipation' was a rising incidence of prostitution. Originally, in the Soviet period, it had been considered a phenomenon that was confined – at least in principle – to capitalism; but in the Gorbachev years its existence was openly acknowledged, and not just as an 'integral part of Moscow's tourist "service"'.[371] The problem took on new dimensions in the postcommunist period, and became increasingly closely associated with organised crime. It was estimated to be the third-largest sphere of criminal activity in terms of the amount of money involved, after gambling and the drugs business.[372] In Moscow, the city's smartest shopping street, Tverskaya, was also the busiest;[373] but, as the daily papers reported, 'for $200 you can have oral sex in the very centre of our motherland – on Red Square'.[374] It was a well-organised trade, worth $30–60 million a month in the early years of the new century, and offering the 'widest possible range of carnal pleasures to suit every taste and wallet'. The cheapest of all were 'station' and 'highway' prostitutes; more expensive and much more common were streetwalkers, who could be found in 'practically every borough of the city', the price depending on location and physical attributes. Streetwalkers worked with pimps, who collected money from clients and then paid off the police; some enterprising officers insisted, in addition, on a 'value-added' and even a 'profits tax'. Then there was 'individual soliciting', based on advertisements in the newspapers and the Internet, and 'sex salons', catering for mid-level businessmen and criminals, where prices varied widely and there were 'surcharges of $10 to $50 for non-traditional types of sex'. At the top end of the market was 'VIP-class prostitution', which was 'over-priced and rather exclusive' but untroubled by the police because of its high-level protection.[375]

As in other societies, there was male as well as female prostitution. Many advertised their services in local papers: 'Sympathetic young man, 16, will place his well-built body in the lustful hands of a woman up to 40. Your every fantasy will become a reality'; or 'Blue-eyed blond, twenty, wants to be the sex toy of an older woman (or two)'; or 'Man, 22, seeks a well-off virgin who would like to become a woman and is in a position to pay for her education'. A suitable candidate, it emerged, would be well dressed, clean-shaven, sweet-smelling and in good physical form, and of course 'his organ must always be in good working order'. Yelena, for instance, was a businesswoman who had divorced a first husband, and lost a second; but a woman had to be 'physiologically satisfied'. So she engaged Vladimir, ten years younger, and treated him as a 'stern mistress'. Irina had parted from her husband, who 'drank like a swine', but she was bringing up a teenager and could afford to engage a lover only once a week. Vera had lost both her legs, but her parents – at what cost she had no idea – had engaged Valerii, a 'high-class professional'. Now she always looked forward to Thursday – 'Valerii day'. Although a relative novelty in Russia, male prostitution of this kind was apparently 'growing more quickly than in other countries'.[376] And it catered for every preference. It was, for instance, a regular practice in the Russian army, according to press reports, with young recruits sent out on the streets to solicit business or delivered to high-ranking clients, including retired generals, and beaten if they refused; there was even a price-list on the Internet that showed the cost of their various 'services'.[377]

And there was under-age prostitution. Sveta, for instance, was just 9 years old and had been abandoned by her mother. A car used to come for her every week and she would spend two or three days at a Moscow address, where several young girls would '"serve" five or six men'. By the mid-1990s this was a 'real social phenomenon, not something out of the ordinary', involving perhaps 20,000 cases a year.[378] The Komsomol newspaper talked to another girl, just out of sixth grade, who was involved in work of this kind, but just with Germans, British and Americans ('I can't stand the smell of Arabs, Negroes or Poles: I'd rather lie under a train than under those guys'). She sometimes obliged Russians, but just 'once in a while'. Many of these unfortunates were picked up at train stations; some were abducted; and some were bought from their parents, who were often alcoholics.[379] There had traditionally been a lot of demand at Black Sea coastal resorts as well as in the cities, but business declined sharply because of the war in Chechnya and the girls had to go elsewhere, some to Moscow, some to St Petersburg and others to Odessa ('there are no punters at all because of that damned war', Lucy, a 'long-legged blonde from Kislovodsk', complained to *Argumenty i fakty*).[380] Prostitution was, however, a 'part of everyday life for most homeless children', whose numbers had been increasing rapidly in the early years of the new century;[381] the Ministry of the Interior estimated that about 17,000 children were engaged in some form of prostitution at this time, but other estimates were much higher – in Moscow alone as many as 50,000.[382]

Prostitution was also a thriving export trade. Using marriage agencies as a cover, girls with 'good physical attributes' were being offered highly paid work abroad, including the opportunity to find a foreign husband or become a photographer's model. At first they went to Yugoslavia, but there was a risk of 'ending up as a slave for some military unit'; more preferred Budapest, in spite of 'fierce competition from the Romanians', because of the large number of Germans from the former GDR who came there on sex tours. The first 'ladies of the night' had gone to Israel, where language was not a problem, and to Greece, because of its easy-going passport regime; they also went to China, where they started as waitresses and were then required to 'entertain the guests'. Russian girls were 'very popular among the hot-blooded Turks', who were also popular with 'our Natashas';[383] 'new Russians', they complained, were 'almost all impotent' because of the 'nervous nature of their business'.[384] The 'richest and most attractive country' was Germany, where Russians were 'creating some serious competition for girls from Eastern Europe', although 'top-quality' girls also went to Sweden, where they worked in expensive hotels and restaurants.[385] Russians were travelling to Asia as well, in the late 1990s, encouraged by lax immigration regimes and corrupt officials; and they were popular with locals, who found they were unusually accommodating: 'in fact', a Colombo businessman told Western journalists, 'they'll do anything'.[386]

Inevitably, there was a price to pay in public health as well as moral terms. Levels of syphilis, in particular, increased spectacularly. There were five new cases in 1990 for every 100,000 Russians; by 2008 there were sixty, although the rate had been declining for some years. So had the rate of gonorrhoeal infection.[387] But the incidence of HIV/AIDS was still increasing in the early years of the new century, with considerable implications for future population numbers, economic performance and social stability.[388] The first officially acknowledged case of HIV infection was in 1987, and the first known AIDS death, of a woman sex worker, was in 1988.[389] Newly diagnosed cases reached a peak in 2001 and then declined, but the total numbers registered with the authorities continued to increase, up more than 300,000 in 2008,[390] and independent estimates suggested that as many as 1.5 million might have become HIV-positive by the end of the decade.[391] This meant that the incidence of infection, in Russia and the other post-Soviet republics, was among the highest in the world outside sub-Saharan Africa.[392] A high rate of HIV infection in turn pushed up the incidence of tuberculosis and other illnesses that took advantage of deficiencies in the immune system; Russian rates were also much higher than in other developed countries in the early years of the new century, at 150 per 100,000 (the US figure was 3, the UK figure 11).[393] Public health issues of all kinds were compounded by deepening social inequalities and chronic underfunding of the state services that had provided some measure of protection in the past.

The whole question of the role of women and public morality was debated in the Duma in the spring of 1997, in the form of a bill that sought to restrict the sale of sex products to a number of specially licensed shops. There were over 4,000 illegal brothels in Moscow alone, deputies were told; sales of sexual products were running at $5 million a month, and about a thousand pornographic journals were in circulation. At the same time the nation's 'golden genetic pool' was being exported to the sex markets of the West. Vladimir Zhirinovsky, always inventive, suggested a different approach: after all, things were 'much calmer' on a nudist beach than on an ordinary one. Often, he pointed out, 'when certain parts are covered, you start to think what might be hidden there'. Wasn't it all a matter of sex education? Or take Russia's Muslim regions; women were covered from head to foot, and 'there's no sex'. As for the charge that there had been 'no sex under the Communists', on the contrary, pointed out a deputy from the other end of the political spectrum, Al'bert Makashov, 'I have three children and five grandchildren already, and we get along fine without your pornography.'[394] Clearly, there would be no early solution to a set of problems that existed in all industrial societies, and which in Russia had become entangled with a number of much more specific difficulties associated with organised crime, uncertain living standards and a loss of moral bearings. It was equally clear that there would be no resolution of such matters until women began to advance their own agenda and press for a more equitable relationship with the wider society than others had yet handed down to them.[395]

Further reading

The widening divisions of the 1990s are considered in Silverman and Yanowitch (2000), and for the Putin years in Pirani (2010). On the 'oligarchs' see, for instance, Klebnikov (2000), Hoffman (2001) and Fortescue (2006). At the other end of the social spectrum, there are good studies of homelessness in Stephenson (2006) and Höjdestrand (2009). On crime, see particularly Volkov (2002) and Rawlinson (2010). Recent studies of the 'woman question' include Hemment (2007), Salmenniemi (2009) and Johnson (2009); Sperling (1999) remains influential. Comprehensive data on social questions of all kinds, including demography, income distribution and crime, are available in English at the website of the State Statistical Committee www.gks.ru/eng.

Fortescue, Stephen, *Russia's Oil Barons and Metal Magnates: Oligarchs and the State in Transition* (Basingstoke and New York: Palgrave Macmillan, 2006).

Hemment, Julie, *Empowering Women in Russia: Activism, Aid, and NGOs* (Bloomington: Indiana University Press, 2007).

Hoffman, David E., *The Oligarchs: Wealth and Power in the New Russia* (New York and Oxford: Public Affairs, 2001).

Höjdestrand, Tova, *Needed by Nobody: Homelessness and Humanness in Post-Socialist Russia* (Ithaca, NY: Cornell University Press, 2009).

Johnson, Janet Elise, *Gender Violence in Russia: The Politics of Feminist Intervention* (Bloomington: Indiana University Press, 2009).

Klebnikov, Paul, *Godfather of the Kremlin: Boris Berezovsky and the Looting of Russia* (New York and London: Harcourt, 2000).

Pirani, Simon, *Change in Putin's Russia: Power, Money and People* (London: Pluto, 2010).

Rawlinson, Paddy, *From Fear to Fraternity: A Russian Tale of Crime, Economy and Modernity* (London: Pluto, 2010).

Salmenniemi, Suvi, *Democratization and Gender in Contemporary Russia* (Abingdon and New York: Routledge, 2009).

Silverman, Bertram, and Murray Yanowitch, *New Rich, New Poor, New Russia: Winners and Losers on the Russian Road to Capitalism* (Armonk, NY: Sharpe, 1997; expanded edn, 2000).

Sperling, Valerie, *Organizing Women in Contemporary Russia: Engendering Transition* (Cambridge and New York: Cambridge University Press, 1999).

Stephenson, Svetlana, *Crossing the Line: Vagrancy, Homelessness and Social Displacement in Russia* (Aldershot and Burlington, VT: Ashgate, 2006).

Volkov, Vadim, *Violent Entrepreneurs: The Use of Force in the Making of Russian Capitalism* (Ithaca, NY: Cornell University Press, 2002).

6 Changing times, changing values

Members of the Holy Synod of the Russian Orthodox Church, 2008 (Novosti)

The Soviet Union had eventually established a public opinion research centre, and it was one of the most important of the variety of agencies that followed the public mood in the early years of the new century. It was generally economic issues that mattered most to ordinary Russians, and there was considerable support for many of the principles that had informed the Soviet system in the past, including its provision of full employment and comprehensive social welfare. Letters to the newspapers were another form of communication with the mass of the society that continued into the postcommunist period, and the authorities themselves placed an increasing emphasis on forms of interaction of this kind, in digital as well as more traditional forms. The postcommunist period had also seen the various churches take an increasingly prominent part in public life; but religious beliefs were vague and internally contradictory, and they had little direct effect on political allegiances.

Just as the Soviet Union – or so its citizens told Western television – 'had no sex', it also had no 'public opinion'. Social consciousness, in the official view, was a reflection of forms of property; in a socialist society, based on public ownership, it was characterised by the 'dominance of Marxist-Leninist ideology in every aspect of the spiritual life of citizens'.[1] In a society of this kind, there was 'sociopolitical and ideological unity', and the views of workers, collective farmers and members of the intelligentsia were 'identical on the basic questions of social development'.[2] It was a unity, moreover, that extended across the nationalities as well as the social groups, genders and generations. Nationalism, the official view insisted, was a 'bourgeois ideology' that developed under capitalism, whose purpose was to set worker against worker.[3] Under Soviet conditions it had been superseded by 'socialist patriotism', a set of beliefs that included 'boundless love for the socialist homeland, a commitment to the revolutionary transformation of society [and] the cause of communism', and by a 'proletarian internationalism' that brought together the peoples of the USSR and of other countries, particularly those under communist rule.[4] All were entitled to express their views; but there were no differences of opinion, and certainly no fundamental differences of interest, that could not be reconciled through the leadership of a broadly based Communist Party.[5]

There could clearly be little scope, in these circumstances, for Soviet social scientists to explore any of the issues that might have exposed the limitations of this basic unity. A centre for the study of public opinion had been established as early as 1960 by a Moscow University philosophy graduate, Boris Grushin, under the auspices of the youth newspaper *Komsomol'skaya pravda*. Taking advantage of the paper's enormous circulation, Grushin and his colleagues used its pages to distribute a series of questionnaires and then publish analyses of their findings. The questions ranged widely, from the causes of war to the best use of free time; patriotism and collectivism were represented among the responses, but so too were alcoholism and delinquency, and there was not a single issue on which there was a uniform opinion.[6] In 1967, however, the newspaper was obliged to close down its operations, and although Grushin was able to establish another centre within the Academy of Sciences, it survived for just a couple of years.[7] Official policies were hardening by this time, in the aftermath of the suppression of the Prague Spring, and the study of public opinion was 'effectively banned';[8] the sociology institute attached to the Academy of Sciences came under heavy pressure, and a hardline director was imposed to restore orthodoxy.[9] Yuri Levada, a Moscow University professor who had published a two-volume set of sociology lectures, was attacked in the party's theoretical journal and forced to resign his position; Grushin himself found it impossible to publish the results of the surveys he had conducted in the Taganrog area in the late 1960s and had four manuscripts rejected by Soviet publishing houses between 1967 and 1981. When he took his study entitled *Soviet Society in Public Opinion Polls* to one of them, the response was 'Are you crazy or what?'[10]

In spite of these restrictions, there were still some indications in officially sanctioned publications that party and people were not quite as 'closely united' as the slogans insisted. Grushin's study of the Taganrog area, for instance, was finally published in 1980, although it had to have a co-author from the Central Committee apparatus. Entitled *Mass Information in a Soviet Industrial Town*, it was able to identify a number of shortcomings in the regime's self-image, including a considerable disparity between the mostly negative letters that local newspapers received and the mostly positive articles they published.[11] A legal scholar, Rafael' Safarov, was able to undertake a parallel investigation of the relationship between citizens and local government, based on surveys in Moscow and the nearby city of Kalinin (present-day Tver). Safarov found that the existing forms through which public opinion could influence public decisions were 'not always effective'; members of the public were much less likely than officials themselves to suggest that government decisions took public opinion into account, and nearly a third reported that the decisions that were taken locally were often at odds with the preferences of those who actually lived there.[12] Workers, similarly, were supposed to be the 'masters of production'; but as empirical inquiries established, they were often reluctant to play a part in the management, or even the discussion, of enterprise affairs.[13] For attentive readers, it was clear that there were many tensions of this kind between official orthodoxies and the world in which they actually lived; indeed, it was for this reason that wits demanded an 'ear and eye' hospital, as they 'heard one thing, but saw something completely different'.

Not even the Soviet system, in fact, could operate in an informational vacuum. Local organisations of the Communist Party had been conducting their own inquiries, in some cases since the mid-1960s,[14] and there were repeated calls for a centre or institute that could conduct investigations of this kind on a more systematic basis.[15] In 1986, in his first address to a party congress, Gorbachev pointed out that no laws had yet been drafted to provide for the nationwide discussions that were mentioned in the Constitution, and he went on to urge that better use be made of all the means that were available for 'eliciting public opinion and quickly and sensitively responding to the people's needs and attitudes'.[16] *Perestroika*, he insisted, could only succeed if ordinary people were persuaded to identify with it; equally, public policy would only be soundly based if it took account of the realities of daily life, and not just abstract principles. The party leadership, indeed, began to call directly for the 'use of sociological research in the practice of decision-making', and for a public that was 'better informed about the main questions of social development'.[17] Public opinion had certainly become legitimate by the late 1980s – official sources insisted that its role was already 'difficult to overestimate'[18] – and an infrastructure had been established for its study that was expanded very much further in the postcommunist period. What, so far as these methods could establish them, were the concerns of ordinary Russians over a turbulent couple of decades in which their country had undergone a fundamental change in its forms of ownership and political management?

Public opinion and its study

The Communist Party had committed itself to a national public opinion centre as early as 1983, when a plenary meeting of the Central Committee agreed that a 'feedback mechanism' was needed of a kind that would allow the party to take account of changes in the public mood. It was time, officials insisted, to move from individual, ad hoc inquiries to a broader framework, perhaps even the 'organisation of a centre for the study of public opinion'. The resolution that was adopted went still further, providing for the establishment of an 'all-union centre for the study of public opinion' that would be located within the Institute of Sociology of the Academy of Sciences.[19] Gorbachev, at an early stage, had identified the need for a closer and more interactive relationship with the society over which he ruled. How, he asked a group of writers in June 1986, could they monitor their own activities? The answer was 'most of all through *glasnost*", but also through a 'responsible opposition' of the kind that existed in parliamentary democracies.[20] Speaking to the 19th Party Conference in 1988, Gorbachev pointed to the need, under conditions of single-party rule, for a 'constantly operating mechanism for the comparing of opinions, of criticism and self-criticism in the party and in society', or in other words a 'permanent and constructive political dialogue' of a kind that would involve the 'study and taking account of public opinion', and he reminded delegates of the damage that had been done in environmental and other matters when proposals had gone ahead without the 'broadest possible consultation'. No-one, the Conference acknowledged in its resolutions, could have a 'monopoly on truth'.[21]

A national public opinion centre had already been established the previous year, under the direction of the sociologist Tat'yana Zaslavskaya.[22] The Centre, in the first instance, was concerned with the study of public attitudes on 'social and economic issues', and it was sponsored by the All-Union Council of Trade Unions as well as the State Committee on Labour and Social Questions. The purpose of its work, Zaslavskaya explained in an interview in March 1988, was to 'provide the most accurate possible advice to the organisations that are responsible for making decisions'. The decisions themselves might often be well founded. But were they transmitted in their original form to those who would have to carry them out? And what did the broader public think of them?[23] The Centre's first survey, on the election of managers by the workforce, was published shortly afterwards,[24] and its bulletin, 'Public Opinion in Figures', began to appear in 1989. The Centre – better known by its Russian initials VTsIOM – soon built up a Moscow staff of about a hundred, with regional offices elsewhere in Russia or the other republics, and by the late 1990s it was interviewing nearly a quarter of a million of its fellow-citizens every year in more than 170 nationally representative surveys as well as exercises of a more commercial character.[25] Its findings were not always welcome in the Kremlin, which in effect took it over in 2003, but the original staff were able to continue their work as the Levada Centre, taking the name of the inspirational figure who had directed its work from 1992 up to his death – at his desk in the Centre itself – in 2006.[26]

VTsIOM was soon followed by other services. They included Vox Populi, established two years later by Boris Grushin, who had been the All-Union Centre's first deputy director;[27] it was best known for its 'political Olympus', a league table of the 100 most influential politicians based on the judgements of well-placed commentators, and normally published in the newspaper *Nezavisimaya gazeta*. Its work was continued in later years by another body, the Agency for Political and Economic Communications, with results that appeared in the same paper. It was Vladimir Putin who generally led the ratings throughout the first decade of the new century, even after he had stepped down from the presidency; he was followed by Dmitri Medvedev, and then by Finance Minister Aleksei Kudrin and Deputy Prime Minister Igor Sechin. As well as leading state officials, the list of the country's twenty most influential politicians in the early months of 2010 included the newly elected Patriarch of the Orthodox Church and three leading businessmen – Gazprom chief executive Aleksei Miller, Alisher Usmanov of Metallinvest and Oleg Deripaska (his fellow oligarch Roman Abramovich was in the top twenty-five).[28] The Public Opinion Foundation also emerged from within VTsIOM, in 1992; it remained close to the Kremlin but also carried out commissions for government ministries and the larger corporations, and issued a regular bulletin as well as occasional collections of its findings on particular subjects (such as Russian attitudes towards the United States before and after 9/11).[29]

Surveys were the best way of establishing the distribution of opinion across a heterogeneous and changing society; but, in part because the society was changing so rapidly and because there was still some reluctance to express views on public issues (or even, with the increase in crime, to open the front door),[30] they were often ambiguous and – at least initially – a poor guide to future behaviour ('Why', asked *Segodnya* after the December 1995 election results were announced, 'does Russia never vote the way it's supposed to?'[31]). Telephone surveys were particularly problematic because less than half the population had access to a receiver, and the only census that was available in the early postcommunist years, conducted in 1989, was increasingly irrelevant as hundreds of thousands became refugees or changed their address for other reasons (a new census was conducted in 2002, but its adequacy was vigorously contested; another was held in October 2010, after initially being postponed until 2013).[32] As elsewhere, it was only surveys that could provide a representative impression of the public mood, but they were best interpreted within a context that took proper account of the ways in which ordinary citizens were inclined to conceive of their own problems, on the basis of their own experience. And this, in turn, could be gathered from letters to the newspapers, from the wider world of cultural expression and behaviour itself, as well as from methodologies that were more familiar in a Western context. Russia, the poet Tyutchev had insisted, could not be 'understood', it could 'only be believed in'; and some of the questions that were being considered in the early postcommunist years, such as what it meant to be a Russian in the first place, were resistant to almost any form of conventional inquiry.[33]

What, as far as surveys could establish them, were the main concerns of ordinary Russians across two decades of far-reaching change? For the most part, they had little to do with political philosophy, constitutional design or Russia's place in a very different world, or even the crisis in culture and public morality: most Russians were more concerned about how they were to earn a living in an unfamiliar and more difficult economic environment (see Table 6.1). In the late 1990s it was delays in the payment of wages and salaries that came first in the list of public concerns (only a third of those who were asked in 1998 had received the previous month's salary in full and on time).[34] The conflict in Chechnya was another concern, but it became an increasingly marginal one over the course of the Putin presidency as federal authority was gradually restored and the loss of life abated; and steadily diminishing numbers thought they would be the victim of a terrorist act of some kind. There were even fewer worries about crime or unemployment, at least until the international financial crisis at the end of 2008 moved it sharply up the national agenda. The other preoccupations were more enduring, and they were dominant in the early years of the new century: above all, the rapid increases that were taking place in the cost of living, and in the poverty and social inequality with which they were associated. There were some new concerns as well, such as the problem (or so it appeared) of absorbing the increasing numbers who had decided to move to Russia from one of the newly independent Soviet republics, or from one part of the country to another.

What about the economic changes to which Russians had been committed by their government even before the end of communist rule? To begin with, the popular view was broadly supportive of 'market reform'; but as its consequences became apparent, including unemployment and higher prices, ordinary Russians became increasingly disillusioned (see Figure 6.1). By the early years of the new century, there were more who thought the 'economic reforms' should be continued than who thought they should be abandoned; but they were never a majority (in 2008, 38 per cent), and the largest group of all was undecided (40 per cent, in the same year).[35] There was certainly no aversion to state control, which had been a part of the daily lives of ordinary Russians since prerevolutionary and not just Soviet times. What, for instance, should be owned and managed by the state, and what should be in the hands of private firms and individuals? An overwhelming majority, by the end of Putin's second presidential term, thought energy, heavy industry, transport, education and health should be run by government exclusively. There was otherwise a preference for joint ownership, for instance in telecommunications, banking, agriculture and the media; but in no single instance was there more than marginal support for wholly private ownership, and even in the case of newspapers there were many more who thought they should be run by government itself rather than private owners. These results were very similar to those that had been obtained almost a decade earlier, and in other inquiries.[36] The Russian ideal, it seemed, was very close to the New Economic Policy that had existed in the Soviet 1920s, in

Table 6.1 **The main concerns of ordinary Russians in the 2000s**

	2000	2001	2002	2003	2004	2005	2006	2007	2008	2009	2010
Rising prices	83	66	70	71	75	71	70	64	82	76	72
Poverty	–	59	61	61	58	53	51	52	45	56	51
Increasing unemployment	51	34	34	40	35	39	34	30	25	51	38
Economic crisis, fall in output	39	30	31	32	37	33	29	28	29	38	36
Corruption, bribery	30	23	23	23	32	24	25	27	27	28	33
Drug addiction	–	37	32	27	26	29	29	25	29	26	32
Environmental pollution	22	19	17	20	19	17	24	22	23	18	31
Income inequalities	38	26	28	31	29	27	30	32	35	30	29
Crisis in morality and culture	26	24	26	24	26	22	24	28	26	26	28
Inaccessibility of medical care	–	25	30	30	31	29	31	32	31	27	26
Increasing crime	53	41	43	39	27	29	29	28	27	22	21
Cost of education	–	26	25	27	28	27	28	26	26	16	20
Official arbitrariness	–	–	–	10	10	9	10	9	10	13	18
Weakness of state power	16	11	14	11	15	11	11	9	9	9	13
Rudeness and cruelty of police	–	–	–	–	8	6	8	9	9	12	12
Increasing immigration	–	–	–	–	–	7	10	9	12	11	11
Terrorist threats at home	16	11	15	15	17	15	10	6	4	5	10
Military actions in Chechnya	48	22	17	11	12	7	4	4	2	9	8
Incidence of AIDS	–	–	–	–	7	6	5	8	7	6	6
Worsening of ethnic relations	13	8	9	5	8	4	10	7	5	5	6
Delays in salaries and pensions	19	9	10	9	7	4	5	3	4	6	5

Source: adapted from www.levada.ru/press/2007080201.print.html, 2 August 2007, last consulted 10 September 2010; figures for 2000 are from *Monitoring obshchestvennogo mneniya*, no. 5, 2000, pp. 66–7, and for 2008–10 from www.levada.ru/press/2010090805.html, last consulted 10 September 2010. Up to six responses were permitted; n = 1,600; rounded percentages. Responses are shown whenever 10 per cent or more indicated accordingly in any year; missing values mean the option was not presented. Corresponding figures for the 1990s are shown in Stephen White, *Russia's New Politics* (Cambridge and New York: Cambridge University Press, 2000), p. 188.

which the state had taken control of strategic resources but allowed a regulated private sector to operate in the sectors that were most closely connected with the daily needs of ordinary citizens.[37]

As for the changes that had actually taken place over the postcommunist years, opinion was divided about their effects: 36 per cent thought they had gained, 37 per cent thought

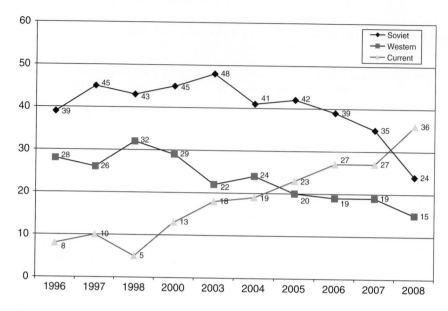

Figure 6.1 Political system preferences, 1996–2008
Source: adapted from Levada Centre figures as reported in *Vestnik obshchestvennogo mneniya*, no. 5, 2008, p. 5. The question was 'Which political system do you think is the best?'; respondents were allowed to choose 'The Soviet system as it existed before the 1990s', 'Democracy as in the Western countries' or 'The current system'; rounded percentages.

they had lost and the remainder found it hard to say. But more than half (55 per cent) thought the country was 'going in the right direction' by the end of the Putin presidency, nearly twice as many as the 29 per cent who took the opposite view (this was a considerable change on the Yeltsin years).[38] And increasing numbers were satisfied with their own position. In 2008, for instance, 12 per cent thought they lived 'well' or even (another 1 per cent) 'very well', and 60 per cent – more than ever before – thought they had at least an 'average' standard of living, although there were still substantial numbers who thought they lived 'badly' (21 per cent) or 'very badly' (5 per cent).[39] Average incomes, in the same year, were 6,452 roubles a month (about $255 at the prevailing rate of exchange); additional earnings raised this figure considerably, to 12,013 roubles (about $475) a month, which was less than what was thought to be necessary to 'live normally' (17,529 roubles), but well above a 'subsistence minimum' (6,771 roubles).[40] And more Russians than ever before were just feeling good. As many as 10 per cent described their mood as 'excellent' when they were asked in the summer months of 2008, and another 57 per cent said it was 'normal and stable'; there were more who thought they would live better in a year's time than who thought they were likely to live worse; and an overwhelming 84 per cent saw themselves, accurately or otherwise, as part of the 'middle stratum' of society.[41]

Russians, not surprisingly, were increasingly positive about the political system that appeared to have brought about this steady improvement in their daily lives. During the

Table 6.2 **Russians and their economy, 1994–2010**

	94	96	98	00	01	02	03	04	05	06	07	08	10
What is the economic position of Russia as a whole?													
Good/very good	1	1	2	2	1	3	2	4	5	8	8	16	10
Middling	14	21	12	26	29	37	33	41	38	45	47	48	47
Bad/very bad	69	68	77	61	60	51	53	44	45	34	31	23	34
What is the economic position of your town or rural district?													
Good/very good	2	3	3	4	4	6	3	6	7	8	10	14	11
Middling	30	30	24	38	35	39	37	38	39	39	42	41	42
Bad/very bad	53	57	66	47	50	49	50	47	47	41	39	37	41
What is the economic position of your family?													
Good/very good	6	5	4	5	6	7	4	8	8	9	11	13	13
Middling	48	43	39	48	54	52	51	55	54	56	57	60	58
Bad/very bad	44	50	54	44	39	38	41	34	36	32	31	26	27

Source: adapted from *Vestnik obshchestvennogo mneniya*, no. 3, 2008, pp. 78–9, and www.levada.ru (rounded percentages); the results are for May in every year except 2008 (June) and 2010 (December).

Bulletin of generally known opinions

early postcommunist years, it was generally the 'Soviet system' that had the most support, but the 'current system' became increasingly popular as the Putin presidency advanced, and latterly it was the most popular option of all; support for a 'Western system', never substantial, dropped even further (see Figure 6.2). The 'Soviet system', admittedly, had varied considerably over time, and in some other surveys respondents were given a more discriminating set of questions that allowed them to choose a 'more democratic Soviet system' as well as other options. This was the most popular choice of all, in 2010, with nearly 33 per cent support; the 'political system that exists today' was the first choice of 25 per cent, but another 14 per cent wanted the 'Soviet system as it existed in our country before *perestroika*', which meant that nearly half of all respondents favoured some kind of Soviet system (just 14 per cent wanted 'Western democracy'). These were the views of the whole society; males and females differed very little in their preferences, but education, living standards and age all had an effect, and of the kind that might have been expected. Those who thought they were 'poor' or 'very poor', for instance, were more than twice as likely to favour a 'Soviet' option as those who thought they lived 'well' or 'very well'; and over-60s – an increasing proportion of the population – were twice as enthusiastic as the under-30s.[42]

Russians were regularly asked another question, which was the kind of alternatives they might prefer to the system they actually had (which, some argued, was itself increasingly 'Soviet').[43] Whatever their abstract preferences, most Russians did not think the communist system should simply be reintroduced (25 per cent supported a change of this kind, a much larger 66 per cent were against). Nor was there much support for the idea that it would be 'better to get rid of the Duma and elections and choose a

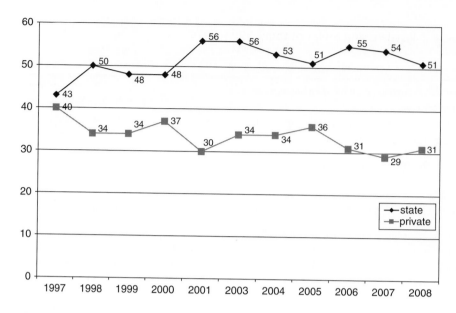

Figure 6.2 Economic system preferences, 1997–2008
Source: adapted from Levada Centre figures as reported in *Vestnik obshchestvennogo mneniya*, no. 5, 2008, p. 5. The question was 'Which economic system do you think is the best?'; respondents were allowed to choose 'one based on state planning and redistribution' or 'one based on private property and market relations'; rounded percentages.

single, strong leader' (32 per cent were in favour, 58 per cent were opposed). Nearly two-thirds (64 per cent) agreed largely or entirely with the view that democracy 'had some shortcomings, but was better than other political systems' (21 per cent disagreed), and other alternatives were even less popular: just 8 per cent supported military rule, and 7 per cent the restoration of a monarchy. But there were modest levels of commitment in every direction. Only 28 per cent, for instance, were prepared to assign themselves to a political philosophy of any kind – left, right or centre. Not much more than a third (36 per cent) had any interest in politics. About the same proportion (35 per cent) followed political news in the newspapers at least several times a week; less than half felt any degree of attachment to a political party. And even fewer felt able to offer an opinion about the larger changes that were taking place in public life – such as the respective merits of a party-list system of the kind that was introduced in 2005 as compared with a system based on single-member constituencies.[44]

What, then, about the future? Opinions were divided here as well (Table 6.3), but there was strong support for a more assertive role for the state in economic and social matters, if not necessarily a return to the Soviet system; older people, villagers and those on lower incomes were particularly likely to take such a view, but they expressed a broader consensus. In the early 1990s, a Western scholar concluded that what ordinary Russians actually wanted was a 'socialism that worked' rather than a complete change of system.[45]

Table 6.3 **Which way forward (2008)?**

	All	M	F	<30	50+	Moscow	Villages	Low income	High income
Return to the Soviet system	11	11	10	5	16	3	19	22	6
Change the direction of reform, strengthen the role of the state in the economy and social security	44	42	45	36	46	44	37	39	46
Continue reforms and reduce the role of the state	14	16	13	18	12	16	11	10	17
Rapidly and decisively complete reforms already initiated	20	21	19	27	16	25	20	17	23
Hard to say	12	10	13	14	10	11	13	11	9

Source: adapted from *Vestnik obshchestvennogo mneniya*, no. 2, 2008, pp. 110, 112; rounded percentages; n = 1,600.

The evidence of the early years of the new century suggested a very similar conclusion: in the words of the head of the national public opinion centre, ordinary people wanted to 'live as if under capitalism, but work as if under Brezhnev'. Russians, as he put it, wanted their country to

remain a presidential republic, with a multiparty system (even if one party is fine, people think there should be an alternative). At the same time the state should continue to be secular, and interfere less in the personal lives of citizens, and occupy an independent and worthy position in the world. We would like to retain a variety of forms of property, and certainly not eliminate private property. This is a consensus position, even communists support it. Finally, the state should be social. Nobody wishes to move towards a model under which the state distances itself from social needs and concerns, and from social guarantees. This is also a consensus position, even for liberals. What should change? We would like to strengthen morality, so as to rein in a ruling stratum that has got out of control. To achieve the equality of all before the law, and break the connection between businessmen and officials. And in the economy we passionately want the major corporations, above all those that extract raw materials, to belong to the state; we don't believe in private initiative in this sector of the economy. We also want to become less dependent on high oil prices and restore progressive taxation, and while retaining a free health and education system, make them cheaper to run and improve their quality and accessibility.[46]

The international financial crisis that began to affect Russia directly in the later months of 2008 had obvious implications for these various predispositions. As elsewhere, it tended to reinforce the preference for a state that would protect ordinary citizens by guaranteeing their employment, supporting those who were all the same forced out of their jobs, and holding prices down for everyone. Some 61 per cent thought Russia was still 'going in the right direction' in September 2008, but only 41 per cent took the same view six months later (and no more than 48 per cent in the early months of 2010). The ratings of the country's political leaders began to slip downwards at about the same time, although they remained very high: 83 per cent 'approved' of President Medvedev in September 2008, and 68 per cent still did so the following April; Putin lost even less of his earlier support, down from 88 to 76 per cent over the same period, after which they both recovered.[47] But more than two-thirds, in another Levada Centre inquiry, said they were buying cheaper food and other necessities than they had done before; about half of those who were asked said they were just about able to cope with the higher prices they were being charged, a quarter admitted they had 'real difficulty' in doing so.[48] Most strikingly of all, a massive 86 per cent, in the late spring of 2009, had begun to worry about losing their job, and 70 per cent thought unemployment was likely to increase; relatively few had been obliged to accept a shorter working week or unpaid holidays, but 25 per cent had experienced mass sackings at their place of work over the previous three months, and even more (29 per cent) thought there was a serious risk that something of the kind would take place in the future.[49]

Although it was sometimes forgotten, the great majority of Russians had opted for a 'reformed USSR' when they were allowed to express an opinion about it in the referendum that took place in March 1991, and although the level fluctuated, about two-thirds of those who were asked in a succession of surveys over the years that followed were inclined to think it was a 'great misfortune' their old state no longer existed.[50] It was certainly clear why they might regret its passing: in particular, its unexpected demise was – or at least it appeared to be – the most obvious reason for the economic difficulties that ordinary Russians had been experiencing.[51] The weekly paper *Argumenty i fakty* went out into the streets in the mid-1990s to ask ordinary Russians to put their responses into their own words. The first person they talked to, a young man temporarily out of work, was 'for the USSR, however stupid that might sound'. Yelena, a businesswoman, was against – it could 'only mean the return of psychiatric prisons, lies and censorship'. But Ruslan from Tajikistan wanted 'everything to be like it was before'. Sergei from Moscow thought the three 'Slavic brothers' were 'simply fated to live together'. A visitor from Grozny was 'for the Soviet Union, naturally'. And Boris, a down-and-out, had a simple explanation: 'When there was a USSR, I had a flat. Now there is no USSR – and I've no flat either.'[52] The largest proportion of those who were asked in the late 1990s to identify their 'homeland', in fact, told interviewers it was the USSR (28 per cent), more than the proportion who thought it was Russia (27 per cent), and nearly as many thought it was the region in which they lived.[53]

What were the best and what were the worst features of the Soviet system? The evidence of successive surveys is set out in Table 6.4.[54] Consistently, it was guaranteed employment that was seen as its most positive feature. But there was also approval for the way in which the Soviet system had maintained a working relationship among the various nationalities, and economic stability was also important. Substantial numbers, in addition, approved of the way in which the Soviet system had maintained a measure of

Table 6.4 **The 'best' and 'worst' features of the Soviet system, 1993–2010**

'Best' features					'Worst' features				
	1993	2001	2005	2010		1993	2001	2005	2010
Job security	29	27	31	28	Too much bureaucracy	32	26	27	21
Interethnic peace	24	24	20	17	Human rights	17	9	14	10
Economic stability	22	20	17	17	Corruption	15	12	8	12
Law and order	12	11	13	13	None	13	12	10	9
More equality	7	11	14	17	Pollution	12	8	7	6
None	7	2	2	2	Economic stagnation	11	18	25	28

Source: 1993, 2001, 2005 and 2010 Russian surveys, rounded percentages; 'don't knows' and non-responses account for residuals. Respondents were asked to identify one positive and one negative feature from a list provided and could suggest alternatives.

social equality and public order. There were in fact very few who thought it had no positive features at all. There was a substantial measure of agreement, at the same time, about the features of the old regime that were least acceptable. By 2010, it was 'economic stagnation' that was its main shortcoming, followed by 'excessive bureaucracy'. Corruption was in third place throughout, ahead of human rights; environmental pollution was mentioned by rather fewer, and about one in ten, in successive surveys, thought the Soviet system had no faults at all. Looking at the pattern of responses over the best part of two decades, there had been a striking increase in the proportion who thought the social equality of the Soviet period was to be commended, although it still came behind security of employment. Among the negative features of the Soviet system, increasing numbers drew attention to its failure to develop economically – which was the main criticism that was advanced by the Putin leadership – and rather fewer were concerned about its bureaucracy or human rights performance.

Substantial numbers, indeed, continue to insist it would have been better if the Soviet system had remained, and in the form it had acquired before *perestroika*. About half of those who were asked by the Levada Centre in January 2005, for instance, thought it 'would have been better if everything had stayed the way it was before 1985'. Why? Because 'we were a big, united country', and 'there was order' (both 26 per cent); in addition, there was 'certainty in the future' (24 per cent) and 'prices were low and stable' (20 per cent). As for *perestroika* itself, just 22 per cent, at the end of 2009, thought it had been a positive development; more than twice as many (52 per cent) took the opposite view.[55] Without it, 35 per cent believed things would have 'slowly improved', and 36 per cent thought it would have been possible to 'avoid bitter conflicts and upheavals' and remain a 'single great country'.[56] Even those who thought *perestroika* had been necessary thought it should all the same have been implemented in a different way, 'without destroying the socialist system' (33 per cent) or by 'firmly developing market relations

Table 6.5 **Evaluating the October revolution, 1990–2010**

With which of the following opinions about the October revolution are you most in agreement?

	1990	1997	2001	2002	2003	2004	2005	2007	2010
It stimulated economic and social development	24	26	27	27	32	27	31	31	29
It opened a new era in Russian history	22	23	32	33	20	30	26	24	29
It slowed down development	19	19	18	19	19	16	16	17	14
It was a catastrophe for the peoples of Russia	13	16	12	9	14	14	15	9	9
Hard to say	22	17	11	13	15	13	13	19	19
Imagine the October revolution was taking place at the moment. What would you do?									
I would actively support the Bolsheviks	23	15	22	23	19	15	17	17	–
I would somewhat support the Bolsheviks	26	16	19	20	16	18	17	13	–
I would try to keep out of it	12	27	24	28	22	26	28	23	–
I would struggle against the Bolsheviks	5	7	6	8	9	8	7	6	–
I would go abroad	7	15	13	16	14	15	14	18	–
Hard to say	27	20	16	5	21	19	17	24	–

Source: adapted from www.levada.ru/press/2007110104.html, 1 November 2007, last accessed 20 September 2010, and www.levada.ru; rounded percentages.

in the economy but not rushing the development of democracy, (19 per cent).[57] Looking back even further, it was the industrialisation of the late 1920s and 1930s that was most favourably evaluated of all the stages through which the country had developed in the twentieth century, followed by the moves towards constitutional government in the late tsarist period and then the Khrushchev 'thaw' of the 1950s and early 1960s; *perestroika* was seen as the most damaging period that Russia had experienced throughout the entire century, followed closely by the transition to a market economy in the 1990s and the collectivisation of agriculture in the 1930s.[58]

The October revolution itself, for most Russians, was a result of the 'difficult position' in which working people had found themselves at the time (57 per cent), or of the 'weakness' of the Provisional Government (35 per cent), rather than the 'extremism of political adventurers' (17 per cent). And more than half, in October 2007, thought it had 'opened a new era in the history of the Russian peoples' or 'given a stimulus to economic and social development' (see Table 6.5), which was rather more than had taken this view in 1990. Lenin was the figure of the time who aroused the greatest sympathy (27 per cent), although his popularity was diminishing; he was followed by secret police chief Felix Dzerzhinsky, and then Joseph Stalin. It was Stalin, on the other hand, towards whom most Russians had the greatest antipathy (29 per cent), followed by Leon Trotsky (13 per cent).[59] And what if there was another October revolution? Some 17 per cent said they would

Table 6.6 **The characteristics of Soviet and postcommunist rule, 1998–2005**

Soviet rule, 1970s–1980s				Postcommunist rule, 1990s–2000s			
	1998	2001	2005		1998	2001	2005
Close to the people	36	30	34	Criminal, corrupt	63	50	62
Legal	32	22	28	Remote, alien	41	34	42
'Our own', familiar	32	24	26	Irresolute	32	25	29
Bureaucratic	30	26	30	Weak, powerless	31	21	20
Strong, firm	27	25	30	Short-sighted	28	17	25
Short-sighted	23	14	21	Bureaucratic	22	24	39
Authoritative, respected	21	21	24	Parasitic	18	12	15
Secretive, closed	17	4	13	Illegal	13	10	16
Just	16	16	11	Unprofessional	13	7	12
Honest, open	14	11	13	Limited	12	4	8
Criminal, corrupt	14	13	12	Educated, intelligent	6	12	13

Source: adapted from *Ekonomicheskie i sotsial'nye peremeny*, no. 3, 1998, p. 57 and *Vestnik obshchestvennogo mneniya* no. 1(81), January–February 2006, p. 10, showing all qualities that were reported by at least 10 per cent of respondents in any year. Respondents were invited to identify respective qualities from a list provided; figures show rounded percentages.

support the Bolsheviks in these hypothetical circumstances, and another 13 per cent would at least cooperate with them, which was many more than the 6 per cent who said they would support the Whites, although still larger numbers thought they would remain on the sidelines or emigrate (the flow of opinion over time is shown in the lower panel of Table 6.5). In Russia at least, the changes that had taken place were clearly more complicated than a 'transition to democracy'. The revolution was after all indigenous; it was the Soviet leadership that had led the struggle for national survival during the Second World War, and the end of the Soviet system had been followed by a sharp fall in living standards. Ordinary Russians, for such reasons, generally spoke about the 'collapse of the union' in 1991 and avoided more complex value judgements.

Russians have also been asked to suggest the characteristics they associate with their current regime, and with the Soviet system of the 1970s and 1980s (see Table 6.6, which is once again based on the regular surveys of the All-Russian Centre for the Study of Public Opinion and subsequently the Levada Centre). Popular images of both systems, in fact, had changed relatively little over the years. Communist rule, in spite of its lack of fully or – until its final years – even partly competitive elections, was thought to have many virtues. It was admittedly bureaucratic, as well as short-sighted and secretive. But its positive features were more apparent. It was 'close to the people', 'legal' and 'our own' (*nash*) – in other words, accessible, indigenous and (for ordinary Russians) legitimate. Postcommunist rule, by contrast, was associated with crime and corruption more than anything else, and by a very considerable margin; but it was also remote, irresolute, weak

Table 6.7 **Changes since communist rule, 2001–2010**

	Somewhat / much better			The same as before			Somewhat / much worse		
	2001	2005	2010	2001	2005	2010	2001	2005	2010
Religious freedom	79	85	79	12	11	13	2	2	4
Freedom of speech	77	75	72	12	18	19	5	5	5
To join any organisation	76	77	74	10	13	16	3	4	4
To take part in politics	69	75	68	17	17	21	4	3	6
Freedom from illegal arrest	24	42	44	34	33	30	19	17	17
Ability to influence government policy	14	19	27	47	44	41	28	33	27
Equal and fair treatment from government	–	11	19	–	38	38	–	44	36

Source: 2001, 2005 and 2010 Russian surveys, rounded percentages; 'don't knows' and non-responses account for residuals. The question about equal treatment was not asked in 2001; a question about freedom of travel (better for 48 per cent, worse for 30 per cent) was not asked in 2005 or 2010. The question wording was: 'Compared with the Soviet period, have the following become easier or more difficult?'; options were respectively 'For everyone to freely resolve questions of his/her religious life', 'To join any organisation', 'To decide freely whether or not to take part in political life', 'For everyone to freely express what they think', 'People can live without worrying about illegal arrest', 'For ordinary people to influence government policy' and 'Government deals with all citizens equally and fairly'.

(less so under Putin than under Yeltsin), short-sighted and more bureaucratic – by 2005 – than the communist system it had replaced. Indeed, the postcommunist system had hardly any positive features, in this inquiry; it was also parasitic, illegal (in spite of its independent courts and competitive elections) and incompetent. Overall, in nearly every respect the late Soviet system was more positively evaluated than the postcommunist system that had replaced it; the 'only, not very significant exception' was in the 'educated and intelligent' quality of its leadership, where the two sets of results were virtually identical – and equally unflattering.[60]

The Soviet period could also be compared with the period that succeeded it in terms of the individual liberties it made available (see Table 6.7; these responses are from surveys conducted by the author and associates, further details of which are provided on pp. 457–8). There was little doubt, for ordinary Russians, that they had more opportunity to practise a religion after 1991 than in the late communist period, and to express their opinions in any way they chose. Similarly, they thought it was easier to decide whether or not to join an organisation, and whether or not to take part in politics itself (during the communist years, it was often remarked, everything that was not banned had in practice been compulsory). As well as this, there was greater freedom to travel if they could afford to do so. In other words, individual liberties appeared to be better protected: the right to express opinions in whatever form, to worship and to decide for themselves whether or

Table 6.8 **Comparing the Soviet system and the West in retrospect**

	'In the USSR'		'In the West'		'The same'	
	2000	2008	2000	2008	2000	2008
The employment system	78	61	11	14	3	8
The education system	70	66	14	11	4	8
Science	64	55	16	14	6	14
Culture and art	61	54	16	14	6	13
The healthcare system	56	52	28	23	3	8
Social security	51	44	29	29	3	8
Observance of civil rights	35	29	41	37	4	10
Life of ordinary people as a whole	49	38	29	30	6	10

Source: adapted from *Vestnik obshchestvennogo mneniya*, no. 6, 2008, p. 88. Note: based on Levada Centre surveys (n = 1,600, rounded percentages); 'don't knows' account for residuals. The question wording was: 'Speaking of the life of ordinary people in the 1970s and 1980s, where was it better – in the USSR or the West?'

not to join the public organisations that in the past had been an all but obligatory requirement of citizenship. But there was no comparable change in the relationship between ordinary people and their institutions of government – at least, as they perceived it. For instance, substantial numbers thought they were better protected against the risk of illegal arrest, but even larger numbers thought there had been no change, or even a regression. Remarkably, ordinary people thought they had no more influence over the making of public policy than they had enjoyed in the communist period, in spite of the introduction of competitive elections, the rule of law and freedom of speech, although the largest proportion of all thought there had simply been no change. And most remarkably of all, ordinary people thought they were actually *less* likely to be treated fairly and equally by government than they had been in Soviet times.

In what respects had the Soviet system been a better one 'for ordinary people' than its Western counterpart, and in what respects had it been worse? For most Russians, looking back, the way that ordinary people had lived in the Brezhnev years had actually been an improvement on the life that ordinary people had experienced in the Western societies of the time (see Table 6.8). The West was clearly more effective in protecting the civil liberties of individual citizens; but in other respects the Soviet system was seen as anything up to six times more satisfactory than its Western counterparts. The differences were most striking in relation to education, but the superiority of the Soviet system was almost as apparent in its perceived ability to generate employment, and in its policies on science, literature and art. The Soviet system was also superior, in retrospect, in its healthcare and social security. In the early 1990s the West had been the model to emulate; by the start of the new century, the Levada Centre concluded, it was the Soviet system that had become the new paradigm, and in spite of a slight fall in popularity, it 'remain[ed] the ideal for Russians in an absolute majority of parameters'. These somewhat idealised views of their own past, in turn, helped to strengthen the tendency towards international isolation, and towards a more distanced view of Western culture in particular. By 2008, only 11 per cent wanted to return to the Soviet model of development; twice as many (22 per cent) favoured the 'common path of European civilisation'; but a steady 60 per cent believed Russia should 'advance along its own special path'.[61]

Many of these competing narratives of the Russian and Soviet past were apparent in the periodic attempts that were made to find the country's 'most outstanding leader'. Vladimir Putin was well ahead, in the surveys that were conducted in the early years of the new century, of those who were regarded with 'admiration, respect or sympathy': 78 per cent opted for the Russian President, ahead of Lenin and Andropov (both on 47 per cent), Nicholas II and Brezhnev (both on 39 per cent), and Joseph Stalin (36 per cent).[62] And he came fifth, behind Pushkin, Peter the Great, Stalin and Lenin, among the 'outstanding people of all times and peoples'.[63] Lenin and Stalin were indeed among the most consistently successful in all such exercises. In one of the most elaborate, the competition that was organised in late 2008 by national television for a 'Name of Russia', the eventual winner was Alexander Nevsky, the prince of Novgorod and saint of the Orthodox Church who had saved Russia from the Teutonic knights in the thirteenth century. He was followed by Petr Stolypin, the early twentieth-century prime minister who was particularly associated with the consolidation of private agriculture, and then by Stalin and Pushkin, each of them with more than half a million votes.[64] There were some who suspected the hand of the Kremlin in this outcome, and particularly in the way in which Stalin, the early leader, had been kept down to third place by a very narrow margin.[65] The survey agencies that asked the same question typically found that it was Peter the Great who had the most support, followed again by Lenin and Stalin.[66]

The flow of political communication

Petitioning the authorities was a tradition that went back to medieval times, when a bucket was lowered from a window in the Old Kremlin Palace in which supplicants could lodge a note of their concerns.[67] It developed in the Soviet period into one of the principal forms of communication between regime and society. The Council of People's Commissars, in the early postrevolutionary years, received about 10,000 letters a year, many of which were taken into account in the elaboration of government decrees; citizens could also address themselves to the reception offices of the Communist Party Central Committee.[68] Lenin's own postbag was itself a substantial one, including many items that directly challenged official policies.[69] They were, he told a colleague, 'real human documents' without which 'not a single one of [his] speeches' would have been complete.[70] The postbag of the major newspapers was even larger: the peasant paper *Krest'yanskaya gazeta*, for instance, received more than 5 million letters over the ten years from 1923 to 1933 as its readers sought advice, appealed for assistance or reflected on a socialism that was 'like the building of the Great Wall of China, which had swallowed up a lot of energy but to no obvious effect'.[71]

During the 1920s and 1930s, as the emphasis of state policy shifted from discovering what popular preferences might be to mobilising the masses towards the achievement of objectives that had already been centrally determined, 'work with letters' began to receive rather less attention. The elected soviets lost whatever democratic content they had originally possessed; newspapers devoted more space to record-breaking economic achievements than the legitimate complaints of citizens; and the style of party leadership became increasingly remote and hierarchical.[72] The Stalin Constitution, published in draft for national discussion, was considered by more than 400,000 workplace meetings with more than 36 million citizens in attendance, who among them suggested over 154,000 changes.[73] The new family legislation of 1936, however, was a better indicator of the use that was made of communications from ordinary citizens at this time. A sharply retrogressive measure, it was intended to strengthen marriage and (among other things) outlawed abortion. A few letters appeared pointing out that 'lack of living space' was often the real problem; but the published correspondence as a whole, together with the editorial coverage, was overwhelmingly favourable. It later emerged that the great majority of letters had in fact opposed the new law but that only a few had been published, while every single communication in favour had been selected. 'The Boss says we must have more children' was the simple explanation.[74]

Letters and other forms of communication from ordinary citizens began to receive more attention during the Khrushchev period, as dictatorship mellowed into consultative authoritarianism. A Central Committee resolution of 1967 made clear that letters were 'one of the main forms of strengthening and broadening the links between party and people';[75] the first comprehensive legislation was adopted the following year,[76] and then in 1977 the new Soviet constitution established the right of citizens to submit proposals and criticisms to public bodies, and to lodge complaints against the actions of officials.[77] The discussion of the Constitution that took place over four months in the summer of 1977 showed both the strengths and the limitations of the exercises of this kind that were staged during the late Soviet period. More than four-fifths of the adult population were reported to have taken some part in the discussion, and letters arrived in an 'unending flow' at party headquarters; they had, Brezhnev reported, overwhelmingly said 'yes, this is the Basic Law we have been waiting for'.[78] Only much later did it emerge that the letters that had been received at this time, while generally supportive, had also raised all kinds of awkward issues. Why, for instance, was there no choice of candidate at elections? Why had the CPSU been given a political monopoly in Article 6 of the Constitution? Why did party and state officials in many places have a 'special, semi-secret service facility' that was beyond the reach of other citizens, a 'personal communism' where they could 'satisfy their needs cheaply and abundantly'? And why had Brezhnev been given two Hero of the Soviet Union awards thirteen years after hostilities had formally concluded?[79]

Gorbachev had given particular attention to letters from the public during his party career, and he made frequent reference to them after he had been elected General Secretary, sometimes quoting directly. In April 1985, for instance, he noted that party members had been asking why officials held the same posts for years on end,[80] and in Kyiv in early 1989 he quoted from some of the complaints that had reached him about the food supply.[81] He was asked, during a visit to what was still Leningrad in October 1987, if letters from ordinary people actually reached him. Yes they did, he replied; he tried to read as many as possible and took others home with him for further consideration.[82] A substantial part of the presidential postbag came from abroad, particularly from Germany, Sweden and the United States.[83] The singer Paul McCartney wrote to suggest the release of a special album of rock-and-roll numbers; Americans suggested building a bridge from Alaska to Siberia ('we could then visit friends of ours on both sides'), asked for his help in completing college assignments and offered to take the Gorbachev family to Disneyland.[84] Many others raised the same theme as a letter from which the President had quoted at a press conference during his visit to the United States in 1987: if the family of man did not learn to live together, a 17-year-old girl had written to him, they would surely die together.[85] Gorbachev responded directly to an appeal from a retired US admiral when he announced his moratorium on nuclear testing in 1985,[86] and he used his correspondence once more when he was seeking to end the Soviet military presence in Afghanistan, circulating his Politburo colleagues with a 'flood of letters' from soldiers asking why they had been sent, and from mothers pleading to have their sons brought home.[87]

Gorbachev's postbag remained a substantial one, even in the last year of his presidential rule: more than 220,000 letters from various parts of the Soviet Union, and a further 70,000 from abroad (of which more than 40 per cent came from the United States). A special group, including lawyers and economists, had been established within the Presidential Administration to deal with this massive inflow. The 'most significant' of the letters, about 1,500 every year, were handed to the President personally, the remainder were used to prepare a weekly overview, 'The Post of the USSR President'. It began with a statistical summary and an indication of the main concerns that had been raised in that week's communications. In the first week of October 1991, for instance, there had been 'numerous telegrams' about the possible transfer of the Kurile islands to Japan, and from veterans who were 'angered by the renaming of Leningrad' (it had reverted to St Petersburg after a local referendum); over the year as a whole, by far the largest volume of correspondence had been concerned with relations among the various nationalities. As well as summaries, the weekly digest also contained extracts from the letters themselves: from the mother whose son had died in Afghanistan who would 'strangle [the President] with her own hands', or from the St Petersburg pensioner whose ration cards had been stolen ('there was nothing like this even during the blockade').[88] Gorbachev himself told interviewers that he began and ended each day by reading correspondence of this kind,[89] and as late as August 1991 he still read 'a proportion' of everything he received.[90]

There was a still more substantial flow of communications into party headquarters, where they were seen as a 'sensitive barometer of public opinion'.[91] More than half a million arrived every year during the 1970s, rising to more than a million in 1988 at the time of the 19th Party Conference.[92] In order to deal with this heavy correspondence, the Central Committee established a Letters Department in 1978, which was later merged with the General Department.[93] Many of the letters required no particular response, such as the one from a captain in the Far Eastern fleet who wrote to inform 'our leader and wise mentor' that the steamer under his command, the *Captain Lyutikov*, had 'worthily fulfilled the tenth five-year plan'. A man in his mid-sixties who had lived through all the five-year plans and knew for himself the horror of war, Mukhin wanted the party leader to know that he had seen his fellow-citizens overcome every challenge thanks to the 'eternal youth of our Motherland, which inspires new energies and belief in the justice of our cause'. From the other end of the country, party member I. Il'in of Archangel wrote in to thank Brezhnev for such 'necessary, simply indispensable books as *Little Land*, *Renewal*, and *Virgin Land*' (the party leader's ghost-written memoirs), and for his 'immeasurable contribution to the cause of world peace'.[94] But as *perestroika* ran into difficulties, the letters became increasingly disillusioned and outspoken:[95] more of them were from the poor, increasing numbers were openly anti-communist,[96] and it was discontent of various kinds that predominated in the selection that was circulated to the delegates that attended the CPSU's 28th Congress in 1990.

Life, a party member and invalid complained, had 'become unbearable'. There was nothing in the shops, the shelves were empty and they lived on vegetables from their allotment, macaroni and milk.[97] The most basic goods, reported a veteran from Khabarovsk, had started to disappear: sugar, tea, matches, soap, washing powder and toothpaste.[98] In the Sverdlovsk region it was 'impossible to buy painkillers'.[99] They had been 'waiting for five years for an improvement in their life', wrote a Mr Zhuravlev from Tambov, but there was 'still no real change', just shelves in the shops that were getting 'emptier and emptier'.[100] The general view, in these circumstances, was 'categorically against a transition to the market by raising retail prices'.[101] The market, wrote equipment workers from the Moscow region, was 'just the latest robbery of the working class'.[102] A mother from Krasnoyarsk warned that her family was 'practically starving' with prices at their existing level.[103] Five years of *perestroika*, wrote a Mr Anosov from the Kemerovo region, had been 'five years of belt tightening' for ordinary people.[104] The 'shelves were bare' in the shops, there were no socks (you couldn't, after all, 'put statistics on your feet') and the health service was in a 'catastrophic state'.[105] Mrs Kolomnikova, a metalworker from Zlatoust, took her concerns directly to the party newspaper. She came back from work exhausted, she told *Pravda*, but there was nothing in the shops; sometimes things were so bad she just went into the bathroom to cry, turning on the shower so that her husband and children would be unable to hear her. When would the slogans about social justice finally become a reality?[106]

The same themes were reflected throughout the press, with many individual titles receiving up to half a million letters a year in the late 1980s: the weekly paper *Argumenty i fakty* received 480,000 in 1989, the trade union daily *Trud* (Labour) about 475,000, *Pravda* itself 473,000 and *Izvestiya* 350,000.[107] A substantial staff had to be engaged to deal with these massive postbags: about ninety at *Trud*, and about seventy at *Izvestiya*.[108] Relatively few letters could be published in full, but *Trud* was one of the papers that could devote an entire issue every month, apart from foreign news, to communications from its readers;[109] and *Izvestiya*, in 1987, began to publish special articles based on readers' letters – readers were even described, in a published collection, as the paper's 'main correspondent'.[110] Letters could sometimes propose initiatives, even if they had presumably been authorised in advance (it was in a weekly paper, for instance, that the first public call was made for the restoration of Solzhenitsyn's Soviet citizenship; and it was a letter from a Saratov worker that had asked 'How long are we going to put up with drunkenness?', just weeks before the Gorbachev leadership launched its ill-fated campaign[111]). Letters were also passed on to party headquarters: like the one from a Tambov war veteran, who complained to *Pravda* that the people in the countryside who harvested the grain could find no bread in their locality; or from a Kishinev widow, who asked how she was supposed to survive on a pension of 55 roubles a month; or from a Mr Ledentsov of the Kirov region, who wondered how it was that they had been constructing socialism for seventy years, but there was nothing to buy in the shops.[112] Newspapers made a telephone line available for those who wished to report their concerns directly; and the larger ones maintained reception offices that dealt with thousands of individual representations.[113]

Letters maintained their significance into the postcommunist period; they were, Yeltsin explained, one of the 'seven channels' by which he kept in touch with the opinions of ordinary people.[114] Every day up to 1,500 letters reached the Russian President, dealing with a 'broad spectrum' of problems. A 'department of letters and the reception of citizens' with a staff of a hundred was set up in the Presidential Administration to deal with these communications,[115] and it reported to him regularly; it prepared an analytic overview every week, as well as briefings on particular subjects. About 80 per cent of all the letters made enquiries of some kind – for instance, about the social benefits to which war veterans were supposedly entitled; 11 per cent were complaints; 4 per cent were proposals for some kind of improvement in public life; and there were also 'quite a few' letters, usually anonymous, written in 'uncensored terms'. In all, about 350,000 letters arrived every year, raising matters from the state of the Tolstoy Museum at Yasnaya Polyana to a student dormitory in Voronezh; the information they provided, the head of the letters department explained, was 'much broader and more varied' than could possibly be obtained by stopping a thousand people in the street and asking them to say something into a microphone.[116] The President, in addition, gave interviews to the newspapers that were based on his responses to their readers' letters;[117] he occasionally replied directly;[118] and about 25,000 citizens were received every year by a member of the presidential staff.[119]

Communications of this kind became even more frequent during the Putin presidency – there were well over half a million letters a year by this time, and up to 120 visitors a day at the reception office in central Moscow. 'I place my hope in God and Vladimir Putin', 75-year-old Raisa Gorelova told journalists as she arrived with a bag full of family photographs, identity papers and a few yellowed pages from a book on Soviet heroes of the Second World War, one of them her brother. She was seeking a grant so that she could move to the same town as her relatives, rather than the city to which the government had allocated her when she fled ethnic tension in Central Asia. Once petitioners got through the door, they lined up at two windows where clerks recorded their names and other details, and the nature of their concern. Then they sat in a corridor waiting to be called into a private office to be interviewed by an official, usually for about fifteen minutes. 'From the homeless to Academicians, they all come to our offices', explained department head Mikhail Mironov. 'We have to find not just a common language, but also solutions to their problems.' In addition, Mironov and his aides sent the President and his key officials a two-page summary every Saturday of the letters and petitions the office had received over the week. About 70 per cent were complaints about entitlements of various kinds, such as housing and pensions; many of these were passed on to lower-level agencies, others led to phone calls to government ministries. And when the President visited one of the republics or regions, he would bring with him a 'thick file of popular comments on the governor's performance'.[120]

Mironov was asked by *Argumenty i fakty* if the President read letters from ordinary citizens. 'Yes of course', he replied. Some that raised important social issues went straight onto his desk, and Putin had replied personally to a number of his correspondents, including war veterans and children. A young woman from Sochi, for instance, had invited the President to her wedding; he could hardly attend in person but sent his congratulations and a present (the happy couple reciprocated with a selection of wedding photographs).[121] In another case that was reported in the press, the President had intervened personally to ensure that there was air transport to take Muslim pilgrims on the Hajj. In yet another, he had called for an investigation after workers at a machinery factory in Khabarovsk had complained that equipment was being sold off to the management at bargain prices (a criminal prosecution followed).[122] Letters came from more than a hundred foreign countries, as well as from Russia itself; it was these letters that were most likely to raise environmental or human rights concerns.[123] Within Russia there were some regions that generated a particularly heavy postbag, not just the big cities but (for instance) Krasnodar, Rostov and Irkutsk. There was good reason for this – the first two were in the southern federal district, where there were serious and continuing difficulties with criminality, employment and the settlement of migrants. Irkutsk, in Siberia, more often generated letters about environmental matters, although the number of such communications fell significantly after the President ordered an oil pipeline to be located further from Lake Baikal than had originally been intended in an apparent response to these expressions of public dissatisfaction.[124]

Letters to the President often raised individual cases of injustice or maladministration, as in the sad story that came from the parents of a young conscript who had lost his life in

Chechnya. His patrol had been ambushed and soon ran out of ammunition, after which it defended itself – as long as it could – with knives. The corpse was handed over two days later, after a ransom had been paid, and the bereaved parents themselves received 10,000 roubles (about $350) by way of compensation. But why was this so much less than the hundreds of thousands of roubles that had been paid to the families of the Kursk victims, whose submarine had sunk in the Baltic in August 2000? The dead man's father had worked as a tractor driver before the tragedy, and his mother had a job as well; but afterwards everything went wrong – the bereaved mother was hospitalised, both parents lost their employment, and the local hospital (where treatment would have been free) closed down. Their daughter, meanwhile, was a schoolteacher in Moscow but had been unable to get hold of the documents that would have allowed her to register with the authorities. Could Vladimir Vladimirovich possibly find her a room in a communal flat, even though he had 'so many things' to take care of? Another letter came from a pensioner in his mid-sixties who had a thousand dollars in his bank account, which would be enough for a decent funeral. But according to the law, it would be six months before his grieving relatives could access the funds; they could get $300 relatively quickly, but only if they produced a notarised death certificate. Would this be enough? (And how much would be spent on the funeral of the Russian President himself, when the time came?)[125]

Tat'yana D'yakonova, a 66-year-old pensioner, wrote to the President about her water supply, which had collapsed and flooded her neighbours one January day. More than a year later, she was still living in more or less 'cave conditions', without hot or cold. Local officials just 'fed her with promises', suggesting she try to contact the President. In the end, she did so – and a day later the supply had been restored! Up to this point she had been obliged to carry four buckets of water daily up to her fifth-floor apartment, and once a week visited friends to have a bath. 'All of this in one of the biggest metropolitan cities in the world, in the 21st century!'[126] There were many other typical concerns. For instance, why were local authorities across the country just beginning to repair the heating systems in apartment buildings as the first winter frosts arrived? Why, in industrial cities like Chelyabinsk, were the metallurgical and chemical factories that caused the most environmental damage still inside the city boundaries, and the trees and bushes on its parks and squares being systematically removed? And what about a better system of benefits for families that had larger numbers of children?[127] But Russians wrote to the President about 'literally everything', Mironov explained in another interview: for instance, just after Putin's first election in 2000 there had been a 'real flood of letters all asking to be sent a portrait' (he had been able to satisfy nearly every request), and two years later there had been more than 110,000 latters in the week in which the President had celebrated his fiftieth birthday.[128]

Russians could also write to the government, now headed by the former president. The numbers were much smaller, but steadily increasing: there were just over 83,000 communications of various kinds in 2008, half as many again as the year before. This included eight or nine thousand individual visits to the government's reception office, which was also an increase on earlier years; 9 had been received by a deputy prime minister in person, and more than 250 by individual ministers or heads of government services. There were electronic as well as written and oral communications; and there were letters that had been forwarded by the Presidential Administration, by the Duma and other bodies. More than a third of the communications to the government were addressed directly to the prime minister, and many of them, as was traditional, came from groups of signatories rather than individual citizens. For instance, from the Far East, where feelings had been running high about the imposition of new and higher duties on the import of Japanese cars, which would have an effect on the employment of all who transported and serviced them. But more often than anything else, it was housing, communal services and social security matters that gave the most cause for concern – for instance, the increasing charges that were being made for services of this kind, and the particular problems of parents with young children. The letters, in fact, raised all kinds of issues, from constitutional reform to the short war with Georgia in August 2008; a certain proportion, inevitably, were from citizens with an 'unstable psychology', but otherwise they all received attention.[129]

There were still further means of reaching the attention of the national leadership. One of the most distinctive, during the Putin years, was the 'direct line' that was organised with the entire society through a series of nationwide call-in television broadcasts. At the first, a year after his accession, the Russian President answered questions online for three different internet services.[130] There was an even greater public response when the second took place over the main television channels at the end of 2001; more than 2 million questions and comments were submitted by telephone and in other ways, a 'dialogue with the country' that was apparently without international precedent.[131] There were further 'direct lines' in the later years of Putin's presidency, except in 2004, which was the year of his re-election (see Table 6.9). The 'direct line' that took place in October 2007 was the last and the longest, at more than three hours; there were two and a half million questions from all over the country as well as from an outside broadcast unit in Kazakhstan, and Putin managed to reply to more than sixty of them.[132] One of the questions was from a disabled man who had been obliged to undergo annual medical tests to obtain his prosthetic limbs; another was from a mother who had received almost no governmental assistance in bringing up her eight children; another was from a man who lived on an island in the Russian Far East who was unable to get a job on the mainland because of transport difficulties. Putin promised that all these and other problems would be resolved, mostly by special presidential decrees. Nor did he forget to congratulate the Russian football team on their unexpectedly decisive win over England the previous evening, the first since 1988 (against what was then the USSR).[133] The exercise continued, in similar form and at even greater length, after his move to the premiership.[134]

In parallel, a network of reception offices began to develop across the country from the summer of 2008, organised by United Russia but in the name of Vladimir Putin, who had

Table 6.9 **Putin's 'direct lines', 2001–2010**

	Questions	Answers	Duration
[As President]			
24 Dec 2001	400,000	47	2 hrs 20 mins
19 Dec 2002	1,400,000	51	2 hrs 37 mins
18 Dec 2003	1,500,000	69	2 hrs 50 mins
[2004: not conducted]			
27 Sept 2005	1,000,000	60	2 hrs 54 mins
25 Oct 2006	2,300,000	52	2 hrs 54 mins
18 Oct 2007	2,500,000	68	3 hrs 02 mins
[As Prime Minister]			
4 Dec 2008	2,200,000	72	3 hrs 08 mins
3 Dec 2009	'more than 2,000,000'	82	4 hrs 02 mins
16 Dec 2010	'more than 2,000,000'	90	4 hrs 26 mins

Source: adapted from *Izvestiya*, 5 December 2008, p. 3, 4 December 2009, p. 1, and 17 December 2010, p. 1) (slightly different figures appear in other sources.

become party leader after he had stepped down as head of state. By the end of the year, there were branches in all the republics and regions, and about 2,500 at local level. Reception offices did not necessarily provide a means of reaching the leadership in person, but Putin attended the opening of the first of them, in Nizhnii Novgorod in July 2008;[135] their purpose, he told party activists, was to 'help particular people with their questions, problems, and perhaps misfortunes', and to 'analyse the whole mass of communications and identify the key problems that require attention'.[136] It was certainly a mechanism that allowed the changing public mood to be recorded. In March 2009, for instance, as the international financial crisis deepened, there were many more who came to express their concern about shorter working weeks, cuts in pay and sackings, and about the problems they were encountering with banks and home loans, as well as to make the usual complaints about housing. Some of the biggest industrial centres were experiencing a shortage of subsidised medicines, a consequence of the cutbacks that were taking place at the massive factories that underpinned the social services of the cities in which they were located. Taken as a whole, complaints that were connected in one way or another with declining living standards had increased by up to a quarter. As well as providing a way in which the authorities could at least appear to be taking account of the concerns of ordinary people, a network of reception offices of this kind also allowed the national party leadership to compare the experience of daily life across the regions and to draw conclusions about the performance of their respective chief executives.[137]

Putin's successor, Dmitri Medvedev, arranged to visit the presidential reception office in central Moscow at least twice a year to meet letter-writers in person, and to give instructions to governors and ministers – where appropriate, by video conferencing. In

April 2009, for instance, he agreed to organise a meeting in the Kremlin of all the Heroes of the Soviet Union on the occasion of the seventy-fifth anniversary of the establishment of the country's highest distinction, to establish a museum on the site of the world's first atomic energy station in Obninsk and to issue a commemorative badge on the fiftieth anniversary of the student construction brigades that had responded to Khrushchev's call to settle the 'virgin lands' of Kazakhstan.[138] In July he met two visitors in person and arranged for pedestrian crossings, the removal of sulphur from a river port, the extension of water and gas supplies to two isolated villages and the construction of a working model of the plane in which the aviator Chkalov had completed a celebrated non-stop flight from Moscow to North America over the North Pole in 1937.[139] The reception office had a facility for mothers and children, disabled access and a first-aid clinic as well as a waiting room; visitors were received from Tuesdays to Saturdays from 9.30 in the morning until 4.45 in the afternoon. A specially equipped studio on the upper floor with a massive screen and satellite connections allowed the President, whenever he wished, to interact directly not just with Muscovites but with the entire society.[140]

Medvedev made a more distinctive contribution to the flow of political communication when he opened a blog on the presidential website in October 2008. At first, it was limited to a series of recorded video messages – for instance, on 'recreation and the development of mass-participation sport'. But from January 2009, it became possible to leave comments on these communications, and a special domain, *blog.kremlin.ru*, was created for the purpose.[141] He read the comments, Medvedev told journalists, and intended to respond individually to some of them.[142] He went a step further later in the year by establishing a 'virtual community', a 'logical extension' of his videoblog. 'Thanks to the "Live Journal" I will interact more actively with other users of the Web', he promised (he had already been dubbed 'the digital president'). Videos and posts would be copied here from the Kremlin website, and registered users would be able to discuss them more freely. Already many politicians, including some oppositionists, were making use of these new opportunities. Medvedev himself would follow the discussion closely, his press secretary told journalists, although he would not often be able to respond in person.[143] Other staff members reported that the presidential blog was consulted by as many as 90,000 daily and that it attracted even larger audiences than interviews on the main television channels.[144] It was 'increasingly becoming a reception office for complaints to the President about the mistakes and unfairness of officials in the Russian regions', commented *Komsomol'skaya pravda*; ordinary people knew this was a way of reaching the President without passing through the hands of a 'provincial bureaucracy' that was likely to sanitise anything it sent on to a higher authority.[145]

Letters to the editor in the postcommunist years

Letters to the newspapers, clearly, had a different function in a political system in which alternatives could be directly articulated by opposition parties at elections. But Russian newspapers continued their 'work with letters' into the postcommunist period, and they remained a central feature of Russia's, and for some time the world's, bestselling paper, the weekly *Argumenty i fakty*, where the editorial day began with the 'enormous bags of mail' that had come in from readers.[146] There were, it appeared, four main kinds of correspondent. The 'irreconcilables', usually of advanced years, wanted to disagree with what the paper had to say; the 'analysts', usually over 50, had their own ideas for the improvement of the society in which they lived; and there were the 'fighters for justice', usually over 30, who were concerned with matters like the poor quality of the food that was provided in kindergartens. Others still had purely personal concerns: El'vira from Tyumen wanted the paper to send her an electric milking machine, Viktor from Orsk wondered where he could find an egg incubator, Oksana and Valerii from Kostroma wanted to get married but were short of the roubles they needed for the reception and hoped other readers could help. And there were individual but well-intentioned citizens like Mr Polevik of Moscow, who had observed a 'large collection of condoms of various sizes' floating down the river and wondered 'which institution (?!) abuses sex and throws these objects into the river' (it was letters of this kind, the paper explained, that it received with the greatest satisfaction).[147]

The letters that appeared in *Argumenty i fakty* in the early postcommunist years raised all kinds of public issues – sometimes, indeed, the entire newspaper was devoted to them. How much, for instance, did the presidents of the CIS states earn? (Yeltsin, it emerged, was not the best paid.)[148] What about Yeltsin himself: was it true that his father had served in Kolchak's anti-Bolshevik army during the civil war? (No, but he and his brother had suffered political persecution in the late 1930s.)[149] Many letters in the summer of 1996 warned of the dangers of a Communist victory at the forthcoming presidential election: would the 'Berezka' shops come back, where Soviet goods had been sold for foreign currency? Would soap operas on television be banned? And would sausage keep as long as four years, until the following round of elections had taken place?[150] Other questions reflected an understandable curiosity about the economic changes that were taking place over the same period. What, for instance, was an '*off-shornaya zona*'?[151] What was a 'golden share' in a company?[152] What were 'notebook computers', and where could you buy them?[153] Could an elderly woman bequeath her apartment to her cat? (She could, so far as the law was concerned.)[154] How could you open a licensed brothel?[155] Where could former prisoners invest their vouchers?[156] What had the leadership done with their own? (The head of the privatisation committee, Anatolii Chubais, had yet to make up his mind.)[157] And could you sell your body in advance of your death, asked a Mr Ivanov of Moscow region, who was trying to survive on a 'small pension'?[158]

Letter-writers had personal questions as well. It was to the press, for instance, that Russians turned to find out if they could take a dog on the underground, if they could buy a place in a graveyard with their privatisation voucher, if the Russian government had an astrological service, and if the presidents of the CIS states had been born under a particular sign of the zodiac.[159] And some had still more intimate concerns. Which men, for instance, were the most sexually potent, asked Galya from Novgorod, for whom it was 'very important'? (Finns, apparently, had the highest sperm counts per cubic centimetre.)[160] And how much did it cost to engage the services of a prostitute? (No more than a few roubles or a glass of port wine on Komsomol Square, where three of Moscow's main railway stations were located, the paper reported, but hundreds of dollars in an Intourist hotel and even more for 'special services', like a lesbian show or a bisexual act; foreigners apparently thought these charges were excessive.)[161] An anguished 'L. K.' wrote in from the oil town of Tyumen to report that his wife was 'constantly complaining that he wasn't very ...' and yet he wasn't old, what could be done to improve his performance? (He was advised at all costs to 'avoid monotony'.)[162] 'A. K.' of Izhevsk had lost an important part of his anatomy in a car crash two years earlier 'and now what can I do? I can't even masturbate' (the paper explained that 'artificial members' could be obtained in sex shops and even at the chemist's).[163] 'Kh. A.' from the Bashkir capital Ufa had a rather different problem. He used to have two wives, and got on well with both of them; but now they had turned against him. Perhaps the paper could help him 'win back the favour of at least one of them' so that he could 'have some comfort in his old age?'[164]

Russians raised a still wider range of personal concerns in their letters during these early postcommunist years. How, for instance, could women lose weight? Polina from Penza had given up: 'diets are no use; in the evening all the same I fill myself up'.[165] Others were more successful: a 13-year-old girl from Chelyabinsk claimed to have lost 20 kilograms in a single month by sticking to juice and porridge, and a correspondent from St Petersburg recommended apples – one for breakfast, two for lunch and three for dinner. A more exotic proposal came from a reader in Uzbekistan, who told the magazine *Rabotnitsa* that women in her republic drank their own urine: 'It keeps us thin and makes our complexion smooth.'[166] There was Lena, aged 16, who wondered what she could do about her hair, which was falling out in great quantities.[167] Others were interested in various forms of cosmetic surgery. Was it dangerous, for instance, to have silicone breast implants? (Not at all, the operation could be done in Russia itself and 'to great effect'.)[168] Was it safe to take a flight in such circumstances, or would they burst? (The paper was reassuring.)[169] And how did women with large busts manage with such a 'heavy load'?[170] A male correspondent, N. Z. of Moscow, had a rather different problem: he was a necrophile. Dead dogs no longer satisfied him, and he was going to look for employment in a morgue; but were his activities illegal? (Apparently not, but he was advised to find a psychiatrist at the earliest opportunity as many who began like him with cats and dogs went on to commit much more serious offences.)[171]

There were particular difficulties in reconciling a changing personal morality with the views of older generations, and indeed a shortage of living space in general (what could you do, for instance, if your grown-up children wanted to use your apartment for their sexual encounters? When you were reaching the 'most interesting moment' and there was the sound of a key in the door?[172]) A husband and wife wanted to know what 'swinging' was. And N. Z. of Novosibirsk had 'no idea what to talk about in bed with your lover – not the cost of living presumably?'[173] Another enquiry was prompted by Sergei Mikhalkov's prize-winning film *Burnt by the Sun*, in which 'it was not he who was on top of his wife, but she on him!' In twenty years, wrote Mr Akulov from Krasnoyarsk, he and his wife had never thought of trying 'Mikhalkov sex'; could the paper please tell them about 'Gaidar sex' and 'Zhirinovsky sex' as well?[174] But another correspondent had no sex life at all because her husband washed very infrequently and the smell in the house was unbearable.[175] And some wanted advice about less conventional relationships. L. P. of Lipetsk, for instance, wanted to know 'Can a woman love another woman?'[176] Thirteen-year-old Olga wrote in similar terms to share the 'problem, even misfortune' that she was obsessed with a female singer.[177] There were girls who were in love with their brothers ('unfortunately, he loves me too').[178] L. M. of Nizhnii Novgorod wanted to know if two cousins, 'secretly in love', could get married, as aristocrats used to do (it all depended how closely they were related).[179]

Most often of all, readers were simply curious. Had Graham Greene, for instance, been a spy? (He had.)[180] Did cosmonauts, after a long time in space, have dreams in which they were flying?[181] And a married pair of cosmonauts had been sent into space by the United States: a reader wanted to ask the 'delicate question' whether they had made love in these weightless conditions, 'at least for scientific purposes?'[182] Other readers asked what pets government leaders had; and N. G. of Arzamas wanted to know if cats could manage without sex, as he lived on the eighth floor of an apartment building and never let his pet outside the building.[183] What, asked other curious readers, did priests earn? And did prostitutes get pensions?[184] What was President Bush's pension? In which films had Ronald Reagan acted, and where in Russia could they be seen? And had any US states ever tried to become independent?[185] What was a 'computer virus'?[186] Was it true that Michael Jackson had a skin disease, and that he had already died?[187] And that a Russian émigré had designed the US one dollar bill? (It was.)[188] If there was no longer a USSR, asked still further readers, what was to become of Heroes of the Soviet Union?[189] And what could be done about alimony payments from a former partner who was living in a different Soviet republic that had now become an independent state?[190] Was Turkish tea radioactive?[191] Had Lenin magically transmitted his soul to Mikhail Gorbachev?[192] Was Jesus Christ a Jew or not?[193] And when He came again, would He take His believers and if so, what about the rest?[194]

The same kinds of personal, sometimes intimate, issues were being raised in the early years of the new century. 'M. V.' of Tambov, for instance, whose husband was in prison, had sent him a sex toy that had been confiscated because items of this kind were 'not allowed'. But there was no provision of this kind in the prison regulations. Why were prisoners, in effect, being encouraged to engage in homosexual relations? (A prison official explained that materials of a 'pornographic character' were not permitted, but the Duma had been unable to agree on a definition and it was good that such a 'piquant theme' was being ventilated in the pages of the country's most popular newspaper.)[195] Dmitri Aleshin of Syktyvkar wrote in to complain that he had bought a packet of condoms 'just in case', but at the 'most important moment' it had turned out that they were 'ridiculously small'. What condoms should he buy to make sure he had the 'right size'? (The paper consulted a group of prostitutes, who agreed that Chinese, Japanese and Russian condoms were generally the shortest and American the longest.)[196] Why, asked another correspondent, was a big bust thought to be attractive, but not a big bottom? A well-endowed woman would presumably have no difficulty nourishing an infant; but if that was true, why were models with slim figures held up as the ideal of female beauty? (The paper replied that to consider childbirth by looking at a large bottom was 'the same as thinking that a television with a big screen would have better programmes'.)[197] Why was it illegal to have sex in public parks, asked an indignant I. Nikolaev of Moscow? 'We weren't bothering anyone, and it will soon be summer again.'[198] And why did the Orthodox Church insist on total celibacy during Lent? (The Church explained that it considered such questions 'individually' and that the prohibition did not apply to newly-weds or to couples who had been separated for a long time.)[199]

But more often than not, Russians were still just curious. Why, for instance, did ballerinas live so long? How many cars were there in Putin's garage, and was he allowed to drive them himself? ('Very rarely.') How did President Medvedev spend his 220,000 roubles a month? (Increasingly on charity.)[200] And where had all the UFOs gone, asked a Kaliningrad reader. (She was assured that they were 'still being regularly spotted'.)[201] How much did it cost to preserve Lenin in his tomb on Red Square? (About $100,000 a year.)[202] How soon would they be able to speak to the dead? (The paper was not encouraging.)[203] Would you turn into a homosexual if you drank too much beer? (No, but your chances of paternity might be reduced.)[204] What was the best age to get married? (26 for a woman and between 27 and 31 for a man, the paper suggested.)[205] How much had J. K. Rowling been paid for the sale of her 'Harry Potter' books in Russia? (The exact figure was a 'commercial secret' but the paper had no doubt it would have 'five zeros – in foreign currency, naturally'.)[206] Was it true that film star Leonardo DiCaprio was of Russian origin? (Yes it was; so were Sylvester Stallone, Michael Douglas and Harrison Ford.) And that he had an ongoing relationship with a Russian model? (So, at the time, did Mel Gibson and one of the Rolling Stones.)[207] What would Judas's thirty pieces of silver be worth in current prices? (About $4,000.)[208] Who was Mrs Putin's dress designer? (She preferred 'exclusively Russian fashion' but kept the names to herself.)[209] And was the President himself ever sick? (Yes, but never to such an extent that he was unable to perform his official duties.)[210]

There were also correspondents who wanted to raise public issues of various kinds, and sometimes in indignant tones. Why, for instance, were deputies not prosecuted for fighting in the Duma, as ordinary people would be if they conducted themselves in the same outrageous manner?[211] And why were the lists of candidates for almost all the political parties full of sportsmen, officials and businessmen, asked D. Khrenov from Voronezh, but he had heard of just a single milkmaid and a single former worker? (The former head of the Central Electoral Commission explained that a professional parliament had replaced the soviets of people's deputies and there was no evidence that workers' interests were better represented by workers themselves; the paper itself disagreed with him – in what way was a well-qualified worker, farmer, teacher or doctor a less appropriate member of the legislature than a newly successful businessman or manager who was 'cut off from life', not to speak of 'concert artists and footballers?')[212] Why did nobody live in the Kremlin, unlike the White House? (Officials explained that it was unsuitable for residential purposes.)[213] And why did Solzhenitsyn only meet foreigners? His wife had told reporters that the writer was 'hard at work' and that interviews 'distracted him'. But why then had he given a lengthy audience to a German magazine? And why was he so reluctant to talk to his own people – perhaps he was afraid he would not be heard? (The writer himself had no fear he would not be heard in his own country, his wife explained, but Russian policy was being 'very tendentiously' interpreted by the Western media and nobody else was trying to correct their misapprehensions.)[214]

Other correspondents raised still further issues. Why, for instance, were railway fares going up so rapidly?[215] Why were all the public toilets so dirty, from Pskov to Magadan?[216] And what could you do if you had lost your employment: like Mrs Zaitseva of Kaliningrad, who had voted for the new Russian president but found herself forced out of the bank at which she had worked for many years at the same time as her husband lost his job in the automobile industry?[217] Others still wanted to know how they could reduce roadside advertising.[218] And what about a ban on genetically modified foods? (Greenpeace activists and the Academy of Medical Sciences explained that it would 'do more harm than good' as the equipment available was quite insufficient and controls would have to be applied to all the food that came from abroad, the only result of which would be that supply became uncertain and prices much higher.)[219] Why, asked others, were Moscow and St Petersburg universities no more than 'outsiders' in the latest list of the world's top higher educational institutions?[220] Why did the Russian government 'treat its people like cattle', when all the flights to Sochi were cancelled for several hours to facilitate a group of officials after an international economic forum?[221] Was it true that officials and Duma deputies were still taking their holidays in Courchevel in spite of the economic crisis, and that in the Duma itself the cost of meals had been frozen and the sums available for foreign trips had been increased? (Prices in the Duma restaurant had actually gone up, the paper was told, the budget for foreign trips had been reduced, and deputies themselves had sustained 'heavy losses'.)[222]

The Constitution of 1993 had already made reference to communications from citizens in Article 33, which established that citizens had the 'right to appeal personally, and also to send individual and collective communications to state bodies and organs of local government'. The flow of communications of all kinds increased steadily: up to 2000 there had been somewhat more than a million letters to government at all levels, but there were more than 2.6 million in 2003, and on the 'most cautious estimates' at least 10 million a year to local government bodies.[223] A new framework for all such matters was introduced in 2006 in a law 'on the procedure for considering communications from citizens'. Not only Russian but also foreign citizens were to be allowed to submit their 'appeals, proposals, announcements and complaints'; they would receive a written response that dealt with the substance of their communication, and if they were dissatisfied, could appeal against it. The law, in addition, prohibited the persecution of citizens for any attempt to 'restore or defend their own rights, freedoms and legitimate interests', or those of others. Anonymous letters, however, would not be considered, nor any that raised issues on which a court had already pronounced judgement, nor any that used abusive language or threatened the life, wellbeing or property of an official or any members of their family. All communications of whatever kind had to be registered, and up to thirty days would be allowed for a response; government bodies would be allowed up to fifteen days to provide whatever documentation was required. At least on paper, matters had moved some distance forward.[224]

But there were still many cases, as there had been in the Soviet period, in which letter-writers themselves were victimised for raising an issue with the authorities – forced to leave their job 'at their own request' and move elsewhere, threatened with legal action, or given to understand that they might even have placed themselves at risk of physical injury. Part of the problem was that a complaint was likely to be sent back – in spite of the provisions of the law – to the authorities in the district from which it had originated, who might themselves have been the object of the complaint. Or it might be given to a junior official to deal with, who would be well aware that his or her long-term interests would be better served by protecting superiors than by taking the side of ordinary citizens. All of this showed how little influence the President could actually command in daily life throughout the country, commented a writer in *Argumenty i fakty*, and how much 'open resistance' to his authority continued to exist at the regional and local level. 'Complaining about your problems to the authorities, federal, regional or local, was always a thankless, pointless, and sometimes risky occupation in our country', added a film director. 'That's what it was in the Soviet years, and so it remains in contemporary Russian society. And I honestly don't believe it will ever change. Government in our country was always on one side, the people on the other. Ordinary mortals had better get used to the idea that in Russia you can only rely on yourself.'[225]

The life hereafter

Russians lost a state and a ruling party in 1991. But more than this, they lost a belief system that had defined their entire existence. Whether or not they had internalised its values, Marxism–Leninism explained the place that Russians occupied in the world in which they lived: their place in their own society, and the place of the USSR itself in a wider process of global change. It had been an official ideology for more than two generations, and by 1989, when the last Soviet census was conducted, fewer than 5 per cent had been born before the October revolution and fewer still had any conscious memory of a non-socialist society.[226]

Russia, before the revolution, had been an overwhelmingly Orthodox and Christian country; the churches retained their legal existence after 1917, and believers enjoyed the right to practise under successive constitutions. Official theory, however, suggested that 'superstitions' of this kind would gradually disappear along with the attitudes and values that arose from 'pre-socialist socioeconomic formations', and that a 'materialist world outlook' would take their place.[227] Nor, it seemed, was this a misplaced confidence. Studies of religious behaviour found that levels of observance had fallen from 80 per cent at the end of the 1920s to 50 per cent by the late 1930s and to 10–20 per cent by the 1960s;[228] by the end of the 1970s, levels of observance had fallen still further, to 8–10 per cent, and skilled workers, farm staff and the intelligentsia were 'almost entirely free of religious convictions'.[229] There were certainly variations from year to year: but the general tendency was clear, and this was the 'elimination of religion as a result of socioeconomic and cultural changes'.[230]

   The evidence, in fact, was much less straightforward than these figures suggested. For a start, it had simply become more difficult to practise, as about two-thirds of the churches that were active before the revolution had simply been closed (as late as 1997 there were just over 8,000 Orthodox communities for the whole of the Russian Federation but more than 27,000 towns or villages for them to serve, and 'for many Russians, the journey from home to the nearest church took many hours, or even days').[231] Those who were young and better educated, on top of this, had every reason to conceal their faith if they had career ambitions of any kind (which was one of the reasons for the predominance of women and the elderly among those who attended services). Even so, 'something like 70 million' defined themselves as believers,[232] which was more than three times the membership of the Communist Party. At the same time, it had become increasingly apparent that believers as well as atheists had a remarkably diffuse and contradictory set of personal philosophies. Believers, for a start, had an 'almost 100 per cent ignorance' of the Scriptures and were quite ready to accept that it was possible to lead a good life without a belief in God; many, indeed, thought religion was positively harmful. At the same time almost half the atheists who were questioned in the late Soviet years thought it was impossible to live without a belief in some kind of God, and the same proportion were unwilling to support a campaign against the levels of 'religious superstition' that still remained.[233] Other non-believers displayed icons in their homes, marked their graves with crosses and observed church holidays 'out of habit or respect for their elders and relatives'.[234]

   The end of communist rule brought about an end to a situation in which believers had been restricted in their expression of faith, and sometimes penalised. But there had been considerable changes in the public role of religion in the late Soviet years, and in any case there were many respects in which church teaching could find common ground with Marxism–Leninism, including a commitment to family life, a strong and united Russia, and peace with other nations and nationalities. The Orthodox Church, in particular, was bound to favour a greater degree of freedom for its own worshippers; but it was ambiguous about liberal democracy, which was not to be understood as the right to make unreasonable demands, and hostile to Western influence, including that of other churches – 'spiritual aggression', in the words of one of the most outspoken of its leaders, that could result in 'moral degeneration the like of which the much-suffering Russian people have never known before'.[235] Church leaders, indeed, were willing to allow their organisations to be used to marginalise any who were publicly critical of state policy or of the treatment of believers in particular, and they were closely associated with the promotion of a relationship with other nations that was virtually the same as the government's own 'Leninist peace policy'.[236] At the same time it was the only institution that commanded a high level of public confidence; it offered a belief system that was the only coherent alternative to Marxism–Leninism; it had publications, property and staff; and its commitment to a particular leader, or a particular set of policies, had enormous potential influence in an unstable political environment.[237]

There had been few indications at the outset that the Gorbachev leadership was one in which there was likely to be a reconciliation between church and state.[238] The General Secretary himself, visiting Tashkent in November 1986, had called for a 'decisive and uncompromising struggle with religious phenomena', and was particularly scathing about party officials who campaigned for communist values but took part themselves in religious ceremonies.[239] A different line began to emerge soon afterwards, taking its cue from an unsigned article on 'socialism and religion' that appeared in the party's theoretical journal *Kommunist* in March 1988. Ostensibly a reconsideration of church–state relations during the early years of Soviet rule, the article went on to call for a much more general reassessment of the place of religion in a socialist society. The existence of millions of believers, it pointed out, was 'a reality', and everything must be done to avoid 'primitivism' in dealing with them.[240] The new line became still clearer after a meeting between Gorbachev and the hierarchy in April 1988 on the occasion of the millennium of the Orthodox Church, in which the Soviet leader spoke of the 'universal norms and customs' both sides had in common and invited believers as well as atheists to join together in the 'common great cause of the restructuring and renewal of socialism'; he drew particular attention to the way in which the Church had been taking a more active part in official public organisations, such as the Children's Fund and the Cultural Fund.[241] The Patriarch, for his part, described the Party Programme as 'highly humane' and 'close to the Christian ideal'.[242]

It was certainly clear that there had been significant changes in the position of believers and their churches by the late communist period. Gorbachev, it emerged, had himself been baptised, and his mother was a regular worshipper.[243] An early gesture of some importance was the return of the Danilov monastery in Moscow to the Orthodox Church; refurbished, it played a central role in the millennium celebrations a few years later. Other property, including the Kremlin cathedrals, had been returned by the end of the decade, and thousands of new churches had opened all over the country.[244] Another first was the meeting between Gorbachev and the Pope, which took place in December

1989; the following year diplomatic relations were formally established between the USSR and the Holy See.[245] Religious believers, even priests, began to appear in the print and electronic media, the first religious leaders were elected to the Soviet parliament in 1989 (some of them in open competition with other candidates) and a religious presence began to establish itself in educational and charitable work, including the first prison chaplaincies since 1917.[246] The first religious services took place in the Kremlin cathedrals in January 1990, and the first religious broadcasts went out over state television;[247] a year later, establishing another precedent, the Orthodox Christmas was celebrated as a public holiday.[248] By the winter of 1990–1, religious broadcasts, phone-ins and faith healing sessions were already 'common occurrences', and in April 1991 the first Orthodox radio station began regular transmissions.[249]

The last months of communist rule, in 1990 and 1991, extended the liberties of believers still further through a series of more formal measures. The Law on Property, approved in 1990, gave the churches full rights of ownership,[250] and a Law on Freedom of Conscience, adopted later in the year, established the right of believers to propagate their faith and of parents to give their children a religious upbringing (which had up to this point been illegal if the children were under 18 years old). The churches themselves were given the right to take part in public life and to establish their own newspapers, although not political parties; and they were allowed to establish their own schools and colleges.[251] The Communist Party had meanwhile changed its rules in 1990 to allow believers to join its ranks;[252] religion, the Secretariat explained, was based on 'general human, moral and cultural values', and the party's aim was not to offend the susceptibilities of believers but to enlist them in 'joint action for the renewal of socialist society'.[253] The Soviet parliament, in one of its last acts, adopted a 'declaration of the rights and freedoms of the individual' that included a guarantee of religious belief and practice.[254] The same guarantees were included in a declaration of rights and freedoms that was approved by the Russian parliament in November 1991;[255] and then in December 1993 the new constitution took matters still further, guaranteeing the 'right to profess, individually or jointly with others, any religion, or to profess no religion, to freely choose, hold and disseminate religious or other beliefs, and to act in accordance with them' in an article that could not be amended by parliamentary vote.[256]

Acting within the framework of this legislation, religious groups and believers more generally had come to play a central role in Russian public life by the early 1990s. The Patriarch was the first to speak at the inauguration of the newly elected president in July 1991, and Yeltsin himself made it known that he attended a religious service 'about once a month'.[257] Both he and the Soviet prime minister, Valentin Pavlov, had attended the Easter service in the Epiphany Cathedral earlier in the year, among a 'gaggle of senior officials who stood gamely, if somewhat sheepishly, at the front of the church, occasionally bowing and fiddling with candles in an attempt to show that they were not totally unfamiliar with the Orthodox rites'.[258] Religious parties had begun to establish themselves in the late 1980s, and several of them contested the 1993 and 1995 parliamentary elections: in 1995 a Christian-Democratic Union and a Muslim movement presented their own lists of candidates, and a Party of the Orthodox, a Russian Christian-Democratic Party and a Russian Christian-Democratic Movement took part as members of a larger pre-election bloc. Symbolically, the largest change of all was the reappearance in central Moscow of the Cathedral of Christ the Saviour. Built in the nineteenth century to commemorate the defeat of Napoleon, it was destroyed by the Soviet authorities in 1931 but reconstructed on the basis of the original design (it was symbolic in other ways that a new commercial facility was constructed underneath it on an even more impressive scale).[259] 'Never before', commented *Izvestiya* in April 1995, had the church's 'participation in the political life of the country [been] so conspicuous'.[260]

Just as the Soviet system reflected a distinctive blend of Marxism and Russian traditions, so too the Russian Orthodox Church combined more general Christian values with a number of particular characteristics. The Orthodox Church had been a state church that was all but identical with citizenship itself in prerevolutionary Russia, and it was more closely associated with the work of government than was the case in the countries that belonged to the Western Christian tradition and especially those that had experienced the church–state conflicts of the Reformation. There was a fairly loose understanding of 'membership', and religious belief was more closely associated with participation in a community of believers than with a formal doctrine.[261] The church stood for values that were not of this world, and it could hardly accept restrictions on the rights of believers or the sequestration of its property. But there were reconciliations at moments of national crisis, such as the Second World War, and there were associations of several other kinds: the party leadership, in practice, made nominations to leading positions, some members of the hierarchy regarded it as their patriotic duty to report to the KGB,[262] and in the postcommunist period it began to enjoy official favour as the 'national' church as compared with unregistered and, still more so, foreign denominations and sects.[263] It was certainly clear, by the early years of the new century, that this was the organised faith of the great majority of Russian believers, and that it was the only one with a genuinely national presence; the new Patriarch, Kirill, elected in January 2009, had a national presence of his own through a weekly television programme, *Words of a Pastor*, and was soon (like his predecessor) rated one of the country's 'most influential politicians'.[264]

There had been a substantial change in the formal position of the churches even before the end of Soviet rule, and the early postcommunist years saw a rapid increase in the number of parishes in which more than sixty different denominations organised their worship (Table 6.10); the Orthodox Church, on which we concentrate in this discussion, was by far the largest. But what had been taking place in the wider society? Were there more believers than before, and were they more active in their expression of faith? Levels of religiosity had certainly stabilised by the late 1990s after what some commentators described as an 'explosion' in the late communist period, but this left more than half the population as self-identified believers, compared with just 10 per cent in the late

Table 6.10 **The main religious denominations, 1996–2010**

	1996	2000	2004	2008	2010
All denominations	13,073	17,427	21,664	22,866	22,507
Russian Orthodox Church	7,195	9,236	11,525	12,586	12,435
Muslims	2,494	3,098	3,537	3,815	3,862
Pentecostalists	351	678	1,355	1,581	1,313
Baptists	677	807	979	903	857
Evangelical Christians	248	430	698	703	668
Seventh Day Adventists	222	368	646	608	577
Jehovah's Witnesses	129	305	386	400	407
Jews	80	130	267	286	284
Old Believers	164	211	284	283	269
Roman Catholic Church	183	236	248	240	222
Lutherans	141	201	219	228	212
Buddhists	124	176	192	200	198
Presbyterian Church	129	185	176	179	170
Methodists	48	67	105	111	106

Source: adapted from *Rossiiskii statisticheskii yezhegodnik*, various years, showing all denominations that had at least 100 congregations or other institutions in 2009.

Table 6.11 **Russians and their religions, 1991–2010**

	1991	1996	2000	2002	2003	2004	2005	2007	2010
Are you a religious person? If so, which religion?									
Orthodox	–	44	52	57	61	57	59	66	70
Not religious	–	43	35	34	30	32	30	23	21
Islam	–	3	4	5	5	4	6	3	4
Other / Hard to say	–	10	9	5	5	8	5	8	5
How often do you attend religious services?									
At least once a month	5	7	–	8	6	–	–	8	8
At least once a year	20	17	–	18	30	–	–	34	32
Do not attend	65	60	–	59	46	–	–	39	45
How much confidence do you have in the church and religious organisations?									
Complete confidence	–	39	38	40	40	43	44	40	52

Source: adapted from 'Religiya i tserkov'' at www.levada.ru/religion.html, last accessed 31 January 2010.

1980s.[265] About two-thirds described themselves as 'Orthodox' in a general sense, but not necessarily as believers (see Table 6.11); about 60 per cent could be considered 'believers', according to a variety of investigations, and about 40 per cent had been baptised.[266] Believers, as in other societies, were disproportionately female and somewhat more

Table 6.12 **Russians and their religion in comparative perspective**

	Russia	UK	USA	India	Nigeria	Mexico
'I have always believed in God'	42	46	79	92	98	82
'I pray regularly'	22	28	67	86	95	63
'I regularly attend an organised religious service'	7	21	54	52	91	58
'I don't believe death is the end'	54	54	74	51	79	55
'God (a higher power) created the universe'	55	52	85	89	95	83
'A belief in God (a higher power) makes for a better person'	81	56	82	91	96	80

Source: adapted from an ICM survey (in Russia n = 1000), fieldwork January 2004, consulted at http://news.bbc.co.uk/1/shared/spl/hi/programmes/wtwtgod/pdf/wtwtogod.pdf, last accessed 20 September 2010; figures show agreement in rounded percentages.

numerous in the older age-groups, although the young were more religious than the middle-aged (two different kinds of religiosity appeared to be involved, a more formal and traditional belief on the part of older generations and a more individual and emotional attachment in the case of younger age-groups).[267] Believers, in addition, were likely to have lower levels of education than the average, and lower incomes; surprisingly perhaps, levels of belief were lowest of all in medium-sized towns, rather higher in the countryside, but highest of all in Moscow and St Petersburg.[268]

Patterns of observance were another matter again. On the major church festivals, attendances were high: more than 80 per cent of the entire population at the time of the Orthodox Easter.[269] But there were very few who attended church on a more regular basis. No more than 8 per cent of the adult population took part in a ceremony at least once a month, according to the 2010 survey evidence,[270] a level of attendance that was among the lowest internationally (see Table 6.12),[271] and so low that for the overwhelming majority it failed to satisfy the normal requirements of church membership.[272] Believers, by the same token, were unlikely to pray on a regular basis, or to observe even the most important church festivals.[273] And what they actually believed in was equally confused. Only a minority, for instance, believed in heaven and hell, or in life after death.[274] Believers, at the same time, were more likely than others to give credence to a whole series of supernatural phenomena that had no place in any conventional Christianity. They were more likely than agnostics or atheists to tell interviewers that Oriental wisdom played a 'large role in their life'; they were more likely at the same time to believe in the transubstantiation of souls, and in extrasensory perception. Believers, similarly, were more likely than others to believe in telepathy, astrology, the evil eye and the abominable snowman; and they were more likely than atheists (although slightly less likely than agnostics) to believe in flying saucers.[275] Conversely, atheists were generally 'positive' or 'very positive' in their attitude to Orthodoxy; substantial proportions thought the church provided answers to moral questions, and that it satisfied spiritual needs.[276]

Across the whole society, including those who regarded themselves as religious as well as those who did not, perhaps the clearest conclusion of all was the 'paradoxical and contradictory nature' of Russian religious belief.[277] For a start, very large numbers believed in various forms of superstition – in omens (63 per cent), apparitions (59 per cent) or the evil eye (66 per cent). Fewer believed in miracles (40 per cent) and fewer still in life after death (33 per cent) or the life eternal (29 per cent).[278] As many as 80 per cent, in surveys that took place in the early years of the new century, identified themselves as Orthodox, but no more than 59 per cent believed in God, 44 per cent thought of themselves as 'believers' and only 27 per cent believed in life after death; by contrast, 43 per cent believed in astrology and black magic.[279] Believers, not surprisingly, were more likely than others to believe in God, but they were also more likely to believe 13 was an unlucky number and that the stars determined their destiny, and they were more likely to believe in telepathy, astrology and flying saucers.[280] Believers, in fact, were 'inclined to believe in everything: from the belief that a black cat brings bad luck, to a belief in the President'.[281] And Christians were by no means exceptional in the 'extremely contradictory' nature of their beliefs. Among the much smaller Buddhist community, for instance, only 60 per cent believed in the transubstantiation of souls, which was a central tenet of their belief, but 25 per cent of Muslims did so, although it was entirely incompatible with the religion to which they nominally subscribed; so did 16 per cent of Catholics and Jews, and 13 per cent of Protestants.[282]

Given these amorphous and heterogeneous beliefs, it was not surprising that there were few direct associations between religiosity and Russian politics. In our 2010 survey, for instance, the overwhelming majority (83 per cent) defined themselves as Orthodox; among those who had voted for United Russia in the 2007 Duma election the proportion was 86 per cent, and among Communist voters 81 per cent. It was those who had not voted at all who were a little different, with just under 75 per cent identifying themselves as Orthodox. Across the entire sample, just over 8 per cent attended a church at least once a month; among those who had voted for United Russia it was 9 per cent and among those who had voted for the Communists it was just under 8 per cent. Non-voters were again the exception, with just 6 per cent regular attenders. There were slight differences in left–right self-placement: among those who identified themselves as Russian Orthodox, the largest number assigned themselves to the centre (13 per cent); among atheists, the largest numbers were on the left (11 per cent). But the great majority had no political orientation of any kind. Nor were there obvious differences on a range of policy options. Monthly attenders, for instance, were somewhat more likely to favour restrictions on the media; they were more enthusiastic about state control of the economy, and about the Putin presidency. But on their attitude to democracy in general, 13 per cent entirely agreed that it 'had its shortcomings but was better than any alternative'; exactly the same proportion of the entire sample – and of those who identified themselves as Orthodox – took the same view.[283]

The Orthodox Church, on the other hand, had some influence in defining the legislative context within which it operated, and to its own advantage. A new law that appeared to discriminate against other religions was vetoed by President Yeltsin in June 1997, but approved by the Duma on a further reading and by a majority such that Yeltsin had no alternative but to sign it. The new law[284] excluded 'non-traditional' churches from educational activities, publishing literature or visiting hospitals and prisons unless they could prove they had been active in Russia for at least fifteen years; the law did not make clear how claims of this kind were to be established, and the advantages it gave to Islam, Buddhism and Judaism as well as Orthodoxy were of a kind that were difficult to reconcile with the equality of all religious organisations before the law (art. 14 of the Constitution) and guarantees of freedom of conscience (art. 28). Minority religions, in turn, found it more difficult to defend their position when local officials used a variety of pretexts to restrict their ability to operate. The US State Department's Commission on International Religious Freedom, which regularly monitors such matters, acknowledged in its 2009 report that the Russian government 'generally respected' the freedom of conscience of ordinary citizens, but added that there were indications that some Islamic and non-traditional churches, including Jehovah's Witnesses, were treated with less understanding, and there were increasingly frequent references in official documents to the country's 'spiritual security', which was usually understood to include the Orthodox Church at the expense of some Protestant and newer religious denominations – sometimes described as 'totalitarian sects'.[285]

Church attenders, it emerged, did in fact have distinctive attitudes on many issues that were part of the postcommunist political agenda. Regular attenders, as in other societies, were typically more 'conservative' than their counterparts outside the church: they were more favourable to law and order, and more likely to believe that children should be taught respect for authority; they were more positive towards Nicholas II, but also Stalin; they were more prepared than others to ban 'harmful' books, and to isolate AIDS victims; and they were less favourable to the market and multiparty politics.[286] Believers, equally, were more positive towards a single Slavic state incorporating Russia, Ukraine and Belarus and more inclined to believe that Russia should be declared an Orthodox state with particular privileges for members of the national church.[287] The most religious, across the postcommunist world more generally, were more likely than others to say that 'the new rich should be jailed' and that a woman's place was in the home.[288] Believers, at least in Russia, were more anti-communist than the population as a whole (they were the most hostile towards socialism as a doctrine and to former party officials in government posts); but they were also more likely to favour order above democracy and to support a planned rather than market economy, and they were less committed to the rule of law and human rights.[289] Believers were also more likely to express hostility towards minorities such as the Chechens and gypsies, particularly if they were regular worshippers.[290]

All the same, there were several circumstances that combined to make religion a marginal influence in Russian public life in the early postcommunist years. For a start, there was a loose association between affiliation and belief. There was an even looser association between belief and attendance – generally, in comparative terms, the variable that had the most powerful direct influence on political attitudes and beha-viour;[291] and levels of attendance, as we have seen, were very low as compared with other developed societies. Many took a positive view of the role of religion in society and welcomed the more prominent place the churches had been assuming; but there was evidence that the Orthodox Church in particular was losing some of the trust it had earlier enjoyed, and its moral standing was not improved by reports of its association with the Soviet regime in the past (as the former Patriarch, who had his own KGB cover name, explained to *Izvestiya*, 'Defending one thing, it was necessary to give something else'),[292] or by reports of corruption and immorality.[293] For believers and non-believers alike, there was almost as much faith in the Pope as in the Patriarch, and the writer Solzhenitsyn (until his death in 2008) carried far more authority in matters of belief and morality than either of them.[294] But it was equally true that very few of the parties or presidential candidates had sought to mobilise support on a denominational basis. It was likely, if any attempted to do so, that this would strengthen nationalist and broadly authoritarian opinion within the society, and in public policy; but support for these positions was increasing already for reasons that had nothing to do with religion, and religious belief as such appeared to make little contribution towards them. In a world of rival and often conflicting faiths, the loose association between religious belief and politics in postcommunist Russia was a positive element in a society that was already deeply divided.

Further reading

The evolution of Soviet and Russian sociology, including the study of public opinion, is considered in Weinberg (2004). On public opinion in the 1990s, see the review in Wyman (1997), and for later years Carnaghan (2007). Up-to-date figures, often incorporating lengthy time series, are available in English at www.russiavotes.org (which draws on Levada Centre data) and in periodic issues of the *New Russia Barometer* from 1992 onwards (there is a full listing at www.abdn.ac.uk/cspp, and an overview of trends in Rose 2004). On religion, see, for instance, Davis (2003), Knox (2005), Garrard and Garrard (2008) and Papkova (2011). On Russian Islam, which is not directly discussed in the chapter, see, for instance, Hahn (2007) and Dannreuther and March (2009). There is a helpful collection of translated papers in Balzer (2010).

Balzer, Marjory Mandelstam, ed., *Religion and Politics in Russia: A Reader* (Armonk, NY, and London: Sharpe, 2010).

Carnaghan, Ellen, *Out of Order: Russian Political Values in an Imperfect World* (University Park: Pennsylvania State University Press, 2007).

Dannreuther, Roland, and Luke March, *Russia and Islam: State, Society, and Radicalism* (London and New York: Routledge, 2009).

Davis, Nathaniel, *A Long Walk to Church: A Contemporary History of Russian Orthodoxy*, 2nd edn (Boulder, CO, and Oxford: Westview, 2003).

Garrard, John, and Carol Garrard, *Russian Orthodoxy Resurgent: Faith and Power in the New Russia* (Princeton, NJ, and Oxford: Princeton University Press, 2008).

Hahn, Gordon, *Russia's Islamic Threat* (New Haven, CT, and London: Yale University Press, 2007).

Knox, Zoe, *Russian Society and the Orthodox Church: Religion in Russia after Communism* (London and New York: RoutledgeCurzon, 2005).

Papkova, Irina, *The Orthodox Church and Russian Politics* (Oxford and New York: Oxford University Press, 2011).

Rose, Richard, *Russian Responses to Transformation: Trends in Public Opinion since 1992* (Aberdeen: Centre for the Study of Public Policy, University of Aberdeen, SPP 390, 2004).

Weinberg, Elizabeth, *Sociology in the Soviet Union and Beyond: Social Inquiry and Social Change*, 2nd edn (Aldershot and Burlington, VT: Ashgate, 2004).

Wyman, Matthew, *Public Opinion in Postcommunist Russia* (London: Macmillan and New York: St Martin's, 1997).

7 Russia and the wider world

Defence Minister Serdyukov reviews the troops on Red
Square, May 2010 (Novosti)

The USSR had repudiated the capitalist system, but it became closely
engaged in the affairs of the international community and occupied an
important position as a member of the United Nations Security Council
quite apart from its great size and military might. There was a closer
association with the 'other democracies' during the Yeltsin presidency, but it
became increasingly clear that a change of government did not necessarily
mean that more enduring sources of division had been eliminated. In the
Putin and Medvedev years, in part as a reaction, there was a stronger
emphasis on relations with the other post-Soviet republics, and with Asia.
There was also a greater willingness to assert Russia's distinctive interests,
for instance in the face of 'coloured revolutions' elsewhere in post-Soviet
space. But in what way? Discussions among Russian politicians and
commentators in the Putin–Medvedev years suggested at least three
different answers: a 'liberal Westernising' strategy, a 'fundamentalist
nationalist' alternative and a 'pragmatic nationalist' position that appeared
to be close to the position of the governing authorities themselves.

For a country of its size and population, the Soviet Union had always been rather isolated from the rest of the international community. In part, at least, this reflected the influence of geography. With their broad and open frontiers, its Russian core territories had been invaded and occupied many times by outside powers. The Russian capital, Moscow, was burned down twice by the Tatars, seized by the Poles in the seventeenth century and Napoleon in the nineteenth, and almost taken again by the Germans during the Second World War. Foreigners, reflecting this uncertain relationship, were required to live in special residential areas and were treated with a good deal of suspicion by ordinary Russians as well as government officials; the national heroes were figures like Alexander Nevsky and Mikhail Kutuzov, who had led the defence of the motherland against invading armies. Russian liberals were often impressed by Western constitutionalism, as compared with their own autocracy; they travelled abroad, conducted their business in French and saw their country as a somewhat wayward member of a common European civilisation. Conservatives and nationalists, on the other hand, were more inclined to see Russia as a country with a unique history and culture, and one that should look to its own traditions for an appropriate form of social organisation; their views were supported by an Orthodox church that was all but coterminous with Russian nationhood, and which helped to promote a feeling that Russians were a 'special people' with a particular civilisational destiny.[1]

The Bolshevik leaders, after 1917, could hardly associate themselves with the notion of a divine mission; and yet many of the attitudes towards the outside world that had flourished in the tsarist period were still influential.[2] It had always been a Russian ambition, for instance, to acquire warm-water ports to the south, and to develop a network of client states in Eastern Europe as a means of strengthening the country's defences against the other continental powers. Russia, equally, had been an Asiatic as well as a European power since at least the sixteenth century, when the first of a series of raids began to bring Siberia under imperial control. By the end of the nineteenth century, most of Central Asia and the Caucasus had been annexed, together with Sakhalin and the Manchurian coast; there were even ambitions to become the dominant power in the Pacific until the fleet was destroyed in an epic battle with the Japanese in 1905. The Russian army, reflecting these far-flung responsibilities, was the 'largest on the European continent',[3] and military spending represented a disproportionately heavy burden on the state budget.[4] Feelings of isolation and insecurity, combined with a belief that Russia represented a special and perhaps unique Eurasian civilisation, carried over after 1917 into a Marxist–Leninist ideology that saw the USSR as an embattled champion of world socialism, a view that appeared to be confirmed as foreign armies sought to overthrow the Soviet government immediately after the revolution by assisting their domestic opponents, and then once again invaded in June 1941.

But for all these tendencies towards isolation, the postrevolutionary period saw the USSR integrate itself ever more closely into the common affairs of a larger global community. The new regime, certainly, might repudiate capitalism; but it had to coexist with other states with which there was no alternative but to enter into a series of practical arrangements – first of all about prisoners of war, and then about postal communications, transport and trade. Trade, in turn, was unlikely to prosper outside an established legal framework; and so agreements of this kind led naturally to full diplomatic relations, first with the smaller border states such as Finland and Estonia; then, in the 1920s, with Britain, Italy, France, Germany and Japan; and finally, in the early 1930s, with the United States, Belgium, Spain and the newly established states of Eastern Europe. The USSR maintained diplomatic relations with only 35 foreign states as late as the mid-1930s, which was less than half the membership of the international community at the time, but by the end of the Second World War it had diplomatic relations with 52 (which was nearly three-quarters), and by the end of the 1980s it maintained relations with 144, which was 85 per cent of a much larger global total.[5] The USSR, similarly, was not a party to the Versailles peace settlement, but it returned to conference diplomacy when its top-hatted representatives appeared at Genoa in 1922;[6] and although the Soviet government had initially been hostile to the League of Nations, describing it as a 'Holy Alliance of capitalists for the suppression of the workers' revolution',[7] the USSR became a member in 1934 and helped to found the United Nations in 1945, with a permanent seat on its Security Council. The USSR was extending its range of trading partners at the same time, from 45 foreign states in 1950 to 145 in the late 1980s,[8] and there were closer links at the popular level: there were more tourists, sportsmen and exchange students at Soviet universities, and more foreign books were being translated into Russian than ever before.[9]

The postcommunist Russian government, after 1991, inherited the international prerogatives as well as the debts and other responsibilities of its Soviet predecessor. Russia was the only one of the former Soviet republics to remain a nuclear power, and the agreed successor to the permanent seat on the United Nations Security Council that the USSR had enjoyed since its foundation. But the new Russia had to accommodate itself to a world in which it was no longer a superpower, and in which – at least initially – its economic weakness mattered more than a stockpile of rusting missiles. There were other challenges, particularly in the relationships that had to be negotiated with the republics of the USSR that had also become independent states and for which the ambiguous term 'near abroad' came into use. Large numbers of Russians found they had become residents of these new states; many had Russian citizenship, and many more were Russian-speakers with strong links with the society from which they had originated. Clearly, the sovereignty of other states had to be respected; but no Russian government could remain indifferent to the fate of its nationals in these circumstances, particularly when their civil rights were being infringed. Equally, there was a new and apparently more congenial international environment after 1991; but the Western powers were still organised in NATO, and the expansion of the alliance into Central and Eastern Europe that began shortly afterwards threatened a new division of the continent that, for many Russians, prejudiced their security almost as seriously as the hostile confrontation of the Cold War period.[10] Under Putin and his successor, taking advantage of the leverage afforded by their massive natural resources and high oil prices, Russian diplomats in the early years of the new century found they had more opportunity to assert their own priorities in these matters and the international environment became more competitive – sometimes, indeed, more confrontational.

'New thinking' in foreign policy

Gorbachev's early pronouncements had given little indication that one of the central features of his administration would be its emphasis on 'new thinking' in international affairs. An address to an ideology conference in December 1984 – in effect, a manifesto to the Central Committee members who would soon be deciding on the succession – stressed the need for 'fundamental change through accelerated economic development', and pointed to *glasnost'* and self-management as the most effective means of achieving it. The section on foreign policy was much more orthodox; it spoke of two 'opposing systems' and accused capitalism of resorting to 'wars and terror' in order to further its policy of 'social revenge'.[11] But a different tone was already emerging, and there were signs of it in an address that Gorbachev gave to British members of parliament later the same month. In the speech Gorbachev made clear his wish for renewed dialogue and cooperation, above all in relation to the threat of a nuclear war in which there could be 'no winners'. This, moreover, was just an example of the kind of issue that required the concerted action of states with different social systems. Another was the need to resolve regional issues peacefully; others were protection of the environment, the global supply of energy and natural resources, and the struggle against famine and disease. The atomic age, Gorbachev suggested, required a 'new way of political thinking', above all a recognition that the peoples of the world lived in a 'vulnerable, rather fragile but interconnected world'; this dictated a 'constructive dialogue, a search for solutions to key international problems [and] for areas of agreement'.[12]

Gorbachev's speech on his election as General Secretary in March 1985 laid its main emphasis on domestic priorities but also called for better relations with the 'great socialist community', particularly China, and for 'peaceful, mutually advantageous cooperation' with the capitalist world, leading if possible to an agreement that would bring about the complete elimination of nuclear arms and with them the threat of nuclear war.[13] His address to the Central Committee in April 1985 – the first full statement of his objectives as party leader – called for 'stable, proper and, if you like, civilised interstate relations based on a genuine respect for international law'. The unity of the socialist states and their military-strategic parity with the NATO countries must at all costs be preserved, but there was no 'fatal inevitability of confrontation'. On the contrary, neither side wanted a war, and there were 'new progressive and demo-cratic forces' in the capitalist countries that shared the Soviet commitment to the peaceful resolution of differences.[14] In a speech to French parliamentarians the following October, Gorbachev laid particular emphasis on the ever-growing interdependence between countries in environmental as well as military and economic terms; he also emphasised the need to develop cultural contacts, and to avoid extending ideological differences to the conduct of interstate relations.[15] His address a few days later to the Central Committee balanced these remarks with more familiar assurances about the 'further strengthening of the positions of existing socialism' and criticism of the 'reactionary, aggressive forces of imperialism'.[16]

Gorbachev's address to the 27th Party Congress in February 1986 was relatively short of surprises in terms of foreign policy; there was nothing, at any rate, to compare with the unilateral moratorium on nuclear testing that had been announced a few weeks earlier. It did, however, make clear the extent to which the Soviet approach to international affairs had changed since the simple dichotomies of the Brezhnev era. Capitalism, certainly, was a system plagued by problems and crises, and based on 'antagonistic contradictions' between social groups and individual capitalist states. Beyond these differences, however, lay a group of rather larger issues in relation to the pollution of the environment and the depletion of the world's natural resources. These were problems no group of states could resolve by itself; and there were many others. No single group of states, for instance, could deal with the 'corruption and vandalisation' that had been taking place in the cultural sphere. Nor could capitalist or socialist states deal by themselves with the threat of a nuclear catastrophe, or the difficulties that were facing the developing countries. Gorbachev invited the major capitalist countries to undertake a 'sober, constructive assessment' of problems of this kind, based if nothing else on their common need for self-preservation. The course of history and of social progress, he told the delegates, required the establishment of 'constructive, creative interaction among states and peoples on the scale of the entire planet'. Whatever their differences, both capitalist and socialist countries had to appreciate that they lived in an 'interdependent, in many ways unitary world' in which they must cooperate for their common benefit.[17]

This 'new thinking' was set out more fully over the months that followed. The 'Delhi declaration' of November 1986, for instance, committed the Soviet leader to a 'non-violent' as well as nuclear-free world.[18] A new defence doctrine began to take shape at the same time: it was intended to be non-offensive in character and to give other states no reason to fear for their own security. The Soviet leader had already taken several unilateral initiatives towards this end, among them the decision, in April 1985, to freeze the deployment of SS-20 missiles in Europe,[19] and the moratorium on all underground nuclear testing that began on 6 August 1985, the anniversary of Hiroshima.[20] Gorbachev added a more elaborate proposal in January 1986, calling for the 'complete elimination of nuclear weapons throughout the world' by the end of the century as a means of overcoming the 'negative, confrontational tendencies that [had] been building up in recent years', as well as for the 'complete elimination' of chemical weapons and of the means for their manufacture.[21] A commitment to these objectives was written into the new Party Programme, which was adopted shortly afterwards, and a similar commitment was made to 'reasonable sufficiency' in military matters as part of a move towards the establish-ment of an 'all-embracing system of international security'.[22] Nor were these simply doctrinal changes: there were accompanying cuts in military spending and troop num-bers and much more information was made available on the military budget and on troop and weapons deployments, which themselves became more overtly defensive.[23]

An even bolder statement of the 'new thinking' came in the Soviet leader's address to the General Assembly of the United Nations in December 1988. In the speech Gorbachev expressed his personal support for the UN as a body that had 'increasingly manifested its ability to act as a unique international centre in the service of peace and security', and reiterated his belief that the most important issues that faced the international commu-nity were global rather than regional in character. The French and Russian revolutions, he suggested, had made an enormous contribution in their time to human progress, but they lived in a rather different world in which universal human values must have priority. This meant a common search for a new kind of global action, less dependent on military force and free of ideological prejudice. In more practical terms, Gorbachev pointed to the need for a greater measure of agreement on the reduction of all forms of armaments and on the elimination of regional conflicts. But the United Nations itself should play a greater role in matters such as Third World development, environmental assistance and the peaceful use of outer space. And more needed to be done to strengthen international law, particularly in relation to human rights. Most spectacularly of all, the Soviet leader suggested moves to convert the 'arms' into a 'disarmament economy', and he announced himself a reduction of 500,000 in the size of Soviet armed forces over the following two years, together with changes in the structure of the forces that remained (including the withdrawal of a large number of tanks) so that their purposes became even more clearly defensive.[24]

In the end, there was virtually no aspect of Soviet foreign policy that remained unchanged. Most notably, there was a steady improvement in relations with the United States after a summit in November 1985 brought Gorbachev face to face with Ronald Reagan, a Republican president who had become notorious for his description of the USSR as an 'evil empire'. Unexpectedly, they established a continuing dialogue, and in December 1987 went on to sign an Intermediate Nuclear Force (INF) treaty that eliminated an entire category of nuclear arms – land-based missiles of intermediate and shorter range – and established more rigorous on-site verification procedures.[25] In July 1991, meeting in Moscow, Gorbachev and Reagan's successor George Bush went even further, concluding a strategic arms reduction treaty that made the first substantial cuts in the weapons available to each side.[26] Gorbachev had evidently hoped to sustain communist rule in Eastern Europe by encouraging the election of fellow reformers, but in the end he had to accept the defeat of governments throughout the region and the dissolution of Comecon and the Warsaw Treaty Organisation, which between them had provided the economic and military basis for Soviet relations with Eastern Europe throughout the post-war period.[27] Speaking to the Central Committee in December 1989, Gorbachev professed to welcome the 'positive changes' that had taken place, presenting them as a response to *perestroika* in the USSR itself and claiming that they represented 'democratisation' and the 'renewal of socialism'.[28] But in any case, he asked the 28th Party Congress in 1990, what was the alternative? 'Tanks once again?'[29]

The USSR, meanwhile, had moved to normalise its relations with other states. The 'limited contingent' that had been sent to maintain a friendly regime in Afghanistan was withdrawn, after multilateral negotiations, in February 1989.[30] Relations with Cuba underwent a comparable transition in September 1991 when 11,000 Soviet troops were brought home after Gorbachev had met the US Secretary of State, but without any prior consultation with the Havana government.[31] Gorbachev's speech to the 27th Party Congress in 1986 was the first in modern times to make no mention of the need to assist 'national liberation' movements in the developing countries;[32] the Party Programme that was adopted at the same congress committed the USSR to no more than to 'do what it could' to assist socialist-oriented states in the developing world,[33] and authoritative commentaries made it clear that the USSR preferred the peaceful settlement of regional conflicts to the 'export of revolution'.[34] The USSR, meanwhile, established diplomatic relations with the Vatican, with Israel and with the Afrikaner state in South Africa;[35] it signed a Paris Charter in November 1990 which confirmed that East and West were 'no longer adversaries' and was taken to mark the symbolic end of the Cold War;[36] and then in 1991 the Soviet government supported international action in the Gulf against an Iraqi regime with which it had for many years sustained a friendship and cooperation treaty.[37] By the end of the Gorbachev years, there were few respects in which the USSR had not become an entirely 'normal' member of the world community it had originally made every effort to overthrow.

Yeltsin and the West

Boris Yeltsin had given little attention to foreign policy in his earlier career, or in his campaign for the Russian presidency. He had made a few trips abroad, to Germany, Nicaragua and Luxembourg, but as a member of an official delegation; and when he visited the United States in 1989 as a newly elected member of the Soviet parliament, the Bush administration, still supportive of Gorbachev, kept him at arm's length and there was no more than a brief and informal meeting with the US President.[38] Once he had been elected to the newly established Russian presidency, however, Yeltsin took an increasingly prominent role. Immediately after his victory in June 1991, he made a four-day visit to the United States in which he appeared to have persuaded President Bush that in future he would have to 'deal with Gorbachev, but also with Russia'.[39] And when Bush visited Moscow the following month to sign the strategic arms reduction treaty, he held separate talks with Yeltsin as well as President Nazarbaev of Kazakhstan before travelling on to Kyiv to address the Ukrainian parliament. When Secretary of State James Baker visited in mid-December, it was clear that Yeltsin had become the dominant figure, and Russian officials were pressing impatiently for full diplomatic relations (a dozen other countries had recognised Russia as an independent state by 25 December, although the USSR was still formally in existence and Gorbachev was still president).[40] Yeltsin himself referred to the 'former USSR' at the press conference that took place at the end of Baker's visit,[41] and his foreign minister used the same term in an address a few days later.[42]

The Russian government had always included a foreign minister, reflecting the fiction that all the republics were sovereign states that had established a voluntary union. But an independent Russian foreign policy had begun to acquire some reality even before the USSR had disappeared, based on the declaration of sovereignty that its parliament had adopted in June 1990. There were agreements with the other Soviet republics that incorporated a reciprocal recognition of sovereignty, and then in January 1991 a treaty was signed with Estonia that defined both states as 'subjects of international law'.[43] Later in the year, within what was still the USSR, Russian negotiators reached still more far-reaching agreements on the establishment of 'diplomatic relations' with Bulgaria,[44] and on relations with Italy and the Federal Republic of Germany that were based on the 'principles of international law'.[45] By the end of the year, with the agreement of the other republics that had now formed the Commonwealth of Independent States, Russia had taken over the Soviet seat in the United Nations as well as its permanent place on the Security Council, and had also assumed the financial and treaty obligations of the USSR as its successor state under international law. The new head of what had been the Soviet Foreign Ministry was Andrei Kozyrev, who had been Russian foreign minister since October 1990. As he explained in a New Year message, he was no longer the director of a 'detachment of revolutionary sword-bearers' but of a 'staff of democratically minded people who [knew] and well [understood] the interests and concerns of their own people'.[46]

Yeltsin himself lost no time in underlining the changes that had taken place in what was still the world's largest state, with its second most formidable concentration of military might. In January 1992 he announced that Russian nuclear weapons would no longer be trained on targets in the United States,[47] and then followed this with a more comprehensive statement in which he announced a series of unilateral reductions in nuclear and conventional arms.[48] At the end of the month, Yeltsin visited the United Nations to address a Security Council summit; emphasising that he saw the Western powers 'not just as partners, but as allies', he made clear that the new Russia would play its full part in the maintenance of world peace and put forward his own proposal for a global security system based on America's Strategic Defence Initiative and Russia's own military technologies.[49] While Yeltsin was in the United States, he held an unofficial meeting with President Bush at which he declared that relations between the two states had 'entered a new era'. Bush himself acknowledged that they had met 'not as adversaries, but as friends',[50] and as the second day of their meeting was Yeltsin's birthday he handed over an autographed pair of cowboy boots to 'my friend Boris' (the boots, it emerged, were too small, but Yeltsin kept them anyway as a souvenir).[51] The 'Camp David declaration' that was issued at the end of their discussions confirmed that relations between the two countries would in future be based on 'friendship and partnership' and that the presidents themselves would seek to 'eliminate the remains of the hostile period of the "cold war", including steps to reduce their strategic arsenals'.[52]

A new framework of relations began to acquire more definite contours over the months that followed. An agreement on the 'bases of relations' had already been concluded with Russia's close neighbour Finland.[53] In April 1992 Yeltsin signed a treaty on friendly relations with the Czech and Slovak Republic (which was the former Czechoslovakia but not yet two separate states), and another with Poland, that superseded the alliances of the communist period.[54] In June there was a formal treaty on cooperation with Canada, and in August another treaty on friendly relations, this time with Bulgaria.[55] A treaty on the 'principles of relations' with the United Kingdom followed in November;[56] it was the first treaty of its kind to be concluded between the two states since 1766. Russia and Britain were now 'allies', Yeltsin told the British Parliament in a warmly applauded address; and at a subsequent news conference, he announced that the Queen had accepted an invitation to visit Russia (a royal visit had been agreed three years earlier but had not yet taken place). It had, in fact, been Yeltsin himself who had authorised the destruction of the Ipat'ev house in which the tsarist royal family – who were the Queen's relatives – had been shot; but they had talked 'like old friends', he told journalists.[57] It was Yeltsin's first official visit to the United Kingdom, and he was the first Russian leader to visit the Stock Exchange rather than the tomb of Karl Marx; his wife, in a 'fashionable emerald green suit with power shoulders', was meanwhile 'stealing the show, a natural in front of the cameras. Hillary Clinton look out!'[58]

The first formal summit between the Russian President and his US counterpart took place in June 1992 in Washington. 'The abyss has ended', Yeltsin told journalists as he stepped off his plane.[59] Secretary of State Baker, who spoke in reply, described the two nations as united in a 'democratic partnership'.[60] He was not coming across the Atlantic with his hand out for assistance, Yeltsin explained, but so that he could 'extend a hand to the President', and the summit saw a series of agreements that began to place Russian–American relations on an entirely new footing. The two presidents approved the basic principles of an unprecedented arms reduction agreement that went far beyond the Strategic Arms Reduction Treaty (START) that Bush and Gorbachev had negotiated the previous year;[61] they also signed a charter that was designed to establish a 'firm foundation for Russian–American relations of partnership and friendship',[62] and there were more specific agreements on the development of a global nuclear security system and the opening of new consulates in Seattle and Vladivostok (the two presidents signed thirty-five joint documents altogether).[63] Yeltsin, addressing the US Congress on 17 June, obtained an enthusiastic response to his message that the 'communist idol' had 'collapsed for good';[64] it was an occasion to which his speechwriters attached even more importance than to his meeting with President Bush, and they 'worked day and night' to get it right (as *Pravda* reminded its readers, the Russian President had actually played a leading part in maintaining the 'communist bondage' he was now deploring).[65]

A further summit, in Moscow in January 1993, saw the framework agreement of the previous summer develop into the START II treaty, under which Russia and the United States each undertook to dismantle two-thirds of their strategic nuclear warheads; the original START treaty, signed in 1991, had called for a cut of just 30 per cent (Table 7.1 shows the entire sequence). Yeltsin described the agreement as a 'major step towards the realisation of humanity's age-old, historic dream of disarmament' and as a 'Christmas present for the whole of humanity' that would allow them to 'pass on a safer world to [their] children, the children of the 21st century'. Its conclusion in just a few months, as compared with the fifteen years it had taken to negotiate its predecessor, was evidence in itself that a 'real revolution' had taken place in relations between the two powers.[66] And he urged the newly elected US president, Bill Clinton, to take part in a 'working meeting on neutral territory to discuss all questions' as soon as he had been inaugurated,[67] or indeed to 'seize the baton' and visit Russia itself.[68] The treaty had still to be approved by the other post-Soviet nuclear powers, as well as by the Russian parliament (which took until the end of the decade to formalise its consent after three earlier votes had been postponed);[69] but Kazakhstan ratified START I in 1992,[70] Belarus did so in 1993,[71] and Ukraine followed in 1994, after its prior conditions had been met, and acceded at the same time to the Nuclear Non-Proliferation Treaty.[72] All nuclear weapons had been removed from Ukrainian territory by the summer of 1996, leaving Russia as the sole nuclear power among the fifteen former Soviet republics.[73]

The first summit between Yeltsin and the new American president took place at Vancouver in April 1993. There was a comprehensive declaration in which both presidents declared their commitment to a 'dynamic and effective Russo-American partnership' – Yeltsin himself suggested their relations were those of 'partners and future allies'[74] – but the main emphasis was on economic assistance to a new and still fragile postcommunist government. Clinton committed the United States itself to a package of financial support valued at $1.6 billion, about half of which represented unilateral aid and the other half of which was in the form of credits, and he promised to seek a more substantial response from the leading industrial nations of the G7.[75] It was the start, Clinton promised, of a 'new democratic partnership'; the Russian President himself spoke of the development of a 'special relationship'.[76] The Canadian Prime Minister, who also met the Russian President, offered $200 million of unilateral aid;[77] and later in the year, reflecting US pressure as well as the views of its other members, the G7 approved a package of multilateral assistance that was valued at more than $43 billion.[78] A new military doctrine, adopted by presidential decree at the end of the year, consolidated the changes that had taken place in East–West relations by declaring that no country was to be regarded as an adversary of the new Russia, although it qualified an earlier commitment to refrain from the first use of nuclear weapons and made provision for the use of the armed forces in domestic conflicts not just within the Russian Federation but also in the other former Soviet republics.[79]

Table 7.1 **The major East–West arms treaties**

The *Test Ban Treaty of 1963* (text in *SDD*, vol. 23 (Moscow 1970), pp. 44–6) prohibited the testing
of nuclear weapons on or above the surface of the earth, but was not signed by China or France.
It was superseded by the Comprehensive Test Ban Treaty of 1996 (text in *DV*, no. 10, 1996,
pp. 38–59, and no. 11, 1996, pp. 46–62), which was ratified by the Russian Federation in 2000 but
has not yet entered into force (*BMD*, no. 8, 2000, pp. 85–8).

The *Non-Proliferation Treaty of 1968* (text in *SDD*, vol. 26 (Moscow 1973), pp. 45–9) required each
signatory nuclear power to undertake not to transfer such weapons or their control or means
of manufacture to other states, and obliged non-nuclear signatories not to receive, manufacture
or 'otherwise acquire' such weapons. The treaty was not signed by Israel, India and Pakistan,
among others; it did, however, include a general commitment to disarmament negotiations.

The *Anti-Ballistic Missile (ABM) Treaty of 1972* restricted the construction of defensive missile
systems to protect against nuclear ballistic weapons attack (text in *SDD*, vol. 28 (Moscow 1974),
pp. 31–5). The United States announced its unilateral withdrawal from the treaty in December
2001; its decision took effect in June 2002.

The *'Interim Agreement on Offensive Missiles' (SALT I)*, also agreed in 1972, placed numerical limits
on land-based intercontinental nuclear missiles, submarine-launched ballistic missiles and
strategic bombers; it had a duration of five years, during which a further agreement was to be
negotiated (text in *SDD*, vol. 28 (Moscow 1974), pp. 35–7).

SALT II, its successor, was signed in 1979, but ratification was delayed because of Soviet reluctance
to allow on-site verification and was then rejected by the US Senate in the more difficult
international environment that followed the Soviet intervention in Afghanistan at the end of that
year; its provisions were nonetheless respected by both sides until 1986. The treaty provided
for equal numbers of strategic nuclear weapons launchers or heavy bombers in the arsenals of
both superpowers; limits were placed on the number of warheads on a MIRVed missile and on the
deployment of new types of missiles (text in *Pravda*, 19 June 1979, pp. 1–2).

The *Intermediate-Range Nuclear Forces (INF) Treaty of 1987* eliminated all INF systems, mostly in
Europe but also in Asia; this meant a cut in nuclear arsenals, not just a limit on their further
increase, and was accompanied by particularly rigorous verification procedures (text in *SMD*,
vol. 43 (Moscow 1990), pp. 58–137).

The *Conventional Armed Forces in Europe (CFE) Treaty* was signed by NATO and Warsaw Pact
representatives in November 1990 (text in *Pravda*, 21 November 1990, pp. 3–4). It set limits for
the major weapons and equipment systems to be held by both blocs, and also specified a regime of
notification and verification, on-site inspections and monitoring of destruction.

The *START I (Strategic Arms Reduction) Treaty*, signed in July 1991, reduced the number of delivery
systems (land-based and submarine-based intercontinental ballistic missiles, plus strategic
bombers) to 1,600 each, and to a maximum of 6,000 warheads; a separate agreement limited the
permitted number of submarine-launched cruise missiles (text in *DV*, no. 19, 1991, pp. 7–34). It
expired on 5 December 2009.

Its successor, *START II*, was signed in January 1993 by Boris Yeltsin on behalf of a newly
independent Russian Federation; it specified a cut of about two-thirds in stocks of
long-range, land-based missiles with multiple warheads within ten years (text in *DV*, nos. 1–2,
1993, pp. 19–24). It was ratified by the United States in 1996 and by Russia in 2000, but never
came into force, even though its provisions continued to be observed. On 14 June 2002, the day
after the United States withdrew from the ABM Treaty, Russia announced that it would no longer
consider itself bound by these commitments (*Kommersant*, 15 June 2002, p. 4).

Table 7.1 (cont.)

The *Strategic Arms Reduction (SORT or Moscow) Treaty*, signed in May 2002, committed the two
parties to limit their nuclear arsenals to 1,700–2,200 operationally deployed warheads each (text
in *BMD*, no. 8, 2003, pp. 67–8; it was due to expire on 31 December 2012).

The *New Strategic Arms Reduction Treaty* that was signed in Prague in April 2010 committed both
parties to reduce their nuclear arsenals still further, to 1,550 operationally deployed warheads and
700 delivery systems over a period of seven years (*Izvestiya*, 9 April 2010, p. 2).

Note: BMD = *Byulleten' mezhdunarodnykh dogovorov*; DV = *Diplomaticheskii vestnik*; SDD = *Sbornik
deistvuyushchikh dogovorov, soglashenii i konventsii, zaklyuchennykh SSSR s inostrannymi
gosudarstvami* (later *Sbornik mezhdunarodnykh dogovorov SSSR (SMD)*); SZ = *Sobranie
zakonodatel'stva Rossiiskoi Federatsii*.

President Clinton paid his first official visit to Russia in January 1994, where the two
presidents agreed that their relations had evolved into a 'mature strategic partnership'.
There were twelve formal agreements, including an undertaking that the strategic
missiles held by each side would no longer be targeted on any other party. There
was also a public recognition that the rights of Russian-speakers in the Baltic republics
should be protected.[80] As in Vancouver, Yeltsin called Clinton 'my friend Bill', and
Clinton entertained the Russian President and his guests to a recital on the saxophone –
'a simple but agreeable tune' – and was 'genuinely touched' by the response.[81] In June
Yeltsin was the guest of the European Union in Corfu, where he signed an agreement on
partnership and cooperation (it came into effect three years later),[82] and then in August
he was in Berlin with 'my friend Helmut' to take part in a ceremony marking the
departure of the last Russian troops from what had originally been the Soviet zone of
Germany.[83] Russian troops had already left Lithuania, and the last troops left Latvia and
Estonia, ahead of schedule, at the end of the month.[84] In September there was another
summit meeting with President Clinton, their fifth in eighteen months, at which the two
presidents agreed a 'partnership for economic progress' that was designed to reduce the
tariff barriers that had hindered bilateral trade;[85] the Russian President addressed the UN
General Assembly in the course of his visit, calling for the conclusion of a comprehensive
nuclear test ban by the end of the year and further steps to limit nuclear arsenals with a
view to the eventual elimination of the entire 'balance of terror'.[86]

Another Russian–US summit took place in Moscow in May 1995 in connection with
the celebration in the Russian capital of the fiftieth anniversary of the Allied victory in
Europe.[87] There were six joint declarations, although there was no attempt to disguise the
fact that there had been 'differences of approach' to a whole series of questions, among
them the sale of nuclear facilities to Iran (Yeltsin insisted on their 'wholly peaceful
character') and the expansion of NATO rather than the development of a more broadly
conceived security framework that could extend across the entire Euro-Atlantic region.[88]
Yeltsin addressed the UN General Assembly again on the organisation's fiftieth anniversary

in October 1995, repeating his call for a more comprehensive framework of European security rather than the expansion of existing alliances so as to avoid the danger of a 'new confrontation'.[89] He also met Bill Clinton for their ninth summit, where the main question on the agenda was the deteriorating situation in Bosnia.[90] There were further summits in April 1996[91] and at Helsinki in the spring of 1997, when the two presidents explored the ways in which Russia might be persuaded to accept NATO enlargement and in which they could jointly promote nuclear disarmament.[92] When they met again in Moscow in September 1998, it was their fourteenth summit, although the least productive because Russia was enmeshed in the governmental crisis that stemmed from the sacking of Prime Minister Kirienko and Clinton himself was engaged in a domestic scandal;[93] the two presidents moved forward on disarmament, including the outlines of a START III, but there were 'no major breakthroughs'.[94]

The early postcommunist years saw not only the establishment of a different relationship with the major Western powers, but also a Russia that was a full and nominally equal member of the international community. Gorbachev, in 1991, had been the first Soviet leader to attend a meeting of the G7 industrial powers, but not as a formal participant. Yeltsin was an invited guest the following year and attended the Naples summit in 1994; the summit that took place in 1997 was the first to be described as a meeting of the G8, and in 2006 the summit took place for the first time in Russia itself, in Putin's home town of St Petersburg. Russia was in turn a member of the larger association, the Group of Twenty (G20), that took over the work of the G8 from 2009 onwards and involved the larger developing countries in its activities.[95] Russia had meanwhile led the other former Soviet republics into the World Bank and the International Monetary Fund (Soviet membership had been agreed in 1944 but never ratified),[96] and then the European Bank for Reconstruction and Development (EBRD).[97] Membership of the Council of Europe in 1996 confirmed Russia's return to the European community of nations,[98] and two years later the Duma ratified the European Convention on Human Rights, although capital punishment was still on the statute book (its application was suspended indefinitely).[99] The new Russian government also applied to join the General Agreement on Tariffs and Trade (soon to become the World Trade Organization), although its application did not proceed further,[100] and it joined the Asian-Pacific Economic Cooperation Group in 1997 in spite of the open misgivings of some of its existing members.[101]

The 'Iron Curtain' that Churchill identified in his Fulton speech of 1946 had separated two rival ideologies and the states that were associated with them. The end of communist rule had eliminated some of the causes of that division, but – it became increasingly clear – not all of them. The developed Western countries, in Foreign Minister Kozyrev's earliest policy statements, were Russia's 'natural allies', based on their shared commitment to democracy, human rights and the market; he looked forward to 'fruitful cooperation', particularly with the United States, and saw no reason to fear it would attempt to become the 'sole superpower', imposing its views on other nations.[102] Russian foreign policy, Kozyrev insisted, should avoid 'ideological schemas and messianic ambitions on a global scale in favour of a realistic assessment of Russia's own needs'; their aim should be the 'thoroughgoing transformation of society'[103] and the entry, on this basis, into the 'club of first-class powers of Europe, Asia and America'.[104] The interests of the new Russia and of the other democracies, he suggested elsewhere, were 'substantially the same',[105] and he called for them to engage in a broader 'humanisation of international politics' that would base itself on the universal observance of human rights.[106] Russia, Yeltsin himself explained, was 'no longer the main power centre of an enormous communist empire', and in the long run Russians would themselves discover that a world in which they could engage in 'mutually advantageous cooperation' served their interests much better than the hostile confrontation of earlier years.[107]

The new approach was set out more fully in a set of 'basic principles of a concept of the foreign policy of the Russian Federation' that was finally approved in the spring of 1993. Russia, it pointed out, was still a great power, with a special responsibility for the creation of a new system of relations among the states that had formerly been part of the Soviet Union. Russia, moreover, was a state that still needed to defend its vital interests, which meant that it should resist the subordinate position it had been accorded in the international economy and intervene in local conflicts near its own borders. The greatest importance of all was attached to relations with the former Soviet republics, and to the efforts that might be undertaken to encourage their reintegration. These included the establishment of a collective security system, a common boundary and a special role for Russia in maintaining public order within that boundary that would legitimate the presence of Russian troops on the territory of the other republics. Further abroad, Russia and the United States had a common interest in the prevention of regional conflict and nuclear proliferation, although their interests in other respects did not always coincide. And there should be 'balanced and stable relations' with the countries of the Asia-Pacific region, especially China, Japan and India.[108] At least two features of the new concept attracted particular attention: the emphasis that was given to the former Soviet republics of the 'near abroad', and the open acknowledgement that Russia had a distinctive set of interests that might not always accord with those of the Western democracies.[109]

Kozyrev was still insisting, in the spring of 1994, that there was 'no sensible alternative to partnership', and he continued to look for the support of Russia's 'natural friends and allies, the democratic states and governments of the West'.[110] Views of this kind, however, were clearly difficult to reconcile with the 'basic principles' (which had been prepared under the auspices of the Security Council rather than the foreign ministry), and they were also difficult to reconcile with the views of the Russian electorate, which had given the largest share of the party-list vote to the Liberal Democratic Party in the 1993 Duma election, and then to the Communist Party – also assertively nationalist – two years later. Western leaders, in these circumstances, began to take a more cautious view of their relationship with the new Russian government, still more so when Yeltsin launched a war in Chechnya at the end of 1994 with what appeared to be an elementary disregard of the human rights to which it had made such a public commitment. Already, Kozyrev warned, the honeymoon in relations with the United States was 'coming to an end', and he moved closer to his nationalist opponents by warning that there might be circumstances in which it would be necessary for Russia to use military force to defend its 'compatriots abroad', particularly ethnic Russians in the Baltic republics.[111] Kozyrev won a seat in the new Duma in December 1995 and resigned his ministerial office so that he could take it up, but his position was becoming increasingly isolated and Yeltsin had several times made clear his own dissatisfaction (a decree authorising the foreign minister's dismissal had, apparently, already been signed).[112] In the end he became a 'ritual sacrifice' to the new Duma.[113]

At their most radical, Kozyrev's critics accused him of an alliance with the 'prince of darkness', facilitating the efforts of a West that wanted a 'weak and degraded Russia' that would be an 'easy prey to overseas companies and banks'.[114] Others argued that he had suffered a 'crushing defeat' in the policies he had pursued, such as preventing the expansion of NATO,[115] and that he had subordinated Russia's own interests to a vacuous 'partnership' that had simply allowed the United States to expand its global hegemony without the financial compensation that had originally been promised.[116] These were extreme charges, but there was a much wider degree of support for a more moderate 'pragmatic nationalist' position that was concerned to assert Russia's right of independent action, and to protect the domestic economy and culture in the face of the West's overwhelming superiority.[117] This meant, first of all, a multipolar world, not one that was dominated by a single superpower. Yeltsin had already made clear, in a speech to senior officials in the foreign ministry, that he was dissatisfied with the heavy emphasis it had been placing on relations with the Western countries,[118] and he insisted that more attention be given to the other post-Soviet republics as well as Russian-speakers who now lived outside the national territory.[119] There was support within the foreign policy community more generally for a shift of orientation towards the 'near abroad' and the neighbouring states of southern and eastern Asia, partly because of the disillusioning experience of their early dealings with the West, but also because of Russia's own 'Eurasianism' and the trading opportunities that appeared to be available in countries with less demanding domestic markets.[120]

Kozyrev's successor was Yevgenii Primakov, a man of a different generation who had spent a long career in the service of the Soviet state and had 'never made any secret of his mistrust of the West, above all the United States'.[121] As the new foreign minister made clear in interviews, he would be mounting a more vigorous defence of Russia's 'national-state interests' and looking for an 'equal' partnership with the Western powers within a foreign policy that would itself be more broadly diversified. Russia, he insisted, had not lost the Cold War but helped to bring it to an end, and there could be no talk of 'victors and vanquished'. Russia, moreover, was still a 'great power' and should have a foreign policy that 'correspond[ed] to her status'.[122] This meant, as it had for Yeltsin, 'correcting the "bias" towards the West' and giving more attention to relations with Belarus and

China, and to Russian-speakers in other countries.[123] Kozyrev had been born to Russian parents in Brussels, spoke Spanish and Portuguese as well as English, and had graduated from the Moscow State Institute of International Relations – the normal training ground for diplomats. Primakov, by contrast, had been born in Kyiv but grew up in the Georgian capital Tbilisi, and knew Arabic as well as Georgian and English; he had graduated from the Institute of Oriental Studies and worked for many years as a *Pravda* journalist with a specialisation in foreign and particularly Arab affairs.[124] He moved into academic life in the 1970s as deputy director of an influential think-tank, the Institute of the World Economy and International Relations of the Academy of Sciences, moving again in the Gorbachev years to become speaker of the lower house of parliament, a member of the Central Committee and a non-voting member of the Politburo.

A very similar approach was taken by his successors, both of them professional diplomats: Igor Ivanov, who became foreign minister in 1998 when Primakov himself moved to the premiership, and Sergei Lavrov, who followed him. Ivanov was a specialist on the West European countries, particularly Spain, where he had served as Russian ambassador in the early 1990s before rejoining the central apparatus of the foreign ministry; he promised there would be 'no radical changes' during his stewardship and drew attention to the support that current policies had been able to secure from the 'broadest possible spectrum of political forces and public opinion'.[125] He made some effort to extend this shared understanding during his term as foreign minister, meeting all the Duma faction leaders at the earliest opportunity and maintaining the 'broadest possible contacts' with the printed and broadcast media.[126] Lavrov, who succeeded him in March 2004, was another graduate of the Moscow State Institute of International Relations who had spent a decade as Russia's permanent representative in the United Nations and was apparently reluctant to leave.[127] Speaking at a press conference a few days after his appointment, he drew attention once again to the 'nationwide consensus' that had developed in relation to the promotion of Russian interests and emphasised the 'continuity' that properly prevailed in all matters of this kind. Like Ivanov, he pointed out that the formulation of foreign policy was in any case a matter for the President; it was the job of the foreign ministry to offer advice, on its own behalf or in consultation with other government departments, and then implement his decisions.[128]

Russia and the West under Putin and Medvedev

With the departure of Yeltsin and Kozyrev, it became increasingly apparent that there were still many issues that divided postcommunist Russia and its Western counterparts. Surprisingly, perhaps, they included espionage. As early as 1992, four Russian representatives had to be expelled from Belgium on the grounds that their activities had been 'incompatible with their status',[129] and four were ordered out of France in what was described as the 'biggest espionage case ever in the field of nuclear technology'.[130] Then in January 1993, as Yeltsin and Bush were clinking glasses in the Kremlin, a senior official from the office of the Russian military attaché in Washington was presented with similar charges and required to leave.[131] Relations with the United States were not improved by the much more serious disclosure in February 1994 that a senior CIA official and his wife, Aldrich and Maria Ames, had been spying for the USSR and then for the Russian Federation since the mid-1980s, betraying the identities of the Americans' top agents and receiving very large payments for doing so (the agents themselves were executed or imprisoned).[132] The Russians themselves announced the arrest of a senior defence official in 1996 on charges of spying for British intelligence, and each side eventually expelled four diplomats (two of the British representatives had been about to leave and both sides were trying – newspapers reported – to 'preserve decorum').[133] The following year came the arrest of Harold Nicholson, who had been working for the Russians since the early 1990s in Malaysia and then in the CIA training centre in Virginia and was the 'highest-ranking CIA officer ever charged with espionage'.[134]

The most spectacular case of its kind was in November 2006, when a former KGB operative, Alexander Litvinenko, died in a London hospital after ingesting a fatal dose of the radioactive isotope Polonium-210 at a meeting with two other former agents who had flown in from Moscow to see him, Dmitri Kovtun and Andrei Lugovoi.[135] Speculation continues about the extent to which an operation of this kind could have been undertaken without the knowledge and support of the Russian authorities, or at least of dissident elements within their security services. Litvinenko himself, in a deathbed statement, accused Putin directly;[136] the British government demanded that Lugovoi be sent back to London to answer charges in a British court;[137] the Russian authorities pointed out that their Constitution did not allow the extradition of citizens to other jurisdictions;[138] Putin, in Helsinki for an EU–Russia summit, acknowledged that a death was 'always a tragedy' but described the deathbed statement as a 'political provocation' and questioned its authenticity.[139] The whole affair, explained an aide who was 'no believer in conspiracy theories', looked like a 'well-rehearsed campaign to discredit the Russian government and the Russian President'.[140] It was certainly difficult to see how a murder of this kind could be to the Kremlin's advantage; but Litvinenko had been working closely with its arch-enemy Boris Berezovsky, and it could not be excluded that his former associates might have decided to administer exemplary punishment to a defector from their ranks, or that the murder might be connected with the commercial intelligence all three former officers had apparently been providing to Western companies.[141]

Relations with the United Kingdom were already deteriorating, following an extraordinary report on Russian television in January 2006 – confirmed by the Federal Security Service – that four British diplomats had been engaged in espionage and that one of them had been channelling funds to local non-governmental organisations (NGOs) using a hollowed-out 'rock', fitted with batteries and a transmitter, that allowed him to communicate remotely with his Russian contacts.[142] All of this, argued the head of the FSB in a lengthy interview in October 2007, was part of a much larger and well-funded plan to destabilise the entire country, making use of the parliamentary elections that were due to take place at the end of that year and of the presidential elections that would take place the following spring, when Putin would be obliged to stand down at the end of his second consecutive term. In addition to the unusually versatile rock, Patrushev mentioned a James Bond-style communication device hidden in a laptop charger and sophisticated software that allowed agents to use their computers without leaving any trace on the hard disk. British intelligence, he went on, had been particularly active, not only in security matters but also in relation to domestic politics. Their methods ranged from bribery and blackmail to offers of immunity from prosecution, and they made use of the large émigré community in London while cooperating closely with the CIA and their counterparts in the Baltic republics, Poland and Georgia in conducting operations in Russia itself. In fact, complained Patrushev, British agents were the most intrusive of all, followed by Turkish intelligence, who were trying to foment divisions in Russia's Muslim regions.[143]

Relations worsened still further when the Russian authorities began to target the British Council in apparent retaliation for the diplomatic expulsions that had followed the death of Alexander Litvinenko. In December 2007 the Foreign Ministry issued a warning that the Council's entire operation had been in violation of Russian tax laws and the Vienna Convention on Diplomatic Relations, and that its regional offices would have to close by the end of the year.[144] The St Petersburg office reopened in mid-January – its activities, embassy staff insisted, had been entirely legitimate – but the ambassador was called in to receive a formal complaint about this 'deliberate provocation'[145] and the two regional offices, in St Petersburg and Yekaterinburg, were obliged to discontinue their activities a few days later.[146] On the face of it, the Council was an independent body that supported the teaching of English and other forms of cultural exchange; but it was widely suspected (as Dmitri Medvedev put it in an interview shortly before his election) of engaging in 'many other activities that aren't so widely advertised'.[147] Russian concerns, some of which were certainly exaggerated, had to be understood within the wider context of political instability across the entire post-Soviet region in the early years of the new century, above all the 'coloured revolutions' that had ousted established governments in Georgia (in 2003), Ukraine (in 2004) and Kyrgyzstan (in 2005; the new government was itself overthrown by another insurgency in 2010). From a Kremlin perspective, these were hardly isolated events: they had a common scenario and a common paymaster, and their common objective was to consolidate the victory the West appeared to have secured at the end of the Cold War by incorporating large parts of postcommunist Europe and even former Soviet republics within its sphere of influence (and ideally within its military alliances).[148]

There were differences with the United States as well as Britain over Iraq, where a widely supported military offensive had brought an end to the invasion of Kuwait in the first Gulf War of 1990–1 but left the Iraqi dictator Saddam Hussein undisturbed.[149] His continued unwillingness to allow UN weapons inspectors to carry out inquiries to their own satisfaction led to punitive sanctions in December 1998 of a kind that were difficult to reconcile with international law, and tensions began to mount again in the early years of the new century. The Kremlin had opposed unilateral military action in the past, and it resisted further sanctions unless they were specifically authorised by the Security Council (where Russia, as one of its permanent members, could exercise a veto). Military action would be 'unwarranted', Putin declared in January 2003; it would undermine efforts to counter global terrorism; and diplomatic efforts had in any case 'not been exhausted'.[150] A joint Franco-German-Russian statement, issued the following month while Putin was visiting Paris, went even further, opposing the use of force so long as the UN's weapons inspectors were continuing their investigations.[151] Meeting the German Chancellor in Moscow two weeks later, Putin made clear that Russia would refuse to accept a new UN resolution that opened the way to the automatic use of force; they were 'ready to talk, but not to fight'.[152] And Foreign Minister Ivanov, in London at the beginning of March, insisted that there was 'no real need for a new resolution', although they would be prepared to consider 'any steps' if the international inspectors required more support. Russia would 'certainly oppose any resolution whose aim was to justify, directly or indirectly, the use of force'.[153]

When war began a few days later, the Kremlin's response was even more critical. As the Russian President put it in an official statement, the NATO bombing campaign had been launched in spite of global public opinion, and contrary to international law and the UN Charter. There could be no justification for any action of this kind, whether it was charges that Iraq had supported international terrorism (of which the Kremlin had no evidence) or a wish to change the Iraqi government, for which there was no legal authority. Nor was there any need for such action – Iraq posed no danger to its neighbours or other countries, as it was weakened economically and militarily after a ten-year embargo, and international weapons inspectors were continuing their work. Resolution 1441, in the Russian view, had not sanctioned the use of force but was rather a means of allowing the UN weapons inspectors to complete the task with which they had been entrusted. The action that had been taken, Putin went on, was a 'major political mistake', not only in humanitarian terms, but also in the threat it represented to the international order. If some felt able to impose their will on others, without regard to national sovereignty, not a single state anywhere in the world could feel secure; hostilities must come to an end as quickly as possible, and the whole matter must be transferred to the UN Security Council.[154] For Foreign Minister Ivanov, speaking to the Duma the following day, the US-led military action had certainly been 'unlawful';[155] the Duma itself condemned the action more forthrightly as a 'violation of the UN Charter and of the generally accepted principles and norms of international law' and demanded an immediate end to 'US aggression'.[156]

A more carefully modulated response emerged a couple of weeks later when Putin spoke to a group of journalists after a meeting in Tambov, 300 miles south-east of Moscow. Everything that had taken place, he told them, including the loss of innocent lives, confirmed the wisdom of the efforts that had been made to achieve a peaceful resolution. All the same, for 'political and economic reasons' Russia had no interest in a US defeat; their interests would be better served by transferring the dispute into a United Nations framework, and the sooner this happened, 'the better it [would] be for all concerned'. It was not, commentators noted, a popular choice – public opinion would have preferred more unambiguous support of a country that was a long-standing Russian ally in the face of what appeared to be a breach of international law. It did, however, reflect the fact that Russia had a considerable stake in any post-Saddam settlement. The total value of Russian oil contracts with the former regime had been estimated at about $30 billion, and the Iraqi debt to Russia was approximately $8 billion. The United States would clearly be taking responsibility for the allocation of rights for oil production after the war had ended, so that Russia could 'lose everything' unless it maintained a working relationship with the government that would be taking such decisions. Even if the United States and its partners lost the war, Saddam would be unable to fulfil the terms of Iraq's oil contracts with Russia, not least because international sanctions would still be in place. So the only scenario under which Russia could be assured of a presence in the Iraqi fuel and energy industry of the future was a US victory. It was, commented *Izvestiya*, an 'utterly pragmatic' decision.[157]

A much larger issue was the security architecture of a postcommunist Europe, and particularly the expansion of NATO.[158] Yeltsin had in fact suggested, as early as December 1991, that Russia itself might seek admission (the USSR had applied for membership in 1954 but in rather different circumstances),[159] and in a joint declaration after a visit to Warsaw in August 1993 he accepted that a Polish application for membership would 'not be in conflict with the process of European integration, including the interests of Russia'.[160] In October, however, he sent a letter to Western leaders arguing against the early admission of the East European states, suggesting instead that NATO and the Russian government provide for their collective security on a different and more comprehensive basis.[161] It was in these circumstances that the US government proposed a 'Partnership for Peace', in effect a counter-proposal that would allow the countries of the region to form an association with NATO but one that stopped short of full membership.[162] A NATO summit in January 1994 approved the Partnership proposal and at the same time ruled against early admission for the East European countries.[163] Russia, its representatives made clear, would join the Partnership for Peace, but Yeltsin insisted on a 'special agreement' that took account of Russia's 'place and role in world and European affairs and [of] our country's military power and nuclear status';[164] Kozyrev signed the Partnership agreement on this basis in June, together with a brief 'protocol' that identified Russia's 'unique and important contribution commensurate with its weight and responsibility as a major European, world and nuclear power'.[165]

The possible expansion of NATO itself was more controversial. Kozyrev was very concerned that the new Partnership should 'not stimulate NATO-centrism among the alliance's policy-makers or NATO-mania among impatient candidates for membership',[166] and Yeltsin warned a meeting of what had become the Organization for Security and Co-operation in Europe (OSCE) the following December that plans to expand the Alliance raised the danger of a 'cold peace' in place of the 'cold war' that had just concluded. It would, he suggested, be far better to establish a more comprehensive framework based on the OSCE itself, with responsibility for human rights throughout the continent including the rights of Russian minorities in other countries. It could also have a peace-keeping capacity, in which Russia would be ready to play its part. NATO had been created in the Cold War era; but the European states were partners, no longer adversaries, and it would be dangerous to isolate any one of them.[167] Russia, he told journalists, could 'not accept NATO's boundaries moving right up to the border of the Russian Federation', bringing back the system of blocs that had so recently been dismantled, and any move of this kind would be regarded as a 'threat to Russia's security'.[168] The speech was widely seen as 'one of Moscow's toughest international statements since the fall of communism',[169] but in the event the meeting agreed there could be no Russian veto on future admissions, and there was little the Russian authorities could do to resist a process to which most of the East European countries were already committed even though they continued to deplore an expansion that might lead to a 'new confrontation'.[170]

These rather different perspectives were both apparent in the 'founding act' that was signed in Paris in May 1997 by the Russian President and the leaders of all the NATO member countries.[171] Yeltsin himself saw the new treaty as the 'basis for an equitable and stable partnership that [took] into account the security interests of each and every signatory',[172] and the government newspaper *Rossiiskie vesti* argued that their negotiators had prevented an 'anti-Yalta', a 'military and political division of the continent by NATO from a position of brute strength and total disregard for Russian interests'.[173] Other commentators were less persuaded, seeing the new treaty as a logical consequence of Russia's defeat in the Cold War and of its military and economic weakness, with no firm guarantees from the Western signatories that they would not at some point move their military infrastructure still closer to Russian borders and admit former Soviet republics as new members.[174] Alexander Lebed', the outspoken general who had been Secretary of the Security Council, went even further, describing the treaty as evidence of the 'complete failure of the policy of Yeltsin and his regime', with the probable result that the country's 'main strategic partners' in the future would be Asian powers like India and China.[175] Yeltsin himself, in a rhetorical flourish, announced at the signing ceremony that he had also decided as a goodwill gesture to remove warheads from all the missiles that had been targeted on other signatory nations; aides had to remind him that Russian nuclear missiles had not been targeted on the major NATO members for some years – in the case of the United States at least, not since 1994.[176]

The NATO summit that took place in Madrid in July 1997, acting on the basis of this understanding, agreed to admit Hungary, Poland and the Czech Republic as new members, with others to be considered at a later stage. 'Madrid', declared the NATO Secretary-General, was 'not the end but only the beginning of the alliance's expansion', and he mentioned Slovenia and Romania as strong candidates for future membership with a further more ambiguous reference to the Baltic states.[177] Primakov, for his part, insisted the decision was the 'biggest mistake in Europe since the end of World War II',[178] and foreign ministry spokesmen explained that it was at odds with the task of creating a 'single security space in the Euro-Atlantic region' within which 'equal security for all states would be guaranteed'.[179] East Europeans themselves, however, appeared to prefer the guarantees that were available through an alliance that already existed to the uncertain prospect of a new framework that would include Russia as an equal participant, and even former Soviet republics that were not at this time being considered for membership (like Ukraine) began to establish a direct relationship.[180] Russian isolation was deepened by the decision of the European Union, at its Luxembourg summit in December 1997, to begin talks on the admission of Poland, the Czech Republic, Hungary, Slovenia and Estonia, with others to be considered in a second wave.[181] The effect of both decisions was indeed to create the 'new dividing lines' the Russian authorities had repeatedly deplored, and they opened up the possibility that the line might move even further to the east as other postcommunist countries began to reconsider their international affiliations now they were in a position to do so.

In the event, the initial enlargement of NATO in 1999 – when the Czech Republic, Hungary and Poland became members on the Alliance's fiftieth birthday – was followed by two further rounds: in March 2004, when the three Baltic republics, Bulgaria, Romania, Slovakia and Slovenia joined as new members, and in April 2009, when they were followed by Albania and Croatia. The European Union was expanding at the same time: in May 2004, when eight of these countries (the Czech Republic, Hungary, Poland, Slovakia, Slovenia and the three Baltic republics) became full members, as well as Malta and Cyprus; and then again in January 2007, when they were joined by Bulgaria and Romania. A wider 'Europe' meant new tariff barriers and restrictions on movement where they had not existed before; the position of the Russian exclave of Kaliningrad became especially problematic as it was separated from the rest of the national territory by Lithuania, which was now part of the European Union. But a working arrangement was negotiated, and trade relations continued to expand; after the 2004 enlargement, indeed, more than half of Russia's total turnover was with the EU member countries. Taken as a whole, the EU was not regarded as a 'threat', and neither official nor public opinion saw any serious danger to Russian interests from the accession of new, even post-Soviet nations. A few, indeed, called for Russia itself to become a member.[182] The difficulties were increasingly on the other side, as the EU acquired new member states that had emerged from the Soviet orbit with every reason to be suspicious of the intentions of their massive neighbour even if it claimed to be postcommunist; this was one of the reasons it took so long to negotiate a successor to the Partnership and Cooperation Agreement of 1994, which formally expired in 2007 although it continued to operate as long as neither side denounced it.

The further expansion of NATO was much more controversial, and particularly the possible admission of two more post-Soviet republics, Georgia and Ukraine. The circumstances, however, were rather different. Public opinion, at least in Ukraine, was generally hostile to the idea of NATO membership, and accession – the Ukrainian government itself agreed – could not take place unless it had been approved by a national referendum. The Western countries, for their own part, had no wish to prejudice their far more important relationship with Moscow, or to assume the responsibility that would be placed on them to defend the entire territory of a member state with an unpredictable leadership if it were to become engaged in, or even precipitate, a military conflict with Russia (such as the short-lived conflict between Russia and Georgia that took place in August 2008, a conflict the Georgians themselves appeared to have initiated).[183] In the end the Alliance agreed at its Bucharest summit in April 2008 that the two countries would at some point become NATO members, but it stopped short of an 'action plan' that would have been the first step towards membership; in practice, this appeared to mean that the question of a formal association would be postponed indefinitely.[184] The Alliance, in any case, had issues of its own to resolve, including the willingness and ability of its members to conduct military action beyond their own borders (particularly in Afghanistan), and to sustain a level of defence spending in its European member countries that would allow them to balance the overwhelming might of the United States.[185]

Another source of dispute was the American plan to locate a new missile defence system in Central Europe, having meanwhile withdrawn from the 1972 anti-ballistic missile treaty. It was certainly difficult to see this as a logical location for a system that was meant to protect the US mainland against an attack from 'rogue states', such as Iran or North Korea. And as Putin made clear in his 2007 parliamentary address, it was a development that posed a 'direct threat' to Russian interests. Indeed, it raised the wider issue of the Conventional Forces in Europe treaty that had been signed in 1990, which placed serious restrictions on Russia's ability to deploy its own forces on its own territory. Russia had ratified the treaty and begun to implement it, but the Western signatories were still refusing to do so until Russian troops had been withdrawn from Georgia and Transnistria under the terms of the agreement that had been reached at Istanbul in 1999. The two agreements, Putin insisted, were entirely unrelated in terms of international law. Meanwhile, the Western countries themselves had been establishing military bases along the Russian frontier and were planning to locate their anti-missile defences in Poland and the Czech Republic; NATO's new members, including Slovakia and the Baltic republics, were in any case not bound by a treaty that had been signed before they became independent states. Putin made clear that in these circumstances Russia would be suspending its own participation in the treaty, at least until all the NATO member countries had begun to implement it, and he called for a more general discussion with the OSCE as well as NATO about security issues that concerned the entire continent.[186]

Putin had already told journalists at one of his regular press conferences that there would be an 'extremely effective response' to the anti-missile defences that were being proposed for Central Europe, including a future generation of offensive weapons against which such defences would have 'absolutely no effect',[187] and speaking to the press in May 2007, First Vice-Premier Sergei Ivanov announced the successful testing of an intercontinental ballistic missile that would be 'capable of overcoming any existing or future missile defence systems'.[188] The new missile, according to Western analysts, carried multiple independent warheads, making it almost impossible to shoot down; it could hit targets thousands of miles away; and it had sophisticated navigation systems that allowed the warheads to lock on to different targets.[189] Putin also warned, in February and again in October 2007, that Russia would consider withdrawing from the 1987 INF treaty unless other countries were included within its provisions. The Kremlin, it appeared, was particularly concerned by the development of mid-range nuclear arsenals in China, Pakistan and India, but also regarded the treaty as disadvantageous as it did not include US naval cruise missiles or the British and French nuclear arsenals.[190] All of this, commentators suggested, represented the 'worst arms control dispute of the post-Cold War era'. Comparisons were made with the Euromissiles crisis of the 1980s, when the deployment of cruise weapons on the European continent had led to widespread public demonstrations;[191] Putin himself suggested a parallel with the Cuban missile crisis of 1962, when the whole world had stood on the brink of nuclear war.[192]

Putin's successor, Dmitri Medvedev, used his first parliamentary address in November 2008 to announce another retaliatory step: that short-range Iskander surface-to-surface missiles would be installed in Kaliningrad, adjoining Poland and Lithuania. These were the first nuclear-capable weapons to be stationed along the NATO–Russian border since the end of the Cold War; the announcement, in what did not appear to be a coincidence, had been made on the same day as the official declaration of the result of the US presidential election. In addition, three rocket divisions would be maintained in a state of military readiness, instead of being stood down and eventually dissolved, and there would be 'radioelectronic suppression' of the new anti-missile defences the United States had been planning to establish. These, Medvedev explained, were measures that had simply been 'forced on them' by partners who had refused to consider their alternative proposals.[193] But there were also more positive gestures, particularly the reiterated invitation to consider a 'regional pact' that could replace the treaties of the Cold War years,[194] or alternatively a legally enforceable European security treaty that could supplement if not replace the NATO alliance.[195] This was at first sight another version of the pan-European security framework, excluding the United States, that had been a long-standing Kremlin objective. But it found support among some of the West European leaders,[196] and it was accompanied by more broadly conceived proposals to establish financial institutions that could take the place of the US-dominated system that had so comprehensively failed in the international economic crisis that began in late 2008.

A rather different approach began to develop after Barack Obama had taken office in January 2009 and signalled a fresh start. The new administration, promised Vice-President Joseph Biden, would 'push the reset button' in the bilateral relationship;[197] the Kremlin, for its part, dropped the idea of installing missiles in Kaliningrad, amid

Table 7.2 **Defence forces, selected countries, c.2010**

	Russia	USA	China	UK	France
Total personnel	1.027 m	1.580 m	2.285 m	175,000	353,000
Estimated reservists	20 m	865,000	510,000	199,000	70,000
Paramilitaries	449,000	0	660,000	0	0
Nuclear warheads	4834	2702	186	160	300
Defence expenditure (million $)	58.6	607	84.9	65.3	65.7
Percentage of GDP	3.5	4.0	1.9	2.4	2.3

Source: The Military Balance, vol. 110 (2010), pp. 462–3 and 465 (personnel); figures for deployed nuclear warheads and defence expenditure in US dollars at current prices and exchange rates are taken from the *SIPRI Yearbook 2009* (Oxford and New York: Oxford University Press, 2009), pp. 182 and 346; GDP figures relate to 2007.

indications that the new administration would not be 'rushing through its plans' to install the new defence system.[198] Obama's first visit to Russia took place in the summer; there was an 'understanding' on moves towards a new agreement on strategic weapons, but the main result, *Izvestiya* suggested, was a 'change in the climate of relations'.[199] In September 2009 the US President moved much further to meet Kremlin concerns by announcing that the plan to locate anti-missile defences in the Czech Republic and Poland had been abandoned on the grounds that the scheme was unduly expensive and irrelevant to the country's real security needs, which now placed more emphasis on Iran.[200] The decision opened the way to a new arms reduction treaty to succeed START I, which formally expired in December 2009, and an agreement to this effect was concluded in April 2010 – accompanied by a Russian declaration that the agreement would be valid as long as the development of US anti-missile defences did not represent a threat to its security.[201] Putin continued to insist that systems of this kind would be destabilising wherever they were located, and a new Military Doctrine, approved in February 2010, identified NATO expansion as the country's main external threat, together with the attempts that were being made to give the Alliance a new range of 'global functions' that were at odds with international law and US missile defence plans that threatened global stability.[202] (Current numbers of troops and weapons in the major world powers are shown in Table 7.2.)

A comprehensive if (some thought) unduly combative statement of the Russian view of the East–West relationship as of the end of the Putin presidency came in his address to the 43rd Munich Conference on Security Policy in February 2007.[203] The speech certainly avoided 'excessive politeness'; indeed it was a sustained attack on the notion of a unipolar world in which there was 'one centre of authority, one centre of force, one centre of decision-making'. A model of this kind was harmful to the state that sought to impose it as well as to the other members of the world community. And it had 'nothing in common with democracy', on which Russia was continually being lectured. This was not just unacceptable, it was also unrealistic in the contemporary world. And yet attempts were being made – there was no need to say by whom – to introduce it. Unilateral and frequently illegal actions had resolved no problems. Instead, a quite unprecedented use of military force and a disregard for international law had plunged the world into new conflicts, in which more people had been dying than ever before. International law was itself being increasingly modelled on the legal system of a single country. It was that country, the United States, that had 'overstepped its national borders in every way', and was attempting to impose its economic, political, cultural and educational policies on the rest of the world. Nobody could feel safe in this kind of situation; so more and more countries acquired the kinds of weapons systems that could protect them, and other security threats such as terrorism became more widespread.

It was time, Putin went on, to seek a more 'reasonable balance between the interests of all participants in the international dialogue', in a world in which countries like India and China between them accounted for more of the world's GDP than the United States, and the four BRIC nations (Brazil, Russia, India and China) for more than the European Union. All of this would strengthen the forces of multipolarity and help to make the use of force a 'really exceptional measure'. It was understandable that states should sometimes be concerned about developments that were taking place in the domestic politics of other members of the world community. But peaceful means were available to deal with them, as they had been in the evolution of Russia itself from communist rule. 'Why should we start bombing and shooting now at every available opportunity?' There was only one institution that could sanction the use of force when other methods had been unavailing, and that was the United Nations – not NATO, and not the EU. Considerations of this kind were relevant to the discussions that were taking place on disarmament, including the development of 'new, destabilising high-tech weapons' and the militarisation of outer space. Any attempt to extend a missile defence system to Europe would be particularly unfortunate. Who needed the next step in what 'would be, in this case, an inevitable arms race?' There was no serious threat to Europe from any of the 'so-called problem countries', such as North Korea. And how could it make sense for them to attack North America in any case by launching ballistic missiles over Europe?

Putin was also critical of the plans that were being made to expand the NATO alliance, which had 'nothing to do with the modernisation of the Alliance itself or with ensuring security in Europe'. Against whom was it directed? What about the assurances that had been given at the time of German reunification that no NATO armed forces would be stationed further to the east? Russia had made its own contribution to the fall of the Berlin Wall; now the West was 'trying to impose new dividing lines and walls on us'. There were further hard-hitting comments on nuclear non-proliferation, and on the way in which the OSCE had begun to intervene in the domestic affairs of its member nations. But in his conclusion Putin returned to the global issues with which he had begun, particularly the gap in development between rich and poor nations, and the ways in which the rich countries tied assistance to their own companies while at the same time denying access to their own highly subsidised markets. All of this raised the level of social tension in the countries that were excluded and inevitably resulted in the growth of extremism, terrorism and local conflict. In the case of a region such as the Middle East, where there was 'increasingly the sense that the world at large is unfair', it could lead to global destabilisation. If nothing else, the speech was a reminder of the truth of a celebrated observation by Lord Palmerston that Russians liked to repeat: that states had no eternal friends or enemies, but only eternal interests.[204] The experience of the early postcommunist years made it clear that interests of this kind would not necessarily be any easier to reconcile even if they no longer had a philosophical foundation.

The CIS and the East

Issues of a rather different kind were involved in Russian relations with the other states that had formerly been Soviet republics, and with the 'far abroad' in Asia. A referendum that took place in March 1991, although the three Baltic republics, Armenia, Georgia and Moldova refused to participate, had produced a substantial majority in favour of the retention of the USSR as a 'renewed federation' (Gorbachev himself claimed it was a mandate for a 'renewal and strengthening of the union state'),[205] and in June a new version of a union treaty that took account of the vote was sent to the Supreme Soviet and to republican parliaments for their consideration.[206] On 12 July the new treaty was approved by the Supreme Soviet, and on 24 July Gorbachev was able to announce that nine of the fifteen republics had reached a more general accommodation.[207] As published in the central press on 15 August, it specified that a new 'Union of Sovereign States' would be established in which defence, foreign policy, energy, communications, transport and budgetary matters would be decided 'jointly' by the centre and the republics, but that in all other matters republican laws would have precedence over those of the union as a whole.[208] Addressing the nation on television at the start of August, Gorbachev confirmed that the new treaty would be signed first by Russia, Kazakhstan and Uzbekistan at a ceremony later in the month, and went on to describe it as the 'decisive stage' in the transformation of a multinational state into a 'democratic federation of equal soviet sovereign republics' that would continue to be a 'great world power'.[209]

It was this version of the union treaty that was to have been signed by Russian and other representatives on 20 August – a weakening of central authority that the attempted coup, launched the previous day, had been intended to prevent. In the event, the coup discredited the draft treaty and led directly to a series of declarations of republican independence that by the end of the year had led to the dissolution of the USSR itself. Ukraine was the first to declare its independence, on 24 August; Moldova followed on 27 August and Azerbaijan on 30 August.[210] The Belarusian head of state, Nikolai Dementei, who had supported the coup, resigned on 25 August, shortly after which the republican parliament voted to declare the republic's 'political and economic independence'.[211] The Uzbek parliament voted similarly on 31 August; so did Kyrgyzstan; Tajikistan voted for independence on 9 September, Armenia on 23 September, Turkmenistan on 27 October and Kazakhstan on 16 December.[212] The three Baltic republics had meanwhile been allowed to secede, restoring the independence they had never properly lost;[213] and Georgia had declared its newly independent status in April, following elections at which nationalists had been overwhelmingly successful.[214] By the end of the year, Russia was the only republic that had not adopted a declaration of this kind; but it had affirmed its sovereignty on 12 June 1990 in a resolution adopted by the First Congress of People's Deputies that provided for the precedence of its own laws over those of the USSR as a whole, and had gradually taken over the functions of the all-union government within its own boundaries.[215]

Republican declarations generally took a similar form, including a change of name (they became 'republics' rather than 'Soviet socialist republics') and an assertion of ownership over the property and government institutions that were located on their respective territories. Their leaders resigned from the CPSU, which by this time had been banned in most of the republics (in some cases, particularly in Central Asia, it simply changed its name but continued to be a dominant presence in national life under the same leadership).[216] The newly independent republics also became more assertive in matters of defence and foreign policy, applying (in most cases) to join the United Nations and (more generally) seeking to establish their own armed forces. The draft union treaty was clearly superseded by these developments; as the Kazakh president, Nursultan Nazarbaev, told the Supreme Soviet in September 1991, only a much looser confederation would satisfy the aspirations of the republics that still wished to conclude some kind of association.[217] In the end, ten of them – including some that had declared independence – agreed a joint statement which indicated that a 'union of sovereign states' of the kind Gorbachev had proposed would be established. Gorbachev, for the time being, would remain president, but he would rule through a Council of State on which all the participating republics would be represented. Management of the economy would be entrusted to an inter-republican committee headed by the Russian prime minister; the old Soviet parliament would be replaced by a new two-chamber assembly; and in due course a new constitution would be presented for approval, leading to presidential and perhaps more general multiparty elections the following year.[218]

These were intended to be no more than interim arrangements, and further negotiations took place in which Gorbachev sought to develop the basis of a more substantial association. An economic union was established by eight of the former republics on 18 October (Moldova and Ukraine added their signatures the following month),[219] and later, on 14 November, nine of the original fifteen republics (excluding the Baltic republics, Georgia, Armenia and Moldova) reached agreement on another version of the 'union of sovereign states'. This agreement, like those that had preceded it, envisaged a directly elected presidency and a bicameral legislature; central authority, however, would be limited to those spheres of activity that had been specifically delegated to it by the members of the union.[220] A draft of this new version of a union treaty, the fifth and final, appeared in the central press in late November.[221] Gorbachev announced that it would be sent to republican parliaments for their consideration and hoped it would be signed by the middle of the following month;[222] he himself regarded publication of the treaty as a 'collective initialling',[223] and in early December he issued an appeal to the parliaments of the various republics urging them to give it their formal support. It would, he promised them, be a 'new Union', a 'confederal democratic state' based on two key principles: self-determination, sovereignty and independence, together with partnership, cooperation and mutual assistance. None of their problems would be successfully resolved if the process of disintegration was allowed to advance any further.[224]

A referendum in Ukraine on 1 December, however, had already resulted in a majority of over 90 per cent in favour of a fully independent status,[225] and this appears to have convinced Yeltsin that it would be pointless to pursue the goal of political union any further (he was personally in favour of the Union, he had told journalists, but 'could not conceive of a Union without Ukraine').[226] The Russian government, in the event, recognised the Ukrainian decision and looked forward to a 'new partnership';[227] and on 8 December, at a country house in the Belovezh forest outside Minsk, the three Slavic republics – Russia, Belarus and Ukraine – concluded an agreement establishing an entirely new entity, the Commonwealth of Independent States. The new commonwealth was not a state and it did not have a capital, but it would nonetheless provide for the unified control of its nuclear weapons, a coordinated approach to transport, customs, migration, organised crime and the environment, and a 'common economic space'. The USSR, as a subject of international law and a geopolitical reality, was declared no longer in existence, and the norms of other states, 'including the former USSR', were explicitly repudiated.[228] There were serious questions about the constitutionality of any such agreement, as we have already noted (p. 25), and Gorbachev, welcoming some 'positive elements', called for it to be considered by republican parliaments and perhaps to be the subject of another referendum.[229] But in the end the three leaders decided they could take a decision of this kind without additional formality as their republics had been the founding members of the USSR, together with a Transcaucasian Federation that no longer existed,[230] and on 12 December the Russian parliament overwhelmingly endorsed their action.[231]

The new commonwealth declared itself open to other Soviet republics, as well as to states elsewhere that shared its objectives. On 21 December, in the Kazakh capital Alma-Ata, a further agreement was signed by the three original members and by eight of the nine other republics – Armenia, Azerbaijan, Kazakhstan, Kyrgyzstan, Moldova, Tajikistan, Turkmenistan and Uzbekistan (Georgia adhered two years later). The declaration[232] committed those who signed it to recognise the independence and sovereignty of other members, to respect human rights including those of national minorities, and to observe existing boundaries. Relations among the members of the Commonwealth were to be conducted on an equal, multilateral basis, but it was agreed to endorse the principle of unitary control of strategic nuclear arms and the concept of a 'common economic space'. The USSR as such was held to have 'ended its existence', but the members of the Commonwealth pledged themselves to discharge the obligations that arose from the 15,000 or so international agreements to which it had been a party.[233] The heads of the member states also agreed that Russia would take the seat at the United Nations formerly occupied by the USSR, and that a framework of interstate and inter-governmental consultation would be established.[234] Gorbachev resigned as president on 25 December, retaining a salary, a staff of twenty and two cars;[235] at 7.38 the same evening the Soviet flag above the Kremlin was replaced by the Russian tricolour;[236] and on 26 December the upper house of the parliament of a Union that no longer existed voted a formal end to the treaty that had originally established it.[237]

The new commonwealth remained a loose and ambiguous framework.[238] Its inter-governmental institutions provided an opportunity for discussion rather than executive action; its decisions were often disregarded; its members traded increasingly with other states; and they concluded bilateral and multilateral agreements among themselves that were generally of greater practical significance. Indeed, they went to war: for instance, in the continuing dispute between Armenia and Azerbaijan over the predominantly Armenian enclave of Nagorno-Karabakh (there had been 20,000 deaths and over a million refugees by the time a cease-fire was declared in 1994),[239] or in the short-lived military conflict in August 2008 between Russia and Georgia over the status of two breakaway regions, Abkhazia and South Ossetia.[240] The CIS member states had committed themselves to a 'common economic space' but not necessarily to the rouble, and in the end they all established currencies of their own. There were continuing tensions between republics, such as Ukraine, that were still suspicious of any form of supranational authority, and others – particularly in Central Asia – that were net beneficiaries of their relations with the other members (particularly Russia) and much more enthusiastic about a greater degree of integration. Turkmenistan moved to associate status in 2005 in order to accommodate its 'positive neutrality' and did not sign the Charter, which was the formal test of membership;[241] nor did Ukraine, although it took part in CIS activities; and Georgia withdrew in 2008, immediately following the five-day war.[242] The CIS nonetheless survived, which suggested it had some enduring value for its remaining members; it was perhaps best understood as the largest and most nominal of the frameworks that associated the former Soviet republics, allowing them to pursue more particular interests as they saw appropriate.

The new commonwealth, indeed, became an increasingly complex structure as it sought to advance the continuing business of what had formerly been a closely inte-grated union of Soviet republics (by the early years of the new century it was the basis for more than seventy different interstate and intergovernmental organisations).[243] A Charter had been approved in January 1993, although only seven of the ten states that were present agreed to sign it and only two of them without reservation; it insisted on the 'sovereign equality' of all the CIS members but at the same time committed them to a variety of forms of cooperation including human rights, foreign policy, transport and communications, health and social policy, and the common maintenance of their external borders.[244] A more far-reaching 'concept for the further development of the CIS' was approved in October 2007, extending its responsibilities to migration, crime and drugs trafficking, terrorism and the protection of cultural treasures, although only four members – Russia, Kyrgyzstan, Belarus and Armenia – signed all the documents that had been agreed and Georgia refused to sign most of them.[245] The intentions of the Russian leadership itself remained obscure. Speaking in 2005, Putin insisted that the CIS had been 'created for the purpose of a civilised divorce';[246] and yet the CIS member countries, if not the organisation that united them, were always the first item in any statement of foreign policy objectives (the 2008 Foreign Policy Concept, for instance, spoke of bilateral and multilateral cooperation with the CIS member states as a 'priority area of Russia's foreign policy',[247] and President Medvedev spoke of the former Soviet republics as an area of 'privileged interests' in an extended statement on the principles of Russian foreign policy later the same year).[248]

The importance that was attached to relations with the CIS member countries reflected the extent to which they were still united by much more than their common Soviet history. Not least, the former Soviet republics were a crossnational human community. More than a third of all Russians, on the evidence of our 2010 survey, had several relatives (22 per cent), or at least one (12 per cent), in another CIS member country. Equally, not much less than half (41 per cent) had made at least one visit to Ukraine, a quarter (25 per cent) had visited Belarus and 23 per cent had visited at least one of the Baltic republics, as compared with 6 per cent who had ever visited Germany, 5 per cent who had ever visited Poland and fewer than 3 per cent who had ever visited the United States. Human linkages of this kind were matched by a strong commitment to the restoration of the same kind of relationships that had existed among the republics in Soviet times, or at least a move in that direction. Nearly a quarter (22 per cent) of all Russians, on the evidence of the same survey, were committed to the formation of a single state that would include all the members of the CIS, and another 43 per cent thought there should at least be closer cooperation (just 3 per cent thought there should be less cooperation than before, or that the CIS should be dissolved). Another third (32 per cent) thought Belarus, in particular, should become an integral part of the Russian Federation itself. Not surprisingly, it was those who had relatives in other CIS countries and had visited them most frequently who were the most enthusiastic about a closer union, and the most likely to deplore the demise of the USSR itself; but they expressed a general consensus.[249]

Relations among the CIS member countries – and with others outside its ranks – were regulated by a complex, changing and overlapping network of bilateral and multilateral agreements. For the most part, they dealt with economic matters, reflecting the need to regulate a whole series of issues that arose directly from the dissolution of what had been a highly centralised system of ownership and management. A (1) *CIS Economic Court* was established quickly, in May 1992.[250] A more elaborate (2) *Economic Union* was established in September 1993 in a treaty initialled by nine of the CIS member states; Turkmenistan joined at the end of the year, and Ukraine became an associate member in 1994.[251] Its general principles were reminiscent of those of the Treaty of Rome that had established the European Union, but it had little relationship to the circumstances of the time and few of its decisions were carried into practical effect.[252] A (3) *Customs Union* was established in January 1995 by Russia and Belarus, joined later by Kazakhstan, Kyrgyzstan and Tajikistan; its first objective was a free trade area, and then a single customs territory.[253] The agreement was extended in March 1996 into a more far-reaching (4) *Treaty on the Deepening of Integration in Economic and Humanitarian Spheres* among the same five countries,[254] and then in February 1999 it became the basis of a still more elaborate (5) *Treaty on the Customs Union and Single Economic Space* with the same five states as members.[255] Other forms of association had meanwhile been developing among the Central Asian republics, which had formed a Central Asian Economic Community in 1994 that later (in 2001) became the Organisation of Central Asian Cooperation; Russia became a member in 2004, and the entire organisation became part of the Eurasian Economic Community that had meanwhile come into existence.[256]

The (6) *Eurasian Economic Community* had been established in October 2000 as a means of advancing the customs union and single economic space.[257] Initially, it had the same five member states: Belarus, Kazakhstan, Kyrgyzstan, Russia and Tajikistan; Uzbekistan joined in 2006.[258] Together, these six states accounted for about 94 per cent of the territory of the entire CIS, and 73 per cent of its total population.[259] The idea of a community of this kind went back, according to its General Secretary, to a lecture the Kazakh president, Nursultan Nazarbaev, had given in 1994 on the formation of a 'Eurasian union of states';[260] it developed, according to *Izvestiya*, into the 'most effective integrating structure in post-Soviet space', with a range of banking, parliamentary, judicial and other institutions as well as its own intergovernmental agencies in Moscow.[261] There were continuing difficulties in deepening the integration of economies that were at rather different stages of development, with rather different approaches to the question of 'reform'.[262] All the same, Russia's abundance of energy resources, on top of the associations that had developed over the Soviet period, provided an obvious basis for cooperation, and it was accepted that an 'inner core' of Russia, Belarus and Kazakhstan might advance more rapidly towards a common customs area, allowing other members to follow as they found it appropriate to do so.[263] 'Already', commentators suggested, the new Eurasian Economic Community had 'significantly exceed[ed] the effectiveness of all [other] integrating associations'; it might even become a counterpart to the European Union on the territory of the former USSR, to which other neighbouring Eurasian states might be attracted (after all, as *Izvestiya* reminded its readers, the EU had itself acquired its present form 'not in a single day. And not in a single year').[264]

Less obviously successful was the (7) *Single Economic Space* (SES), formed by an agreement in 2003 that had been signed by Belarus, Kazakhstan and Ukraine as well as

Russia,[265] and which was in effect an attempt to relaunch the economic union that had been established ten years earlier. Ukraine was a full member of the SES from the outset – indeed its president had been the first to call for the new organisation[266] – but it was a somewhat detached member, as the only one that was not also a part of the CIS and the Eurasian Economic Community, and it accepted the decisions of the SES only insofar as they were consistent with the Ukrainian Constitution.[267] The aims of the SES, once again, had much in common with those of the European Union: to move initially towards a free trade area, and then towards a common territory on which goods and services, capital and labour would all be allowed to choose their own location. But there was little movement in this direction, not least because the Ukrainian leadership, after the election of Viktor Yushchenko to the presidency at the end of 2004, became increasingly disposed to regard the SES as a Russian initiative that would make it more difficult to achieve the country's newly affirmed objective of Euro-Atlantic integration.[268] Indeed, it began to appear possible that the other members might proceed further, with Ukraine a nominal participant or entirely excluded (a customs union that was concluded in November 2009 certainly led in this direction), or that the SES as a whole might eventually merge with the Eurasian Economic Community.[269] Meanwhile, the SES itself existed 'only juridically': the agreements on which it was based remained in force, but nothing was done to implement them.[270]

There was rather more reality in the (8) *Collective Security Treaty*, and still more so in the formal organisation that was established on its basis in the early years of the new century. The original collective security treaty had been signed in Tashkent in May 1992 by six of the CIS member countries, later joined by three others, all of which pledged themselves to 'refrain from the application or the threat of force in interstate relations' and to come to the assistance of any member of the alliance in the event of external aggression.[271] Initially, the practical significance of this commitment was that the other states (particularly Russia) became heavily involved in supporting the Tajik government against domestic insurgents, and in resisting incursions by armed militants from neighbouring Afghanistan that might extend the influence of Islamic fundamentalism. However, there were continuing differences among its member states, including a dispute between Russia and Georgia about the status of Abkhazia, ongoing tensions between Uzbekistan and Tajikistan, and a suspended military conflict between Armenia and Azerbaijan about the status of Nagorno-Karabakh. Azerbaijan, Georgia and Uzbekistan withdrew from the treaty when its initial period of validity came to an end in 1999, but the other states agreed to extend it indefinitely,[272] and the treaty itself began to develop an increasingly dense network of intergovernmental coordination. A council of defence ministers was established in 2000, the following month an agreement on weapons procurements came into effect and in May 2001 an agreement was signed that set up a 1,600-strong rapid reaction force for the Central Asian region with its base in the Kyrgyz capital Bishkek.[273]

In May 2002 it was agreed to establish a new and more integrated framework of cooperation, and the following October the Collective Security Treaty Organisation

(CSTO) was set up for this purpose at a meeting in the Moldovan capital Chisinau;[274] after ratification by all of the participants, it came into force in September 2003.[275] The CSTO was intended to 'increase the effectiveness' of the treaty by assisting its members to strengthen their collective peace and security, and to defend their independence, territorial integrity and sovereignty without intervening in matters that properly belonged to the jurisdiction of national governments. Current business was to be handled by a central Secretariat, headed by a General Secretary based in Moscow (the first incumbent was Nikolai Bordyuzha, an army general who had been head of the Russian Presidential Administration and of the Security Council for some months in the late 1990s). The Secretariat was supervised by a Council of the respective heads of state, which took ultimate responsibility for the deployment of the CSTO's military forces. The CSTO, as before, was particularly active in Central Asia, dealing with instability beyond its collective boundaries (in Afghanistan, Iraq and potentially Iran) and helping local governments maintain themselves against newer as well as more traditional threats to their security such as 'international terrorism and extremism, the illegal circulation of narcotics and psychotropic substances, arms [and] illegal immigration'.[276] It was evidently for reasons of this kind that Uzbekistan decided to reaffiliate in 2006, some months after it had brutally suppressed a domestic insurgency in the city of Andijan.[277]

There were further developments in 2007, bringing about what a Russian newspaper called an 'almost revolutionary transformation' that was turning the CSTO into a 'powerful politico-military structure for maintaining order in post-Soviet space'.[278] The most important single change was the formation of a collective peace-keeping force that Russia had been seeking to establish since 2003, of a kind that would provide a legal basis for the deployment of its own troops throughout the territory of the entire organisation. The agreement made it easier at the same time for other members of the alliance to obtain Russian military equipment at domestic prices, not just for their armed forces but also for internal security. Changes of this kind meant that the CSTO was becoming much more than the 'amorphous organisation' that had originally been created, and much more of an agency through which the Russian authorities could seek to influence developments in the other post-Soviet republics; this made it an even more welcome guarantee for incumbent elites against external or domestic challenge.[279] The Foreign Policy Concept of 2008 described the CSTO as a 'key instrument for supporting stability and maintaining security on the territory of the CIS',[280] and the Security Strategy of 2009 described it in similar terms as a means of dealing with 'regional challenges and threats of a military-political or military-strategic nature'.[281] Of potentially still greater significance, there was increasingly close cooperation between the CSTO and the Eurasian Economic Community,[282] initially on matters such as illegal migration, narcotics and transport, but opening the possibility (at least for some commentators) that the two might at some time in the future become a single organisation with a common membership.[283]

Relations with the largest and most important of Russia's CIS partners, Ukraine, were complicated by a dispute over control of the Black Sea fleet, with Yeltsin insisting that the

Table 7.3 **Patterns of international membership, 2010**

	CIS	EurAsEC	SES	CU	CSTO	SCO	GUAM
Russia	X	X	X	X	X	X	
Ukraine	X*		X				X
Belarus	X	X	X	X	X		
Georgia	1993–2009						X
Armenia	X				X		
Azerbaijan	X						X
Moldova	X						X
Kazakhstan	X	X	X	X	X	X	
Tajikistan	X	X			X	X	
Turkmenistan							
Kyrgyzstan	X	X			X	X	
Uzbekistan	X	X			X	X	
China						X	

Note: CIS = Commonwealth of Independent States; EurAsEC = Eurasian Economic Community; SES = Single Economic Space; CU = Customs Union (in effect from January 2010); CSTO = Collective Security Treaty Organisation; SCO = Shanghai Cooperation Organisation; GUAM = Georgia, Ukraine, Armenia and Moldova (an organisation that was formally established in 2001 and of which Uzbekistan was a member until 2005, when it was known as GUUAM).
*Ukraine had ratified the founding documents of the CIS, but not the Charter, and was formally a 'participant' rather than a 'member'.

fleet 'was, is and will continue to be Russian' but the Ukrainian authorities insisting that all troops in the republic, other than strategic nuclear forces, accept their orders and take an oath of allegiance.[284] Relations were also complicated by the issue of Crimea, whose predominantly Russian population favoured a greater degree of autonomy or even separation; the entire region had become a part of Ukraine as late as 1954, when Khrushchev chose to mark the 300th anniversary of Ukraine's unification with Russia with a gesture that many Russians – including the then mayor of Moscow, Yuri Luzhkov – regarded as illegitimate,[285] and which was denounced by the Russian parliament in 1992.[286] Nearly a quarter of the entire republican population, including most of eastern Ukraine and the industrial Donbass, was Russian speaking, and there were as many as 20 million visits a year in each direction.[287] President Kuchma, in an interview in early 1997, blamed Russia's 'prejudiced attitude' for the continuing difficulties in their relationship,[288] and it was not until May of that year that the Russian President was able to make an official visit. When he did so it was to sign a treaty of friendship, cooperation and partnership that appeared to place relations between the two countries on a new and more amicable footing.[289] The treaty contained a commitment to the inviolability of international boundaries (which meant that there would be no Russian encouragement of secessionist movements by fellow nationals), and there were guarantees for the cultural rights of national minorities, including radio and television transmissions in their respective languages.[290]

The relationship remained a difficult one, particularly after Viktor Yushchenko had won the Ukrainian presidency at the end of 2004 after the popular upheaval of the 'Orange revolution' had forced a re-run of the second round of the election. Putin had offered his open support to the candidate who was seen as more pro-Russian, Viktor Yanukovych, visiting the republic shortly before the first round to make a live television broadcast in which he failed to mention his main opponent, and again before the second round;[291] and he congratulated Yanukovych prematurely when first reports of the heavily manipulated ballot suggested he had been successful.[292] Not surprisingly, relations became increasingly confrontational, above all in relation to the provision of gas and the terms under which it crossed Ukraine to Western Europe. The dispute became a full-blown crisis in January 2006, when Gazprom cut off its supply after it had proved impossible to reach an agreement on the price that was to be paid and on the settlement of the bill for earlier deliveries.[293] There was a repeat performance in January 2009, which again was settled quickly, but not before the dispute had led to the suspension of supplies to most of the European Union member countries as well as Ukraine itself.[294] The effect was to encourage the efforts the EU countries were already making to diversify their sources of supply (as matters stood, Russia supplied about a quarter of EU gas consumption and about half of its imports, 80 per cent of which came through Ukraine in pipelines);[295] it also reduced their enthusiasm for any action by the Ukrainian authorities – such as moving closer to NATO – that might unnecessarily antagonise the Kremlin.

It was an indication of the poor state of the relationship that when Viktor Chernomyrdin stepped down as Russian ambassador in June 2009, it was announced that his successor would not be taking up his responsibilities until a new Ukrainian president had taken office. Yushchenko's policies, Medvedev complained in an open letter, had been 'anti-Russian'. He drew particular attention to the support the Ukrainian President had offered to the Georgian leadership in its August 2008 offensive on South Ossetia, including the provision of armaments, and his apparent determination to move Ukraine towards NATO membership in spite of the wishes of Ukrainians themselves, as well as continuing disagreements about the status of the Black Sea fleet. The Russian President also expressed concern about the disruption of energy supplies, the property rights of Russian investors, the celebration of Ukrainians who had become Nazi auxiliaries during the Second World War, the attempt to represent the Soviet famine of 1932–3 as a 'genocide of the Ukrainian people' and the continued marginalisation of the Russian language in public life.[296] The Ukrainian President, in his reply, insisted that part of the blame for the worsening of relations between the two countries lay on the Russian side and described as 'without foundation' the reports that Ukraine had provided the Georgians with armaments.[297] There was some hope of an improvement in relations when Yushchenko was replaced by Yanukovych in the closely fought presidential election that took place in January and February 2010, and in April an agreement was reached on the long-term future of the naval base at Sevastopol; all the same, there were likely to be continuing tensions between a newly independent state that was determined to assert its own priorities and a Russian leadership that continued to regard it, in the last resort, as subordinate.

Among the other Soviet republics, Russia enjoyed particularly close relations with Belarus, where Alexander Lukashenko had won an overwhelming victory in presidential elections in the summer of 1994 and then gone on to establish a firm, sometimes repressive ascendancy.[298] Lukashenko, a former collective farm chairman who had become prominent as an anti-corruption campaigner, was a strong supporter of closer relations with Russia and had acquired some notoriety as the only member of the Belarusian parliament who had voted against ratification of the Belavezh agreement that had dissolved the USSR in December 1991.[299] But there was a real basis for the association in terms of language, religion and family ties (nearly 53 per cent, in our 2009 survey, had at least one close relative who lived in Russia, and 38 per cent had at least one relative in another CIS republic).[300] Apart from this, Belarus had traditionally been the 'workshop' of a closely integrated Soviet economy, it commanded the main East–West transport routes and its air defence systems were a vital part of Russia's own security. In February 1995 Lukashenko and Boris Yeltsin signed a treaty of friendship and cooperation during a state visit by the Russian President to a republic that he described as Russia's 'closest partner'; Lukashenko, for his part, noted that the republic saw its future 'only on the basis of a deeper integration with Russia'.[301] In March a statement from the Belarusian President ruled out membership of NATO;[302] and in May 1995 a referendum gave overwhelming support to the resumption of closer cultural and economic ties, the reinstatement of Russian as an official language, the restoration of the Soviet-era flag and an extension of presidential powers.[303]

Relations between the two countries moved much further in March 1996 with the conclusion of a 'treaty of the four' (Russia, Belarus, Kazakhstan and Kyrgyzstan) that provided for the 'deepening of [their] integration in the economic and humanitarian spheres', and more particularly the creation of a 'single economic space', the harmonisation of legislation, minimum standards of social assistance across all the member states and an 'agreed foreign policy', and at some point in the future the creation of a 'community of integrated states'. It was described by the four presidents at the signing ceremony as an 'epochal' agreement for a group of states that were 'joined by a common historical fate'; it was to be valid for five years with automatic extension, and open to other states that wished to join it.[304] Then in April Russia and Belarus together concluded a treaty that established a 'deeply integrated ... Community', with wide-ranging powers including a common foreign policy, shared use of 'military infrastructure', a common power grid and eventually a common currency.[305] For President Yeltsin, the treaty strengthened his appeal to Russian nationalist opinion in the run-up to the presidential elections of the summer; for President Lukashenko it had obvious economic advantages. Lukashenko was able to secure popular support for a further extension of his powers and of his presidential term at a referendum in November 1996;[306] Western governments expressed reservations about the result and about the President's increasingly authoritarian methods, but Prime Minister Chernomyrdin congratulated him on a 'real victory'.[307]

A more far-reaching agreement was signed in April 1997, converting the Community of the two states into a formal Union.[308] The treaty, the two presidents declared, was an 'historic event' that had 'taken to a new level the process of unification of two friendly peoples and the integration of our states'. Both states, they announced, were firmly opposed to NATO's eastward expansion, which could only lead to a 'dangerous confrontation'. The two presidents undertook to unify their countries' respective legislation, and every effort would be made to synchronise their economic and taxation policies with a view to the introduction of a common currency. Social benefits would gradually be equalised so that living standards increasingly converged; and there might be a joint citizenship of the Community that the two states had already established.[309] A statute approved the following May, after public discussion, made a series of more specific provisions, including a single citizenship of the new Union.[310] And in December 1998 both leaders took a further step, calling for a more far-reaching union that would continue to respect their individual sovereignties. Again, many of the more detailed provisions were to be agreed at a later stage, including the dismantling of customs barriers and tax, currency and monetary harmonisation; but there would be joint agencies of government, and equal rights for the citizens of one state on the territory of the other. The agreement, Yeltsin declared, opened a 'new page' in the history of relations between the two countries; they would 'enter the 21st century together', added Lukashenko, 'and God willing, as a single state'.[311]

A single state, indeed, was formally established a year later, when the two presidents concluded a treaty that was held to represent a 'new stage in the process of unifying the peoples of both countries in a democratic law-based state'. The new union state would be established 'in stages', as economic and social circumstances allowed. Both of its members retained their full sovereignty, but there would be a 'single economic space', unified transport and energy systems, common legislation on foreign investment, military coordination, and (in due course) a single currency with a single emission centre. The union state would be governed by a Supreme State Council consisting of the heads of state, prime ministers and parliamentary speakers of each of the participants; current business would be in the hands of a Standing Committee, headed by a State Secretary (the first to hold this position was Yeltsin's former head of staff, Pavel Borodin).[312] But the union state, in the event, made little further progress. On the Belarusian side, there was support for closer economic cooperation, but not if it meant the sacrifice of state sovereignty; on the Russian side there was more support for a single state in which the larger state would obviously have the dominant role, and for a single currency that would be the Russian rouble, with its emission centre in Moscow.[313] There was also a personal element. Yeltsin and Lukashenko had enjoyed a close, even intimate relationship; Putin placed more emphasis on the promotion of Russian interests and offered the Belarusian leader a formal handshake rather than a Slavic bear hug at their first official meeting.[314]

As with Ukraine, there were particularly sharp differences on matters of energy supply and transportation. Belarus depended almost entirely on Russia for its gas, and for most of its oil. Accordingly, it had an obvious interest in paying Russian domestic (or at least lower) prices, rather than those that prevailed on world markets. It had another obvious interest in maintaining its ownership of the distribution network, and maximising the income it received from the oil pipelines that ran across the national territory. An open dispute about the prices that should be paid for such facilities broke out at the end of 2006, finally settled in mid-January 2007 after Belarusians had spent a couple of weeks shivering in the winter cold.[315] Supplies were suspended once again in January 2010 in similar circumstances.[316] But there was a larger divergence in the philosophy of economic management, with Russians committed to the principles of market capitalism and Belarusians more inclined to favour a 'socially oriented economy' of a broadly Chinese kind, one that (Lukashenko suggested) had been more successful in practice.[317] The Russian Foreign Policy Concept spoke of continuing to create the conditions for the 'effective construction of a Union State through the steady transfer of relations between [the two countries] to market principles in the process of the formation of a single economic space';[318] but it was always unlikely that there could be an 'equal' partnership between two countries whose population, territory and resources were so very different, and for this, if no other reason, it was just as unlikely there would ever be a 'union state' of the kind that had been originally envisaged.[319] Indeed, there was some evidence that Belarus was already 'leaving Russia' in the early years of the new century,[320] and cultivating a wider range of European associations.[321]

By the early years of the new century, Russian relations with the other former Soviet republics had become a complex network of associations that reflected a variety of short-term and more enduring circumstances, ranging from a nominal unity with Belarus to an open military conflict with Georgia.[322] Ordinary Russians shared the same range of opinions. There was little doubt, at this level, that the former Soviet republics should have overall priority, and it was former Soviet republics that were most likely to be regarded as Russia's natural allies – although they also included some of the countries that were seen as Russia's most determined opponents, in Georgia and the Baltic (see Table 7.4). Friendliest of all at the end of the first decade of the new century was the other member of the 'union state', Belarus, followed by Kazakhstan, with its substantial population of Russian-speakers and pro-Russian leadership. Armenia, Azerbaijan, Kyrgyzstan, Uzbekistan, Tajikistan, Turkmenistan and Moldova were also seen as positively disposed, although not necessarily more so than China, Germany or India. Understandably, Georgia (under the leadership of Mikheil Saakashvili, widely believed to have precipitated the short war of 2008 with the covert support of the United States) was seen as the most hostile foreign country, closely followed by the United States, Ukraine and the Baltic republics. It was striking that the end of the Cold War had not

Table 7.4 Russia's friends and foes, 2009

'Friends'		'Foes'	
Belarus	50	Georgia	62
Kazakhstan	38	USA	45
China	18	Ukraine	41
Germany	17	Latvia	35
Armenia	15	Lithuania	35
India	12	Estonia	30
Cuba	11	Poland	10
Azerbaijan	10	Afghanistan	7

Source: adapted from 'Druz'ya i vragi Rossii', 10 June 2009, at www.levada.
ru/press/2009061001.html, last accessed 20 September 2010. The question
wording was: 'Name five countries that you consider: Russia's closest friends
and allies; those that are the most unfriendly or hostile towards Russia.'
Figures are shown in rounded percentages for all the countries that were
mentioned by at least 10 or 7 per cent of respondents respectively (n=1,600).

significantly altered the image of the United States, and by extension NATO, as essentially hostile; there was much less concern about 'the West' and a broadly positive
attitude towards 'Europe'.

The Soviet relationship with Asia was dominated by the relationship with a still
communist China, with which the USSR had shared the world's longest land border as
well as an ideology and system of government.[323] The Chinese authorities were clearly
distressed by the gradual relaxation of communist control in the USSR and Eastern
Europe, but in visits to Beijing by Gorbachev in May 1989, and to Moscow by premier
Li Peng in 1990 and by party leader Jiang Zemin in May 1991, both sides agreed to
preserve normal relations and to accept differences in their 'ways and means of pursuing
reforms within the framework of the socialist choice'.[324] The collapse of the USSR at the
end of 1991 placed Russo-Chinese relations on a new basis, as the postcommunist
Russian government was at least nominally committed to human rights as they were
understood in other countries, while the Chinese insisted that human rights were a
domestic matter and in any case that they could be understood only in the context of
their own history, in which basic human needs had always occupied a more prominent
place.[325] Yeltsin made a first visit to China in December 1992, where he called for a 'new
era' in relations between the two countries,[326] but his visit was cut short by the need to
assist in the formation of a new Russian government; and a planned visit to Japan did not
take place at all because of continuing differences over the fate of the southern Kurile
islands that Japan regarded as its 'northern territories' (in the end the two states agreed to
'make every effort' to conclude a peace treaty that would regulate all aspects of their
relations by the year 2000, but failed to do so).[327]

The Chinese leadership appeared to have taken the view that communist rule had come to an end in the USSR because of the weakness and indecision of the Soviet leadership,[328] but they refrained from public criticism of their Russian counterparts. Russian ministers, for their part, made no comment on the state of human rights in China (as Gorbachev had remarked about the Tiananmen Square massacre of 1989, 'We cannot interfere and give advice').[329] In September 1994 Jiang Zemin made another official visit to Moscow, this time to a postcommunist Russia, developing what both countries had agreed to describe as a 'constructive partnership'; as it was defined in a declaration that was signed during the visit, this meant 'equitable, non-ideologised relations constructed on the basis of good-neighbourliness, friendship and mutual advantage'.[330] Relations moved to a qualitatively new level during President Yeltsin's visit to Beijing in 1996, as part of a more assertive and less pro-Western orientation in Russian policy more generally. The two countries, it was agreed, had established 'relations of equal partnership, based on trust, that [were] aimed at strategic cooperation in the 21st century'.[331] In their joint communiqué, Yeltsin committed Russia once again to the Chinese positions on Taiwan and on Tibet, while the Chinese endorsed Russian policy towards Chechnya (an 'internal affair of Russia') and the expansion of NATO. Both sides also agreed to deplore the 'hegemonism' of, in effect, the United States; and in what was a symbolic as well as a practical move, a 'hot line' was installed between the two capitals.[332]

The Chinese President visited Russia once again in April 1997, signing an elaborate declaration on a 'multipolar world and the formation of a new world order' and concluding an agreement on arms reductions along the common borders of the two countries and of Kazakhstan, Kyrgyzstan and Tajikistan in which the leaders of those states also took part.[333] A fifth summit between the two presidents took place in China later in the year; neither state, it was noted, pursued any 'hegemonistic or expansionist aims', and by this time 'virtually all issues' that related to their common border, still not entirely demarcated, had been agreed.[334] Yeltsin was able to make a friendly visit to the Russian community in Harbin, most of whom had fled their home country in the 1920s, and a Russo-Chinese committee of friendship, peace and development was set up to 'strengthen the traditions of Russo-Chinese partnership, trust and good neighbourliness'.[335] Reviewing progress at the end of his first full year as foreign minister, Primakov drew particular attention to the 'significant progress' that had been made in relations with China;[336] but while both sides could agree to deplore the 'hegemonism' of a single power, the Chinese remained reluctant to underwrite Russian plans for a joint system of Asian security, and bilateral trade remained (in the words of Russian Vice-Premier Boris Nemtsov) 'laughable for two great countries'.[337] Indeed, there were moments in the late 1990s, with liberal Westernisers in the ascendant, when the relationship with Japan began to appear almost as important, although there was little sign of progress in the ongoing territorial dispute, and bilateral trade was also modest.[338]

A rather different emphasis became apparent with the election of Vladimir Putin and a rebalancing of priorities that attached more weight to relations with the CIS and traditional allies, including those (like China and Cuba) that were still under communist rule. Relations advanced considerably in the summer of 2001 with the conclusion of a full-scale 'treaty on good neighbourliness, friendship and cooperation' between the two countries, with a twenty-year period of validity. Although its provisions – in terms of mutual non-aggression, respect for international law, the development of trade and cultural relations – were relatively conventional, it had additional symbolic significance as the first bilateral treaty of its kind for more than fifty years.[339] Three years later, the lengthy border was finally demarcated.[340] Trade was meanwhile increasing substantially, to such an extent that China, by the end of the decade, had become Russia's largest single supplier as well as one of its most important export markets.[341] The relationship, it was generally argued, was no more than a pragmatic accommodation that did not supersede enduring differences in interests and values, an 'axis of convenience' that did not suggest there was a common vision of the international order or of their respective places within it; but it appeared to be a 'largely effective relationship in its own right' and was arguably the 'greatest Russian foreign policy achievement of the post-Soviet period'.[342] It was an indication of the importance of the relationship to the Kremlin that President Dmitri Medvedev's first foreign trip was to China, just a couple of weeks after he had taken office, with a stopover in Kazakhstan on the way out.[343]

Russo-Chinese relations were underpinned by their joint commitment to the Shanghai Cooperation Organisation (SCO), a development of the 'Shanghai Five' (including Kazakhstan, Kyrgyzstan and Tajikistan) that had been established in that city in 1991 and which had acquired a more formal status in 1996.[344] The SCO itself came into existence in 2001 when these five countries, together with Uzbekistan, agreed to move towards a 'higher level of cooperation' through a new organisation that would help to develop a 'new democratic, fair and rational political and economic international order', and which would give more particular attention to regional security including the struggle against terrorism, separatism and extremism, and to the illegal trade in arms and narcotics and illegal migration.[345] The declaration that announced its establishment insisted that the new organisation was not directed against 'third states and regions' (in other words, the United States and its allies) but was an 'international organisation of a new type', imbued with what was described as the 'Shanghai spirit' of 'mutual trust, mutual benefit, equality, reciprocal consultation, respect for the diversity of cultures [and the] aspiration towards common development' (these were in fact very close to China's own 'five principles of peaceful coexistence', which dated from 1955).[346] A Charter, adopted in 2002, set out the new organisation's operating principles and management structures.[347] India, Pakistan, Iran and Mongolia had observer status from the summer of 2005, and the combined population of members and observers, 3 billion at this point, was more than half the population of the entire planet.[348]

The SCO acquired an increasingly overt military dimension after it began to organise joint manoeuvres, first of all in 2005 with Russia and China and then involving all six members of the alliance in 2007. For Russian commentators, this was part of an 'overall plan to transform the SCO into a politico-military bloc in Central Asia that [would] defend Russian interests and counter the growing penetration of the United States into that region'.[349] For other commentators, there '[had] to be some sort of counterweight to the claims of the USA and NATO to world supremacy'; Russia was 'responding to America's drive for global hegemony in various ways, and imparting a military-political direction to the SCO [was] just one of them'.[350] And yet this was still some distance short of an eastern NATO. For a start, there was no early prospect of a unified military force or strategic doctrine. Nor was there a common external front: Uzbekistan ended the agreement by which it had hosted a US military base in 2005, but Kyrgyzstan allowed the one at Manas to remain after the Americans had offered to increase their payment and rename it a 'transfer centre'.[351] Russia and China themselves had historically been military rivals, even opponents, and took a very different view of the possible admission of new members, such as India or Iran, that might alter the internal dynamics of the alliance. The three Central Asian states, for their part, had reason to be cautious about the regional superpowers, although for the moment the offer of unconditional support for their autocratic regimes seemed preferable to the US insistence on democratisation.[352] If the SCO were to seek a more active role and a larger membership, it was likely that these internal differences would become even more significant.

Competing narratives

Although Putin and Medvedev's assertive approach was clearly dominant in the early years of the new century, there was still a diversity of opinion about the position that Russia should adopt in its relations with the wider world. Perhaps the most fundamental was the long-standing division between those who regarded Russia as a unique civilisation that should seek its 'own path' towards the future, and those who saw Russia as part of a wider and more advanced European community. In the nineteenth century, the former became known as 'Slavophiles' and the latter as 'Westernisers'; the terms of the debate were set by philosopher Petr Chaadaev, who insisted in a celebrated series of letters in the 1830s that the Russian past and present were worthless and that there was no alternative but to seek reunion with the great body of European civilisation, including the Catholic Church. The Slavophiles could be seen as a 'reply to Chaadaev';[353] Russia, they believed, would more readily find salvation within its own distinctive traditions and should not import ideas and institutions from an alien and degenerate West.[354] Much later, something of this difference underlay the bitter struggle between Stalin (prepared, if necessary, to build 'socialism in a single country') and his Trotskyite opponents, who looked to the more developed countries of Europe to complete a transition to socialism that a backward Russia could only initiate. Later still, it was a central distinction in the elite debate about the place a postcommunist Russia should occupy in a rather different international environment, in which the key issue was 'whether Russia should follow the path of the West or ... pursue its own unique path while taking into account its own putatively unique historical and geographical uniqueness'.[355]

Others have suggested at least one further element in the debate, one that was associated with the interests of the state itself whether or not Russia was seen as a unique civilisation or as part of a much wider community of values. To conceive of those interests was of course no easy matter in a state that was unavoidably engaged in the geopolitics of the entire Eurasian landmass, from small and stable European democracies on the one hand to a vast and rapidly developing China on the other, and from friendly and non-aligned countries to what the rest of the world regarded as 'rogue states' in North Korea and possibly Iran, with further and more particular difficulties where territorial issues had still to be resolved (most notably with Japan, where the dispute about the Kuriles or 'northern territories' dated from the end of the Second World War). Nor were 'national interests' exclusively or even primarily a matter of relations with foreign states. As successive administrations conceived of them in the early postcommunist years, they involved a great deal more: from the Russian language to the environment, from demography to the Orthodox Church, and from science and technology to education, culture and public health. Above all, as the national security strategy defined it in 2009, the 'national interest' meant a stable and prosperous Russia, one that provided for the rights and freedoms and the 'quality and level of life' of its citizens as well as for the territorial integrity and security of the state itself; and increasingly, foreign and security policy was designed to promote that objective.[356] The main elements of these various positions are shown in Table 7.5.

At one extreme, in all frameworks of this kind, were the pro-Western liberals who had exercised considerable influence during the years of the Yeltsin presidency, but who had become a marginal presence in public life under Putin and his successor.[357] For 'Liberal Westernisers', as we shall call them in this discussion, Russia was unquestionably a part of Europe in its history, culture and mentality, and its natural affinity was with the Western countries with which it formed (in Kozyrev's words) 'one – democratic – community'.[358] In this view, Russia should emulate European standards to the greatest extent possible while developing trade and other forms of association, moving eventually (in some versions) towards full membership of the EU and even NATO. Russia, they believed, should also join the World Trade Organization and play a cooperative part in the full range of international organisations. They did so 'not for cost–benefit reasons, but because they [identified] with European values and [believed] Russia should adopt them';[359] in addition, there were strong grounds for cooperation in the face of new challenges to the international system, including Islamic fundamentalism and transnational crime. Liberal Westernisers were supportive of the Commonwealth of Independent States, but on a pragmatic basis, and they believed Russia should abandon its historical great-power illusions about having a 'special role' as a bridge between Europe and Asia in favour of developing its European orientation. Domestically, they also favoured a market economy, an effective rule of law and liberal-democratic political institutions, both for

Table 7.5 Russian foreign policy orientations: a schematic representation

	Liberal Westerniser	Pragmatic Nationalist	Fundamentalist Nationalist
Russia?	A European country	Mostly but not entirely European	Eurasian or unique
EU?	Closer relations, membership perspective	Practical cooperation	Practical cooperation, but seen as hostile
NATO?	Closer relations, membership perspective	Practical cooperation	A threat
USA?	Closer relations	Practical cooperation, but interests do not always coincide	An even greater threat
CIS?	Sceptical, but retain where of practical value	A vital national interest, further integration desirable	Ineffective, but further integration desirable
WTO?	Join at earliest opportunity	Join in medium term	An agency of Western control
International orientation?	Europe and the USA	Multi-vector	Multi-vector, tilted towards the East
Supported by?	Liberal intellectuals, some ministers, some parties (esp. Yabloko and the URF / Right Cause)	Presidency and most of government, party of power (United Russia), business (especially natural resource companies)	Orthodox Church, *silovik* elements in presidency and government, some parties (esp. CPRF, Liberal Democrats)

their own sake and because they would make it easier to integrate with other European societies.

Views of this kind were represented to some extent among parliamentarians, but to a much greater extent among the experts and commentators who were a part of Russia's foreign policy community and contributed substantially to its discourse. For Vladislav Inozemtsev, for instance, a professor at the Higher School of Economics and editor of the left-leaning journal *Svobodnaya mysl'* (Free Thought), Russia was a 'European country in its history and traditions, which [was] naturally oriented towards Europe'. Over the early years of the new century, it would 'cease to be an Asian power, and [would] have an even closer relationship with Europe'. There was no harm in entertaining larger ambitions, for Inozemtsev, but if they were serious about realising such ambitions, there was 'only one "polygon" for that – the European one'. Indeed more than this, a return to Europe could be Russia's 'national idea', and not as some kind of thirtieth member of the European Union 'but as a force able to transform the Old World, to rejuvenate it, and give the European Union qualitatively new geopolitical and geoeconomic dimensions'. Russia's geopolitical and military resources, combined with Europe's technology and global presence, 'would make Eurussia the undoubted world leader'. And Europe could help to transform Russia itself, encouraging a greater awareness of the rule of law and of the rights of individual citizens. It was time, he argued, to abandon the positions that had traditionally been taken by both sides, and to accept that neither Russia nor Europe would be able to cope by themselves with the challenges of a new century.[360]

For Westernisers like Inozemtsev, there were still larger, civilisational choices. If Russia moved in a Eurasian direction, they suggested, the results could well be tragic. It would mean an association with the other members of the Shanghai Cooperation Organisation, which was evidently attempting to 'consolidate "Eurasian space"' and achieve a degree of relative economic independence. But the countries that were members of the SCO were very loosely associated, and conducted no more than 8 per cent of their trade with other members. Moreover, any grouping of this kind would be dominated by China, which had 80 per cent of its combined population, 74 per cent of its GDP and a level of military spending that was second only to that of the United States. Nor had there been any sign that the Beijing leadership was willing to take into account the interests of its 'partners' in domestic or foreign policy, for instance in preventing river-borne pollution. If there was any further 'integration' on this basis, Inozemtsev warned, Russian leaders would in effect become the 'secretaries of the Moscow regional committee of the Communist Party of China' – there would be no room for them in its Politburo.[361] Nor was it likely that there would be any salvation in Russia's new-found importance as an energy supplier. Energy superpowers were 'unknown to history', and there was a 'very sceptical view in the West of the very possibility of the successful and stable development of countries that [sought] to base their economic success on the strengthening of the raw materials sector'; the United States in particular did not see Russia as a 'real competitor', aware of its dependence on the oil pipeline.[362]

Inozemtsev wrote elsewhere that Russia had been 'squeezed between two poles' since the demise of the USSR. On one side was a united Europe with nearly 500 million citizens and 16 per cent of world exports; on the other was China, with 1.3 billion people and more than 8 per cent of world trade. Russia itself was in the middle, with no more than 2.4 per cent of the world's population and 2.5 per cent of world exports, and most unlikely to become an independent pole of attraction. 'Only a blind man' could fail to see the way in which the other former Soviet republics were moving towards the European Union on the one hand – the Baltic states, Ukraine, Moldova and Georgia – or else towards China – Kyrgyzstan, and to some extent Uzbekistan and Turkmenistan. Sooner or later Russia would have to make its own choice, and it would hardly be in favour of China, because in these circumstances it would become no more than the 'vassal' of a more powerful and authoritarian neighbour with whom they had little cultural affinity. In Inozemtsev's own view, Russia in the twenty-first century should be a 'free European state' and part of its 'great civilisation'. Nor was this an illusory prospect. For all the talk of a 'separate path', Russians were 'voting in favour of Europe with their roubles and their feet, not against it': the EU already provided more than half of Russia's imports and more than 80 per cent of the SCO's foreign investment, and it was European countries in which nearly half of all Russians chose to take their foreign holidays. On top of this, ordinary people were far more favourably disposed towards 'Europe' than the United States or China, and they automatically associated 'European' with anything that suggested a higher standard of living.[363]

Another, broadly 'Liberal Westerniser' view came from Timofei Bordachev, also a professor at the Higher School of Economics and director of research for the influential Council on Foreign and Defence Policy. In this case, he argued in a 2009 book, it was the external challenges that were faced by Russia and the European Union together that suggested a 'package of agreements in the interests of their common security'. One of these challenges was the 'anarchy' that had come to prevail in world affairs, with a series of powers that were no longer willing to abide by the established rules of the game; another was their wish to find a balanced rather than subordinate relationship with the United States; a third was the still wider issue of globalisation, and its implications for the role of government in all countries. All of this suggested the possibility of a 'strategic union' instead of the 'zero-sum' competition that had taken place since the end of the Cold War.[364] Russia, for Bordachev, had 'no constant and reliable allies'. But Russia and the EU member countries were naturally interdependent: the European Union as an enormous and stable market with a way of life that could well serve as a model for Russia's own social and economic modernisation, and Russia a country that commanded an immense wealth of natural resources. All of this suggested that Russia and Europe should combine their strengths in a 'big deal' – 'energy in exchange for fully fledged common institutions combined with a common view of the problems of international security' – that in the long run might lead to a greater degree of peace and stability throughout Eurasia.[365]

What we have called 'Fundamentalist Nationalists' were at the opposite end of the foreign policy spectrum, and closer to the Slavophiles in their inspiration.[366] For Fundamentalist Nationalists, Russia was at least as much an Asian as a European power, and it had a distinctive civilisation that was not simply different from but arguably superior to that of other European and Western countries. Fundamentalist Nationalists, accordingly, attached a great deal of importance to the re-establishment of Russian hegemony within the territory that had formerly constituted the Soviet Union, and they favoured the greatest possible strengthening of the Commonwealth of Independent States and of the other structures that brought together the former Soviet republics. They also leaned towards Asia in terms of their foreign policy priorities, not simply as a counterbalance to the 'West' but also because of their belief in strong or even authoritarian government and in a pattern of state-led development that was more often to be found in the other countries of the continent. They were correspondingly hostile towards the EU as well as NATO, and indeed Western Christianity; straightforward nationalists thought they were aiming at the break-up of the Russian state, Communists saw them as instruments by which the United States was attempting to turn their country into a 'raw materials appendage', and Orthodox believers regarded them as a threat to their historic religion and way of life. Fundamentalists liked to think of issues of this kind in geopolitical terms and were much attracted to the idea of a 'global chessboard' on which all such rivalries were apparently being played out.[367]

The Fundamentalist Nationalist view was set out most comprehensively in the voluminous writings of the Eurasianist leader Alexander Dugin, which became still more significant because of the prominence they were given – clearly not by accident – in the pro-government press.[368] For Dugin, Russia was not a European but a Eurasian country, 'a synthesis of Eastern, Asian and West European characteristics' that 'should be compared with Europe itself or with India as a civilisation'.[369] Its direct opponent was the United States, whose aim was to see Russia 'weak, obedient, dependent and subordinate', perhaps even divided up and placed under 'external management'.[370] The United States, in Dugin's view, had ended its unspoken agreement not to intervene on the territory of the former Soviet Union at the end of the Cold War and had declared a 'geopolitical jihad': it was currently moving into the Northern Caucasus and the Volga basin, using the same 'orange' methods it had perfected elsewhere in the region.[371] As a result, Russian influence in post-Soviet space had become 'even more tightly constricted' and the prospect of Eurasian integration had become 'even more problematic'. Now 'orange revolutions' in Belarus and Kazakhstan were the immediate objective, with the same intention: 'to prevent the reintegration of post-Soviet space'.[372] The obvious response, for Fundamentalist Nationalists, was to emphasise multipolarity and to seek the support of all who rejected American domination: in Dugin's words, of 'all the countries of East and West that . . . reject[ed] the the hegemony of the USA, unipolarity and the so-called "benign empire"'.[373]

Writing in early 2008, Dugin still conceived of the United States as Russia's 'No. 1 threat', with a 'global domination model' that was based on the 'desovereignisation of the world's countries'. Russia, in his view, should contain this threat by meeting it symmetrically. For the moment, there was no prospect in Russia itself of an 'orange revolution' with a 'new pro-US liberal-democratic successor coming to power'. But the United States would 'do everything it [could] to set Medvedev against Prime Minister Putin – that is to say, to divide the elites and arouse separatist sentiments among ethnic minorities'.[374] The high price of oil and gas on world markets, in Dugin's view, gave Russia an opportunity to redress the international balance by developing an advanced modern economy, based on leading-edge technologies and the defence industry.[375] Similar views were advanced by Mikhail Margelov, chair of the foreign affairs committee of the Federation Council and a sometime member of the council of Dugin's International Eurasian Movement, who saw the 'balance between its Western and Eastern vectors' as the 'main sign of an independent Russian foreign policy'. This meant better relations with India and China as well as the strengthening of the Shanghai Cooperation Organisation and the Single Economic Space, and the return of Russia to Central Asia, but without withdrawing from Europe, where both sides had an interest in cooperation.[376] There was a similar emphasis on the need to restore a 'Eurasian balance' in the writings of Natal'ya Narochnitskaya, for some time deputy chair of the Duma's foreign affairs committee,[377] and of others who shared her belief in Russia's distinctive historical mission.

Fundamentalist Nationalist assumptions were widely shared by communist as well as nationalist members of the political class, for instance in the statements of Yuli Kvitsinsky, a senior diplomat in the Soviet period and later a Communist deputy in the Duma. The United States, for Kvitsinsky and many of his colleagues, was advancing a 'claim to world leadership, attempting to export democracy by force, imposing an economic and political diktat with the aim of realising its national interests, and showing an unwillingness to observe the norms and principles of international law and to respect the UN Charter'.[378] Fundamentalist Nationalists, such as Kvitsinsky, were particularly concerned by NATO's open declaration that it was willing to act outside the territory of its member nations: 'however you interpret it, that's a claim to the right of aggression'. Any realistic Russian foreign policy had to make provision for cooperation with NATO. But Washington and its NATO allies were trying to oblige Russia to act in accordance with their far-reaching global and regional ambitions. 'That's a dead end', commented Kvitsinsky, 'as it does not secure the position of Russia as a great power.'[379] Party leader Zyuganov claimed that the United States and its allies were attempting to construct nothing less than a 'super-empire' in which they would take possession of the 'most important natural resources and bridgeheads in Europe, in the Arab East, in the Caucasus and in Central Asia'. Now that they had achieved the break-up of the USSR, their next move would be to divide up and subordinate Russia itself, condemning the Eastern Slavs to a 'humiliating, semi-colonial existence' and eventually 'extinction'.[380]

Opinion of this kind was also well represented in academic circles. The eminent and otherwise broadly 'liberal' economist Nikolai Petrakov, for instance, claimed that American foreign policy was a new form of colonialism, a 'democratic colonialism' that sought to impose democratic institutions by undemocratic and sometimes military means. It deliberately encouraged small parties, which undermined the stability of governments in the post-Soviet region and made them easier to overthrow (as in Serbia, Georgia and Ukraine). It openly funded NGOs with an 'exclusively Western orientation'. And in economic matters, it promoted policies that were intended to turn countries such as Russia into a 'primitive, as far as possible raw materials and mono-cultural economy'. The effect was to enrich a 'tiny elite' and place power in the hands of a 'state-wide corrupt oligarchy'. Why indeed should the West want a free and democratic Russia that would immediately become a serious competitor on world markets? Instead of this, the West had established a 'destructive system of pseudocapitalism with all its characteristic flaws: corruption, crime, theft, the mass homelessness of children and adults, fantastic sickness and mortality levels'.[381] Two other economists who had been associated respectively with the Communist Party and the left-nationalist party Rodina, Sergei Glaz'ev and Mikhail Delyagin, took a similar view, arguing that a strategy that depended on the high price of oil would turn Russia into a 'raw materials appendage'.[382] Delyagin drew the same lesson from the international financial crisis that began in late 2008; so did many others.[383]

A third position, 'Pragmatic Nationalism', developed initially as a response to the Western-oriented policies that were being followed by Yeltsin and Kozyrev and then became dominant under the Putin presidency. Pragmatic Nationalists supported the broad principles of democracy, although not necessarily the particular form in which they were expressed in Western countries. They also supported the principles of the market economy, although they were generally in favour of state ownership of strategic resources. At the same time, they shared some common ground with Fundamentalists in their belief in Russia's great-power status and the legitimacy of its presence in other former Soviet republics. For Pragmatic Nationalists, Russia's vital interests encompassed the geopolitical space of the former Soviet Union, and they believed the international community should recognise Russia's particular responsibility for guaranteeing its stability; they did not think it was realistic to attempt to reconstitute the USSR but supported the fullest possible reintegration of its former members. Pragmatic Nationalists believed above all that policy towards the West, including the EU and NATO, should be based on a realistic assessment of Russia's national interests. The United States was not a friend, but not an enemy either, just a partner with which there should be as much cooperation as possible while accepting that there would also be disagreements. Pragmatic Nationalists favoured a diversification of foreign policy more generally, giving more attention to former Soviet allies and the newly industrialised countries of Asia and the Middle East in order to give them more leverage in their dealings with the West.

Views of this kind were not limited to the Kremlin administration: they extended very widely across the political elite, including almost all of those who associated themselves with its ruling party. The then Moscow mayor, Yuri Luzhkov, for instance, in an extended statement on 'We and the West' in the government newspaper, argued that the new century would see a very different international order, one in which there would be major 'geopolitical mainlands' with new supranational politico-economic systems, global common markets and larger mega-regions of cultural and informational communication. The powers that would prevail in this kind of world would be those that had their 'own global integration project', one that allowed them to develop and strengthen their positions. At the same time, although it was certainly a part of European civilisation, it was simply 'impossible' for Russia to join the integration project of the European Union, and any attempt to do so would end badly for both sides. Russia, first of all, should seek to integrate post-Soviet space and the world of its compatriots. But Russia had a much more important and indeed unique position. It had enormous resources, including energy, of a kind that was typical for the countries of the global South. In addition, it had the industrial, military and above all cultural and historical experience that was characteristic of the developed West. All of this made Russia a 'bridge between different world civilisations' and a country whose contribution to world politics could provide the basis for a wider global stability.

Pragmatic Nationalists were sceptical of the West's good intentions and resentful of their judgements on Russian politics. Even though Russia was clearly a European nation and part of its history and culture, the other continental countries, Luzhkov went on, still regarded it with a 'mix of attraction and fear'. Nothing had changed, in this respect, since Nikolai Danilevsky had written his celebrated study of *Russia and Europe* in the late nineteenth century. Russia, insisted Luzhkov, was still democratising, but in its own way, taking account of its own culture and circumstances. The idea of the 'end of history', he suggested, had led the West to see its own society as the 'highest achievement of civilisation', with other countries seeking to 'catch up' and some of them unable to do so. The same 'geopolitical egoism' had led the West to ignore the legitimate interests of the rest of the world, intervening whenever it chose to do so on the basis of 'humanitarian' considerations and spreading democracy by force just as the Soviet Union had in earlier times sought to extend the influence of communism. The essence of the situation with which the United States and perhaps some other forces found it hard to reconcile themselves, suggested Luzhkov, was that Russia had 'returned to the political arena'. There was no 'empire of evil' and Russia itself was no 'authoritarian monster', just a country that was more conscious of its national interests than it had been in the recent past and just as ready to defend them as the United States or anywhere else. And in particular, unwilling to allow the West to continue to have virtually unrestricted access to its natural resources.[384]

Pragmatic Nationalists had little confidence in the good intentions of the West, and in some cases they could take an almost paranoiac view of an outside world in which an expansionist China and Islamic fundamentalism appeared to have joined hands with the United States in a conspiracy that aimed not just to diminish Russian influence but to break up the state itself.[385] These views evidently carried some weight in the Kremlin itself if the statements of Vladislav Surkov, first deputy head of the Presidential Administration, were representative. For Surkov, there were two groups of foreign countries: those that saw Russia as a valued member of the international community, an important market, a good neighbour and a reliable ally. The other group were 'still living out the phobias of the cold war'. They regarded Russia as a 'potential enemy', credited themselves with the 'nearly bloodless collapse of the Soviet Union' and were 'trying to build on that success'; their immediate objective was to 'destroy Russia and fill its enormous geographic space with numerous unviable quasi-state entities'. They had found allies in Russia itself – in the North Caucasus, for instance, where attempts had been made to break up southern Russia since the nineteenth century. And they had the support of a 'fifth column of left- and right-wing radicals' who had appeared in Russia itself, 'pseudoliberals and authentic Nazis' who had 'more and more in common', and who had the same foreign financial support and the same hatred of their own country.[386] It was Putin himself, in one of his presidential addresses, who noted that there were outside forces that wanted to 'deprive our country of its economic and political independence', and who were responsible for the 'increase in the flow of money from abroad for direct interference in our internal affairs'. In earlier times, he went on, colonial powers had spoken of their 'civilising role'; the same aims were still being pursued, but this time using 'democratising slogans'.[387]

The Kremlin's own 'Pragmatic Nationalist' position was set out in the programmatic statements that were issued at various times under different presidencies. The revised version of the Foreign Policy Concept that appeared in July 2008 reflected and consolidated the position that had been developed over the Putin years. As well as a 'positive trend' that had seen Russia establish a more influential position in world affairs, there had also been a series of more negative developments. Overall, the key foreign policy objectives were:

(i) to 'ensure national security, to preserve and strengthen its sovereignty and territorial integrity, to achieve strong positions of authority in the world community that best meet the interests of the Russian Federation';

(ii) to 'create favourable external conditions for the modernisation of Russia', including 'transformation of its economy along innovative lines, enhancement of living standards, consolidation of society [and] strengthening of the foundations of the constitutional system';

(iii) to 'influence global processes to ensure the formation of a just and democratic world order, based on collectivism in finding solutions to international problems and the supremacy of international law, first of all the provisions of the UN Charter';

(iv) to 'promote good-neighbourly relations with bordering states';

(v) to 'search for agreement and coinciding interest with other states and international associations';

(vi) to 'provide comprehensive protection of the rights and legitimate interests of Russian citizens and compatriots abroad';

(vii) to 'promote an objective image of the Russian Federation globally as a democratic state committed to a socially oriented market economy and an independent foreign policy'; and

(viii) to 'promote and propagate the Russian language and the culture of the Russian peoples in foreign states, representing a unique contribution to the cultural and civilisational diversity of the contemporary world and to the development of an intercivilisational partnership'.[388]

All of these were political positions, rather than fixed groups of individuals. As we have seen, they often had their origin in much older views about the kind of relationship that Russia should sustain with the outside world, particularly the other countries of the European continent. But individuals could modify their position, as Kozyrev himself had done, and they could move between institutions that might have rather different interests to defend. So these positions were not necessarily absolute, or monolithic. Equally, the entire spectrum could shift, as it did in the immediate aftermath of the NATO bombing campaign in Yugoslavia in 1999, when there were demonstrations outside Western embassies in Moscow; or in a rather different direction, following the 11 September 2001 attacks on New York and Washington DC.[389] No less important, the increasing authority of the Kremlin itself made a difference: the influence it commanded at any time in relation to the foreign ministry and other institutions, or the extent to which it could dominate the legislature through its sponsored party, United Russia. The net effect, in the early years of the new century, was to weaken Liberal Westernisers and strengthen the Pragmatic Nationalists, who themselves had moved rather closer towards the Fundamentalist Nationalists. The international crisis that began in late 2008 seemed if anything to have added to these tendencies, as once again a malevolent West could be seen as the source of the problem and the entire crisis could be represented as a cunning device whose real objective was to undermine a stubbornly independent but resource-rich competitor.[390]

The 2008 Concept took as its point of departure a 'new Russia', one that exerted a 'substantial influence on the development of a new architecture of international relations' and which had helped to ensure that the 'threat of full-scale war, including a nuclear one, [had] been diminished'. At the same time it faced new challenges and threats, including terrorism, organised crime, global poverty, illegal migration and climate change. The West was losing its ability to dominate these processes and was doing its best to 'contain' its Russian competitor by political and psychological means. But there could be no way forward that involved 'coercive measures with the use of military force in circumvention of the UN Charter and Security Council', whose effect was to undermine the principles of international law and extend conflict even more widely, not least in Russia's 'immediate geopolitical environment'. The Concept was very firmly opposed to any attempt that might be made to diminish the sovereignty of individual states, or any 'arbitrary interference in the internal affairs of sovereign states'. Russia's foreign policy, in this connection, was 'balanced and multidirectional', reflecting the 'geopolitical position of Russia as the largest Eurasian power [and] its status as one of the leading states of the world and a permanent member of the UN Security Council'. Its priorities in addressing global problems would include an increase in the effectiveness of the United Nations, the strengthening of international law and international security, greater cooperation in economic, environmental and humanitarian matters, and better projection in the wider world of its own foreign policy positions.[391]

So far as individual regions were concerned, the development of bilateral and multilateral cooperation with the CIS member states was still a 'priority area of Russia's foreign policy'. This meant, first of all, that every effort would be made to establish a more effective 'union state' with Belarus. It also meant the promotion of a customs union and common economic space with Belarus and Kazakhstan within the Eurasian Economic Community, and transforming the Collective Security Treaty Organisation into a 'key instrument for supporting stability and ensuring security on the territory of the CIS'. A particular priority was the support of compatriots in the other former Soviet republics, especially in the Baltic republics, where Russia attached 'fundamental importance' to the rights of their Russian-speaking minorities. Within the wider European context, Russia's main objective was to create a 'truly open, democratic system of regional collective security and cooperation' that would ensure the 'unity of the Euro-Atlantic region, from Vancouver to Vladivostok' and bring to an end the 'bloc approaches' of earlier years. A new European security treaty remained a key objective; beyond that, a 'genuinely unified Europe without dividing lines through equal interaction between Russia, the European Union and the United States'. Russia itself was the 'biggest European state, with a multinational and multiconfessional society and a centuries-old history'. The Council of Europe should meanwhile be strengthened and better relations established with the European Union, moving on from the 'common spaces' that had been agreed in 2003 to a partnership treaty and eventually a visa-free regime.[392]

The Concept looked forward to the 'progressive development' of relations with NATO within the framework of the Russia–NATO Council, not just to enhance stability within their respective territories but also to strengthen their joint response to 'common threats' such as terrorism, the spread of weapons of mass destruction and narcotics. Russia, however, was still opposed to any further expansion of the alliance, particularly to Ukraine and Georgia, and to any plans that might be made to bring NATO's infrastructure closer to Russia's own borders. Every effort would be made to establish a 'strategic partnership' with the United States and to eliminate the differences that still existed; in the long run the relationship should ideally be underpinned by a 'solid economic foundation', and by the development of a 'culture of the management of differences on the basis of pragmatism and a balance of interests'. The Concept also referred to the 'ever-increasing significance' of the Asia-Pacific Region and its relevance for the development of Siberia and the Russian Far East. The Russian–Chinese strategic partnership should be strengthened further, and the economic relationship expanded so that it matched the high level of political understanding that had been achieved. There was another 'strategic partnership' with India, and there should be 'good-neighbourly' relations with Japan in spite of the still-unresolved disputes that had been inherited from the past. Extended reference was made to the regional conflicts in Afghanistan and the Middle East; there was finally a rather cursory discussion of relations with Africa and Latin America, including a 'strategic partnership' with Brazil (an inventory of the key statements of this kind since Putin's accession is shown in Table 7.6).[393]

President Medvedev offered his own interpretation of the general principles of Russian foreign policy in a statement that appeared shortly after the conclusion of the five-day war with Georgia in August 2008. There were 'five principles', he explained, on which the country's foreign policy would be based.

- The first was the supremacy of international law, which 'defines relations between civilised peoples'.
- The second was the principle of a multipolar world; Russia could 'not recognise a world order in which all decisions are taken by one country, even such a major country as the USA'; such a world would be 'unstable and prone to conflicts'.

Table 7.6 The key Russian foreign policy documents (since 2000)

National security

The *2000 National Security Concept* ('Kontseptsiya natsional'noi bezopasnosti Rossiiskoi
  Federatsii')

Text in *Sobranie zakonodatel'stva Rossiiskoi Federatsii* (*SZ*), no. 2, item 170, 10 January 2000.

English translation in Andrei Melville and Tatiana Shakleina, eds., *Russian Foreign Policy in
  Transition: Concepts and Realities* (Budapest and New York: CEU Press, 2005), pp. 129–46.

Superseded by the *2009 National Security Strategy* for the period to 2020 ('Strategiya natsional'noi
  bezopasnosti Rossiiskoi Federatsii do 2020 goda').

Text in *SZ*, no. 20, item 2444, 12 May 2009, and online at www.mid.ru.

Defence

The *2000 Military Doctrine* ('Voennaya doktrina Rossiiskoi Federatsii')

Text in *SZ*, no. 17, item 1852, 21 April 2000.

English translation in Melville and Shakleina, eds., *Russian Foreign Policy in Transition*,
  pp. 105–28.

Superseded by the *2010 Military Doctrine* ('Voennaya doktrina Rossiiskoi Federatsii', 5 February
  2010).

Text in *Rossiiskaya gazeta*, 10 February 2010, p. 17, and online at www.mid.ru.

Foreign policy

The *2000 Foreign Policy Concept* ('Kontseptsiya vneshnei politiki Rossiiskoi Federatsii')

Text in *Rossiiskaya gazeta*, 11 July 2000, p. 5.

English translation in Melville and Shakleina, eds., *Russian Foreign Policy in Transition*, pp. 89–104,
  and in *International Affairs* (Moscow), vol. 46, no. 5 (2000), pp. 1–14.

The *2008 Foreign Policy Concept* ('Kontseptsiya vneshnei politiki Rossiiskoi Federatsii') was
  intended to 'supplement and develop' the Concept of 2000.

Text in *Mezhdunarodnaya zhizn'*, nos. 8–9, 2008, pp. 211–39, and online at www.mid.ru with
  English, French and German translations.

English translation in *International Affairs* (Moscow), vol. 54, no. 8 (2008), pp. 25–31.

- Russia, thirdly, would not seek confrontation with anyone and did 'not intend to isolate itself'; on the contrary, Russia would 'develop as much as possible [its] friendly relations with Europe and the USA and other countries of the world'.
- A fourth principle had 'unconditional priority', which was the 'defence of the lives and dignity of Russian citizens, wherever they [were] located', and of Russian entrepreneurs abroad.
- And there was a fifth principle, which related to the interest that Russia would continue to take in the affairs of countries that lay beyond its own borders. Like other states, Russia had 'regions of our privileged interests', within which there were countries with which they had traditionally maintained friendly relations and in which they intended to remain active; nor were these simply the countries with which Russia had a common border.[394]

Whatever the regime and whatever its leadership, there were certain 'constants' in Russian foreign policy that were imposed by geography if nothing else.[395] But constants of this kind were consistent with a range of policy prescriptions: indeed over the course of the twentieth century, Russia had been an ally of the Western powers in both global conflicts, but their principal adversary duing the years of Cold War; during the post-communist years there had been 'naïve Westernism' under Kozyrev and Yeltsin, and then a more confrontational position under Putin and Medvedev. Broadly speaking, those who favoured a closer relationship with the West shared many of its liberal-democratic values and wished to promote them in their own society. Those who preferred a more distanced view of the West placed more emphasis on Russia's relations with its eastern neighbours and at the same time were more sceptical about 'democracy', at least as it was understood elsewhere; they were also more committed to a traditional interpretation of international law, in which the sovereignty of an individual state could not legitimately be violated. Understood in this way, foreign policy was a projection of domestic politics; but at the same time, domestic politics reflected the international environment – whether the price of oil was rising or falling, and whether the Western powers were pressing the advantage they appeared to have secured at the end of the Cold War or constructing a larger and more balanced system of international security that would take the place of earlier divisions. It was not only Russians that had to make choices about the kind of international order they wished to see in these circumstances, and it was not only Russians that would be affected by their decisions.

Further reading

There are several well-documented and up-to-date accounts of Russian foreign policy. Malcolm, Pravda, Allison and Light (1996) is still valuable, especially for its classification of foreign policy thinking. Mankoff (2009) is more recent; so is the new edition of Donaldson and Nogee (2009). I particularly like Tsygankov (2010), which is more 'constructivist' in approach. De Haas (2010) considers the whole range of security policy. Allison, Light and White (2006) includes a chapter on foreign policy decision-making and deals with public opinion, as do the studies listed in note 322. Pursiainen (2000) and Thorun (2009) place Russian foreign policy behaviour within the wider context of international relations theory, and Rieber (1993, extended in 2007) offers a provocative analysis of long-term 'persistent factors in Russian foreign policy'. There is a comprehensive range of documentation, much of it available in English, on the website of the Ministry of Foreign Affairs (www.mid.ru).

Allison, Roy, Margot Light and Stephen White, *Putin's Russia and the Enlarged Europe* (Oxford: Blackwell and Chatham House, 2006).

De Haas, Marcel, *Russia's Foreign Security Policy in the 21st Century: Putin, Medvedev and After* (Abingdon and New York: Routledge, 2010).

Donaldson, Robert H., and Joseph L. Nogee, *The Foreign Policy of Russia: Changing Systems, Enduring Interests*, 4th edn (Armonk, NY, and London: M. E. Sharpe, 2009).

Malcolm, Neil, Alex Pravda, Roy Allison and Margot Light, *Internal Factors in Russian Foreign Policy* (Oxford and New York: Oxford University Press for the RIIA, 1996).

Mankoff, Jeffrey, *Russian Foreign Policy: The Return of Great Power Politics* (Lanham, MD: Rowman & Littlefield, 2009).

Pursiainen, Christer, *Russian Foreign Policy and International Relations Theory* (Aldershot and Burlington, VT: Ashgate, 2000).

Rieber, Alfred J., 'Persistent factors in Russian foreign policy: an interpretive essay', in Hugh Ragsdale, ed., *Imperial Russian Foreign Policy* (Washington, DC: Woodrow Wilson Center Press and Cambridge and New York: Cambridge University Press, 1993), pp. 315–59.

'How persistent are persistent factors?', in Robert Legvold, ed., *Russian Foreign Policy in the Twenty-First Century and the Shadow of the Past* (New York and Chichester: Columbia University Press, 2007), pp. 205–78.

Thorun, Christian, *Explaining Change in Russian Foreign Policy* (Basingstoke and New York: Palgrave Macmillan, 2009).

Tsygankov, Andrei P., *Russia's Foreign Policy: Change and Continuity in National Identity*, 2nd edn (Lanham, MD: Rowman & Littlefield, 2010).

8 What kind of system?

St Basil's Cathedral and Red Square (Stephen White)

If it was no longer 'communist', did that mean that a newly independent Russia had become a 'democracy'? Or at least, that it was 'in transition'? Competitive elections, freedom of speech and a commitment to the rule of law appeared to suggest a positive answer. But elections came increasingly to be regulated by the authorities themselves, freedom of speech (at least on television) became increasingly restricted, and there was little reality to a rule of law if judges were corrupt and high-ranking officials and rich businessmen were effectively outside its scope. Another view was that postcommunist Russia was an 'authoritarian' system; but so were many other countries that lay in a large and heterogeneous 'grey zone' between Western-style democracy and naked dictatorship. There appeared to be strong arguments in these circumstances for avoiding the term 'democracy' altogether and focusing instead on mechanisms of accountability and their effectiveness in Russia as compared with other countries.

Just as the October revolution in 1917 was a landmark in world history, so too the end of communist rule in its country of origin appeared to be a turning-point, and not just in Russia. For Boris Yeltsin, speaking just after the attempted coup had collapsed, the Soviet people had 'thrown off the chains of seventy years of slavery'.[1] The defeat of the coup, he wrote in his memoirs, was actually much more than this: it meant the end of the twentieth century itself, when in just three days, between 19 and 21 August 1991, 'one century finished and another began'.[2] For his finance minister, Yegor Gaidar, the most obvious comparison was with the classic revolutions of the past; the end of communist rule in Russia, he thought, had been a 'revolution comparable in its influence on the historical process to the Great French Revolution, the Russian revolution of 1917 and the Chinese revolution of 1949'.[3] *Izvestiya*, writing just after the collapse of the coup, thought democracy itself had 'taught the people not to be silent': a reference to Pushkin's *Boris Godunov*, in which local townspeople had been invited to hail the False Dmitri as their new ruler but had famously refused to respond, and which had served since that time as a metaphor for Russia's long-suffering but (it seemed) eternally passive citizenry.[4] Gorbachev's still larger view was that the society itself had changed: it was more educated, more diverse and more accustomed to the political freedoms it had acquired during the years of *perestroika*, and for these reasons it would never accept the reimposition of authoritarian structures.[5] For some, indeed, it was the 'end of history' itself, after seventy years in which liberal democracy had faced a real alternative.[6]

The experience of the early postcommunist years suggested a less extravagant verdict. For a start, many of the same people were still in power, even if they no longer called themselves communists. They had very similar privileges, and often the same buildings and facilities. There was little popular control over the actions of government, in spite of elections that were nominally competitive. Political parties and associations of all kinds were weak and poorly supported, if they were not directly sponsored by the regime itself. The rule of law was routinely flouted. And the Russian state, apparently on the verge of disintegration under Boris Yeltsin, had become a centralised 'power vertical' that was strongly reminiscent of its Soviet predecessor. This was no longer communism, which had come to an end in a meaningful sense in the late 1980s; but neither was it democracy, at least in its classic Western form. It was, for some of its own citizens, a new system entirely: a '*nomenklatura* democracy' that left ordinary people with as little influence as before over those who ruled them;[7] or in Grigorii Yavlinsky's phrase, a 'criminal oligarchy with a monopolistic state'.[8] Or in the words of a Russian constitutionalist, writing in the Putin years, an 'unstable balance between democracy and authoritarianism' that could be seen as a 'contemporary variant of the "enlightened absolutism"' of the late eighteenth century.[9]

For Western scholars there were no less serious challenges. There was widespread agreement, by the early years of the new century, that it was time to 'abandon the transition paradigm'[10] and its underlying assumption that countries that were no longer communist-ruled would necessarily assume the political forms of their Cold War adversaries. But if this was no longer a 'transition to democracy', how else was it to be characterised? What kind of system was it that had taken the place of communist rule in the large and heterogeneous 'grey zone' that had developed between straightforward dictatorship and liberal democracy as it had conventionally been understood? There was certainly no shortage of suggestions. To begin with, it seemed to be no more than a matter of the rate of change (after all, it had taken a long time for democratic institutions to become established in the Western countries themselves). But increasingly it became clear that it was a matter of the direction as well as the rapidity of change, and that postcommunist Russia and other countries in the 'grey zone' might be more satisfactorily understood in terms that did not necessarily assume a 'democratic' destination. For some, a better label was 'competitive authoritarianism';[11] for others, it was 'semi-authoritarianism',[12] or simply 'authoritarianism'.[13] Or, as the Putinist system passed from one presidency to another, 'consolidated authoritarianism'.[14] And there were even more imaginative proposals: such as a 'form of third world patrimonialism with Bonapartist tendencies',[15] or 'West European feudalism as it existed between the ninth and twelfth centuries' – how else could one make sense of a system in which power and property were 'closely intertwined', officials constructed 'fiefdoms' and the most powerful people were 'not elected officials but the friends of the President (or the king, if we examine the past)'?[16]

The Russian authorities, for their part, insisted on their commitment to 'democracy' but made clear it would be a particular kind of democracy, one that took account of Russia's distinctive geography and culture. It would not, Putin explained in his address at the turn of the millennium, be a 'second edition of, say, the US or Britain, where liberal values [had] deep historic traditions', but one that was better suited to a country in which 'the state and its institutions and structures [had] always played an exceptionally important role'.[17] In the first instance, this appeared to mean that Russia would be a 'managed democracy', a form of government that was more appropriate, in the view of Kremlin advisers, to a country that was undergoing far-reaching social and economic change and in which Western-style institutions – such as political parties – had not yet established themselves.[18] During Putin's second presidential term, a more considered response began to emerge: the notion of a 'sovereign democracy', one that took account of universal values but at the same time (in Putin's words) allowed Russians to find their 'own path to the construction of a democratic, free and fair society and state'. He was 'convinced', Putin told the Russian parliament, 'that in contemporary Russia the values of democracy [were] no less important than the aspiration to achieve economic success or social wellbeing'.[19] But he rejected the attempt that was being made, for transparently political purposes, to represent the strengthening of Russian statehood as some kind of 'authoritarianism'; on the contrary, a commitment to democratic values was 'dictated by the will of our people and by the strategic interests of the Russian Federation itself'.[20] The essence of 'sovereign democracy', in this interpretation, was that states should be able to make their own decisions in any matters of this kind, and not have them imposed from outside.

In the end, it was hardly definitions that would resolve the matter, but substantive issues that were related to the distribution of political power. If politics was the organised choice of alternatives, a choice that was made in Russia (as in other developed societies) by a mass electorate, what mattered was less the words that were used – 'authoritarian', 'democratic' or whatever else – than the relationship between those who made such choices and those who had responsibility for carrying them out. There had, in turn, to be mechanisms through which relationships of this kind could be articulated: such as the opportunity to replace the political leadership at regular and competitive elections, and to seek to influence it in other ways at other times. The question then became: what were the *mechanisms of government* that were available in early postcommunist Russia, how effective were they and how did their effectiveness compare with the operation of similar mechanisms in other countries? Whatever the system was called, how did it provide for a mass electorate to express their views, influence the governing authorities and hold them periodically to account? The more effective those mechanisms, the more widely political power would be distributed and the more likely the actions of government would advance a shared national agenda; the less effective, the more political power would be centralised and the greater the danger (not least under Russian conditions) that it would be used to benefit those who were themselves in government and to repress any who sought to challenge the wisdom of their decisions.

The Russian 'transition'

At the outset, it hardly seemed that the kind of process that was taking place in what had been the communist world would present any kind of analytical difficulty. East Europeans had overthrown their communist leaderships in the *annus mirabilis* of 1989, the Soviet republics had followed suit two years later. Some, including the three Baltic republics, had gone on to join the EU, and even NATO. There were new constitutions and competitive elections with a multiplicity of parties. And there were new leaderships that were overtly committed, like Boris Yeltsin's, to 'democracy' and the rule of law. The academic literature made sense of these developments initially as a 'transition to democracy',[21] part of a wider process that had originated in the Iberian peninsula and would eventually extend worldwide. In one influential formulation, what had been taking place in the communist world was part of a 'third wave' of democratisation that had started with the overthrow of the Portuguese dictatorship in 1974 and then swept on through Spain and Greece, reaching Eastern Europe at the end of the 1980s. Over the whole period, democratic had replaced authoritarian governments in about thirty countries in Europe, Asia and Latin America in what seemed to be an 'almost irresistible global tide moving on from one triumph to another'. By the end of the decade, similar changes were taking place in the Baltic republics, and there was some prospect that the process might extend to Russia itself in what would represent the 'single most dramatic gain for democracy since the immediate post-World War II years'.[22]

For others, it was not so much a third as a 'fourth wave' that was sweeping through Eastern Europe and the USSR at the end of the 1980s. The changes that had taken place in Southern Europe and Latin America, it was argued, had not directly influenced the communist world, and the proximity in time was simply a coincidence. Not only this, the process itself was different: in particular, in the USSR and the other communist-ruled countries there had been no balance of political forces of a kind that had led in other cases to a negotiated transition, and then a set of rules by which all could agree to abide in the future. In Eastern Europe, on the contrary, there had been an asymmetric distribution of power at the moment of transition that had allowed a dominant party to impose a set of rules that operated to its own advantage, a pattern that 'resulted in unconsolidated, unstable partial democracies and autocracies'.[23] There was a still more fundamental difference, which was that the 'democratisation' that had taken place in the other countries of the third wave had been limited to their political regimes. In Russia and the communist world, there had been a more far-reaching 'triple transition' that had affected forms of ownership and national boundaries as well as the institutions of government. This meant that the attempt to analyse them in terms of patterns that had been established elsewhere was bound to be 'unsuitable and misleading', as they had experienced a combination of changes that was 'unique and unprecedented'.[24]

However they were labelled, 'wave' interpretations rested on a determinism that was oddly reminiscent of the official Soviet doctrine that all countries would eventually become 'socialist'. Human values, it was assumed, were essentially the same, Western democracy was a universal means of realising them, and once recalcitrant governments had been removed – if necessary by force – there would be a natural community of purpose that would take the place not just of East–West but of Christian–Muslim and other long-standing divisions. It was not only scholars who shared many of these assumptions but also Western policy-makers, and particularly the neoconservatives who were dominant during the George W. Bush presidency. The 'Statement of Principles' of the Project for the New American Century, for instance, issued in 1997, called for a foreign policy that 'boldly and purposefully promote[d] American principles abroad', which among other things meant a readiness to 'challenge regimes hostile to our interests and values' and to 'promote the cause of political and economic freedom'. The signatories included several of the most influential members of the Bush administration, including Defense Secretary Donald Rumsfeld and his deputy Paul Wolfowitz as well as the President's own brother, Florida governor Jeb Bush, and 'end of history' theorist Francis Fukuyama.[25] The assumptions that underpinned such approaches had much in common with those of neoliberal economics: there were no 'special countries', the laws involved were as universal as the laws of physics, and references to 'history' and 'culture' were a form of special pleading that often concealed a vested interest.

As the new century advanced, these assumptions came under increasingly close scrutiny. There was certainly little evidence that the removal of dictatorial governments in countries like Iraq or Afghanistan had allowed 'democracy' to take its place (or indeed advanced US interests); all that had happened was that pre-existing divisions had acquired a capacity to express themselves through competitive elections as well as other ways, and that public order of any kind had become even more difficult to sustain.[26] Nor was it clear that in countries like Russia it had been enough for a communist party to leave power if all that happened was that it was replaced by an 'inverted bolshevism' that once again imposed its priorities from the top and repressed any who sought to oppose them. As well as 'waves of democracy', Huntington had pointed out, there were 'reverse waves' that 'eliminated some but not all of the transitions to democracy of the previous democratization wave'.[27] Indeed, in another influential interpretation, there had been nothing less than a 'democratic roll-back' in the early years of the new century, with military coups in Pakistan and Thailand and clear evidence of regression under nominally elected leaderships in Nigeria and Venezuela as well as Russia. Many other states, apart from this, had 'remained firmly authoritarian', including China, Vietnam, Saudi Arabia and Egypt, and some nominal democracies elsewhere were 'at risk of collapsing' (Bangladesh) or 'seriously deteriorating' (the Philippines).[28] The 'third wave', it had become clear, was 'only part of the story. The remainder [was] a tale of authoritarianism in the age of democratization.'[29]

In Russia itself, it appeared at first that the forward march of history had simply been 'delayed'[30] and that the transition might be more 'protracted' than had originally been expected;[31] democracy itself might have been 'derailed'[32] or somehow failed to 'strike roots'.[33] What had 'gone wrong', asked the *Journal of Democracy*, as the Yeltsin presidency drew to a disappointing conclusion.[34] But interpretations of this kind rested on a reading of the early postcommunist years that had itself become increasingly difficult to justify. It had, after all, been during the Yeltsin era that a super-presidency had been established, replacing the approximate balance of power between executive and legislature that had prevailed up to this point. And it was during these years that the tools of media management and 'administrative resource' had been developed, first of all in an attempt to prevent Yeltsin being defeated in 1996 (it was the only presidential election in which the decision went to a second round), and then to ensure there would be no possibility of a serious challenge at any time in the future.[35] Even before this, it was clear that Russians themselves had been misusing their new liberties. The most successful party in the 1993 party-list election was the Liberal Democrats, led by the right-wing populist Vladimir Zhirinovsky – a party that had openly supported the attempted coup in August 1991 and opposed the dissolution of the USSR at the end of that year; the most successful in the two following elections was the Communist Party of the Russian Federation, whose aim was the restoration of soviet rule and, on a voluntary basis, of the USSR itself.

Nor was it clear that the 'democrats' were really democrats. Yeltsin himself, in the view of those who knew him best, had no coherent philosophy other than the 'ideology of power itself'.[36] He had crushed the elected parliament by force of arms in 1993, in what was a clear breach of the Constitution that prevailed at the time and of the solemn vow he had made to uphold it; he then withdrew the promise he had made to stand for re-election the following year, before his first term had been completed. Nor did the 'democrats' appear to have an overriding commitment to the ballot box if it was likely to hand a victory to their political opponents, which was a real prospect in the 1996 presidential contest. As Yeltsin's bodyguard and confidant, Alexander Korzhakov, told journalists at the time, elections were 'a Western idea. Why risk everything just to have some people put pieces of paper into something called a ballot box?'[37] When Igor Malashenko, the head of independent television, joined the Yeltsin campaign team, he found it an 'incredible organisation, where half of the members wanted the poll to take place and the other half did not'.[38] Decrees had apparently been drafted dissolving the parliament, banning the Communist Party and cancelling the entire exercise; Yeltsin's own staff, in private briefings, meanwhile made clear that he would refuse to leave the presidency if he was defeated by a Communist, although he was prepared to give way to another candidate.[39] Russia, certainly, was still a long way short of satisfying the 'Huntington test', of a twofold change of regime through the ballot box.[40]

The self-declared democrats were also prepared to deal uncompromisingly with any who challenged their authority, whatever the rule of law might have provided. Yeltsin and his supporters, for a start, made every effort to suppress the Communist Party to which they themselves had recently belonged – banning it after the collapse of the attempted coup in a manner the Constitutional Court later found illegitimate, seizing its property and appropriating its bank accounts.[41] The bombing of the Russian parliament in October 1993 was another moment that showed how limited was the acceptance of a set of civilised 'rules of the game'. According to the former Prosecutor General, Aleksei Kazannik (who was himself a Yeltsin supporter), after the storming of the White House a scenario was outlined to him by which he would 'investigate the October events for three or four days, charge all those held under Articles 102 and 17, that is, with conspiracy to murder', and then turn them over to a military rather than a civilian court. The case, Kazannik told *Komsomol'skaya pravda*, 'was supposed to last for two or three days and everyone was supposed to be sentenced to death . . . The President's team put a lot of pressure on us.'[42] In the event he resisted, and there was nothing Yeltsin could do when the Duma voted to exercise its right to grant an amnesty in February 1994 to all who had been involved in the events of August 1991 and September–October 1993.[43]

Putin's election to the presidency in 2000 and the changes that followed made it even more difficult to argue that this was still an 'emerging democracy'. He rode to victory on the back of a war in Chechnya that was being prosecuted with little regard for individual liberties and might have been started deliberately.[44] He began to strengthen the 'power vertical', subordinating the regions to a set of overarching federal districts that coincided very closely with the country's military administration. The scope for electoral contestation was sharply reduced, particularly after the Beslan hostage-taking crisis in September 2004. A new ruling party was confected, headed by Putin himself, and it quickly established a dominant position in elected bodies at all levels, making it a simple matter to amend the Constitution whenever the Kremlin wished to extend its already overwhelming powers. The media were subordinated, governors became agents of the Presidential Administration rather than representatives of the regions that had formerly elected them, and the oligarchs were forced into exile or else obliged to continue their activities on the Kremlin's terms in a system that was increasingly reminiscent of its Soviet predecessor. Speaking to Western journalists in 2007, Putin presented himself as a 'pure and absolute democrat' – the first since Mahatma Gandhi; it was a 'real tragedy' he was 'alone'.[45] But taken as a whole, the system he had constructed looked more like a 'transition to autocracy'[46] than the move to Western-style democracy that had at one time been so confidently predicted.

Arguably, in fact, what had taken place was a transition to a new and distinctive 'Putinist system'[47] that had a number of defining characteristics:

- an electoral system that effectively placed the authorities beyond reach (unlike the classic Western arrangement, in which the 'rules were known and the outcome was uncertain', in Russia it was the outcome that was known in advance and the rules that were unpredictable[48]);
- a system of party politics that was increasingly dominated by a single organisation, sometimes called the 'party of power', that was the functional equivalent of the Communist Party of the Soviet years;
- a disproportionately powerful 'superpresidency' or at least 'superexecutive', whether or not authority was concentrated in the hands of a single person or shared between a duumvirate; and
- a political regime that dominated the entire society in a manner that again was often reminiscent of the way in which the Communist Party had played a 'leading role' in the Soviet period, and which extended to the mass media (especially television), the legal system and at least the key sectors of the economy (especially those that were concerned with natural resources).

It was a system, moreover, that appeared to be capable of reproducing itself (there was certainly no sign of difficulty when the presidency passed from Putin to Medvedev in 2008); and it was a system that was to be found in some of the other post-Soviet republics such as Azerbaijan and Kazakhstan, where the incumbent authorities made it equally clear that there could be a nominal choice at elections but that no serious challenge to their continuing dominance would be permitted.

The Putinist system had one further characteristic that made it more than a simple reproduction of the Soviet system it had succeeded: the presence at all levels of the system of senior officials with a military or security background, known collectively as the *siloviki*. According to the most authoritative estimates, no more than 8 per cent of those who held leadership positions in the Gorbachev years had a background of this kind, but 25 per cent in the early Yeltsin years and 42 per cent by the end of Putin's second presidential term, in 2008.[49] This was the proportion of 'declared' *siloviki*; there were many others who made no reference of this kind in their official biographies but had unexplained career gaps, and had served in security-related occupations. Former Prime Minister Mikhail Fradkov, for instance, had graduated from the Moscow Machine Construction Institute in 1972. A year later he was working at the Soviet embassy in India, having somehow acquired excellent English, in a position that led contemporaries to conclude he must have been monitoring technical developments for the KGB; his later career was associated with arms exports and the tax police before he 'returned' to foreign intelligence after standing down from the premiership. And there were many other examples.[50] This was hardly a complete explanation of the authoritarian direction that Russian politics had taken after Putin's accession to the presidency, nor did it imply that the *siloviki* themselves were a single group with a common agenda.[51] But it did reflect Putin's own career background, and it was certainly consistent with the kinds of terms in which leading officials discussed political opposition, the centralisation of state power, access to information, and relations with the outside world.

From this perspective there had been no fundamental break with communist rule, still less with much longer-standing patterns in which a strong state had dominated a weak society, with decisive change coming from above and little more than token resistance from ordinary citizens. Russia, it had to be remembered, had always been 'a society apart in the European community'.[52] In particular, it had established representative government much later than in other European countries. Its first parliament, the State Duma, had come into existence as late as 1905, with a limited range of powers and a franchise that had been extended to no more than 2 or 3 per cent of adults at a time when 20–30 per cent enjoyed the right to vote in France, Germany, the United Kingdom and the United States.[53] Political parties and trade unions of any kind were illegal until the same date and operated thereafter on a severely restricted basis (they could not exist at all if their aims and objectives were judged to represent a threat to public morals, and the police could close their meetings at any time if they appeared likely to 'incite hostility between one section of the population and another').[54] There was a detailed and intrusive censorship (although it allowed the publication of Marx's *Capital* on the grounds that 'few will read it and even fewer will understand it'),[55] and even after 1906 the press was treated in a manner that 'would have been considered intolerable in a Western country'.[56] From this point of view there had been no radical break, not just between Soviet and postcommunist Russia, but between either of them and centuries of authoritarian rule.

It had, in fact, been a very curious 'transition'. For a start, many of the decisive changes had taken place during the last years of Soviet rule, with a communist party still in power. Freedom of conscience had been formally secured through the law of October 1990 that gave parents the right to give their children a religious upbringing and allowed the churches to establish their own schools and publications (see p. 254). A media law of June 1990 abolished censorship and established the right of all citizens to 'express opinions and beliefs [and] to seek, select, receive and disseminate information and ideas in any form'; in particular, it confirmed that citizens had the 'right of access to information from foreign sources, including direct television and radio broadcasts, and the press'.[57] A start had been made on ownership through the legislation on property that had been approved in 1990, and a July 1991 law on privatisation that provided for the transfer of up to half the assets of state-owned industry into the hands of individuals or cooperatives by the end of the following year.[58] Above all, there had been competitive elections since the adoption of new legislation in December 1988, and in 1990 the existence of multiparty politics had been formally recognised with the reformulation of Article 6 of the Constitution and the adoption of a new law on political parties and mass organisations.[59] A more general declaration of the 'rights and freedoms of the individual', adopted by the Soviet parliament in September 1991 and then by the Russian parliament two months later, guaranteed the right to own property and engage in business as well as equality before the law, freedom of movement, and freedom of speech and assembly.[60]

When, in fact, had a communist system become a postcommunist one? There was no doubt about the moment of transition in the former East Germany: it was the night of 9 November 1989, when the Berlin Wall was breached in a dramatic development that had enormous symbolic importance for the whole of a divided continent. Nor was there much doubt about the moment of transition in Romania. As late as November 1989, there had been little obvious threat to party leader Nicolae Ceauşescu at the Communist Party's 14th Congress, and his six-hour speech was interrupted no fewer than 125 times by standing ovations (these owed something to a man in the control room who switched on pre-recorded applause at the appropriate moments). But on 21 December, as demonstrations spread across the country, a rally in the capital turned against him and he was obliged to flee party headquarters the following morning on a helicopter so overloaded that one of the crew had to sit on his lap. He was captured shortly afterwards, put on trial and executed in a grisly spectacle, broadcast later on television, that left no doubt the change of government had been irreversible.[61] Most other East European countries had a reasonably clear turning-point, such as the moment when a communist government resigned and a largely or entirely postcommunist administration took its place: in Poland in August 1989, following a general election at which Solidarity had been overwhelmingly successful, or in Czechoslovakia the following December, after widespread public demonstrations. But when was the moment at which Russians had rejected the Soviet system and chosen another?

Had it, for instance, been August 1991, when the hardline coup had been defeated by the Russian parliament and the newly elected Russian president? But the coup had not been led by the CPSU leadership: the conspirators were party members of senior standing, but they headed government agencies rather than the party itself and included no current members of the Politburo or Secretariat. Their first action, indeed, had been to detain the party leader in his Crimean retreat; the first demand of those who resisted the coup was for his release, and for the Soviet Constitution to be respected. Yeltsin, no longer a party member by this time, had been joined on a tank in front of the White House by his vice-president, Alexander Rutskoi, who was a Communist, and nearly 90 per cent of the parliament that supported the Russian President against the self-styled 'State Emergency Committee' had been Communists at the time of their election. Russians themselves, certainly, were not inclined to see the events around the White House as a decisive moment in the establishment of democratic rule. Just 8 per cent, looking back in 2010, saw the defeat of the coup as a 'victory of the democratic revolution' (the figures had changed very little over the intervening period); much larger numbers saw it as 'no more than an episode in the struggle for power within the top leadership' (43 per cent), or simply a 'tragedy' (36 per cent).[62] And when Russians were asked what they would do if there was another attempt to seize power in the same way, 16 per cent said they would side with Yeltsin and his supporters but 21 per cent said they would support the State Emergency Committee; still larger numbers identified with neither side (35 per cent), or had no opinion of any kind (28 per cent).[63]

Perhaps, then, the decisive moment was the end of the USSR in December 1991? But actually, as a concept, it remained extremely popular. A very large majority had approved the establishment of a 'renewed federation' in the March 1991 referendum, and it was to have been inaugurated on 20 August. The conspirators who prevented its conclusion had been attempting to defend a viable and more centralised union in what they conceived as their patriotic duty, not to dissolve it. Equally, the coup itself was followed by a series of agreements on various forms of cooperation among the republics that were still committed to a formal association. In October, most of them agreed to form an economic union; and in November they established a Union of Sovereign States with a single president, a single parliament and a single citizenship.[64] The decisive moment appears to have been the Ukrainian referendum of 1 December, at which there was an overwhelming vote in favour of the declaration of independence the republican parliament had adopted the previous August.[65] But the USSR remained immensely popular as a concept in Russia itself, where it had the support of up to 75 per cent of the adult population,[66] and there was strong support for the moves that were made over the years that followed to develop a framework of association between Russia and the other republics that might eventually lead to the formation of another unitary state (the parliamentary vote that approved the dissolution of the USSR had meanwhile been rescinded).[67]

Was the banning of the Communist Party, then, the decisive moment? But this was an illegal act, as the Constitutional Court ruled the following year. The Communists, meanwhile, were able to reconstitute their national organisation and went on to win third place in the party-list election that took place at the end of 1993, moving up to first place in 1995 and 1999 and second place in the two following elections. And it was striking, compared with East-Central Europe, how many members of the communist leadership of the past had managed to retain a presence in the new regime. The first postcommunist prime minister in Eastern Europe, Tadeusz Mazowiecki, had been a Solidarity activist and political prisoner; so had the new Polish president, Lech Wałęsa. The new Hungarian prime minister, József Antall, and the new Czechoslovak president, Václav Havel, had also been political prisoners in the communist period. The Czechoslovak parliamentary speaker was Alexander Dubček, who had been party leader in 1968 but was then forced to resign and earn his living as a forestry worker. Russia's first postcommunist president, by contrast, had been a Communist for thirty years and a member of the ruling Politburo. His prime minister, Viktor Chernomyrdin, had been a member of the Soviet government as well as the Central Committee; Yevgenii Primakov, who headed the government from 1998 until the following year, was another former member of the Politburo. Vladimir Putin himself had been a party member up to the moment of the August coup, and never formally resigned (he simply 'took his membership card and put it in a drawer').[68] Indeed virtually every senior official, in the early postcommunist years, had been a party member and in many cases an office-holder. How could it be otherwise when there had been no other form of legitimate political activity up to the end of the 1980s?

Elements of continuity were even stronger at the regional level, where the typical party first secretary had simply moved sideways to become head of the local executive and ran the same region from the same building in much the same way. Within Yeltsin's Presidential Administration, about three-quarters had their origins in the communist *nomenklatura*, which meant that their appointments were of a kind that had required the approval of the relevant level of the party apparatus; within the Russian government it was a similar proportion, at the regional level even larger.[69] Others moved into banking and private business, using their party connections and working initially within the 'Komsomol economy' that had developed around the party's youth organisation in the late Soviet years. Indeed, for some the nature of the Russian transition was precisely that it had allowed an elite whose position depended on their control of office, but who were now obliged to seek the support of an unpredictable electorate, to 'convert' their political influence into the more enduring forms of advantage that were made available by private property.[70] 'Privileges', as Trotsky had already pointed out in the late 1930s, 'have only half their value if they cannot be transmitted to one's children.' But the ability to do so was 'inseparable from the right of property'. This meant that it would not be enough for the ruling group (as he termed it, the bureaucracy) to bring back ranks and decorations; they would 'inevitably' have to bring back private property itself, as the only secure foundation for their position. The victory of the bureaucracy would accordingly mean their 'conversion into a new possessing class'.[71]

In all of these events, moreover, there was very limited popular involvement – compared, at least, with the 'people power' that had been on display in Eastern Europe and the Baltic republics. Journalists estimated that perhaps 50,000 had ignored the curfew in Moscow and rallied outside the White House in support of the parliamentary resistance on 20 August 1991 (rather larger numbers – 9 per cent of the city's entire population – 'remembered' having done so a year later).[72] But there was no indefinite strike, as Yeltsin had demanded. There was little action of any kind in the other republics, which took the view that a state of emergency in Russia had no legal force outside the republic's own boundaries. And the numbers involved, even in the Russian capital, were far smaller than the numbers that had taken part in the popular movements in Eastern Europe and in some of the other Soviet republics. In Armenia, up to a million had demonstrated on the streets of Yerevan in early 1988 to demand the return of Nagorno-Karabakh.[73] In the Baltic republics, as many as 2 million had joined hands in a gesture of defiance on the fiftieth anniversary of the Nazi–Soviet Pact in August 1989.[74] In Czechoslovakia, an estimated three-quarters of the entire population had taken part in the political strike that was called in November 1989;[75] and in what was still the German Democratic Republic, hundreds of thousands had taken to the streets in weekly demonstrations.[76] Russians, electing their republican parliament the following spring, returned more Communist Party members than ever before.[77]

Issues of institutional design

Formally, at least, the Constitution of December 1993 had marked a significant step forward. The new Russia was to be a 'democratic, federative, law-based state' (art. 1). People themselves, and their rights and freedoms, were the 'supreme value' (art. 2) and the only legitimate source of political authority (art. 3). The state itself was based on a separation of powers, with an executive, legislature and judiciary that were independent of each other (art. 10). It was a constitution that committed the new state to 'ideological pluralism', 'political diversity' and 'multiparty politics' and prohibited a 'compulsory ideology' of any kind (art. 13). The new Russia would be secular, with churches separate from the state, and no religion could be official or compulsory (art. 14). A whole chapter dealt with the rights and freedoms of the individual, including equality before the law and equal rights for men and women as well as 'equal opportunities to exercise them' (art. 19). There were guarantees of personal inviolability and privacy (art. 22). There was freedom of movement, within and across national boundaries (art. 27), and freedom of conscience, including the right to 'choose, hold and propagate religious and other views and act in accordance with them' (art. 28). Press freedom was guaranteed, censorship prohibited (art. 29). There was freedom of association (art. 30) and peaceful assembly (art. 31). In the courts, similarly, all had the right to a defence counsel (art. 48) and had to be presumed innocent until they were proven guilty (art. 49).

There were some provisions, indeed, that went further than established practices in many of the Western liberal democracies. One of them was a commitment to freedom of information that gave ordinary citizens the right to see 'documents and materials that directly [affected] their rights and freedoms' unless the law – in practice, security considerations – dictated otherwise (art. 24). There was a more general commitment to the 'universally acknowledged principles and norms of international law', and the international treaties into which Russia had entered were to be regarded as a part of its own legal system. In the event of any divergence, the provisions of the international treaty were to have precedence (art. 15), which was a remarkable qualification of national

sovereignty. And there were economic guarantees of a kind that had additional reso-
nance in a country that had experienced more than seventy years of communist rule. The
right of private property was protected by law, including the right to hold and dispose of
property and to pass it on by inheritance (art. 35); there were more specific provisions that
guaranteed the right to engage in 'entrepreneurial or any other economic activities not
prohibited by law' (art. 34), and to the private ownership of land on a basis that would be
established by subsequent legislation (art. 36). All these rights, moreover, were
entrenched: in other words, they could not be considered by the Federal Assembly and
could not be amended without a complicated procedure involving a constitutional
assembly and (normally) a referendum (art. 135).

At the same time, there were grave weaknesses in Russia's new institutional design. For
a start, it had been unilaterally imposed, which meant that it became 'Yeltsin's constitution' – at least initially – rather than a more broadly supported framework within which
all of Russia's political forces might be willing to compete for popular support. And it had
been adopted by a 'national vote' rather than a referendum conducted in accordance with
the relevant legislation, which made it clear that a majority of the entire electorate (not
just of voters) must be in favour if a proposition was to be accepted.[78] The chairman of the
Constitutional Court, Valerii Zor'kin, wrote at the time that the vote on the Constitution
could 'not in the least be regarded as a referendum' but as a 'national opinion poll, with
no direct legal consequences'; years later, lawyers were still debating if a 'constitution
could be legitimate that had been adopted illegitimately'.[79] Still more important, the new
constitution, in the form in which it was adopted in December 1993, was seriously
unbalanced, a 'triangle with a single corner'.[80] Formally, there was a separation of
powers. The president had powers in relation to the Duma and the Duma had powers in
relation to the president, both of which were protected from abuse by an independent
judiciary. But the president's powers were extraordinarily extensive, in theory and
practice: in particular, the power to dismiss the government, as Yeltsin did five times
between March 1998 and August 1999 and as Putin did twice (in February 2004 and
September 2007), without reference to public or parliamentary opinion. It was because of
these far-reaching powers that Russia was often held to have not just a presidential but a
'super-', even 'hyper-presidential' system.[81]

The Duma also enjoyed a direct mandate, but its influence over the executive was very
limited. Its 'consent' was needed for the appointment of a new prime minister, but if
consent was withheld three times in a row, it was automatically dissolved. And although
it could pass a vote of no confidence in the government as a whole, if it did so twice in
three months the president was not obliged to nominate a new administration; the Duma
could once again be dissolved and a new election be held. In addition, the president had
the authority to dismiss the entire government at any time, for any reason. And while the
possibility of impeachment existed, it could be pursued only with a great deal of
difficulty. Under the 1993 Constitution, any action of this kind could only take place in
the event of treason or a crime of similar gravity, after the Supreme Court and the

Constitutional Court had both confirmed there was a basis for proceeding, and after two-thirds of the entire membership of both houses of parliament had voted in favour on the initiative of a third of the State Duma (art. 93). Even when the president was unable to exercise power effectively because of bad health or other reason, as had occasionally been the case under Boris Yeltsin, the office remained a disproportionately powerful one. Presidential elections, in these circumstances, became a contest for the state itself, the Constitution became a set of rules of the game that those who held power found most congenial, and parliamentary elections had only marginal significance – certainly, they had nothing to do with 'winning power'. It was, in other words, a textbook example of the 'perils of presidentialism'.[82]

On the face of it, a more balanced set of constitutional arrangements had come into effect in the spring of 2008 with the formation of the Putin–Medvedev (or was it Medvedev–Putin?) 'tandem'. Putin himself, speaking to the foreign press later in the year, pointed out that the prime minister was now the leader of a party that had an overall majority in the Duma and claimed this was a sign of the 'increased influence of parliament'. But the 'final word remain[ed] with the President'.[83] Medvedev, for his part, insisted that a parliamentary republic was simply not appropriate for Russia, at this time or in the foreseeable future, although it could be considered again in 'two or three hundred years' time'.[84] Russia, he told interviewers, had 'always developed around a strong executive authority. These lands have been gathered over the centuries, and they can't be governed any other way.'[85] Russia, he remarked elsewhere, was a 'presidential republic with a "strong" executive, and it [had] to stay the same if it [was] to remain a Russian Federation'.[86] For some, the example of Ukraine was instructive: the changes that had taken place after the 'Orange revolution' at the end of 2004 had strengthened the prime minister as against the president, but left unclear who really determined (in particular) foreign and defence policy; the result was indecision and a continuous struggle for personal ascendancy. Any change of this kind would be 'fatal for Russia', insisted the speaker of the upper house, Sergei Mironov. Why should they create an unnecessary division of this kind when it would clearly lead to the same kind of 'uncompromising confrontation between President, Supreme Rada [parliament] and premier'?[87]

The 'tandem' was in any case some distance from a French semi-presidential system, with a prime minister who could (and sometimes did) represent an oppositional party, and who had to command a majority in the assembly as well as the confidence of the president in a system in which the parties themselves were autonomous and the elections genuinely competitive. So long as the entire process, in Russia, was controlled from above by the governing authorities, there was little prospect of a parliament that could hold them effectively to account. All that had taken place, from this perspective, was a redistribution of responsibilities within a small and self-recruiting group of leaders who were all the beneficiaries of a system in which state officials were increasingly engaged in the management of the largest companies as well as government itself – in effect, of 'Russia Incorporated'. It mattered little, from this perspective, if the Constitution was amended in December 2008 to require the government to present an annual report to parliament;[88] or if the election law was modified the following May so that one or two seats in the 450-seat parliament were allocated to parties that had reached more than 5 but less than 7 per cent of the popular vote;[89] or if an entirely new law sought to ensure that smaller parliamentary parties had some access to the state-owned media.[90] It was far more important that the parliament itself would in future be elected for a five-year and the president for a six-year term of office;[91] on top of the abolition of single-member constituencies and the direct election of governors, the effect was to open up an even wider gap between ordinary citizens and the government that claimed to represent them.

There was at least one other mechanism that was available to ordinary citizens who wished to contribute to the wider government of the society in which they lived: the 'Public Chamber' that was established in 2005 as part of the package of constitutional changes that followed the Beslan hostage-taking crisis of September 2004.[92] As Putin explained in his address to an enlarged meeting of the Russian government a few days later, the Public Chamber would be a 'platform for broad dialogue' in which civic initiatives of all kinds could be discussed, and 'no less important', a 'place for the conduct of a public evaluation of the key state decisions and draft laws that concern the development perspectives of the entire country and have broad national significance'. As well as this, it would provide a kind of 'civic supervision of the work of the state apparatus, including the law enforcement and specialised agencies'.[93] A bill was presented to the Duma in December 2004 to bring these proposals into effect; there was considerable opposition – a Communist deputy called it a 'figleaf covering the authoritarianism that [was] running rampant in the country and the State Duma'; another deputy claimed outlying areas were under-represented and that there should be 'one person from each region'[94] – but it was carried in the end by a very large majority with the support of United Russia and Liberal Democrat deputies and signed into law in April 2005.[95]

Formally speaking, the Public Chamber provided for 'interaction' between the wider society and government bodies at all levels so that they could take more adequate account of the 'needs and interests' of citizens, and of their rights and freedoms and those of public associations, and at the same time improve the public oversight of executive action (art. 1). In particular, it was intended to provide a means by which ordinary citizens could be engaged in the implementation of state policy, and by which civic initiatives of national significance could be assisted; it would offer an expert assessment of draft legislation and suggest priorities in relation to the state support of associations of whatever kind that were seeking to develop a Russian civil society (art. 2). Its decisions were in the form of recommendations, rather than legislation (art. 17), and it also issued an 'annual report about the state of civil society in the Russian Federation' (art. 22). The Public Chamber had 126 members, made up in three ways. A first 42 were nominated by the Russian President; these members chose another 42, representing national public organisations; and both of these together elected the remaining 42, chosen from among those who had been nominated to represent inter-regional and regional public organisations (arts 6 and 8). The first meeting of the Public Chamber took place in January 2006, at which the President expressed the hope that it would become a 'platform for reconciling positions on major aspects of government policy';[96] further work was entrusted to a series of seventeen commissions, all but two of them headed by presidential nominees.[97]

The Public Chamber's early actions, in the event, 'showed more boldness and independence than critics of the body [had] predicted'.[98] It was too late for the entire Chamber to consider the restrictions that had already been introduced on the activities of non-governmental organisations, but individual members had expressed their misgivings at the time and there were calls at the first meeting for the President to send draft legislation of this or any other kind to the Chamber for preliminary evaluation.[99] A delegation was sent to investigate the circumstances in which an army private, Andrei Sychev, had been brutally maltreated at the Chelyabinsk Tank Academy;[100] an appeal was issued in support of two physicists who appeared to have fallen victim to the 'spymania of the FSB';[101] and three commissions held a joint meeting to consider the ethnic disturbances that had taken place in the Karelian town of Kondopoga.[102] According to the Chamber itself, its members had taken an active part in all kinds of public issues in the first years of its existence: for instance, drawing the attention of the national government to the plan to drive an oil pipeline through protected nature reserves in the vicinity of Lake Baikal (the pipeline was relocated), and pushing for the gambling business to be restricted.[103] The Chamber held four or five plenary meetings a year, and there were occasional meetings with the President himself.[104] It was also represented throughout the federation: by 2010 there were Public Chambers in about two-thirds of the country's republics and regions, in six of the seven federal districts, and in many of its individual towns and cities.[105]

The Public Chamber, all the same, had been a Kremlin initiative, and its leading officials made clear from the outset that they would be 'oriented towards government and above all the President' in their activities. 'In the history of Russian civil society', the Chamber's Secretary, the eminent scientist Yevgenii Velikhov, told a press conference, 'there [had] been pages of confrontation with the authorities. We will work in harmony with the President, the Presidential Administration, the State Duma and the government.'[106] Political parties were not represented in the Chamber, and individual members were required to suspend their affiliation for as long as they took part in the work of the Chamber in order to preserve its disinterested character; nor could they form any kind of association on the basis of their national, religious or regional allegiances (art. 11). It had a small staff of its own, which was formally part of the Presidential Administration; indeed it was often unclear what contribution had been made by the Chamber itself, as distinct from the efforts of its individual members and of the organisations they represented.[107] On the face of it, the Russian public had secured another agency through which their various concerns could be expressed outside the constraining framework of party politics. In practice, it served as much to contain as to articulate the concerns of the wider society, and it was more likely to reinforce the cynicism that discouraged ordinary citizens from entering public life in the first place and 'reproduce the patterns of Russian officialdom that it was supposed to monitor and control'.[108]

The establishment of the Public Chamber had to be seen as part of a wider series of changes, following the Beslan crisis but not necessarily in response to it, that had the effect of strengthening the Kremlin's already dominant position in relation to the society over which it ruled. There were increasingly tight restrictions on the operation of non-governmental organisations of all kinds, especially in the legal changes that were approved in January 2006 before the Public Chamber had held its first meeting; these made it even more difficult to access foreign funds and imposed a burdensome new system of registration (the Kremlin was evidently concerned to prevent the use that had apparently been made of NGOs in the 'coloured revolutions' that had taken place elsewhere in Eurasia).[109] At the same time the law on the referendum was repeatedly modified, first of all in an entirely new statute, approved in June 2004, that prohibited any exercise of this kind within a year of a parliamentary or presidential election and made it more difficult to collect the signatures that would be necessary to initiate it.[110] An amendment in 2008 restricted the questions that could be posed in this way and excluded any that related to the 'exclusive competence of federal bodies of state power'.[111] New legislation on 'extremism', approved in 2002 and extended in 2007, meanwhile gave the authorities an additional set of powers by which they could marginalise their political opponents at the same time as they attempted to deal with the increasing numbers of individuals and organised groups that had been engaging in racist or xenophobic violence.[112]

Checking executive authority: parties, media and the courts

Not simply did the Russian authorities have far-reaching executive powers; it was also relevant that countervailing forces of all kinds were poorly developed. There was no shortage of political parties, but the authorities regulated them closely under an increasingly restrictive law and made sure their own 'party of power' – latterly, United Russia – was normally dominant. It took the largest share of the vote in the 2003 election and almost two-thirds in 2007, which gave it enough seats to push through constitutional as well as other forms of legislation whenever it chose to do so. It was just as dominant throughout the regions and republics, whose chief executives were nominated by the Russian President from the end of 2004 and could be removed at any time if he 'lost confidence' in them.[113] A registration exercise had meanwhile reduced the numbers of parties themselves by about half, ostensibly because they had failed to demonstrate a minimum level of membership but – at least in the view of those that were disappointed – for political reasons as well (see p. 54). And yet how else, other than by a functioning party system, were Russian voters to be given an organised choice of political alterna-tives? There were trade unions as well, and they repeatedly made clear they could bring millions onto the streets on 'days of action'. But levels of membership were a fraction of what they had been in the Soviet period, and in any case the trade union leadership had a substantial stake in the status quo through the range of properties they managed and the salaries their leading officials were able to command.[114]

The press might have represented another check on executive authority, but its circulation had fallen dramatically since the late Soviet years and its ownership was increasingly in the hands of Kremlin-friendly oligarchs. A very few titles – among them *Novaya gazeta*, a thrice-weekly paper supported by the *New York Times* and ex-President Gorbachev – offered an alternative view, and there were some national dailies that permitted a diversity of opinion, such as the mildly liberal *Nezavisimaya gazeta*, the business papers *Kommersant* and *Vedomosti* (which was foreign-owned), and the long-established and serious-minded *Izvestiya* (at least until state-controlled Gazprom acquired a controlling interest in 2005). But their circulations were hardly of a kind that could represent even a potential challenge to Kremlin authority (respectively 40,000, 113,000, 75,000 and 150,000 copies daily at the start of 2010 in a country of more than 140 million). *Komsomol'skaya pravda* had the largest circulation of all (660,000 copies daily), but it was strongly pro-government and in any case devoted much of its attention to celebrity news and scandal from home and abroad rather than serious reporting and analysis. All the printed media, apart from this, were heavily dependent on state subsidies as well as government printing, distribution and transmission facilities. The result was that whole areas of the political agenda remained in partial or total obscurity: such as human rights abuses in the North Caucasus, government corruption, organised crime, and non-accidental injury in police custody.

Television was a more potent influence, given the size of its audience (Table 8.1), but for this reason it was even more closely monitored. The state itself had a controlling interest in the flagship First Channel (as many as 78 per cent, in our 2010 survey, claimed to watch its news programmes regularly), and it owned the second channel (Rossiya) outright. State-owned Gazprom had a controlling interest in the third channel, NTV; the Bank of Russia had a controlling interest in two other channels, REN-TV and the Fifth Channel; and the Moscow city administration owned TV-Centre, which gave its primary attention to developments in the capital. The largest radio stations, Mayak and Rossiya, were also state-owned; a lively independent, Ekho Moskvy ('Echo of Moscow'), was less conformist, although majority ownership was in the hands of Gazprom. Indeed two-thirds of the country's 2,500 television stations were completely or partially owned by the federal or local governments.[115] The result was that, across all platforms, it was a 'neo-Soviet model' that predominated. A much wider range of information was available than had been the case in Soviet times, and there was more freedom to criticise the authorities. But criticism had little practical effect because of the absence of political structures that might have taken it further, and there were new problems, such as commercial pressures

Table 8.1 Patterns of media consumption, 2010

How often do you . . .

	regularly	sometimes	rarely	never
Read national newspapers?	20	38	29	12
Read local newspapers?	24	35	28	13
Watch national television?	76	18	5	2
Watch local television?	57	28	10	4
Consult the Internet?	23	16	14	46

Source: 2010 Russia survey, rounded percentages.

and the rise of organised crime, that imposed their own constraints. The outcome was a media that was once again a 'tool for the elites rather than a watchdog of the masses'.[116]

Newer communication technologies were of course available, but their reach was much less than in other developed nations. About a quarter of all adults had regular internet access, but there were many more users in the Western countries, relative to population, and many more had telephone landlines, although Russia was ahead of the United States in mobile phone ownership.[117] And the internet was closely monitored, not just for evidence of criminal activity but also for political dissent. By law, service providers were required to set up dedicated lines that routed all private traffic to the security agencies, allowing them to monitor e-mail communications and broader patterns of activity. It was not clear that a warrant would necessarily be sought or obtained in all cases of this kind, and there were many other cases in which electronic communications had clearly been used to identify and punish those who had engaged in even minor forms of political contestation. In Omsk, for instance, police ordered the administrators of a popular internet forum to provide the personal details of any participants who had posted comments critical of the city authorities; and sanctions were taken against service providers and individual bloggers for 'inciting extremism' and 'hatred and enmity' towards regional governments.[118] The muck-raking website Kompromat.ru was removed for the entire period before the 2008 presidential election, apparently by a '[single] phone call'.[119] All the same there were much greater opportunities to exchange views and information over the internet than through the established media, in whatever form; particularly important was an 'elite internet', including electronic periodicals that circulated widely among senior officials, academics and professionals.[120]

It was also clear that independent-minded journalists would be at some risk if they inconvenienced the rich and powerful. We have already mentioned the landmark case of Anna Politkovskaya, shot dead in October 2006 in what appeared to be a contract killing that made headlines across the world; her outspoken writings on the Chechen war, and on the Putin system as a whole, had made her a lot of enemies. But she was one of very many examples of attacks on journalists, some of them from her own newspaper, *Novaya gazeta* (see, pp. 198–9). In November 2008 a former colleague, now the editor of a local paper in the Moscow suburb of Khimki, was assaulted near his home and left unconscious; he had been a persistent opponent of the local administration, criticising its plans to drive a new road through a local forest and demolish a war memorial that stood in its way.[121] Another casualty was *Kommersant*'s military correspondent, Ivan Safronov, who leapt out of a fifth-floor window in the block of flats in which he lived in an apparent case of suicide, but following his discovery of sensitive information about Russian arms sales to Iran and Syria that could have embarrassed senior officials.[122] Yet another was a campaigning journalist in Rostov-on-Don who lost his life in June 2009 after suffering serious head injuries in what the authorities claimed was a domestic dispute, but which his colleagues had no doubt was premeditated murder.[123] The following November a Kaliningrad television journalist fell to her death from the fourteenth floor after winning a legal battle to regain control of her independent-minded channel; in January 2010 a Tomsk journalist died in hospital from the injuries he had sustained while in police custody and without regaining consciousness.[124]

Given Russia's enormous territorial extent, political campaigning was in practice conducted by television; and since television was effectively controlled by the authorities themselves, this meant that election coverage was overwhelmingly concerned to show the Kremlin in a positive light and its opponents more negatively, if at all. The most extensive study of its kind was undertaken by the Centre for Journalism in Extreme Situations, which is affiliated to the Russian Union of Journalists, over the period leading up to the 2007 Duma and 2008 presidential elections. They found that between 1 October and 22 November 2007 United Russia had 19.2 per cent of prime-time news coverage on the First Channel, ten times as much as for its leading competitor, the Communist Party (1.9 per cent). On the second channel, wholly state-owned Rossiya, the proportions were similar: United Russia had 20.2 per cent, followed by the Liberal Democrats with 3.7 per cent. It was very similar on the commercial channel NTV, with 19.1 per cent devoted to United Russia and 3.8 per cent to its nearest competitor, the broadly pro-Kremlin A Just Russia. And it was very similar, once again, during the period before the presidential election: Dmitri Medvedev had 25.9 per cent of prime-time news coverage on Rossiya, 32.4 per cent on the First Channel and a massive 43.3 per cent on NTV; his closest opponent, Gennadii Zyuganov, had 6.8 per cent, 3.1 per cent and 1.4 per cent respectively. The Centre concluded that the state channels 'had not carried out their legal obligation to create equal conditions for all the candidates' and had been 'prejudiced in favour of Dmitri Medvedev, both in the amount of time that had been allocated to him and in the tone of its coverage'; NTV had also been 'obviously biased'.[125]

Russia was not alone in the attempts that were made by its government to manipulate the published and electronic media. But it was certainly an extreme case, by the latter stages of the Putin presidency. Freedom House's regular survey found that freedom of the press in Russia had been in decline over the entire period, with the Kremlin 'relying on Soviet-style media management to facilitate a sensitive political transition and deflect responsibility for widespread corruption and political violence'. The Constitution nominally provided for freedom of speech and of the press, but a 'politicized and corrupt court system' had been used to harass and prosecute the few remaining journalists who dared to maintain their independence. In one representative case, two journalists from Bashkortostan who had accused the local authorities of corruption were convicted under the comprehensive provisions of the law on extremism, given suspended prison sentences and banned from working as journalists for a year (the paper itself was closed down). There was additional pressure on journalists about the way in which they reported what was by now a deepening economic crisis; prosecutors warned the media against 'damaging' news reports, Putin publicly told journalists not to report anything 'unpatriotic', and all sections of the media were instructed to avoid the word 'crisis' in their coverage. Indeed the police and security forces sometimes assaulted journalists who were simply carrying out their professional duties, as in December 2008, when they destroyed the equipment of the television and newspaper journalists who had been covering local protests against increases in car import tariffs.[126]

Many of the same concerns were identified in a parallel exercise conducted by the Paris-based organisation Reporters without Borders, which concluded in its 2010 report that most Russians had 'very little chance of hearing independent views' on their television and that opposition figures and government critics had 'no access to nationwide stations'.[127] Reporters without Borders was particularly critical of media coverage during the period that had preceded the election of Dmitri Medvedev and Putin's move to the premiership in 2008, which had seen 'new obstacles' to the work of journalists on top of those with which they had contended for a decade or more. The way in which the economic crisis was being handled also came in for criticism. In some regions, such as Sverdlovsk, matters of this kind had been placed in the hands of the Federal Security Bureau; and journalists and their newspapers had found themselves pursued by the courts because (for instance) of their publication of an analysis of the crisis that drew explicit comparisons with the violent disturbances that had taken place at Novocherkassk in 1962, or their investigation of the accounts of a number of finance companies. Another case was the journalist Natal'ya Morar', a Moldovan citizen working for the independent weekly *New Times*, who had investigated the Kremlin's secret funding of the United Russia campaign during the period before the December 2007 Duma election and then found herself unable to return after she had made a trip abroad.[128]

Both Freedom House and Reporters without Borders published a statistical index of press freedom that allowed some comparative judgements to be made. Nearly twenty years after an independent and apparently postcommunist Russia had been established, its level of press freedom, on these measures, was among the lowest in the world (see Table 8.2). Indices of this kind were typically compiled by independent experts and specialists from the countries concerned, using a detailed checklist.[129] Their conclusions were certainly unambiguous. For Freedom House, Russia stood at 175 out of the 196 countries that were included in the exercise in 2010, just above Saudi Arabia but below

Table 8.2 Indices of press freedom, selected countries, 2010 (rankings)

	Japan	USA	UK	Ukraine	India	Russia	China	(n)
Reporters without Borders	11	20	19	131	122	140	171	178
Freedom House	21	24	26	108	72	175	181	196

Source: adapted from the 'Press Freedom Index' sponsored by Reporters without Borders and maintained at www.rsf.org, and from Freedom House's 'Freedom of the Press' index maintained at www.freedomhouse.org.

the Democratic Republic of the Congo and Tajikistan; the Scandinavian countries were at the top of the list, and North Korea at the bottom.[130] Reporters without Borders put Russia at 140 out of the 178 countries that were included in their 'Press Freedom Index' in the same year, below Iraq and Ethiopia; the Scandinavian countries (with the Netherlands and Switzerland) were again at the top, with Eritrea at the bottom.[131] Another comparative exercise, the Media Sustainability Index, was less comprehensive in its global coverage but dealt with similar issues, using similar methods of assessment. On a scale of 0 (the lowest) to 4 (the best), Russia in 2010 was rated 1.45 (the same as Tajikistan); this signified an 'unsustainable mixed system', with 'segments of the legal system and government opposed to a free media', and represented a clear decline over the decade.[132]

The rule of law

It was perhaps most fundamental of all that the rule of law remained uncertain. Judges, formally speaking, were 'independent and subject only to the Constitution of the Russian Federation and federal law' (art. 120); they were 'irremovable' (art. 121) and 'inviolable' (art. 122). But the Constitutional Court, which was supposed to regulate the behaviour of the president as well as of the highest levels of government, was appointed on the president's own nomination, subject to the approval of the upper house of parliament. Judges in the Supreme Court and the Supreme Arbitration Court were appointed in the same way; judges in other federal courts were appointed by the president directly (art. 128). Under the previous constitution, up to 1993, the Constitutional Court had been elected by the Congress of People's Deputies, and it had countermanded the president's decisions on several important occasions.[133] As long as the appointment of judges was (in practice) in the hands of government, it was unlikely the courts would defend the rights of ordinary citizens if they were infringed by the authorities themselves, and unlikely that individual ministers would be held to account for their actions and if necessary for any wrongdoing. The central theme of Dmitri Medvedev's various addresses to the nation, even before he became president, was 'legal nihilism': the disregard of law, and the damage that was done to the economy and to public life by its routine violation

> ## Table 8.3 **The Russian judicial system: an outline**
>
> The Russian judiciary is divided into three branches. Most ordinary business is heard in *courts of general jurisdiction* in urban and rural districts, or at regional level, all of which are subordinate to the Supreme Court (art. 126 of the Constitution). Their decisions may be appealed only to the immediately superior court unless a constitutional issue is involved. A *commercial (arbitrazh) court system* under the Supreme Arbitration Court (art. 127 of the Constitution) constitutes a second branch of the judicial system; it deals with cases that involve business disputes between legal entities (companies) and between legal entities and the state. The *Constitutional Court* (art. 125 of the Constitution), as well as constitutional courts in a number of administrative entities, represents the third branch of the judicial system.
>
> In addition, *justices of the peace* in local areas deal with criminal cases involving maximum sentences of less than three years and with some civil cases; they operate in all regions except Chechnya. The *Procuracy* (art. 129 of the Constitution) is a further and distinctively Russian institution, originally established by Peter the Great, that is responsible for supervising the implementation of legislation across the entire state system; the Procurator General is appointed and dismissed by the Federation Council on the representation of the President.

Source: adapted from US Department of State, *2009 Human Rights Report: Russia* (2010); the judicial system is ultimately based on the Constitution, arts 118–31.

(see p. 106). But until the administration of justice was more clearly separated from government itself, there would hardly be a qualitative improvement.

It was certainly the view of outside observers that the judicial system as a whole 'did not consistently act as an effective counterweight to other branches of government' (a basic outline is provided in Table 8.3). Judges, for a start, were 'subject to influence from the executive, military, and security forces, particularly in high-profile or politically sensitive cases'. Judges, apart from this, were regularly bribed by officials and others, in spite of an increase in their salaries that was intended to reduce if not eliminate this form of abuse. About seventy judges had to be removed from their positions every year for reasons of this kind, and approximately 300 warnings were issued for a variety of offences including unreasonable delays in processing cases, alcohol-related and other lapses of behaviour, and conflicts of interest or corruption. Nor was there an adequate system of protection for witnesses who might often be invited to give evidence against defendants with powerful criminal connections; nearly half of all those who appeared in cases of this kind were reported to have suffered threats or violence, and few were even aware of the arrangements that were available to ensure their personal security.[134] According to the Council of Europe in a 2009 report that was based on interviews with judges, prosecutors, defence lawyers and defendants, judges routinely received intimidating phone calls from their superiors instructing them how to rule in specific cases (what was sometimes called 'telephone justice'), and there was a heavy emphasis on delivering convictions at any cost.[135]

There were additional issues about the Constitutional Court itself, which was meant to ensure the integrity of the legal order as a whole. Its independence was certainly diminished when the law on which it operated was amended in 2009 so that its chairman and two deputy chairmen were appointed in future by the upper house of parliament on the nomination of the President, instead of being elected by secret ballot from among the judges themselves.[136] In addition, two of the Court's nineteen members were obliged to leave their positions when they made public their concern about the pressures to which the judicial system as a whole had been subjected. One, Anatolii Kononov, left the Court entirely, the other, Vladimir Yaroslavtsev, stood down from the Council of Judges, which was responsible for disciplinary matters. Yaroslavtsev, who retained his position on the Court itself, had told the Spanish paper *El Pais* that the security organs were as dominant as they had been in the Soviet period, that the courts themselves had become an 'instrument of the executive' and that their decisions were 'made in the Presidential Administration'. Kononov, who had defended his colleague in an interview in a weekly paper, was then obliged to resign his own position after the other judges had called on him to do so; apart from the offending interview, he had repeatedly used his right to state a 'special [in other words, dissenting] opinion' about the Court's decisions.[137]

It was also clear that individual citizens and even their legal representatives would have little support if they took action of which the authorities at any level of the system disapproved. Lawyer Inna Yermoshkina, for instance, had not been unduly bothered when she found a group of police officers waiting at the entrance to her building as she returned home one evening in May 2008. But when the plainclothes officers surrounded Yermoshkina and her husband and a uniformed officer ordered their arrest, she realised things were rather more serious than she had first imagined. She was handcuffed, placed in a police car and assaulted; her husband was meanwhile escorted up to their apartment, where the police confiscated documents she had gathered about relatives of senior city and government officials, supposedly in connection with a fraud investigation. 'That will teach you not to step on the toes of important people', she was told. The source of her difficulties was evidently the attempt Yermoshkina had been making to combat the corruption that had become rampant in the granting of licences to practise as notaries. Relatively few were issued, so that earnings were very high, and Yermoshkina had threatened to undermine a lucrative business by complaining that too many of the licences were being given to the relatives of powerful officials instead of lawyers who were well qualified but politically unconnected. Or to those who were willing to pay a bribe of up to $500,000, with every expectation they would be able to recover their investment in less than a year and 'after that it's all profit'.[138]

Another case, and one that attracted international attention, was when Sergei Magnitsky died in a Moscow prison in November 2009 after his pleas for medical treatment had been refused. Magnitsky, a lawyer in his late thirties, had been a key witness in an acrimonious legal battle over alleged tax fraud between the Russian government and Hermitage Capital Management, which was based in London and had previously been the country's top investment fund. Hermitage's co-founder, William Browder (ironically, the grandson of an American Communist leader), had accused corrupt officials of using Heritage and other companies to submit false returns in order to defraud Russian taxpayers of hundreds of millions of dollars in a scandal that embraced senior police officers, judges, government bureaucrats, bankers and the mafia. Magnitsky was arrested as a suspect, and kept for a year in a squalid prison cell. In a lengthy affidavit sent to the Prosecutor General he had complained about his treatment and how his numerous requests to see a doctor had been refused, even when he was obviously in pain (Magnitsky had developed pancreatitis while in custody and the death was officially attributed to a ruptured abdominal membrane).[139] Friends and colleagues believed the lawyer had deliberately been denied treatment so as to persuade him to testify against Browder and his company. An investigation followed; but for Western journalists, the death was a 'grim reminder of the costs of clashing with powerful vested interests in a country where campaigning journalists and human rights activists are often murdered with impunity'.[140]

The other side of the coin was that senior officials and their families had little to fear even if their actions led to the injury or loss of life of innocent members of the public. People like the son of the defence minister, Sergei Ivanov, who ran down and killed an elderly pedestrian in 2005 but avoided prosecution (he could have spent five years in prison).[141] There was another storm of controversy when the Mercedes sedan of a senior LUKoil executive crashed head-on into a Citroën hatchback in central Moscow in February 2010, killing a prominent gynaecologist and her daughter-in-law. Police immediately blamed the Citroën, claiming it had pulled illegally into the oncoming lane, but an alternative version soon emerged from the testimony of eyewitnesses, who insisted on exactly the opposite. The police initially showed little interest, refusing to issue an accident report (which was a legal requirement) and claiming that nearby video cameras had been pointing in the wrong direction; but none of the footage they had recorded was made available. The company meanwhile made clear it would refuse to pay compensation, even if it was found guilty; the LUKoil executive, Anatolii Barkov, who had himself sustained minor injuries, had been head of its security department and was thought to have the kind of connections with high-level state officials that placed him effectively outside the rule of law. For many ordinary Russians, the entire episode was further evidence that the notoriously corrupt police were 'little more than a force to protect the country's strong from ordinary citizens'.[142]

It was for reasons of this kind that the courts and law enforcement in general had a rather poor public reputation (see also pp. 203–4). Levels of distrust of the police were particularly high: two-thirds of those who were asked by the Levada Centre in early 2010 had little or no confidence in them, exactly the opposite of the position in Western Europe and the United States. In Moscow, not a single respondent could be found who was 'definitely' prepared to trust the police; only 1 per cent were 'inclined' to do so. And would the courts defend the rights of ordinary citizens if they were the victim of abuse at the hands of the police? Just 29 per cent, in January 2010, had at least some confidence they would be assisted; 54 per cent took the opposite view.[143] Were the courts, indeed, actually independent of government? Only 8 per cent, according to the Levada Centre's surveys, thought so; 12 per cent thought they were controlled by the federal government and another 17 per cent that they were controlled by the local authorities. The largest proportion of all, 37 per cent, thought they were simply corrupt ('anyone who has money can get the kind of decision they want'). And a substantial majority (68 per cent) did not believe the law offered them any protection, more than anything else because it was 'not written for everybody' and allowed too many of the rich and powerful to ignore it whenever it suited them to do so.[144]

If the Russian courts offered no solution, there were admittedly some other ways in which ordinary citizens could secure their rights – or at least attempt to do so. One of these was the 'Plenipotentiary on Human Rights in the Russian Federation', or ombudsman, that had been established in its present form in 1997 on the classic Swedish model.[145] The first ombudsman was Communist deputy and law professor Oleg Mironov, who had been appointed in 1998; he was succeeded in 2004 by Vladimir Lukin, one of those who had founded the Yabloko party in the early 1990s. The ombudsman was appointed and dismissed by the lower house of the Russian parliament, although the president was one of those who had the right to make a nomination under Article 7 of the law. An eligible candidate had to be at least 35 years old, with appropriate qualifications and experience (art. 6); the ombudsman could hold office for a maximum of two consecutive five-year terms (art. 10) but could not engage in politics or belong to a political party (art. 11). The purpose of the office, according to the law, was to ensure that the 'rights and freedoms of citizens' were properly respected by state and local government bodies, and by those who worked for them (art. 1). The ombudsman was 'independent and not subordinate to any state bodies or officials' (art. 2) and could not be brought before the courts without the consent of the Duma itself (art. 12); the powers of the office remained valid even in the event of a wartime or emergency situation (art. 4).

The human rights commissioner was required by the law to present an annual report to the president and other bodies, which had to be published in the government newspaper *Rossiiskaya gazeta* (art. 33). Lukin, in the report he presented in 2009 on his work over the previous year, argued that Russian legislation on the matters with which he was concerned was more or less satisfactory, but added that there were 'serious problems' about its implementation. This concerned the most fundamental of all rights, the right to life, particularly in the armed forces, where more than 700 had lost their lives in peaceful circumstances by suicide and in other ways. There were other problems in relation to the rights that had supposedly been guaranteed by the Constitution in respect of citizenship, freedom of movement and the ability to choose a place of residence. Lukin concluded that the experience of the previous five years allowed no 'unambiguous or, still more so, final conclusions about the situation with regard to the rights and freedoms of the individual in our country', but for all its shortcomings, this was still a 'country of developing democracy'.[146] The ombudsman dealt with approximately 30,000 submissions in a typical year;[147] the kinds of issues that were raised most frequently were the environment, human rights in the armed forces, migration, the rights of children, violence against women, crime and corruption, rights at the workplace and in prisons, national and religious intolerance, and care for the victims of terrorism.[148]

Russian commentators accepted that there were serious limitations on the powers of the newly established office. The ombudsman had no right to initiate legislation, and very little opportunity to appeal to the Constitutional Court; there was also an unclear relationship between the federal ombudsman and the corresponding offices that had been established in most of the Russian regions.[149] Lukin himself, in his annual report, acknowledged that his dealings with government bodies had become 'more businesslike and, consequently, more productive', but the same kinds of offences were still being committed, and there had been a 'weak and indifferent' response from the wider society to his regular communications.[150] Russian human rights activists, for their part, took the view that the ombudsman had been 'generally effective as an official advocate for many of their concerns, despite and within the legal constraints on his position'.[151] And he was certainly prepared to take positions that were unpopular with the authorities, such as drawing attention to the 'disbalance' that had prevailed in all sections of the media during the period before the December 2007 Duma election, and the arbitrary way in which pro-regime demonstrations had been approved while those of a less supportive nature had been banned or disrupted.[152] All the same, the office remained 'primarily consultative and investigatory, without powers of enforcement', and there was a much less satisfactory position in the regions and republics, where the effectiveness of those who held the analogous office 'varied significantly'.[153]

Another way in which individual citizens could seek recourse was through the European Court of Human Rights, based in Strasbourg, which was the judicial arm of the Council of Europe. The Court's judgements were binding on all its member states, including Russia, and its machinery allowed citizens to sue their own state for any violation of the provisions of the European Convention for the Protection of Human Rights and Fundamental Freedoms, which had been ratified by Russia in 1998, provided they had first of all exhausted the remedies that were available through their national court system.[154] Increasing numbers of Russians were soon availing themselves of these new opportunities – more than 33,000 over the decade that followed, which was more than a quarter of all the cases that had come before the Court and the largest number from any individual member state. Cases took some time to reach a conclusion, but there were 273 judgements against the Russian authorities in 2009, leading to fines or other sanctions. The compensation and legal fees that were specified in these judgements were generally paid promptly, but there was less evidence that changes had been made in domestic practice to ensure that cases of the same kind did not occur in future, and no access was permitted to the domestic case files relating to alleged gross violations in Chechnya, which generated a substantial proportion of the caseload.[155]

Most of the judgements against Russia were concerned with the failure to implement domestic court decisions in non-criminal cases, and many others dealt with the excessive length of judicial proceedings. Cases of this kind also originated from other Council members. What distinguished Russia was the judgements that concerned the right to life and the prohibition of torture and degrading punishment, almost all of which related to Chechnya, in most of which the Court found the rights in question had been violated and that the Russian authorities had failed to investigate them adequately. In addition, the Court 'repeatedly found that prison or jail conditions in other parts of Russia could also amount to inhuman treatment or torture'.[156] The Court did exercise some influence in other ways, particularly through the use that was made of its rulings to determine cases in Russia's own court system.[157] There was less satisfaction with its rulings on Chechnya, where no serious effort appeared to have been made to bring the perpetrators to justice even when they were known and had been named in its judgements. And in a 'new and very troubling trend' the Russian authorities had 'flatly contested' several of the Court's judgements, 'apparently in order to justify closing investigations and refusing to bring charges against perpetrators'. For the families affected, monetary compensation was often less important than the need to see justice being done and to obtain further information about those who had disappeared.[158]

Assessing Russian democracy and human rights

Freedom of expression was one of a number of human or civil rights that appeared to be poorly protected in postcommunist Russia. Several bodies monitored the performance of the international community in these respects in the early years of the new century; one of the most systematic was Amnesty International, a non-governmental organisation established in the early 1960s whose particular concern was the treatment of peaceful protest. According to its statute, Amnesty has a 'vision of a world in which every person enjoys all of the human rights enshrined in the Universal Declaration of Human Rights and other international human rights instruments'. Amnesty works through national branches and a much wider network of individual members, drawing for the most part on their subscriptions and taking great care to avoid financial support of any kind that might compromise its independence. It seeks not only to identify and document human rights abuses, particularly the arrest and maltreatment of 'prisoners of conscience' who have refrained from the advocacy of violence, but also to mobilise international opinion, typically through letter-writing campaigns, so that abuses are remedied and innocent victims released from incarceration. It publishes an annual report as well as a whole series of statements on individual countries and human rights concerns, drawing on a full-time staff and periodic field visits.[159]

Amnesty deliberately reports no kind of score or ranking; nor does it assume that the established Western democracies are necessarily beyond reproach. In the United

Kingdom, for instance, Amnesty drew attention in its 2008 report to the way in which individuals continued to be returned to states where they would face a real risk of torture on the basis of nothing more than unenforceable 'diplomatic assurances'. It also believed that secrecy in the implementation of counterterrorism measures was leading to 'unfair judicial proceedings', and drew attention to 'continued failures of accountability for past violations', including 'alleged state collusion in killings in Northern Ireland'.[160] The United States, Amnesty reported, was still holding hundreds of foreign nationals at its naval base in Guantánamo, the vast majority without charge and without the ability to challenge the legality of their detention. The Central Intelligence Agency continued to follow policies of secret detention and interrogation, and a number of videotapes of these interrogations, which might have provided incriminating evidence, had been destroyed. On top of this there were 'serious failings' in the policies that had been introduced in order to address the problem of sexual violence against Native American women; there was evidence of discrimination in a variety of areas, including policing, the operation of the criminal justice system and housing rights; and the death penalty was still applied (Amnesty is opposed to capital punishment under any circumstances).[161]

But although there was no explicit comparison, it was clear from successive reports that there was much more to worry about in postcommunist Russia. The situation in the North Caucasus was a cause of particular concern.[162] During 2006, for instance, Amnesty found that extrajudicial executions, enforced disappearances and abductions, arbitrary detention and torture were all continuing, particularly in Chechnya and Ingushetia. Those who sought justice in Russian courts, or before the European Court of Human Rights, were intimidated by officials, and defence lawyers were harassed. 'Serious violations including torture' were also reported in North Ossetia and Dagestan.[163] The same issues were highlighted in its report on 2007, which also reported trials in which convictions had been based on the forcibly extracted 'confessions' of the accused. In Ingushetia there were at least six cases in which local residents had been shot dead by law enforcement officers, witnesses claiming they had been summarily executed. Investigations into human rights abuses were 'often ineffectual, and suspended for failure to identify any suspect'. There was no comprehensive list of disappeared persons, no exhumation of mass graves and no fully functioning forensic laboratory carrying out autopsies; '[v]ery few cases reached trial'.[164] It was much the same in following years, with 'continuing reports of human rights violations' including 'arbitrary detention, torture and ill-treatment, and extrajudicial executions'.[165]

Amnesty was equally concerned about the steady erosion of opportunities to express alternative opinions and call the authorities to account. The restrictions that had been imposed on NGOs, for instance, 'were legally imprecise, allowing arbitrary implementation and disproportionate penalties, and [had] diverted resources from substantive programmes'. The amendments that had been made to the law on extremism had outlawed reasonable comment and were likely to 'restrict and punish the activities of civil society organizations and other government critics'. Journalists were 'intimidated, faced with groundless criminal proceedings and attacked'; human rights activists were 'subjected to administrative harassment and some received anonymous death threats'. There were bans on demonstrations, which 'did not appear to be legitimate or proportionate restrictions of freedom of assembly', and peaceful protestors were detained even if they had given the authorities advance notice of their intentions as the law required.[166] In later reports Amnesty found that government representatives and the state media had 'repeatedly accused human rights defenders and members of the opposition movement of working for foreign interests and being "anti-Russian"'; they had been 'subjected to harassment and intimidation'; and criminal charges, such as using unlicensed computer software or inciting hatred, had been taken out against them on a selective and arbitrary basis.[167]

Further abuses had taken place during the five-day war with Georgia in the late summer of 2008. On Amnesty's evidence more than 600 people, most of them civilians, had lost their lives in the conflict. The Russian army had pushed Georgian forces out of South Ossetia – which was legally part of a foreign state, whatever its residents might have wished – and occupied parts of Georgia proper, defining it as a 'buffer zone', until early October. By the end of the year, the Georgian authorities were reporting that up to 25,000 South Ossetians had been unable to return to their homes and were facing long-term displacement. Russian air and artillery attacks had mostly affected Georgian military positions outside built-up areas, but villages and towns had also been hit, and there were reports that some of the bombardment might have been aimed deliberately at civilians or civilian infrastructure. Russian forces, according to Amnesty, had also failed to restrain militia groups loyal to the South Ossetian authorities, who had carried out large-scale pillaging and arson in a number of predominantly Georgian settlements in the disputed territory.[168] The Georgians, according to Amnesty, had also been guilty of serious violations of human rights. They had not taken the appropriate precautionary measures in the assault on the South Ossetian capital that had initiated the conflict, and used Grad missiles that were difficult to target accurately; 'dozens of civilians' had lost their lives as a result.[169]

Amnesty had additional concerns about the administration of justice, including conditions in Russian prisons. Trial procedures did not always meet international standards, and in some cases with a political context the treatment of suspects had amounted to persecution. The right of suspects to legal representation had repeatedly been violated. In prisons themselves there had been reports of torture and ill-treatment from all over the country. The methods employed included 'beatings, electric shocks, suffocation with plastic bags and being forced to stay in painful positions for prolonged periods', and there were threats of further punishment unless prisoners acknowledged their 'guilt' and signed fabricated 'confessions'.[170] There had been reports of rape while in custody, and some detainees had been denied the medical treatment they had obviously required. A number of Ingush men had apparently been abducted from their homes and kept at a secret detention centre in the Moscow region run by the Ministry of Defence. Prisoners in several Russian prisoner colonies had protested at their conditions of detention, which could sometimes be described as inhuman or degrading treatment. Riots and hunger strikes had been reported from several prison colonies in the Urals and the Volga region; prisoners complained about beatings and ill-treatment by prison officials and by other detainees, and four prisoners had died while they were being moved to a different place of incarceration.[171]

The same kinds of concerns appeared in other reports, such as those produced by the New York-based organisation Human Rights Watch. Originally founded in 1978 to monitor the Soviet Union's compliance with the commitments that had been made three years earlier in the Final Act of the Helsinki Conference on Security and Cooperation in Europe, and then enlarged in the late 1980s by a series of mergers, Human Rights Watch is 'dedicated to protecting the human rights of people around the world' and aims particularly to 'prevent discrimination, to uphold political freedom, to protect people from inhumane conduct in wartime, and to bring offenders to justice'.[172] Like Amnesty, it produces an annual report as well as the results of more specific investigations. And like Amnesty, it found much that was troubling in the new Russia (as well, of course, as in other states worldwide). The election of Dmitri Medvedev, they concluded, had not resulted in improvements in the rule of law or the environment for civil society, with the government 'continuing to crack down against independent groups and activists'. The amendments that had been made to the law on extremism allowed almost any kind of action to be designated accordingly, and the law was itself being used to initiate proceedings against NGOs and the independent media, including internet sites and blogs. All of this was part of what appeared to be a determined effort to 'weaken – in some cases beyond recognition – the checks and balances needed for an accountable government'.[173]

Human Rights Watch shared Amnesty's concern about the North Caucasus, where there were continuing violations of a whole series of basic rights. In Chechnya, they found, federal agencies had come to play a less prominent role and law enforcement had been taken over by local forces loyal to President Ramzan Kadyrov, who 'dominate[d] law enforcement and security operations and commit[ed] grave human rights abuses'. There were fewer forced disappearances than in the past, but they remained a 'key feature of the conflict', with as many as 5,000 cases since the conflict had begun in 1999. And reports of torture, particularly in the unofficial detention centres that were run by Kadyrov's loyalists, were increasing in number. There was no adequate means by which ordinary citizens could protect their rights through the Russian courts, and accordingly 'hundreds of victims of abuse' had been applying to the European Court in Strasbourg, which had issued 'landmark rulings' that the Russian government had been guilty of violating the right to life and the prohibition of torture.[174] The 'counterterrorism operation' in Chechnya had supposedly been concluded in April 2009, but there was a 'growing atmosphere of intimidation' and the insurgency was spreading into nearby Dagestan and Ingushetia, where the law enforcement agencies had been guilty of 'serious human rights abuses including summary and arbitrary detentions, acts of torture and ill-treatment, enforced disappearances, and extrajudicial executions'.[175]

Human Rights Watch also shared Amnesty's concern about the sanctions that had been applied to all kinds of independent political action. During the period before the 2007 Duma election, for instance, the agencies of law enforcement had 'beat[en], detained, and harassed activists participating in and planning peaceful political protests', and the series of demonstrations that had become known as 'dissenters' marches' had been banned or severely restricted. When they nonetheless took place, for instance in Moscow in April 2007, they had been broken up by police and special forces. Activists and observers had been prevented from travelling to Samara to take part in another march, timed to coincide with an EU–Russia summit, and 'excessive force' was used to disperse the dissenters' marches that took place in Moscow and St Petersburg the following November.[176] Meanwhile the Russian government was 'tightening controls over civil society through new legislation, interference with peaceful assembly, and harassment of NGOs and government critics'. There were increasing numbers of on-site investigations and in some cases documents and equipment were seized, forcing the organisations concerned to suspend their operations or close down entirely. Even after the law was modified in 2009 – in what was hardly a coincidence, just before Barack Obama's first visit – Russian and foreign NGOs continued to be subject to 'excessive, unwarranted government scrutiny and interference'.[177]

All human rights organisations were increasingly concerned about a rising incidence of xenophobia and intolerance. There were more than a hundred such attacks in 2006, according to Human Rights Watch, including the violent riots in the Karelian town of Kondopoga that had also concerned members of the Public Chamber, where local citizens had attacked residents from the Caucasus and hundreds had fled the city in fear of their lives. A 'gay and lesbian pride march' in May 2006 was banned by the Moscow mayor, who called it 'satanic'; two protest rallies were called to resist this challenge to freedom of expression and assembly, but those who took part were attacked by '[h]undreds of anti-gay protestors, including skinheads, nationalists, and Orthodox followers', who kicked and beat the participants and 'chanted threats'.[178] Migrant workers, most of them from other former Soviet republics, were another group whose rights were routinely infringed. There were as many as 9 million of them, mostly engaged in construction projects in the big cities, where they faced abuses that included 'confiscation of passports, denial of contracts, non-payment or delayed payment of wages, and unsafe working conditions'; some employers used violence or the threat of violence against any who complained about non-payment. The police frequently used document inspections to extort money from visible minorities of all kinds, including migrant workers, and many were physically abused or forced to work for free.[179]

Amnesty, Human Rights Watch and (among others) the US State Department in its annual reports on human rights around the world avoid any explicit comparison between one country and another, still more so any attempt to attach a numerical value to their respective performance.[180] A rather different approach is taken by Freedom House of

New York, which has been producing its Comparative Survey of Freedom since the early 1970s and which aims to provide an 'annual evaluation of political rights and civil liberties anywhere in the world', expressed in two seven-point scales. For Freedom House, political rights were the 'extent that the people [had] a choice in determining the nature of the system and its leaders', and civil liberties were the 'freedoms to develop views, institutions and personal autonomy apart from the state'; both of these were derived from a more detailed and continuously revised checklist of criteria. Based on these scores, countries could be classified as 'free' (if they averaged between 1 and 2.5), 'partly free' (between 3 and 5) or 'not free' (between 5.5 and 7). One of the main criticisms of the survey was that it took no account of levels of development, which would obviously have some bearing on a country's ability to deliver a given level of human rights performance; later surveys took some account of this by providing additional contextual information. All the same, it remained an exercise that privileged individual and 'liberal' under-standings of human rights of a kind that were most strongly associated with the countries of the developed and Christian West.[181]

It was clear, on these criteria, that the end of communist rule had brought about no dramatic or lasting improvement (see Figure 8.1). The USSR, in the Brezhnev years, had

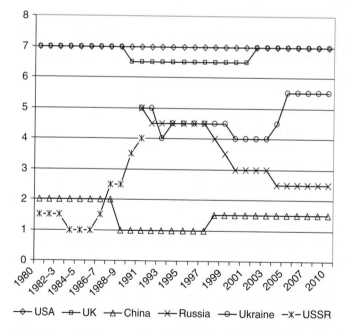

Figure 8.1 Freedom House ratings, selected countries (1980–2010)
Source: adapted from www.freedomhouse.org; scores average 'political rights' and 'civil liberties', and have been scaled from 7=top to 1=bottom.

been 'not free', but in 1990, while still under communist rule, it was judged to have become 'partly free'. The new union treaty that was under consideration at this time, Freedom House explained, was based on human rights and the creation of a democratic state based on popular representation and the rule of law. All the fifteen republics had declared some form of sovereignty, and the Soviet parliament had adopted laws guaranteeing freedom of the press and freedom of conscience.[182] Russia, as a Soviet republic, had a higher score, and so did early postcommunist Russia, but it never became more than 'partly free' in terms of the Freedom House survey, and its rating was already falling as the decade advanced. In 2004, at the end of Putin's first presidential term, the score fell again, this time into the 'not free' category, and at the start of 2011 Russia was still considered 'not free', with a score of 6 for political rights and 5 for civil liberties; this placed it just above Iran and Rwanda, at exactly the same point on the scale as Angola, Cambodia, Egypt, Yemen and several other Asian or African countries. Of the fifteen former Soviet republics, only the Baltic states were considered 'free' at this time. Armenia, Moldova, Georgia, Kyrgyzstan and Ukraine were 'partly free'; all the others, including Russia, were 'not free'.

Freedom House also produced an annual report, which made clear some of the reasons for this undistinguished showing. The Duma election in December 2007, in its view, had marked a 'new low in the Kremlin's manipulations of the political process'. Access for outside observers had been 'sharply restricted', and the campaign environment had favoured Kremlin-sponsored parties, which had won the 'vast majority of seats'. Not only this, but Putin had announced that he intended to remain on the political stage after his second presidential term came to an end in 2008, advantaging the figures from the security agencies that had been appointed to top positions in the government and state-owned enterprises and setting Russia on a 'firmly authoritarian course'. There were 'strict limits' on opposition parties, public demonstrations, the media and NGOs, and no serious attempt had so far been made to address Russia's extensive corruption.[183] Freedom House reported the following year that the 2008 election had been 'manipulated . . . to install a designated successor' and that the Medvedev administration had 'continue[d] to implement Putin's authoritarian restrictions on media coverage and the activities of non-governmental organizations, particularly those with foreign funding'; a separate report found press freedom in further decline, with the Kremlin 'relying on Soviet-style media management to facilitate a sensitive political transition and deflect responsibility for widespread corruption and political violence'.[184]

Democracy and 'sovereign democracy'

The Russian authorities themselves had little time for external judgements, and even less for exercises that placed them at a systematic disadvantage. These, after all, were 'Western' judgements. And consciously or otherwise, they reflected the assumptions of

Western liberal democracy: in their focus on the individual rather than the collective, on procedural form rather than substantive outcome, and on formal rights as against social and economic performance. Both East and West had agreed at various times to a common set of criteria, most notably the Universal Declaration of Human Rights of 1948. But the Universal Declaration was itself a compromise, embracing individual liberties as well as the social and economic rights that were more heavily emphasised in the communist countries. The classic 'liberal' freedoms were all there, including equality before the law, freedom of movement, and freedom of thought and conscience, based on a government that had been constituted by 'periodic and genuine elections'. So, however, were the social and economic rights to which the USSR and its allies attached no less importance, including the right of everyone to work, to social security, and to 'a standard of living adequate for the health and wellbeing of himself and of his family'. Predictably, Western countries attached most importance to their comprehensive range of individual rights; the communist world (and some Catholic and Islamic countries) laid more emphasis on the extent to which they provided full employment and a comprehensive system of social welfare.

At first, it had seemed that Russia and the other postcommunist countries would take the same view of these matters as their Western counterparts now that they were no longer obliged to commit themselves to Marxism–Leninism. Hadn't the Cold War come to an end? Wasn't this supposed to represent the end of ideological differences of any fundamental kind between Russia and the 'other democracies'? But Russia and the other former Soviet republics, as we have already noted, had developed in rather different ways over long periods of time. For the most part, they had not experienced Roman law, with its insistence on the rights of private property, and they had no more experience of feudalism, which in its 'classic' Western form had provided a framework of reciprocal obligations that could develop into a rule of law. They shared a Christian religion, but it was Eastern or Orthodox Christianity, in which church and state were more closely associated and the individual conscience was less securely protected. In one influential interpretation, the Slavic or Orthodox Christian world was a distinct 'civilisation', and one in which it was much less likely that liberal democracy would develop and be sustained than in the Christian West.[185] None of this made it impossible for Russia and the other post-Soviet republics to move in a 'democratic' direction; but it meant that they were likely to do so more slowly and irregularly, or not at all, and in either case it was likely to be in a way that reflected their distinctive values and traditions.

There was accordingly some basis for Putin to insist, from the outset of his presidency, that Russia would and should not attempt to be a

second edition of, say, the US or Britain, where liberal values have deep historic traditions. Our state and its institutions and structures have always played an exceptionally important role in the life of the country and its people. For Russians, a strong state is not an anomaly to be got rid of. Quite the contrary, it is a source of order and the main driving force of any change.

Russians, Putin explained in his address at the turn of the millennium, had come to value the benefits of democracy, the rule of law, and personal and political freedom. But they were 'alarmed by the obvious weakening of state power' and looked forward to a 'certain restoration of the guiding and regulating role of the state, proceeding from Russia's traditions as well as the current state of the economy' – traditions that were collective rather than individual, and in which it was assumed that improvements in living standards would be the result of government policy rather than the efforts of individual citizens.[186] 'From the very beginning', Putin told a group of journalists shortly afterwards, 'Russia was created as a supercentralised state. That's practically laid down in its genetic code, its traditions, and the mentality of its people.'[187]

Putin was equally clear that Russia was and would remain a democratic country, but one that would choose its own way of realising the democratic ideal. The experience of the 1990s, as he put it in his millennium address, had 'eloquently demonstrate[d] that a genuinely successful renewal of our homeland without excessive costs [could] not be achieved by the simple transfer to Russian soil of abstract models and schemes taken from foreign textbooks', nor by the 'mechanical copying of other nations' experience'.[188] Russia, he explained in his 2005 presidential address, had shared the common experience of other European countries, extending human rights, broadening the franchise, protecting the weak and emancipating women, sometimes taking the lead in these developments. And Russia had chosen democracy

for itself, by the will of its own people. It started out on this path itself and, observing all the generally accepted democratic norms, will itself decide in what way – taking account of its historical, geopolitical or any other specific features – it can guarantee the realisation of the principles of freedom and democracy. As a sovereign country Russia can and will decide for itself on the stages and conditions of any movement along this path.[189]

It was a democracy, he told Slovak television, that would 'be adapted to the realities of contemporary Russian life, to our traditions and our history. And we will do this ourselves.'[190]

What was most distinctive in this vision was that the choice of political form should be for Russia alone, and that it should avoid anything that weakened the state and allowed it to be manipulated from outside. This was a view that was widely shared by the defence and security officials we have already identified, collectively known as the *siloviki*, who had become an increasingly influential component of the leadership during the Putin years, and who appeared to have set themselves the task of preventing another state collapse that would leave Russians themselves a 'stateless people and a "dead" civilisation'.[191] But it also reflected a broader and quite understandable response to the break-up of the Soviet Union at the start of the 1990s and then the near collapse of the Russian state that had taken place under the Yeltsin presidency. Communism, Putin explained in his millennium address, had achieved a great deal; but Russians had paid an 'outrageous price' for a social experiment that had left them 'lagging consistently behind the economically advanced countries'.[192] The Soviet state was a different matter, and Putin went as far in his 2005 presidential address as to describe its disintegration as the 'greatest geopolitical catastrophe of the century'. Tens of millions of Russian citizens had found themselves outside their native territory, and an 'epidemic of collapse' had threatened to overwhelm Russia itself. Savings had been devalued; old ideals had been rejected; and many institutions had been dissolved or replaced much too hastily.[193]

Concerns of this kind were greatly strengthened when a series of governments in the post-Soviet area were overthrown in the mid-2000s in what became known as the 'coloured revolutions'. Putin and those who shared his thinking were in no doubt that the entire process had been engineered in Washington, and that it was designed to shift as many of the remaining post-Soviet republics as possible into the Western sphere of influence and ideally into its military and economic alliances. The 'Orange revolution' in Ukraine at the end of 2004 was particularly important. This was the largest of the other post-Soviet republics, with a long common border and a substantial proportion of its citizens who were Russians by language or nationality; but in spite of Putin's open support for his opponent, it was the pro-Western candidate, Viktor Yushchenko, who eventually became president after extended and (as Moscow saw it) externally financed street demonstrations (see p. 298). Putin made clear, shortly afterwards, that he would not allow other countries to turn Russia into an 'amorphous state formation' that could be manipulated from outside in the same kind of way.[194] And it was this experience that appears to have been the most direct inspiration for the restrictions that were increasingly imposed on Russian NGOs and public life in general,[195] as well as the attempt that began to be made to develop a coherent narrative of the larger purposes of the Putin presidency.

Gradually, particularly in the writings of presidential adviser Vladislav Surkov, an elaboration of this distinctively Putinist set of objectives began to take shape. It received the name 'sovereign democracy', understood as a form of rule that combined general democratic principles with the ability to take decisions without deferring to the views of other powers – in other words, a real rather than a nominal sovereignty. Surkov had already set out his views in a widely noted interview in September 2004, shortly after the Beslan hostage-taking crisis. In the outside world, he told *Komsomol'skaya pravda*, there were two groups of people: those who wanted a strong and prosperous Russia as a 'good neighbour and reliable ally', and those who were trying to build on what they saw as their success in undermining the Soviet Union and whose aim was to 'destroy Russia and fill its enormous territory with numerous unviable quasi-state formations'. The second group, unfortu-nately, had allies inside Russia itself, including the 'supercritical mass of criminality' that had developed in the Northern Caucasus, and this had allowed them to develop all kinds of 'doubtful political projects'. Surkov called this second group a 'fifth column of left and right radicals', a combination of 'fake liberals and genuine Nazis' who had much in common including their foreign sponsorship and their hostility not just to a Putinist Russia (which was how they represented themselves) but to Russia itself.[196]

The new term, 'sovereign democracy', came into public use in the spring of 2005, in a journalist's commentary on Putin's presidential address of that year. But there was 'no particular effort to conceal that behind this and many analogous publications stood Surkov and his colleagues'.[197] Surkov himself first used the term in February 2006 in a speech to party activists.[198] Sovereign democracy, he explained elsewhere, was 'a form of the political life of a society in which the governing authorities, their organs and actions are chosen, formed and directed by the Russian nation in all its variety and integrity in order to achieve material welfare, freedom and fairness for all the citizens, social groups and peoples that compose it'. There was nothing specifically Russian about the term, Surkov pointed out; it had been widely used by leading politicians in the United States and the European Union. Why was there any need for adjectives at all, he asked? Why not just democracy, or the absence of democracy? But there were many societies that had called themselves democracies and had yet restricted the rights of women, ethnic minorities and other groups. Was that the same kind of democracy as they had in the contemporary world? And if not, how could they manage without some kind of additional descriptor? His own proposal simply made clear that they were 'on the side of a community of sovereign democracies (and the free market) and against any kind of global dictatorship (or monopoly)'.[199]

'Sovereign democracy' had its opponents as well as its supporters. Deputy Premier Sergei Ivanov, a figure with a background in defence and security, was one of the most positive, declaring sovereign democracy the 'quintessence of our internal order, implying the right of citizens to determine their country's policies themselves and to protect that right from outside pressure by any means, including the use of force'. It was one of a 'triad of national values', including a strong economy and military power. There was no democracy in the abstract; all democratic states had their own particular features, and indeed it was one of the main democratic values that states could make these choices for themselves.[200] Russia, explained the pro-Kremlin commentator Vyacheslav Nikonov, could not accept the role of a 'backward pupil' being called to account for some kind of 'unsatisfactory homework'. They were 'not pupils, and the wisdom of the teachers of democracy [was] very much in question against the background of Iraq, thousands of people who had been arrested and detained without trial or investigation in Guantánamo and other prisons, mass eavesdropping on their own citizens without the authority of a court, and so forth'. No-one would define Russia's fate for it, nor would they allow any attempt to influence its political development from outside. Sovereign democracy, in this sense, meant the 'recognition of the right of every people to development free of external interference, and the primacy of international law'.[201]

Others were less convinced. Former Prime Minister Yevgenii Primakov, for one, was 'categorically opposed' to the use of a term of any kind that could 'lead to the denial of such general human values as the separation of powers, freedom of choice and so on'.[202] Writing elsewhere, he professed to understand why Surkov had chosen to call their democracy 'sovereign': it was a way of underlining that Russian democracy was exercised within its own state boundaries. Surkov, presumably, had also wished to emphasise the independent nature of the Russian form of democracy, and the inadmissibility of any attempt to impose a different model from outside. But it was a term that had major shortcomings. Not least, it could be used by critics in other countries, who could represent it as a departure from generally accepted democratic principles. And the term itself was 'very doubtful'. Could there be a 'non-sovereign democracy', and if so, what would it look like? In any case, sovereignty in the modern world was far from absolute, as states routinely delegated many of their powers to supranational bodies such as the United Nations. There could even be circumstances (if the Security Council allowed) in which a country could represent such a threat to regional or global security that external intervention into its domestic affairs would be justified. Why, apart from this, did Surkov limit his comparisons to Western models of democracy when other models were available, such as India or some of the moderate Islamic states?[203]

For others, 'sovereign democracy' was nothing less than a throwback to the Soviet period, when there had been such terms as 'socialist democracy' and 'people's democracy'; it was 'absolutely meaningless' in itself.[204] And there were still more pointed criticisms, including the charge that the new doctrine was simply an attempt to obscure the grossly unequal nature of Russia's postcommunist society. It was less Surkov's 'nationalisation of the future' and rather more a 'privatisation of the present', argued the economist and former presidential candidate Sergei Glaz'ev. Russia had one of the lowest levels of spending on social security of any country in the world; it was using its oil to supply NATO, and the proceeds to support the dollar; the only increase in 'freedom' had been the freedom of government from any kind of democratic accountability.[205] Rather more important, Dmitri Medvedev, at this time Ivanov's counterpart as first deputy prime minister, was also opposed to the new orthodoxy – or at least to the way in which it had been formulated. Playing games with definitions, he thought, was always a doubtful exercise. 'Sovereign democracy', in this respect, was 'far from ideal'; it would have been more appropriate to speak of 'genuine democracy', or of 'democracy within a comprehensive state sovereignty'. And it left a 'strange aftertaste', suggesting they had in mind some kind of 'different, non-traditional democracy' that would create an unfortunate impression, not least in other countries.[206]

Surkov, speaking a month later, declared himself less interested in the term itself and rather more in what it represented. Only a people who had some overall idea of who they were and where they were going could develop organically. And only if they developed their own discourse, a 'national ideology' that was acceptable at least to the majority and ideally to all, would they be taken seriously in the wider world. Sovereign democracy was just the first step in this process, and it made no claim to represent the 'truth in the final instance'.[207] They were 'not in some kind of philology club', he told a United Russia meeting in September 2006. It hardly mattered what terms they used, or how they were used; it was the substance of 'sovereign democracy' that alone concerned him. This meant a set of policies that would give Russia back her status as a major world power that was independent in reality and not just on paper, and an economy that was not over-dependent on the export of natural resources. Almost all the world's countries had some reference to sovereignty in their constitutions; but only a few dozen had the military and economic capability that allowed them to make their own decisions, instead of simply carrying out instructions that came from outside their national boundaries. 'Do we want to be a self-sufficient country', asked Surkov, 'or should we rely on other, more powerful nations for help? Who said that we should stop trying to be a sovereign people?'[208]

United Russia was revising its party programme at about this time, and different views were being expressed about whether the concept of sovereign democracy should be incorporated as a part of its official ideology. In the event the congress adopted a 'programmatic declaration' in December 2006 that called for a 'strategy of qualitative renewal of the country on the principles of sovereign democracy' and went on to define it in terms that were clearly reminiscent of those Surkov had been proposing.[209] In the words of the declaration, the party's strategy was a 'qualitative renewal of the country as a sovereign democracy', which meant

- the 'right of a people to make its own choice on the basis of its own traditions and law';
- the 'opportunity to take an effective part in the formation of a fair world order';
- the 'identity of external and domestic security';
- the 'condition of our historical competitiveness, that is the right publicly to formulate and stand up for our national-state interests';
- and the 'unconditional recognition of universal democratic values while accepting a variety of national models for their realisation'.[210]

Sovereign democracy was also a feature of the party manifesto at the Duma election a year later, where it was related to the 'inalienable right of the free Russian people to define their historical fate independently and use the national wealth in the interests of the entire nation and every citizen'.[211]

Medvedev took the opportunity of a visit to the World Economic Forum at Davos in January 2007 to restate his objections, speaking (for this part of his address) in English. Russia, he told the gathering, had been through all kinds of crises during the twentieth century. Now they were constructing new institutions, based on the 'fundamental principles of fully-fledged democracy'. Democracy, he repeated, had 'no need of additional definitions'; it meant a market economy, the rule of law and the accountability of government to the society as a whole. And not one undemocratic state had ever prospered, as 'freedom [was] better than non-freedom'.[212] Speaking a few days later at a meeting of youth organisations in Moscow, he emphasised the common ground that all the same united the two leaders. As Medvedev explained, he and Surkov had simply been having a 'friendly conversation'; he was prepared himself to accept a variety of definitions, and in any case definitions were not the issue. His own preference was for the 'classic' formulation he had been taught in university, which was a 'universal construction'. But the differences between himself and Surkov on the matter had been no more than 'terminological'. There was in fact very general agreement that democracy could 'only be effective in conditions of fully-fledged state sovereignty'; equally, that sovereignty in the sense of a government that was independent inside and outside its own frontiers could 'only achieve results under a democratic political regime'.[213]

Putin himself, throughout the discussion, had remained studiously neutral. Meeting the United Russia Duma fraction in July 2006, he congratulated them on their elaboration of the notion of a Russia that would develop as a 'sovereign democratic state'.[214] But asked about sovereign democracy at his regular meeting with Western journalists the following September, he told them he preferred to leave the task of defining the new concept to the 'experts' and did not interfere in their work.[215] A year later, he was more dismissive: sovereign democracy, he now suggested, was a 'controversial term', and one that confused two elements: sovereignty was an attribute of Russia's relations with other countries, and democracy a matter of its domestic politics.[216] When United Russia held its 11th Congress at St Petersburg in December 2009, with Putin now party leader, its official ideology became a 'Russian conservatism', although one that would be based on the country's 'own history, culture and spirituality' and which would also seek to strengthen its 'sovereignty'.[217] Whatever their apparent divergences, it was reasonable to conclude that Russia's political class was actually agreed on the fundamentals: that a meaningful democracy was one in which government decisions could be taken without being unduly influenced by the outside world; that this was more likely to be achieved in a country that was economically and militarily strong; and that any attempt to articulate an alternative was unhelpful, unpatriotic and possibly subversive.

Russians and 'democracy'

Russians themselves were largely outside this discussion; indeed, it was not entirely clear they had a single or coherent view of the kinds of issues that were involved. Did ordinary Russians, for instance, wish to live in a 'democracy'? On the evidence of a succession of national surveys, a substantial majority wished to do so (as many as 70 per cent took this view in 2010, more than four times as many as those who were against it: Table 8.4). But this was in response to a question that simply asked, yes or no, if respondents were in favour of an undefined 'democracy' for their country, and gave no indication of their strength of feeling. Nearly as many (67 per cent) agreed with the more grudging Churchill proposition, that democracy 'had its faults, but it [was] better than any other form of government'; all the same, only 13 per cent 'agreed entirely', and 21 per cent took the opposite view. A different but related question asked respondents if they agreed that a 'strong leader was better than any laws'; in this case there were more who preferred the 'authoritarian' to the 'democratic' option, perhaps influenced by the apparent success of the Putin presidency.[218] This was the opposite of the position in the established

Table 8.4 **Russians and 'democracy', 2005–2010**

	2005	2006	2007	2008	2009	2010
Does Russia need democracy?						
Yes, Russia needs democracy	66	56	67	62	57	70
No, a democratic form of government is not for Russia	21	27	17	20	23	17

Source: adapted from 'Predstavleniya rossiyan o demokratii', 15 October 2009, at www.levada.ru/press/
2009101501.print.html, last accessed 20 September 2010, and (for 2010) from the author's survey;
rounded percentages.

democracies, such as Britain, the United States and Japan, where a 'strong leader who does not bother with parliament and elections' was rejected by two or three to one.[219]

What, moreover, was the 'democracy' Russians thought they supported? The standard definitions in the academic literature were hardly any different from those in Western textbooks. Democracy, in one 'short dictionary of political language', was a

form of the political organisation of society based on the principles of popular rule (the creation of representative bodies of government), political pluralism and multiparty politics, the equality of all before the law, [and] observance of the constitutional rights and freedoms of citizens.[220]

In the *Great Juridical Dictionary*, published in a third edition in 2007, democracy was to be understood as a

form of state structure based on the recognition of such principles as the supremacy of the constitution and laws, popular rule and political pluralism, the freedom and equality of citizens, [and] the inalienability of human rights.

In a modern society, this meant the

rule of the majority while protecting the rights of the minority, the elective nature of the main state bodies, recognition of the rights and political freedoms of citizens and of their equal rights, the supremacy of the law, constitutionalism [and] the separation of powers.[221]

It was, however, accepted that there was no 'no generally recognised understanding that [suited] everybody'.[222]

For ordinary Russians, 'democracy' had a rather different meaning; or at any rate, its various components were weighted rather differently (Table 8.5). According to the survey evidence of early 2010, it was more likely to be associated with 'order and stability' than anything else, followed closely by the various freedoms of expression. Another very substantial proportion identified it with economic prosperity (in 2008 and 2009 this was the most popular response), and a smaller but still substantial minority defined it as 'strict conformity with the law'. Relatively few associated democracy with the direct election of government officials, an essential part of any form of representative democracy, and very

Table 8.5 What, in your view, is 'democracy' (1996–2010)?

	1996	2000	2004	2008	2009	2010
Order and stability	29	28	29	41	37	29
Freedom of speech, expression and conscience	24	37	44	46	38	28
Economic prosperity	24	33	31	47	39	23
Strict observance of the law	21	29	24	26	29	17
Direct election of all government leaders	9	15	18	15	13	8
Opportunity for people to do what they like	8	10	6	7	7	5
Empty talk	14	10	11	3	5	5
Protection of minority rights	3	5	6	5	7	2
Majority rule	2	6	3	3	3	1
Anarchy and powerlessness	7	6	6	2	3	1

Source: adapted from 'Chto takoe demokratiya i nuzhna li ona Rossii?', 21 January 2010, www.levada.ru/press/2010012105.print.html, last accessed 20 September 2010 (several responses were permitted) and (for 2010) from the author's survey (one response required); don't knows and non-responses account for residuals.

Table 8.6 What are the positive and negative features of 'democracy' (2006)?

'Positive' features		'Negative' features	
A fair system of government with the equal participation of all citizens	27	Windbaggery, demagogy	19
Guarantees that government will respect the rights and freedoms of citizens	27	A form of government suitable for 'normal countries', but not for us	12
Opportunity to criticise the authorities at all levels	13	Chaos, disorder, anarchy	11
Separation of powers and accountability of government to citizens	9	A system of government that has shown its inadequacy in Russia	10
Free competition of political parties for the support of the voters	9	The lack of a firm hand in government, dispersion of responsibility	8

Source: adapted from 'Predstavleniya rossiyan o demokratii', as Table 8.4 above.

few indeed associated it with the protection of minority rights (on other evidence Russians had little attachment to the rights of drug addicts or homosexuals, or even their right to exist, although they were more understanding about alcoholics and the congenitally disabled).[223] However they understood it, what did ordinary Russians think were the positive and negative features of 'democracy' as a form of government? For substantial numbers, it was at least a 'fair system' and one that was likely to ensure that government respected the 'rights and freedoms of citizens'; but at the same time, it was a system that was prone to 'windbaggery', and one that was perhaps better suited to 'more normal countries' than Russia (Table 8.6). There were other, more hostile judgements.

Table 8.7 What kind of democracy does Russia need (2005–2010)?

	2005	2006	2007	2008	2009	2010
A special kind that accords with national traditions	45	48	47	45	43	52
The same as in the developed countries of Europe and America	24	18	22	20	23	21
The kind that existed in the USSR	16	13	10	13	14	14
Russia does not need democracy	6	10	7	8	7	6

Source: as Table 8.4.

Table 8.8 What would be the most suitable political system for Russia (2010)?

The Soviet system, but in a different, more democratic form	33
The political system that exists today	25
The Soviet system that we had before *perestroika*	14
Democracy of the Western kind	14
Don't know/no answer	14

Source: Russia 2010 survey; a single response was invited to a list of options; rounded percentages.

Whether or not they regarded 'democracy' as desirable, did ordinary Russians think their own government could be characterised in this way? Just 4 per cent, in our 2010 survey, thought Russia could already be seen as an 'established democracy'. Another 25 per cent regarded Russia as a country that was at least moving towards democracy, and rather larger numbers (35 per cent) thought Russia was 'more democratic than it was before'; but 19 per cent thought it had been 'more democratic in the Soviet period'. If they were to be allowed to choose their own form of democratic government, what would it be? There was no more than modest support for the form that existed in the developed countries of Europe and America; some favoured 'the kind of democracy that had existed in the USSR', but the most popular option of all, with the support of more than a half of all respondents in our 2010 survey, was a kind of democracy that reflected Russia's own traditions (Table 8.7). If the choice was not 'a form of democracy' but simply a form of government, it was in fact a 'Soviet' system of some kind that found the most support, especially if it was a (perhaps mythical) 'more democratic' Soviet system (Table 8.8). Predictably, the straightforwardly 'Soviet' option had twice as much support among the over-60s as among the under-30s; under-30s, even so, were more likely to favour a 'democratic' Soviet system than a Western-style democracy.

Most Russians were more interested in how they were to make a living than in abstractions such as the label that should be attached to their political system;[224] and as we suggested at the start of this chapter, definitions in any case were hardly the issue. What, we asked, were the *mechanisms* of government, how effective did they appear to be and how did they compare with similar mechanisms in other countries? Russians themselves were certainly under no illusion that the end of communist rule had of itself handed them a means by which they could hold their government effectively to account. How much respect did they think was accorded to their human rights, we asked in our 2010 survey. About a quarter thought 'a great deal' (2 per cent) or at least 'some' (23 per cent); but far larger numbers thought 'not very much' (37 per cent) or 'none at all' (36 per cent). Large numbers thought public officials 'rarely' (30 per cent) or 'hardly ever' (53 per cent) treated citizens equally, perhaps because 'the majority' (39 per cent) or 'almost all of them' (33 per cent) were corrupt. And an overwhelming 86 per cent were largely (41 per cent) or entirely (45 per cent) in agreement that it was 'very difficult for ordinary people to secure their legal rights'.

Russians, similarly, had little faith that they could exercise much influence over the government that spoke in their name. Just 14 per cent, in early 2010, thought they had at least some degree of influence in matters of this kind; 85 per cent took the opposite view, a level that was remarkably consistent except for the short periods when election campaigns were taking place.[225] Why was this? For 47 per cent, it was because officials were 'only interested in the views of their immediate superiors and ignore[d] the opinions and needs of ordinary citizens'; another 21 per cent thought government was simply failing to communicate with the wider public about its activity, but 18 per cent thought it was because 'elections, referendums and free discussions' had come to play an 'increasingly marginal role in society'. The outcome, at any rate, was that (in the words of the Levada Centre) a 'majority of Russians [felt] a significant degree of alienation from the state', with substantial numbers who thought they had no means of influencing its decisions; as a result, 'government' and 'people' were like 'autonomous subjects, with little relationship to each other'. Indeed, most ordinary Russians did their best to avoid any kind of contact with government if they could possibly do so (62 per cent), and very few (19 per cent) were prepared to take a more active part in public life in order to attempt to influence its decisions – more often than not, because they thought it would have not the slightest effect (34 per cent).[226]

It was, of course, a universal that citizens did not believe their views were taken sufficiently into account by those who governed them. A substantial Western literature has identified a deepening disenchantment with established forms of politics worldwide: turnouts in national, local and European elections have been falling, the membership of political parties has been declining, levels of distrust in government and those who exercise it have been increasing, and there has been a more general increase in disaffection with civic institutions of all kinds, including the churches, the banks and the agencies of law enforcement as well as parliaments and those who hold seats in them.[227] The view of Russians themselves was that they had much in common, in these respects, with their counterparts in Western Europe and North America. But rightly or wrongly, they thought they had even less influence than citizens in those other countries (Table 8.9). More than half, in Russia itself, thought they had 'no influence at all' over the

Table 8.9 Comparing political influence in Russia and the West, 2010

	to a significant extent	to some extent	to an insignificant extent	not at all
In Russia	2	17	25	53
In the West	8	22	17	38

Source: Russia 2010 survey; rounded percentages. The question wording was 'To what extent can people like you directly influence the actions of central government?'; and 'To what extent can people like you directly influence the actions of central government in Western countries such as Great Britain, Germany and the United States?'

actions of government. In 'Western countries such as Great Britain, Germany and the United States', just over a third thought ordinary citizens had no influence at all, but almost as many (30 per cent) thought ordinary citizens had 'some' or even a 'significant degree of influence' over the actions of their elected government.

CONCLUSION

In the end, it was for Russians themselves to decide what kind of 'democracy', or any other political philosophy, they wished to adopt as the basis of their postcommunist system. What could less readily be discounted was the accumulating evidence that the distribution of power in the years after Putin's accession had shifted so far towards the central authorities that the achievement of other objectives was in peril. It was understandable, after the near-collapse of the federation during the Yeltsin years, that later presidents would place a heavy emphasis on the effectiveness of government, which meant in practice the powers of the federal authorities in Moscow. It was understandable that they would have popular support in doing so, given the sharp fall in living standards that had accompanied the years of Yeltsinite 'reform'. And it was predictable that they would continue to have popular support in the years that followed, given high rates of economic growth that in turn were based on record oil prices on world markets. A larger argument could indeed be constructed in favour of a process of state-led 'modernisation' along the lines set out in President Medvedev's address of September 2009, 'Russia, Forward!' (who had ever suggested 'backwards'?), his speech two months later to the Federal Assembly, and United Russia's commitment in its new programme to an 'increase in the competitiveness of the economy on the basis of the realisation of a strategy of innovative development'.[228]

But the system of government that consolidated itself during the Putin–Medvedev years was centralised to such an extent that it generated problems of its own. If power was concentrated in the centre, it was the central authorities themselves that would be held responsible for any shortcomings. If institutions were weak, there would be little attachment to the decisions they generated unless they seemed of individual and short-term benefit. If the parliament was wholly compliant, laws would be poorly scrutinised and ministerial incompetence would not be exposed in good time. If the courts were unduly influenced by politicians or even corrupt, those who could afford to do so would try to secure the decisions they wanted by exercising their influence or paying the going rate instead of accommodating themselves to the rule of law, and foreigners would put their money somewhere safer. And if political parties were another branch of state power, they would disproportionately recruit careerists. This was certainly true of United Russia, if Putin himself was to be believed. Speaking in November 2007, he complained that the party was 'not an ideal political structure', that it lacked a 'stable ideology [or] principles for which the overwhelming majority of members would be prepared to assert themselves', and that because it was so close to government it attracted 'all kinds of hangers-on'.[229] How could it be otherwise, if a single party monopolised the positions that conveyed political influence and economic reward?

There was no indication that there would be a resolution of these issues under the Medvedev presidency. And if there was going to be, it would be difficult to do without some of the mechanisms that had been developed in Western liberal democracies to deal with the same kinds of problems. The separation of powers would have to become a real one, so that courts became independent of government. A more even balance would have to be found between an overpowerful executive and a parliament that was supposed to represent the interests of the public as a whole so that the country as a whole would find its decisions acceptable. And elections themselves would have to become more genuine contests, without unreasonable barriers to participation and with independent institutions that could monitor their conduct. The Russian tradition was indeed one in which the state had normally been strong and paternalistic. But it had other elements as well – the city assemblies that had met in the late medieval years; the self-governing peasant communities that Marx had seen as the harbinger of a communist society; the limited experience of parliamentary government that had accumulated in the early years of the twentieth century. If Russian politics was to be more effective in the future, it was likely that it would draw on these indigenous traditions as well as the experience of other countries, and that they would be used to strengthen the accountability of government to those who gave it the authority to rule.

Further reading

An influential early discussion of the 'problems of democratic transition and consolidation' was Linz and Stepan (1996); the account of postcommunist Eastern Europe was perhaps its least satisfactory section. An 'end to the transition paradigm' was signalled by Carothers in the *Journal of Democracy* (2002) and much of the subsequent discussion has taken place in the same location. On 'competitive authoritarianism', see particularly Levitsky and Way (2010), and on the 'durability of nondemocracy' Rose, Mishler and Munro (2011). The problem of a 'superpresidency' is examined in Fish (2005). The place of *siloviki* within the leadership was set out in Kryshtanovskaya and White (2003) and has been developed at book length in Soldatov and Borogan (2010); other contributions to the debate are listed in note 51. Human rights performance is most easily followed through the annual reports of Amnesty International (www.thereport. amnesty.org), Human Rights Watch (www.hrw.org) and the US Department of State's *Country Reports on Human Rights* (www.state.gov), which gives close attention to rule-of-law issues. Freedom House's annual and more occasional reports are available at-www.freedomhouse.org. Weiler (2004) is the most recent book-length study of human rights in Russia; Gilligan (2010) deals with the special issue of Chechnya. On the politics of the media, see particularly Oates (2006) and Mickiewicz (2008), and the annual monitoring of Freedom House and Reporters without Borders (www.rsf.org). On 'sovereign democracy' and what has followed it, see Evans (2008); the more recent discourse of 'modernisation' has not yet been discussed at length in the English-language literature.

Carothers, Thomas, 'The end of the transition paradigm', *Journal of Democracy*, vol. 13, no. 1 (January 2002), pp. 5–21.

Evans, Alfred B., Jr, *Power and Ideology: Vladimir Putin and the Russian Political System* (The Carl Beck Papers in Russian and East European Studies of the University of Pittsburgh, no. 1902, 2008).

Fish, M. Steven, *Democracy Derailed in Russia: The Failure of Open Politics* (Cambridge and New York: Cambridge University Press, 2005).

Gilligan, Emma, *Terror in Chechnya: Russia and the Tragedy of Civilians in War* (Princeton, NJ, and Oxford: Princeton University Press, 2010).

Kryshtanovskaya, Ol'ga, and Stephen White, 'Putin's militocracy', *Post-Soviet Affairs*, vol. 19, no. 4 (October–December 2003), pp. 289–306.

Levitsky, Steven, and Lucan A. Way, *Competitive Authoritarianism: Hybrid Regimes after the Cold War* (Cambridge and New York: Cambridge University Press, 2010).

Linz, Juan J., and Alfred Stepan, *Problems of Democratic Transition and Consolidation: Southern Europe, South America, and Post-Communist Europe* (Baltimore and London: Johns Hopkins University Press, 1996).

Mickiewicz, Ellen, *Television, Power, and the Public in Russia* (Cambridge and New York: Cambridge University Press, 2008).

Oates, Sarah, *Television, Democracy, and Elections in Russia* (Abingdon and New York: Routledge, 2006).

Rose, Richard, William Mishler and Neil Munro, *Popular Support for an Undemocratic Regime: The Changing Views of Russians* (Cambridge and New York: Cambridge University Press, 2011).

Soldatov, Andrei and Irina Borogan, *The New Nobility: The Restoration of Russia's Security State and the Enduring Legacy of the KGB* (New York: PublicAffairs, 2010).

Weiler, Jonathan, *Human Rights in Russia: A Darker Side of Reform* (Boulder, CO, and London: Lynne Rienner, 2004).

Notes

1 From communist to postcommunist rule

1. Calculated from *Narodnoe khozyaistvo SSSR za 70 let: yubileinyi statisticheskii sbornik* (Moscow: Finansy i statistika, 1987), various pages.
2. *XXIV S"ezd Kommunisticheskoi partii Sovetskogo Soyuza 30 marta – 9 aprelya 1971 goda: stenograficheskii otchet*, 2 vols. (Moscow: Politizdat, 1971), vol. I, p. 482.
3. A. A. Gromyko and B. N. Ponomarev, eds., *Istoriya vneshnei politiki SSSR, 1917–1980*, 2 vols. (Moscow: Nauka, 1981), vol. II, p. 666. Gromyko expressed very similar views to the 24th Party Congress in 1971: 'There is not a single question of any significance that can be resolved without the Soviet Union or in spite of it' (*XXIV S"ezd*, vol. I, p. 482).
4. *Vestnik MGU: nauchnyi kommunizm*, no. 2, 1990, p. 90.
5. *Voprosy istorii KPSS*, no. 10, 1989, p. 18 (reporting the testimony of K. T. Mazurov).
6. *XXV S"ezd Kommunisticheskoi partii Sovetskogo Soyuza 24 fevralya – 5 marta 1976 goda: stenograficheskii otchet*, 3 vols. (Moscow: Politizdat, 1976), vol. II, pp. 309–10.
7. *Vedomosti Verkhovnogo Soveta SSSR*, no. 19, 1976, item 318; *Pravda*, 7 May 1976, p. 1.
8. *Leonid Il'ich Brezhnev: kratkii biograficheskii ocherk* (Moscow: Politizdat, 1976), p. 4.
9. *Pravda*, 17 November 1977, p. 1.
10. *Vedomosti Verkhovnogo Soveta SSSR*, no. 8, 1978, art. 117.
11. *Pravda*, 22 April 1979, p. 1; *ibid.*, 26 April 1979, p. 2 (the recipient was Alexander Chakovsky).
12. *XXVI S"ezd Kommunisticheskoi partii Sovetskogo Soyuza 23 fevralya – 3 marta 1981 goda: stenograficheskii otchet*, 3 vols. (Moscow: Politizdat, 1981), vol. I, p. 110 (Viktor Grishin).
13. Yu. V. Aksyutin, ed., *L. I. Brezhnev: materialy k biografii* (Moscow: Politizdat, 1991), p. 276.
14. *XXVI S"ezd*, vol. II, p. 242.
15. *Pravda*, 20 December 1981, p. 2.
16. On state awards see Dmitrii Volkogonov, *Sem' vozhdei*, 2 vols. (Moscow: Novosti, 1995), vol. II, p. 69; the comparison with Zhukov is from Zhores Medvedev, *Andropov: His Life and Death*, rev. edn (Oxford: Blackwell, 1984), pp. 103–4. On the foreign awards see Aleksandr Maisuryan, *Drugoi Brezhnev* (Moscow: Vagrius, 2004), p. 433.
17. Roy Medvedev in *Rabochii klass i sovremennyi mir*, no. 6, 1988, p. 155.
18. *Pravda*, 19 May 1982, p. 2; it had originally appeared in a Kursk youth paper, *Komsomolets*, on 1 January 1924. A television broadcast showed a Politburo member pointing out the rediscovered poem to the Soviet leader, although he appeared not to recognise it (*The Times*, 20 May 1982, p. 14).
19. Roy Medvedev in *Moskovskie novosti*, no. 37, 1988, p. 8; Brezhnev's clinical death and subsequent degeneration was also recalled by his personal photographer (*Izvestiya*, 10 July 2009, p. 5). Medvedev, in his still-incomplete biography, noted that the Soviet leader had suffered several other heart attacks after which he had 'several times' to be brought back to life (*Lichnost' i epokha: politicheskii portret L. I. Brezhneva*, vol. I (Moscow: Novosti, 1991), pp. 5–6). Another well-placed source, foreign policy adviser Georgii Arbatov, dated Brezhnev's serious illness from December 1974; after that he 'ruled' but did not govern (*Znamya*, no. 9, 1990, p. 216). Marshal Akhromeev recalled similarly that after his heart attack in 1976 Brezhnev had 'stopped working as head of state and party' (S. F. Akhromeev and G. M. Kornienko, *Glazami marshala i diplomata* (Moscow: Mezhdunarodnye otnosheniya, 1992), p. 15). Brezhnev's doctor, Evgenii Chazov, ascribed 'fatal influence' to an attractive nurse with whom the Soviet leader had latterly established a 'special relationship' (*Zdorov'e i vlast'* (Moscow: Novosti, 1992), p. 117; Vladimir Medvedev, *Chelovek za spinoi* (Moscow: Russlit, 1994), p. 151). A wider selection of memoirs appears in *Leonid*

Brezhnev v vospominaniyakh, razmyshleniyakh, suzhdeniyakh (Rostov-on-Don: Feniks, 1998).

20. A. S. Chernyaev, *Moya zhizn' i moe vremya* (Moscow: Mezhdunarodnye otnosheniya, 1995), p. 437; and on the Czechoslovakian experience in 1981, Medvedev, *Chelovek za spinoi*, pp. 101–2.

21. *Argumenty i fakty*, no. 43, 1996, p. 9.

22. A. M. Aleksandrov-Agentov, *Ot Kollontai do Gorbacheva* (Moscow: Mezhdunarodnye otnosheniya, 1994), p. 273. M. S. Dokuchaev, a member of the KGB division that ensured the security of Soviet leaders, notes that Brezhnev had attempted to resign in 1979: *Moskva. Kreml'. Okhrana* (Moscow: Biznes-Press, 1995), pp. 173–4; so did a member of the Kremlin guard, Sergei Krasikov (*Vozle vozhdei* (Moscow: Sovremennik, 1997), p. 425). Dmitri Volkogonov, however, suggests that Brezhnev was simply trying to manoeuvre his closest colleagues into another public declaration of the Soviet leader's 'irreplaceability' (*Sem' vozhdei*, vol. II, p. 79).

23. M. S. Gorbachev, *Zhizn' i reformy*, 2 vols. (Moscow: Novosti, 1995), vol. I, p. 217. Brezhnev's foreign policy adviser, A. M. Aleksandrov-Agentov, recalled that Politburo meetings 'began to last just an hour, or forty-five minutes' (*Ot Kollontai*, p. 273); so did trade union leader Stepan Shalaev (*Izvestiya Tsentral'nogo komiteta* [hereafter *TsK*] *KPSS*, no. 2, 1989, p. 246); *Pravda* editor Viktor Afanas'ev recalled meetings lasting 'an hour or two, not more' (*4-ya vlast' i 4 genseka* (Moscow: Kedr, 1994), p. 38), and Moscow party leader Viktor Grishin meetings that were latterly of an hour and a half's duration (*Ot Khrushcheva do Gorbacheva. Politicheskie portrety pyati gensekov i A. N. Kosygina. Memuary* (Moscow: Askol, 1996), p. 5). Yegor Ligachev, who as Tomsk first secretary occasionally took part in Politburo meetings, recalled that they lasted forty minutes or so in the late Brezhnev years, but 'hours, without a break' under his successor (E. K. Ligachev, *Predosterezhenie* (Moscow: Pravda Internashnl, 1998), p. 52). Memoirs agree that the later Brezhnev was very different from the General Secretary of earlier years: for Afanas'ev there were 'two Brezhnevs' (*4-ya vlast'*, p. 30); Georgii Arbatov, similarly, knew 'two Brezhnevs – one before and one after his illness' (*Zatyanuvsheesya vyzdorovlenie (1953–1985 gg.): svidetel'stvo sovremennika* (Moscow: Mezhdunarodnye otnosheniya, 1991), p. 288); and Gromyko noted that

Brezhnev had 'not [been] able to work' for the last two or three years of his administration (*Kommunist Belorussii*, no. 4, 1990, p. 51). Even Gorbachev conceded that the Brezhnev of the late 1960s and early 1970s was 'nothing like the cartoon figure' he later became (*Zhizn' i reformy*, vol. I, p. 124).

24. Akhromeev and Kornienko, *Glazami*, p. 15.

25. Yuri Churbanov, *Ya rasskazhu vse, kak bylo . . .*, 2nd edn (Moscow: Nezavisimaya gazeta, 1993), p. 1.

26. Medvedev, *Lichnost' i epokha*, pp. 97–101; and for the view that he had become the 'second person in the party', Medvedev, *Chelovek za spinoi*, p. 119 (similarly Roy Medvedev in *Moskovskie novosti*, no. 46, 1997, p. 18).

27. Medvedev, *Andropov*, pp. 93–6. Tsvigun's obituary appeared in *Pravda*, 21 January 1982, p. 2. Rumours of suicide were strengthened by the fact that Brezhnev, his brother-in-law, was not among the signatories; confirmation that his death was by suicide appears in the memoirs of Brezhnev's bodyguard (Medvedev, *Chelovek za spinoi*, p. 148).

28. Medvedev, *Andropov*, pp. 93–6.

29. Dusko Doder, *Shadows and Whispers: Power Politics inside the Kremlin from Brezhnev to Gorbachev* (New York: Random House, 1986), p. 62; Fisheries Minister Alexander Ishkov was obliged to resign over the caviare scandal (*Pravda*, 7 February 1979, p. 6), and a deputy minister was executed for bribe-taking (*ibid.*, 27 April 1982, p. 3).

30. N. I. Ryzhkov, *Desyat' let velikikh potryasenii* (Moscow: Kniga, prosveshchenie, miloserdie, 1995), p. 56.

31. Doder, *Shadows and Whispers*, pp. 94–5 (the report of Medunov's dismissal 'in connection with a transfer to other work' appeared in *Pravda*, 24 July 1982, p. 2); on the dismissal of the manager of Gastronom No. 1, see *Moskovskaya pravda*, 14 April 1983, p. 3 (the arrests had taken place the previous November and December, just before the death of the party leader: *Argumenty i fakty: Moskva*, no. 52, 2007, p. 47, which examines the case in retrospect). Brezhnev's daughter found a biographer in Stanley Landau, *Galina Brezhnev and Her Gypsy Lover* (London: Quartet, 1989); she died in the summer of 1998 (*Izvestiya*, 2 July 1998, p. 7). The manager of Gastronom No. 1, with whom she had been associated, was executed in the summer of 1984 (*Vechernyaya Moskva*, 13 July 1984, p. 2).

32. *Pravda*, 12 November 1982, p. 1.

33. Yu. V. Andropov, *Izbrannye rechi i stat'i*, 2nd edn (Moscow: Politizdat, 1983), pp. 209–18. Biographies include Zhores Medvedev, *Andropov*; Roy Medvedev, *Gensek s Lubyanki* (Nizhnii Novgorod: Leta, 1993); and Jonathan Steele and Eric Abraham, *Andropov in Power* (Oxford: Martin Robertson, 1983).

34. Gorbachev discusses their relations during this period in *Zhizn' i reformy*, vol. I, pp. 241–6.

35. *Pravda*, 11 February 1984, p. 1. Andropov's doctor later reported that the General Secretary had read about 400 pages a day although he had the use of only one eye, and that he remained lucid even after his liver, lungs and kidneys had stopped functioning: *Moskovskie novosti*, no. 8, 1991, p. 11.

36. Gorbachev, *Zhizn' i reformy*, vol. I, pp. 234, 248–9. Viktor Grishin, in his own memoirs, insisted that Andropov had 'never included Gorbachev in the inner circle of party leaders', still less identified him as a successor (*Ot Khrushcheva do Gorbacheva*, p. 66, similarly p. 70); Ligachev, however, is equally insistent that Gorbachev was seen as a possible leader at this time (*Predosterezhenie*, pp. 57–8), and this view is more widely supported in the memoir literature.

37. Gorbachev, *Zhizn' i reformy*, vol. I, pp. 248–50.

38. *Pravda*, 14 February 1984, p. 1. There was no real alternative to the election of Chernenko, in the view of Vitalii Vorotnikov, as he was already the 'second person' in the leadership (*A bylo eto tak . . . Iz dnevnika chlena Politbyuro TsK KPSS* (Moscow: Sovet veteranov knigoizdaniya, 1995), p. 37).

39. *Pravda*, 16 February 1984, p. 1.

40. See, for instance, *The Observer* (London), 19 February 1984, p. 12; Medvedev, *Andropov*, p. 226. Subsequent memoirs have disputed that Gorbachev had, in fact, a formal position of this kind: Ryzhkov, *Desyat' let*, p. 57, and similarly Vorotnikov, *A bylo eto tak*, pp. 39–40. Ligachev, however, recalled that it was Chernenko's own proposal that Gorbachev should chair the Secretariat during his leadership and that he should occupy on this basis the 'unofficial second post in the upper party hierarchy' (*Predosterezhenie*, p. 65).

41. *Pervaya sessiya Verkhovnogo Soveta SSSR (odinnadtsatyi sozyv) 11–12 aprelya 1984 goda: stenograficheskii otchet* (Moscow: Izvestiya, 1984), pp. 38–42.

42. See particularly the film *Young Years on the Border*, which recorded Chernenko's 'courage and fortitude' in the border guards service: *Izvestiya*, 1 December 1984, p. 4. Chernenko's lack of personality is noted in Mark Galeotti, *Gorbachev and His Revolution* (London: Macmillan, 1997), p. 41.

43. *Pravda*, 1 March 1985, p. 1.

44. *Trud*, 12 March 1985, p. 2.

45. For the decision see *Trud*, 12 March 1985, p. 1; and for the views of regional party secretaries, Gorbachev, *Zhizn' i reformy*, vol. I, p. 266. According to a well-placed observer, Grigorii Romanov was Gorbachev's only real challenger at the Politburo meeting that preceded the plenum, not Viktor Grishin (Valerii Legostaev in *Obozrevatel'*, no. 15, 1994, pp. 138–9). Dokuchaev (*Moskva. Kreml'. Okhrana*, pp. 205–6) claims that Romanov had at first proposed Grishin, but this version is not supported by other accounts or by the secretary's minutes (Centre for the Preservation of Contemporary Documentation (TsKhSD), *fond* 89, *perechen'* 36, doc. 16, 11 March 1985). According to Ligachev, Grishin had clearly been angling for the succession, but he had been outmanoeuvred by Foreign Minister Gromyko who stood up at once and proposed Gorbachev, followed by Prime Minister Tikhonov and all the other members (*Predosterezhenie*, p. 109). Gromyko, whose intervention was clearly decisive, had discussed the position beforehand with his son Anatolii and Alexander Yakovlev and had agreed to take the initiative (Anatolii Gromyko, *V labirintakh Kremlya: vospominaniya i razmyshleniya syna* (Moscow: Avtor, 1997), pp. 94–6). Ryzhkov (*Desyat' let*, pp. 74–6) confirms that there was no opposition to Gorbachev's election; Kunaev recalls that all including he were in favour ('O moem vremeni', part 3, *Prostor*, no. 12, 1991, pp. 2–44, at pp. 3–4); so does Vorotnikov (there was 'no discussion [and] no alternative candidates, still less a struggle': *A bylo eto tak*, p. 57); and so does Gorbachev himself, although he had already told his wife that they '[couldn't] go on living like this' (*Zhizn' i reformy*, vol. I, pp. 265 and more generally 265–72). His wife also recalled this memorable phrase: R. M. Gorbacheva, *Ya nadeyus'* (Moscow: Novosti, 1991), p. 14. According to Ligachev, local party first secretaries were prepared to force the nomination of Gorbachev at the plenum if the Politburo had recommended otherwise (*Predosterezhenie*, pp. 108–9). Gromyko's speech is reported in the official record (*Materialy vneocherednogo Plenuma*

Tsentral'nogo komiteta KPSS 11 marta 1985 goda (Moscow: Politizdat, 1985), pp. 6–8). According to Eduard Shevardnadze's recollections, he added that Gorbachev had a 'nice smile and an iron hand' ('O proshedshem i budushchem', *Druzhba narodov*, no. 11, 2006, p. 128), although this remark does not appear in the published proceedings.

46. I owe this anecdote to Archie Brown. Marshal Sokolov commented similarly, leaving the Kremlin: 'at last we have a leader' (Akhromeev and Kornienko, *Glazami*, p. 35).

47. M. S. Gorbachev, *Izbrannye rechi i stat'i*, 7 vols. (Moscow: Politizdat, 1987–90), vol. II, p. 129.

48. For Nikolai Ryzhkov, for instance, the origins of *perestroika* dated 'from the beginning of 1983, when Andropov directed us – a group of Central Committee officials, including myself and Gorbachev – to prepare some basic principles of economic reform' (quoted from the interview in M. Nenashev, *Poslednee pravitel'stvo SSSR* (Moscow: Krom, 1993), p. 23). Andropov, he wrote elsewhere, was the real initiator of *perestroika*, and the word itself had been in use as early as the 1976 Party Congress (*Desyat' let*, pp. 80, 81). For Gorbachev's adviser Georgii Shakhnazarov, on the other hand, Andropov's programme was 'limited to the perfection of the system' (*Tsena svobody: reformatsiya Gorbacheva glazami ego pomoshchnika* (Moscow: Rossika/Zevs, 1993), p. 34). Gorbachev, too, believed Andropov was a 'man of his time, and one of those who was unable to break through the barrier of old ideas and values' (*Zhizn' i reformy*, vol. I, p. 247).

49. See Mark Zlotnik, 'Chernenko's program', *Problems of Communism*, vol. 31, no. 6 (November–December 1982), pp. 70–5. Chernenko's speech to people's controllers of October 1984 and his election address of February 1985 are especially relevant in this connection: *Pravda*, 6 October 1984, pp. 1–2, and 23 February 1985, pp. 1–2.

50. *Spravochnik partiinogo rabotnika*, issue 23 (Moscow: Politizdat, 1983), p. 99; Andrei Kirilenko, a Politburo and Secretariat member who was Brezhnev's exact contemporary, left the leadership at the same time 'for health reasons and at his own request'.

51. *Ibid.*, issue 24, 2 parts (Moscow: Politizdat, 1984), part 1, p. 9. Vorotnikov's subsequent appointment is in *Pravda*, 25 June 1983, p. 1.

52. *Spravochnik partiinogo rabotnika*, issue 24, part 1, p. 63. M. S. Solomentsev moved at the same time to full Politburo membership, and

KGB head Viktor Chebrikov became a candidate.

53. His obituary appeared in *Pravda*, 22 December 1984, p. 1.

54. These biographical details have been drawn from *Sostav tsentral'nykh organov KPSS, izbrannykh XXVI s"ezdom partii* (Moscow: Politizdat, 1982), and *Izvestiya TsK KPSS*, no. 1, 1989, pp. 9–31.

55. *Pravda*, 18 December 1982, p. 2.

56. *Literaturnaya gazeta*, 18 May 1988, p. 13.

57. *Spravochnik partiinogo rabotnika*, issue 24, part 1, p. 9. Medunov was later expelled from the CPSU itself: *Pravda*, 24 March 1989, p. 2.

58. *Izvestiya*, 9 November 1984, p. 6.

59. *Literaturnaya gazeta*, 18 May 1988, p. 11; his wife's suicide is reported in T. Gdlyan and E. Dodolev, *Mafiya vremen bezzakoniya* (Yerevan: Izdatel'stvo AN Armenii, 1991), p. 113, and his son's loss of position in *Dokumenty TsK VLKSM 1983* (Moscow: Molodaya gvardiya, 1984), p. 13.

60. Medvedev, *Andropov*, pp. 97–8.

61. *Pravda*, 31 December 1988, p. 3; and for his loss of state honours, *Izvestiya*, 25 July 1989, p. 8. On the Uzbek cotton scandal, see Arkadii Vaksberg, *The Soviet Mafia* (London: Weidenfeld & Nicolson, 1991), and T. Gdlyan and N. Ivanov, *Kremlevskoe delo*, 2nd edn (Moscow: Gramota, 1996).

62. *Izvestiya*, 16 January 1988, p. 3.

63. *Istochnik*, no. 2, 1994, pp. 71–3.

64. *Izvestiya*, 25 July 1989, p. 8, and 29 September 1989, p. 3.

65. *Pravda*, 7 January 1988, p. 1.

66. Brezhnev was assessed 'negatively' or 'very negatively' by 89 per cent of respondents and positively by just 7 per cent, in a Moscow telephone poll; Stalin was assessed positively by 13 per cent and negatively by 37 per cent (Lenin, at this time, was evaluated positively by 94 per cent and negatively by just 1 per cent: *Argumenty i fakty*, no. 5, 1989, p. 4). Similar results were reported in *Soviet Weekly*, 18 February 1989, p. 6, and in *Dialog*, no. 2, 1990, p. 5. Brezhnev's grandson is quoted from *Moskovskie novosti*, no. 38, 1988, p. 10.

67. *Radio Liberty Research Report* RL 92 (21 February 1983) and *Pravda*, 28 December 1982, p. 3.

68. *Spravochnik partiinogo rabotnika*, issue 24, part 2, pp. 95–9.

69. For instance *Pravda*, 7 January 1985, p. 1. Gorbachev himself paid tribute in December 1984: *Izbrannye rechi i stat'i*, vol. II, p. 92. On Stakhanov's unhappy fate see *Trud*, 31 August 1988, pp. 1–2; an entirely uncritical

obituary appeared in *Pravda*, 6 November 1977, p. 8.

70. *Pravda*, 6 May 1984, pp. 1–2; *Literaturnaya gazeta*, 13 June 1984, p. 2.

71. *The Times*, 4 September 1982, p. 4 (direct dialling); the new law on the Soviet frontier was published in *Pravda*, 26 November 1982, pp. 1–3. On postal restrictions see *The Times*, 19 November 1982, p. 8.

72. In a Presidium decree the sanctions of the law were extended to the conduct of 'anti-Soviet agitation and propaganda' with funds or resources provided by 'foreign organisations': *Vedomosti Verkhovnogo Soveta SSSR*, no. 5, 1984, item 168, 30 January 1984.

73. *The Times*, 22 May 1983, p. 7 (Vladimov's deprivation of citizenship was reported in *Vedomosti Verkhovnogo Soveta SSSR*, no. 33, 1983, item 520); and *The Times*, 20 January 1983, p. 5.

74. *Vedomosti Verkhovnogo Soveta SSSR*, no. 29, 1984, item 515, and no. 51, 1983, item 797. Other cases were reported in *ibid.*, nos. 17, 23, 26, 29 and 35, items 315, 418, 474, 516 and 625 respectively, 1984.

75. *Keesing's Contemporary Archives*, 1984, p. 33120; *The Observer*, 10 February 1985, p. 19.

76. The first such report appeared in *Pravda*, 11 December 1982, p. 1. For a detailed analysis of such reports up to 1988, see John Löwenhardt, 'Politbyuro zasedaet: reported and secret meetings of the Politburo of the CPSU', *Nordic Journal of Soviet and East European Studies*, vol. 5, no. 2 (1988), pp. 157–74.

77. *Pravda*, 1 February 1983, pp. 1–2, and 30 April 1984, pp. 1–2.

78. *Ibid.*, 19 June 1983, pp. 1, 3. For a full study, see Darrell P. Slider, 'Reforming the workplace: the 1983 Soviet Law on Labour Collectives', *Soviet Studies*, vol. 37, no. 2 (April 1985), pp. 173–83.

79. *Pravda*, 21 October 1984, p. 2.

80. *Ibid.*, 15 June 1983, p. 3, and 16 June 1983, p. 3. (The Centre came into existence at the end of 1987: see Chapter 6.)

81. See *Plenum Tsentral'nogo komiteta KPSS 14–15 iyunya 1983 goda: stenograficheskii otchet* (Moscow: Politizdat, 1983).

82. *Pravda*, 11 December 1982, p. 1, and 9 January 1983, p. 3.

83. *The Times*, 14 February 1983, p. 10.

84. Yu. Korolev, *Kremlevskii sovetnik* (Moscow: Olimp, 1995), p. 226.

85. Andropov, *Izbrannye rechi i stat'i*, pp. 245–6. For a full discussion of these and related changes, see Alfred B. Evans, *Soviet Marxism-Leninism: The Decline of an Ideology* (Westport, CT: Praeger, 1993).

86. Andropov, *Izbrannye rechi i stat'i*, pp. 286–7, 212 (November 1982).

87. K. U. Chernenko, *Narod i partiya yediny: izbrannye rechi i stat'i* (Moscow: Politizdat, 1984), p. 246. Chernenko expressed similar sentiments in his 'Na uroven' trebovanii razvitogo sotsializma', *Kommunist*, no. 18, 1984, pp. 3–21.

88. See his articles in *Voprosy filosofii*, no. 10, 1982, pp. 16–29, and no. 2, 1984, pp. 116–23.

89. Gorbachev, *Izbrannye rechi i stat'i*, vol. III, p. 269. For further discussion of this important debate, see Ernst Kux, 'Contradictions in Soviet socialism', *Problems of Communism*, vol. 33, no. 6 (November–December 1984), pp. 1–27, and Stephen White and Alex Pravda, eds., *Ideology and Soviet Politics* (London: Macmillan, 1988), chs. 1 and 5.

90. *Materialy vneocherednogo Plenuma*, pp. 7–8.

91. Tsentr po khraneniyu sovremennoi dokumentatsii, Moscow, *fond* 89, *perechen'* 36, doc. 16, 11 March 1985 (also published in *Istochnik*, no. 0, 1993, pp. 66–75); Gorbachev provided the same assurance on matters of foreign policy at the Politburo meeting that took place on 21 March 1985 (Vorotnikov, *A bylo eto tak*, p. 60).

92. *Materialy vneocherednogo Plenuma*, p. 9.

93. Gorbachev referred to the 20th Congress as the starting point of reform in his opening speech at the 28th Party Congress in 1990 (*XXVIII S''ezd Kommunisticheskoi partii Sovetskogo Soyuza, 2–13 iyulya 1990 goda: stenograficheskii otchet*, 2 vols. (Moscow: Politizdat, 1991), vol. I, p. 87) and stressed its impact in his memoirs (*Zhizn' i reformy*, vol. I, pp. 83–5). A more general account of the flow of political generations is provided in Evan Mawdsley and Stephen White, *The Soviet Elite: The CPSU Central Committee and its Members, 1917–1991* (Oxford and New York: Oxford University Press, 2000).

94. Gorbachev, *Zhizn' i reformy*, vol. I, pp. 42–51. Gorbachev travelled frequently between the south and Moscow at the end of the 1940s; 'with my own eyes', as he recalled, 'I saw the destruction of Stalingrad, Rostov, Khar'kov, Orel, Kursk, Voronezh' (*Perestroika i novoe myshlenie dlya nashei stany i dlya vsego mira* (Moscow: Politizdat, 1987), pp. 37–8).

95. Gorbachev, *Zhizn' i reformy*, vol. I, pp. 37–8.

96. *Ibid.*, p. 62.

97. Zdeněk Mlynář, 'Il mio compagno di studi Mikhail Gorbaciov', *L'Unità*, 9 April 1985, p. 9.
98. Gorbachev, *Zhizn' i reformy*, vol. I, pp. 64–5.
99. The outstanding biography, generally very sympathetic to its subject, is Archie Brown, *The Gorbachev Factor* (Oxford and New York: Oxford University Press, 1996). See also Zhores Medvedev, *Gorbachev*, rev. edn (Oxford: Blackwell, 1988); Dev Murarka, *Gorbachev* (London: Hutchinson, 1988); Strobe Talbott, intro., *Mikhail S. Gorbachev: An Intimate Biography* (New York: Time, 1988); Dusko Doder and Louise Branson, *Gorbachev: Heretic in the Kremlin* (London: Macdonald, 1990); Gerd Ruge, *Gorbachev: A Biography* (London: Chatto and Windus, 1991); Martin McCauley, *Gorbachev* (London and New York: Longman, 1998); and Mark Sandle, *Gorbachev: Man of the Twenty-First Century?* (London: Hodder Arnold, 2008). The possibility that Gorbachev might have found a position in the KGB on graduation is reported in *Argumenty i fakty*, no. 41, 1992, p. 4; nothing came of it because his family had spent some time under German occupation during the Second World War.
100. Gorbachev, *Zhizn' i reformy*, vol. I, pp. 67–71.
101. *Ibid.*, pp. 38–42; Gorbachev's paternal grandfather had spent two years in prison. Gorbachev first referred to his family's experience of Stalinism in *Pravda*, 1 December 1990, p. 4.
102. Talbott, *Gorbachev*, pp. 198–202. Raisa's memoirs were published as *Ya nadeyus'*; for a biography see Urda Juergens, *Raisa* (London: Weidenfeld & Nicolson, 1990).
103. Gorbachev, *Izbrannye rechi i stat'i*, vol. V, p. 486; Medvedev, *Chelovek za spinoi*, p. 272.
104. Gorbachev, *Izbrannye rechi i stat'i*, vol. V, pp. 58–9.
105. *Izvestiya*, 24 March 1989, p. 3.
106. *Izvestiya TsK KPSS*, no. 5, 1989, pp. 57–60.
107. *Ibid.*, no. 8, 1989, p. 66.
108. *Pravda*, 11 December 1984, pp. 1–2 (full text in *Izbrannye rechi i stat'i*, vol. II, pp. 75–108).
109. *Pravda*, 21 February 1985, p. 2 (full text in *Izbrannye rechi i stat'i*, vol. II, pp. 117–28).
110. Gorbachev, *Izbrannye rechi i stat'i*, vol. 2, pp. 152–67.
111. *Spravochnik partiinogo rabotnika*, issue 26 (Moscow: Politizdat, 1986), pp. 15–16. KGB chairman Viktor Chebrikov moved at the same time from candidate to full Politburo membership. For a full record of appointments and dismissals over the entire Soviet period, see Stephen White, *The Soviet Leadership: Politburo, Orgburo and Secretariat of the CPSU, 1919–1991*, 2nd edn (Manchester: Lorton House, 1994).
112. *Spravochnik partiinogo rabotnika*, vyp. 26, p. 38. The other new Central Committee secretary was Lev Zaikov, first secretary of the Leningrad regional party organisation. Romanov, in the event, survived into his eighties (his death was reported in *Izvestiya*, 4 June 2008, p. 3).
113. *Tret'ya sessiya Verkhovnogo Soveta SSSR (odinnadtsatyi sozyv) 2–3 iyulya 1985 goda: stenograficheskii otchet* (Moscow: Izvestiya, 1985), pp. 8, 12. Outgoing Foreign Minister Gromyko was shocked by the appointment: Gromyko, *V labirintakh Kremlya*, p. 101. Shevardnadze himself was 'taken aback' when he was telephoned by Gorbachev and told to come to Moscow where the appointment was being considered; as he told the Politburo, he had no relevant experience and in any case the post had traditionally been held by a Russian, who could more obviously be seen to represent the interests of the mass of the population ('O proshedshem i budushchem', p. 127).
114. *Vedomosti Verkhovnogo Soveta SSSR*, 1985, no. 48, item 907. Tikhonov retired from the Politburo the following month: *Spravochnik partiinogo rabotnika*, issue 26, p. 39. Two other Brezhnevites, Viktor Grishin and Konstantin Rusakov, retired from the Politburo and Secretariat respectively early the following year: *ibid.*, issue 27 (Moscow: Politizdat, 1987), p. 121.
115. These and other details are taken from *Izvestiya TsK KPSS*, no. 1, 1989, pp. 9–31.
116. Roy Medvedev in *Pravda*, 30 May 1989, p. 2.
117. *Spravochnik partiinogo rabotnika*, issue 28 (Moscow: Politizdat, 1988), p. 32; the circumstances of Kunaev's expulsion are set out in *Izvestiya TsK KPSS*, no. 2, 1989, p. 44.
118. *Spravochnik partiinogo rabotnika*, vyp. 28, p. 31.
119. *Izvestiya TsK KPSS*, no. 8, 1990, p. 4.
120. *Kommunist*, no. 13, 1988, p. 11.
121. *Pervyi s"ezd narodnykh deputatov SSSR 25 maya – 9 iyunya 1989 goda: stenograficheskii otchet*, 3 vols. (Moscow: Izdanie Verkhovnogo soveta SSSR, 1989), vol. I, p. 44.
122. *Pravda*, 31 March 1989, p. 2.
123. The term had already been employed in the 1977 'Brezhnev' constitution and had been used as early as 1874 by the radical writer Nikolai Chernyshevsky, who noted – with

some accuracy – that it was a 'bureaucratic expression thought up to replace "freedom of speech"' (*Arkhiv Marksa i Engel'sa*, vol. XI (Moscow: Ogiz/Gospolitizdat, 1948), pp. 190–1; I owe this reference to my colleague James D. White). For a full account see Alec Nove, *Glasnost' and After* (Boston: Unwin Hyman, 1989); Anna Lawton, *Kinoglasnost: Soviet Cinema in Our Time* (Cambridge and New York: Cambridge University Press, 1992); on television, Ellen Mickiewicz, *Split Signals* (New York: Oxford University Press, 1988); Walter Laqueur, *The Long Road to Freedom: Russia and Glasnost* (London: Unwin Hyman, 1989); and David Wedgwood Benn, *From Glasnost to Freedom of Speech* (London: Pinter, 1992).

124. Gorbachev, *Izbrannye rechi i stat'i*, vol. II, p. 131.

125. *Sovetskaya Rossiya*, 24 November 1985, p. 1.

126. *Ibid.*, 5 January 1986, p. 3.

127. Gorbachev, *Izbrannye rechi i stat'i*, vol. III, p. 181.

128. *Ibid.*, vol. V, p. 408.

129. *Ibid.*, vol. III, p. 162, and vol. V, p. 401 (November 1987).

130. *Ibid.*, vol. IV, p. 373.

131. *Ibid.*, vol. V, pp. 397–402.

132. *Pravda*, 6 February 1988, p. 1 (a copy of the Court's decision appeared in *Izvestiya TsK KPSS*, no. 1, 1989, p. 121); Bukharin's readmission into the Communist Party was reported in *Pravda*, 10 July 1988, p. 1, and into the Academy of Sciences in *ibid.*, 21 October 1988, p. 2.

133. An early reassessment by V. Ivanov in *Sovetskaya Rossiya*, 27 September 1987, p. 4, noted Trotsky's willpower and personal courage but also emphasised his arrogance and lack of principle. A fuller account by N. A. Vasetsky, 'L. D. Trotsky: politicheskii portret', *Novaya i noveishaya istoriya*, no. 3, 1989, emphasised Trotsky's 'contradictory' character: valuable where he had acted as a party and state leader, but not where his 'personal ambitions' had led him into conflict with the party line (p. 165). The first of Trotsky's own writings to be reprinted were, predictably, his studies of Lenin (*Ogonek*, no. 17, 1989, pp. 3–7); for a full bibliography see Ian D. Thatcher, 'Recent Soviet writings on Leon Trotsky', *Coexistence*, vol. 27, no. 3 (September 1990), pp. 141–67.

134. Yuri Polyakov as quoted in *The Guardian* (London), 10 October 1987, p. 7; *Moskovskie novosti*, no. 48, 1988, pp. 8–9 (Medvedev

gave a figure of 40 million 'victims of Stalinism' in an interview in *Argumenty i fakty*, no. 5, 1989, pp. 5–6, at p. 6). The official KGB figures were 3.8 million 'victims' of Stalinism between 1930 and 1953, of whom 786,098 had been shot (*Pravitel'stvennyi vestnik*, no. 7, 1990, p. 11); this is close to the figure of 3.1 million sentenced on political grounds – of whom 749,421 had been condemned to death – that is reported from state archives in *Sotsiologicheskie issledovaniya*, no. 7, 1996, p. 6. For reviews of the emerging evidence, see J. Arch Getty and Robert T. Manning, eds., *Stalinist Terror: New Perspectives* (Cambridge and New York: Cambridge University Press, 1993), and R. W. Davies, *Soviet History in the Yeltsin Era* (London: Macmillan and New York: St Martin's, 1997).

135. *Izvestiya*, 12 September 1988, p. 4, 27 November 1988, p. 3, and 25 January 1989, p. 1 (number of victims); and more generally, David R. Marples, 'Kuropaty: the investigation of a Stalinist historical controversy', *Slavic Review*, vol. 53, no. 2 (Summer 1994), pp. 513–23.

136. On the Memorial Society and popular memory, see Nanci Adler, *Victims of Soviet Terror: The Story of the Memorial Movement* (Westport, CT: Praeger, 1993), and Kathleen E. Smith, *Remembering Stalin's Victims: Popular Memory and the End of the USSR* (Ithaca, NY: Cornell University Press, 1996).

137. See Vladimir Treml, 'Perestroyka and Soviet statistics', *Soviet Economy*, vol. 4, no. 1 (January–March 1988), pp. 65–94, and Tim Heleniak and Albert Motivans, 'A note on glasnost' and the Soviet statistical system', *Soviet Studies*, vol. 43, no. 3 (1991), pp. 473–90.

138. For the text of the law, see *Vedomosti S"ezda narodnykh deputatov SSSR i Verkhovnogo Soveta SSSR*, no. 29, 1990, art. 492; on the operation of censorship, see A. V. Blyum, 'Zakat glavlita: kak razrushalas' sistema sovetskoi tsenzury – dokumental'naya khronika 1985–1991 gg.', *Kniga: issledovaniya i materialy*, vol. 71 (1995), pp. 168–87, and T. M. Goryacheva *et al.*, eds., *Istoriya sovetskoi politicheskoi tsenzury: dokumenty i kommentarii* (Moscow: Rosspen, 1997).

139. *Izvestiya*, 22 April 1989, p. 6.

140. *Materialy XIX Vsesoyuznoi konferentsii Kommunisticheskoi partii Sovetskogo Soyuza 28 iyunya – 1 iyulya 1988 goda* (Moscow: Politizdat, 1988), pp. 35–7.

On democratisation the most satisfactory
account is Michael E. Urban with Vyacheslav
Igrunov and Sergei Mitrokhin, *The Rebirth of
Politics in Russia* (Cambridge and New York:
Cambridge University Press, 1997).

141. For the text of the law, see *Vedomosti
Verkhovnogo Soveta SSSR*, no. 49, 1988,
art. 729.

142. *Materialy XIX Vsesoyuznoi konferentsii*,
pp. 145–8.

143. *Materialy XIX Vsesoyuznaya konferentsiya
Kommunisticheskoi partii Sovetskogo
Soyuza, 28 iyunya – 1 iyulya 1988 g.:
stenograficheskii otchet*, 2 vols. (Moscow:
Politizdat, 1988), vol. I, p. 337 (G. I.
Zagainov); on the membership, see *Izvestiya
TsK KPSS*, no. 7, 1989, p. 113. Developments
in the party more generally are considered in
Ronald J. Hill, 'The CPSU: from monolith to
pluralist?', *Soviet Studies*, vol. 43, no. 2
(1991), pp. 217–35; Stephen White,
'Rethinking the CPSU', *ibid.*, no. 3 (1991),
pp. 405–28; E. A. Rees, ed., *The Soviet
Communist Party in Disarray* (London:
Macmillan, 1992); Graeme Gill, *The Collapse
of a Single-Party System* (Cambridge and
New York: Cambridge University Press,
1994); Stephen White, 'Communists and
their party in the late Soviet period', *Slavonic
and East European Review*, vol. 72, no. 4
(October 1994), pp. 644–63; Stephen White,
'The failure of CPSU democratization', *ibid.*,
vol. 75, no. 4 (October 1997), pp. 681–97
(both of these studies make extensive use of
the recently available party archives);
Jonathan Harris, *Subverting the System:
Gorbachev's Reform of the Party's Apparat,
1986–1991* (Lanham, MD: Rowman &
Littlefield, 2004); and Atsushi Ogushi, *The
Demise of the Soviet Communist Party*
(Abingdon and New York: Routledge, 2008).

144. Gorbachev, *Zhizn' i reformy*, vol. I, p. 270;
Gorbachev did employ the term in his
address to the April 1985 Central Committee
plenum (*ibid.*, p. 279), and it was
incorporated into the Programme and Rules
that were adopted at the 27th Party Congress
in 1986 (*Materialy XXVII S"ezda
Kommunisticheskoi partii Sovetskogo
Soyuza* (Moscow: Politizdat, 1986),
pp. 122, 188).

145. For this term see, for instance, Gorbachev,
Izbrannye rechi i stat'i, vol. IV, p. 110.

146. *Materialy Plenuma Tsentral'nogo Komiteta
KPSS, 5–7 fevralya 1990 g.* (Moscow:
Politizdat, 1990), p. 125 (I. I. Mel'nikov). The
text of the declaration as adopted at the

Plenum is in *ibid.*, pp. 353–82, and as
adopted at the Congress in *Materialy XXVIII
S"ezda Kommunisticheskoi partii
Sovetskogo Soyuza* (Moscow: Politizdat,
1990), pp. 77–98.

147. To quote the Leningrad party leader, Boris
Gidaspov, in *Pravda*, 27 July 1991, p. 4; the
text of the new draft Programme appeared in
ibid., 8 August 1991, pp. 3–4, and also in
Kommunist, no. 12, 1991, pp. 3–15.
According to ethnographer Valerii Tishkov,
the reference to a 'communist perspective'
had originally been omitted entirely and was
included in the interests of compromise
(*Izvestiya*, 8 August 1991, p. 4). For a
discussion see Neil Robinson, 'Sign of the
times: the last draft of the CPSU Programme
and the crisis of party power, 1990–91',
Slovo, vol. 5, no. 1 (1992), pp. 32–42, and
Mark Sandle, 'The final word: the draft Party
Programme of July/August 1991', *Europe-
Asia Studies*, vol. 48, no. 7 (November 1996),
pp. 1131–50.

148. *Pravda*, 26 July 1991, p. 2.

149. *XXVIII S"ezd*, vol. II, pp. 196–7 (*Short
Course*); *Pravda*, 26 October 1990, p. 2
(railway timetables). Gorbachev, his adviser
Anatolii Chernyaev explained, 'genuinely
believed in the formula: socialism is the
creation of the masses. Let them create it.
And we'll see what happens'
(A. S. Chernyaev, *1991 god: dnevnik
pomoshchnika Prezidenta SSSR* (Moscow:
Terra/Respublika, 1997), p. 24).

150. Gorbachev, *Izbrannye rechi i stat'i*, vol. IV,
pp. 308–9.

151. *Ibid.*, vol. II, p. 154.

152. *Ibid.*, vol. III, pp. 181–3.

153. *Pravda*, 26 June 1990, p. 2.

154. *Ibid.*, 9 October 1990, p. 1.

155. *Ibid.*, 16 November 1990, p. 3.

156. See Mikhail Gorbachev, *Avgustovskii putch:
prichiny i sledstviya* (Moscow: Novosti,
1991), p. 9 (Gorbachev spoke here of his
'betrayal'); Raisa Gorbacheva is quoted on
Boldin from Chernyaev, *1991 god*, p. 189.

157. *Izvestiya*, 20 December 1990, p. 6.

158. *Komsomol'skaya pravda*, 3 August 1991,
p. 3.

159. *Sovetskaya Rossiya*, 23 July 1991, p. 1.

160. *Pravda*, 13 August 1989, p. 4, and *Izvestiya*,
16 August 1991, p. 2. Yakovlev expressed
similar views in an interview the same day
that appeared in *Literaturnaya gazeta*,
28 August 1991, p. 2.

161. Anatolii Sobchak noted his 'complete
surprise' in his *Khozhdenie vo vlast'*, 2nd edn

(Moscow: Novosti, 1991), p. 275. Gorbachev may possibly have given reason to believe he would support the introduction of a state of emergency provided he had to take no direct responsibility for it (see, for instance, Amy Knight, 'The coup that never was: Gorbachev and the forces of reaction', *Problems of Communism*, vol. 40, no. 6 (November–December 1991), pp. 36–44, at pp. 39–40); about 6 per cent of the Soviet public, indeed, saw him as the 'chief instigator' of the coup (*Argumenty i fakty*, no. 36, 1991, p. 1). A detailed chronology and documentation of the coup is available in *Putch: khronika trevozhnykh dnei* (Moscow: Progress, 1991); see also *Avgust-91* (Moscow: Politizdat, 1991), which is more 'Gorbachevian' in tone; M. K. Gorshkov and V. V. Zhuravlev, eds., *Krasnoe ili beloe? (Drama avgusta-91: fakty, gipotezy, stolknoveniya mnenii)* (Moscow: Terra, 1992); and Yu. Kazarin and B. Yakovlev, eds., *Smert' zagovora: belaya kniga* (Moscow: Novosti, 1992), which reflects the position of the Moscow city administration. There are also several journalists' accounts: Giulietto Chiesa, *Cronaca del golpe rosso* (Milan: Baldini and Castoldi, 1991); Martin Sixsmith, *Moscow Coup* (London: Simon & Schuster, 1991); and the relevant chapters of David Remnick, *Lenin's Tomb* (New York: Random House, 1993). Contemporary testimony is collected in Victoria Bonnell, Ann Cooper and Gregory Freidin, *Russia at the Barricades: Eyewitness Accounts of the August Coup* (Armonk, NY: Sharpe, 1993), and in Viktor Maslyukov and Konstantin Truevtsev, eds., *V avguste 91-go: Rossiya glazami ochevidtsev* (Moscow and St Petersburg: Limbus-Press, 1993). Gorbachev's own account is his *Avgustovskii putch*. For discussions see Richard Sakwa, 'The revolution of 1991 in Russia: interpretations of the Moscow coup', *Coexistence*, vol. 29, no. 4 (December 1992), pp. 335–75, and John B. Dunlop, *The Rise of Russia and the Fall of the Soviet Empire* (Princeton, NJ: Princeton University Press, 1993).

162. Gorbachev, *Avgustovskii putch*, pp. 18–23 (Gorbachev later told a television audience rather later that if he had not gone on holiday to Foros in August 1991, 'the Soviet Union would have survived': *Argumenty i fakty*, no. 50, 2008, p. 5).

163. *Izvestiya*, 20 August 1991, p. 1.

164. *Pravda*, 20 August 1991, pp. 1–2.

165. *Izvestiya*, 20 August 1991, p. 1.

166. *Ibid.*

167. *Ibid.*, 29 August 1991, pp. 4, 8 (Pavlov admitted later that he 'probably had a sip': *ibid.*, 10 October 1991, p. 7).

168. *Putch*, pp. 19–20.

169. *Izvestiya*, 21 August 1991, pp. 1–2 (the paper reported that 'more than 70,000 Muscovites' had taken part in the demonstration: *ibid.*, p. 1).

170. *Ibid.*, 26 August 1991, p. 6 (whether an order was actually given to attack remains unclear: see Knight, 'The coup that never was', p. 40).

171. On Luk'yanov as 'chief ideologist', see *Izvestiya*, 22 August 1991, p. 4; his arrest is reported in *ibid.*, 2 September 1991, p. 1. For Luk'yanov, writing subsequently, this was not a coup but a 'desperate attempt to save the social order that had been established by the USSR Constitution' (*Perevorot mnimyi i nastoyashchii* (Moscow: Manuskript, 1993), p. 12). Bessmertnykh's unconvincing press conference is in *Pravda*, 22 August 1991, p. 5.

172. Gorbachev's initial assessment appeared in *Pravda*, 23 August 1991, p. 2; he later named three Central Committee secretaries, Andrei Girenko, Galina Semenova and Yegor Stroev, who had refused to support the conspirators and emerged as 'mature politicians and honest people': *Zhizn' i reformy*, vol. II, p. 575.

173. *Izvestiya*, 26 August 1991, p. 2.

174. *Vedomosti S"ezda narodnykh deputatov RSFSR i Verkhovnogo Soveta RSFSR*, no. 35, art. 1149, 23 August 1991.

175. *Ibid.*, art. 1164, 25 August 1991.

176. *Ibid.*, no. 45, 1991, art. 1537, 6 November 1991.

177. The declaration establishing the CIS appeared in *Rossiiskaya gazeta*, 10 December 1991, p. 1; the text of the agreement is in *ibid.*, 11 December 1991, p. 1.

178. *Vedomosti S"ezda narodnykh deputatov RSFSR i Verkhovnogo Soveta RSFSR*, no. 51, arts. 1798 and 1799, 12 December 1991. For the view that the full Congress of People's Deputies should have considered the matter, see Boris Lazarev in *Vestnik Rossiiskoi Akademii nauk*, no. 7, 1993, p. 612; for the view that there should have been a referendum, see A. S. Tsipko in G. A. Bordyugov, ed., *Rossiiskaya imperiya, SSSR, Rossiiskaya Federatsiya: istoriya odnoi strany?* (Moscow: Rossiya molodaya, 1993), p. 95. The jurist and deputy Viktor Sheinis commented that the December 1991 agreement between the three Slavic leaders

was 'outside any constitutional procedure' and that the decision to end the USSR was 'ratified by a Supreme Soviet that had no competence to decide accordingly' (*Gosudarstvo i pravo*, no. 12, 1997, p. 65). See also Z. Stankevich, *Istoriya krusheniya SSSR: politiko-pravovye aspekty* (Moscow: Izdatel'stvo Moskovskogo Universiteta, 2001), and P. P. Kremnev, *Raspad SSSR: mezhdunarodno-pravovye problemy* (Moscow: Zertsalo-M, 2005). The agreement, indeed, was formally repudiated by the Duma in March 1996, although its decisions had no practical effect. A first resolution rescinded the Russian Supreme Soviet resolution of 12 December 1991 that had denounced the 1922 treaty of union; a second 'confirm[ed] the juridical force' of the March 1991 referendum and declared the agreement to establish the CIS – which had not been ratified by the 'supreme organ of state power of the RSFSR', the Congress of People's Deputies – without legal foundation insofar as it concerned the continued existence of the USSR (*SZ*, no. 13, items 1274 and 1275, 15 March 1996).

179. *Rossiiskaya gazeta*, 24 December 1991, p. 1.
180. *Pravda*, 20 December 1991, p. 5.

2   Voters, parties and parliament

1. The fullest available discussion of Soviet and early postcommunist electoral behaviour is Stephen White, Richard Rose and Ian McAllister, *How Russia Votes* (Chatham House, NJ: Chatham House, 1997); the early postcommunist years are given particularly close attention in Timothy J. Colton, *Transitional Citizens: Voters and What Influences Them in the New Russia* (Cambridge, MA: Harvard University Press, 2000); later work is noted in the Further Reading section. The development of the electoral system itself up to the early 1990s is considered in Yu. A. Novikov, *Izbiratel'naya sistema Rossii: 90 let istorii* (Moscow: Manuskript, 1996), which reprints the relevant legislation. Sources of electoral data are also noted in the Further reading section. This chapter draws in part on a series of visits to Russia as an official election observer in 1995–6 and 1999–2000, and again in December 2003 and 2007–8.
2. *Izvestiya*, 10 February 1987, p. 1.

3. See Stephen White, 'Reforming the electoral system', in Walter Joyce, Hillel Ticktin and Stephen White, *Gorbachev and Gorbachevism* (London: Cass, 1989), pp. 1–17, and Jeffrey Hahn, 'An experiment in competition: the 1987 elections to the local soviets', *Slavic Review*, vol. 47, no. 2 (Fall 1988), pp. 434–47.
4. For the text see *Vedomosti Verkhovnogo Soveta SSSR*, no. 49, 1988, art. 729.
5. For Ligachev's view see his *Zagadka Gorbacheva* (Novosibirsk: Interbuk, 1992), p. 75. The number of defeats of first secretaries was reported in *Argumenty i fakty*, no. 21, 1989, p. 8; Yeltsin's victory in Moscow (with 89.4 per cent of the vote) was reported in *Moskovskaya pravda*, 28 March 1989, p. 2. Gorbachev told his Politburo colleagues the election was a 'major step in . . . the further democratisation of society', and Alexander Yakovlev argued similarly that it had been a 'referendum for *perestroika*'; but Yuri Solov'ev (who had lost his seat) thought a 'struggle for power' was in progress, and Alexander Luk'yanov called for measures against Memorial and Pamyat', which were 'close to anti-Soviet organisations' (Politburo minutes, 28 March 1989, Chernyaev papers, Gorbachev Foundation, Moscow). Nikolai Ryzhkov recalled Gorbachev's 'delight' but warned himself that the party had 'lost the elections' (*Perestroika: istoriya predatel'stv* (Moscow: Novosti, 1992), pp. 284–5).
6. For the casualties see *Izvestiya*, 28 December 1993, p. 1. Gaidar is quoted from his *Dni porazhenii i pobed* (Moscow: Vagrius, 1996), p. 294. There are several documentary accounts of the confrontation: N. L. Zheleznova, A. G. Panova, A. P. Surkov, comps., *Moskva. Osen'-93. Khronika protivosostoyaniya* (Moscow: Respublika, 1994) favours the presidential position; more critical are A. V. Buzgalin and A. I. Kolganov, eds., *Krovavyi oktyabr' v Moskve: khronika, svidetel'stva, analiz sobytii 21 sentyabrya – 4 oktyabrya 1993 goda* (Moscow: Erebus, 1993), and V. Ya. Vasil'ev, Buzgalin and Kolganov, eds., *Ploshchad' svobodnoi Rossii: sbornik svidetel'stv o sentyabr'skikh-oktyabr'skikh dnyakh 1993 goda v stolitse Rossii* (Moscow: Erebus, 1994). A chronology and commentary is provided in A. Zevelev and Yu. Pavlov, eds., *Raskolotaya vlast'* (Moscow: Rosspen, 1995); there is also a chronology in *Svobodnaya mysl'*, no. 15, 1993, pp. 12–42.
7. Boris Yeltsin, *Zapiski Prezidenta* (Moscow: Ogonek, 1994), p. 347.
8. *Rossiiskie vesti*, 4 March 1993, p. 1.

9. For the result of the 'national vote', see *Rossiiskaya gazeta*, 25 December 1993, p. 1; a more detailed set of results is in *Byulleten' Tsentral'noi izbiratel'noi komissii Rossiiskoi Federatsii*, no. 1(12), 1994, pp. 34–8. Independent observers estimated the real level of turnout at between 38 and 43 per cent (O. G. Rumyantsev, *Osnovy konstitutsionnogo stroya Rossii* (Moscow: Yurist, 1994), pp. 216–17), or in another estimate 46.1 per cent (*Sovetskaya Rossiya*, 7 May 1994, p. 2). Yeltsin's press secretary, Vyacheslav Kostikov, himself witnessed the alteration of the results by the chairman of the Central Electoral Commission, Nikolai Ryabov, a defector from the parliamentary camp who was 'universally regarded as cunning and treacherous' (*Roman s prezidentom* (Moscow: Vagrius, 1997), pp. 266–7). The Constitution entered into force on its official publication on 25 December, but it is considered to have been adopted on the date of the vote, 12 December.

10. The full text of the constitutional amendments appears in *Vneocherednoi tretii s"ezd narodnykh deputatov SSSR 12–15 marta 1990 g.: stenograficheskii otchet*, 3 vols. (Moscow: Izdanie Verkhovnogo Soveta SSSR, 1990), vol. III, pp. 192–207.

11. *Materialy Plenuma Tsentral'nogo Komiteta KPSS, 5–7 fevralya 1990 goda* (Moscow: Politizdat, 1990), pp. 9–10; the Platform for the 28th Party Congress that was approved at the plenum, 'Towards a humane, democratic socialism', made clear that elections should be a 'terrain of honest competition of the representatives of all sections of society', and that the development of society did 'not exclude the creation of parties' (*ibid.*, p. 365).

12. For the text of the law, see *Vedomosti S"ezda narodnykh deputatov SSSR i Verkhovnogo Soveta SSSR*, no. 42, 1990, art. 840.

13. *Argumenty i fakty*, no. 24, 1992, p. 8; the number of activists is estimated in *Izvestiya*, 20 April 1992, p. 2. There were an estimated 1,200 parties or movements at this time: *ibid.*, 11 June 1992, p. 2.

14. *Sobranie zakonodatel'stva Rossiiskoi Federatsii* [hereafter *SZ*], no. 21, 1995, art. 1930. By 1998 'over three thousand' parties had registered under its auspices (*Argumenty i fakty*, no. 20, 1998, p. 24); there were ninety-five parties that were organised on a national basis, and 154 public movements (*Nezavisimaya gazeta*, 20 November 1998, p. 1).

15. *Nezavisimaya gazeta*, 7 October 1993, p. 2, and Yu. G. Korgunyuk and S. E. Zaslavsky,

Rossiiskaya mnogopartiinost' (stanovlenie, funktionirovanie, razvitie) (Moscow: Indem, 1996), pp. 191–2. For a full account of the 1993 elections, see Jerry F. Hough, 'The Russian election of 1993: public attitudes toward economic reforms and democratization', *Post-Soviet Affairs*, vol. 10, no. 1 (January–March 1994), pp. 1–37; Stephen Whitefield and Geoffrey Evans, 'The Russian election of 1993: public opinion and the transition experience', *ibid.*, pp. 38–60; Ralph S. Clem and Peter R. Craumer, 'The politics of Russia's regions: a geographical analysis of the Russian election and constitutional plebiscite of December 1993', *Post-Soviet Geography*, vol. 36, no. 2 (February 1995), pp. 67–86; Richard Sakwa, 'The Russian elections of December 1993', *Europe-Asia Studies*, vol. 47, no. 2 (March 1995), pp. 195–227; Matthew Wyman, Stephen White, Bill Miller and Paul Heywood, 'Public opinion, parties and voters in the December 1993 Russian elections', *ibid.*, no. 4 (June 1995), pp. 591–614; Ralph S. Clem and Peter R. Craumer, 'A rayon-level analysis of the Russian election and constitutional plebiscite of December 1993', *Post-Soviet Geography*, vol. 36, no. 8 (October 1995), pp. 459–75; White, Rose and McAllister, *How Russia Votes*, chs. 6 and 7; Peter Lentini, ed., *Elections and Political Order in Russia* (Budapest: Central European University Press, 1995); and Jerry F. Hough and Timothy J. Colton, eds., *Growing Pains: The 1993 Russian Duma Election* (Washington, DC: Brookings, 1998). For a more sceptical view, see Michael E. Urban, 'December 1993 as a replication of late-Soviet electoral practices', *Post-Soviet Affairs*, vol. 10, no. 2 (April–June 1994), pp. 127–58.

16. Boris Grushin, 'Fiasko sotsial'noi mysli', *Mir mnenii i mneniya o mire*, no. 5, 1994, p. 9; the All-Russian Public Opinion Centre's last published poll appeared in *Segodnya*, 30 November 1993, p. 1. Russia's senior pollster, Yuri Levada, acknowledged later that his own organisation had 'underestimated the influence of the opposition and the role of provincial attitudes (of the "backwoods") in the overall results' (*Sotsiologicheskii zhurnal*, no. 4, 1997, p. 225).

17. *Izvestiya*, 15 December 1993, p. 2; *Vechernyaya Moskva*, 13 December 1993, p. 1.

18. See A. G. Beloborodov *et al.*, *Vybory deputatov Gosudarstvennoi Dumy. 1995. Elektoral'naya statistika* [hereafter *Vybory 1996*] (Moscow: Ves' mir, 1996), p. 11. The possibility of a

'world record' was suggested in *Segodnya*, 18 August 1995, p. 2.

19. *Vybory 1996*, pp. 154, 152.

20. *Ibid.*, p. 80 (there were 329 fewer candidates by the day of the election).

21. *Izvestiya*, 14 October 1995, p. 4; for the increasing cost see *ibid.*, 18 October 1995, p. 2.

22. *Rossiiskie vesti*, 16 December 1995, p. 1.

23. *Segodnya*, 27 December 1995, p. 3.

24. *Moskovskaya pravda*, 21 December 1995, p. 1.

25. *Segodnya*, 20 December 1995, p. 1; the party's share of the vote in the single-member constituencies was just 6.2 per cent: *Vybory 1996*, p. 154. For more detailed accounts of the 1995 election, see Stephen White, Matthew Wyman and Sarah Oates, 'Parties and voters in the 1995 Russian Duma election', *Europe-Asia Studies*, vol. 49, no. 5 (July 1997), pp. 767–98; Richard Rose, Evgeny Tikhomirov and William Mishler, 'Understanding multi-party choice: the 1995 Duma election', *ibid.*, pp. 799–823; and Laura Belin and Robert W. Orttung, eds., *The Russian Parliamentary Elections of 1995: The Battle for the Duma* (Armonk, NY: Sharpe, 1997). Spatial aspects are given close attention in Ralph S. Clem and Peter R. Craumer, 'The geography of the Russian 1995 parliamentary election: continuity, change, and correlates', *Post-Soviet Geography*, vol. 36, no. 10 (December 1995), pp. 587–616. Two studies by Russian scholars deal with electoral politics from 1993 to 1996: Vladimir Gel'man and Grigorii V. Golosov, eds., *Elections in Russia, 1993–1996: Analyses, Documents and Data* (Berlin: Edition Sigma, 1999), and Vladimir Gel'man, Grigorii Golosov and Yelena Meleshkina, eds., *Pervyi elektoral'nyi tsikl v Rossii 1993–1996 gg.* (Moscow: Ves' mir, 2000).

26. See Stephen White and Ian McAllister, 'Reforming the Russian electoral system', *Journal of Communist Studies and Transition Politics*, vol. 15, no. 4 (December 1999), pp. 17–40.

27. *Rossiiskaya gazeta*, 18 January 2000, p. 1.

28. *Monitoring obshchestvennogo mneniya*, no. 2, 2000, p. 56.

29. *Rossiiskaya gazeta*, 10 August 1999, p. 1; and for the Stepashin interview, *Komsomol'skaya pravda*, 13 August 1999, p. 6.

30. *Izvestiya*, 5 November 1999, p. 1.

31. See Stephen White, Sarah Oates and Ian McAllister, 'Media effects and Russian elections, 1999–2000', *British Journal of Political Science*, vol. 35, no. 2 (April 2005), pp. 191–208.

32. The 1999 election is considered more fully in Richard Sakwa, 'Russia's "permanent" (uninterrupted) elections of 1999–2000', *Journal of Communist Studies and Transition Politics*, vol. 16, no. 3 (September 2000), pp. 85–112; Richard Rose, Neil Munro and Stephen White, 'Voting in a floating party system: the 1999 Duma election', *Europe-Asia Studies*, vol. 53, no. 3 (May 2001), pp. 419–43; Timothy J. Colton and Michael McFaul, *Popular Choice and Managed Democracy: The Russian Elections of 1999 and 2000* (Washington, DC: Brookings, 2003); and Vicki L. Hesli and William M. Reisinger, eds., *The 1999–2000 Elections in Russia: Their Impact and Legacy* (Cambridge and New York: Cambridge University Press, 2003). See also Maikl Makfol, Nikolai Petrov and Andrei Ryabov, eds., *Rossiya v izbiratel'nom tsikle 1999–2000 godov* (Moscow: Gendal'f, 2000), which draws on the resources of the Carnegie Moscow Center; Vladimir Gel'man, Grigorii Golosov and Yelena Melekhina, eds., *Vtoroi elektoral'nyi tsikl v Rossii 1999–2000 gg.* (Moscow: Ves' mir, 2002), which reflects the work of scholars grouped around the European University in St Petersburg; and on spatial aspects, Ralph S. Clem and Peter R. Craumer, 'Regional patterns of political preference in Russia: the December 1999 Duma elections', *Post-Soviet Geography and Economics*, vol. 41, no. 1 (January–February 2000), pp. 1–29.

33. *Rossiiskaya gazeta*, 30 December 2003, p. 1. For a fuller account see Ralph S. Clem and Peter R. Craumer, 'Redrawing the political map of Russia: the Duma election of December 2003', *Eurasian Geography and Economics*, vol. 45, no. 4 (June 2004), pp. 241–61; Richard Sakwa, 'The 2003–2004 Russian elections and prospects for democracy', *Europe-Asia Studies*, vol. 57, no. 3 (May 2005), pp. 369–98; and Vladimir Gel'man, ed., *Tretii elektoral'nyi tsikl v Rossii, 2003–2004 gody* (St Petersburg: Yevropeiskii universitet v Sankt-Peterburge, 2007).

34. *Vybory deputatov Gosudarstvennoi Dumy Federal'nogo Sobraniya Rossiiskoi Federatsii. 2003. Elektoral'naya statistika* (Moscow: Ves' mir, 2004; hereafter *Vybory 2003*), pp. 51, 192.

35. *Ibid.*, p. 193.

36. *Ibid*, p. 49.

37. *Kommersant*, 26 December 2003, p. 3. On the use of the term 'locomotive' (*parovoz*), see Gasan Guseinov, *D. S. P. Materialy k russkomu slovaryu obshchestvenno-politicheskogo yazyka XX veka* (Moscow: Tri kvadrata, 2003), p. 371.

38. *Rossiiskaya gazeta*, 14 September 2004, pp. 1, 3.

39. 'O vyborakh deputatov Gosudarstvennoi Dumy Federal'nogo Sobraniya Rossiiskoi Federatsii', *SZ*, no. 21, item 1919, 18 May 2005. The current version of the law, incorporating all subsequent changes, may be consulted at the Central Electoral Commission's website, www.cikrf.ru.

40. See Ian McAllister and Stephen White, 'Voting "against all" in postcommunist Russia', *Europe-Asia Studies*, vol. 60, no. 1 (January 2008), pp. 67–87; for the amendment to the law, see *SZ*, no. 29, item 3125, 12 July 2006.

41. *SZ*, no. 18, item 2118, 26 April 2007.

42. In the words of party leader Boris Gryzlov: *Rossiiskaya gazeta*, 17 October 2007, p. 1. Putin expressed himself in similar terms in a speech in Krasnoyarsk: *Kommersant*, 14 November 2007, p. 3.

43. *Rossiiskaya gazeta*, 2 October 2007, p. 1 (the nomination was overwhelmingly approved the following day).

44. *Ibid.*, 29 October 2007, p. 1; for the candidate numbers see *ibid.*, 30 October 2007, p. 2.

45. *Ibid.*, 22 November 2007, pp. 2–3.

46. *Kommersant*, 29 November 2007, p. 4.

47. United Russia leader Boris Gryzlov, for instance, speaking in Berlin, warned that they were 'taking very seriously the threat of the country's being destabilised from outside' (*Nezavisimaya gazeta*, 20 November 2007, p. 2).

48. *Rossiiskaya gazeta*, 30 November 2007, p. 1.

49. *Izvestiya*, 5 December 2007, p. 2.

50. The Kremlin had apparently made clear to lower-level officials that a turnout of at least 60 per cent would be expected: Vitalii Ivanov, *Partiya Putina: istoriya 'Yedinoi Rossii'* (Moscow: Olma, 2008), p. 306. A daily paper quoted 'party sources who wish to remain anonymous' to the effect that regional leaders had been given oral briefings in which 'target figures' for the share of the vote that should be won by particular parties, in the first instance United Russia, had been identified (*Nezavisimaya gazeta*, 20 July 2007, p. 1).

51. *Nezavisimaya gazeta*, 3 December 2007, p. 3.

52. *Izvestiya*, 4 December 2007, p. 3. A fuller account appears in Ian McAllister and Stephen White, '"It's the economy, comrade!" Parties and voters in the 2007 Russian Duma election', *Europe-Asia Studies*, vol. 60, no. 6 (August 2008), pp. 937–63.

53. OSCE Parliamentary Assembly, 'Russian Duma elections "not held on a level playing field", say parliamentary observers',

3 December 2007, www.oscepa.org, last accessed 3 July 2008.

54. *Izvestiya*, 19 November 2007, p. 2.

55. The 'Golos' (Voice) Foundation visited more than 20,000 polling stations on 2 December and set up a hotline for voters to report violations. Of the 4,000 calls they received, 23 per cent related to restrictions placed on observers at polling stations, 22 per cent were complaints about illegal campaigning, 15 per cent cited voter list violations, 9 per cent said voter privacy was not observed and 4 per cent complained of some form of payment for votes (*Moscow Times*, 5 December 2007, p. 3; the full report may be consulted at www.golos.org).

56. 'Osoboe mnenie chlena TsIK Rossii Kolyushina Ye. I.', *Vestnik Tsentral'noi izbiratel'noi komissii Rossiiskoi Federatsii* no. 19(222), 2007, pp. 24–8. Kolyushin also noted that, oddly in a country with a declining population, the number of officially registered electors had increased by nearly 1.7 million since the figure that had been reported on 1 July of the same year (p. 27).

57. Clifford J. Levy, 'Kremlin rules. Putin's iron grip on Russia suffocates his opponents', *New York Times*, 24 February 2008, pp. 1, 14.

58. *Sunday Telegraph*, 26 November 2007, p. 37.

59. *Kommersant*, 26 November 2007, p. 3 (there was no reference to his arrest or Boris Nemtsov's detention in St Petersburg on national television: *ibid.*).

60. *Guardian*, 26 November 2007, p. 16.

61. *Moscow Times*, 4 December 2007, p. 3.

62. *Guardian*, 4 December 2007, p. 2. The Communist leader, Gennadii Zyuganov, claimed similarly that the entire exercise had been the 'dirtiest [and] most irresponsible' since the demise of the Soviet Union (*The Times*, 3 December 2007, p. 31); the liberal leader, Grigorii Yavlinsky, described the manipulation as 'unprecedented' (*Moscow Times*, 5 December 2007, p. 3). An exceptionally rigorous econometric analysis (Mikhail Myagkov, Peter C. Ordeshook and Dimitri Shakin, *The Forensics of Election Fraud: Russia and Ukraine* (Cambridge and New York: Cambridge University Press, 2009)) found that 'upwards of 10 million suspect or fraudulent votes' had been cast in the election and that 'anywhere between 20 and 25 percent of United Russia's vote [had been] won in a way that would not pass muster in an established or transitional democracy' (pp. 136–7).

63. Just 28 per cent identified themselves in this way in the author's 2008 survey; 40 per cent

rejected the terms of the question ('no one', 'no interest') and 32 per cent opted for 'don't know' or refused to answer. Just 56 per cent of Russians could locate themselves on a left–right scale in the mid-1990s, leading Colton to conclude that ideologies of this kind can 'not yet assume a prominent place in interpretations of the mass politics of the Russian transition' (*Transitional Citizens*, p. 148).

64. See Ol'ga Kryshtanovskaya, *Anatomiya rossiiskoi elity* (Moscow: Zakharov, 2005), pp. 154–5.

65. *Izvestiya*, 31 March 2003, p. 3.

66. See, for instance, S. M. Khenin, '"Partiya vlasti": shtrikhi k portretu', *Politiya*, no. 1(3) (Spring 1997), pp. 28–35; Hans Oversloot and Reuben Verheul, 'The party of power in Russian politics', *Acta Politica*, vol. 35, no. 2 (Summer 2000), pp. 123–45; Regina Smyth, 'Building state capacity from the inside out: parties of power and the success of the president's reform agenda in Russia', *Politics and Society*, vol. 30, no. 4 (December 2002), pp. 555–78; Sergei Ustimenko and Andrei Ivanov, '"Partiya vlasti" v sovremennoi Rossii: retrospektiva i perspektiva', *Vlast'*, no. 8, 2003, pp. 6–12; L. I. Glebova, 'Partiya vlasti', *Polis*, no. 2, 2004, pp. 85–92; and Zoe Knox, Peter Lentini and Brad Williams, 'Parties of power and Russian politics: a victory of the state over civil society?', *Problems of Post-Communism*, vol. 53, no. 1 (January–February 2006), pp. 3–14. A 'party of the state' is defined by Paul Cammack as 'a political party (or coalition of parties) that is subordinated to the executive in that it endorses and promotes the programme of the executive, rather than generating the programme to which the executive adheres, and which builds political support for the government by administering or directly benefiting from the systematic orchestration of clientelism by the state' ('Globalization and the death of liberal democracy', *European Review*, vol. 6, no. 2 (May 1998), pp. 249–63, at p. 258).

67. 'O politicheskikh partiyakh', *SZ*, no. 29, item 2950, 11 July 2001; for the 2004 revision see 'O vnesenii izmenenii v Federal'nyi zakon "O politicheskikh partiyakh"', *ibid.*, no. 52, 2004, art. 5272, 20 December 2004. The current version of the law may be consulted at the Central Electoral Commission website www.cikrf.ru.

68. On this murky subject see most recently Kenneth Wilson, 'Party finance in Russia: has the 2001 law "On political parties" made a difference?', *Europe-Asia Studies*, vol. 59, no. 7 (November 2007), pp. 1089–113.

69. See *SZ*, no. 30, item 3600, 22 July 2008 (converted at prevailing exchange rates: on the same date one US dollar bought 23.44 roubles). As of the date of the original law on 11 July 2001, the relevant minimum salary – on 1 March of the preceding year – was 83.49 (redenominated) roubles and one US dollar bought 29.23 roubles (*Rossiiskaya gazeta*, 11 July 2001, p. 2).

70. For these changes see respectively *SZ*, no. 30, item 3104, 21 July 2005, and *ibid.*, no. 30, item 3600, 22 July 2008.

71. See www.cikrf.ru/politparty/finance/svodn_otchet.jsp; accounts are displayed from 2005 onwards. The 2008 party accounts were also made available in published form: see *Vestnik Tsentral'noi izbiratel'noi komissii Rossiiskoi Federatsii*, no. 4, 2009, pp. 179–81.

72. *Izvestiya*, 29 November 2003, p. 3.

73. See *ibid.*, 2 February 2007, p. 3. He made the same point when speaking to the party congress later in the year: *ibid.*, 2 October 2007, p. 2.

74. The fullest and most useful account is Ivanov, *Partiya Putina*; a shorter, updated version was published as *'Yedinaya Rossiya': kratkaya istoriya partii* (Moscow: Yevropa, 2009). See also Regina Smyth, Anna Lowry and Brandon Wilkening, 'Engineering victory: institutional reform, informal institutions, and the formation of a hegemonic party regime in the Russian Federation', *Post-Soviet Affairs*, vol. 23, no. 2 (April–June 2007), pp. 118–37, which focuses on the use of public money via a ruling party to sustain a 'single-party cadre regime'; Ora John Reuter and Thomas F. Remington, 'Dominant party regimes and the commitment problem: the case of United Russia', *Comparative Political Studies*, vol. 42, no. 4 (April 2009), pp. 501–26; and Darrell Slider, 'How united is United Russia? Regional sources of intra-party conflict', *Journal of Communist Studies and Transition Politics*, vol. 26, no. 2 (June 2010), pp. 257–75.

75. *Kommersant*, 16 April 2008, p. 1.

76. Ivanov, *Partiya Putina*, p. 97.

77. Manifest Vserossiiskoi politicheskoi partii 'Yedinstvo i Otechestvo'–Yedinaya Rossiya, *Put' natsional'nogo uspekha* (Moscow 2003), various pages.

78. Quoted in Ivanov, *Partiya Putina*, p. 95.

79. *III S"ezd politicheskoi partii 'Yedinaya Rossiya'* (Moscow 2003), p. 6.

80. *Rossiiskaya gazeta*, 13 November 2003, p. 11.

81. In a survey fielded in early October 2007, for instance, fully 59 per cent said they had first heard about the 'Putin plan' when they were asked about it by the interviewer: 'Chto takoe "Plan Putina"?', 11 October 2007, at www.bd.fom.ru/report/cat/pres/putin_/d074122, last accessed 20 September 2010.

82. V. V. Putin, *Izbrannye rechi i vystupleniya* (Moscow: Knizhnyi mir, 2008), pp. 447–8 (this phrase did not appear in the contemporary press reports that were consulted). Putin himself complained that the party was 'not an ideal political structure', that it lacked a 'stable ideology [or] principles' and that because it was so close to government it attracted 'all kinds of hangers-on' (*Rossiiskaya gazeta*, 14 November 2007, p. 1).

83. *Rossiiskaya gazeta*, 9 November 2007, p. 14.

84. Ivanov, *Partiya Putina*, p. 248.

85. *Vremya novostei*, 24 September 2007, p. 2.

86. Ivanov, *Partiya Putina*, p. 281.

87. *Rossiiskaya gazeta*, 14 November 2007, p. 18.

88. Several studies of the party's origins and development are available including Joan Barth Urban and Valerii D. Solovei, *Russia's Communists at the Crossroads* (Boulder, CO: Westview, 1997); Luke March, *The Communist Party in Post-Soviet Russia* (Manchester and New York: Manchester University Press, 2002); A. Ye. Volokhov, *Noveishaya istoriya Kommunisticheskoi partii: 1990–2002* (Moscow: Impeto, 2003); and Luke March, 'Power and opposition in the former Soviet Union: the communist parties of Moldova and Russia', *Party Politics*, vol. 12, no. 3 (May 2006), pp. 341–65. Sergei Pluzhnikov and Dmitrii Shevchenko, *Zyuganov.net: tainaya istoriya KPRF 1990–2008 godov* (Moscow: Stolitsa-Print, 2008), is a detailed but undocumented 'secret history'.

89. Quoted from O. Prokhanov, ed., *Kto est' kto v Rossii: spravochnoe isdanie* (Moscow: Olimp/Eksmo-Press, 1998), pp. 262–4. The fullest biography is Anatolii Zhitnukhin, *Gennadii Zyuganov* (Moscow: Molodaya gvardiya, 2007); a selection of autobiographical and other writings is collected in translation in Gennadii Zyuganov, *My Russia: The Political Autobiography of Gennady Zyuganov*, ed. Vadim Medish (Armonk, NY: Sharpe, 1997). A recent article argues that the influence on Zyuganov's thinking of Russian conservative Slavophils such as Danilevsky and Leont'ev is 'hard to exaggerate' and that the influence of Western geopolitical theorists such as Mackinder and Mahan has also been

'significant', both of which helped to explain the party leader's shift from the language of class to that of civilisations (N. V. Rabotyazhev and E. G. Solov'ev, 'Ot Lenina k Danilevskomu: metamorfozy geopoliticheskikh vozzrenii KPRF', *Polis*, no. 2, 2007, pp. 124–36, at pp. 126, 127). Zyuganov was also the author of an 'open panegyric' on Stalin (*Stalin i sovremennost'* (Moscow: Molodaya gvardiya, 2009); the description is from the review in *Svobodnaya mysl'*, no. 1, 2009, p. 209).

90. Quotations are from the version of the 1995 Programme that appears in *IV S"ezd Kommunisticheskoi partii Rossiiskoi Federatsii, 19–20 aprelya 1997 goda. Materialy i dokumenty* (Moscow: ITRK SPPP, 1997), pp. 74–92. For the revised version of the programme that was adopted in 2008, see *Pravda*, 11 April 2008, pp. 4–5 (draft), and *ibid.*, 9 December 2008, pp. 2–3 (final text).

91. As Zyuganov told a plenary session of the Central Committee that was held immediately after the presidential election, 'the majority of party members are past or approaching retirement age; older people make up about 85 per cent of the organisation's membership, while people under 30 account for only 5 to 7 per cent' (*Kommersant*, 24 March 2008, p. 3); on other evidence Communist members were typically 59 years old, compared with an average of 42 among their United Russia counterparts (*Izvestiya*, 11 June 2008, p. 3). The Communist electorate, by contrast, appeared to over-represent those of late adult rather than pensionable age: see D. Roderick Kiewiet and Mikhail G. Myagkov, 'Are the Communists dying out in Russia?', *Communist and Post-Communist Studies*, vol. 31, no. 1 (March 2002), pp. 39–50.

92. *Rossiiskaya gazeta*, 9 November 2007, p. 12.

93. It did, however, win four single-member constituency seats in 2003. The party's origins and development are considered in Oleg Manikhin, *Rossiiskaya demokraticheskaya partiya 'YABLOKO': kratkii istoricheskii ocherk* (Moscow: Integral-Inform, 2003; also available on the party's website), and in David White, 'Going their own way: the Yabloko party's opposition to unification', *Journal of Communist Studies and Transition Politics*, vol. 21, no. 4 (December 2005), pp. 462–86; White, *The Russian Democratic Party Yabloko: Opposition in a Managed Democracy* (Aldershot and Burlington VT: Ashgate, 2006); and the same author's 'Victims of a managed democracy? Explaining the electoral

decline of the Yabloko party', *Demokratizatiya*, vol. 15, no. 2 (Spring 2007), pp. 209–29.

94. *Programma Rossiiskoi demokraticheskoi partii 'Yabloko' – 'Demokraticheskii manifest'. Ustav Politicheskoi partii 'Rossiiskaya demokraticheskaya partiya "Yabloko"'* (Moscow: EPITsentr, 2002), various pages; the revised version that was adopted by the party's 13th Congress in June 2006 – which is in these respects identical – may be consulted at www.yabloko.ru/Union/programma.html, last accessed 20 September 2010.

95. *Parlamentskaya gazeta*, 9 November 2007, p. 14.

96. *Kommersant*, 23 June 2008, p. 1 (Yavlinsky became a member of the party's newly established Political Committee at the same congress; it had responsibility for policy and finance and his effective influence within the party had not necessarily diminished).

97. *Rossiiskii liberal'nyi manifest (Programma politicheskoi partii 'Soyuza pravykh sil')* (Moscow: SPS, 2002), *passim*.

98. Putin appeared on the national television news on 13 December 1999, receiving and apparently endorsing the URF's massive programme for economic reform, and the party backed him in the subsequent presidential contest. Putin, Kirienko told national television, had met party leaders earlier the same day and 'supported many of the key points' of their economic programme (*BBC Summary of World Broadcasts* SU/3718 B/2, 15 December 1999).

99. *Novye izvestiya*, 25 March 2004, p. 2. Khakamada later withdrew from political life entirely: *Kommersant*, 19 May 2008, p. 3.

100. *Vremya novostei*, 30 May 2005, p. 4.

101. *Parlamentskaya gazeta*, 9 November 2007, p. 5.

102. *Kommersant*, 17 November 2008, p. 8; Belykh's resignation was reported in *ibid.*, 27 September 2008, p. 1. Leonid Gozman, a senior URF official, explained to journalists that the party had been finding it difficult to cover its current expenses and the cost of its free publicity at the time of the Duma election, which had to be repaid if a party won less than 3 per cent of the vote (*ibid.*); opening the congress at which the URF itself agreed to dissolve, he did not conceal that the new party had been set up 'with the collaboration of the Kremlin' (*ibid.*, 17 November 2008, p. 4). In any case, suggested Dmitri Oreshkin, a party that represented the interests of business had

little alternative but to work with any government that actually existed (*Nezavisimaya gazeta*, 1 October 2008, p. 3). Belykh himself joined Gary Kasparov's militantly oppositional Other Russia (*ibid.*, 29 September 2008, p. 1) and was then nominated to the governorship of Kirov region by President Medvedev (*Kommersant*, 19 December 2008, p. 3). The party's history from its establishment to the merger is reviewed in Kirill Benediktov, *'Soyuz pravykh sil': kratkaya istoriya partii* (Moscow: Yevropa, 2009). Following the merger, the URF continued as a 'movement' (*Nezavisimaya gazeta*, 21 April 2009, p. 1).

103. See, for instance, *Izvestiya*, 14 April 1994, p. 2. It was certainly the case that the party's founding documents had been published by the CPSU's own publishing house (*Liberal'no-demokraticheskaya partiya Sovetskogo Soyuza: dokumenty i materialy* (Moscow: 'with the participation of Politizdat', 1991). The former KGB chairman, Vladimir Kryuchkov, on the other hand, denied the direct assistance of his own organisation (*Lichnoe delo*, 2 vols. (Moscow: Olimp/Ast, 1996), vol. II, p. 13), and Gorbachev could neither confirm nor deny it (*Izvestiya*, 13 January 1994, p. 1). The party's own version of its development is available in Aleksei Mitrofanov, *Istoriya LDPR: Istoki i fakty* (Moscow: n.p., 2007; the author himself defected to A Just Russia in 2007) and in Aleksandr Andreev, *Kratkaya istoriya LDPR: ot avgustovskogo putcha do smeny karaula, 1990–2007 gody* (Moscow: Izdanie LDPR, 2008; also available on the party website www.ldpr.ru).

104. For the comparison see Vladimir Solovyov and Elena Klepikova, *Zhirinovsky: The Paradoxes of Russian Fascism*, trans. Catherine A. Fitzpatrick in collaboration with the authors (London: Viking, 1995), p. 161; he was also described as a 'comic opera dictator, more Charlie Chaplin than Adolf Hitler' (*ibid.*, p. 97). There are several other studies of the LDPR leader, including Vladimir Kartsev with Todd Bludeau, *!Zhirinovsky!* (New York: Columbia University Press, 1995).

105. *Izvestiya*, 12 February 1992, p. 3.

106. *Pravda Zhirinovskogo*, no. 6, 1993, in Vladimir Zhirinovsky, *Politicheskaya klassika*, vol. V (Moscow: LDPR, 1997), p. 138. The party leader expressed himself in similar terms the following year: *Pravda Zhirinovskogo*, no. 5(28), 1994, in

Zhirinovsky, *Politicheskaya klassika*, vol. VI (Moscow: LDPR, 1997), p. 145. There is a full collection of such statements in Graham Frazer and George Lancelle, *Zhirinovsky: The Little Black Book* (London: Penguin Books, 1994), p. 111.

107. *Washington Times*, 15 December 1993, p. A12.

108. *Programma LDPR: ustav LDPR* (Moscow: Izdatel'stvo Liberal'no-demokraticheskoi partii, 2006), various pages.

109. *Rossiiskaya gazeta*, 8 November 2007, p. 12.

110. To quote the title of Ye. Malkin, Ye. Suchkov and V. Khomyakov, 'Bespartiinaya Rossiya', *Svobodnaya mysl'*, no. 2, 2009, pp. 17–30. The rapid turnover of parties, up to the end of the Yeltsin period, led others to suggest that Russia had a 'floating party system': see Richard Rose, Neil Munro and Stephen White, 'Voting in a floating party system: the 1999 Duma election', *Europe-Asia Studies*, vol. 53, no. 3 (May 2001), pp. 419–43.

111. In the classic account of electoral volatility, defined as the 'net change within the electoral party system resulting from individual vote transfers', Pedersen himself acknowledges the difficulties that arose from the 'fluidity of the party system', including 'party splinterings and party mergers of various kinds', which meant that problems of comparability over time and across countries could 'not be entirely eradicated' (Mogens N. Pedersen, 'The dynamics of European party systems: changing patterns of electoral volatility', *European Journal of Political Research*, vol. 7, no. 1 (March 1979), pp. 1–26, at pp. 3, 5). Additional difficulties arise in the Russian case, up to 2007, from the participation of blocs of parties and other entities; from the need to take account of the parallel single-member constituency contests, involving independent as well as party-sponsored candidates; and from the need to take account of the substantial vote 'against all', which was a valid ballot-paper option until the same date.

112. Several recent accounts of the development of Russian party politics are available, including Henry E. Hale, *Why Not Parties in Russia? Democracy, Federalism, and the State* (Cambridge and New York: Cambridge University Press, 2006); Kenneth Wilson, 'Party-system development under Putin', *Post-Soviet Affairs*, vol. 22, no. 4 (October–December 2006), pp. 314–48; Yu. G. Korgunyuk, *Stanovlenie partiinoi sistemy v sovremennoi Rossii* (Moscow: INDEM/

Moskovoskii gorodskoi pedagogicheskii universitet, 2007); Stephen White, 'Russia's client party system', in Paul Webb and Stephen White, eds., *Party Politics in New Democracies* (Oxford and New York: Oxford University Press, 2007; rev. paperback edn, 2009), pp. 21–52; Vladimir Gel'man, 'Party politics in Russia: from competition to hierarchy', *Europe-Asia Studies*, vol. 60, no. 6 (August 2008), pp. 913–30; Dmitrii Chizhov, *Rossiiskie politicheskie partii: mezhdu grazhdanskim obshchestvom i gosudarstvom* (Moscow: Rosspen, 2008); and G. M. Mikhaleva, *Rossiiskie partii v kontekste transformatsii* (Moscow: Knizhnyi dom 'Librokom', 2009). G. Belonuchkin and V. Pribylovsky, eds., *Yest' takie partii: putevoditel' izbiratelya* (Moscow: Panorama, 2008), is a detailed guide to all the parties that presented candidates in the 2007 Duma election. There are still very few studies of local party politics in the postcommunist period; see, however, Derek S. Hutcheson, *Political Parties in the Russian Regions* (New York: RoutledgeCurzon, 2003), which focuses on the middle Volga; Grigorii Golosov, *Political Parties in the Regions of Russia* (Boulder, CO: Lynne Rienner, 2004); and the same author's *Rossiiskaya partiinaya sistema i regional'naya politika 1993–2003* (St Petersburg: Izdatel'stvo Yevropeiskogo universiteta v Sankt-Peterburge, 2006).

113. Putin's approval rating, according to the Levada Centre, varied between 85 and 86 per cent in the first four months of 2008; Medvedev's fluctuated between 70 and 83 per cent over the remainder of the year (see www.levada.ru/prezident.html, last accessed 28 February 2009).

114. See, for instance, Ol'ga Gryaznova, 'Otnoshenie zhitelei Rossii k pravookhranitel'nym organam: obzor issledovanii poslednykh let', *Vestnik obshchestvennogo mneniya*, no. 2(82), March–April 2006, pp. 32–46 (and pp. 203–4, 346–7).

115. Vladimir Shlapentokh, 'Trust in public institutions in Russia: the lowest in the world', *Communist and Post-Communist Studies*, vol. 39, no. 2 (June 2006), pp. 153–74.

116. The only case in which political parties have not been the least trusted civic institution appears to have been when respondents were asked, on a single occasion, to express their confidence in a list that included the investment funds that had (for the most part)

defrauded ordinary citizens of the vouchers they had obtained as a result of the privatisation of state property (Richard Rose, *Getting Things Done with Social Capital: New Russia Barometer VII* (Glasgow: Centre for the Study of Public Policy, University of Strathclyde, 1998), p. 59). See also G. L. Kertman, 'Status partii v rossiiskoi politicheskoi kul'ture', *Polis*, no. 1, 2007, pp. 120–31.

117. See Marc Morjé Howard, *The Weakness of Civil Society in Post-Communist Europe* (Cambridge and New York: Cambridge University Press, 2003), pp. 58–60, 67.

118. These figures are taken from my 2010 Russia survey (see Note on surveys).

119. See respectively *Izvestiya*, 5 August 2002, p. 4; *ibid.*, 20 January 2006, p. 3.

120. *Ibid.*, 20 January 2003, p. 3; the later membership figure is in *ibid.*, 11 September 2008, p. 2, and the plan for an 'audit' of the existing membership is noted in *ibid.*, 11 June 2008, p. 3.

121. *Ibid.*, 3 March 2003, p. 1.

122. *Ibid.*, 20 March 2003, p. 3.

123. *Novye izvestiya*, 3 July 2003, p. 1.

124. *Kommersant*, 27 October 2006, p. 2.

125. *Ibid.*, 29 October 2007, p. 1.

126. The classification that follows is based on *Vybory 2003*, p. 235.

127. See Richard Rose, William Mishler and Neil Munro, *Russia Transformed: Developing Popular Support for a New Regime* (Cambridge and New York: Cambridge University Press, 2006), pp. 118–20, 145–6.

128. *Ibid.*, pp. 154, 158–9, 163–5.

129. See, for instance, White, Rose and McAllister, *How Russia Votes*, p. 231.

130. See Stephen White and Ian McAllister, 'Turnout and representation bias in post-communist Europe', *Political Studies*, vol. 55, no. 3 (October 2007), pp. 586–606, at pp. 592–4.

131. See Stephen White and Ian McAllister, 'Putin and his supporters', *Europe-Asia Studies*, vol. 55, no. 3 (May 2003), pp. 383–99, and by the same authors, 'The Putin phenomenon', *Journal of Communist Studies and Transition Politics*, vol. 24, no. 4 (December 2008), pp. 604–28.

132. The classic statement is Donald R. Kinder and D. Roderick Kiewiet, 'Economic discontent and political behaviour: the role of personal grievances and collective economic judgements in Congressional voting', *American Journal of Political Science*, vol. 23, no. 3 (August 1979), pp. 495–527.

133. McAllister and White, '"It's the economy, comrade!"', pp. 949–50, 954.

134. See White, 'Russia's client party system', pp. 29–30.

135. White, Rose and McAllister, *How Russia Votes*, p. 135.

136. Richard Rose and Neil Munro, *Elections without Order: Russia's Challenge to Vladimir Putin* (Cambridge and New York: Cambridge University Press, 2002), p. 148.

137. *Izvestiya*, 10 January 1992, p. 3.

138. These figures are from the author's 2008 survey (see Note on surveys).

139. Parties, for instance, under the legislation of 1906 that governed their activities, could not exist at all if their aims and objectives were judged to represent a threat to public morals, and the police could close their meetings at any time if they appeared likely to 'incite hostility between one section of the population and another' (O. I. Chistyakov, ed., *Rossiiskoe zakonodatel'stvo X–XX vekov*, vol. IX (Moscow: Yuridicheskaya literatura, 1994), pp. 207, 224). Parties had relatively few members under these circumstances – no more than 0.5 per cent of the population during the years before the First World War, and up to 1.5 per cent during the months leading up to the October revolution (V. V. Shelokhaev, chief ed., *Politicheskie partii Rossii. Konets XIX – pervaya tret' XX veka. Entsiklopediya* (Moscow: Rosspen, 1996), p. 9). In spite of these restrictions, more than forty parties were active on a countrywide basis in the early years of the new century, and more than a hundred catered for the Empire's numerous minority nationalities (A. I. Zevelev, Yu. P. Sviridenko and V. V. Shelokaev,, eds., *Politicheskie partii Rossii: istoriya i sovremennost'* (Moscow: Rosspen, 2000), p. 9).

140. Howard, *Weakness of Civil Society*, pp. 11, 58–60; the distinctive nature of postcommunist party politics is also emphasised by Peter Mair, *Party System Change: Approaches and Interpretations* (Oxford and New York: Clarendon Press, 1997), pp. 175–98.

141. Focus groups were conducted in the early months of 2004 in Tula, Odintsovo in the Moscow region, Ryazan, Kolomna in the Moscow region, Novosibirsk, Voronezh, Bryansk, the Komi capital Syktyvkar, the village of Konstantinovo in Ryazan region, and Biisk in Novosibirsk region (for a full account see Stephen White, 'Russians and their party system', *Demokratizatsiya*,

vol. 14, no. 1 (Winter 2006), pp. 7–22). The focus groups that took place in June–July 2008 and January 2010 were conducted by the Institute of Applied Politics in Moscow with the support of the Economic and Social Research Council under grant RES-000-22-2532 to Stephen White and Ian McAllister: two in Moscow, one in Podol'sk in the Moscow region, two in Novomoskovsk in the Tula region, one in Kursk, and (in 2010) one in Kaluga and one in Ul'yanovsk.

142. Our own survey evidence (see Note on surveys) found that United Russia voters were within four percentage points of the entire sample on all relevant variables except for gender (women accounted for 55 per cent of the sample but 64 per cent of United Russia voters). On United Russia voters in the 2007 election, see above.

143. In our 2008 survey, for instance, Communist voters were by far the most likely to have decided 'long before' how they would vote, and the second most likely (after United Russia) to base their vote on their approval of the 'programme and slogans' of their chosen party.

144. According to newspaper reports, Yukos had paid the party $30 million for its places on the list, and individual businessmen anything from $1 million to $3 million for an advantageous position (*Izvestiya*, 23 September 2003, p. 3).

145. *Segodnya*, 20 December 1995, p. 1.

146. For the law on state service, see 'Ob osnovakh gosudarstvennoi sluzhby Rossiiskoi Federatsii', *SZ*, no. 31, item 2990, 31 July 1995 (art. 5.11 specified the 'nonparty' nature of the service); the new law, 'O sisteme gosudarstvennoi sluzhby Rossiiskoi Federatsii', *SZ*, no. 22, item 2063, 27 May 2003, made no provision of this kind in its otherwise very similar Article 3. According to the Law on the Government as originally formulated, ministers were not permitted to hold elected positions in legislative bodies at any level, or to be employed by state bodies, local government or public associations (*ibid.*, no. 51, item 5712, 17 December 1997, art. 11); the reference to public associations was subsequently removed (*ibid.*, no. 24, item 4376, 3 November 2004), allowing ministers, if they wished, to hold paid office in political parties and similar organisations.

147. *Rossiiskaya gazeta*, 17 May 2003, p. 4.

148. For recent reviews of such proposals, see, for instance, Yu. S. Pivovarov, ed., *Konstitutsionno-pravovaya reforma v Rossiiskoi Federatsii* (Moscow: INION RAN, 2000), and V. V. Kireev, *Konstitutsionnaya reforma v Rossiiskoi Federatsii* (Moscow: Izdatel'stvo Moskovskogo Universiteta, 2006).

149. The *locus classicus* is Maurice Duverger, 'A new political system model: semi-presidential government', *European Journal of Political Research*, vol. 8, no. 2 (June 1980), pp. 165–87; see also Robert Elgie, ed., *Semi-Presidentialism in Europe* (Oxford and New York: Oxford University Press, 1999).

150. *Rossiiskaya gazeta*, 1 February 2006, p. 3.

151. There were three disagreements on procedural matters at its very first meeting in 1938, but thereafter unanimity prevailed: *Pervaya sessiya Verkhovnogo Soveta SSSR 12–19 yanvarya 1938 goda: stenograficheskii otchet* (Moscow: Izdatel'stvo Verkhovnogo Soveta SSSR, 1938), pp. 49, 50 and 56.

152. Yuri Korolev, *Kremlevskii sovetnik* (Moscow: Olimp, 1995), p. 160.

153. *Moskovskie novosti*, no. 50, 1988, p. 4.

154. See Stephen White, 'The USSR Supreme Soviet: a developmental perspective', in Daniel N. Nelson and White, eds., *Communist Legislatures in Comparative Perspective* (Albany: State University of New York Press, 1982), ch. 6. On turnover particularly, see Ronald J. Hill, 'Continuity and change in USSR Supreme Soviet elections', *British Journal of Political Science*, vol. 2, no. 1 (January 1972), pp. 47–67 (men, older deputies, and party members were disproportionately likely to be re-elected).

155. For the decision see *Pravda*, 20 August 1986, p. 1. Reformer Yuri Chernichenko claimed that a 'victory' had been achieved in public life with this and a decision to abandon an unpopular plan for a memorial to the Second World War: 'public opinion has won and official opinion has been forced to retreat' (*Sovetskaya kul'tura*, 16 August 1986, p. 3).

156. *Izvestiya*, 19 June 1989, p. 5.

157. *Materialy XIX Vsesoyuznoi konferentsii Kommunisticheskoi partii Sovetskogo Soyuza 28 iyunya – 1 iyulya 1988 goda* (Moscow: Politizdat, 1988), pp. 35–7.

158. The Tatar president, Mintimer Shaimiev, was among those who publicly took this view (*Izvestiya*, 11 June 2008, p. 7); so was the Bashkir president, Murtaza Rakhimov (*ibid.*, 30 June 2008, p. 6), and the Moscow mayor, Yuri Luzhkov (*Moscow News*, no. 46, 21 November 2008, p. 10). Similar views continued to be expressed even after the

President had announced the introduction of the principle of indirect election in his November 2008 address: see, for instance, *Gosudarstvo i pravo*, no. 2, 2009, p. 6.

159. *SZ*, no. 7, item 789, 14 February 2009; the residence requirement that had been introduced in 2007 was dropped at the same time.

160. *Rossiiskaya gazeta*, 30 December 2003, p. 1.

161. *SZ*, no. 1, 2004, item 11, 29 December 2003.

162. Under the Duma's standing orders, as reformulated in October 2007, deputies were entitled to resign from their fraction, but if they did so they would automatically lose their seat (*ibid.*, no. 42, item 4981, 9 October 2007, art. 18).

163. Article 19 of the 1998 Duma 'Reglament', as amended, consulted at www.duma.ru; the standing orders are conveniently reprinted in their entirety, with related documents, in S. A. Avak'yan, comp., *Konstitutsionnoe pravo Rossii: sbornik normativnykh aktov* (Moscow: Vebli, 2007), pp. 580–653.

164. *SZ*, no. 31, item 3823, 31 July 1998, ch. 22.

165. *Vremya novostei*, 31 March 2005, p. 1.

166. As one of the Duma's cleaning ladies told the Moscow evening paper (quoted in the *New York Times*, 19 January 1997, part 4, p. 3).

167. Svetlana Lolaeva and Gleb Cherkasov, *Povsednevnaya zhizn' deputatov Gosudarstvennoi dumy, 1993–2003* (Moscow: Molodaya gvardiya, 2007), pp. 161–2.

168. *Komsomol'skaya pravda*, 1 December 1998, pp. 1–2.

169. *Moskovskii komsomolets*, 28 October 1997, p. 2.

170. *Izvestiya*, 26 May 2005, p. 2. Seats in the Federation Council, after the basis of its composition had been changed in 2000, also became an 'ordinary commodity'; the prevailing price in 2006 was between 3.5 and 5 million dollars (*Moskovskii komsomolets*, 17 May 2006, p. 4).

171. See, for instance, O. N. Bulakov, ed., *Parlamentskoe pravo Rossii* (Moscow: Eksmo, 2006), who notes that the practice began to develop in the spring of 2004, when it was used to discuss the conversion of social benefits into cash payments; it was a practice that deprived oppositional deputies of an opportunity to contribute and reduced open parliamentary activity to behind-the-scenes lobbying (pp. 448–52, at pp. 448, 451).

172. The redrafted budget, for instance, completed all its three readings within a week (*Kommersant*, 28 March 2009, p. 2).

173. *Izvestiya*, 30 December 2003, p. 3.

174. *Rossiiskaya gazeta: nedelya*, 22 November 2007, p. 2.

175. Following a constitutional change recorded in *SZ*, no. 1, 2009, item 1, 30 December 2008; the longer term was to apply to the Duma elected after the amendment had come into effect.

3 Presidential government

1. N. A. Sakharov, *Institut prezidentstva v sovremennom mire* (Moscow: Yuridicheskaya literatura, 1994), notes that 130 of the United Nations' 183 members in 1993 had a presidential form of government (p. 3). On Russia's 'leadership' see Dinmukhamed Kunaev in *Prostor*, no. 12, 1991, p. 39.

2. M. F. Nenashev, *Poslednee pravitel'stvo SSSR* (Moscow: Krom, 1993), p. 26. Yeltsin's first deputy head of staff, Oleg Sysuev, rejected the idea that Yeltsin would be willing to be a 'Queen of England' in a later interview (*Moskovskii komsomolets*, 10 November 1998, p. 2).

3. *Izvestiya*, 15 November 1993, p. 4.

4. *Ibid.*, 6 April 1991, p. 1.

5. This is the central thesis of Stephen Whitefield, *Industrial Power and the Soviet State* (Oxford: Clarendon Press and New York: Oxford University Press, 1993).

6. L. A. Okun'kov, *Prezident Rossiiskoi Federatsii: Konstitutsiya i politicheskaya praktika* (Moscow: Infra.M-Norma, 1996), p. 27.

7. See Philip G. Roeder, 'Varieties of post-Soviet authoritarian regimes', *Post-Soviet Affairs*, vol. 10, no. 1 (January–March 1994), pp. 61–101; and more particularly John Anderson, 'Authoritarian political development in Central Asia: the case of Turkmenistan', *Central Asian Survey*, vol. 14, no. 4 (December 1995), pp. 509–27. The most egregious of these potentates, the Turkmen leader Saparmurad Niyazov, died in 2006 and his bizarre personality cult was quickly dismantled.

8. The classification adopted here is based on Sakharov, *Institut prezidentstva*. For a fuller discussion of presidentialism in the postcommunist context, see Ray Taras, ed., *Postcommunist Presidents* (Cambridge and New York: Cambridge University Press, 1997), and Gerald M. Easter, 'Preference for presidentialism: postcommunist regime change in Russia and the NIS', *World Politics*, vol. 49,

no. 2 (January 1997), pp. 184–211. Of the Baltic republics, Estonia and Latvia had parliamentary rather than presidential systems, while Lithuania had a directly elected executive presidency.

9. For a representative selection of views, see, for instance, Arend Lijphart, ed., *Parliamentary versus Presidential Government* (Oxford and New York: Oxford University Press, 1992); Giovanni Sartori, *Comparative Constitutional Engineering* (London: Macmillan, 1994), part 2; Juan J. Linz and Arturo Valenzuela, eds., *The Failure of Presidential Democracy: Comparative Perspectives* (Baltimore: Johns Hopkins University Press, 1994); and José Cheibub, *Presidentialism, Parliamentarism, and Democracy* (Cambridge and New York: Cambridge University Press, 2007).

10. On these developments see Michael E. Urban, 'Boris El'tsin, democratic Russia and the campaign for the Russian presidency', *Soviet Studies*, vol. 44, no. 2 (1992), pp. 187–207.

11. *Vedomosti S"ezda narodnykh deputatov RSFSR i Verkhovnogo Soveta RSFSR*, no. 2, art. 22, 12 June 1990.

12. *Vtoroi (vneocherednoi) s"ezd narodnykh deputatov RSFSR 27 noyabrya – 15 dekabrya 1990 goda: stenograficheskii otchet*, 6 vols. (Moscow: Respublika, 1992), vol. VI, pp. 242–3 (15 December 1990).

13. *Izvestiya*, 26 March 1991, p. 2.

14. *Tretii (vneocherednoi) s"ezd narodnykh deputatov RSFSR 28 marta – 5 aprelya 1991 goda: stenograficheskii otchet*, 5 vols. (Moscow: Respublika, 1992), vol. V, pp. 154–5 (5 April 1991); and *Izvestiya*, 6 April 1991, p. 3.

15. For the text of the law, see *Vedomosti S"ezda narodnykh deputatov RSFSR i Verkhovnogo Soveta RSFSR*, no. 17, art. 512, 24 April 1991.

16. *Ibid.*, no. 22, art. 776, 24 May 1991.

17. *Ibid.*, no. 34, art. 1125, 21 August 1991.

18. *Shestoi S"ezd narodnykh deputatov Rossiiskoi Federatsii 6–21 aprelya 1992 goda: stenograficheskii otchet*, 5 vols. (Moscow: Respublika, 1992), vol. I, pp. 30–1 (the voting on 6 April was 412 in favour but 447 against placing a vote of confidence on the agenda), and for the resolution vol. II, pp. 289–94 (11 April 1992).

19. *Sed'moi s"ezd narodnykh deputatov Rossiiskoi Federatsii 1–14 dekabrya 1992 goda: stenograficheskii otchet*, 4 vols. (Moscow: Respublika, 1993), vol. I, pp. 536–42, 5 December 1992. The President's powers were further weakened by amendments to the Constitution: *Vedomosti S"ezda narodnykh deputatov Rossiiskoi Federatsii i Verkhovnogo Soveta Rossiiskoi Federatsii*, no. 2, 1993, art. 55, 9 December 1992.

20. *Vos'moi (vneocherednoi) s"ezd narodnykh deputatov Rossiiskoi Federatsii 10–13 marta 1993 goda: stenograficheskii otchet* (Moscow: Respublika, 1993), pp. 414–15 and 415–17, 11 and 12 March 1993.

21. For the broadcast see *Delovoi mir*, 23 March 1993, p. 1; the version that was subsequently published contained no reference to a 'special form of administration' (*Rossiiskaya gazeta*, 25 March 1993, p. 1).

22. *Rossiiskaya gazeta*, 1 April 1993, p. 3. For the text of the resolution, which includes the wording of the questions, see *Vedomosti S"ezda narodnykh deputatov Rossiiskoi Federatsii i Verkhovnogo Soveta Rossiiskoi Federatsii*, no. 14, 1993, art. 501, 29 March 1993.

23. The full results appeared in *Rossiiskaya gazeta*, 19 May 1993, pp. 2–3. For a thorough discussion see Marie Mendras, 'Les trois Russie: analyse du referendum du 25 avril 1993', *Revue française de science politique*, vol. 43, no. 6 (December 1993), pp. 897–939.

24. *Sed'moi s"ezd*, vol. III, pp. 126–31, 10 December 1992. It was 'inevitable', he reflected later, that at the end of the Soviet period there would be a conflict between 'two systems of power' (*Izvestiya*, 10 December 1994, p. 1).

25. *Narodnyi deputat*, no. 12, 1992, pp. 13–14, and no. 13, pp. 7–8. For an extended statement of his views, see R. I. Khasbulatov, *Vybor sud'by* (Moscow: Respublika, 1993), and Khasbulatov, *Velikaya rossiiskaya tragediya*, 2 vols. (Moscow: SIMS, 1994).

26. *Izvestiya*, 12 March 1993, p. 1.

27. *Ibid.*, 9 February 1993, p. 1, and (for the 'collective Rasputin') 10 April 1993, p. 1.

28. *Ibid.*, 5 June 1993, pp. 1–2; similarly *Rossiiskaya gazeta*, 2 June 1993, pp. 3–4.

29. *Rossiiskie vesti*, 14 July 1993, p. 1. The presidential draft appeared in *Izvestiya* and *Rossiiskie vesti*, 30 April 1993, pp. 3–5 and 3–6 respectively, and in *Konstitutsionnyi vestnik*, no. 16, 1993, pp. 65–106, with a discussion; the version agreed by the constitutional conference on 12 July appeared in *Rossiiskie vesti*, 15 July 1993, pp. 3–6. A number of drafts are conveniently reprinted in *Konstitutsii Rossiiskoi Federatsii (al'ternativnye proekty)*, 2 vols. (Moscow: Obozrevatel', 1993), and in S. A. Avak'yan, *Konstitutsiya Rossii: priroda, evolyutsiya,*

sovremennost', 2nd edn (Moscow: Sashko, 2000). A still more comprehensive documentation is available in the proceedings of the constitutional conference (*Konstitutsionnoe soveshchanie: stenogrammy, materialy, dokumenty, 29 aprelya – 10 noyabrya 1993 g.*, 20 vols. (Moscow: Yuridicheskaya literatura, 1995–6)) and in O. G. Rumyantsev, ed., *Iz istorii sozdaniya Konstitutsii Rossiiskoi Federatsii. Konstitutsionnaya komissiya: stenogrammy, materialy, dokumenty (1990–1993 gg.)*, 6 vols. (Moscow: Wolters Kluwer, 2007–10).

30. For the text see *Izvestiya*, 10 November 1993, pp. 3–5.

31. Rita Moore, 'The path to the new Russian constitution', *Demokratizatsiya*, vol. 3, no. 1 (Winter 1995), pp. 44–60, at pp. 55–56.

32. *Izvestiya*, 12 October 1994, p. 4 (similarly *ibid.*, 19 March 1998, p. 2); the 'monarchical' label was used, for instance, by Alexander Rutskoi in *Nezavisimaya gazeta*, 8 May 1993, p. 2.

33. The academic and commentator Sergei Karaganov referred to a 'president-tsar' in an interview in *Nezavisimaya gazeta*, 13 October 1993, p. 1; Gorbachev's opinion is quoted in *The Times*, 29 November 1993, p. 16.

34. The president, in addition, headed the armed forces and could declare a state of war as well as a state of emergency (arts. 87 and 88).

35. Under legislation that was adopted in 1995, a referendum could be initiated by 2 million citizens or by a Constitutional Convention (*Sobranie zakonodatel'stva Rossiiskoi Federatsii* [hereafter *SZ*], no. 42, art. 3921, 10 October 1995).

36. The full text as adopted appeared in *Rossiiskaya gazeta*, 25 December 1993, pp. 3–6, and was reprinted in *Konstitutsiya Rossiiskoi Federatsii: prinyata vsenarodnym golosovaniem 12 dekabrya 1993 goda* (Moscow: Yuridicheskaya literatura, 1993) and subsequent editions. For a set of authoritative 'commentaries' by Russian jurists, see B. N. Topornin, Yu. M. Baturin and R. G. Orekhov, eds., *Konstitutsiya Rossiiskoi Federatsii: kommentarii* (Moscow: Yuridicheskaya literatura, 1994). A dictionary of the 1993 Constitution, including the full text in English, French and German, is available in V. A. Tumanov, V. Ye. Chirkin, Yu. A. Yudin, *Konstitutsiya Rossiiskoi Federatsii: entsiklopedicheskii slovar'*, 2nd edn (Moscow: Nauchnoe izdatel'stvo 'Bol'shaya sovetskaya entsiklopediya', 1997). English-language editions of the Constitution are listed in the Further reading section.

37. The powers and composition of the Presidential Administration are set out in two presidential decrees: 'Ob Administratsii Prezidenta Rossiiskoi Federatsii', *SZ*, no. 13, item 1188, 25 March 2004, and 'Polozhenie ob Administratsii Prezidenta Rossiiskoi Federatsii', *ibid.*, no. 15, item 1395, 6 April 2004, as amended. The administration consisted of fifteen departments in 2010, including a foreign policy department, a domestic politics department, a department for appointments and awards, a department for 'work with the communications of citizens', and a press service; see www.kremlin.ru/articles/podr.shtml, last accessed 28 January 2010. The administration had 'about one thousand five hundred' full-time staff in 2009 (*Izvestiya*, 25 February 2009, p. 2).

38. O. Prokhanov, ed., *Kto est' kto v Rossii: spravochnoe izdanie* (Moscow: Olimp/ EKSMO-Press, 1998), p. 742. Yumashev's influence made him 'effectively equal to the premier' in the view of commentators (see, for instance, *Segodnya*, 3 October 1998, p. 1).

39. 'O pravitel'stve Rossiiskoi Federatsii', *SZ*, no. 51, item 5712, 17 December 1997.

40. See *ibid.*, no. 25, item 2478, 19 June 2004. The provisions of the 1997 law in these respects had already been strengthened in a reformulation of the relevant article that was approved on 31 December 1997 (*ibid.*, no. 1, 1998, item 1, art. 32).

41. Article 29 of the Law on the Government. The present composition of the Presidium is set out in a government decree of 16 May 2008: *ibid.*, no. 20, item 2370.

42. *Kommersant daily*, 24 March 1998, p. 1.

43. *Rossiiskaya gazeta*, 24 March 1998, p. 1.

44. *Moscow News*, no. 11, 1998, p. 1.

45. *Rossiiskaya gazeta*, 28 March 1998, p. 1.

46. *Ibid.*, 3 April 1998, p. 2.

47. The voting was 251 in favour, 25 against: *ibid.*, 25 April 1998, p. 2.

48. *Ibid.*, 15 August 1998, p. 1; Kirienko's interview was in *Moskovskii komsomolets*, 5 August 1998, pp. 1–2 (as the paper noted, Napoleon, who had been the first to speak of a 'first hundred days', had come to a 'bad end').

49. Yeltsin's own health, it appears, was a crucial element in this decision: in the event of incapacity his powers would pass to the prime minister, and there was concern within the Kremlin 'inner circle' that Kirienko would be 'too weak and inexperienced to handle all that': *Newsweek*, 18 January 1999, p. 35.

50. Chernomyrdin's nomination and Yeltsin's broadcast were both reported in *Rossiiskaya gazeta*, 25 August 1998, p. 1.

51. *Segodnya*, 1 September 1998, p. 1 (the voting was 94 in favour, 257 against); *ibid.*, 8 September 1998, p. 1 (this time there were 138 votes in favour).

52. *Rossiiskaya gazeta*, 2 September 1998, p. 1. A report in *Nezavisimaya gazeta* earlier in the year suggested that Our Home is Russia and the Communist Party would both have gained slightly, but that Yabloko would nearly have trebled its vote (22 April 1998, p. 8); another survey reported that the Communist Party would have jumped from the 22.3 per cent it had achieved in the 1995 election to 37.9 per cent (*Argumenty i fakty*, no. 16, 1998, p. 7).

53. *Segodnya*, 12 September 1998, p. 1 (315 were in favour, 63 against).

54. *Obshchaya gazeta*, no. 36, 1998, p. 7.

55. *Rossiiskaya gazeta*, 12 September 1998, p. 1.

56. For the vote see *Segodnya*, 22 August 1998, p. 1; according to a survey reported in *Trud-7*, 4–10 September 1998, some 66 per cent of Russians favoured Yeltsin's immediate resignation (p. 3).

57. *Kommersant daily*, 29 August 1998, p. 1.

58. Oleg Sysuev in *Segodnya*, 28 October 1998, pp. 1–2.

59. *Ibid.*, 17 September 1998, p. 2 (59 per cent of urban residents were reported to approve of the new appointment, with 17 per cent against).

60. The claim that Yeltsin would have been 'unable to win decisively' in the second round of the presidential election unless the 'seven bankers' had persuaded him to ally with Alexander Lebed' was made by Boris Berezovsky in an interview in the *Financial Times*, 1 November 1996, p. 17; the bankers, as far as he recalled, had contributed about $3 billion to the Yeltsin campaign. On privatisation more generally, see pp. 129–35.

61. For a more detailed account of the entire episode, see Peter Reddaway and Dmitri Glinski, *The Tragedy of Russia's Reforms: Market Bolshevism against Democracy* (Washington, DC: United States Institute of Peace Press, 2001), pp. 604–8. Skuratov's own version is in Yuri Skuratov, *Variant drakona* (Moscow: Detektiv Press, 2000).

62. *Rossiiskaya gazeta*, 13 May 1999, p. 1.

63. *Segodnya*, 3 April 1999, p. 2.

64. *SZ*, no. 1, 2000, item 11, 31 December 1999 (an earlier decree simply gave formal notice that he had assumed the responsibilities of acting president: *ibid.*, item 10, 31 December 1999).

65. *Kommersant*, 10 August 1999, p. 3.

66. Boris Yeltsin, *Prezidentskii marafon* (Moscow: AST, 2000), pp. 354–9, 383–4.

67. *Ot pervogo litsa: razgovory s Vladimirom Putinym* (Moscow: Vagrius, 2000), pp. 130–1.

68. *Rossiiskaya gazeta*, 17 August 1999, pp. 1–2.

69. *Ibid.*, p. 1.

70. *Nezavisimaya gazeta*, 2 September 1999, pp. 1–2; here and elsewhere casualty figures are as reported in *Segodnya*, 20 September 1999, p. 2. The final total was 241 dead and 'several hundred' injured: *Izvestiya*, 30 April 2003, p. 10.

71. *Kommersant*, 7 September 1999, pp. 1, 3.

72. *Segodnya*, 10 September 1999, pp. 1, 7; *Nezavisimaya gazeta*, 14 September 1999, pp. 1–2.

73. *Rossiiskaya gazeta*, 14 September 1999, p. 1.

74. *Kommersant*, 15 September 1999, p. 2.

75. *Vremya MN*, 17 September 1999, p. 1.

76. *Segodnya*, 24 September 1999, p. 1, and 25 September 1999, pp. 1–2.

77. *Rossiiskaya gazeta*, 25 September 1999, p. 2.

78. Some 'two-thirds' of the population favoured the mass bombardment of Chechnya following the explosions in Moscow, and 'three-quarters' supported some form of military action: Valerii Fedorov, ed., *Ot Yel'tsina do Putina: tri epokhi v istoricheskom soznanii rossiyan* (Moscow: VTsIOM, 2007), p. 44. There are many accounts of the continuing Chechen conflict, including John B. Dunlop, *Russia Confronts Chechnya: Roots of a Separatist Conflict* (Cambridge and New York: Cambridge University Press, 1998); Matthew Evangelista, *The Chechen Wars: Will Russia Go the Way of the Soviet Union?* (Washington, DC: Brookings, 2002); Valerii Tishkov, *Chechnya: Life in a War-Torn Society* (Berkeley: University of California Press, 2004); Richard Sakwa, ed., *Chechnya: From Past to Future* (London: Anthem Press, 2005); Moshe Gammer, *The Lone Wolf and the Bear: Three Centuries of Chechen Defiance of Russian Rule* (London: Hurst, 2005); John Russell, *Chechnya – Russia's 'War on Terror'* (London and New York: Routledge, 2007); Tony Wood, *Chechnya: The Case for Independence* (London and New York: Verso, 2007); and James Hughes, *Chechnya: From Nationalism to Jihad* (Philadelphia: University of Pennsylvania Press, 2007). The 'anti-terrorist action' was officially concluded in the spring of 2009; since October 1999 an officially estimated 4,000 servicemen had died in the conflict (the Committee of Soldiers' Mothers estimated

twice as many): *Izvestiya*, 17 April 2009, pp. 1–2.

79. *Rossiiskaya gazeta*, 25 September 1999, p. 1.

80. None of the Chechen groups had claimed responsibility for the apartment bombings, from which in any case they had little to gain. The journalist David Satter, among others, concluded that the bombings had been 'organised not by the Chechens' but 'by those who needed another war capable of propelling Putin into the presidency in order to save their corruptly acquired wealth. These could only have been the leaders of the Yeltsin regime itself' (*Darkness at Dawn: The Rise of the Russian Criminal State* (New Haven, CT, and London: Yale University Press, 2003), p. 69). The most elaborate statement of this conspiratorial view is Yuri Felshtinsky and Alexander Litvinenko, *Blowing Up Russia* (London: Gibson Square, 2007).

81. *Trud*, 27 January 2000, p. 2 (VTsIOM survey figures, based in each case on respondents who said they were intending to vote).

82. B. N. Yeltsin, *Ispoved' na zadannuyu temu* (Leningrad: Chas pik, 1990), pp. 17–18.

83. *Izvestiya*, 28 September 1993, p. 4; the incident was also reported in B. N. Yeltsin, *Zapiski Prezidenta* (Moscow: Ogonek, 1994), pp. 121–5.

84. Alexander Korzhakov, *Boris Yel'tsin: ot rassveta do zakata* (Moscow: Interbuk, 1997), p. 78.

85. Yeltsin, *Ispoved'*, various pages. Naina Yeltsin explained how they had met in *Moskovskie novosti*, no. 7, 1997, p. 4. For biographical accounts see Leon Aron, *Yeltsin: A Revolutionary Life* (New York: St Martin's and London: HarperCollins, 2000); Herbert J. Ellison, *Boris Yeltsin and Russia's Democratic Transformation* (Seattle and London: University of Washington Press, 2006); most authoritatively Timothy J. Colton, *Yeltsin: A Life* (New York: Basic Books, 2008); and most recently Boris Minaev, *Boris Yel'tsin* (Molodaya gvardiya, 2010).

86. Yeltsin, *Ispoved'*, p. 58. Yeltsin's speech at the burial was reported in *Izvestiya*, 18 July 1998, p. 1; the Orthodox Church remained doubtful about the 'Yekaterinburg remains', and the Patriarch chose to remain in Moscow.

87. Yeltsin, *Ispoved'*, p. 63.

88. His appointment was reported in *Pravda*, 25 December 1985, p. 2; his successor was Viktor Grishin.

89. *XXVII S"ezd Kommuunisticheskoi partii Sovetskogo Soyuza 25 fevralya – 6 marta 1986 goda: stenograficheskii otchet*, 3 vols.

(Moscow: Politizdat, 1986), vol. I, pp. 140–5.

90. V. I. Vorotnikov, *A bylo eto tak … Iz dnevnika chlena Politbyuro TsK KPSS* (Moscow: Sovet veteranov knigoizdaniya, 1995), p. 167. Ten years later Yeltsin recalled his own action as the 'result of prolonged reflection', based on a belief that *perestroika* would 'only make sense if it affected the party' (*Segodnya*, 28 October 1997, p. 1).

91. *Izvestiya Tsentral'nogo komiteta* [hereafter *TsK*] *KPSS*, no. 2, 1989, pp. 239–41; for the unauthorised version see *Le Monde*, 2 February 1988, p. 6. Yeltsin referred to his preparation for the speech in *Ispoved'*, p. 134. Many different versions of the speech were circulated as a kind of 'samizdat of the *glasnost'* era', and its purported author became a 'hero' (Yekaterina Lakhova, *Moi put' v politiku* (Moscow: Aurika, 1995), pp. 97, 98).

92. Yeltsin, *Ispoved'*, p. 137.

93. *Izvestiya TsK KPSS*, no. 2, 1989, p. 287; Gorbachev's contribution is recorded in Yeltsin, *Ispoved'*, p. 99.

94. *Ispoved'*, p. 143 ('barely conscious'); *Pravda*, 13 November 1987, pp. 1–3. Yeltsin, it appeared to Gorbachev, had simulated a suicide, although he later claimed it had been a hooligan attack (M. S. Gorbachev, *Zhizn' i reformy*, 2 vols. (Moscow: Novosti, 1995), vol. I, p. 374).

95. Korzhakov, *Boris Yel'tsin*, pp. 65, 66.

96. Yeltsin, *Ispoved'*, p. 175.

97. *Materialy Plenuma Tsentral'nogo komiteta KPSS, 15–16 marta 1989 goda* (Moscow: Politizdat, 1989), pp. 5–6.

98. *Moskovskaya pravda*, 28 March 1989, p. 2.

99. *Izvestiya*, 5 March 1990, p. 2.

100. *Sovetskaya Bashkiriya*, 14 August 1990, p. 1.

101. *Materialy Plenuma … 5–7 fevralya 1990 goda*, pp. 68–9.

102. *XXVIII S"ezd Kommunisticheskoi partii Sovetskogo Soyuza, 2–13 iyulya 1990 goda: stenograficheskii otchet*, 2 vols. (Moscow: Izdatel'stvo politicheskoi literatury, 1991), vol. I, pp. 473–4, and vol. II, pp. 500–1.

103. *Argumenty i fakty*, no. 22, 1990, p. 3.

104. *Rossiiskaya gazeta*, 4 November 1993, p. 4; Yeltsin referred again to Peter the Great in his interview in *Argumenty i fakty*, no. 16, 1993, p. 3.

105. *Izvestiya*, 11 June 1992, p. 3.

106. *Pravda*, 10 June 1991, p. 2.

107. Yeltsin, *Zapiski Prezidenta*, pp. 173–4, 181.

108. Lev Sukhanov, *Tri goda s Yel'tsinym* (Riga: Vaga, 1992), pp. 143–50.

109. Viktor Yaroshenko, *Yel'tsin: ya otvechu za vse* (Moscow: Vokrug sveta, 1997), pp. 32–3.

110. Her appointment was reported in *Izvestiya*, 1 July 1997, p. 1; Korzhakov left no doubt of her influence in his *Boris Yel'tsin*, pp. 353–60.

111. Korzhakov, *Boris Yel'tsin*, p. 126.

112. See, for instance, *Argumenty i fakty*, no. 3, 1995, p. 3, and no. 44, 1995, p. 1.

113. Korzhakov, *Boris Yel'tsin*, p. 359.

114. *Argumenty i fakty*, no. 49, 1997, p. 2. Berezovsky's direct access to the Yeltsin family could be exaggerated: Mrs Yeltsin, interviewed in late 1998, had not seen him since the presidential elections and insisted he had 'never visited them at home': *Argumenty i fakty*, no. 41, 1998, p. 3.

115. Yavlinsky quoted in *Dialog*, no. 9, 1998, p. 17, and *Izvestiya*, 1 November 1995, p. 1.

116. *Moskovskie novosti*, no. 36, 1995, p. 5.

117. *Kommersant daily*, 4 November 1995, p. 1.

118. Vyacheslav Kostikov, *Roman s prezidentom* (Moscow: Vagrius, 1997), pp. 10–11, 16. Boris Nemtsov, while first deputy premier, was another who believed his telephone had been tapped (*Izvestiya*, 11 September 1997, p. 1, and similarly in *ibid.*, 20 January 1998, p. 5).

119. Kostikov, *Roman*, pp. 14–15, 20–1.

120. Korzhakov, *Boris Yel'tsin*, p. 253.

121. *Ibid.*, pp. 252–3.

122. *Ibid.*, p. 82.

123. Lakhova, *Moi put'*, p. 146.

124. Kostikov, *Roman*, pp. 65, 84, 128, 300–1, 130, 317, 339, 347.

125. Yegor Gaidar, *Dni porazhenii i pobed* (Moscow: Vagrius, 1996), pp. 60–2, 105–6.

126. Korzhakov, *Boris Yel'tsin*.

127. *Argumenty i fakty*, no. 16, 1994, p. 1.

128. *Nezavisimaya gazeta*, 28 February 1991, p. 2.

129. *Sem' s plyusom*, no. 12 (March 1991), p. 4.

130. *Nezavisimaya gazeta*, 28 February 1991, p. 2; similarly *Moskovskie novosti*, no. 15, 1991, p. 10.

131. *Argumenty i fakty*, no. 38, 1993, p. 2.

132. *Ekonomicheskie i sotsial'nye peremeny: monitoring obshchestvennogo mneniya*, no. 1, 1995, p. 5.

133. *Izvestiya*, 14 December 1994, p. 3. Interior Minister Vyacheslav Plehve had spoken of the need for a 'small, victorious war' in order to head off the pressure for political change in a conversation with General Kuropatkin in January 1904 on the eve of the ill-fated conflict with Japan (Konstantin Dushenko, ed., *Russkie politicheskie tsitaty ot Lenina do Yel'tsina* (Moscow: Yurist, 1996), p. 71).

134. *Kommersant daily*, 10 March 1995, p. 3.

135. *Nezavisimaya gazeta*, 17 February 1996, p. 1.

136. See, for instance, *Izvestiya*, 18 May 1996, pp. 1–2 (conscription and service in Chechnya). Yeltsin's success is largely explained in these terms in Daniel Treisman, 'Why Yeltsin won', *Foreign Affairs*, vol. 75, no. 5 (September–October 1996), pp. 64–77.

137. *Washington Post*, 7 July 1996, p. A22. As in the case of other candidates, Yeltsin's election expenses were reported in the bulletin of the Central Electoral Commission: *Vestnik Tsentral'noi izbiratel'noi komissii Rossiiskoi Federatsii*, no. 18(38), 1996, pp. 20–2.

138. *Nezavisimaya gazeta*, 7 September 1996, p. 1.

139. *Argumenty i fakty*, no. 22, 1996, p. 1; for Berezovsky's comment on Yeltsin 'waking up', see the *Washington Post*, 7 July 1996, p. A22. The thesis that there had been a Yeltsin imposter – or perhaps more than one – was repeatedly put forward during the campaign by the nationalist newspaper *Zavtra*, basing itself on a close study of the number of fingers on the left hand (if all were present it had to be someone else) and the ears; the real Yeltsin had supposedly died before the election and was being preserved in a refrigerator (interview with the journalist and editor of *Duel'*, Yuri Mukhin, in *Zavtra*, 11 December 1997, p. 3). The head of a Duma committee and a 'specialist in falsifications', Alexander Saly, suggested instead that Yeltsin had been replaced after the election, during his heart operation (*Moskovskii komsomolets*, 18 June 1998, p. 1).

140. For the flow of votes between the two rounds, see *Argumenty i fakty*, no. 28, 1996, p. 2.

141. *Vybory Prezidenta Rossiiskoi Federatsii. 1996. Elektoral'naya statistika* (Moscow: Ves' mir, 1996), pp. 190, 192. There is a considerable literature on these watershed elections: see, for instance, on the background Jerry F. Hough, Evelyn Davidheiser and Susan Goodrich Lehmann, *The 1996 Russian Presidential Election* (Washington, DC: Brookings, 1996), and on the outcome Richard Rose and Evgeny Tikhomirov, 'Russia's forced choice presidential election', *Post-Soviet Affairs*, vol. 12, no. 4 (October–December 1996), pp. 351–79; Ralph S. Clem and Peter R. Craumer, 'Roadmap to victory: Boris Yel'tsin and the Russian presidential

elections of 1996', *Post-Soviet Geography and Economics*, vol. 37, no. 6 (June 1996), pp. 335–54; Stephen White, Richard Rose and Ian McAllister, *How Russia Votes* (Chatham House, NJ: Chatham House, 1997), ch. 12; Yitzhak M. Brudny, 'In pursuit of the Russian presidency: why and how El'tsin won the 1996 presidential election', *Communist and Post-Communist Studies*, vol. 30, no. 3 (September 1997), pp. 255–75; David S. Mason and Svetlana Sidorenko-Stephenson, 'Public opinion and the 1996 elections in Russia: nostalgic and statist, yet pro-market and pro-Yeltsin', *Slavic Review*, vol. 56, no. 4 (Winter 1997), pp. 698–717; and Michael McFaul, *Russia's 1996 Presidential Election: The End of Polarized Politics* (Stanford, CA: Hoover Institution Press, 1997).

142. *SZ*, no. 46, item 5701, 5 November 1998.

143. *Rossiiskaya gazeta*, 5 January 2000, pp. 1–2.

144. *Kommersant*, 26 February 2000, p. 1.

145. The 'Open Letter' appeared in *Izvestiya*, 25 February 2000, p. 4, and simultaneously in *Kommersant*, *Komsomol'skaya pravda* and *Trud*, all on p. 3.

146. *Ot pervogo litsa*, pp. 163, 161, 166.

147. *Ibid.*, pp. 135, 136. An English translation appeared as *First Person: An Astonishingly Frank Self-Portrait by Russia's President Vladimir Putin, with Nataliya Gevorkyan, Natalya Timakova, and Andrei Kolsenikov*, trans. Catherine A. Fitzpatrick (London: Hutchinson and New York: Random House, 2000).

148. *Kommersant*, 21 March 2000, p. 1.

149. *Russian Federation: Presidential Election 26 March 2000 – Final Report* (Warsaw: ODIHR, 2000), pp. 21–3.

150. *Monitoring the Media Coverage of the March 2000 Presidential Elections in Russia: Final Report* (Düsseldorf: European Institute for the Media, 2000), pp. 43, 46. For a fuller discussion of the 2000 presidential election, see, for instance, Richard Sakwa, 'Russia's "permanent" (uninterrupted) elections of 1999–2000', *Journal of Communist Studies and Transition Politics*, vol. 16, no. 3 (September 2000), pp. 85–112; Timothy J. Colton and Michael McFaul, *Popular Choice and Managed Democracy: The Russian Elections of 1999 and 2000* (Washington, DC: Brookings, 2003); and Vicki L. Hesli and William M. Reisinger, eds., *The 1999–2000 Elections in Russia: Their Impact and Legacy* (Cambridge and New York: Cambridge University Press, 2003).

The regional dimension is again given close attention in Ralph S. Clem and Peter R. Craumer, 'Spatial patterns of political choice in the post-Yeltsin era: the electoral geography of Russia's 2000 presidential election', *Post-Soviet Geography and Economics*, vol. 41, no. 7 (October–November 2000), pp. 465–82. The work of Russian political scientists based at the European University in St Petersburg is represented in Vladimir Gel'man, Grigorii Golosov and Yelena Melekhina, eds., *Vtoroi elektoral'nyi tsikl v Rossii 1999–2000 gg.* (Moscow: Ves' mir, 2002); Maikl Makfol, Nikolai Petrov and Andrei Ryabov, eds., *Rossiya v izbiratel'nom tsikle 1999–2000 godov* (Moscow: Gendal'f, 2000), draws on the resources of the Moscow Carnegie Center.

151. *Russian Federation: Presidential Election 26 March 2000 – Final Report*, pp. 3–5.

152. *International Observer Mission: Election of President of the Russian Federation 16th June 1996 and 3rd July 1996 – Report on the Election* (Warsaw: ODIHR, 1996), pp. 4–5.

153. *Izvestiya*, 9 January 2004, p. 1.

154. *Kommersant*, 2 February 2004, p. 2 (a whole-page advertisement).

155. *Ibid.*, 11 February 2004, p. 1.

156. *Ibid.*, 6 March 2004, p. 3.

157. *Argumenty i fakty*, no. 7, 2004, pp. 4–9.

158. *Russian Federation: Presidential Election 14 March 2004: OSCE/ODIHR Election Observation Mission Report* (Warsaw: ODIHR, 2004), p. 13.

159. For a fuller account see Christopher Marsh, Helen Albert and James W. Warhola, 'The political geography of Russia's 2004 presidential election', *Eurasian Geography and Economics*, vol. 45, no. 4 (June 2004), pp. 262–79; Richard Sakwa, 'The 2003–2004 Russian elections and prospects for democracy', *Europe-Asia Studies*, vol. 57, no. 3 (May 2005), pp. 369–98; and Vladimir Gel'man, ed., *Tretii elektoral'nyi tsikl v Rossii, 2003–2004 gody* (St Petersburg: Yevropeiskii universitet v Sankt-Peterburge, 2007). A much more sceptical view of the exercise, based on econometric evidence, is taken by Mikhail Myagkov, Peter C. Ordeshook and Dimitri Shakin, *The Forensics of Election Fraud: Russia and Ukraine* (Cambridge and New York: Cambridge University Press, 2009), who conclude that there were 'upwards of 10 million or more suspect votes' and that fraud 'now permeates Russian elections' (p. 137).

160. *Russian Federation: Presidential Election 14 March 2004: OSCE/ODIHR Election Observation Mission Report*, pp. 16, 18.

161. A 'wave of popular support for a third term for Vladimir Putin' had been 'gathering across the country' in late 2007, according to press reports; spokesmen for the Kremlin and United Russia insisted it had been a 'grassroots initiative' (*Kommersant*, 25 October 2007, p. 1), but intercepted documents made clear that regional officials had instructed schools in the Tver region and railway departments in Novosibirsk to make the necessary arrangements (*Guardian*, 31 October 2007, p. 22), and in Grozny the students who came in that morning had been told that 'all classes were cancelled and [that they] should take part in the action in support of Putin' (*Sovetskaya Rossiya*, 27 October 2007, p. 2). An open letter to Putin on behalf of 'more than 65,000 artists, painters, sculptors, graphic designers, craftsmen, set designers and folk artists' appeared in the government newspaper the same month, calling similarly on the Russian leader to remain beyond the end of his second term in March 2008 and signed by four very senior representatives of the cultural intelligentsia (*Rossiiskaya gazeta*, 16 October 2007, p. 2). 'Where are the other 64,996 names?', asked *Sovetskaya Rossiya* (27 October 2007, p. 2), echoing the complaint from a St Petersburg actor that had appeared in the liberal paper *Novaya gazeta* (25 October 2007, pp. 19–20).

162. *Rossiiskaya gazeta*, 15 February 2008, p. 1. The possibility of a third term had been advanced by Magadan Duma as early as 2002, and it found further support among local legislators in 2005 and 2006; Putin himself had ruled out the possibility of a third term as early as June 2003 (*Izvestiya*, 18 January 2007, p. 3). Speaking to Indian journalists in 2007, however, he was less unqualified: the question of a third term, he told them, was one that 'would have to be discussed with the citizens of Russia' (*Moskovskie novosti*, no. 3, 26 January 2007, p. 14).

163. For representative discussions of these alternatives, see, for instance, Roi Medvedev, *Vladimir Putin* (Moscow: Molodaya gvardiya, 2007), pp. 660–70, and Vladimir Solov'ev, *Putin – putevoditel' dlya neravnodushnykh* (Moscow: Eksmo, 2008), pp. 375–415. The call for Putin to become a 'national leader' was associated particularly with party leader Boris Gryzlov: see for instance *Rossiiskaya gazeta: nedelya*, 23 October 2007, p. 5, and *Izvestiya*, 8 November 2007, p. 3.

164. *Rossiiskaya gazeta*, 11 December 2007, p. 1.

165. *Ibid.*, 12 December 2007, p. 1.

166. *Ibid.*, 28 January 2008, p. 3.

167. *Izvestiya*, 29 January 2008, p. 2.

168. *Rossiiskaya gazeta*, 23 January 2008, p. 3.

169. Putin's speech to the State Council appeared in *ibid.*, 9 February 2008, pp. 1–3; for a discussion see pp. 148–9.

170. *Rossiiskaya gazeta*, 16 February 2008, pp. 1, 3–4, at p. 3.

171. *Ibid.*, 28 February 2008, p. 3.

172. *Ibid.*, 4 March 2008, p. 1. There is a close analysis of the sources of Medvedev's as well as Putin's electoral support in Timothy J. Colton and Henry E. Hale, 'The Putin vote: presidential electorates in a hybrid regime', *Slavic Review*, vol. 68, no. 3 (Fall 2009), pp. 473–503. Myagkov, Ordeshook and Shakin argue that the degree of central management had by now become such that to call the exercise an election 'denigrates the meaning of the word' (*Forensics*, p. 6).

173. *Rossiiskaya gazeta*, 4 March 2008, pp. 1–2.

174. *Izvestiya*, 12 May 2008, p. 2 (the report in *Kommersant* on the same date recorded no abstentions or absences of any kind; Putin, either way, had more support from those who voted, or could have voted, than any premier had so far been able to secure).

175. *Izvestiya*, 10 August 1999, p. 1.

176. *Financial Times*, 6 September 2000, p. 11. He had been thrown by a 14-year-old boy on a visit earlier in the year: *Asashi Shimbun*, 24 July 2000, p. 30 (I owe this reference to Dr Atsushi Ogushi). For the textbook, see Vladimir Putin, Vasilii Shestakov and Aleksei Levitsky, *Dzyudo: istoriya, teoriya, praktika* (Archangel: Izdatel'skii dom SK, 2000). In 2007 he made an instructional judo video with Yasuhiro Yamashita, a world judo champion from Japan (*Moscow Times*, 15 April 2008, p. 1).

177. *Ot pervogo litsa*, p. 86. There are full biographies in Richard Sakwa, *Putin: Russia's Choice*, 2nd edn (Abingdon and New York: Routledge, 2008), and in Roi Medvedev's *Vladimir Putin*, 2nd edn (Moscow: Molodaya gvardiya, 2008), extended by the same author's *Vladimir Putin: prodolzhenie sleduet*, 2nd edn (Moscow: Vremya, 2010).

178. *Rossiiskaya gazeta*, 31 December 1999, pp. 4–5, and also in *Nezavisimaya gazeta*, 30 December 1999, p. 4 (an English translation is appended to the text of *First Person*, pp. 209–19).

179. *Komsomol'skaya pravda*, 2 August 2001, p. 11.

180. *Ibid.*, 12 March 2001, pp. 3, 7 (fighting), and 26 June 2001, p. 6.

181. Vera Gurevich, *Vospominaniya o budushchem prezidente* (Moscow: Mezhdunarodnye otnosheniya, 2001), pp. 10, 12 and 9 respectively.

182. *Knizhnoe obozrenie*, 30 September 2002, p. 5.

183. Oleg Blotsky, *Vladimir Putin: istoriya zhizni*, vol. I (Moscow: Mezhdunarodnye otnosheniya, 2002), pp. 59, 61, 216. The second volume appeared later the same year: *Vladimir Putin: doroga k vlasti. Kniga vtoraya* (Moscow: Osmos-Press, 2002); there has, however, been no sign of further instalments.

184. *Obshchaya gazeta*, 24 May 2001, p. 7.

185. *Argumenty i fakty*, no. 49, 2001, p. 5, and no. 16, 2002, p. 4 (watch); and on the bar, *Guardian*, 29 June 2002, p. 16 (it was later closed down: *Izvestiya*, 28 September 2002, p. 1).

186. *RFE/RL Newsline*, 28 August 2002; the group and their director were featured in *Ogonek*, no. 40, 2002, pp. 28–9.

187. This was a play on the President's celebrated promise that he would 'wipe out the terrorists even if they [were] on the john' (*Rossiiskaya gazeta*, 25 September 1999, p. 1).

188. *Argumenty i fakty*, no. 40, 2002, p. 4.

189. Quoted in *Moscow Times*, 11 March 2008, p. 1.

190. *Guardian*, 12 March 2001, p. 14.

191. *St Petersburg Times*, 3 November 2000, p. 1.

192. *Izvestiya*, 29 June 2002, p. 3.

193. *Guardian*, 12 March 2001, p. 14.

194. *Ibid.*, 12 October 2004, p. 4.

195. 'In bed with President Putin', 20 September 2001, accessed at www.english.pravda.ru/fun/2002/09/20/15789.html; this and some of the other examples are drawn from Stephen White and Ian McAllister, 'Putin and his supporters', *Europe-Asia Studies*, vol. 55, no. 3 (May 2003), pp. 383–99, and by the same authors, 'The Putin phenomenon', *Journal of Communist Studies and Transition Politics*, vol. 24, no. 4 (December 2008), pp. 604–28. The 'Putin phenomenon' had been identified even before he assumed the acting presidency: see, for instance, *Izvestiya*, 22 December 1999, p. 4. The

French film star Brigitte Bardot went so far as to call Putin 'the president of my heart' (*ibid.*, 25 September 2009, p. 9).

196. See respectively *Komsomol'skaya pravda*, 22 August 2007, p. 1 (bare chest); *Izvestiya*, 2 September 2008, p. 2 (tiger); *Komsomol'skaya pravda*, 5 August 2009, p. 4 (swim); *Vremya novostei*, 3 August 2009, p. 2 (submarine); *Izvestiya*, 26 August 2010, p. 3 (whale); *ibid.*, 11 August 2010, p. 3 (co-pilot). Putin's status as a 'gay icon' was mentioned in *The Times*, 5 August 2009, p. 29. Was he perhaps 'preparing for the next presidential elections', asked V. Mikhailin of Klimovsk, after the latest of these sequences was made public (*Argumenty i fakty*, no. 33, 2009, p. 7).

197. *Izvestiya*, 27 June 2007, p. 1.

198. *Ibid.*, 9 August 2007, p. 5.

199. *Ibid.*, 27 June 2007, p. 4.

200. *Ibid.*, p. 1.

201. *Ibid.*, 19 July 2007, p. 4.

202. *Ibid.*, 6 October 2008, p. 6.

203. Aleksandr Kolesnichenko, 'Nesting dolls, vodka, and underpants', *Transitions Online*, 5 May 2008, at www.tol.cz/look/TOL, last accessed 15 September 2008.

204. *Izvestiya*, 14 August 2007, p. 2.

205. *Anekdoty pro Putina* (St Petersburg: Izdatel'stvo Bukovskogo, 2001), p. 11.

206. *Moskovskii komsomolets*, 11 December 2007, pp. 1, 4; and on the number of sects, 'Russian sect prays to Putin icons, claims he is the "chosen one"', RIA-Novosti, 11 December 2007, www.rian.ru, last accessed 5 May 2008.

207. See, for instance, Roi Medvedev, *Dmitrii Medvedev: Prezident Rossiiskoi Federatsii* (Moscow: Vremya, 2008), p. 89; *Moscow Times*, 27 February 2008, pp. 1–2. The fullest available biography is Roi Medvedev, *Dmitrii Medvedev: dvoinaya prochnost' vlasti*, 2nd edn (Moscow: Vremya, 2010), which extends the same author's *Dmitrii Medvedev*; for an illuminating series of interviews in a format very similar to Putin's own *First Person*, see Nikolai Svanidze and Marina Svanidze, *Medvedev* (St Petersburg: Amfora, 2008).

208. *Itogi*, no. 16, 16 April 2007, p. 22.

209. His grandfather had been a district first secretary in the Kuban and a party member for more than sixty years who had 'very much believed in socialist ideals' (Svanidze, *Medvedev*, p. 113), and his own father had considered a party career before choosing the life of science (*ibid.*, p. 109). Given

Medvedev's age and occupation, it is likely that he was himself a party member, although not necessarily an active one.

210. *Ibid.*, p. 204.

211. *Argumenty i fakty*, no. 10, 2008, p. 3.

212. These details are based on K. A. Shchegolev, ed., *Kto est' kto v Rossii. Ispolnitel'naya vlast'. Kto pravit sovremennoi Rossiei*, 2nd edn (Moscow: AST/Astrel', 2010), pp. 324–61.

213. *Kommersant*, 15 September 2007, p. 1.

214. *Izvestiya*, 11 December 2007, p. 2.

215. *Itogi*, no. 8, 18 February 2008, p. 22.

216. *Ibid.*, no. 16, 16 April 2007, p. 24.

217. *Moscow Times*, 15 April 2008, p. 1.

218. *Argumenty i fakty*, no. 10, 2008, p. 3.

219. The full text appeared in *Rossiiskaya gazeta*, 16 February 2008, pp. 1, 3–4.

220. *Moskovskie novosti*, no. 75, 1995, p. 5.

221. Kostikov, *Roman*, pp. 53–6; for the calls for a medical inspection, see, for instance, *Moskovskie novosti*, no. 38, 1996, p. 6, and *Kommersant daily*, 11 June 1998, p. 3 (which noted that there had been demands of this kind since May 1992).

222. *Kommersant daily*, 7 September 1996, p. 1. A decree of 19 September 1996 provided for the 'temporary performance of the duties of the President of the Russian Federation' in such circumstances: *SZ*, no. 39, 1996, art. 4533.

223. *Argumenty i fakty*, no. 16, 1993, p. 3.

224. *Nezavisimaya gazeta*, 16 May 1992, p. 2.

225. *Guardian*, 29 March 1993, p. 18.

226. Korzhakov, *Boris Yel'tsin*, pp. 213–18.

227. *Guardian*, 9 September 1994, p. 12.

228. Korzhakov, *Boris Yel'tsin*, pp. 219–20.

229. *Lipetskaya gazeta*, 2 March 1995, p. 2. Yeltsin told voters during the 1996 presidential election that he could 'take a drink' but didn't 'go too far' (*Izvestiya*, 22 May 1996, p. 2). Yeltsin had not emerged at Shannon airport, in fact, because of a heart attack, following which Korzhakov had refused to allow him to leave the aircraft (*Boris Yel'tsin*, pp. 209–10). An official apology to the Irish government followed shortly afterwards (*Izvestiya*, 8 October 1994, p. 1).

230. Interview on Russian television, 14 March 1996, as quoted in the *OMRI Daily Digest*, no. 54, part 1, 15 March 1996.

231. For Yeltsin's sympathetic interest in a restoration of the monarchy, see, for instance, the *Guardian*, 15 October 1994, p. 13, based on statements made during his visit to China in 1992; Yeltsin's interest was shared by the historian Yuri Afanas'ev in *Izvestiya*, 20 June 1997, p. 5.

232. *Segodnya*, 26 December 1997, p. 3. Yeltsin made clear elsewhere that he could 'not agree with proposals for amending the existing Constitution'; in his opinion it had 'proved its viability' and they must 'all learn to live under the present Constitution and make full use of its potential, and only then consider the question of changing it – unhurriedly and with cool heads' (*ibid.*, 1 February 1997, p. 1). Yeltsin, in other statements, remained opposed to any amendment that might 'infringe the President's authority'; he was willing to hold discussions but intended that any working group should 'keep working for as long as possible, and preferably without results'; and there could be no question of changes in the 'basic principles' of the Constitution, or of 'disproportionate powers' for the government (*Izvestiya*, 31 October 1998, p. 1). Yeltsin's refusal to contemplate any reduction in his constitutional powers was reiterated by his press spokesman the following year: *ibid.*, 28 January 1999, p. 1.

233. *Rossiiskaya gazeta*, 31 December 1999, p. 5.

234. 'Nash dolg – berezhno otnosit'sya k Konstitutsii', *Zhurnal rossiiskogo prava*, no. 1, 2004, pp. 3–4. Putin expressed himself in similar terms on many other occasions: for instance, on 12 December 2001, when he insisted that any change in the fundamentals of the Constitution would be a 'direct route to a crisis of government' (*Trud*, 14 December 2001, p. 2); in his 'direct line' in 2005 he told a caller it would be 'inappropriate to have radical changes in legislation, above all in the Constitution of the Russian Federation' (*Rossiiskaya gazeta*, 28 September 2005, p. 3). His repeated rejection of an amendment of the Constitution to allow a third consecutive presidential term (above, n. 162) was consistent with this view.

235. *Obshchaya gazeta*, no. 5, 1997, p. 10.

236. Avak'yan, *Konstitutsiya Rossii*, pp. 215–28.

237. *Rossiiskaya Federatsiya*, no. 14, 1997, pp. 54–5; the opportunity to vote a lack of confidence in individual ministers and the desirability of an easier process of impeachment were proposed in *Gosudarstvo i pravo*, no. 4, 1998, p. 7, and a simpler process of impeachment also in *ibid.*, no. 12, 1997, p. 73.

238. Oleg Kutafin, *Rossiiskii konstitutsionalizm* (Moscow: Norma, 2008), p. 499.

239. Boris Strashun in Strashun, ed., *Konstitutsiya Rossiiskoi Federatsii* (Moscow: Infra.M-Norma, 1997), p. 93.

240. *Gosudarstvo i pravo*, no. 4, 1998, p. 6; for the lack of a 'clear idea', see *Izvestiya*, 31 January 1997, p. 2.

241. This was, for instance, the view of the chair of the Duma's committee on constitutional legislation, Vladimir Pligin (*Vremya novostei*, 30 April 2008, p. 1). On semi-presidentialism see Maurice Duverger, 'A new political system model: semi-presidential government', *European Journal of Political Research*, vol. 8, no. 2 (June 1980), pp. 165–87, which identifies three distinct subtypes; there is a further discussion in Horst Bahro, Bernhard H. Bayerlein and Ernst Veser, 'Duverger's concept: semi-presidential government revisited', *European Journal of Political Research*, vol. 34, no. 2 (October 1998), pp. 201–24, and in Robert Elgie, ed., *Semi-Presidentialism in Europe* (Oxford and New York: Oxford University Press, 1999).

242. Medvedev, *Medvedev: Prezident Rossiiskoi Federatsii*, pp. 81–3.

243. See, for instance, '100 vedushchikh politikov Rossii v sentyabre', *Nezavisimaya gazeta*, 30 September 2008, p. 13 (Putin scored 9.36 out of 10, Medvedev was in second place with 8.51). Putin was normally in the lead thereafter; most Russians, according to the survey evidence, thought power was shared equally between the two men (50 per cent took this view in August 2010, according to the Levada Centre), but 28 per cent thought Putin was the dominant figure and just 13 per cent thought it was Medvedev ('Karta potentsial'nykh vyborov Prezidenta', 2 August 2010, at www.levada.ru, last accessed 10 September 2010).

244. Svanidze and Svanidze, *Medvedev*, pp. 230–1

245. *Versiya*, 25 February 2008, p. 12.

246. *Izvestiya*, 12 December 2007, p. 3.

247. *Ot pervogo litsa*, pp. 167–8. Speaking to journalists in June 2007, Putin reiterated his view that some limitation on the number of presidential terms was necessary but conceded that four years for a single term was 'not very long' (*Izvestiya*, 5 June 2007, p. 4).

248. *Izvestiya*, 2 June 2008, p. 2, reproducing an interview that had appeared in *Le Monde*.

249. According to Federation Council speaker Sergei Mironov, for instance, the Ukrainian experience showed that it would be 'fatal' for Russia to become a parliamentary republic (*Argumenty i fakty*, no. 18, 2008, p. 2).

250. See, for instance, Ol'ga Kryshtanovskaya, 'The Russian elite in transition', *Journal of Communist Studies and Transition Politics*, vol. 24, no. 4 (December 2008), pp. 585–603, at pp. 600–3, and Andrei Kolesnikov, *Razdvoenie VVP: kak Putin Medvedeva vybral* (Moscow: Eksmo, 2008).

251. Putin, as we have noted, consistently rejected the idea that he might change the Constitution and serve a third consecutive term (above, notes 162, 234 and 247). Speaking to journalists in Hannover in the spring of 2005, however, he acknowledged for the first time that the Constitution did not prevent him serving a further term at some point in the future, although he was 'not sure he would want it' (*Izvestiya*, 13 April 2005, p. 3), and responding to a journalist's question after his first 'direct line' as prime minister in December 2008, he was pointedly non-committal about the possibility of a future term in 2012: 'Let's wait until then and we'll see' (*ibid.*, 5 December 2008, p. 2). Speaking to the Japanese media the following year, Putin suggested that it was the economic crisis that would decide which of the two men, he or President Medvedev, would seek election at the next presidential election; again, 'Let's wait and see' (*ibid.*, 12 May 2009, p. 2). There was another strong hint at the annual Valdai meeting with Western journalists and commentators: *ibid.*, 14 September 2009, p. 3 (the two were 'of one blood' and would not be competing against each other in 2012), and in his 'direct line' in December 2009, when he was asked if he would stand for the presidency in the future and promised he would 'think about it' (*Kommersant*, 4 December 2009, p. 3), and again at the Valdai meeting in 2010 (*Rossiiskaya gazeta*, 7 September 2010, p. 3).

252. See, for instance, *Izvestiya*, 26 December 2007, p. 2. Federation Council speaker Sergei Mironov was a particularly enthusiastic advocate of an extended presidential term and more generally of a larger set of proposals to improve the work of elected institutions that was labelled 'Mironov's Plan': *Rossiiskaya gazeta*, 15 September 2007, p. 2.

253. The change was approved by the Duma in third reading on 21 November, and by the upper house five days later (*Izvestiya*, 27 November 2008, p. 2; there were 144 votes in favour and one against). For the text of the amendment, see *SZ*, no. 1, 2009, item 1, 30 December 2008. Medvedev's address is in *Rossiiskaya gazeta: nedelya*, 6 November

2008, pp. 2–8; the proposal to extend the presidential and parliamentary terms is at p. 6.

254. The speaker of the upper house, Sergei Mironov, even speculated that when Putin had been re-elected in 2012, he might serve two further seven-year terms, and then be succeeded again by Dmitri Medvedev: *Moskovskii komsomolets*, 21 January 2008, p. 5. Mironov had already called for Putin to stand again in 2012: *Izvestiya*, 24 July 2007, p. 2.

255. See, for instance, Vladislav Surkov in *Izvestiya*, 12 February 2007, p. 5. Putin himself noted that Roosevelt had won four consecutive elections.

256. Putin referred to this long-standing problem and to the lack of trust that accompanied it in one of his speeches during the Duma election campaign: *Rossiiskaya gazeta*, 14 November 2007, p. 1.

4   From plan to market

1. V. I. Lenin, *Polnoe sobranie sochinenii*, 5th edn, 55 vols. (Moscow: Izdatel'stvo politicheskoi literatury, 1958–65), vol. XXXIX, p. 21.

2. M. S. Gorbachev, *Izbrannye rechi i stat'i*, 7 vols. (Moscow: Politizdat, 1987–90), vol. V, p. 301.

3. *Ibid.*

4. *Ibid.*, vol. V, p. 482.

5. *Ibid.*, vol. II, p. 93.

6. *Ibid.*, p. 154.

7. Valerie Bunce and John M. Echols III, 'Soviet politics in the Brezhnev era: "pluralism" or "corporatism"?', in Donald R. Kelley, ed., *Soviet Politics in the Brezhnev Era* (New York: Praeger, 1980), pp. 1–26, at p. 11. For a more extended statement, see Valerie Bunce, 'The political economy of the Brezhnev era: the rise and fall of corporatism', *British Journal of Political Science*, vol. 13, no. 2 (April 1983), pp. 129–58; Peter Hauslohner, 'Gorbachev's social contract', in Ferenc Fehér and Andrew Arato, eds., *Gorbachev: The Debate* (Cambridge: Polity and Atlantic Highlands, NJ: Humanities Press International, 1989), pp. 84–123; and Linda J. Cook, *The Soviet Social Contract and Why It Failed* (Cambridge, MA, and London: Harvard University Press, 1993).

8. *Pervyi S"ezd narodnykh deputatov SSSR 25 maya – 9 iyunya 1989 goda: stenograficheskii otchet*, 6 vols. (Moscow: Izdanie Verkhovnogo Soveta SSSR, 1989), vol. II, p. 290.

9. Oleg Bogomolov in *Soviet Weekly*, 4 November 1989, p. 15.

10. *Izvestiya Tsentral'nogo komiteta* [herafter *TsK*] *KPSS*, no. 8, 1989, p. 64.

11. See, for instance, Michael Ellman and Vladimir Kontorovich, 'The collapse of the Soviet system and the memoir literature', *Europe-Asia Studies*, vol. 49, no. 2 (March 1997), pp. 259–79, and more fully in Ellman and Kontorovich, eds, *The Destruction of the Soviet Economic System: An Insiders' History* (Armonk, NY: Sharpe, 1998).

12. This was one of the questions asked insistently by former World Bank chief economist and Nobel prize-winner Joseph Stiglitz: in Russia, 'with efficient capitalism replacing moribund and decadent communism, output was supposed to soar. In fact GDP declined 40 percent and poverty increased tenfold. And the results were similar in the other economies making the transition who followed the advice of the US Treasury and the International Monetary Fund. Meanwhile, China, following its own course, showed that there was an alternative path of transition which could succeed both in bringing the growth that markets promised and in markedly reducing poverty' (*The Roaring Nineties: A New History of the World's Most Prosperous Decade* (London: Allen Lane and New York: Norton, 2003), p. 21).

13. S. N. Prokopovich, ed., *Opyt ischisleniya narodnogo dokhoda 50 gubernii Evropeiskoi Rossii v 1900–1913 gg.* (Moscow: Sovet vserossiiskikh kooperativnykh s"ezdov, 1918), p. 26.

14. A. M. Anfimov and A. P. Korelin, eds., *Rossiya 1913 god: statistiko-dokumental'nyi spravochnik* (St Petersburg: Blits, 1995), p. 51.

15. *Ibid.*, p. 327; for the US figure of 89.3 per cent in 1900, see *Historical Statistics of the United States: From Colonial Times to 1970*, 2 vols. (Washington, DC: Bureau of the Census, 1975), vol. I, p. 382; for the UK, Juliet Gardiner and Neil Wenborn, eds., *The Columbia Companion to British History* (New York: Columbia University Press, 1997), p. 473.

16. Calculated from B. R. Mitchell, ed., *International Historical Statistics: Europe, 1750–1993*, 4th edn (London: Macmillan, 1998), and Mitchell, *International Historical Statistics: The Americas, 1750–1993*, 4th edn (London: Macmillan, 1998), various pages.

17. Korelin, ed., *Rossiya 1913 god*, pp. 148, 150.

18. These data are taken from *Narodnoe khozyaistvo SSSR v 1987 godu* (Moscow:

Finansy i statistika, 1988), pp. 5, 8, 13, 14 and 666 (international comparisons).

19. More recent research suggests a loss of 26.6 million lives (Yu. A. Polyakov, intro., *Lyudskie poteri SSSR v period vtoroi mirovoi voiny: sbornik statei* (St Petersburg: Institut rossiiskoi istorii RAN, 1995), p. 41). Chernomyrdin officially confirmed a loss of 27 million in *Izvestiya*, 19 April 1995, p. 1; it had earlier been reported in *Vestnik statistiki*, no. 10, 1990, p. 27.

20. M. S. Gorbachev, *Perestroika i novoe myshlenie dlya nashei strany i dlya vsego mira* (Moscow: Izdatel'stvo politicheskoi literatury, 1987), pp. 37–8.

21. Gorbachev, *Izbrannye rechi i stat'i*, vol. II, pp. 352–3.

22. *Kommunist*, no. 1, 1991, p. 74; for a brief discussion of growth rates, see R. W. Davies, *Soviet Economic Development from Lenin to Khrushchev* (Cambridge and New York: Cambridge University Press, 1998), ch. 5.

23. *Narodnoe khozyaistvo SSSR v 1987 godu*, pp. 58–9.

24. N. Shmelev and V. Popov, *Na perelome: ekonomicheskaya perestroika v SSSR* (Moscow: Novosti, 1989), p. 131.

25. *EKO*, no. 11, 1987, pp. 50–2; Shmelev and Popov, *Na perelome*, pp. 169–71, 181–204. The steady fall in relative plan fulfilment is noted in *ibid.*, p. 131.

26. Shmelev and Popov, *Na perelome*, p. 44.

27. *Voprosy ekonomiki*, no. 3, 1991, p. 59 (there were similar losses of fruit and vegetables; losses of grain ran at 20 per cent, compared with 2 per cent in the USA).

28. Abel Aganbegyan, *The Challenge: Economics of Perestroika* (London: Hutchinson, and as *The Economic Challenge of Perestroika*, Bloomington: Indiana University Press, 1988), p. 2.

29. *Novyi mir*, no. 2, 1987, pp. 181–201. Khanin published slightly different figures in *Kommunist*, no. 17, 1988, pp. 83–90, and in his book *Dinamika ekonomicheskogo razvitiya SSSR* (Novosibirsk: Nauka, 1991); his analysis of Western estimates appeared in Khanin, *Sovetskii ekonomicheskii rost: analiz zapadnykh otsenok* (Novosibirsk: Ekor, 1993). A secret working group that was established within the Institute of the World Economy and International Relations in 1967 reached conclusions at the time that were close to those of the CIA, and which suggested that Soviet utilised national income was 41 per cent of that of the United States (*Mirovaya ekonomika i mezhdunarodnye otnosheniya*,

no. 2, 1997, pp. 139–45, and no. 3, 1997, pp. 138–48, at p. 148). Another working group within the State Statistics Committee calculated that Soviet GNP at the end of the 1980s was actually 37 per cent of that of the United States, not the 64 per cent reported in official sources, and that at the end of its existence it was 'not more than 30 per cent' of the American figure (*Voprosy statistiki*, no. 9, 1996, p. 10).

30. S. S. Shatalin and E. T. Gaidar, *Ekonomicheskaya reforma: prichiny, napravleniya, problemy* (Moscow: Ekonomika, 1989), p. 16; Gorbachev in *Pravda*, 16 March 1989, p. 3.

31. Aganbegyan in *Izvestiya*, 25 August 1987, p. 2, and in *Literaturnaya gazeta*, 18 February 1987, p. 13.

32. Shmelev and Popov, *Na perelome*, p. 50; *Narodnoe khozyaistvo SSSR v 1988 g.* (Moscow: Finansy i statistika, 1989), p. 680.

33. The most satisfactory guide to the economic performance of the later Soviet period is Philip Hanson, *The Rise and Fall of the Soviet Economy: An Economic History of the USSR from 1945* (London and New York: Longman, 2003); for a longer time perspective, see Alec Nove, *An Economic History of the USSR*, 3rd edn (Harmondsworth and New York: Penguin, 1992).

34. V. Perevedentsev in *Rabochii klass i sovremennyi mir*, no. 4, 1988, pp. 57–67.

35. Aganbegyan, *The Challenge*, p. 69.

36. *Vestnik statistiki*, no. 10, 1990, p. 41.

37. G. M. Sorokin, ed., *Intensifikatsiya i effektivnost' sotsialisticheskogo proizvodstva* (Moscow: Nauka, 1988), p. 10.

38. Aganbegyan, *The Challenge*, p. 71.

39. *Ibid.*, p. 72, and on the Noyabr'skoe field Sorokin, ed., *Intensifikatsiya*, p. 11.

40. *XXVII S"ezd Kommunisticheskoi partii Sovetskogo Soyuza, 25 fevralya – 6 marta 1986 goda: stenograficheskii otchet*, 3 vols. (Moscow: Politizdat, 1986), vol. I, p. 236, and vol. II, p. 298. These apprehensions were noted at the time by Peter Frank, 'Gorbachev's dilemma: social justice or political instability?', *The World Today*, vol. 42, no. 6 (June 1986), pp. 93–5.

41. Gorbachev, *Izbrannye rechi i stat'i*, vol. II, pp. 86, 154–5.

42. Leonid Abalkin on Moscow radio in the BBC *Summary of World Broadcasts*, 10 February 1989, SU/0386 B/6; Nikolai Shmelev is quoted from his 'Ekonomika i zdravyi smysl', *Znamya*, no. 7, 1988, pp. 179–84, at p. 179.

43. Gorbachev, *Izbrannye rechi i stat'i*, vol. III, p. 182.
44. *Ibid.*, pp. 199–202.
45. *Ibid.*, pp. 202–23. For the text of the five-year plan, as adopted, see *Vedomosti Verkhovnogo Soveta SSSR*, no. 26, item 481, 19 June 1986.
46. Gorbachev, *Izbrannye rechi i stat'i*, vol. V, pp. 157–9.
47. For the text of the law, see *Vedomosti Verkhovnogo Soveta SSSR*, no. 26, item 385, 30 June 1987. Gorbachev set out the need to move from 'mainly administrative to mainly economic methods of management at all levels' in his speech to the plenum (*Izbrannye rechi i stat'i*, vol. V, pp. 129–85); the five main principles of the new economic mechanism are at p. 165.
48. Gorbachev's speech appeared in *Pravda*, 16 March 1989, pp. 1–4; the Central Committee's resolution on leaseholding is in *ibid.*, 1 April 1989, pp. 1–2.
49. For the text of the law, see *Vedomosti Verkhovnogo Soveta SSSR*, no. 47, item 964, 19 November 1986; the numbers employed – 673,800 – are reported in *Narodnoe khozyaistvo SSSR v 1990 g.* (Moscow: Finansy i statistika, 1991), p. 65.
50. For the text of the law, see *Vedomosti Verkhovnogo Soveta SSSR*, no. 22, item 355, 26 May 1988. It was described as the 'first major step away from the totally state-controlled economy' by F. J. M. Feldbrugge (*Russian Law: The End of the Soviet System and the Role of Law* (Dordrecht: Nijhoff, 1993), p. 267); Yevgenii Yasin, who became minister of economics in the Chernomyrdin government, commented later that 'Literally within a year or two, under the guise of cooperatives, private enterprise was born' (Ellman and Kontorovich, eds., *The Destruction of the Soviet Economic System*, p. 151).
51. *Narodnoe khozyaistvo v 1990 g.*, p. 55 (for a third of those employed it was a second job); future projections appeared in V. F. Yakovlev, ed., *Kooperativy segodnya i v budushchem* (Moscow: Yuridicheskaya literatura, 1989), p. 62, and Leonid Abalkin in *Sovetskaya Rossiya*, 27 July 1988, p. 3.
52. *Spravochnik partiinogo rabotnika*, issue 28 (Moscow: Izdatel'stvo politicheskoi literatury, 1988), p. 50.
53. Ryzhkov, in his report to the Party Congress, specified a growth rate of 5 per cent in the last years of the century and a more modest rate of between 3.5 and 4 per cent in the course of the five-year plan that was to begin that year; the 'Basic Guidelines of the Economic and Social Development of the USSR for 1986–1990 and for the Period to 2000' and the new edition of the Party Programme both promised that national income would 'almost double' by the end of the century. See *XXVII S"ezd*, vol. II, pp. 11 and 14 (Ryzhkov); for the 'Basic guidelines' see *ibid.*, pp. 221–92 (at p. 228), and for the Programme, vol. I, pp. 554–623 (at p. 574). The 12th Five-Year Plan specified an increase of 22.1 per cent in national income between 1985 and 1990, which represented an annual rate of 4.2 per cent as compared with the 3.6 per cent that had been achieved in 1981–5 (*Narodnoe khozyaistvo SSSR za 70 let: yubileinyi statisticheskii sbornik* (Moscow: Finansy i statistika, 1987), p. 55).
54. *Narodnoe khozyaistvo v 1990 g.*, p. 7.
55. *Ekonomika i zhizn'*, no. 5, 1991, p. 9.
56. *Ibid.*, no. 6, 1992, pp. 13–16. For a discussion of these results, see *Vestnik statistiki*, no. 3, 1992, pp. 4–12.
57. *Voprosy ekonomiki*, no. 3, 1991, p. 36.
58. *Materialy Plenuma Tsentral'nogo komiteta KPSS 25 aprelya 1989 goda* (Moscow: Izdatel'stvo politicheskoi literatury, 1989), p. 89.
59. *Pravda*, 26 January 1991, p. 1.
60. *Ibid.*, 2 January 1991, p. 2.
61. Yegor Gaidar, *Dni porazhenii i pobed* (Moscow: Vagrius, 1996), p. 96. Other estimates suggested a budgetary deficit of 22–23 per cent for the former USSR as a whole (*Svobodnaya mysl'*, no. 6, 1992, p. 56); a subsequent and more precise figure for the Russian Federation alone was 31.9 per cent (*Voprosy ekonomiki*, no. 7, 1995, p. 23).
62. For the national debt estimate (of 60 per cent), see *Izvestiya*, 23 January 1992, p. 2.
63. *Pravda*, 8 May 1989, p. 1.
64. *Ibid.*, 16 January 1989, p. 1.
65. *Ibid.*, 21 September 1987, p. 3 (sugar), 23 November 1987, p. 1 (bread), and 22 August 1991, p. 3 (medicine).
66. *Izvestiya*, 30 October 1991, p. 2 (Novosibirsk), and 31 January 1991, p. 2 (sales staff).
67. *Pravda*, 27 April 1989, p. 3.
68. *Ibid.*, 11 July 1989, p. 2.
69. *Izvestiya TsK KPSS*, no. 2, 1991, p. 92.
70. According to the trade union paper *Trud*, the black market already accounted for about 30 per cent of the value of services provided by the state (12 August 1988, p. 2); the appearance of the coupons themselves on the black market was reported in *Pravda*, 1 September 1988, p. 3. For a more general discussion, see *Voprosy ekonomiki*, no. 3,

1990, pp. 110–33, and B. A. Druzhinin, ed., *Tenevaya ekonomika* (Moscow: Ekonomika, 1991).

71. *Klinicheskaya meditsina*, vol. 66, no. 8 (August 1988), pp. 155–7 ('significant exposure'); *Nezavisimaya gazeta*, 26 April 1991, p. 1 (deaths over following decade); *Izvestiya*, 25 April 1996, p. 5 (survivors). The party leadership's attempt to play down the incident was subsequently documented from the archives: see Alla Yaroshinskaya, *Chernobyl': sovershenno sekretno* (Moscow: Drugie berega, 1992).

72. *Izvestiya*, 24 April 1996, p. 5 (resettlement), and 25 April 1996, p. 5 (land).

73. Zhores Medvedev, *Times Higher Education Supplement*, 22 March 1996, p. 20 (economic costs); *Izvestiya*, 25 April 1996, p. 5 (costs for Ukraine). Twenty years later, expert opinion was still widely divided about the long-term effects of the explosion. The National Commission for Radiation Protection in Ukraine claimed that 'at least 500,000 people – perhaps more' had already died of the 2 million who had been officially classified as victims of Chernobyl in Ukraine alone; at the other extreme the United Nations International Atomic Energy Agency and the World Health Organization insisted that only fifty deaths could be directly attributed to the disaster and that at most 4,000 eventually succumbed (*Guardian*, 25 March 2006, p. 17). For a review of the emerging evidence, see David R. Marples, 'Chernobyl: a reassessment', *Eurasian Geography and Economics*, vol. 45, no. 8 (December 2004), pp. 588–607.

74. These details were communicated to journalists by Nikolai Ryzhkov, who headed an emergency commission (*Pravda*, 14 December 1988, pp. 1–2); the eighty-year comparison is in *ibid*., 8 December 1988, p. 12.

75. *Narodnoe khozyaistvo v 1990 g.*, pp. 397, 644–62.

76. *Izvestiya*, 29 July 1991, p. 7 (there were also threats of 'state bankruptcy', *ibid*., 27 August 1991, p. 2); on the rouble see Yevgenii Yasin in *ibid*., 27 August 1991, p. 2). A particularly detailed and contemporary analysis of issues of this kind, prepared for the guidance of Western policy-makers, is available in *A Study of the Soviet Economy*, 3 vols. (Paris: OECD, 1991).

77. *Molodoi kommunist*, no. 2, 1980, p. 69. For discussion of the campaign, see Stephen White, *Russia Goes Dry: Alcohol, State and Society* (Cambridge and New York: Cambridge University Press, 1996).

78. Ye. K. Ligachev, *Zagadka Gorbacheva* (Novosibirsk: Interbuk, 1992), pp. 286–7.

79. V. I. Vorotnikov, Second Russian Revolution interview transcript, 26 May 1990, held in the British Library of Political and Economic Science manuscript division.

80. M. S. Solomentsev, Soviet Elite Project interview transcript, May 1993, held in the Glasgow University Library special collections division.

81. M. S. Gorbachev, *Zhizn' i reformy*, 2 vols. (Moscow: Novosti, 1995), vol. I, p. 340.

82. The budgetary loss was estimated to represent about a tenth of all indirect taxation (Abel Aganbegyan in *Pravda*, 6 February 1989, p. 3); Nikolai Shmelev later dated the collapse of the economy itself to the 'mindless, idiotic anti-alcohol campaign' (*ibid*., 31 October 1992, p. 2).

83. KGB chairman Vladimir Kryuchkov had already presented a dossier of evidence to Gorbachev that appeared to implicate Alexander Yakovlev, the Politburo's leading reformer, as an American agent, recruited when he was an exchange student at Columbia University in the late 1950s. It was clear, he wrote later, that the system could have been reformed, but 'certain forces' had wanted its destruction and they had used all kinds of methods, including financial support for its domestic opponents, to achieve their ends: *Lichnoe delo*, 2 vols. (Moscow: Olimp, 1996), vol. I, pp. 294–309, 264 ('certain forces'), and vol. II, ch. 1. Other views of this kind are reported in Jerry F. Hough, *Democratization and Revolution in the USSR 1985–1991* (Washington, DC: Brookings, 1997), pp. 368–9.

84. Gaidar, *Dni*, pp. 42, 56, 59, 60.

85. *Vedomosti S"ezda narodnykh deputatov SSSR i Verkhovnogo Soveta SSSR*, no. 11, item 164, 6 March 1990.

86. *Sobranie postanovlenii pravitel'stva SSSR*, no. 19, art. 101 (8 August 1990), and no. 24, item 114 (16 August 1990).

87. *Vedomosti S"ezda narodnykh deputatov SSSR i Verkhnovnogo Soveta SSSR*, no. 32, item 904, 1 July 1991.

88. *Ibid*., no. 16, item 442, 2 April 1991.

89. *Pravda*, 4 July 1991, p. 3.

90. Nikolai Ryzhkov, *Perestroika: istoriya predatel'stv* (Moscow: Novosti, 1992), p. 311; he had gone to the rostrum in May 1990, he told *Pravda*, 'as to the scaffold' (4 March 1991, p. 4).

91. *Shestoi S"ezd narodnykh deputatov Rossiiskoi Federatsii 6–21 aprelya 1992 goda:*

stenograficheskii otchet, 5 vols. (Moscow: Respublika, 1993), vol. I, p. 122.

92. *Pyatyi (vneocherednoi) S"ezd narodnykh deputatov RSFSR 10–17 iyulya, 28 oktyabrya – 2 noyabrya 1991 goda: stenograficheskii otchet*, 3 vols. (Moscow: Respublika, 1992), vol. II, pp. 4–29, esp. pp. 4–18.

93. *Vedomosti S"ezda narodnykh deputatov RSFSR i Verkhovnogo Soveta RSFSR*, no. 44, item 1456, 1 November 1991; for the measures see *ibid.*, no. 47, art. 1609, 15 November 1991; no. 46, item 1612, 15 November 1991; and no. 48, item 1675, 25 November 1991.

94. *Ibid.*, no. 52, item 1878, 3 December 1991.

95. *Ekonomicheskaya gazeta*, no. 4, 1993, p. 13.

96. *Rossiiskaya gazeta*, 17 January 1992, pp. 1–2.

97. *Izvestiya*, 28 February 1992, pp. 1–2.

98. *Programma uglubleniya ekonomicheskikh reform v Rossii* (Moscow: Respublika, 1992); it was also carried in full in *Voprosy ekonomiki*, no. 8, 1992 (quotations at pp. 12–13, 17). It was a kind of 'party programme' for reformers, explained *Izvestiya*'s economics editor, Mikhail Berger, designed to 'unite and strengthen the team and its supporters' (25 June 1992, p. 2); it was subsequently to be presented to the Russian Supreme Soviet.

99. J. S. Earle, Roman Frydman and Andrzej Rapaczynski, eds., *The Privatization Process in Russia, Ukraine and the Baltic States* (Budapest: Central European University Press, 1993), p. 39. The same authors identify a 'plethora of often overlapping and conflicting laws and decrees emanating from a number of jurisdictions' (*ibid.*, p. 15), some of which are conveniently collected in *Voprosy ekonomiki*, no. 9, 1992, pp. 75–153. The literature is deeply divided, although more enthusiastic accounts became markedly less numerous after the collapse of the currency in 1998. Among broadly 'positive' interpretations see, for instance, Anders Åslund, *How Russia Became a Market Economy* (Washington, DC: Brookings, 1995); Maxim Boycko, Andrei Shleifer and Robert Vishny, *Privatizing Russia* (Cambridge, MA: MIT Press, 1995); Joseph R. Blasi, Maya Kroumova and Douglas Kruse, *Kremlin Capitalism: The Privatization of the Russian Economy* (Ithaca, NY: Cornell University Press, 1997); Rose Brady, *Kapitalizm: Russia's Struggle to Free its Economy* (New Haven, CT, and London: Yale University Press, 1999); Thane Gustafson, *Capitalism Russian-Style* (Cambridge and New York: Cambridge University Press, 1999); and Andrei Shleifer and Daniel Triesman,

Without a Map: Political Tactics and Economic Reform in Russia (Cambridge, MA: MIT Press, 2000). A more critical view is presented in Lynn D. Nelson and Irina Y. Kuzes, *Property to the People: The Struggle for Radical Economic Reform in Russia* (Armonk, NY: Sharpe, 1994); Nelson and Kuzes, *Radical Reform in Yeltsin's Russia: Political, Economic and Social Dimensions* (Armonk, NY: Sharpe, 1995); Marshall I. Goldman, *Lost Opportunity: What Has Made Economic Reform in Russia So Difficult?* (New York and London: Norton, 1996); Lawrence R. Klein and Marshall Pomer, eds., *The New Russia: Transition Goes Awry* (Stanford, CA: Stanford University Press, 2001); Marshall I. Goldman, *The Piratization of Russia: Russian Reform Goes Awry* (New York and London: Routledge, 2003); and perhaps most devastatingly of all, in the work of Joseph Stiglitz (noted p. 145).

100. For the legislation see *Vedomosti S"ezda narodnykh deputatov RSFSR i Verkhovnogo Soveta RSFSR*, no. 27, art. 927, 3 July 1991; it was amended on 5 June 1992: *ibid.*, no. 28, item 1614. From November 1991 the Committee was chaired by Russia's 'privatisation tsar', Anatolii Chubais.

101. *Ibid.*, no. 27, item. 925, 3 July 1991.

102. *Ibid.*, no. 3, item 92, 28 December 1991, and also in *Rossiiskaya gazeta*, 10 January 1992, pp. 3–4.

103. *Vedomosti S"ezda narodnykh deputatov RSFSR i Verkhovnogo Soveta RSFSR*, no. 3, item 93, 29 December 1991.

104. *Ibid.*, no. 28, item 1617, 11 June 1992.

105. *Ibid.*, no. 35, item 2001, 14 August 1992; a presidential decree had already announced that a system of 'personal privatisation accounts' would be introduced in the fourth quarter of the year (*ibid.*, no. 15, item 825, 2 April 1992).

106. Gaidar, *Dni*, pp. 201–2.

107. Presidential decree of 6 October 1993, *Sobranie aktov Prezidenta i pravitel'stva Rossiiskoi Federatsii*, no. 41, item 3914.

108. *Izvestiya*, 27 January 1993, p. 2.

109. *Ibid.*, 1 October 1992, p. 1.

110. *Ibid.*, 25 August 1992, p. 1; Boycko, Shleifer and Vishny, *Privatizing Russia*, p. 108.

111. *Vedomosti S"ezda narodnykh deputatov Rossiiskoi Federatsii i Verkhovnogo Soveta Rossiiskoi Federatsii*, no. 28, item 1617, 11 June 1992.

112. The second option was selected by 73 per cent of all the firms concerned, and the first

by 25 per cent: Boycko, Shleifer and Vishny, *Privatizing Russia*, p. 98.

113. *Ibid.*, p. 79.

114. *Izvestiya*, 20 August 1992, p. 2; speaking to the Congress of People's Deputies earlier in the year, he had called similarly for 'millions of owners, not hundreds of millionaires' (*Shestoi S"ezd*, vol. I, p. 127).

115. *Rossiiskaya gazeta*, 20 January 1993, p. 6.

116. *Izvestiya*, 6 January 1993, p. 2 (Tyumen'); *ibid.*, 24 December 1992, p. 1 (Yaroslavl').

117. For counterfeiting see, for instance, *ibid.*, 11 March 1993, p. 1; for theft, *Nezavisimaya gazeta*, 8 October 1992, p. 1; for their interception, *Moskovskaya pravda*, 20 March 1993, p. 2.

118. Timothy N. Ash and Paul G. Hare, 'Privatisation in the Russian Federation: changing enterprise behaviour in the transition period', *Cambridge Journal of Economics*, vol. 18, no. 6 (December 1994), pp. 619–34, at p. 626.

119. *Nezavisimaya gazeta*, 11 August 1992, p. 4.

120. Gaidar, *Dni*, p. 201; the choice of face value is noted in Roi Medvedev, *Chubais i vaucher* (Moscow: Impeto, 1997), p. 9.

121. The regulations for investment funds are in *Vedomosti S"ezda narodnykh deputatov Rossiiskoi Federatsii i Verkhovnogo Soveta Rossiiskoi Federatsii*, no. 42, art. 2370, 7 October 1992.

122. *Izvestiya*, 20 February 1993, p. 5, and 24 February 1993, p. 2.

123. Boycko, Shleifer and Vishny, *Privatizing Russia*, p. 101; *Izvestiya*, 10 September 1996, p. 1.

124. Mavrodi was sentenced to four and a half years of imprisonment in April 2007 but was soon released as he had already served most of the sentence; as of 2009 he was ostensibly unemployed. According to *Izvestiya*, he had defrauded as many as 50 million Russians between 1992 and 1995 (30 June 2009, p. 8).

125. *Argumenty i fakty*, no. 49, 1996, p. 5 (later estimates suggested there had been fewer victims (*ibid.*, no. 10, 1997, p. 12). Mavrodi had sent an estimated 70 per cent of the money abroad (*ibid.*, no. 38, 1997, p. 8) and had been officially declared bankrupt by this time (*Izvestiya*, 4 September 1997, pp. 1–2).

126. *Izvestiya*, 8 February 1995, p. 13.

127. *Ibid.*, 30 June 1994, p. 1.

128. Michael Kaser, *Privatization in the CIS* (London: RIIA, 1995), p. 15; *Izvestiya*, 30 June 1994, p. 1.

129. *Sobranie zakonodatel'stva Rossiiskoi Federatsii* [hereafter *SZ*], no. 13, art. 1478,

22 July 1994; for the 1997 privatisation law, see *ibid.*, no. 30, item 3595, 21 July 1997.

130. *Ekonomika i zhizn'*, no. 7, 1999, p. 1.

131. *Rossiiskii statisticheskii yezhegodnik: statisticheskii sbornik* [hereafter *RSYe*] (Moscow: Goskomstat Rossii, 1997), p. 335.

132. *Segodnya*, 2 July 1994, p. 2.

133. See respectively Åslund, *How Russia Became a Market Economy*, p. 266, and Richard Layard and John Parker, *The Coming Russian Boom: A Guide to New Markets and Politics* (New York: Free Press, 1996).

134. Sergei Glaz'ev, *Genotsid: Rossiya i novyi mirovoi poryadok. Strategiya ekonomicheskogo rosta na poroge XXI veka* (Moscow: Astra sem', 1997), p. 29.

135. Sergei Glaz'ev, *Genotsid*, 2nd edn (Moscow: Terra, 1998), pp. 50, 55.

136. *Pravda*, 27 September 1997, p. 1.

137. According to Medvedev there were 'almost two hundred' foreign advisers and heads of section in the State Property Committee alone, provided with exorbitant salaries on the basis of an unpublished decree (*Chubais i vaucher*, p. 8).

138. Glaz'ev, *Genotsid*, pp. 5–6.

139. Tat'yana Zaslavskaya, 'Chelovek v reformiruemom obshchestve', *Obshchestvo i ekonomika*, no. 9, 1995, pp. 3–12, at p. 10.

140. Richard Rose and Evgeny Tikhomirov, *Trends in the New Russia Barometer, 1992–1995* (Glasgow: Centre for the Study of Public Policy, University of Strathclyde, 1995), pp. 48–9.

141. *Ibid.*, p. 33.

142. *Vremya novostei*, 20 December 2006, p. 2. In another poll in 2007, 37 per cent thought all the property that had been privatised at this time should be returned to the state, and another 37 per cent thought this should happen when the privatisation had been illegal (*Izvestiya*, 15 August 2007, p. 9).

143. See A. B. Chubais, 'Itogi privatizatsii v Rossii i zadachi sleduyushchego etapa', *Voprosy ekonomiki*, no. 6, 1994, pp. 4–9, at p. 4. Writing later, Chubais emphasised how important it had been to use the short time window that was available before Yeltsin's extraordinary executive powers came to an end; they had made it with just three hours to spare (A. B. Chubais, ed., *Privatizatsiya po-rossiiski* (Moscow: Vagrius, 1999), p. 80). The post-voucher, monetary phase of privatisation was introduced by presidential decree in July 1994 after the Duma had rejected the proposals in five rounds of voting (Hilary Appel, *A New Capitalist*

Order: Privatization and Ideology in Russia and Eastern Europe (Pittsburgh, PA: University of Pittsburgh Press, 2004), p. 93; the relevant legislation is in *SZ*, no. 13, item 1478, 22 July 1994). Similar points are made in a particularly clear and balanced account by Ri Don Khi, 'Istoriya chekovoi privatizatsii v Rossii. 1991–1994 gg.', *Vestnik Moskovskogo universiteta*, seriya 8: *Istoriya*, no. 3, 2007, pp. 71–84, at pp. 76–8, 81; see also Chrystia Freeland, *Sale of the Century: The Inside Story of the Second Russian Revolution* (London: Little, Brown and New York: Crown Business, 2000).

144. Zaslavskaya, 'Chelovek', p. 5.

145. *Voprosy ekonomiki*, no. 6, 1996, p. 128 (labour productivity had fallen by 1995 to 69.7 per cent of its 1990 level, and in industry to 66.6 per cent of its 1990 level).

146. In most though not all sectors of the economy: *RSYe 2000*, p. 307.

147. Again, in most though not all sectors: *ibid.*, p. 314.

148. *Ibid.*, p. 315.

149. Blasi, Kroumova and Kruse, *Kremlin Capitalism*, pp. 179, 180–1.

150. Vladimir Tikhomirov, 'The second collapse of the Russian economy', *Europe-Asia Studies*, vol. 52, no. 2 (March 2000), pp. 207–36, at p. 222. Joseph Stiglitz, drawing on World Bank research, concluded similarly that privatisation had had 'no positive effect on growth' (*Globalization and its Discontents* (New York and London: Norton, 2002), p. 157); Ash and Hare, basing themselves on a factory-level survey, also found it 'difficult to identify any significant changes in enterprise behaviour as being specifically due to privatisation' ('Privatisation in the Russian Federation', p. 630). Others took a more optimistic view, in some cases reflecting the understandable bias of those who had provided the advice in the first place: see, for instance, Shleifer and Triesman, *Without a Map*, which speaks of a 'remarkable success' while acknowledging that the financial crisis of the late summer of 1998 was already 'call[ing] into question the wisdom of earlier reform tactics' (pp. 1, 19). Many Russian economists, by contrast, were even more outspoken critics of the entire exercise than their Western counterparts. For Nikolai Petrakov and Vilen Perlamutrov, for instance, Russia had become a 'zone of economic catastrophe' ('Rossiya – zona ekonomicheskoi katastrofy', *Voprosy ekonomiki*, no. 3, 1996, pp. 74–83); others

compared the economy in the early 1990s to Grozny at the end of the Chechen war, after 'monetarist "carpet bombing"' (V. Maevsky in his contribution to a discussion reported in *Voprosy ekonomiki*, no. 4, 1995, pp. 4–66, at p. 58).

151. See respectively *Vedomosti S"ezda narodnykh deputatov Rossiiskoi Federatsii i Verkhovnogo Soveta Rossiiskoi Federatsii*, no. 11, item 561, 2 March 1992; and no. 25, item 1427, 14 June 1992.

152. *Nezavisimaya gazeta*, 29 October 1993, p. 1.

153. *Sobranie aktov Prezidenta i pravitel'stva Rossiiskoi Federatsii*, no. 44, art. 4181, 27 October 1993.

154. *RSYe 2000*, pp. 370 (number of commercial farms), 361 (percentage of all agricultural land), 362, 368 (share of value of agricultural output). Agricultural enterprises (including collective and state farms) produced more than 40 per cent of the value of all agricultural output, and individual holdings more than 57 per cent (p. 362).

155. *Ibid.*, p. 368 (88 per cent were doing so in 1998, 54 per cent in 1999).

156. *Kommersant daily*, 2 September 1995, p. 2.

157. *Argumenty i fakty*, no. 8, 1997, p. 5.

158. *SZ*, no. 11, item 1026, 7 March 1996.

159. *Kommersant daily*, 12 March 1996, p. 8.

160. *RSYe 2000*, pp. 16, 382; the output of vegetables, however, had increased.

161. *Pravda*, 27 March 1991, p. 1; *Izvestiya*, 7 October 1991, p. 1.

162. *Vedomosti S"ezda narodnykh deputatov SSSR i Verkhovnogo Soveta SSSR*, no. 31, art. 880, 5 July 1991.

163. *Izvestiya*, 18 July 1991, p. 1.

164. *Ibid.*, 28 April 1991, p. 1 (membership of the IMF had been agreed in 1944 but never ratified); *ibid.*, 17 June 1992, p. 5.

165. *Ibid.*, 18 June 1993, p. 3 (membership was still under discussion more than a decade later).

166. *Ibid.*, 30 April 1992, pp. 1–2.

167. *Ibid.*, 16 April 1993, pp. 1, 3.

168. *Ibid.*, 6 April 1993, p. 3.

169. *Argumenty i fakty*, no. 5, 1993, p. 1; the IMF itself insisted that a larger sum was involved (*Financial Times*, 4 February 1993, p. 8).

170. *Izvestiya*, 5 June 1997, p. 4; *Ekonomika i zhizn'*, no. 43, 1998, p. 4.

171. *Finansovye izvestiya*, 17 April 1997, p. 1; *Izvestiya*, 27 November 1998, p. 1.

172. *Izvestiya*, 6 March 1996, p. 7. On other calculations, about $140 billion had been exported since 1992; this was more than Brazil, Venezuela, Mexico and Peru had lost,

taken together, in the course of their
financial crises in the 1970s and 1980s
(*Rossiiskaya gazeta*, 6 October 1998, p. 2).

173. *Segodnya*, 30 December 1998, p. 1; *Financial Times*, 12 February 1999, p. 2.

174. See respectively *Izvestiya*, 25 April 1997, p. 5, 11 July 1997, p. 2, and 1 August 1997, p. 2.

175. *Nedvizhimost' za rubezhom*, nos. 13–14 (August–September 1996), p. 1.

176. *Izvestiya*, 15 August 1997, p. 8; *The Times*, 6 January 1998, p. 9.

177. *Izvestiya*, 22 May 1998, p. 3.

178. *Sunday Telegraph*, 20 September 1998, p. 28.

179. *World Development Report 2002* (New York: Oxford University Press for the World Bank, 2002), pp. 238–9.

180. *RSYe 2000*, pp. 553 (total investment), 547 (foreign investment share), 552–3.

181. *Ibid.*, p. 308.

182. *Argumenty i fakty*, no. 17, 1995, p. 5.

183. *Izvestiya: ot pyatnitsy do pyatnitsy*, 29 May 1998, p. 1.

184. Quoted in Jerrold L. Schecter, *Russian Negotiating Behavior: Continuity and Transition* (Washington, DC: United States Institute of Peace Press, 1998), p. 146.

185. *Izvestiya*, 11 December 1996, p. 4; similarly *Voprosy ekonomiki*, no. 3, 1997, pp. 129–30.

186. Grigorii Khanin in *Izvestiya*, 7 April 1998, p. 4; see also the critique by Grigorii Yavlinsky, *Finansovye izvestiya*, 5 February 1998, p. 2.

187. *Izvestiya*, 10 June 1998, p. 1, and 11 June 1998, p. 1.

188. See *Finansovye izvestiya*, 29 September 1995, p. 2.

189. Khanin in *Izvestiya*, 7 April 1998, p. 4; for the World Bank estimate, see *Argumenty i fakty*, no. 1–2, 1998, p. 7.

190. *RSYe 2000*, pp. 302, 332–3.

191. *Ibid.*, pp. 16 (the rate of capital investment in 1999 was 22 per cent of the 1990 level), 315.

192. *Ibid.*, p. 608.

193. Russia accounted for 2.1 per cent of world exports in 1990, but 1.3 per cent in 1999, and for 2.5 and 0.5 per cent respectively of world imports in the same years: *ibid.*, p. 630.

194. *World Development Report 2000/2001: Attacking Poverty* (New York: Oxford University Press for the World Bank, 2001), pp. 273–5, 316.

195. *Izvestiya*, 11 December 1996, p. 4. World Bank figures, expressed in terms of purchasing power parity, also put Russian GNP per capita in 1997 below that of Peru, Namibia and Gabon, but above that of

Jordan; no figures for Iraq were reported (*World Development Report 1998/99*, pp. 190–1).

196. *RSYe 2000*, p. 578 (in 1999).

197. *Izvestiya*, 9 January 1998, p. 1; *Trud*, 22 November 1996, p. 6 (cheese, tinned meat and pasta). Up to 60 per cent of all meat and 80 per cent of poultry was imported (*Izvestiya*, 4 November 1998, p. 1).

198. *RSYe 2000*, pp. 582–3 (mineral products were 48 per cent of the value of all exports in 1997 and 44 per cent in 1999).

199. *RSYe 2000*, p. 559.

200. *Izvestiya*, 30 October 1998, p. 4.

201. *Ibid.*, 17 October 1996, p. 1.

202. *Moskovskie novosti*, no. 44, 1996, p. 4.

203. *Izvestiya*, 9 October 1996, p. 2.

204. *Argumenty i fakty*, no. 22, 1998, p. 7.

205. *Ibid.*, no. 9, 1997, p. 6.

206. *RSYe 2000*, pp. 503–4.

207. *Izvestiya*, 22 October 1996, p. 1.

208. *Ibid.*, 19 September 1996, p. 1, and 8 February 1996, p. 1.

209. *Moskovskie novosti*, no. 36, 1996, p. 9.

210. *Rossiiskaya gazeta*, 15 January 1997, pp. 1, 3.

211. *Kommersant daily*, 1 November 1996, p. 10; *Izvestiya*, 15 February 1996, p. 1.

212. *RSYe 2000*, pp. 112, 120 (a year or more).

213. *Financial Times*, 6 February 1997, p. 2.

214. *RSYe 2000*, pp. 108–9.

215. *Nezavisimaya gazeta*, 15 August 1998, p. 1.

216. *Ibid.*, p. 3.

217. *Rossiiskaya gazeta*, 18 August 1998, p. 1.

218. *Trud*, 8 October 1998, p. 1.

219. *Izvestiya*, 30 October 1998, p. 4.

220. 'All my money is gone', he told a German magazine: *Guardian*, 30 December 1998, p. 2.

221. *RSYe 2000*, p. 627.

222. *Ibid.*, p. 578.

223. *Ibid.*

224. *RSYe 2008*, p. 36.

225. *RSYe 2009*, p. 725; for earlier years see *RSYe 2000*, p. 593.

226. *RSYe 2009*, p. 725 (the nickel price is for 2007).

227. *Rossiiskaya gazeta*, 9 February 2008, p. 2.

228. As Putin told his annual press conference: *Komsomol'skaya pravda*, 2 February 2007, p. 2.

229. In the first year of operation, it stood at 106 billion roubles (0.8 per cent of GDP), but by 2008 it had reached 3.8 trillion roubles, or 11.7 per cent of GDP: *RSYe 2008*, p. 643. The Fund was divided in February 2008 into a Reserve Fund and a separate National

Prosperity Fund (*Rossiiskaya gazeta*, 1 February 2008, p. 5).

230. *Kommersant*, 15 September 1998, p. 8; a fuller version appeared in *Voprosy ekonomiki*, no. 6, 1998, pp. 10–67. A set of related proposals was approved by the Council of the Federation, involving an increase in state regulation, a state alcohol monopoly and a limited currency emission (*Nezavisimaya gazeta*, 25 July 1998, p. 3).

231. *Izvestiya*, 20 November 1998, p. 1.

232. *Segodnya*, 29 October 1998, p. 5.

233. *Izvestiya*, 7 October 1998, p. 1.

234. A point made in V. P. Loginov, A. V. Barysheva and Reni Lekach, eds., *Ekonomicheskie reformy v Rossii: itogi pervykh let: 1991–1996* (Moscow: Nauka, 1997), p. 6, and at greater length in Alice Amsden, Jacek Kochanowicz and Lance Taylor, *The Market Meets its Match: Restructuring the Economies of Eastern Europe* (Cambridge, MA, and London: Harvard University Press, 1994).

235. *Nezavisimaya gazeta*, 1 July 1996, pp. 1, 4.

236. Joseph E. Stiglitz, 'Whither reform? Ten years of the transformation', in Boris Pleskovic and Stiglitz, eds., *Annual World Bank Conference on Development Economics 1999* (Washington, DC: World Bank, 2000), pp. 27–56, at pp. 28–32, 46.

237. *Ibid.*, p. 34. Other Nobel economics laureates had already made this point: as R. H. Coase wrote, it made 'little sense for economists to discuss the process of exchange without specifying the institutional setting within which the trading takes place', as developments in Eastern Europe had made 'crystal clear' ('The institutional structure of production', *American Economic Review*, vol. 82, no. 4 (September 1992), pp. 713–19, at p. 718). Or as Douglass C. North put it, 'transferring the formal political and economic rules of Western market economies to third-world and East European economies is not a sufficient condition for good economic performance' ('Economic performance through time', *ibid.*, vol. 84, no. 3 (June 1994), pp. 359–68, at p. 366).

238. As Sachs confessed to Russian interviewers, 'When we undertook the reforms we felt ourselves to be doctors who had been called to someone's sickbed. But when we placed the patient on the operating table and opened him up, we immediately found that his anatomical structure and internal organs were completely different, of a kind we had never encountered in medical school' (*Novoe vremya*, no. 28, 1995, p. 24). A controversial study argued, some years later, that the privatisation programme that had been promoted by Sachs and others had been directly responsible for the 'early deaths of 1m people that could have been prevented' (*Financial Times*, 15 January 2009, p. 3; Sachs responded in *ibid.*, 19 January 2009, p. 6, and the report's authors in *ibid.*, 22 January 2009, p. 8).

239. *World Development Report 1997: The State in a Changing World* (New York: Oxford University Press for the World Bank, 1997), pp. 29–38, at p. 38.

240. The most spectacular case of this kind involved Andrei Shleifer, a Harvard University professor and close friend of then US Treasury Under-Secretary Laurence Summers, who was appointed to advise Russia on its privatisation through a government contract with the university. Shleifer was accused of the improper use of his position, the contract was suspended and then cancelled, and the university was sued for the money that had been spent; it was eventually obliged to pay more than $26 million and Shleifer himself more than $2 million, although he did not admit liability. Summers (who had by this time become president of the university) resigned his position shortly afterwards. See Joseph E. Stiglitz, *Making Globalization Work* (London: Allen Lane and New York: Norton, 2006), p. 332, A remarkable and much more detailed account is available in David McClintick, 'How Harvard lost Russia', *Institutional Investor*, vol. 40, no. 1 (January 2006), pp. 62–90; see also Janine R. Wedel, *Collision and Collusion: The Strange Case of Western Aid to Eastern Europe*, rev. edn (New York: Palgrave, 2001), and the further discussion in Wedel, *Shadow Elite: How the World's New Power Brokers Undermine Democracy, Government, and the Free Market* (New York: Basic Books, 2009).

241. Glaz'ev, *Genotsid*, pp. 80–3, *passim*.

242. US Treasury Secretary Lawrence Summers, for instance, appeared to have 'played an insider role' in the formation of the new Russian government that was announced in the spring of 1997; an 'instructional' letter from Summers to Anatolii Chubais caused particular offence when it was published in the Russian press later in the year (Peter Reddaway and Dmitri Glinski, *The Tragedy of Russia's Reforms: Market Bolshevism*

against Democracy (Washington, DC: United States Institute of Peace Press, 1997), pp. 548, 550, 575; the leaked letter appeared in *Nezavisimaya gazeta*, 26 September 1997, pp. 1–2). The view that the Yeltsin administration consisted largely of Western 'agents of influence' had emerged some years earlier: see, for instance, *Sovetskaya Rossiya*, 21 November 1992, p. 3, and Viktor Ilyukhin in *Pravda*, 5 February 1993, p. 2.

243. *Rossiiskaya gazeta*, 31 December 1999, pp. 4–5.

244. See respectively *Rossiiskaya gazeta*, 11 July 2000, pp. 1, 3; *ibid.*, 4 April 2001, pp. 3–4; and *ibid.*, 19 April 2002, pp. 4–7. The eight presidential addresses are conveniently collected in G. O. Pavlovsky, ed., *Plan Prezidenta Putina: rukovodstvo dlya budushchikh prezidentov Rossii* (Moscow: Yevropa, 2007), with commentaries and related documents; this edition unfortunately adds emphases that are not in the original, provides new titles and occasionally omits part of the text without indication or explanation. Accurate versions of the first six presidential addresses may be found in *Yezhegodnye poslaniya Prezidenta RF Federal'nomu sobraniyu 1994–2005 gg.* (Novosibirsk: Sibirskoe universitetskoe izdatel'stvo, 2006), and they may also be consulted on the presidential website (www.kremlin.ru).

245. *Rossiiskaya gazeta*, 17 May 2003, p. 4.

246. *Ibid.*

247. *Ibid.*, 27 May 2004, p. 3.

248. *Ibid.*, 26 April 2005, p. 3.

249. *Ibid.*, 6 September 2005, p. 3; the full text of the speech appears in V. V. Putin, *Izbrannye rechi i vystupleniya* (Moscow: Knizhnyi mir, 2008), pp. 294–304.

250. 'O Sovete pri Prezidente Rossiiskoi Federatsii po realizatsii prioritetnykh natsional'nykh proektov', *SZ*, no. 43, item 4374, 21 October 2005.

251. *Ibid.*, no. 47, item 4881, 14 November 2005.

252. *Rossiiskaya gazeta*, 11 May 2006, p. 2.

253. *SZ*, no. 29, item 3245, 13 July 2006.

254. The business paper *Vedomosti* compared Putin's speech directly with Brezhnev's contribution to the celebration of the fiftieth anniversary of the October revolution in 1967: *Vedomosti*, 11 February 2008, p. A02.

255. Dmitrii Bulin, 'Vertikal' natsional'nykh proektov', *Svobodnaya mysl'*, no. 10, 2007, pp. 19–32, at pp. 23–4.

256. Leonid Abalkin, 'Razmyshleniya o dolgosrochnoi strategii, nauke i demokratii',

Voprosy ekonomiki, no. 12, 2006, pp. 4–19, at p. 15.

257. Vyacheslav Glazychev, 'Predislovie', in *Prioritetnye natsional'nye proekty: tsifry, fakty, dokumenty* (Moscow: Yevropa, 2006), pp. 3–7, at pp. 6–7. The 'national projects' were to become 'state programmes' from January 2009 (*Izvestiya*, 25 September 2008, p. 2).

258. *Rossiiskaya gazeta*, 9 February 2008, pp. 1–3.

259. *SZ*, no. 47, item 5489, 17 November 2008. A document of this kind had first been called for in July 2006 and had been approved by the government on 1 October: *Vremya novostei*, 26 November 2008, p. 2.

260. *SZ*, no. 48, item 5639, 17 November 2008.

261. *Vremya novostei*, 26 November 2008, p. 2.

262. *Izvestiya*, 15 February 2008, p. 2.

263. *Ibid.*, 29 February 2008, p. 2.

264. *Nezavisimaya gazeta*, 12 May 2008, p. 1.

265. See Stephen Sestanovich, 'Russia by the numbers', *Wall Street Journal*, 17 December 2007, p. A21 (the World Bank estimated Russian gross national income per head in 2007 at $7,560, but $14,400 if expressed in purchasing power parities; the corresponding figures for 'high income' countries were generally very close to each other).

266. *World Development Report 2009* (Washington, DC: World Bank, 2009), various pages, available at http://econ.worldbank.org, where issues for earlier years may also be consulted; last accessed 14 March 2009.

267. *RSYe 2008*, p. 783.

268. *Ibid.*, p. 768; *Narodnoe khozyaistvo SSSR v 1985 g.* (Moscow: Finansy i statistika, 1986), p. 575.

269. *Argumenty i fakty*, no. 12, 2006, p. 10.

270. *Kommersant*, 14 September 2009, p. 2.

271. S. L. Kravets, ed., *Bol'shaya rossiiskaya entsiklopediya: Rossiya* (Moscow: Bol'shaya rossiiskaya entsiklopediya, 2004), p. 121.

272. Yevgenii Primakov, *Mir bez Rossii? K chemu vedet politicheskaya blizorukost'* (Moscow: Rossiiskaya gazeta, 2009), p. 6.

273. The implications of the 'resource curse' for Russia specifically are closely examined in Michael Ellman, ed., *Russia's Oil and Natural Gas: Bonanza or Curse?* (London and New York: Anthem, 2006), and in Vladimir Gel'man and Otar Marganiya, eds., *Resource Curse and Post-Soviet Eurasia: Oil, Gas, and Modernization* (Lanham, MD: Lexington Books, 2010); a more sceptical view is

presented in Pauline Jones Luong and Erika Weinthal, *Oil is Not a Curse: Ownership Structures and Institutions in Soviet Successor States* (Cambridge and New York: Cambridge University Press, 2010). Russian economists argued that the effects of the 'resource curse' were latterly most apparent in the quality of government, particularly freedom of the media and corporate management (S. Guriev and K. Sonin, 'Ekonomika "resursnogo proklatiya"', *Voprosy ekonomiki*, no. 4, 2008, pp. 61–74).

274. See www.transparency.org, various years. The reports are also issued in published form: see, for instance, Transparency International, *Global Corruption Report 2008: Corruption in the Water Sector* (Cambridge and New York: Cambridge University Press, 2008).

275. Larger methodological issues of this kind are considered in Johann Lambsdorff, *The Institutional Economics of Corruption and Reform: Theory, Policy and Evidence* (Cambridge and New York: Cambridge University Press, 2007).

276. *Moscow Times*, 23 April 2008, p. 9.

277. *Daily Telegraph*, 10 December 2008, p. 18. Full results may be consulted on the Transparency International website: 'Bribe Payers Index 2008', at www.transparency.org, last consulted 6 September 2009.

278. *Global Corruption Report 2008*, pp. 311, 308–9; full results may be consulted at *ibid*. For a recent overview of these issues, see, for instance, Leslie Holmes, 'Corruption and organised crime in Putin's Russia', *Europe-Asia Studies*, vol. 60, no. 6 (August 2008), pp. 1011–31.

279. *SZ*, no. 21, item 2429, 19 May 2008.

280. 'Natsional'nyi plan protivodeistviya korruptsii', 31 July 2008, in *Rossiiskaya gazeta*, 5 August 2008, p. 10.

281. *Nezavisimaya gazeta*, 1 October 2008, pp. 1, 4.

282. *SZ*, no. 52, part 1, item 6228, 25 December 2008.

283. *Global Corruption Report 2007* (Cambridge and New York: Cambridge University Press, 2007), p. 347; for the establishment of the Council, see *SZ*, no. 48, item 4657, 24 November 2003.

284. *Izvestiya*, 31 July 2007, p. 1. (Gutseriev later returned to Russia after criminal charges had been dropped: *Moscow Times*, 10 May 2010, p. 1.)

285. *Guardian*, 27 January 2009, p. 6.

286. *Ibid*., 26 July 2008, p. 41

287. See Marshall I. Goldman, *Petrostate: Putin, Power, and the New Russia* (New York and Oxford: Oxford University Press, 2008), pp. 86–7.

288. *Guardian*, 2 July 2008, p. 23.

289. *Ibid*., 25 July 2008, p. 29.

290. *Ibid*., 5 August 2008, p. 2.

291. *Ibid*., 9 September 2008, p. 29.

292. See, for instance, the case of Telenor's investment in the Russian mobile phone business (*Financial Times*, 24 June 2009, p. 24), or the experience of Hermitage Capital Management, headed by William Browder (*ibid*., 7 July 2009, p. 11). The hedge fund, once one of Russia's largest foreign investors, accused a leading Russian investment bank and senior state officials and judges of complicity in alleged tax fraud but found its investigations hampered by what the International Bar Association described as 'state-sponsored intimidation' (*Daily Telegraph*, 31 July 2009, p. B5). IKEA suspended any further investment in Russia because of the 'unpredictable nature of [its] administrative procedures' (*The Economist*, 4 July 2009, p. 61).

293. *Rossiiskaya gazeta*, 11 May 2006, p. 2

294. These connections are set out systematically in (for instance) Goldman, *Petrostate*, pp. 192–4; an earlier analysis is available in A. A. Mukhin, *Nevskii–Lubyanka–Kreml': proekt-2008* (Moscow: Tsentr politicheskoi informatsii, 2005), pp. 16–18.

295. *The Economist*, 29 November 2008, 'Special report on Russia', p. 10.

296. *Guardian*, 24 June 2008, p. 25. There were 'tens of thousands' of such cases annually: *Izvestiya*, 25 March 2009, p. 7.

297. On Russia and crisis see, for instance, the studies by the rector of the Academy of National Economy, A. G. Aganbegyan (*Krizis: beda i shans dlya Rossii* (Moscow: Astrel', 2009)); by the first chairman of the Russian State Bank, Viktor Gerashchenko (*Rossiya i den'gi: chto nas zhdet?* (Moscow: Astrel'/Rus'-Olimp, 2009)); and by the director of the Institute of the Problems of Globalisation, Mikhail Delyagin (*Rossiya dlya rossiyan* (Moscow: Algoritm, 2009), and with Vyacheslav Sheyanov, *Mir naiznanku: chem zakonchitsya ekonomicheskii krizis dlya Rossii?* (Moscow: Kommersant/Eksmo, 2009)).

298. Interview on Italian television, 2 September 2008, at www.un.int/russia/new/MainRoot/docs/warfare/statement020908en2.htm, last accessed 20 September 2010 (this part of the

interview was not included in *Izvestiya*'s report, 3 September 2008, p. 2).

299. *Le Figaro*, 13 September 2008, p. 2.

300. See, for instance, Nikolai Starikov, *Krizis: kak eto delaetsya* (St Petersburg: Piter, 2010).

301. Speech at the 7th International Investment Forum at Sochi, 19 September 2008, at www.premier.gov.ru/events/653.html, last accessed 1 July 2009.

302. It was agreed, for instance, that Russian banks would be lent $950 billion for five years: *Izvestiya*, 8 October 2008, pp. 1, 7.

303. *Ibid.*, 26 February 2009, p. 3.

304. *Daily Telegraph*, 17 November 2008, p. 21.

305. *Vremya novostei*, 18 September 2008, p. 1.

306. The Central Bank's own figures may be consulted at www.crb.ru.

307. *Guardian*, 3 February 2009, p. 22.

308. Food prices increased by nearly 18 per cent in 2008, but for the poorest families by up to 50 per cent: *Izvestiya*, 26 January 2009, p. 7.

309. *Ibid.*, 14 January 2009, p. 7.

310. *Ibid.*, 23 March 2009, p. 7.

311. *Guardian*, 30 October 2008, p. 29.

312. *Moscow Times*, 3 June 2009, p. 3; two more local factories closed down or suspended operations.

313. World Bank in Russia, *Russian Economic Report*, No.17, November 2008, p. 17, at http://siteresources.worldbank.org/INTRUSSIANFEDERATION/Resources/rer17_eng.pdf, last accessed 18 September 2010.

314. *Ibid.*, No. 18, March 2009, various pages.

315. *Ibid.*, No. 19, June 2009, pp. 12–13.

316. *Izvestiya*, 20 March 2009, pp. 1, 10. The revised budget may be consulted in *SZ*, no. 18, item 2156, 28 April 2009.

317. *Kommersant*, 9 December 2008, p. 1.

318. *Ibid.*, 5 February 2009, p. 1.

319. *Izvestiya*, 2 March 2009, p. 2.

320. First Deputy Premier Igor Shuvalov as reported in *ibid.*, 23 March 2009, p. 1, and again in his presentation to the Duma on the government's anti-crisis measures (he assured the deputies that the 'difficult stage' was already behind them and that they had already reached the 'restoration stage': *ibid.*, 17 September 2009, p. 2).

321. Finance Minister Aleksei Kudrin as reported in *ibid.*, 25 March 2009, p. 1.

322. See, for instance, 'Red Square blues', *The Economist*, 6 June 2009, pp. 13–14; or on enduring technological and productivity lags, Raj M. Desai and Itzhak Goldberg, eds., *Can Russia Compete?* (Washington, DC: Brookings, 2008).

323. V. G. Belinsky, *Polnoe sobranie sochinenii*, 13 vols. (Moscow: Izdatel'stvo Akademii nauk SSSR, 1953–9), vol. XII, p. 402.

324. The most sustained statement of this view is Richard Pipes, *Russia under the Old Regime* (London: Weidenfeld & Nicolson and New York: Scribner, 1974); see also Pipes, *Property and Freedom* (London: Harvill and New York: Knopf, 1999).

5   A divided society

1. *Voprosy istorii*, no. 6, 1989, p. 134.

2. A. M. Prokhorov, ed., *SSSR: entsiklopedicheskii spravochnik* (Moscow: Sovetskaya entsiklopediya, 1982), p. 20.

3. According to the 1977 Constitution, the USSR was a 'multinational state' which had been formed 'as a result of the free self-determination of nations and the voluntary association of equal Soviet socialist republics' (art. 70).

4. Borrowings of this kind were not uncommon in the early Soviet period: see Jay Bergman, 'The image of Jesus in the Russian revolutionary movement', *International Review of Social History*, vol. 25, part 2 (1990), pp. 220–48.

5. F. J. M. Feldbrugge, *Russian Law: The End of the Soviet System and the Role of Law* (Dordrecht: Martinus Nijhoff, 1993), p. 301.

6. Yu. V. Andropov, *Izbrannye rechi i stat'i*, 2nd edn (Moscow: Poliizdat, 1983), pp. 194–5.

7. M. S. Gorbachev, *Izbrannye rechi i stat'i*, 7 vols. (Moscow: Politizdat, 1987–90), vol. V, p. 219 (socialist pluralism), vol. VI, p. 205 (pluralism of opinions), 212 (pluralism of interests). There had already been a reference to political pluralism in *Pravda* on 18 January 1985, shortly before Gorbachev's accession (Vadim Pechenev, *Gorbachev: k vershinam vlasti* (Moscow: Gospodin narod, 1991), p. 71).

8. *Rossiiskii statisticheskii yezhegodnik: statisticheskii sbornik* [hereafter *RSYe*] (Moscow: Goskomstat Rossii, 2000), pp. 112, 105 (number of unemployed).

9. *Ibid.*, *RSYe 2000*, p. 155.

10. *Ibid.*, p. 141; for 1990, *RSYe 1996*, p. 116.

11. *RSYe 2000*, p. 155.

12. For international comparisons, see *World Development Report 2000/2001* (Washington, DC: Oxford University Press for the World Bank, 2000), pp. 282–3. The richest 20 per cent of Russians at this time took 53.7

per cent of all income, compared with 43 per cent in the United Kingdom and 46.4 per cent in the United States.

13. *RSYe 2000*, p. 141; *Rossiya v tsifrakh 1998* (Moscow: Goskomstat, 1998), p. 61. For a fuller discussion of emerging inequalities, see Bertram Silverman and Murray Yanowitch, *New Rich, New Poor, New Russia: Winners and Losers on the Russian Road to Capitalism* (Armonk, NY: Sharpe, 1997; expanded edn, 2000).

14. See Richard Rose and Ian McAllister, 'Is money the measure of welfare in Russia?', *Review of Income and Wealth*, vol. 42, no. 1 (March 1996), pp. 75–90.

15. *RSYe 2000*, p. 154.

16. *Ibid.*, p. 165.

17. *Ibid.*, p. 457.

18. *Ibid.*, p. 165. The poor, surveys suggested, spent about 70 per cent of their income on food in the early postcommunist years; parents with large families, and pensioners, spent up to 90 per cent of their income in this way (*Sotsiologicheskie issledovaniya*, no. 3, 1994, p. 66). The same was true in later years: see, for instance, *Izvestiya*, 29 October 2008, p. 8, and 26 January 2009, p. 7.

19. Regional statistics are most comprehensively reported in *Regiony Rossii: informatsionno-statisticheskii sbornik*, 2 vols. (Moscow: Goskomstat Rossii, annually since 1997, latterly in three volumes, with occasional changes of scope and subtitle). For a comprehensive guide to the specialist literature, see John Löwenhardt and Stephen White, comps., *The Russian Regions: A Bibliography* (Pittsburgh, PA: Carl Beck Papers in Russian and East European Studies, University of Pittsburgh, 2007).

20. *RSYe 2000*, pp. 157–8.

21. *Regiony Rossii: statisticheskii sbornik*, 2 vols. (Moscow: Goskomstat, 2001), vol. II, pp. 128–9.

22. *RSYe 2000*, p. 164.

23. *Ibid.*, p. 156.

24. VTsIOM surveys found that 44 per cent had an 'allotment where they [grew] vegetables and fruit' (*Ekonomicheskie i sotsial'nye peremeny: monitoring obshchestvennogo mneniya*, no. 3, 1998, p. 67); The United States Information Agency (USIA) found that Russia had become a 'country of partial subsistence farmers', with 54 per cent reporting that they grew half or more of their own food (*Poverty in Russia*, M-4-99, 12 January 1999), p. 5.

25. *Argumenty i fakty*, no. 11, 1997, p. 2.

26. *Voprosy statistiki*, no. 2, 1997, pp. 30–6; similarly Natal'ya Rimashevskaya, 'Sotsial'nye posledstviya ekonomicheskikh transformatsii v Rossii', *Sotsiologicheskie issledovaniya*, no. 6, 1997, pp. 55–65, at p. 59.

27. *Ekonomicheskie i sotsial'nye peremeny*, no. 4, 1998, p. 58, and no. 3, 1998, p. 31 (earning the most); a similar point is made in Rimashevskaya, 'Sotsial'nye posledstviya', p. 58. USIA surveys found that only 10 per cent of working Russians had a second job or a second source of income, and another 6 per cent that they sometimes had additional income of this kind (*Poverty in Russia*, p. 10). Surveys in Samara, Kemerovo, Lyubertsy and Syktyvar found similarly that the poorest households did not have access to agricultural land, and had neither the time nor the money to grow their own crops; those who did so were richer than average and still spent considerable sums on buying food (*Financial Times*, 11 December 1998, p. 3).

28. *Izvestiya*, 26 January 1996, p. 4; according to another survey, 71 per cent of families had incomes below subsistence level (*Vestnik Moskovskogo Universiteta. Seriya 18. Sotsiologiya i politologiya*, no. 3, 1996, p. 19).

29. *Izvestiya*, 22 April 1998, p. 6.

30. Natal'ya Rimashevskaya in *ibid.*

31. Rimashevskaya, 'Sotsial'nye posledstviya', pp. 55, 57.

32. T. I. Zaslavskaya, 'Problema demokraticheskoi pereorientatsii ekonomiki sovremennoi Rossii', *Obshchestvo i ekonomika*, nos. 1–2, 1997, pp. 51–7, at pp. 54–5.

33. *Izvestiya*, 12 August 1995, p. 5.

34. *Ibid.*, 27 December 1995, p. 7.

35. *Ekonomicheskie i sotsial'nye peremeny*, no. 2, 1997, pp. 78–9. A survey conducted in 2004 (n=1750) found similarly that 'having helpful acquaintances' was perceived as the best way of joining the business elite (65 per cent), although 'having good abilities' (52 per cent) was seen as the second most important requirement. See Alexander Chepurenko, 'The "oligarchs" in Russian mass consciousness', in Stephen White, ed., *Politics and the Ruling Group in Putin's Russia* (Basingstoke and New York: Palgrave Macmillan, 2008), pp. 130–7, at p. 124.

36. Olga Kryshtanovskaya, 'Rich and poor in post-communist Russia', *Journal of Communist Studies and Transition Politics*, vol. 10, no. 1 (March 1994), p. 12. According to a later survey, 64 per cent of Russians were unsure who the oligarchs were: 23 per cent named Boris Berezovsky, 18 per cent Chubais, 17 per cent Chernomyrdin and 8 per cent Yeltsin (*Izvestiya*, 16 June 1998, p. 1).

37. For biographies, see O. Prokhanov, ed., *Kto est' kto: spravochnoe izdanie* (Moscow: Olimp/EKSMO Press, 1998). Vyakhirev was rated the 'most important figure in Russian business' in a reputational study (*Izvestiya: ot pyatnitsy do pyatnitsy*, 29 May 1998, p. 5).

38. *Financial Times*, 1 November 1996, p. 17. Berezovsky identified the other members of the group as Potanin, Khodorkovsky and Gusinsky, who had all been at the Davos meeting, together with Petr Aven and Mikhail Fridman of Al'fa-Bank and Alexander Smolensky of the SBS-Agro Bank; Vladimir Vinogradov of Inkombank (who had also been at Davos) was sometimes included in the list. See Hans-Henning Schröder, 'El'tsin and the oligarchs: the role of financial groups in Russian politics between 1993 and July 1998', *Europe-Asia Studies*, vol. 51, no. 6 (September 1999), pp. 957–88, at pp. 968–70, and more generally David E. Hoffman, *The Oligarchs: Wealth and Power in the New Russia* (New York and Oxford: PublicAffairs, 2001); Phil Hanson and Elizabeth Teague, 'Big business and the state in Russia', *Europe-Asia Studies*, vol. 57, no. 5 (July 2005), pp. 657–80; Ol'ga Kryshtanovskaya and Stephen White, 'The rise of the Russian business elite', *Communist and Post-Communist Studies*, vol. 38, no. 3 (September 2005), pp. 293–307; and Stephen Fortescue, *Russia's Oil Barons and Metal Magnates: Oligarchs and the State in Transition* (Basingstoke and New York: Palgrave Macmillan, 2006). The term 'oligarch' appears to have been first used in the newspaper *Vek* in June 1995, and it became increasingly popular during 1997 ('Slovar' russkogo publichnogo yazyka kontsa XX veka', *Kommersant-vlast'*, no. 24(527), 23 June 2003, pp. 63–78, at p. 71). Berezovsky was rated first as a 'professional lobbyist' in a reputational study reported in *Nezavisimaya gazeta*, 11 April 1998, p. 1; his wealth was estimated by *Forbes* magazine at $3 billion in 1997: *Argumenty i fakty*, no, 30, 1997, p. 8.

39. For a critical biographical study, see Paul Klebnikov, *Godfather of the Kremlin: Boris Berezovsky and the Looting of Russia* (New York and London: Harcourt, 2000).

40. A scheme of Berezovsky's complex commercial interests is set out in *ibid.*, p. 345.

41. *Financial Times*, 31 October 1996, p. 2.

42. *Argumenty i fakty*, no. 44, 1996, p. 6.

43. *Nezavisimaya gazeta*, 3 June 1998, p. 8.

44. *Argumenty i fakty*, no. 44, 1996, p. 6.

45. *Ibid.*

46. *Daily Telegraph*, 10 April 1999, p. P4.

47. *Argumenty i fakty*, no. 44, 1996, p. 6.

48. Klebnikov, *Godfather of the Kremlin*, pp. 38–9.

49. *Izvestiya*, 22 April 1998, p. 6.

50. *Ibid.*, 13 March 1996, p. 7.

51. *Ibid.*, 12 April 1997, p. 4 (cost); *Argumenty i fakty*, no. 20, 1998, p. 7 (competition).

52. *Scotland on Sunday*, 28 December 1997, p. 17.

53. *Sunday Times*, 25 May 1997, Section 1, p. 22.

54. *Living Here*, no. 5, 1996, various pages.

55. Boris Kagarlitsky, *Restoration in Russia*, trans. Renfrew Clarke (London and New York: Verso, 1995), pp. 20–1.

56. *Newsweek*, 19 December 1994, pp. 34–6.

57. *Guardian*, 5 March 1998, Section 2, p. 19.

58. *Argumenty i fakty*, no. 30, 1996, p. 9.

59. *Sunday Times*, 14 May 1995, Section 1, p. 17.

60. *Izvestiya*, 5 August 1997, p. 3.

61. *Sunday Times*, 14 May 1995, Section 1, p. 17.

62. *Izvestiya*, 25 February 2000, p. 4.

63. Television interview, 28 February 2000, BBC SWB SU/3777 B/1, 1 March 2000; similarly in *Segodnya*, 29 February 2000, p. 1.

64. Interview on Mayak, 18 March 2000, BBC SWB SU/3793 B/3, 20 March 2000.

65. *Segodnya*, 20 March 2000, p. 1.

66. *Kommersant*, 12 May 2000, pp. 1, 3.

67. *Ibid.*, 14 June 2000, p. 1 (charges); *Segodnya*, 17 June 2000, pp. 1–2 (release).

68. *Segodnya*, 28 July 2000, p. 1 (charges dropped); *Kommersant*, 28 July 2000, p. 1 (Spain).

69. *Segodnya*, 19 August 2000, p. 1.

70. *Nezavisimaya gazeta*, 5 December 2000, p. 3 (warrant); *Kommersant*, 14 December 2000, pp. 1, 3 (extradition attempt).

71. *Nezavisimaya gazeta*, 17 April 2001, pp. 1, 8. There is a full account of this crucial episode in Laura Belin 'The rise and fall of Russia's NTV', *Stanford Journal of International Law*, vol. 38, no. 1 (2002), pp. 19–42.

72. *Kommersant*, 18 April 2001, pp. 1, 9 (*Itogi*); *Rossiiskaya gazeta*, 18 April 2001, p. 1 (the issue of *Segodnya* that should have appeared the previous day had been suppressed and the editor, Mikhail Berger, given a redundancy notice).

73. *Kommersant*, 21 April 2001, p. 3.

74. *Nezavisimaya gazeta*, 19 October 2001, p. 1. A later attempt to extradite Gusinsky, this time from Greece, was also unsuccessful: *Izvestiya*, 15 October 2003, p. 1.

75. He was removed as CIS Executive Secretary in April 1999 and a warrant for his arrest on charges of 'illegal business activities' and 'money laundering' was issued, although it

76. See particularly his open letter to President Putin, *Kommersant*, 31 May 2000, pp. 1–2, in which he described the reforms as 'anti-democratic' (p. 1).

77. Berezovsky explained his decision at a press conference (*ibid.*, 18 July 2000, p. 3); the Duma accepted his resignation two days later (*ibid.*, 20 July 2000, p. 2).

78. *Ibid.*, 15 November 2000, p. 1.

79. *Nezavisimaya gazeta*, 12 September 2003, pp. 1, 3.

80. *Guardian*, 13 April 2007, p. 1.

81. *Izvestiya*, 30 November 2007, p. 1. There was a further sentence in June 2009, representing a total of thirteen years in all (*ibid.*, 29 June 2009, p. 3). He did, however, remain a member of the Russian Academy of Sciences: *Moscow Times*, 6 March 2009, p. 3.

82. *Vremya novostei*, 3 July 2003, p. 1.

83. *Kommersant*, 27 October 2003, pp. 1–2.

84. *Vremya novostei*, 31 October 2003, pp. 1, 3; *Izvestiya*, 4 November 2003, pp. 1–2 (resignation) and 5 November 2003, pp. 1–2 (new management).

85. *Izvestiya*, 1 June 2005, p. 1; *Kommersant*, 23 September 2005, p. 1 (appeal).

86. *Guardian*, 23 August 2008, p. 35.

87. *Ibid.*, 10 October 2008, p. 28. The interview was conducted by the writer Boris Akunin and published in the Russian edition of *Esquire* magazine; because of the 'highly restricted nature of Khodorkovsky's imprisonment [it] took place by letter over several weeks' (see www.esquire.com/the-side/feature/mikhail-khodorkovsky-interview-esquire, last accessed 20 September 2010).

88. *Rossiiskaya gazeta*, 31 December 2010, p. 3. Khodorkovsky, in spite of his circumstances, was able to issue a remarkable series of political statements from prison. His 'Levyi povorot', published in the business paper *Vedomosti*, called for a return to broadly socialist principles (1 August 2005, p. A5); his 'Levyi povorot-2', later the same year, attacked a 'cosmic alienation between the elite and the people, between government and those it rules' (*Kommersant*, 11 November 2005, p. 8). A third part, 'Novyi sotsializm: levyi povorot-3', appeared in *Vedomosti*, 7 November 2008, p. A5.

89. *Argumenty i fakty*, no. 30, 1997, p. 8.

90. *Izvestiya*, 7 March 2008, p. 9; the full list appeared as 'The world's richest', *Forbes*, 6 March 2008, pp. 62–91.

91. *Izvestiya*, 7 March 2008, p. 9.

92. See '500 milliarderov', *Finans*, no. 7(242), 18–24 February 2008, various pages; there had been 61 the year before.

93. *Forbes*, Russian edition, no. 5(50), May 2008, various pages.

94. For a full biography see Dominic Midgley and Chris Hutchins, *Abramovich: The Billionaire from Nowhere* (London: HarperCollins, 2004; expanded paperback edn, 2005).

95. *Izvestiya*, 4 July 2008, p. 1.

96. *Tribuna*, 23 October 2008, p. 2.

97. The view of *Izvestiya*, 23 December 2008, p. 8. On his original intentions see *ibid.*, 3 July 2003, p. 1.

98. *Izvestiya*, 15 March 2007, p. 9; similarly *Argumenty i fakty*, no. 12, 2007, p. 10. The purchase of Chelsea Football Club in 2003 had cost him £140 million (*Izvestiya*, 4 July 2008, p. 4).

99. *Argumenty i fakty*, no. 12, 2007, p. 10.

100. *Guardian*, 3 November 2008, p. 3.

101. *Ibid.*, 3 November 2008, p. 3, and 16 June 2009, p. 14.

102. What follows is based, unless otherwise stated, on the profiles in the *Sunday Telegraph*, 19 October 2008, p. 26, and *Moscow Times*, 28 April 2008, pp. 12–13.

103. *Guardian*, 31 October 2008, p. 8.

104. *Izvestiya*, 18 September 2007, pp. 1, 10.

105. *Ibid.*, 6 February 2004, p. 1.

106. *Komsomol'skaya pravda*, 13 September 2008, p. 2.

107. *Novye izvestiya*, 17 November 2005, p. 2. There were complaints that the Public Chamber, following the Duma, had become a 'second club of billionaires': Vladimir Novitsky in *Moskovskie novosti*, 2 December 2005, p. 30.

108. *Izvestiya*, 23 December 2008, p. 1 (end of the oligarchs), p. 8.

109. *Ibid.*, 16 February 2009, pp. 1, 7.

110. 'The world's billionaires', *Forbes*, 11 March 2009; *Izvestiya*, 13 March 2009, p. 1.

111. 'The world's billionaires', *Forbes*, 10 March 2010, various pages. On Lisin see the *Guardian*, 16 February 2010, p. 19.

112. *Guardian*, 21 December 2007, pp. 1–2; similarly *Daily Telegraph*, 22 December 2007, p. 1.

113. At his final presidential press conference: *Nezavisimaya gazeta*, 15 February 2008, p. 3. Putin later reported an annual income from all sources of about $150,000, including his KGB pension, and assets that included a 1,500 square metre plot of land and 'a stake in a garage cooperative equivalent to one car seat' (*Kommersant*, 7 April 2009, p. 4).

Top of left column (continuation):
was later withdrawn. See Klebnikov, *Godfather of the Kremlin*, pp. 284–6, 289–90.

114. *The Times*, 7 September 2002, p. 13. A journalist's account of the Russian colony in London and especially of its richest members is available in Mark Hollingsworth and Stewart Lansley, *Londongrad: From Russia with Cash – The Inside Story of the Oligarchs* (London: Fourth Estate, 2009).

115. *Daily Telegraph*, 4 September 2008, p. 8.

116. *Ibid.*, 18 August 2008, p. 14; *Izvestiya*, 18 August 2008, p. 9. The deal later fell through after Prokhorov had paid the deposit: *Guardian*, 19 February 2009, p. 23, and also *Izvestiya*, 20 February 2009, p. 7.

117. *Izvestiya*, 21 March 2008, pp. 1, 11.

118. *Guardian*, 10 October 2007, p. 19.

119. *Izvestiya*, 17 July 2008, p. 5.

120. *Ibid.*, 7 March 2008, p. 1.

121. *Ibid.*, pp. 1, 5; *Moscow Times*, 26 March 2008, pp. 11–12.

122. *Guardian*, 10 October 2005, p. 15.

123. *Moscow Times*, 8 August 2008, pp. 1, 4.

124. *Daily Telegraph*, 29 November 2008, p. 21. For the summer fair see *Izvestiya*, 30 June 2009, p. 5.

125. John Kampfner, 'A tale of two cities', *GQ*, November 2007, pp. 288–95, at p. 294.

126. *Izvestiya*, 16 June 2008, p. 9.

127. See http://news.bbc.co.uk/1/hi/ entertainment/6227341.stm, last accessed 20 September 2010.

128. *Daily Telegraph*, 24 June 2006, p. 11.

129. *Moscow News*, no. 39, 3 October 2008, p. 28.

130. 'Striptease and gentlemen clubs in Moscow', WayToRussia.Net Guide to Russia, at www. waytorussia.net, last accessed 24 December 2008.

131. See www.essortment.com/travel/ nightlifeguide_smun.htm, last accessed 20 September 2010. For another report on Moscow nightlife, with photographs, see Martin Cruz Smith, 'Moscow never sleeps', *National Geographic*, vol. 214, no. 2 (August 2008), pp. 106–33.

132. *Izvestiya*, 12 January 2007, p. 1.

133. *Ibid.*, pp. 1, 4; for the 'castings' see *ibid.*, 11 January 2007, p. 1.

134. *Ibid.*, 12 January 2007, p. 4; for the fall-off see the *Daily Telegraph*, 13 January 2009, p. 17. Increasing numbers were reportedly transferring their loyalties to St Moritz, which was significantly cheaper, or Kitzbühel, where there was a better chance of meeting the European aristocracy (*Izvestiya*, 25 November 2008, p. 8). Another version was that there were just as many highly placed officials as before, but that they were avoiding conspicuous excess (*ibid.*,

19 January 2009, p. 5). It later emerged that Prokhorov's hotel room had been bugged but 'nobody had sex there', according to his lawyer (*ibid.*, 11 March 2009, p. 4).

135. Gleb Bryanski, 'French spoil party for Russia's super-rich ski set', Reuters, 12 January 2007, at www.reuters.com/ article/idUSL1212088220070112, last accessed 20 September 2010.

136. *Izvestiya*, 12 January 2007, p. 5; for 'open tills' see the *Sunday Times*, 21 January 2007, Section 1, p. 20.

137. Bryanski, 'French spoil party'.

138. *Guardian*, 8 February 2007, p. 20.

139. *Sunday Telegraph*, 30 December 2007, p. 11.

140. *Daily Telegraph*, 21 August 2008, p. 18.

141. *Komsomol'skaya pravda*, 19 July 2008, p. 8. A later survey found Russians rated the 'most unpleasant holidaymakers in the world': *Mail Online*, 28 August 2009, last accessed 10 September 2009.

142. *Daily Telegraph*, 15 August 2007, p. 15.

143. *Ibid.*, 21 August 2008, p. 18.

144. *RSYe 1997*, p. 153; *Segodnya*, 16 June 1997, p. 5.

145. *Izvestiya*, 20 February 1997, p. 1.

146. *Guardian*, 18 April 1997, p. 10.

147. *Izvestiya*, 20 February 1997, p. 5.

148. *Ibid.*, 24 October 1997, p. 5.

149. *Ibid.*, 23 October 1997, p. 5.

150. *Argumenty i fakty*, no. 17, 1997, p. 5.

151. *Sunday Telegraph*, 12 October 1997, p. 31.

152. *Izvestiya*, 9 April 1996, p. 1.

153. *Guardian*, 11 July 1998, p. 15; *Izvestiya*, 3 April 1996, p. 5.

154. Charles J. Dick, 'A bear without claws: the Russian army in the 1990s', *Journal of Slavic Military Studies*, vol. 10, no. 1 (March 1997), pp. 1–10, at p. 5.

155. See http://news.bbc.co.uk/1/hi/world/ europe/7425694.stm, last accessed 20 September 2010.

156. *Guardian*, 11 July 1998, p. 15.

157. *Literaturnaya gazeta*, no. 49, 1996, p. 10; see also more generally S. A. Stivenson, *Bezdomnye v sotsial'noi strukture bol'shogo goroda* (Moscow: INION RAN, 1997).

158. *Izvestiya*, 12 April 1996, pp. 1–2, and (for Moscow) *ibid.*, 25 February 1995, p. 1.

159. *Sunday Telegraph*, 12 October 1997, p. 31.

160. *RSYe 2002*, pp. 186, 198.

161. *Argumenty i fakty*, no. 46, 1996, p. 5.

162. *Izvestiya*, 6 May 1993, p. 6.

163. *Ibid.*, 27 January 1993, p. 5.

164. *RSYe 2001*, p. 171.

165. Rimashevskaya, 'Sotsial'nye posledstviya', pp. 56–7.

166. *Nezavisimaya gazeta*, 25 November 1998, p. 8.
167. *Izvestiya*, 30 October 1998, p. 4.
168. *Ibid.*, 1 October 1998, p. 1.
169. *Ibid.*, 30 October 1998, p. 4.
170. *Ibid.*, 24 October 1998, p. 2.
171. *Novye izvestiya*, 19 September 1998, p. 4.
172. *Trud*, 31 October 1998, p. 1.
173. *Ibid.*, 28 October 1998, p. 2.
174. *RSYe 2009*, p. 167.
175. *Ibid.*, p. 195.
176. *Ibid.*, p. 201.
177. *Ibid.*, p. 511.
178. *Ibid.*, pp. 292 (tourism), 167 (income differentials), 175 (real value of pensions) and 167 (numbers living in officially defined poverty).
179. *Ibid.*, pp. 188–9. Levels of poverty were substantially greater in rural as compared with urban areas (p. 191).
180. N. M. Rimashevskaya, 'Bednost' i marginalizatsiya naseleniya', *Sotsiologicheskie issledovaniya*, no. 4, 2004, pp. 33–44, at pp. 38–41, 43. The same term was used by the Communist leader Gennadii Zyuganov (*Na perelome* (Moscow: Molodaya gvardiya, 2009), p. 100).
181. *Izvestiya*, 16 December 2008, p. 10.
182. *Guardian*, 17 March 2009, p. 27.
183. *Argumenty i fakty*, no. 5, 2009, p. 15.
184. *Ibid.*, no. 10, 2009, p. 10 (on the 'person-delegation' see *Izvestiya*, 5 June 2009, p. 2).
185. *Izvestiya*, 25 November 2008, p. 8.
186. *Ibid.*, 11 February 2009, p. 8.
187. *Ibid.*, 3 April 2009, pp. 1, 7, and 16 April 2009, p. 9.
188. *Ibid.*, 16 April 2009, p. 7.
189. *Ibid.*, 11 February 2009, p. 1.
190. *Ibid.*
191. *Argumenty i fakty*, no. 11, 2009, p. 19.
192. *Izvestiya*, 11 February 2009, pp. 1, 5.
193. *Moscow Times*, 23 April 2009, p. 2.
194. *Trud*, 1 June 2009, p. 6.
195. *Izvestiya*, 20 February 2009, p. 26.
196. *Guardian*, 15 March 2007, p. 29.
197. See www.opendemocracy.net/article/russia-theme/russia-life-on-the-poverty-line, 28 May 2008, last accessed 20 September 2010.
198. *Izvestiya*, 8 July 2008, pp. 1, 8.
199. *Ibid.*
200. There is a careful discussion of issues of this kind in O. N. Shkaratan and colleagues, *Sotsial'no-ekonomicheskoe neravenstvo i ego vosproizvodstvo v sovremennoi Rossii* (Moscow: Olma, 2009). The inadequacy of official measures of inequality was particularly vigorously contested by

opposition politicians: for Zyuganov, for instance, the decile ratio was really 30:1 and in Moscow 42:1 (*Na perelome*, p. 101); for Mikhail Delyagin and Vyacheslav Sheyanov it was at least 40:1 (*Mir naiznanku: chem zakonchitsya ekonomicheskii krizis dlya Rossii?* (Moscow: Kommersant/Eksmo, 2009), p. 63).
201. On the calculation of the Index, see, for instance, United Nations Development Programme, *Human Development Report 200: Overcoming Barriers – Human Mobility and Development* (Basingstoke and New York: Palgrave Macmillan, 2009), p. 208. The HDI is not without its critics: see, for instance, Robert V. Horn, *Statistical Indicators for the Economic and Social Sciences* (Cambridge and New York: Cambridge University Press, 1993), pp. 92–5.
202. *Komsomol'skaya pravda*, 2 February 2007, p. 2. Putin repeated the point in an interview with G8 journalists later in the year that was carried by the Russian press the following day, describing the 'huge income gap between the people at the top and the bottom of the scale' as one of the country's 'biggest' problems (*Izvestiya*, 5 June 2007, p. 3).
203. *Izvestiya*, 18 October 1994, p. 5. For a further discussion see, for instance, Stephen Handelman, *Comrade Criminal: Russia's New Mafia* (New Haven, CT, and London: Yale University Press, 1995), and on the later period Robert W. Orttung and Anthony Latta, eds., *Russia's Battle with Crime, Corruption, and Terrorism* (London and New York: Routledge, 2008). Especially insightful are Vadim Volkov, *Violent Entrepreneurs: The Use of Force in the Making of Russian Capitalism* (Ithaca, NY, and London: Cornell University Press, 2002), and Paddy Rawlinson, *From Fear to Fraternity: A Russian Tale of Crime, Economy and Modernity* (London: Pluto, 2010).
204. Tsentr po khraneniyu sovremennoi dokumentatsii, Moscow, *fond* 89, *opis'* 11, d. 131, 14 July 1987.
205. *Narodnoe khozyaistvo SSSR v 1988 g.* (Moscow: Finansy i statistika, 1989), p. 253.
206. *Materialy XXII s"ezda Kommunisticheskoi partii Sovetskogo Soyuza* (Moscow: Gosudarstvennoe izdatel'stvo, 1961), p. 400.
207. *Izvestiya*, 18 October 1994, p. 5.
208. A. I. Dolgova, ed., *Kriminal'naya situatsiya v Rossii i ee izmerenie* (Moscow: Kriminologicheskaya assotsiatsiya, 1996), pp. 4, 13–14 (the number of criminals had doubled over the same period: *ibid.*, p. 5).

Other inquiries suggested that more than 60 per cent of the victims of serious crime did not bother to report it (*Izvestiya*, 2 April 1997, p. 1).

209. On arson, *Prestupnost' i pravonarusheniya (1992–1996): statisticheskii sbornik* (Moscow: MVD RF, 1997), p. 148; on criminal groupings, V. I. Gladkikh, *Prestupnost' v sverkhkrupnom gorode i ee preduprezhdenie organami vnutrennykh del* (Moscow: VNII MID Rossii, 1996), p. 54.

210. *Prestupnost' v Rossii* (Moscow: Tsentr kompleksnykh sotsial'nykh issledovanii i marketinga, 1997), p. 5.

211. *RSYe 2000*, p. 243.

212. *RSYe 1997*, p. 270. Not only were there more murders: there were more unidentified bodies, and nearly twice as many who were 'lost without trace' (Dolgova, ed., *Kriminal'naya situatsiya*, pp. 14–15).

213. *RSYe 2001*, p. 273.

214. *Ibid.*, pp. 273–4.

215. The suspension effectively began with Boris Yeltsin's presidential decree on the 'gradual reduction in the application of the death penalty in connection with Russia's admission to the Council of Europe' (*Sobranie zakonodatel'stva Rossiiskoi Federatsii* [hereafter *SZ*], no. 21, item 2468, 16 May 1996). The 'ultimate measure of punishment' was retained in the new Criminal Code that came into effect in January 1997.

216. N. Zorkaya, ed., *Obshchestvennoe mnenie-2007* (Moscow: Levada-tsentr, 2007), p. 96.

217. Kagarlitsky, *Restoration in Russia*, p. 23.

218. *Argumenty i fakty*, no. 30, 1996, p. 8.

219. *Prestupnost' i pravonarusheniya*, pp. 16–17, 31–2, 36–7.

220. *Ibid.*, pp. 31–2, 62–3.

221. *Voprosy statistiki*, no. 3, 1997, p. 63 (in urban areas); its high levels of poverty and ill health have already been noted (p. 187).

222. *Komsomol'skaya pravda*, 10 November 1994, p. 3.

223. *Problemy bor'by s prestupnost'yu (regional'nyi aspekt)* (Moscow: VNII MVD Rossii, 1996), pp. 34–40.

224. *Prestupnost' i pravonarusheniya*, p. 18.

225. *Izvestiya*, 9 February 1994, p. 5.

226. *Argumenty i fakty*, no. 36, 1996, p. 16.

227. See respectively *Izvestiya*, 18 October 1994, p. 5, and *Financial Times*, 20 March 1997, p. 2.

228. This was the estimate of the Ministry of Internal Affairs (*Izvestiya*, 6 February 1997,

p. 1); Ivan Rybkin, for instance, estimated 45–50 per cent, Grigorii Yavlinsky 70 per cent (*ibid.*, 23 October 1997, p. 4).

229. *Nezavisimaya gazeta*, 1 October 1997, p. 1.

230. *Izvestiya*, 1 March 1997, p. 1. On these parallels see, for instance, Federico Varese, 'Is Sicily the future of Russia? Private protection and the rise of the Russian mafia', *European Journal of Sociology*, vol. 35, no. 2 (1994), pp. 224–58; Stefan Hedlund and Niclas Sundstrom, 'Does Palermo represent the future for Moscow?', *Journal of Public Policy*, vol. 16, no. 2 (May–August 1996), pp. 113–55.

231. *RSYe 2008*, p. 299.

232. Yu. M. Antonyan, *Prestupnost' sredi zhenshchin* (Moscow: Rossiiskoe pravo, 1992), p. 26.

233. *Ibid.*, p. 25.

234. *Prestupnost' i pravonarusheniya*, p. 8.

235. *Izvestiya*, 31 January 1996, p. 2.

236. *Ibid.*, 20 October 1994, p. 5.

237. More than 6,000 such guards had registered their services by April 1994, and 26,000 had obtained licences allowing them to take on security guard or detective duties: *ibid.*, 18 October 1994, p. 5.

238. *Ibid.*, 20 October 1994, p. 5.

239. *Ibid.*, 5 November 1993, p. 3.

240. *The Times*, 26 August 1998, p. 10; and on 'conversations', *Argumenty i fakty*, nos. 22–23, 1992, p. 8.

241. *Izvestiya*, 7 December 1993, p. 6.

242. *Ibid.*, 14 September 1993, p. 5.

243. *Nezavisimaya gazeta*, 9 October 1998, p. 12.

244. *Izvestiya*, 12 April 1997, p. 1 (38,000 and 1,700 respectively).

245. *Daily Telegraph*, 5 November 1998, p. 21; *Guardian*, 19 October 1998, p. 11.

246. There were 'graveyard wars' in St Petersburg in this connection: *Izvestiya*, 17 February 1994, p. 7.

247. *Ibid.*, 18 December 1993, p. 10.

248. *Ibid.*, 6 February 1997, p. 1.

249. *Ibid.*

250. *Ibid.*, 9 April 1996, p. 1.

251. *Guardian*, 1 August 1997, p. 13.

252. *Ibid.*, 6 May 1998, p. 14.

253. See, for instance, *Izvestiya*, 5 August 1992, p. 1.

254. *Guardian*, 22 October 1998, p. 18.

255. *Argumenty i fakty*, no. 30, 1996, p. 8.

256. *Izvestiya*, 21 October 1994, p. 5.

257. *Kommersant daily*, 15 December 1994, p. 14; *Rossiiskaya gazeta*, 10 January 1995, p. 3.

258. *Izvestiya*, 31 March 1998, p. 2, commenting on the election of a former criminal, Andrei

Kliment'ev, to the mayoralty; Kliment'ev was subsequently arrested and sentenced (*ibid.*, 28 May 1998, p. 1). The elected mayor of Leninsk-Kutnetskii in the Kemerovo region had a criminal record and was believed to be implicated in a 'series of murders' (*ibid.*, 19 September 1997, p. 1).

259. *Izvestiya*, 6 January 1996, p. 5.

260. The fourth was reported in *Segodnya*, 28 November 1995, p. 1; Starovoitova (see below) was the sixth.

261. *Izvestiya*, 4 July 1998, p. 1.

262. *Nezavisimaya gazeta*, 15 March 1994, p. 2.

263. *Segodnya*, 22 November 1998, p. 1 (her aide was also killed).

264. *Izvestiya*, 19 March 1997, p. 1.

265. *Ibid.*, 1 March 1997, p. 1.

266. *Segodnya*, 24 May 1996, p. 1.

267. *Kommersant daily*, 5 July 1996, p. 14.

268. *Nezavisimaya gazeta*, 21 October 2002, p. 8.

269. *Ibid.*, 23 June 2009, p. 1.

270. *Kommersant*, 18 December 2008, p. 4.

271. *Izvestiya*, 27 November 2008, pp. 1, 4.

272. There had been many other attacks on less senior judicial officials: *Kommersant*, 26 November 2008, p. 4.

273. *Argumenty i fakty*, no. 48, 1996, p. 7 (there had been 118 such killings).

274. *Izvestiya*, 15 September 2006, pp. 1–2; his bodyguard was also murdered.

275. See www.cpj.org/deadly/, last accessed 30 January 2010.

276. See *Partial Justice: An Inquiry into the Deaths of Journalists in Russia, 1993–2009* (Brussels: International Federation of Journalists, 2009), Preface. According to the IFJ's database, there had been 312 deaths between January 1993 and July 2009 (see www.ifj.org, last consulted 16 July 2010).

277. *Kommersant*, 9 October 2006, pp. 1–2.

278. It appeared posthumously in *Novaya gazeta*, 12 October 2006, p. 2.

279. See the obituary by David Hearst in the *Guardian*, 9 October 2006, p. 36. Politkovskaya's books include, in English, *A Dirty War: A Russian Reporter in Chechnya*, trans. and ed. John Crowfoot (London: Harvill, 2001), *Putin's Russia: Life in a Failing Democracy*, trans. Arch Tait (London: Harvill, 2004 and New York: Metropolitan Books, 2005), and *Nothing But The Truth: Selected Despatches*, trans. Arch Tait (London: Harvill Secker, 2010); her last in Russian was the compendious and posthumous *Za eto* (Moscow: Novaya gazeta, 2007).

280. *Vremya novostei*, 9 October 2006, p. 2.

281. *Ibid.*, 11 October 2006, p. 1.

282. *Izvestiya*, 20 February 2009, pp. 1, 3; the Supreme Court later overturned the acquittal on a technicality (*ibid.*, 26 June 2009, pp. 1, 3).

283. Roman Shleinov, 'Rules of the game', *Index on Censorship*, vol. 36, no. 2 (June 2007), pp. 6–14, at pp. 6, 8, 9–10, 14.

284. *Guardian*, 20 January 2009, p. 16, and *Izvestiya*, 20 January 2009, pp. 1, 3; the early release was noted in *Izvestiya*, 16 January 2009, p. 5.

285. *Izvestiya*, 25 September 2008, p. 1 (the victim was Ruslan Yamadaev).

286. *Kommersant*, 15 January 2009, p. 6 (the victim was Umar Izrailov).

287. *Daily Telegraph*, 31 March 2009, p. 12; *Izvestiya*, 31 March 2009, p. 9 (the victim was Sulim Yamadaev).

288. *Izvestiya*, 17 July 2009, pp. 1, 4; a posthumous article appeared in the *Independent*, 17 July 2009, pp. 1–2. It was rumoured that the Chechen President had an entire list of victims of this kind with more than 200 names on it: Tony Wood, 'The murder list', *London Review of Books*, vol. 31, no. 9 (14 May 2009), p. 14.

289. The trial was reported in *Izvestiya*, 15 April 1992, p. 8, and 16 October 1992, p. 3.

290. See Lyudmila Vinnikova, *Man'yak yavlyaetsya v dozhd': dokumental'naya povest' o prestupnike-man'yake Chikatilo* (Moscow: Argumenty i fakty, 1992); and Richard Lourie, *Hunting for the Devil: The Search for the Russian Ripper* (London: Grafton, 1993). Chikatilo's son was later arrested for rape: *Argumenty i fakty*, no. 9, 1997, p. 13.

291. *Argumenty i fakty*, no. 7, 1997, p. 13.

292. *Ibid.*, no. 9, 1997, p. 13.

293. *Scotland on Sunday*, 19 October 1997, pp. 16–17.

294. *Kuranty*, 12 May 1994, p. 1.

295. *Scotland on Sunday*, 2 November 1997, p. 20.

296. *Evening Times* (Glasgow), 21 July 1997, p. 3.

297. *Herald*, 10 March 1998, p. 10.

298. *Moscow Times*, 28 October 2008, p. 3.

299. The two St Petersburg killers had lured the young girl to an apartment one of them had rented for the day, where they drowned her and then 'ate the body parts because they were hungry' (*Moskovskii komsomolets*, 9 February 2009, p. 7). For the Samara case see *ibid.*, 10 November 2009, p. 3.

300. *Izvestiya*, 23 July 2008, pp. 1, 3.

301. *Guardian*, 25 October 2007, p. 22.

302. See United Nations Development Programme, *Human Development Report*

2007/8 (Basingstoke and New York: Palgrave Macmillan, 2007), pp. 322–5.

303. *Global Peace Index: 2010 Methodology, Results and Findings* (Sydney: Institute of Economics and Peace, 2010, accessed at www.visionofhumanity.org), various pages (the most peaceful country was New Zealand, and the least peaceful Iraq). The Global Peace Index is produced by the Institute for Economics and Peace in Sydney in association with the Economist Intelligence Unit; it combines twenty-three different qualitative and quantitative indicators, in this case the latest available for 2008–9.

304. In what follows I have drawn on Ol'ga Gryaznova, 'Otnoshenie zhitelei Rossii k pravookhranitel'nym organam: obzor issledovanii poslednikh let', *Vestnik obshchestvennogo mneniya*, no. 2(82), March–April 2006, pp. 32–46.

305. *Izvestiya*, 29 April 2009, p. 1; on the background to the case, see *ibid.*, 8 May 2009, pp. 1, 5.

306. *Ibid.*, 29 July 2009, p. 1.

307. *Sunday Herald*, 8 November 2009, pp. 36–7 (attitudes); *Novaya gazeta*, 29 April 2009, p. 1 (dissolution). The call to disband the police entirely was made by Andrei Makarov, a senior United Russia Duma deputy, who made clear he was speaking in a personal capacity (*Kommersant*, 26 November 2009, p. 4), among others.

308. *Izvestiya*, 4 December 2009, p. 2.

309. *Vestnik statistiki*, no. 1, 1992, p. 65.

310. Gorbachev, *Izbrannye rechi i stat'i*, vol. III, p. 266. Statistics on the position of women and the family were reported annually in *Vestnik statistiki*, and as a separate serial publication, *Zhenshchiny i deti v SSSR*; many are conveniently available in Peter Lentini, *Statistical Data on Women in the USSR* (Glasgow: Lorton House, 1994).

311. *Vestnik statistiki*, no. 1, 1992, p. 53.

312. *Ibid.*, pp. 65, 64.

313. *Pravda*, 13 April 1984, pp. 1, 4.

314. *Izvestiya Tsentral'nogo komiteta* [hereafter *TsK*] *KPSS*, no. 6, 1991, p. 28.

315. A. D. Chernev, *229 kremlevskikh vozhdei: Politbyuro, Orgbyuro, Sekretariata tsk Kommunisticheskoi partii v litsakh i tsifrakh* (Moscow: Rodina/Russika, 1996), p. 82. Women were 30.5 per cent of the mass membership of the CPSU in 1990: *Izvestiya TsK KPSS*, no. 6, 1991, p. 27.

316. *Izvestiya TsK KPSS*, no. 6, 1991, p. 28.

317. *Pravda*, 2 June 1989, p. 2.

318. *XIX Vsesoyuznaya konferentsiya Kommunisticheskoi partii Sovetskogo Soyuza, 28 iyunya – 1 iyulya 1988 g.: stenograficheskii otchet*, 2 vols. (Moscow: Politizdat, 1988), vol. II, pp. 78–80.

319. Z. Yankova in N. Solov'ev, Yu. Lazauskas and Z. Yakova, eds., *Problemy byta, braka i sem'i* (Vilnius: Mintis, 1970), p. 43.

320. L. A. Gordon and E. V. Klopov, *Chelovek posle raboty. Sotsial'nye problemy byta i vnerabochego vremeni. Prilozhenie* (Moscow: Nauka, 1972), pp. 11–12.

321. *Pravda*, 9 March 1989, p. 2; see also *ibid.*, 5 March 1988, p. 1.

322. *Izvestiya TsK KPSS*, no. 6, 1991, pp. 34, 32, 37, 38.

323. Gorbachev, *Izbrannye rechi i stat'i*, vol. III, p. 232.

324. M. S. Gorbachev, *Perestroika i novoe myshlenie dlya nashei strany i dlya vsego mira* (Moscow: Politizdat, 1987), pp. 116–17.

325. Gorbachev, *Izbrannye rechi i stat'i*, vol. VI, p. 380.

326. *XIX Vsesoyuznaya konferentsiya*, vol. II, p. 81. A rather different set of figures, suggesting economic reasons were primary, was reported in *Vestnik statistiki*, no. 1, 1992, p. 52.

327. *Soviet Weekly*, 29 July 1989, p. 5.

328. *Ibid.*, 25 November 1988, p. 15.

329. N. Zakharova, A. Posadskaya and N. Rimashevskaya, 'Kak my reshaem zhenskii vopros', *Kommunist*, no. 4, 1989, pp. 56–65.

330. El'vira Novikova in *Moskovskie novosti*, no. 10, 1989, p. 14.

331. *Izvestiya TsK KPSS*, no. 12, 1990, p. 133.

332. *Ibid.*, no. 6, 1991, pp. 25–31.

333. *Soviet Weekly*, 26 November 1988, p. 15.

334. *Izvestiya TsK KPSS*, no. 6, 1991, pp. 25–31.

335. *Ibid.*, no. 12, 1990, p. 134; see similarly *Pravda*, 25 June 1990, p. 5, and *Izvestiya*, 25 November 1990, p. 2.

336. *Izvestiya*, 21 October 1990, p. 2.

337. See *Pravda*, 15 August 1990, p. 4, and *Izvestiya*, 13 May 1990, p. 1.

338. *Izvestiya*, 21 October 1990, p. 2.

339. *Pravda*, 9 December 1990, p. 3; the proposal was supported in *ibid.*, 11 February 1991, p. 4, and in *Izvestiya*, 22 March 1991, p. 7.

340. *Izvestiya*, 25 October 1995, p. 7.

341. The global average for the representation of women in national parliaments was 14 per cent in 2001, and somewhat higher in European and OSCE member countries (Judith Squires and Mark Wickham-Jones, *Women in Parliament: A Comparative*

Analysis (Manchester: Equal Opportunities Commission, 2001), pp. 4–5).

342. *Izvestiya*, 6 March 2009, p. 2.

343. *Vybory v Rossiiskoi Federatsiya. 2007. Elektoral'naya statistika* (Moscow: SitiPressServis, 2008), p. 128.

344. *Sunday Times*, 30 December 2007, p. 20.

345. *Daily Telegraph*, 17 April 2008, p. 17.

346. The paper was *Moskovskii korrespondent*; its offices had already been visited several times by FSB operatives and the editor had been advised to 'beef up his personal security' (www.theotherrussia.org/2008/04/20/ newspaper-suspended-after-steamy-putin-rumor, 20 April 2008, last accessed 20 September 2010). The paper's owner, Alexander Lebedev, described reports that he had been ordered to close it down as 'complete nonsense' (*Kommersant*, 21 April 2008, p. 6).

347. *Metro*, 23 April 2009, p. 1.

348. *Izvestiya*, 25 September 1995, p. 7.

349. *RSYe 2009*, pp. 129, 148; their proportion of the rural unemployed was noted in *Segodnya*, 18 February 1998, p. 3.

350. *RSYe 2009*, p. 137.

351. *Ibid.*, p. 138; *Izvestiya*, 19 February 1998, p. 5 (these estimates were somewhat impressionistic).

352. *RSYe 2009*, p. 218.

353. *Ibid.*, p. 291.

354. *Ibid.*, p. 222.

355. *Izvestiya*, 14 September 1993, p. 5.

356. *Nezavisimaya gazeta*, 9 April 1997, p. 6; other estimates went up to 4 million (*Segodnya*, 24 May 1997, p. 2).

357. *Izvestiya*, 18 June 2009, pp. 1, 5.

358. *RSYe 2009*, p. 112 (there were 8.3 marriages per thousand population in 2008 as compared with the 10.6 that had been recorded in 1980; there were 5.0 divorces, as compared with 3.8 in 1990 and 4.2 in 1980).

359. *Ibid.*, p. 101 (there were 12.1 births per thousand population in 2008 as compared with 13.4 in 1990 and 15.9 in 1980; the death rate was 14.6 in 2008 as compared with 11.2 in 1990 and 11.0 in 1980).

360. *Ibid.*, p. 113 (359,330 arrived from other countries in 2000, but 281,614 in 2008; the peak year was 1994, when 1,146,735 relocated, in nearly all cases from other CIS countries).

361. *Ibid.*, p. 266.

362. *Ibid.*, p. 111.

363. A 'Conception of Demographic Policy to 2025' was issued by presidential decree in 2007: *SZ*, no. 42, item 5009, 9 October 2007.

364. World Population Prospects: The 2008 Revision Population Database, at http://esa. un.org/unpp, various pages, last accessed 31 January 2010.

365. *Izvestiya*, 14 May 2003, p. 1; Amnesty International is quoted from their report, *Violence against Women in the Russian Federation* (2005) at www.amnesty.org/en/ library/info/EUR46/056/2005, last consulted 20 September 2010.

366. *Sunday Telegraph: Stella*, 12 April 2009, pp. 40, 43. Valeriya set out her experience more fully in an autobiography: *I zhizn', i slezy, i lyubov'* (St Petersburg: Azbuka-klassika, 2006).

367. *BBC News*, 26 November 2007, at http://news. bbc.co.uk, last consulted 9 July 2009. There is a comprehensive exchange of experience in Natal'ya Rimashevskaya, ed., *Razorvat' krug molchaniya* (Moscow: URSS, 2005).

368. *Nezavisimaya gazeta*, 28 November 1996, p. 6.

369. Ol'ga Stuchevskaya, 'Kharassment i rossiiskie zhenshchiny', *Vestnik obshchestvennogo mneniya*, no. 4(96), July–August 2008, pp. 43–9, at p. 44.

370. *Daily Telegraph*, 29 July 2008, p. 16.

371. *Izvestiya*, 30 August 1988, p. 6. For a further discussion see Elizabeth Waters, 'Restructuring and the "woman question": perestroika and prostitution', *Feminist Review*, no. 33 (Autumn 1989), pp. 3–19.

372. *Izvestiya*, 14 August 1996, p. 5.

373. Locations in Moscow, and typical charges, were set out in *Argumenty i fakty: Moskva*, no. 24, 1997, p. 14.

374. *Ekspress-gazeta*, no. 41, 1998, p. 1 (I thank Ronald J. Hill for this reference).

375. *Nezavisimaya gazeta*, 23 December 2002, p. 8.

376. *Sobesednik*, no. 36, 1997, pp. 2–3.

377. *Gazeta*, 13 February 2007, p. 6 (based on reports from St Petersburg).

378. *Izvestiya*, 14 August 1996, p. 5.

379. *Komsomol'skaya pravda*, 10 October 1992, pp. 1, 3 (there were 'over a thousand' child prostitutes in Moscow at this time, p. 3).

380. *Argumenty i fakty*, no. 31, 1996, p. 4.

381. *Segodnya*, 24 May 1997, p. 2. There was another report in *Argumenty i fakty*, no. 36, 1996, p. 7.

382. *Global Monitoring Report on the Status of Action against Commercial Exploitation of Children: The Russian Federation* (Bangkok: End Child Prostitution, Child Pornography and the Trafficking of Children for Sexual Purposes, 2006; available online at www. ecpat.net), p. 11.

383. *Komsomol'skaya pravda*, 12 May 1993, p. 3.
384. *Argumenty i fakty*, no. 9, 1997, p. 9.
385. *Komsomol'skaya pravda*, 12 May 1993, p. 3.
386. *Sunday Telegraph*, 11 January 1998, p. 28.
387. *RSYe 2009*, p. 271.
388. See, for instance, *Averting AIDS Crises in Eastern Europe and Central Asia: A Regional Support Strategy* (Washington, DC: World Bank, 2003), pp. 13–14 and elsewhere.
389. Judyth L. Twigg, ed., *HIV/AIDS in Russia and Eurasia*, 2 vols. (Basingstoke and New York: Palgrave Macmillan, 2006), vol. I, pp. 10–11, which provides a comprehensive assessment. For more recent overviews see John M. Kramer, 'Drug abuse and HIV/AIDS in Russia', in Stephen White, ed., *Media, Culture and Society in Putin's Russia* (Basingstoke and New York: Palgrave Macmillan, 2008), pp. 226–45, and Alexandra V. Orlova, 'The Russian "war on drugs": a kinder, gentler approach?', *Problems of Post-Communism*, vol. 56, no. 1 (January–February 2009), pp. 23–34. The first AIDS case, according to newspaper reports, was of a military interpreter in Africa, arising from a homosexual encounter (*Rossiiskaya gazeta*, 8 September 2004, p. 10). On his return he infected his wife, who gave birth to an infected child, who in turn infected dozens more women and children while being treated in hospital (*Trud*, 3 May 2006, p. 6).
390. *RSYe 2009*, p. 269.
391. *Moscow News*, no. 49, 12 December 2008, p. 5.
392. *Human Development Report 2007/8*, pp. 257–9.
393. *Ibid.*
394. *Argumenty i fakty*, no. 9, 1997, p. 5; a similar report appeared in *Obshchaya gazeta*, no. 11, 1997, p. 8.
395. Perhaps the most striking example of successful female activism in the early years of the new century was the Committee of Soldiers' Mothers; the fullest study is Amy Caiazza, *Mothers and Soldiers: Gender, Citizenship, and Civil Society in Contemporary Russia* (New York and London: Routledge, 2002).

6   Changing times, changing values

1. L. A. Onikov and N. V. Shishlin, eds., *Kratkii politicheskii slovar'* (Moscow: Politizdat, 1978), p. 264.
2. L. F. Il'ichev, ed., *Filosofskii entsiklopedicheskii slovar'* (Moscow: Sovetskaya entsiklopediya, 1983), p. 449.
3. L. A. Onikov and N. V. Shishlin, eds., *Kratkii politicheskii slovar'*, 6th edn (Moscow: Politizdat, 1989), p. 350.
4. Onikov and Shishlin, *Kratkii politicheskii slovar'* (1978), pp. 289, 308–9.
5. *Ibid.*, pp. 159–62.
6. B. A. Grushin, *Mneniya o mire i mir mnenii* (Moscow: Izdatel'stvo politicheskoi literatury, 1967), p. 175. The full report appeared as Grushin and V. V. Chikin, *Ispoved' pokoleniya* (Moscow: Moldaya gvardiya, 1962), based on the 17,466 responses that had been received (p. 5). For discussions see Elizabeth Weinberg, *Sociology in the Soviet Union and Beyond: Social Inquiry and Social Change*, 2nd edn (Aldershot and Burlington, VT: Ashgate, 2004), pp. 79–101, and B. Z. Doktorov, *Ottsy-osnovateli: istoriya izucheniya obshchestvennogo mneniya* (Moscow: Tsentr sotsial'nogo prognozirovaniya, 2006), pp. 413–17.
7. O. Prokhanov, ed., *Kto est' kto v Rossii: spravochnoe izdanie* (Moscow: Olimp/EKSMO-Press, 1998), pp. 183–4. Grushin's own account is in his 'General'nyi proekt "Obshchestvennoe mnenie" (POM). Institut filosofii i IKSI AN SSSR (1967–1974)', *Vestnik obshchestvennogo mneniya*, no. 6(86), November–December 2006, pp. 55–62.
8. *Sotsiologicheskie issledovaniya*, no. 7, 1993, p. 7.
9. On these developments see M. G. Pugacheva, 'Institut konkretnykh sotsiologicheskikh issledovanii Akademii nauk SSSR, 1968–1972 gody', *Sotsiologicheskii zhurnal*, no. 2, 1994, pp. 158–72, and more generally Vladimir Shlapentokh, *The Politics of Sociology in the Soviet Union* (Boulder, CO: Westview, 1987).
10. *Ogonek*, no. 12, 1988, p. 20. Grushin, born in Moscow in August 1929, died in September 2007 with his most ambitious project still incomplete. For an obituary see 'In memoriam. Pamyati B. A. Grushina', *Vestnik obshchestvennogo mneniya*, no. 5(91), September–October 2007, p. 65, and also David Wedgwood Benn in the *Independent*, 22 October 2007, p. 39; there is a fuller discussion of his work in Doktorov, *Ottsy-osnovateli*, pp. 399–437. Only two volumes (the second in two parts) were published of his projected four-volume compendium of Russian public opinion over four leaderships: *Chetyre zhizni Rossii v zerkale oprosov obshchestvennogo mneniya: ocherki massovogo*

soznaniya rossiyan vremen Khrushcheva, Brezhneva, Gorbacheva i Yel'tsina (Moscow: Progress-Traditsiya, 2001–6).

11. B. Grushin and L. A. Onikov, *Massovaya informatsiya v sovetskom promyshlennom gorode* (Moscow: Politizdat, 1980), p. 414 (67 per cent of letters to the local paper were largely or entirely negative, but 69 per cent of the articles it published were largely or entirely positive).

12. R. A. Safarov, *Obshchestvennoe mnenie i gosudarstvennoe upravlenie* (Moscow: Yuridicheskaya literatura, 1975), pp. 145, 121, 159.

13. See, for instance, Murray Yanowitch, ed., *Soviet Work Attitudes: The Issue of Participation in Management* (White Plains. NY: Sharpe and Oxford: Martin Robertson, 1979).

14. See Darrell P. Slider, 'Party-sponsored public opinion research in the Soviet Union', *Journal of Politics*, vol. 47, no. 1 (February 1985), pp. 209–27.

15. V. S. Korobeinikov, *Piramida mnenii* (Moscow: Molodaya gvardiya, 1981), pp. 176, 173, 182. The establishment of an institute of this kind had been proposed in a letter to the party and state leadership from Andrei Sakharov and others (*Posev*, no. 7, 1970, p. 40); Safarov also called for a greater degree of attention to public opinion, and to its systematic investigation (*Pravda*, 25 September 1981, pp. 2–3).

16. M. S. Gorbachev, *Izbrannye rechi i stat'i*, 7 vols. (Moscow: Politizdat, 1987–90), vol. III, p. 241. Legislation on the 'national discussion of important questions of state life' was approved the following year: 'O vsenarodnom obsuzhdenii vazhnykh voprosov gosudarstvennoi zhizni', *Vedomosti Verkhovnogo Soveta SSSR*, no. 26, item 387, 30 June 1987.

17. *Spravochnik partiinogo rabotnika*, issue 29 (Moscow: Izdatel'stvo politicheskoi literatury, 1989), pp. 322–5.

18. Onikov and Shishlin, eds., *Kratkii politicheskii slovar'* (1989), p. 378.

19. *Plenum Tsentral'nogo Komiteta KPSS 14–15 iyunya 1983 goda: stenograficheskii otchet* (Moscow: Izdatel'stvo politicheskoi literatury, 1983), pp. 40, 200. The Centre, it was agreed in a July 1987 resolution adopted jointly by the Central Committee, the Soviet government and the All-Union Council of Trade Unions, would in fact be established under the auspices of the All-Union Council and the State Labour Committee, and it would

'systematically conduct surveys of the population on the most important social-economic themes' (*O korennoi perestroike upravleniya ekonomikoi: sbornik dokumentov* (Moscow: Politizdat, 1988), p. 242).

20. *Détente*, no. 8 (Winter 1987), pp. 11–12.

21. *Materialy XIX Vsesoyuznoi konferentsii Kommunisticheskoi partii Sovetskogo Soyuza, 28 iyunya – 1 iyulya 1988 g.* (Moscow: Politizdat, 1988), pp. 69, 26, 144.

22. In spite of the changes that had taken place in official thinking, Levada recalled, it was only Zaslavskaya's 'enormous scholarly and public authority' together with the 'organisational talent and enthusiasm' of Grushin that had made it possible: Yu. A. Levada, 'Dvadtsat' let raboty Vserossiiskogo tsentra izucheniya obshchestvennogo mneniya', *Sotsiologicheskii zhurnal*, no. 4, 1997, pp. 221–7, at p. 221. Zaslavskaya herself had been greatly impressed by the Institut für Demoskopie in West Germany, which she had visited in 1972 and again in 1989, but refused to take on the organisational responsibilities unless Boris Grushin was her deputy: 'Kak rozhdalsya VTsIOM', *Ekonomicheskie i sotsial'nye peremeny: monitoring obshchestvennogo mneniya*, no. 1, 1998, pp. 8–11, at pp. 8–9. Grushin's own account of the establishment of VTsIOM is in his 'Na dal'nikh i blizkikh podstupakh k sozdaniyu VTsIOMa', *Vestnik obshchestvennogo mneniya*, no. 5 (91), September–October 2007, p. 55; Zaslavskaya's fullest account is in her memoirs: T. I. Zaslavskaya, *Izbrannoe*, 3 vols. (Moscow: Ekonomika, 2007), vol. III, chs. 9 and 10. For an overview of its work and a full selection of articles from its bimonthly (later quarterly) bulletin, see L. Gudkov, B. Dubin and Yu. Levada, eds., *Obshchestvennyi razlom i rozhdenie novoi sotsiologii: dvadtsat' let monitoringa* (Moscow: Novoe izdatel'stvo, 2008).

23. *Pravda*, 18 March 1988, p. 4.

24. *Moskovskie novosti*, no. 35, 1988, p. 10. The first four surveys, in 1988, were essentially 'pilots', Zaslavskaya recalled; the 'first serious exercise' was at the start of 1989, a 2500-N survey directed by Yuri Levada on what Russians thought of the 'New Year' (*Izbrannoe*, vol. III, p. 604).

25. *Ekonomicheskie i sotsial'nye peremeny*, no. 5, 1998, p. 45. For a convenient guide to its early findings, see *A Catalogue of VCIOM Surveys, 1989–1996* (Glasgow: University of Strathclyde, Centre for the Study of Public Policy, SPP 281, 1997).

26. On Levada's career and influence, see, for instance, Boris Dubin, 'Obraz i obrazets: pamyati Yuriya Levady (1929[*sic*]–2006)', *Sotsiologicheskii zhurnal*, no. 1, 2007, pp. 186–7, and the wider symposium that appeared in *ibid.*, no. 1, 2008, pp. 109–49. An English-language obituary appeared in *The Times*, 21 November 2006, p. 57. VTsIOM's two most important early studies were Yu. A. Levada, ed., *Yest' mnenie! Itogi sotsiologicheskogo oprosa* (Moscow: Progress, 1990), and A. A. Golov *et al.*, *Sovetskii prostoi chelovek: opyt sotsial'nogo portreta na rubezhe 90-kh godov* (Moscow: Mirovoi okean, 1993). Levada's own writings are collected in Yu. A. Levada, *Ot mnenii k ponimaniyu: sotsiologicheskie ocherki, 1993–2000* (Moscow: Moskovskaya shkola politicheskikh issledovanii, 2000), and *Ishchem cheloveka: sotsiologicheskie ocherki, 2000–2005* (Moscow: Novoe izdatel'stvo, 2006).

27. Vox Populi lasted from 1989 up to 1999; its findings were issued in a regular newsletter, *Mir mnenii i mneniya o mire*.

28. *Nezavisimaya gazeta*, 1 February 2010, p. 6.

29. The Foundation (*Fond 'Obshchestvennoe mnenie'*) maintains a website at www.fom.ru (in Russian, but some English-language material is also available). On attitudes to the United States, see T. Vorontsova and A. Danilova, eds., *Amerika – vzglyad iz Rossii: do i posle 11 sentyabrya* (Moscow: FOM, 2001); other collections of its 'sociological observations' include A. A. Oslon, Ye. S. Petrenko, G. S. Batygin, G. L. Kertman and I. A. Klimov, eds., *Desyat' let sotsiologicheskikh nablyudenii* (Moscow: FOM, 2003); A. A. Chernyakov, ed., *Sotsiologicheskie nablyudeniya, 2002–2004* (Moscow: FOM, 2005); and A. A. Chernyakov, ed., *Obraz myslei i obraz zhizni: sotsiologicheskie nablyudeniya* (Moscow: FOM, 2008).

30. *Sotsiologicheskie issledovaniya*, no. 6, 1993, p. 39.

31. *Segodnya*, 28 December 1995, p. 3. The 1993 result, for Boris Grushin, was nothing less than a 'fiasco' (*Mir mnenii i mneniya o mire*, no. 5, 1994, p. 9). A fuller discussion is available in A. V. Dmitriev and Zh. T. Toshchenko, 'Sotsiologicheskii opros i politika', *Sotsiologicheskie issledovaniya*, no. 5, 1994, pp. 42–51; Vladimir Shlapentokh, 'The 1993 Russian election polls', *Public Opinion Quarterly*, vol. 58, no. 4 (Winter 1994), pp. 579–602; and William L. Miller, Stephen White and Paul Heywood, 'Twenty-five days to go: measuring and interpreting the trends in public opinion during the 1993 Russian election campaign', *ibid.*, vol. 60, no. 1 (Spring 1996), pp. 106–27. The 1995 election is considered in the same context in Ye. G. Andryushchenko, A. V. Dmitriev and Zh. T. Toshchenko, 'Oprosy i vybory 1995 goda', *Sotsiologicheskie issledovaniya*, no. 6, 1996, pp. 3–17. Survey-based forecasts later became much more accurate, but serious methodological issues remained: for a post-mortem on the 2007 experience, see Denis Volkov and Aleksei Grazhdankin, 'Chto oznachaet skhodstvo i razlichie predvybornogo prognoza Levada-Tsentra i ofitsial'nykh rezul'tatov TsIK?', *Vestnik obshchestvennogo mneniya*, no. 2, 2008, pp. 44–8.

32. For representative criticisms of the 2002 census, see, for instance, *Izvestiya*, 19 October 2002, p. 1, and 14 November 2002, p. 4; there were calls for the entire exercise to be declared invalid (*Moskovskie novosti*, no. 22, 2003, p. 24). There is a more extended analysis in Valerii Tishkov, ed., *Na puti k perepisi* (Moscow: Aviaizdat, 2003); Tishkov, director of the Institute of Ethnography of the Academy of Sciences, was a particularly outspoken critic. For the announcement of the postponement of the 2010 census to 2013, for financial reasons, see *Nezavisimaya gazeta*, 21 September 2009, p. 3; Putin announced the restoration of the original census date shortly afterwards (*Vremya novostei*, 2 November 2009, p. 1).

33. For a comprehensive review of survey findings in the early postcommunist years, see Matthew Wyman, *Public Opinion in Postcommunist Russia* (London: Macmillan and New York: St Martin's, 1997). There are several critical discussions of the experience of polling in the Russian context, including John P. Willerton and Lee Sigelman, 'Public opinion research in the USSR: opportunities and pitfalls', *Journal of Communist Studies*, vol. 7, no. 2 (June 1991), pp. 217–34; James L. Gibson, 'Survey research in the past and future USSR: reflections on the methodology of mass opinion surveys', *Research in Micropolitics*, vol. 4 (1994), pp. 87–114; and James Alexander, 'Surveying attitudes in Russia: a representation of formlessness', *Communist and Post-Communist Studies*, vol. 30, no. 2 (June 1997), pp. 107–27. Two important and methodologically innovative studies are James Alexander, *Political Culture*

in Post-Communist Russia: Formlessness and Recreation in a Traumatic Transition (Basingstoke: Macmillan / New York: St Martin's, 2000), and Ellen Carnaghan, *Out of Order: Russian Political Values in an Imperfect World* (University Park: Pennsylvania State University Press, 2007).

34. *Ekonomicheskie i sotsial'nye peremeny*, no. 5, 1998, pp. 57, 89.

35. *Vestnik obshchestvennogo mneniya*, no. 3, 2008, p. 79.

36. In a study based on surveys carried out in the early 1990s, for instance, Miller and colleagues found strong support for the view that farming, motor car and computer manufacturing, newspapers and television should be 'run mainly by the state, rather than mainly as private businesses': William L. Miller, Stephen White and Paul Heywood, *Values and Political Change in Postcommunist Europe* (Basingstoke: Macmillan and New York: St Martin's, 1998), p. 112.

37. M. K. Gorshkov, 'Rossiiskii mentalitet v sotsiologicheskom izmerenii', *Sotsiologicheskie issledovaniya*, no. 6, 2008, pp. 100–14, at pp. 108–9.

38. *Vestnik obshchestvennogo mneniya*, no. 2, 2008, p. 111.

39. *Ibid.*, no. 3, 2008, p. 78

40. *Ibid.*, p. 101.

41. *Ibid.*, pp. 78–9.

42. There figures are drawn from the 2010 Russia survey (see Note on surveys).

43. See, for instance, Silvana Malle, 'Soviet legacies in post-Soviet Russia: insights from crisis management', *Post-Communist Economies*, vol. 21, no. 3 (September 2009), pp. 249–82; Andrew C. Kuchins, 'Why Russia is so Russian', *Current History*, vol. 108, no. 720 (October 2009), pp. 318–24; Ol'ga Kryshtanovskaya and Stephen White, 'The Sovietization of Russian politics', *Post-Soviet Affairs*, vol. 25, no. 4 (October–December 2009), pp. 283–309.

44. These figures are drawn from the 2008 Russia survey (some 41 per cent were unable to express a view on whether party lists of single-member constituencies gave them more political influence). Some of the complexities of non-responses in the Russian context are examined in Ellen Carnaghan, 'Alienation, apathy, or ambivalence? "Don't knows" and democracy in Russia', *Slavic Review*, vol. 55, no. 2 (Summer 1996), pp. 325–63, and Adam J. Berinsky and Joshua A. Tucker, '"Don't knows" and public opinion

towards economic reform: evidence from Russia', *Communist and Post-Communist Studies*, vol. 39, no. 1 (March 2006), pp. 73–99.

45. James L. Gibson, 'Political and economic markets: changes in the connections between attitudes toward political democracy and a market economy within the mass culture of Russia and Ukraine', *Journal of Politics*, vol. 58, no. 4 (November 1996), pp. 954–84, at pp. 965–6.

46. Valerii Fedorov, 'Zhit' kak pri kapitalizme, a rabotat' kak pri Brezhneve', *Izvestiya*, 6 December 2007, p. 6.

47. 'Otsenki rossiiskikh liderov i polozheniya del v strane', 30 April 2009, www.levada.ru/press/2009043003.html, last accessed 20 September 2010. Medvedev's rating had improved to 77 per cent and Putin's to 80 per cent by February 2010: 'Fevral'skie reitingi odobreniya i otsenki polozheniya del v strane', 4 March 2010, at www.levada.ru/press/2010030404.html, last accessed 20 September 2010.

48. 'Ekonomicheskaya situatsiya v strane glazami rossiyan', 25 May 2009, at www.levada.ru/press/2009052500.html, last accessed 20 September 2010.

49. 'Rynok truda v otvetakh rossiyan', 26 May 2009, at www.levada.ru/press/2009052602.html, last accessed 20 September 2010.

50. Dobson, *Is Russia Turning the Corner?*, p. 32. Between 55 and 75 per cent of those who were asked 'regretted' the demise of the USSR, in Levada Centre surveys between 1992 and 2009; in November 2009, 60 per cent 'regretted' the demise of the USSR and fewer than half as many (28 per cent) did not: 'Rossiyane o raspade SSSR i budushchem SNG', 21 December 2009, at www.levada.ru/press/2009122101.print.html, last accessed 20 September 2010.

51. Richard Rose and Christian Haerpfer, *New Russia Barometer III: The Results* (Glasgow: University of Strathclyde, Centre for the Study of Public Policy, SPP 228, 1994), p. 41 (4 per cent thought the disintegration of the USSR had affected their living standards for the better, but 76 per cent thought they had been affected for the worse).

52. *Argumenty i fakty*, no. 12, 1996, p. 1.

53. USIA, *Opinion Analysis*, 23 December 1996, pp. 1–3.

54. Miller, White and Heywood, *Values and Political Change*, pp. 86–7 (see also Chapter 8).

55. Yuri Levada, 'Dvadtsat' let spustya: perestroika v obshchestvennom mnenii i v

obshchestvennoi zhizni', *Vestnik obshchestvennogo mneniya* no. 2, 2005, pp. 8, 9, 11. The figures for December 2009 are taken from 'Epokha i lichnost' M. Gorbacheva v glazakh rossiyan', 11 March 2010, at www.levada.ru/press/2010031101.print.html, last accessed 20 September 2010.

56. N. Zorkaya, ed., *Obshchestvennoe mnenie – 2005* (Moscow: Levada-tsentr, 2005), p. 169.

57. Mikhail Gorshkov and Vladimir Petukhov, 'Perestroika glazami rossiyan: 20 let spustya', in *Proryv k svobode: o perestroike dvadtsat' let spustya (kriticheskii analiz)* (Moscow: Al'pina Biznes Buks, 2005), pp. 376, 380.

58. M. K. Gorshkov, *Rossiiskoe obshchestvo v usloviyakh transformatsii: mify i real'nost' (sotsiologicheskii analiz), 1992–2002 gg.* (Moscow: Rosspen, 2003), pp. 382, 384.

59. Adapted from www.levada.ru/press/2007110104.html, 1 November 2007, last accessed 20 September 2010; rounded percentages.

60. Yuri Levada in *Vestnik obshchestvennogo mneniya*, no. 1, 2006, p. 10.

61. Aleksei Levinson, 'Mif tretii: "osobyi put"', *Vestnik obshchestvennogo mneniya*, no. 6, 2008, pp. 80–8, at pp. 88, 80.

62. *Izvestiya*, 12 May 2006, p. 2.

63. Levada Centre data, 1 September 2008, at www.levada.ru/press/2008090104.print.html, last accessed 20 September 2010.

64. *Izvestiya*, 29 December 2008, p. 1.

65. *Guardian*, 29 December 2008, p. 18.

66. Lyubov' Borusyak, 'Proekt "Imya Rossii" kak novyi uchebnik istorii', *Vestnik obshchestvennogo mneniya*, no. 5, 2008, pp. 58–66, at p. 62.

67. *The Times*, 12 July 1982, p. 1. For a fuller discussion of the evolution of letter-writing and petitioning over the Soviet period, see Gregory L. Freeze, *From Supplication to Revolution: A Documentary Social History of Imperial Russia* (Oxford and New York: Oxford University Press, 1988); Sheila Fitzpatrick, 'Supplicants and citizens: public letter-writing in Soviet Russia in the 1930s', *Slavic Review*, vol. 55, no. 1 (Spring 1996), pp. 78–105; Fitzpatrick, 'Signals from below: Soviet letters of denunciation of the 1930s', *Journal of Modern History*, vol. 68, no. 4 (December 1996), pp. 831–66; Fitzpatrick, ed., 'Petitions and denunciations in Russia from Muscovy to the Stalin era', *Russian History*, vol. 24, nos. 1–2 (Spring–Summer 1997); and A. K. Sokolov, ed., *Golos naroda: pis'ma i otkliki ryadovykh sovetskikh grazhdan o*

sobytiyakh 1918–1932 gg. (Moscow: Rosspen, 1997).

68. E. N. Roshchepkina, 'O rabote s pis'mami grazhdan v pervye gody sovetskoi vlasti (1917–1924 gg.)', *Sovetskie arkhivy*, no. 6, 1979, p. 23.

69. See particularly *Novyi mir*, no. 6, 1992, pp. 281–300.

70. Lev Karpinsky in *Vospominaniya o V. I. Lenine*, vol. IV (Moscow: Politizdat, 1969), p. 283.

71. *Neizvestnaya Rossiya: XX vek*, vol. III (Moscow: Istoricheskoe nasledie, 1993), pp. 200, 222.

72. Obkom first secretaries, in fact, 'were often quite responsive to appeals from ordinary people' at this time (Fitzpatrick, 'Supplicants and citizens', p. 104). For a more general account, see V. K. Romanovsky, 'Pis'ma rabochikh kak istochnik dlya izucheniya sotsial'nogo oblika rabochego klassa 20-kh godov', *Vspomogatel'nye istoricheskie distsipliny*, vol. 21 (1990), pp. 54–65.

73. See Ye. B. Pashukanis and P. V. Tumanov, eds., *Vsenarodnoe obsuzhdenie proekta Konstitutsii Soyuza SSR* (Moscow: Partizdat, 1936; a copy of this rare item is held in the Russian State Library), p. xi, which also provides a digest of the amendments organised by article. Archive sources indicate still higher figures: over 623,000 meetings with over 42 million participants, who among them generated 169,739 proposals (Lewis Siegelbaum and Andrei Sokolov, eds., *Stalinism as a Way of Life: A Narrative in Documents* (New Haven, CT, and London: Yale University Press, 2000), p. 162). There is a broader discussion in *ibid.*, pp. 158–206; Ellen Wimberg, 'Socialism, democratism and criticism: the Soviet press and the national discussion of the 1936 draft constitution', *Soviet Studies*, vol. 44, no. 2 (1992), pp. 313–32; and V. A. Syrkin, 'Massovyi istochnik po istorii sovetskoi derevni', *Otechestvennye arkhivy*, no. 5, 1996, pp. 54–7. The edition of the Constitution edited by Anna Louise Strong (*The New Soviet Constitution* (New York: Henry Holt, 1937)) shows variations in translation and changes in the final text; it is conveniently reprinted in the second and third editions of Sidney Webb and Beatrice Webb, *Soviet Communism: A New Civilisation* (London: Longmans, 1937 and 1944).

74. Robert C. Tucker, *Stalin in Power: The Revolution from Above, 1928–1941* (New York and London: Norton, 1990), pp. 356–8.

75. For the text see 'Ob uluchshenii raboty po rassmotreniyu pisem i organizatsii priema trudyashchikhsya', *Partiinaya zhizn'*, no. 18, 1967, pp. 8–10, at p. 8.

76. For the text see 'O poryadke rassmotreniya predlozhenii, zayavlenii i zhalob grazhdan', *Vedomosti Verkhovnogo Soveta SSSR*, no. 17, art. 144, 12 April 1968; the decree was expanded in scope in 1980 (*ibid.*, no. 11, art. 192, 4 March 1980).

77. See respectively Articles 49 and 58. Another resolution on the party's own 'work with letters' was adopted after the 26th Party Congress in 1981: *Partiinaya zhizn'*, no. 8, 1981, pp. 9–11.

78. L. I. Brezhnev, *Leninskim kursom: rechi i stat'i*, vol. VI (Moscow: Politizdat, 1978), p. 518.

79. G. I. Zlokazov, 'Konstitutsiya SSSR 1977 g.: "nesvoevremennye" mysli sovremennikov', *Voprosy istorii KPSS*, no. 10, 1990, pp. 72–85, at pp. 73–7; a rather different picture had been given by the specialist literature that appeared at the time (see V. P. Smirnov, *Referendum v pechati* (Moscow: Mysl', 1978)). The number of proposals that had been received in the course of the discussion was rather arbitrarily determined: Supreme Soviet staff thought it was about 300,000, Central Committee staff thought it had been 600,000 and Brezhnev simply decided 'let's say 400,000' (Yuri Korolev, *Kremlevskii sovetnik* (Moscow: Olimp, 1995), p. 197).

80. Gorbachev, *Izbrannye rechi i stat'i*, vol. II, p. 164.

81. *Pravda*, 24 February 1989, p. 2.

82. *Ibid.*, 13 October 1987, p. 1.

83. *Izvestiya*, 7 August 1991, p. 1.

84. Lloyd S. Fischel, ed., *Dear Mr Gorbachev* (Edinburgh: Canongate, 1990), p. 187; V. Korotich and S. Koen, intro., *Amerikantsy pishut Gorbachevu* (Moscow: Progress, 1988), pp. 247, 102, 300.

85. Gorbachev, *Izbrannye rechi i stat'i*, vol. V, p. 497.

86. Fischel, ed., *Dear Mr Gorbachev*, pp. xv–xvi, 6.

87. Diego Cordovez and Selig S. Harrison, *Out of Afghanistan: The Inside Story of the Soviet Withdrawal* (Oxford and New York: Oxford University Press, 1995), p. 247.

88. *Narodnyi deputat*, no. 1, 1992, pp. 118–23.

89. *Pravda*, 19 September 1990, p. 2.

90. *Izvestiya*, 7 August 1991, p. 1. Staff found he 'lost interest' as his post became increasingly hostile, but the head of his staff still placed 'a couple of dozen' on his desk every day: V. I. Boldin, *Krushenie p'edestala: shtrikhi k portretu M. S. Gorbacheva* (Moscow: Respublika, 1995), p. 254.

91. S. M. Gurevich, *Rabota s pis'mami v redaktsii* (Moscow: Vysshaya shkola, 1991), p. 7.

92. *Spravochnik partiinogo rabotnika*, issue 21, pp. 503–4; and for 1988, *Izvestiya Tsentral'nogo komiteta* [hereafter *TsK*] *KPSS*, no. 4, 1990, p. 157.

93. See *Partiinaya zhizn'*, no. 17, 1979, pp. 22–30.

94. *Ibid.*, pp. 26–7.

95. See, for instance, *Izvestiya TsK KPSS*, no. 4, 1990, pp. 157–62, and no. 9, 1990, pp. 35–54 (which quotes numerous extracts from the letters themselves); both surveys noted the 'politicisation' of the party's postbag (pp. 157 and 35 respectively).

96. *Ibid.*, no. 9, 1990, pp. 133, 134.

97. *Ibid.*, no. 7, 1990, p. 21.

98. *Ibid.*

99. *Ibid.*

100. *Ibid.*

101. *Ibid.*, p. 22.

102. *Ibid.*, no. 9, 1990, p. 39.

103. *Ibid.*

104. *Ibid.*, p. 40.

105. *Ibid.*, p. 41.

106. *Pravda*, 25 May 1989, p. 1.

107. Gurevich, *Rabota s pis'mami*, pp. 35, 24, 25, 23. *Pravda*'s postbag was 473,201 in 1989: *Pravda*, 6 January 1990, p. 3.

108. Gurevich, *Rabota s pis'mami*, p. 23.

109. *Ibid.*, p. 45.

110. *Ibid.*, p. 46; for the 'main correspondent' see Yu. Rytov, ed., *Komandirovka po pros'be chitatelei* (Moscow: Izvestiya, 1985), p. 6. A selection of letters to the paper since 1917 appeared in L. Tolkunov, ed., *Ot glavnogo korrespondenta* (Moscow: Izvestiya, 1970).

111. *Knizhnoe obozrenie*, no. 32, 1988, p. 15 (there were further letters of support in the following issue); on alcoholism, see *Pravda*, 23 March 1985, p. 3 (the campaign itself is considered in Stephen White, *Russia Goes Dry: Alcohol, State and Society* (Cambridge and New York: Cambridge University Press, 1996)).

112. *Argumenty i fakty*, no. 24, 1996, p. 12. A survey of letters to a range of newspapers and journals in the late 1980s found that there had in fact been a general belief that the society needed 'not radical reform, but only a few changes' (*Svobodnaya mysl'*, no. 7, 1993, p. 80). Equally, the archives suggested, there had been 'few' letters in support of Solzhenitsyn after the 1974 decision to expel him: *Svobodnaya mysl'*, no. 6, 1992, pp. 81–5, at p. 81.

113. Gurevich, *Rabota s pis'mami*, p. 54; *Pravda*, for instance, received over 3,000 visitors in 1990: *ibid.*, 4 January 1991, p. 4.

114. *Izvestiya*, 11 June 1992, p. 3.

115. The entire department was reorganised in 2004, when it became a 'Board of the Presidency of the Russian Federation for Work with Citizens' Appeals'; its main responsibilities were to consider oral and written communications, to provide an overall analysis and to ensure that appropriate action was taken. See *Sobranie zakonodatel'stva Rossiiskoi Federatsii* [hereafter *SZ*], no. 35, item 3609, 24 August 2004. It was reorganised again in 2010, when it became a 'Board of the Presidency of the Russian Federation for Work with the Appeals of Citizens and Organisations' (*Rossiiskaya gazeta*, 24 February 2010, p. 17).

116. *Rossiiskie vesti*, 16 March 1994, p. 2.

117. See, for instance, *Argumenty i fakty*, no. 42, 1992, pp. 1–2; *Trud*, 6 October 1992, pp. 1–2.

118. There were 300 letters in 1996–7 that secured a response of this kind: *Argumenty i fakty*, no. 3, 1998, p. 5.

119. *Ibid.*

120. *St Petersburg Times*, 17 May 2002, internet edition. Born in 1939, Mironov had a background in Komsomol work and then (from 1978 to 1991) in the apparatus of the USSR Council of Ministers, after which he moved to the letters department in the Presidential Administration and then (in 1995) became head of the reconstituted Board (see K. A. Shchegolev, ed., *Kto est' kto v Rossii. Ispolnitel'naya vlast'. Kto pravit sovremennoi Rossiei*, 2nd edn (Moscow: AST-Astrel', 2009), p. 330). He was replaced in 2009 by Mikhail Mikhailovsky, a former deputy governor of St Petersburg who had been a member of the Federation Council and then of the Presidential Administration (*Kommersant*, 9 June 2009, p. 3); he was reappointed to the reorganised Board the following year (*Rossiiskaya gazeta*, 2 March 2010, p. 2).

121. *Argumenty i fakty*, no. 17, 2001, p. 4.

122. *Izvestiya*, 16 March 2006, p. 2.

123. 'O chem pishut Prezidentu Putinu?', 13 October 2002, at www.utro.ru/articles/20021013150906105408.shtml, last accessed 20 September 2010.

124. *Parlamentskaya gazeta*, 20 November 2006, p. 1.

125. *Guardian*, part 2, 10 March 2004, pp. 6–7.

126. *Moskovskii komsomolets*, 18 May 2007, pp. 1, 3.

127. *Rossiiskaya gazeta*, 8 November 2007, p. 4.

128. 'O chem pishut Prezidentu Putinu'.

129. 'Otchet ob obrashcheniyakh grazhdan, postupivshikh v Pravitel'stvo Rossiiskoi Federatsii v 2008 godu', 20 March 2009, at www.government.ru, last accessed 14 April 2009.

130. *Nezavisimaya gazeta*, 7 March 2001, p. 3.

131. *Rossiiskaya gazeta*, 25 December 2001, p. 1. The 'direct line' the following year was published in its entirety: *Vladimir Putin: razgovor s Rossiei: stenogramma 'Pryamoi linii s Prezidentom Rossiiskoi Federatsii V. V. Putinym' ('Pervyi kanal', telekanal 'Rossiya', radio 'Mayak', 'Radio Rossii'), 19 dekabrya 2002 goda* (Moscow: Olma-Politizdat, 2003). For an analysis of the linguistic content of Putin's presidential 'direct lines', see Lara Ryazanova-Clarke, *Putin's Nation: Discursive Construction of National Identity in Direct Line with the President* (Helsinki: Slavica Helsingiensia, 2008). Commenting on the 2005 'direct line', *Trud* observed that Putin had been the 'first world leader' to submit himself so directly to the questions of the entire society (28 September 2005, p. 1).

132. *Rossiiskaya gazeta: nedelya*, 19 October 2007, p. 2 (which reported 69 responses).

133. *Ibid.*, pp. 2–13, at pp. 5, 6, 3–4, 2 (football).

134. For the first such exercise, see *Rossiiskaya gazeta*, 5 December 2008, pp. 1, 3; for the second see *Izvestiya*, 4 December 2009, pp. 1–2.

135. Mikhail Babich, 'Obshchestvennye priemnye – barometr obshchestvennogo mneniya', 17 December 2008, at www.edinoros.ru, last accessed 13 August 2009.

136. Vitalii Ivanov, *'Yedinaya Rossiya': kratkaya istoriya partii* (Moscow: Yevropa, 2009), p. 166.

137. *Kommersant*, 17 April 2009, p. 3. The reception offices had their origin in the corresponding facilities that had been established by Dmitri Medvedev in February 2008, in his capacity as a candidate for the presidency; however, they did not appear to have passed on their caseload, and it was often unclear what practical results had been achieved (*Nezavisimaya gazeta*, 1 September 2008, p. 1). *Izvestiya* found a 'businesslike and welcoming atmosphere' when it visited the United Russia reception office at 39 Kutuzov Avenue in Moscow, where seven or eight staff received visitors between 10 a.m.

and 6 p.m.; as elsewhere, it was housing that generated the largest volume of enquiries (16 October 2008, Moscow supplement, pp. 1–2).

138. *Izvestiya*, 10 April 2009, p. 1.

139. *Ibid.*, 16 July 2009, p. 2.

140. *Ibid.*, 10 April 2009, p. 2.

141. *Kommersant*, 13 January 2009, p. 3.

142. *Izvestiya*, 3 February 2009, p. 2.

143. *Ibid.*, 22 April 2009, pp. 1–2 (the presidential blog may be consulted at community. livejournal.com/blog_medvedev). Initial experience was somewhat mixed; in particular, moderators had to 'work non-stop' to eliminate obscenities and other inappropriate postings (*Moscow Times*, 23 April 2009, p. 3).

144. *Izvestiya*, 1 June 2009, p. 2.

145. *Komsomol'skaya pravda*, 18 May 2009, p. 4.

146. *Izvestiya*, however, made clear that it would be giving less prominence to its postbag in the future: 2 January 1992, p. 3.

147. *Argumenty i fakty*, no. 37, 1996, p. 2.

148. *Ibid.*, nos. 38–39, 1992, p. 1.

149. *Ibid.*, no. 47, 1993, p. 12.

150. *Ibid.*, no. 24, 1996, p. 16.

151. *Ibid.*, no. 9, 1995, p. 16.

152. *Ibid.*, no. 34, 1993, p. 8.

153. *Ibid.*, no. 2, 1994, p. 16.

154. *Ibid.*, no. 9, 1993, p. 16.

155. *Ibid.*, no. 43, 1993, p. 8.

156. *Ibid.*, no. 10, 1993, p. 12.

157. *Ibid.*, no. 8, 1993, p. 12.

158. *Ibid.*, no. 23, 1993, p. 12.

159. *Ibid.*, nos. 38–39, 1992, p. 13; no. 41, 1992, p. 1; nos. 38–39, p. 2; and no. 41, 1992, p. 5.

160. *Ibid.*, no. 43, 1993, p. 8.

161. *Ibid.*, no. 10, 1992, p. 8.

162. *Ibid.*, no. 5, 1992, p. 7.

163. *Ibid.*, nos. 38–39, 1992, p. 9.

164. *Ibid.*, no. 34, 1993, p. 12.

165. *Ibid.*, no. 14, 1993, p. 8.

166. *The Times*, 22 September 1992, p. 10.

167. *Argumenty i fakty*, no. 39, 1993, p. 8.

168. *Ibid.*, nos. 38–39, 1992, p. 9.

169. *Ibid.*, no. 15, 1998, p. 24.

170. *Ibid.*, no. 9, 1993, p. 16.

171. *Ibid.*, no. 43, 1993, p. 8.

172. *Ibid.*, no. 48, 1995, p. 12; similarly no. 4, 1996, p. 1.

173. *Ibid.*, no. 15, 1996, p. 13, and no. 43, 1993, p. 8.

174. *Ibid.*, no. 6, 1996, p. 1.

175. *Ibid.*, no. 30, 1994, p. 13.

176. *Ibid.*, no. 38, 1994, p. 13.

177. *Ibid.*, no. 4, 1993, p. 6.

178. *Ibid.*, no. 37, 1993, p. 5.

179. *Ibid.*, no. 6, 1996, p. 16.

180. *Ibid.*, no. 5, 1995, p. 16.

181. *Ibid.*, no. 13, 1995, p. 16.

182. *Ibid.*, nos. 38–39, 1992, p. 15.

183. *Ibid.*, no. 41, 1994, p. 16, and no. 34, 1993, p. 13.

184. *Ibid.*, no. 43, 1993, p. 4, and no. 43, 1993, p. 8.

185. *Ibid.*, no. 6, 1993, p. 12, no. 41, 1992, p. 5, and nos. 38–39, 1992, p. 3.

186. *Ibid.*, no. 17, 1993, p. 8.

187. *Ibid.*, no. 17, 1993, p. 12.

188. *Ibid.*, no. 14, 1993, p. 12.

189. *Ibid.*, nos. 38–39, 1992, p. 2.

190. *Ibid.*, no. 9, 1994, p. 16.

191. *Ibid.*, no. 3, 1993, p. 12.

192. *Ibid.*, nos. 38–39, 1992, p. 11.

193. *Ibid.*, no. 17, 1993, p. 5; similarly nos. 38–39, 1992, p. 3.

194. *Ibid.*, no. 17, 1993, p. 12.

195. *Ibid.*, no. 16, 2000, p. 11.

196. *Ibid.*, no. 22, 2000, p. 16.

197. *Ibid.*, no. 31, 2007, p. 10.

198. *Ibid.*, no. 11, 2002, p. 24.

199. *Ibid.*, no. 13, 2002, p. 24.

200. See respectively *ibid.*, no. 18, 2009, p. 48; no. 15, 2009, p. 56; and no. 16, 2009, p. 2.

201. *Ibid.*, no. 43, 2002, p. 18.

202. *Ibid.*, p. 24.

203. *Ibid.*, p. 26.

204. *Ibid.*, no. 45, 2003, p. 20.

205. *Ibid.*, no. 9, 2003, p. 21.

206. *Ibid.*, no. 43, 2002, p. 12.

207. See respectively *ibid.*, no. 22, 2003, p. 22, and no. 34, 2009, p. 48.

208. *Ibid.*, no. 45, 2003, p. 28.

209. *Ibid.*, no. 8, 2003, p. 26.

210. *Ibid.*, no. 16, 2003, p. 1.

211. *Ibid.*, no. 10, 2003, p. 24.

212. *Ibid.*, no. 40, 2007, p. 7.

213. *Ibid.*, no. 48, 2008, p. 64.

214. *Ibid.*, no. 31, 2007, p. 10 (as we note below, the writer died shortly afterwards, in 2008).

215. *Ibid.*, no. 7, 2009, p. 7.

216. *Ibid.*

217. *Ibid.*, no. 11, 2009, p. 14.

218. *Ibid.*, no. 40, 2007, p. 7 (local authorities, it appeared, already had the necessary powers).

219. *Ibid.*

220. *Ibid.*

221. *Ibid.*

222. *Ibid.*, no. 10, 2009, p. 10.

223. *Parlamentskaya gazeta*, 20 November 2006, p. 1.

224. 'O poryadke rassmotreniya obrashchenii grazhdan Rossiiskoi Federatsii', *SZ*, no. 19, item 2060, 2 May 2006.

225. *Argumenty i fakty*, no. 32, 2009, pp. 8–9.

226. Calculated from *Itogi Vsesoyuznoi perepisi naseleniya 1989 goda* (Minneapolis: EastView, 1992), vol. II, part 1, pp. 13–14.

227. See, for instance, V. T. Syzrantsev, ed., *Kratkii slovar'-spravochnik agitatora i politinformatora* (Moscow: Politizdat, 1977), p. 225.

228. V. D. Kobetsky, 'Issledovanie dinamiki religioznosti naseleniya v SSSR', in V. D. Sherdakov, ed., *Ateizm. Religiya. Sovremennost'* (Leningrad: Nauka, 1973), pp. 126–7, 129. According to the census that was conducted in 1937 but whose results were suppressed at the time, 42.9 per cent of the population aged over 16 were atheist, 42.3 per cent were Orthodox and 14.8 per cent subscribed to other faiths (calculated from Yu. A. Polyakov, ed., *Vsesoyuznaya perepis' naseleniya 1937 g.: kratkie itogi* (Moscow: Institut istorii AN SSSR, 1991), pp. 106–7).

229. *Pravda*, 30 March 1979, pp. 2–3.

230. Sherdakov, ed., *Ateizm*, p. 129.

231. *Rossiiskii statisticheskii yezhegodnik: statisticheskii sbornik* [hereafter *RSYe*] (Moscow: Goskomstat Rossii, 1997), pp. 47, 50–1; Nathaniel Davis, *A Long Walk to Church: A Contemporary History of Russian Orthodoxy* (Boulder, CO: Westview, 1995), p. xi.

232. This was the authoritative estimate of Konstantin Kharchev, Chairman of the Council on Religious Affairs attached to the USSR Council of Ministers: 'Sovest' svobodna', *Ogonek*, no. 21 (21–28 May 1988), pp. 26–8, at p. 26.

233. *Materialy mezhvuzovskoi nauchnoi konferentsii po probleme vozrastaniya aktivnosti obshchestvennogo soznaniya v period stroitel'stva kommunizma* (Kursk: Kurskii gosudarstvennyi pedagogicheskii institut, 1968), pp. 361–2.

234. S. I. Tereshchenko, ed., *Gor'kaya balka. Kompleksnoe sotsiologicheskoe issledovanie kolkhoza imeni V. I. Lenina* (Stavropol': Stavropol'skoe knizhnoe izdatel'stvo, 1972), pp. 114–16.

235. *Sovetskaya Rossiya*, 29 August 1992, p. 2.

236. See particularly Nickolas Lupinin, 'The Russian Orthodox Church', in Lucian Leustean, ed., *Eastern Christianity and the Cold War, 1945–1991* (London and New York: Routledge, 2010), pp. 19–39.

237. For a discussion of the entire Byzantine tradition, see Michael Angold, ed., *Cambridge History of Christianity*, vol. V: *Eastern Christianity* (Cambridge and New York: Cambridge University Press, 2006). On the Soviet and Russian experience in particular, see, for instance, John Anderson, *Religion, State and Politics in the Soviet Union and Successor States* (Cambridge and New York: Cambridge University Press, 1994); Davis, *A Long Walk*; and Jane Ellis, *The Russian Orthodox Church: Triumphalism and Defensiveness* (London: Macmillan and New York: St Martin's, 1996). More recent studies are listed in the Further reading section.

238. See, for instance, the two-page article entitled 'Increasing the effectiveness of atheistic propaganda' in *Pravda*, 13 September 1985, pp. 2–3.

239. *Pravda Vostoka*, 25 November 1986, p. 1.

240. *Kommunist*, no. 4, 1988, pp. 121–2.

241. Gorbachev, *Izbrannye rechi i stat'i*, vol. VI, pp. 201–3.

242. *Izvestiya*, 9 April 1988, p. 3.

243. For Gorbachev's baptism see *Izvestiya TsK KPSS*, no. 8, 1989, p. 66; for his mother's church attendance, see Michael Bordeaux, *Gorbachev, Glasnost and the Gospel* (London: Hodder and Stoughton, 1990), p. 24. A different account is provided by Davis, *A Long Walk*, who visited Privol'noe in 1991 and noted that the village church had been destroyed many years earlier (p. 253).

244. *Pravda*, 29 November 1991, p. 1 (Kremlin cathedrals), and *Izvestiya*, 7 February 1991, p. 3 (return of monasteries). Over 4,000 new Orthodox churches were opened between 1985 and 1990: *Otechestvennye arkhivy*, no. 1, 1995, p. 61.

245. *Pravda*, 16 March 1990, p. 6.

246. *Izvestiya*, 7 June 1994, p. 5 (chaplaincies). On charity work see Anne White, 'Charity, self-help and politics in Russia, 1985–91', *Europe-Asia Studies*, vol. 45, no. 5 (1993), pp. 787–810, and Melissa L. Caldwell, 'The politics of rightness: social justice among Russia's Christian communities', *Problems of Post-Communism*, vol. 56, no. 4 (July–August 2009), pp. 29–40.

247. *Pravda*, 30 December 1989, p. 3, and 4 February 1991, p. 6.

248. *Izvestiya*, 7 January 1991, p. 1.

249. Anderson, *Religion, State and Politics*, p. 171.

250. For the text see 'O sobstvennosti v SSSR', *Vedomosti S"ezda narodnykh deputatov SSSR i Verkhovnogo Soveta SSSR*, no. 11, 1990, item 164, 6 March 1990.

251. For the text see 'O svobode sovesti i religioznykh organizatsiyakh', *ibid.*, no. 41,

1990, item 813, 1 October 1990.
A corresponding Russian law was adopted on 25 October 1990: 'O svobode veroispovedanii', *Vedomosti S"ezda narodnykh deputatov RSFSR i Verkhovnogo Soveta RSFSR*, no. 21, 1990, item 240.

252. *Materialy XXVIII s"ezda Kommunisticheskoi partii Sovetskogo Soyuza* (Moscow: Politizdat, 1990), rule 2, pp. 108–9.

253. Tsentr po khraneniyu sovremennoi dokumentatsii, Moscow, *fond* 89, *perechen'* 20, document 66, April 1991.

254. *Vedomosti S"ezda narodnykh deputatov SSSR*, no. 37, 1991, item 1083.

255. *Vedomosti S"ezda narodnykh deputatov RSFSR*, no. 52, 1991, item 1865.

256. Article 28 of the 1993 Constitution.

257. *Izvestiya*, 10 July 1991, p. 1, and 11 June 1992, p. 3 (Yeltsin).

258. *New York Times*, 8 April 1991, p. A6.

259. *Nezavisimaya gazeta*, 31 December 1994, p. 13. The varied fortunes of the cathedral over time are examined in Konstantin Akinsha and Grigorij Kozlov, *The Holy Place: Archaeology, Ideology and History in Russia* (New Haven, CT, and London: Yale University Press, 2007).

260. *Izvestiya*, 4 April 1995, p. 5.

261. For a clear presentation of Orthodox teaching, see, for instance, Timothy Ware, *The Orthodox Church*, new edn (Harmondsworth and New York: Penguin, 1993).

262. According to documents that are now available, three Metropolitans played a key role in the Kremlin's ideological battle with the West, reporting directly to KGB handlers. Metropolitan Yuvenalii of Krutitsy, former head of the Orthodox Church's external relations department, worked under the cover name Adamant, using his influential position within the World Council of Churches to attack as 'falsehoods and lies' reports of the arrests of Orthodox priests and the destruction of churches in the Soviet Union. Filaret of Kiev was another church leader with a KGB cover name, who was active (for instance) during the Gorbachev–Reagan summit at Iceland in 1987 where, as his KGB handler reported, he 'fulfilled the task of providing religious circles in the West with objective information and impressed upon them the need for positive action in support of the peaceful initiatives of the Soviet Union' (*Scotland on Sunday*, 5 July 1998, p. 11). According to M. V. Shkarovsky, the CPSU had been conducting a 'cadres

policy' in the Orthodox Church since the 1950s: *Russkaya pravoslavnaya tserkov' i Sovetskoe gosudarstvo v 1943–1964 godakh* (St Petersburg: Dean + Adia-M, 1995), p. 11.

263. For perceptions of the 'privileged' position of the Orthodox Church, see, for instance, *Sotsiologicheskie issledovaniya*, no. 5, 1994, p. 10 (17 per cent of Orthodox believers themselves agreed with this view).

264. For his election see *Izvestiya*, 28 January 2009, p. 1; for the rating see, for instance, *Nezavisimaya gazeta*, 1 February 2010, p. 6 (Kirill at this time stood at No. 6).

265. For the 'explosion' see Levada, ed., *Sovetskii prostoi chelovek*, p. 217; a figure of 10 per cent of believers in 1988 is reported in L. M. Mitrokhin, ed., *Religiya i politika v postkommunisticheskoi Rossii* (Moscow: Institut filosofii RAN, 1994), p. 35. The stabilisation of levels of religious belief is suggested in, for instance, *Svobodnaya mysl'*, no. 11, 1998, p. 95, and levels of trust were falling after 1993 (p. 96), although there is evidence of a continuing increase in levels of Orthodox affiliation (Stephen White and Ian McAllister, 'The politics of religion in postcommunist Russia', *Religion, State and Society*, vol. 25, no. 3 (September 1997), pp. 235–52, at p. 242, based on survey data collected between 1991 and 1996).

266. On the numbers of 'believers', see V. I. Garadzha, *Sotsiologiya religii* (Moscow: Aspekt Press, 1996), p. 226. Somewhat lower figures are reported in other sources; the national public opinion research centre, for instance, found a level of 47.5 per cent (*Ekonomicheskie i sotsial'nye peremeny: monitoring obshchestvennogo mneniya*, no. 1, 1998, p. 81). For baptisms see *ibid.* (37 per cent had been baptised and 5.7 per cent had baptised themselves).

267. Boris Dubin in *ibid.*, no. 6, 1996, pp. 15–16.

268. See the VTsIOM data reported in *Svobodnaya mysl'*, no. 11, 1998, p. 99.

269. *Ibid.*, p. 103.

270. 2010 Russia survey.

271. In the United Kingdom, for instance, the corresponding figure was 19 per cent (*Social Trends*, no. 36 (London: Stationery Office, 2006), p. 200); in the United States, Gallup found that 42 per cent claimed to attend church once a week or almost as frequently (Frank Newport, 'No evidence bad times are boosting church attendance', 17 December 2008, at www.gallup.com, last accessed 17 April 2010). There were lower levels of at least monthly attendance in every one of the

nineteen countries that were represented in the European Social Survey, from Denmark at 9 per cent to Poland at 75 per cent, although Orthodox (and Catholic) countries were generally more likely to have high levels of attendance than others (*Social Trends*, no. 36, p. 200).

272. *Svobodnaya mysl'*, no. 11, 1998, p. 99.

273. Mitrokhin, ed., *Religiya i politika*, p. 49 (22 per cent of self-identified believers reported praying on a regular basis; 14 per cent observed Lent).

274. *Ibid.*, p. 49 (just 25 per cent believed in heaven and hell); only 45 per cent of believers, in another survey, believed in life after death (*Svobodnaya mysl'*, no. 1, 1997, p. 80).

275. Mitrokhin, ed., *Religiya i politika*, p. 50. For the evil eye and abominable snowman, see Lyudmila Vorontsova and Sergei Filatov, 'The changing pattern of religious belief: *perestroika* and beyond', *Religion, State and Society*, vol. 22, no. 1 (March 1994), pp. 89–96, at pp. 89–90.

276. *Svobodnaya mysl'*, no. 1, 1997, p. 81.

277. Mikhail Mchedlov, 'Religioznaya identichnost' i sotsial'nye predpochteniya', *Svobodnaya mysl'*, no. 4, 2006, pp. 101–15, at pp. 104–5.

278. 'Vo chto veryat rossiyane?', 18 July 2008, at www.levada.ru, last accessed 18 August 2009.

279. D. E. Furman and Kimmo Kaariainen, 'Religioznaya stabilizatsiya: otnoshenie k religii v sovremennoi Rossii', *Svobodnaya mysl'*, no. 7, 2003, pp. 19–32, at p. 24.

280. *Ibid.*, p. 25; L. M. Vorontsova, S. B. Filatov and D. E. Furman, 'Religiya v sovremennom massovom soznanii', *Sotsiologicheskie issledovaniya*, no. 11, 1995, pp. 81–91, at p. 87.

281. Furman and Kaariainen, 'Religioznaya stabil'nost'', p. 25; similarly D. E. Furman and Kimmo Kaariainen, *Religioznost' v Rossii v 90-e gody XX – nachale XXI veka* (Moscow: OGNI TD, 2006), pp. 46–51.

282. M. M. Mchedlova, 'Rol' religii v sovremennom obshchestve', *Sotsiologicheskie issledovaniya*, no, 12, 2009, pp. 77–84, at p. 78.

283. 2010 Russia survey.

284. 'O svobode sovesti i o religioznykh ob"edineniyakh', *SZ*, no. 39, item 4465, 26 September 1997.

285. See www.state.gov/g/drl/rls/irf/2009/127333.htm, last accessed 1 March 2010, which lists numerous examples. Issues of religious freedom in Russia and other countries are also monitored by the Oslo-based organisation Forum 18: see www.forum18.org. The National Security Concept adopted in early 2000 referred to the 'negative influence of foreign religious organisations and missionaries' (*SZ*, no. 2, item 170, 10 January 2000, pp. 691–704, at p. 700), and the Information Security Doctrine adopted later in the year referred directly to 'totalitarian religious sects' (*Rossiiskaya gazeta*, 28 September 2000, pp. 4–6, at p. 5).

286. See, for instance, Mark Rhodes, 'Religious believers in Russia', *RFE/RL Research Report*, vol. 1, no. 14, 3 April 1992, pp. 60–4.

287. *Svobodnaya mysl'*, no. 8, 1996, p. 118.

288. Miller, White and Heywood, *Values and Political Change*, pp. 260–3.

289. L. M. Vorontsova and S. B. Filatov, 'Religioznost' – demokratichnost' – avtoritarnost'', *Polis*, no. 3, 1993, pp. 141–8, at pp. 144–5.

290. *Ekonomicheskie i sotsial'nye peremeny*, no. 6, 1996, p. 17; believers were similarly persuaded that non-Russians 'had too much influence'.

291. See, for instance, Anthony Heath, Bridget Taylor and Gabor Toka, 'Religion, morality and politics', in Roger Jowell, Lindsay Brook and Lizanne Dowds, eds., *International Social Attitudes: The 10th BSA Report* (Aldershot: Dartmouth, 1993), pp. 57–8.

292. *Independent*, 7 January 1998, p. 12. Subsequent reports, based upon KGB documents left behind in Estonian archives, identified the Patriarch as a 'fully fledged KGB spy' who had used his connections to secure his rapid advancement (*Guardian*, 12 February 1999, p. 18). A similar view is taken in John Garrard and Carol Garrard, *Russian Orthodoxy Resurgent: Faith and Power in the New Russia* (Princeton, NJ and Oxford: Princeton University Press, 2008), who identify Aleksii as 'one of the KGB's best and brightest operatives' (p. 36).

293. See, for instance, the reported homosexual murder in *Moskovskii komsomolets*, 27 September 1997, p. 1.

294. *Svobodnaya mysl'*, no. 5, 1994, p. 54.

7   Russia and the wider world

1. Russians, as Isaiah Berlin put it, combined a sense of the West as 'enviably self-restrained, clever, efficient, and successful: but also as

being cramped, cold, mean, calculating, and fenced in, without capacity for large views or generous emotion' (*Russian Thinkers* (London: Hogarth Press and New York: Viking, 1978), p. 181). For the wider context see, for instance, Paul Dukes, *October and the World* (London: Macmillan and New York: St Martin's, 1979).

2. See, for instance, Ivo J. Lederer, ed., *Russian Foreign Policy: Essays in Perspective* (New Haven, CT, and London: Yale University Press, 1962); Robert H. Donaldson and Joseph L. Nogee open their substantive discussion of this subject, *The Foreign Policy of Russia: Changing Systems, Enduring Interests*, with a chapter on 'the tsarist roots of Russia's foreign policy' (4th edn (Armonk, NY, and London: M. E. Sharpe, 2009), ch. 2).

3. John L. H. Keep, *Soldiers of the Tsar: Army and Society in Russia, 1462–1874* (Oxford: Clarendon Press and New York: Oxford University Press, 1985), p. 145.

4. Walter M. Pinter, 'The burden of defense in Imperial Russia, 1725–1914', *Russian Review*, vol. 43, no. 3 (October 1984), pp. 231–59.

5. Stephen White and Stephen Revell, 'Revolution and integration in Soviet international diplomacy 1917–1991', *Review of International Studies*, vol. 25, no. 4 (October 1999), pp. 641–54.

6. See Stephen White, *The Origins of Detente: The Genoa Conference and Soviet–Western relations, 1921–1922* (Cambridge and New York: Cambridge University Press, 1985).

7. *Pervyi kongress Kominterna* (Moscow: Partiinoe izdatel'stvo, 1933), p. 199.

8. *Vneshnyaya torgovlya SSSR v 1987 g.: statisticheskii sbornik* (Moscow: Finansy i statistika, 1988), p. 4.

9. Half a million tourists visited the USSR in 1950, for instance, but there were ten times as many, over 5 million, in the late 1980s (*Pravda*, 24 September 1988, p. 3). In 1956 there were 4,648 translations of books in English into one of the Soviet languages (normally Russian); twenty years later there were more than eighteen times as many, 84,304 (United Nations *Statistical Yearbook 1959* (New York: United Nations, 1959), p. 575, and *Statistical Yearbook 1978* (New York: United Nations, 1979), p. 944).

10. An introductory guide to some of the relevant literature is provided in the Further reading section.

11. M. S. Gorbachev, *Izbrannye rechi i stat'i*, 7 vols. (Moscow: Izdatel'stvo politicheskoi literatury, 1987–90), vol. II, pp. 99 and 99–103, *passim*.

12. *Ibid.*, pp. 109–16.

13. *Ibid.*, p. 131.

14. *Ibid.*, pp. 167–72.

15. *Ibid.*, pp. 460, 466–7.

16. *Ibid.*, vol. III, p. 9.

17. *Ibid.*, pp. 183–96.

18. For the text see *Spravochnik partiinogo rabotnika*, issue 27 (Moscow: Politizdat, 1987), pp. 342–4.

19. *Pravda*, 8 April 1985, p. 1.

20. *Ibid.*, 30 July 1985, p. 1.

21. *Ibid.*, 16 January 1986, pp. 1–2.

22. *Materialy XXVII S"ezda Kommunisticheskoi partii Sovetskogo Soyuza* (Moscow: Izdatel'stvo politicheskoi literatury, 1986), p. 179; Gorbachev spoke of 'reasonable sufficiency' at the 27th Party Congress (*Izbrannye rechi i stat'i*, vol. III, p. 248), and the Warsaw Treaty Organisation made its commitment shortly afterwards: *Pravda*, 12 June 1986, pp. 1–2.

23. Cuts in military spending and personnel were approved by the Supreme Soviet Presidium in March 1989 (*Pravda*, 22 March 1989, p. 1); the first useful figures for Soviet and WTO troop and weapons numbers were reported in early 1989 (*ibid.*, 30 January 1989, p. 5, and 19 April 1989, p. 4), and the first meaningful figures for Soviet defence expenditure in May 1989 (*ibid.*, 30 May 1989, p. 2).

24. Gorbachev, *Izbrannye rechi i stat'i*, vol. VII, pp. 184–202.

25. For the text see *Sbornik mezhdunarodnykh dogovorov SSSR*, vol. 43 (Moscow: Mezhdunarodnye otnosheniya, 1990), no. 4413, pp. 58–137.

26. For the text see Ministerstvo inostrannykh del Rossiiskoi Federatsii, *Vneshnyaya politika Rossii: sbornik dokumentov, 1990–1992* (Moscow: Mezhdunarodnye otnosheniya, 1996), no. 23, pp. 65–105.

27. The dissolution of the Council for Mutual Economic Assistance (Comecon) was reported in *Izvestiya*, 28 June 1991, p. 6, and of the Warsaw Treaty Organisation in *ibid.*, 2 July 1991, p. 5.

28. *Materialy Plenuma Tsentral'nogo Komiteta KPSS, 9 dekabrya 1989 goda* (Moscow: Izdatel'stvo politicheskoi literatury, 1989), pp. 18–19.

29. *XXVIII S"ezd Kommunisticheskoi partii Sovetskogo Soyuza 2–13 iyulya 1990 goda: stenograficheskii otchet*, 2 vols. (Moscow: Izdatel'stvo politicheskoi literatury, 1991), vol. II, p. 199. A substantial literature, much of it drawing upon archives or interviews, includes (on Soviet–American relations

during this period) Michael Beschloss and Strobe Talbott, *At the Highest Levels: The Inside Story of the End of the Cold War* (London: Little, Brown, 1993); Raymond L. Garthoff, *Détente and Confrontation: American–Soviet Relations from Nixon to Reagan*, rev. edn (Washington, DC: Brookings, 1994); Garthoff, *The Great Transformation: American–Soviet Relations and the End of the Cold War* (Washington, DC: Brookings, 1994); and Don Oberdorfer, *From the Cold War to a New Era: The United States and the Soviet Union, 1983–1991* (Baltimore, MD: Johns Hopkins University Press, 1998). On Soviet relations with Eastern Europe, see particularly Jacques Levesque, *The Enigma of 1989: The USSR and the Liberation of Eastern Europe* (Berkeley: University of California Press, 1997); on relations with Germany and the rest of Europe, Philip Zelikow and Condoleezza Rice, *Germany Unified and Europe Transformed: A Study in Statecraft* (Cambridge, MA: Harvard University Press, 1995), and Angela Stent, *Russia and Germany Reborn: Unification, the Soviet Collapse, and the New Europe* (Princeton, NJ: Princeton University Press, 1999). An insider's view of Gorbachev's foreign policy as a whole is available in Andrei Grachev, *Gorbachev's Gamble: Soviet Foreign Policy and the End of the Cold War* (Cambridge and Maldon, MA: Polity, 2008).

30. *Pravda*, 16 February 1989, p. 1; the background to the decision is considered in Diego Cordovez and Selig S. Harrison, *Out of Afghanistan: The Inside Story of the Soviet Withdrawal* (New York: Oxford University Press, 1995).

31. *Izvestiya*, 12 September 1991, p. 1. The wider background is considered in Mervyn J. Bain, *Soviet–Cuban Relations, 1985 to 1991: Changing Perceptions in Moscow and Havana* (Lanham, MD: Lexington Books, 2006).

32. Gorbachev, *Izbrannye rechi i stat'i*, vol. III, pp. 256–7.

33. *Materialy XXVII s"ezda*, p. 174.

34. See, for instance, *Pravda*, 14 November 1986, pp. 2–3, and 10 July 1987, p. 4.

35. Ambassadorial relations with the Vatican were established in 1990 (*Pravda*, 16 March 1990, p. 6) and were restored with Israel in 1991 (*Izvestiya*, 19 October 1991, p. 1); consular relations with South Africa were restored the following month (*ibid.*, 11 November 1991, p. 1).

36. The signatories were the thirty-four members of the Conference on Security and

Cooperation in Europe (*Pravda*, 22 November 1990, pp. 1, 3); there was also a treaty on conventional forces in Europe: *ibid.*, 24 November 1990, pp. 3–4.

37. Why, asked Gorbachev, had the United States, which had itself invaded Grenada and Panama, been allowed to expatiate about the rights of man? (*Pravda*, 28 February 1991, p. 2). His statement on the outbreak of the war, however, emphasised that everything must be done to bring it to an end in cooperation with other governments and the United Nations (*ibid.*, 18 January 1991, p. 1), and foreign ministry statements took the same line (see, for instance, *ibid.*, 13 December 1990, p. 5).

38. *Izvestiya*, 14 September 1989, p. 4.

39. *Ibid.*, 21 June 1991, p. 4.

40. *Diplomaticheskii vestnik*, no. 1, 1992, p. 36. In addition, the United Kingdom had recognised the new Russian government on 24 December, and Germany on 25 December (*ibid.*, p. 33); by 10 January 116 states had done so: *ibid.*, nos. 2–3, 1992, p. 33.

41. *Ibid.*, no. 1, 1992, pp. 24–5, 15–16 December 1991.

42. *Ibid.*, p. 28, 23 December 1991; Russia took over the USSR's seat in the United Nations, also prematurely, on 24 December: *ibid.*, p. 13.

43. *Vneshnyaya politika Rossii 1990–92*, no. 8, pp. 29–33.

44. *Ibid.*, no. 28, p. 111.

45. See respectively *Diplomaticheskii vestnik*, no. 1, 1992, pp. 14–18; *Vestnik ministerstva vneshnykh snoshenii*, no. 24, 1991, p. 13.

46. *Izvestiya*, 2 January 1992, p. 3; also in *Diplomaticheskii vestnik*, nos. 2–3, 1992, pp. 3–5.

47. *Pravda*, 29 January 1992, p. 5.

48. *Vneshnyaya politika Rossii 1990–92*, no. 80, pp. 185–90.

49. *Ibid.*, no. 91, pp. 214–18.

50. *Rossiiskaya gazeta*, 3 February 1992, p. 3.

51. *Izvestiya*, 3 February 1992, p. 4; on the boots see Aleksandr Korzhakov, *Boris Yel'tsin: ot rassveta do zakata* (Moscow: Interbuk, 1997), p. 60.

52. The declaration was printed in *Rossiiskaya gazeta*, 3 February 1992, p. 3, and also in *Diplomaticheskii vestnik*, nos. 4–5, 1992, p. 12, 1 February 1992. After the UN summit Yeltsin went on to Canada, where he signed a declaration of friendship and cooperation, and then visited France, where he signed a fully-fledged treaty (see respectively *Vneshnyaya politika Rossii 1990–92*, no. 95, pp. 226–8, and no. 106, pp. 248–55).

53. *Vneshnyaya politika Rossii 1990–92*, no. 73, pp. 173–6.

54. See respectively *ibid.*, no. 149, pp. 329–35, and no. 175, pp. 381–7.

55. See respectively *ibid.*, no. 201, pp. 445–51, and no. 223, pp. 495–9.

56. *Ibid.*, no. 256, pp. 555–60.

57. *Izvestiya*, 11 November 1992, p. 1. When the visit took place two years later – the first by a reigning British monarch since 1917 – the Russian President and his assistants all wore dinner jackets for the first time in their lives (Vyacheslav Kostikov, *Roman s prezidentom* (Moscow: Vagrius, 1997), p. 131); the visit was reported in *Izvestiya*, 19 October 1994, p. 1.

58. *The Times*, 10 November 1992, p. 1.

59. *Izvestiya*, 16 June 1992, p. 1. The most comprehensive analysis of the developing relationship is James M. Goldgeier and Michael McFaul, *Power and Purpose: U.S. Policy towards Russia after the Cold War* (Washington, DC: Brookings, 2003).

60. *Izvestiya*, 16 June 1992, p. 1

61. *Vneshnyaya politika Rossii 1990–92*, no. 196, pp. 437–8 (it was ratified by the Supreme Soviet later in the year: *Pravda*, 5 November 1992, p. 1).

62. *Vneshnyaya politika Rossii 1990–92*, no. 195, pp. 431–7.

63. See respectively *ibid.*, no. 197, pp. 438–9, and no. 198, pp. 439–40; the total number of agreements is given in *Diplomaticheskii vestnik*, nos. 13–14, 1992, p. 3.

64. *Vneshnyaya politika Rossii 1990–92*, no. 194, pp. 426–7.

65. Vyacheslav Kostikov, *Roman s prezidentom* (Moscow: Vagrius, 1997), pp. 51, 57 (they hoped particularly to eclipse the influence that Gorbachev had enjoyed); *Pravda*, 3 February 1992, p. 4.

66. *Rossiiskaya gazeta*, 4 January 1993, p. 1.

67. *Izvestiya*, 4 January 1993, p. 4.

68. *Diplomaticheskii vestnik*, nos. 1–2, 1993, pp. 26, 19.

69. *Rossiiskaya gazeta*, 15 April 2000, p. 1. The legislation, as approved by the Federation Council and signed by the President, is in *Sobranie zakonodatel'stva Rossiiskoi Federatsii* [hereafter *SZ*], no. 19, item 2022, 4 May 2000.

70. *Izvestiya*, 20 November 1993, p. 1.

71. Belarus also ratified the Nuclear Non-Proliferation Treaty: *ibid.*, 6 February 1993, p. 2.

72. *Segodnya*, 5 February 1994, p. 4; *Nezavisimaya gazeta*, 18 November 1994, p. 1.

73. *Segodnya*, 4 June 1996, p. 1.

74. *Diplomaticheskii vestnik*, nos. 7–8, 1993, p. 18.

75. See respectively *ibid.*, p. 17, and *Izvestiya*, 6 April 1993, p. 1.

76. *Izvestiya*, 6 April 1993, p. 3.

77. *Diplomaticheskii vestnik*, nos. 7–8, 1993, p. 18.

78. *Nezavisimaya gazeta*, 10 July 1993, p. 1.

79. See *Sobranie aktov Prezidenta i Pravitel'stva Rossiiskoi Federatsii*, no. 45, item 4329, 2 November 1993. The text was not appended but appeared in abbreviated form in *Krasnaya zvezda*, 19 November 1993, pp. 3–4 (a 'detailed summary of 21 of the 23 pages of the original') and other central newspapers; an 'exposition' also appeared in *Diplomaticheskii vestnik*, nos. 23–24, 1993, pp. 6–16. For a discussion see Mary E. Glantz, 'The origins and development of Soviet and Russian military doctrine', *Journal of Slavic Military Studies*, vol. 7, no. 3 (September 1994), pp. 443–80, and Charles J. Dick, 'The military doctrine of the Russian Federation', *ibid.*, pp. 481–506.

80. *Diplomaticheskii vestnik*, nos. 3–4, 1994, pp. 11–18.

81. Korzhakov, *Boris Yel'tsin*, p. 236.

82. *Diplomaticheskii vestnik*, nos. 15–16, 1994, pp. 29–59; the agreement eventually came into force at the start of December 1997: *ibid.*, no. 12, 2007, pp. 53–4. Yeltsin also visited Spain in April and the Italian Prime Minister visited Moscow in October, in both cases concluding a formal treaty of friendship and cooperation: see respectively *ibid.*, nos. 9–10, 1994, pp. 7–11, and nos. 21–22, 1994, pp. 9–14.

83. *Ibid.*, nos. 19–20, 1994, pp. 3–6; Yeltsin referred in these familiar terms only to his American and German counterparts (Korzhakov, *Boris Yel'tsin*, p. 339).

84. *Izvestiya*, 30 August 1994, p. 4 (they had left Lithuania exactly a year earlier).

85. *Diplomaticheskii vestnik*, nos. 19–20, 1994, pp. 10–19.

86. *Ibid.*, pp. 7–10, at p. 8.

87. *Ibid.*, no. 6, 1995, pp. 9–15.

88. *Ibid.*, p. 9.

89. *Ibid.*, no. 11, 1995, pp. 55–6.

90. *Ibid.*, p. 10.

91. *Ibid.*, no. 5, 1996, p. 15.

92. *Ibid.*, no. 4, 1997, pp. 4–11.

93. Clinton had been accused of a sexual relationship with Monica Lewinsky, a White House intern, which he initially denied; however, he was then faced with charges of perjury and the obstruction of justice. He was finally acquitted by the Senate in February 1999.

94. *Nezavisimaya gazeta*, 3 September 1998, p. 1. The documents adopted at the summit were published in *Diplomaticheskii vestnik*, no. 10, 1998, pp. 12–23.

95. The G20 summit in Pittsburgh in 2009 agreed to meet in future at the level of leaders rather than finance ministers and declared in its final communiqué: 'We designate the G20 to be the main forum for our international economic cooperation' (*Guardian*, 26 September 2009, p. 34). What had taken place, commented *Rossiiskaya gazeta*, was the 'institutionalisation of this international forum' (28 September 2009, p. 2).

96. *Izvestiya*, 17 January 1992, p. 5, and 28 April 1992, p. 1.

97. The EBRD was established in 1990 (*Izvestiya*, 10 April 1990, p. 4) and began its operations in 1991; membership procedures were completed for the three Baltic republics in November 1991, and for Russia and the other eleven post-Soviet republics in December 1992 (see www.ebrd.com/about/basics/dates.htm, last accessed 21 January 2010).

98. Membership was approved by 164 votes to 35 with 15 abstentions: *Izvestiya*, 27 January 1996, p. 1.

99. For the legislation see *SZ*, no. 14, item 1514, 30 March 1998; the text of the Convention, with its associated annexes, was printed in the *Byulleten' mezhdunarodnykh dogovorov* [hereafter *BMD*], no. 7, 1998, pp. 3–45.

100. *Izvestiya*, 18 June 1993, p. 3.

101. *Ibid.*, 27 November 1997, p. 1.

102. *Ibid.*, 2 January 1992, p. 3.

103. *Voprosy istorii*, no. 1, 1994, p. 4

104. *Rossiiskie vesti*, 3 December 1992, p. 2.

105. 'Russia and human rights', *Slavic Review*, vol. 51, no. 2 (Summer 1989), pp. 287–93, at p. 289; he had advocated this view as early as August 1995: Andrei Kozyrev, *Preobrazhenie* (Moscow: Mezhdunarodnye otnosheniya, 1995), p. 211.

106. 'Russia and human rights', p. 293.

107. *Izvestiya*, 22 February 1992, p. 3.

108. The 'basic principles' were approved by presidential directive on 23 April 1993 (not located in *Sobranie aktov Prezidenta i Pravitel'stva Rossiiskoi Federatsii* and apparently unpublished). An earlier draft appeared in a special issue of *Diplomaticheskii vestnik*, nos. 1–2, 1993, pp. 3–23, conveniently reprinted in T. A. Shakhleina, ed., *Vneshnyaya politika i bezopasnost' sovremennoi Rossii. 1991–2002. Khrestomatiya v chetyrekh tomakh* (Moscow: Rosspen, 2002), vol. IV, pp. 19–50. The extensive summary that appeared in *Nezavisimaya gazeta*, 29 April 1993, pp. 1, 3, has normally been regarded as authoritative.

109. The formulation of the 'basic principles' is closely analysed by Margot Light, 'Foreign policy thinking', in Neil Malcolm, Alex Pravda, Roy Allison and Margot Light, *Internal Factors in Russian Foreign Policy* (Oxford and New York: Oxford University Press for the RIIA, 1996), pp. 61–70.

110. *Izvestiya*, 11 March 1994, p. 3.

111. *Nezavisimaya gazeta*, 19 April 1995, p. 1; journalists claimed to distinguish a 'late Kozyrev' in these speeches as compared with the 'early' and more pro-Western Kozyrev (*Preobrazhenie*, p. 53). He was similarly a strong supporter of the Chechen campaign, siding with the President and abandoning his former colleagues in Russia's Choice: *Moskovskie novosti*, no. 63, 1994, p. 6.

112. For the decree see O. Prokhanov, ed., *Kto est' kto v Rossii: spravochnoe izdanie* (Moscow: Olimp/EKSMO-Press, 1998), p. 320. Kozyrev had already been criticised by Yeltsin at a press conference (*Rossiiskie vesti*, 9 September 1995, p. 3); the following month the President was 'still dissatisfied' with the performance of the foreign ministry but had not found a 'fitting candidate' to replace the minister himself: *ibid.*, 21 October 1995, p. 9.

113. Kostikov, *Roman s prezidentom*, p. 71.

114. *Zavtra*, no. 1, November 1993, p. 1.

115. *Nezavisimaya gazeta*, 10 December 1994, p. 1.

116. *Ibid.*, 16 November 1995, pp. 1, 5.

117. For these distinctions see Light, 'Foreign policy thinking'.

118. According to Primakov in the course of his first news conference, Yeltsin believed there had been a 'disbalance' in their foreign relations in this respect (*Diplomaticheskii vestnik*, no. 2, 1996, p. 4); there is no reference to this term in the report of Yeltsin's address to the foreign ministry (*ibid.*, no. 1, 1996, p. 4).

119. *Ibid.*, no. 4, 1995, p. 3.

120. See, for instance, *Segodnya*, 20 October 1995, p. 3.

121. *Izvestiya*, 11 September 1998, p. 1.

122. *Diplomaticheskii vestnik*, no. 2, 1996, pp. 3, 4.

123. *Rossiiskaya gazeta*, 10 January 1997, p. 2.

124. See respectively Prokhanov, ed., *Kto est' kto*, pp. 320, 523; an official biography of Primakov appeared in *Diplomaticheskii vestnik*, no. 1, 1996, p. 3. He had been a committed supporter of *perestroika* in the

Gorbachev years but was already in disagreement with the 'Americanocentrism' by which its success was to be judged by the extent to which the US government approved of it (*Znamya*, no. 6, 1989, pp. 185, 192).

125. *Izvestiya*, 28 October 1998, pp. 1, 6.
126. *Nezavisimaya gazeta*, 30 September 1998, p. 6.
127. *Ibid.*, 11 March 2004, p. 5.
128. *Diplomaticheskii vestnik*, no. 4, 2004, pp. 9, 15.
129. *Izvestiya*, 13 April 1992, p. 4.
130. *Ibid.*, 26 October 1992, p. 4.
131. *Ibid.*, 5 January 1993, p. 3.
132. *Nezavisimaya gazeta*, 24 February 1994, p. 1.
133. *Kommersant*, 21 May 1996, p. 4.
134. *Guardian*, 10 March 1999, Section 2, p. 3.
135. For a full discussion see especially Martin Sixsmith, *The Litvinenko File: The True Story of a Death Foretold* (London: Macmillan and New York: St Martin's, 2007); Alex Goldfarb with Marina Litvinenko, *Death of a Dissident: The Poisoning of Alexander Litvinenko and the Return of the KGB* (London: Simon & Schuster and New York: Free Press, 2007); and Zhores Medvedev, *Polonii v Londone: po sledam rassledovaniya Skotlend-Yarda* (Moscow: Molodaya gvardiya, 2008).
136. *Kommersant*, 25 November 2006, p. 1.
137. A formal request for extradition was made by the Crown Prosecution Service on 28 May 2007 but rejected by the Russian Prosecutor General, who nonetheless offered his 'legal assistance' to the British investigation: *Kommersant*, 6 July 2007, p. 4.
138. Prosecutor General Yuri Chaika in *Gazeta*, 6 December 2006, p. 1.
139. *Kommersant*, 25 November 2006, p. 3.
140. *Ibid.*
141. Four Russian diplomats were eventually obliged to leave London as a sign of official displeasure (*Kommersant*, 17 July 2007, p. 1); there was a symmetrical response from the Kremlin three days later (*ibid.*, 20 July 2007, p. 1).
142. *Nezavisimaya gazeta*, 24 January 2006, pp. 1, 9.
143. *Argumenty i fakty*, no. 41, 2007, pp. 9–10.
144. *Kommersant*, 13 December 2007, p. 1.
145. *Rossiiskaya gazeta*, 15 January 2008, p. 8.
146. *Kommersant*, 19 January 2008, p. 4.
147. *Itogi*, no. 8, 18 February 2008, p. 24.
148. For a full review see David Lane and Stephen White, eds., 'Rethinking the "coloured revolutions"', a special issue of the *Journal of Communist Studies and Transition Politics*, vol. 25, nos. 2–3 (June–September 2009); and also Donnacha Ó Beacháin and Abel Polese, eds., *The Colour Revolutions in the Former Soviet Republics: Successes and Failures* (London and New York: Routledge, 2010). The Kremlin's response is considered in more detail in Vladimir Shlapentokh, 'Perceptions of foreign threats to the regime: from Lenin to Putin', *Communist and Post-Communist Studies*, vol. 42, no. 3 (September 2009), pp. 305–24, and Jeanne L. Wilson, 'The legacy of the color revolutions for Russian politics and foreign policy', *Problems of Post-Communism*, vol. 57, no. 2 (March–April 2010), pp. 21–36. Kremlin attempts to anticipate these challenges are considered in Thomas Ambrosio, *Authoritarian Backlash: Resistance to Democratization in the Former Soviet Union* (Farnham and Burlington, VT: Ashgate, 2009); official attitudes are reflected in two short studies from a Kremlin-sponsored publishing house: Georgii Pochentsov, *Grazhdanskoe sambo: kak protivostoyat' 'tsvetnym revolyutsiyam'* (Moscow: Yevropa, 2005), and Vitalii Ivanov, *Antirevolyutsioner: pochemu Rossii ne nuzhna 'oranzhevaya revolyutsiya'* (Moscow: Yevropa, 2006). The externally orchestrated nature of the 'coloured revolutions' is emphasised in Natal'ya Narochnitskaya, ed., *Oranzhevye seti: ot Belgrada do Bishkeka* (St Petersburg: Aleteya, 2008).
149. I draw here on my contribution to the comprehensive analysis in Rick Fawn and Raymond Hinnebusch, eds., *The Iraq War: Causes and Consequences* (Boulder, CO, and London: Lynne Rienner, 2006).
150. *Vremya novostei*, 29 January 2003, p. 6.
151. *Diplomaticheskii vestnik*, no. 3, 2003, pp. 38–9 (the statement was dated 10 February 2003).
152. *Trud*, 28 February 2003, p. 4.
153. *Kommersant*, 5 March 2003, p. 10.
154. *Rossiiskaya gazeta*, 21 March 2003, p. 2.
155. *Kommersant*, 22 March 2003, p. 1.
156. *Rossiiskaya gazeta*, 22 March 2003, p. 3.
157. *Izvestiya*, 4 April 2003, p. 1.
158. For a more general discussion, see, for instance, Martin Smith, *Russia and NATO since 1991* (New York and London: Routledge, 2005); Aurel Brown, *NATO-Russian Relations in the Twenty-First Century* (London and New York: Routledge, 2008); and Vincent Pouliot, *International Security in Practice: The Politics of*

NATO-Russia Diplomacy (Cambridge and New York: Cambridge University Press, 2010).

159. *Diplomaticheskii vestnik*, no. 1, 1992, pp. 12–13. A recent archive-based study throws light on this earlier application: N. Kochin, 'A history of two notes, or why the USSR did not become a NATO member', *International Affairs* (Moscow), vol. 55, no. 2, 2009, pp. 177–91.

160. *Segodnya*, 27 August 1993, p. 1.

161. *Izvestiya*, 2 October 1993, p. 4.

162. *Segodnya*, 26 October 1993, p. 5.

163. *Diplomaticheskii vestnik*, nos. 13–14, 1994, pp. 32–3.

164. *Nezavisimaya gazeta*, 7 April 1994, p. 1.

165. *Diplomaticheskii vestnik*, nos. 13–14, 1994, pp. 30–1.

166. Andrei Kozyrev, 'The lagging partnership', *Foreign Affairs*, vol. 73, no. 3 (May–June 1994), pp. 59–71, at p. 65.

167. *Diplomaticheskii vestnik*, no. 1, 1995, pp. 4–5, 5 December 1994.

168. *Rossiiskaya gazeta*, 8 December 1994, pp. 1–2.

169. *Nezavisimaya gazeta*, 7 December 1994, p. 1.

170. This was Yeltsin's term, speaking at a Helsinki summit: *Rossiiskaya gazeta*, 18 March 1997, pp. 1–2.

171. *Diplomaticheskii vestnik*, no. 6, 1997, pp. 4–10.

172. *Ibid.*, pp. 3–4.

173. *Rossiiskie vesti*, 28 May 1997, p. 3.

174. Andranik Migranyan in *Nezavisimaya gazeta*, 27 May 1997, pp. 1–2.

175. *Izvestiya*, 28 May 1997, p. 4.

176. *Nezavisimaya gazeta*, 28 May 1997, p. 1; *Izvestiya*, 28 May 1997, p. 1.

177. *Segodnya*, 10 July 1997, p. 4.

178. *New York Times*, 9 July 1997, p. A1.

179. *Rossiiskaya gazeta*, 11 July 1997, p. 4.

180. *Kommersant-daily*, 10 July 1997, p. 2.

181. For a discussion of the background to the decision, see, for instance, Wolfram Kaiser and Jürgen Elvert, *European Union Enlargement: A Comparative History* (London and New York: Routledge, 2004); Neill Nugent, ed., *European Union Enlargement* (Basingstoke and New York: Palgrave Macmillan, 2004); and Allan F. Tatham, *Enlargement of the European Union* (Alphen aan den Rijn and Austin, TX: Kluwer Law, 2009).

182. Sergei Karaganov, the chairman of the Council for Foreign and Defence Policy, and Konstantin Kosachev, the chairman of the Foreign Affairs Committee of the Duma, for instance, both argued for Russian membership in the medium or longer term (perhaps up to thirty years): *Vek*, 25 October 2002, p. 5. For a more comprehensive analysis, see, for instance, Roy Allison, Margot Light and Stephen White, *Putin's Russia and the Enlarged Europe* (Oxford: Blackwell and Chatham House, 2006); Ted Hopf, ed., *Russia's European Choice* (New York and Basingstoke: Palgrave Macmillan, 2008); Jackie Gower and Graham Timmins, eds., 'The European Union, Russia and the shared neighbourhood', a special issue of *Europe-Asia Studies*, vol. 61, no. 10 (December 2009); and Hiski Haukkala, *The EU–Russia Strategic Partnership: The Limits of Post-Sovereignty in International Relations* (London and New York: Routledge, 2010). A Russian perspective is available in N. N. Yemel'yanova, *Rossiya i Yevrosoyuz: sopernichestvo i partnerstvo* (Moscow: Mezhdunarodnye otnosheniya, 2009), and Sergei Karaganov and Igor' Yurgens, eds., *Rossiya vs Yevropa: protivostoyanie ili soyuz?* (Moscow: Astrel'/Rus'-Olimp, 2010).

183. According, at least, to a subsequent European Union investigation: *Guardian*, 1 October 2009, p. 23. The causes and consequences of the short-lived conflict are given detailed consideration in Svante E. Cornell and S. Frederick Starr, eds., *The Guns of August 2008: Russia's War in Georgia* (Armonk, NY: Sharpe, 2009), and Paul B. Rich, *Crisis in the Caucasus: Russia, Georgia and the West* (Abingdon and New York: Routledge, 2009). Ronald D. Asmus, *A Little War that Shook the World* (Basingstoke and New York: Palgrave Macmillan, 2010), reflects Georgian perspectives.

184. *Daily Telegraph*, 4 April 2008, p. 20.

185. For a selection of assessments, see, for instance, Michael Clarke, 'Unhappy returns', *The World Today*, vol. 65, no. 4 (April 2009), pp. 13–15; Karl-Heinz Kamp, 'A new NATO strategy: just what is it for?', *ibid.*, vol. 65, no. 10 (October 2009), pp. 24–5; Zbigniew Brzezinski, 'An agenda for NATO: toward a global security web', *Foreign Affairs*, vol. 88, no. 5 (September–October 2009), pp. 2–20; and Wallace J. Thies, *Why NATO Endures* (Cambridge and New York: Cambridge University Press, 2009).

186. *Rossiiskaya gazeta*, 27 April 2007, pp. 4–5. Russian participation in the treaty was formally suspended in late November, ending NATO inspection of its military sites and restrictions on the deployment of

conventional weapons west of the Urals (*SZ*, no. 49, item 6037, 29 November 2007).

187. *Izvestiya*, 2 February 2007, p. 4.
188. *Vremya novostei*, 30 May 2007, p. 1.
189. *Guardian*, 30 May 2007, p. 1.
190. *Ibid.*, 13 October 2007, p. 22; Putin had already indicated Russian dissatisfaction with the terms of the treaty in his Munich speech of 10 February 2007 (pp. 287–8).
191. *Ibid.*, 20 February 2007, p. 19.
192. *Novye izvestiya*, 29 October 2007, p. 2.
193. *Rossiiskaya gazeta: nedelya*, 6 November 2008, p. 7.
194. *Kommersant*, 6 June 2008, p. 3.
195. *Ibid.*, 9 October 2008, p. 3. A draft treaty of this kind had first been proposed by Dmitri Medvedev in a speech in Berlin on 5 June 2008 and was published on the foreign ministry website (www.mid.ru) on 29 November 2009 after the Russian Foreign Minister had distributed a copy to the entire OSCE membership: *Novye izvestiya*, 1 December 2009, p. 2.
196. The French president, Nicolas Sarkozy, was one of those who declared himself in favour of the establishment of such a framework (*Kommersant*, 9 October 2008, p. 3).
197. *Nezavisimaya gazeta*, 9 February 2009, p. 1.
198. *Daily Telegraph*, 29 January 2009, p. 16; the announcement itself was reported in *Nezavisimaya gazeta*, 29 January 2009, p. 1.
199. *Izvestiya*, 9 July 2009, p. 2.
200. *Ibid.*, 18 September 2009, p. 1.
201. *Ibid.*, 9 April 2010, pp. 1–2.
202. Putin's warning was in *ibid.*, 30 December 2009, p. 1. Plans to build a scaled-down missile defence shield in Romania by 2012 were reported in the *Daily Telegraph*, 5 February 2010, p. 18, and 8 February 2010, p. 15. For the new Military Doctrine, see *Rossiiskaya gazeta*, 10 February 2010, p. 17; a new policy statement on nuclear proliferation was announced at the same time but not made public. The 2009 security strategy had already identified the attempt by 'a number of leading countries' to achieve 'military supremacy, primarily in nuclear forces' as one of the main challenges that the country was likely to face in coming years, together with a growing competition for resources in the Arctic as well as the Middle East, Central Asia and the Caspian Sea ('Strategiya natsional'noi bezopasnosti Rossiiskoi Federatsii do 2020 goda', *SZ*, no. 20, item 2444, 12 May 2009).
203. *Rossiiskaya gazeta*, 12 February 2007, pp. 1–2; an authorised translation is conveniently provided in *Problems of Post-Communism*, vol. 55, no. 2 (March–April 2008), pp. 40–4.
204. Palmerston was British foreign secretary and then prime minister in the middle of the nineteenth century. As he put it in his speech to the House of Commons, 'We have no eternal allies, and we have no perpetual enemies. Our interests are eternal and perpetual, and those interests it is our duty to follow' (*Hansard's Parliamentary Debates*, 3rd series, vol. 97, col. 122, 1 March 1848).
205. *Izvestiya*, 10 April 1991, p. 1. The vote in favour of a 'renewed federation' was 76 per cent, on a turnout of 80 per cent: *ibid.*, 28 March 1991, pp. 1, 3.
206. For the text see *Pravda*, 27 June 1991, p. 3.
207. See respectively *ibid.*, 13 July 1991, p. 2, and 25 July 1991, p. 1; an Armenian representative was also in attendance. All that remained, according to the Soviet President, was the question of federal taxation.
208. *Ibid.*, 15 August 1991, p. 2, and also *Izvestiya*, 15 August 1991, pp. 1–2. The text, with a substantial body of documentation drawn in part from the Gorbachev archives, is reproduced in *Soyuz mozhno bylo sokhranit': belaya kniga* (Moscow: Aprel'-85, 1995), pp. 186–99.
209. *Pravda*, 3 August 1991, p. 1. Moldova subsequently announced that it would not be signing the union treaty (*Izvestiya*, 9 August 1991, p. 2), but Belarus and Kazakhstan confirmed that they would do so (*ibid.*, 10 August 1991, p. 1).
210. See respectively *Pravda*, 26 August 1991, p. 2 (Ukraine); *Izvestiya*, 27 August 1991, p. 3 (Moldova); and *Pravda*, 31 August 1991, p. 1 (the Azerbaijani Supreme Soviet confirmed the vote in October (*ibid.*, 19 October 1991, p. 1), and it was endorsed by a referendum with 99.6 per cent in favour at the end of the year (*Izvestiya*, 8 January 1992, p. 2)).
211. *Nezavisimaya gazeta*, 27 August 1991, p. 3.
212. See respectively *Pravda*, 2 September 1991, p. 2 (Uzbekistan and Kyrgyzstan; in a referendum in Uzbekistan later in the year there was over 98 per cent support for independence: *Izvestiya*, 31 December 1991, p. 1); and *Narodnaya gazeta*, 10 September 1991, p. 1 (Tajikistan). Armenia voted in the same sense in September following a referendum in which independence had been approved by 99.3 per cent (*Pravda*, 24 September 1991, p. 1); so did Turkmenistan (*ibid.*, 28 October 1991, p. 1) and Kazakhstan (*Izvestiya*, 17 December 1991, p. 1).

213. *Izvestiya*, 6 September 1991, pp. 1–2.
214. There was a 98.9 per cent vote in a 30 March 1991 referendum in favour of the restoration of full independence, which had been proclaimed by the Georgian parliament on 9 April 1991 (*ibid.*, 2 April 1991, p. 1, and 9 April 1991, p. 1).
215. *Vedomosti S"ezda narodnykh deputatov RSFSR i Verkhovnogo Soveta RSFSR*, no. 2, 1990, art. 22.
216. In Uzbekistan, for instance, the Communist Party became the People's Democratic Party, with the Communist leader Islam Karimov unanimously elected its new leader: *Pravda*, 2 November 1991, p. 1.
217. *Ibid.*, 3 September 1991, p. 1.
218. *Vedomosti S"ezda narodnykh deputatov SSSR i Verkhovnogo Soveta SSSR*, no. 37, 1991, art. 1082, 5 September 1991.
219. *Izvestiya*, 19 October 1991, p. 1; the text was published in *Rossiiskaya gazeta*, 22 October 1991, p. 2. Moldova and Ukraine initialled it as well on 6 November 1991: *Izvestiya*, 7 November 1991, p. 1.
220. *Izvestiya*, 15 November 1991, p. 1. Georgia and Armenia later announced they would not be taking part (*ibid.*, 18 November 1991, p. 1, and 23 November 1991, p. 1); Yeltsin, however, was 'firmly convinced' there would be a union, the only question was how many of the republics would belong to it (M. S. Gorbachev, *Dekabr'-91: moya pozitsiya* (Moscow: Novosti, 1992), p. 9).
221. *Izvestiya*, 25 November 1991, p. 3.
222. *Pravda*, 26 November 1991, p. 1.
223. *Ibid.*, 27 November 1991, p. 1; the USSR Supreme Soviet approved the draft but suggested that the president be not directly elected: *Izvestiya*, 5 December 1991, p. 2.
224. *Izvestiya*, 3 December 1991, p. 2. The establishment of the 'Union of Sovereign States' was approved by the USSR Supreme Soviet after 'brief debates' in both houses (*Izvestiya*, 4 December 1991, p. 2). The resolutions adopted are in *Vedomosti Verkhovnogo Soveta SSSR*, no. 50, 1991, item 1413, 3 December 1991 (Council of Republics), and item 1418, 4 December 1991 (Council of the Union).
225. The vote in favour was 90.3 per cent: *Pravda*, 6 December 1991, p. 1.
226. *Izvestiya*, 29 November 1991, p. 3.
227. *Ibid.*, 5 December 1991, p. 1.
228. The declaration establishing the CIS appeared in *Rossiiskaya gazeta*, 10 December 1991, p. 1; the text of the agreement is in *ibid.*, 11 December 1991, p. 1. The agreement was ratified by Ukraine but with significant amendments (for instance, there would be 'consultation' rather than 'coordination' in foreign policy: *Izvestiya*, 12 December 1991, p. 1); it was also ratified by Belarus (*ibid.*) and by Russia (*ibid.*, 13 December 1991, p. 1). A comprehensive collection of documents is available in Zbigniew Brzezinski and Paige Sullivan, eds., *Russia and the Commonwealth of Independent States: Documents, Data and Analysis* (Armonk, NY: Sharpe, 1997).
229. *Pravda*, 13 December 1991, p. 1; Gorbachev's television address of the evening of 9 December was published in *Izvestiya*, 10 December 1991, p. 2.
230. Kozyrev, *Preobrazhenie*, pp. 171–2.
231. *Vedomosti S"ezda narodnykh deputatov RSFSR i Verkhovnogo Soveta RSFSR*, no. 51, 1991, art. 1798, 12 December 1991; the Russian parliament voted at the same time to withdraw from the 1922 Union Treaty (*ibid.*, no. 1799, 12 December 1991; see p. 25).
232. *Rossiiskaya gazeta*, 24 December 1991, p. 1. Gorbachev, in a letter to the participants, had proposed a 'Commonwealth of European and Asian States' and emphasised the need for common citizenship and economic coordination (*Izvestiya*, 20 December 1991, pp. 1–2).
233. *Izvestiya*, 19 December 1991, p. 1.
234. *Ibid.*, 23 December 1991, p. 2.
235. *Ibid.*, 25 December 1991, p. 1.
236. *Izvestiya*, 26 December 1991, p. 1 (slightly different times were reported in other sources; my thanks to Conor O'Clery for clarifying these developments).
237. *Pravda*, 27 December 1991, p. 1. The Union Treaty provided for withdrawal, but not for dissolution, and any changes were the 'exclusive competence of the Congress of Soviets of the Union of Soviet Socialist Republics' (S. S. Studenikin, ed., *Istoriya sovetskoi konstitutsii (v dokumentakh) 1917–1956* (Moscow: Gosudarstvennoe izdatel'stvo yuridicheskoi literatury, 1957), p. 398). On these legal issues see also p. 25 and note 178, p. 379–80.
238. For an up-to-date review, see Mark Kramer, 'Russian policy towards the Commonwealth of Independent States: recent trends and future prospects', *Problems of Post-Communism*, vol. 55, no. 6 (November–December 2008), pp. 3–19. A wide range of documentation is available on the CIS website, www.cis.minsk.by; a

comprehensive collection of data is collected in E. M. Kozhin *et al.*, eds., *Sodruzhestvo nezavisimykh gosudarstv: yubileinyi spravochnik* (Moscow: Izdatel'stvo Moskovskogo universiteta and CheRo, 2007), and in the annual CIS statistical handbook *Sodruzhestvo nezavisimykh gosudarstv v … godu: statisticheskii yezhegodnik* (Moscow: Statkomitet SNG, annual). There is a substantial secondary literature, mostly in Russian: see particularly Ye. I. Pivovar, *Postsovetskoe prostranstvo: al'ternativy integratsii. Istoricheskii ocherk* (St Petersburg: Aleteiya, 2008); Yu. V. Kosov and A. V. Toropygin, *Sodruzhestvo Nezavisimykh Gosudarstv: instituty, integratsionnye protsessy, konflikty* (Moscow: Aspekt Press, 2009); I. I. Klimin, *Sodruzhestvo nezavisimykh gosudarstv: proshloe, nastoyashchee, budushchee* (St Petersburg: Nestor, 2009); and A. N. Bykov, *Postsovetskoe prostranstvo: strategii integratsii i novye vyzovy globalizatsii* (St Petersburg: Aleteiya, 2009).

239. *Izvestiya*, 5 May 1994, p. 1.

240. On the conflict itself see Cornell and Starr, *Guns of August 2008*, and Rich, *Crisis in the Caucasus*. Russia recognised Abkhazia and South Ossetia as independent states on the conclusion of hostilities (*SZ*, no. 35, 2008, items 4011 and 4012 respectively, 26 August 2008). The international community responded more cautiously; the two new states were recognised promptly by Nicaragua (*Vremya novostei*, 5 September 2008, p. 5) and a year later Venezuela (*Kommersant*, 11 September 2009, p. 1), but not – at least initially – by Belarus or China. For a full study of the background, see A. A. Zakharov and A. G. Areshev, *Priznanie nezavisimosti Yuzhnoi Osetii i Abkhazii: istoriya, politika, pravo* (Moscow: Izdatel'stvo MGIMO, 2008).

241. See Luca Anceschi, *Turkmenistan's Foreign Policy: Positive Neutrality and the Consolidation of the Turkmen Regime* (London and New York: Routledge, 2009).

242. *Nezavisimaya gazeta*, 13 August 2008, p. 1.

243. Kosov and Toropygin, *Sodruzhestvo*, pp. 18–19, 29.

244. *Rossiiskaya gazeta*, 12 February 1993, p. 6.

245. Pivovar, *Postsovetskoe prostranstvo*, p. 53; the text of the 'Concept' is reprinted on pp. 217–26.

246. *Nezavisimaya gazeta*, 28 March 2005, p. 2.

247. 'Kontseptsiya vneshnei politiki Rossiiskoi Federatsii', 12 July 2008, in *Mezhdunarodnaya zhizn'*, nos. 8–9, 2008, pp. 211–39, at p. 229.

248. *Rossiiskaya gazeta*, 1 September 2008, p. 1.

249. 2010 Russia survey.

250. *BMD*, no. 9, 1994, p. 5. An agreement on the status of the court was signed in July 1992 by Armenia, Belarus, Kazakhstan, Kyrgyzstan, Russia, Tajikistan and Uzbekistan, but not by Turkmenistan or Ukraine; Moldova signed with reservations (*ibid.*, pp. 4–8; Azerbaijan and Georgia were not represented).

251. Kosov and Toropygin, *Sodruzhestvo*, p. 217; for the text of the treaty, see *BMD*, no. 1, 1995, pp. 3–10, 24 September 1993.

252. Bykov, *Postsovetskoe prostranstvo*, p. 75.

253. For the text of the treaty, see *BMD*, no. 10, 1995, pp. 31–6, 6 January 2005. Kazakhstan's accession is recorded in *ibid.*, no. 6, 1995, pp. 11–12, 20 January 1995; Kyrgyzstan's – as part of a wider agreement – in *ibid.*, no. 8, 1997, p. 4, 29 March 1996; and Tajikistan's in *ibid.*, no. 11, 2002, pp. 33–8, 26 February 1999.

254. For the text of the treaty, see *ibid.*, no. 8, 1997, pp. 3–8, 26 March 1996; Tajikistan joined in 1998.

255. For the text of the treaty, see *ibid.*, no. 12, 2001, pp. 3–19, 26 February 1999.

256. Pivovar, *Postsovetskoe prostranstvo*, p. 87.

257. For the text of the treaty, see *BMD*, no. 5, 2002, pp. 9–15, 10 October 2000.

258. *Ibid.*, no. 6, 2006, pp. 5–6, 25 January 2006.

259. *Izvestiya*, 31 January 2008, p. 5.

260. *Ibid.*

261. *Ibid.*, 25 March 2008, p. 14.

262. Pivovar, *Postsovetskoe prostranstvo*, p. 100.

263. Bykov, *Postsovetskoe prostranstvo*, p. 85.

264. Pivovar, *Postsovetskoe prostranstvo*, p. 100. Armenia appeared likely to join the Community at some point in the future and already attended its meetings as an observer: Bykov, *Postsovetskoe prostranstvo*, p. 85. For 'not in a single day', see *Izvestiya*, 31 January 2008, p. 5.

265. For the text see Pivovar, *Postsovetskoe prostranstvo*, pp. 303–7. Russia's ratification of the agreement is in *SZ*, no. 17, item 1589, 19 September 2004.

266. Bykov, *Postsovetskoe prostranstvo*, p. 86.

267. Pivovar, *Postsovetskoe prostranstvo*, p. 105.

268. *Ibid.*, pp. 110–11.

269. *Ibid.*, pp. 111–12; the conclusion of a customs union by Russia, Belarus and Kazakhstan, effective from 1 January 2010, was intended to lead to a single economic space by 2012 (*Kommersant*, 28 November 2009, p. 1).

270. Kosov and Toropygin, *Sodruzhestvo*, p. 61.
271. *Izvestiya*, 16 May 1992, p. 1. For the text of the treaty, see *BMD*, no. 12, 2000, pp. 6–8, 15 May 1992. The original six members were Armenia, Kazakhstan, Kyrgyzstan, Russia, Tajikistan and Uzbekistan; they were joined by Azerbaijan, Belarus and Georgia in 1993 (Pivovar, *Postsovetskoe prostranstvo*, p. 74).
272. *BMD*, no. 12, 2000, p. 9.
273. Pivovar, *Postsovetskoe prostranstvo*, pp. 75–6.
274. For the text of the treaty, see *BMD*, no. 3, 2004, pp. 3–9, 7 October 2002.
275. The Russian ratification is recorded in *SZ*, no. 3, item, 163, 26 May 2003.
276. Article 8 of the treaty (*BMD*, no. 3, 2004, p. 4).
277. Formally, according to President Karimov, Uzbekistan had suspended its membership in 1999 and in 2006 had simply decided to reactivate it: *Kommersant*, 24 June 2006, p. 2.
278. *Ibid.*, 8 October 2007, p. 9.
279. *Ibid.*
280. 'Kontseptsiya vneshnei politiki', p. 230.
281. 'Strategiya natsional'noi bezopasnosti Rossiiskoi Federatsii do 2020 goda', at p. 6418.
282. Pivovar, *Postsovetskoe prostranstvo*, pp. 81–2.
283. Bykov, *Postsovetskoe prostranstvo*, p. 85.
284. *Rossiiskaya gazeta*, 10 January 1992, p. 1.
285. Luzhkov set out his views in *Argumenty i fakty*, no. 50, 1996, p. 3, and no. 51, p. 5. There is a full discussion of the Crimean issue in Gwendolen Sasse, *The Crimean Question: Identity, Transition, and Conflict* (Cambridge, MA: Harvard University Press for the Harvard Ukrainian Research Institute, 2007).
286. *Rossiiskaya gazeta*, 25 May 1992, p. 1.
287. *Diplomaticheskii vestnik*, no. 7, 1997, p. 42.
288. *Nezavisimaya gazeta*, 20 February 1997, p. 3.
289. *Diplomaticheskii vestnik*, no. 7, 1997, pp. 35–41.
290. *Ibid.*, pp. 41, 42; Russia was to lease Sevastopol for twenty years, with the possibility of extension; the wider security framework, in line with Russian preferences, was to be based on the OSCE.
291. *Kommersant*, 27 October 2004, p. 9 (broadcast) and 13 November 2004, p. 2.
292. *Ibid.*, 23 November 2004, p. 1.
293. *Ibid.*, 10 January 2006, p. 1 (the agreement was concluded on 4 January).
294. The settlement was reported in *ibid.*, 20 January 2009, p. 1.
295. *Guardian*, 2 January 2009, p. 4. On the wider implications of energy in politics of the post-Soviet region and beyond, see, for instance, Andrei Kokoshin, *Mezhdunarodnaya energeticheskaya bezopasnost'* (Moscow: Yevropa, 2006), and Margarita Balmaceda, *Energy Dependency, Politics and Corruption in the Former Soviet Union: Russia's Power, Oligarchs' Profit and Ukraine's Missing Energy Policy, 1995–2006* (London and New York: Routledge, 2007).
296. *Izvestiya*, 12 August 2009, pp. 1–2.
297. *Ibid.*, 14 August 2009, p. 3.
298. He won 80.1 per cent of the vote in the second round: *ibid.*, 12 July 1994, p. 1. For more recent developments see Stephen White, Elena Korosteleva and John Löwenhardt, eds., *Postcommunist Belarus* (Lanham, MD: Rowman & Littlefield, 2005); there is a particularly insightful treatment of the international context in Grigorii Ioffe, *Understanding Belarus and How Western Foreign Policy Misses the Mark* (Lanham MD: Rowman & Littlefield, 2008).
299. There is a substantial and well-informed biography: Aleksandr Feduta, *Lukashenko: politicheskaya biografiya* (Moscow: Referendum, 2005).
300. 2009 Belarus survey.
301. *Diplomaticheskii vestnik*, no. 3, 1995, p. 37.
302. Speaking in Brussels in March 1995, Lukashenko made clear his view that NATO enlargement would 'not help to strengthen stability in the region and in the world as a whole. The Belarusian people, who [had] suffered so much in European and world wars, [could] not approve any action directed towards the strengthening of military confrontation [or] on the location of a large quantity of arms on the borders of the republic' (*Sovetskaya Belorussiya*, 10 March 1995, pp. 1, 3, at p. 3).
303. *Nezavisimaya gazeta*, 16 May 1995, p. 1.
304. *Izvestiya*, 30 March 1996, p. 1; for the text see *Diplomaticheskii vestnik*, no. 4, 1996, pp. 56–60.
305. For the text see *Diplomaticheskii vestnik*, no. 5, 1996, pp. 39–42.
306. *Izvestiya*, 26 November 1996, p. 2 (about 70 per cent had voted for the new constitution).
307. *Nezavisimaya gazeta*, 29 November 1996, p. 3.
308. *Diplomaticheskii vestnik*, no. 4, 1997, pp. 41–3.
309. *Ibid.*, pp. 40–1. Other states could join the new Community and it was of indefinite duration (p. 42).

310. *Ibid.*, no. 6, 1997, pp. 30–9.

311. *Rossiiskaya gazeta*, 26 December 1998, p. 1.

312. For the text of the treaty, see *SZ*, no. 7, 2000, item 786, 8 December 1999; it came into force on 26 January 2000.

313. Pivovar, *Postsovetskoe prostranstvo*, p. 72.

314. Interview with journalist Alexander Feduta, Minsk, 30 May 2000.

315. *Vedomosti*, 15 January 2007, p. 3.

316. *Nezavisimaya gazeta*, 12 January 2010, p. 1.

317. *Izvestiya*, 5 June 2009, p. 9.

318. 'Kontseptsiya vneshnei politiki', p. 230.

319. As David Marples argues in 'Is the Russia–Belarus Union obsolete?', *Problems of Post-Communism*, vol. 55, no. 1 (January–February 2008), pp. 25–35. Russian policy towards Belarus is considered in A. Suzdal'tsev, 'Formirovanie rossiiskoi politiki v otnoshenii Belorussii (2005–2008 gg.)', *Mirovaya ekonomika i mezhdunarodnye otnosheniya*, no. 3, 2009, pp. 64–74.

320. Leonid Zaiko, 'Ot zhelaemogo k deistvitel'nomu', *Rossiya v global'noi politike*, vol. 4, no. 1 (January–February 2006), pp. 172–80, at p. 172.

321. *Izvestiya*, 14 May 2009, p. 4; there was particular annoyance in the Kremlin that Belarus was continuing to withhold recognition from Abkhazia and South Ossetia. The European Union, for its own part, agreed at its Council in September 2008 to review its policies towards Belarus, and earlier restrictions on travel for its leading officials began to be relaxed. For a review of these developments, see Sabine Fischer, ed., *Back from the Cold? The EU and Belarus in 2009* (Paris: Institute for Security Studies, Chaillot Paper No. 119, 2009).

322. There is a developing literature on Russians' perceptions of their international environment, including William Zimmerman, *The Russian Public and Foreign Policy: Russian Elite and Mass Perceptions, 1993–2000* (Princeton, NJ, and Oxford: Princeton University Press, 2002), extended in Zimmerman, 'Slavophiles and Westernizers redux: contemporary Russian elite perspectives', *Post-Soviet Affairs*, vol. 21, no. 3 (July–September 2005), pp. 183–209; V. A. Kolosov, ed., *Mir glazami rossiyan: mify i vneshnyaya politika* (Moscow: Obshchestvennoe mnenie, 2003), which draws on the work of the Public Opinion Foundation; John O'Loughlin and Paul F. Talbot, 'Where in the world is Russia?', *Eurasian Geography and Economics*, vol. 46, no. 1 (January–February 2005), pp. 23–50; John O'Loughlin, Gearóid Ó Tuathail and Vladimir Kolossov, 'The geopolitical orientations of ordinary Russians', *Eurasian Geography and Economics*, vol. 47, no. 2 (March–April 2006), pp. 129–52; and Richard Rose and Neil Munro, 'Do Russians see their future in Europe or the CIS?', *Europe-Asia Studies*, vol. 60, no. 1 (January 2008), pp. 49–66.

323. The whole range of Russian policy towards Asia under the Putin presidency is considered in S. G. Luzyanin, *Vostochnaya politika Vladimira Putina: vozvrashchenie Rossii na 'Bol'shoi vostok' (2004–2008 gg.)* (Moscow: Vostok-Zapad, 2007). On Russian relations with China, see particularly Bobo Lo, *Axis of Convenience: Moscow, Beijing, and the New Geopolitics* (London: Chatham House and Washington, DC: Brookings Institution Press, 2008), and also Jeanne Wilson, *Strategic Partners: Russian–Chinese Relations in the Post-Soviet Era* (Armonk, NY, and London: Sharpe, 2004); Natasha Kuhrt, *Russian Politics toward China and Japan: The El'tsin and Putin Periods* (New York and London: Routledge, 2006); and James Bellacqua, ed., *The Future of China–Russia Relations* (Lexington: University Press of Kentucky, 2010).

324. The communiqué issued at the end of Gorbachev's visit emphasised 'non-interference in each other's internal affairs' (*Pravda*, 19 May 1989, p. 1); Li Peng's visit was reported in *ibid.*, 27 April 1990, p. 6, and Jiang Zemin's in *ibid.*, 16 May 1991, pp. 1, 5 (the final communiqué was in *ibid.*, 20 May 1991, p. 5).

325. *Izvestiya*, 18 March 1992, p. 4.

326. *Ibid.*, 17 December 1992, p. 1.

327. *Ibid.*, 4 November 1997, pp. 2, 3; the Moscow declaration on Russo-Japanese relations was published in *Rossiiskaya gazeta*, 14 November 1998, p. 2.

328. *Izvestiya*, 1 February 1994, p. 5.

329. *Pravda*, 6 July 1989, p. 2.

330. *Segodnya*, 2 September 1994, p. 3.

331. *Diplomaticheskii vestnik*, no. 5, 1996, p. 18.

332. *Ibid.*, pp. 16–21.

333. *Ibid.*, no. 5, 1997, pp. 19–21 (declaration), 18 (arms agreement).

334. *Ibid.*, no. 12, 1997, pp. 9–10.

335. *Izvestiya*, 12 November 1997, p. 3 (Harbin); *Diplomaticheskii vestnik*, no. 12, 1997, pp. 17–19.

336. *Rossiiskaya gazeta*, 10 January 1997, p. 2.

337. *Izvestiya*, 26 June 1997, p. 1.

338. Lo, *Axis of Convenience*, p. 122.

339. *BMD*, no. 8, 2002, pp. 56–62.

340. *Vremya novostei*, 15 October 2004, p. 1; the text of the agreement is in *BMD*, no. 11, 2004, pp. 76–9, 14 October 2004 (it took effect from 2 June 2005).

341. *Rossiiskii statisticheskii yezhegodnik: statisticheskii sbornik* [hereafter *RSYe*] (Moscow: Rosstat, 2009), pp. 704–5.

342. Lo, *Axis of Convenience*, pp. 3, 174.

343. *Rossiiskaya gazeta*, 24 May 2008, p. 1.

344. *Izvestiya*, 27 April 1996, p. 1. There is a developing literature on the SCO, for the most part in Russian: see, for instance, I. N. Komissina and A. A. Kurtov, *Shankhaiskaya organizatsiya sotrudnichestva: stanovlenie novoi real'nosti* (Moscow: Rossiiskii institut strategicheskikh issledovanii, 2005); A. V. Botlyako, ed., *Shankhaiskaya organizatsiya sotrudnichestva: vzaimodeistvie vo imya razvitiya* (Moscow: Institut Dal'nego Vostoka RAN, 2006); M. L. Titarenko, ed., *Shankhaiskaya organizatsiya sotrudnichestva: k novym rubezham razvitiya* (Moscow: Institut Dal'nego Vostoka RAN, 2008); and Enrico Fels, *Assessing Eurasia's Powerhouse: An Inquiry into the Nature of the Shanghai Cooperation Organisation* (Bochum: Winkler, 2009).

345. *Diplomaticheskii vestnik*, no. 7, 2001, pp. 27–9.

346. *Ibid.*, p. 28. On the 'five principles' see Lo, *Axis of Convenience*, p. 233, note 43.

347. *BMD*, no. 1, 2007, pp. 8–17.

348. *Izvestiya*, 27 October 2005, p. 2. By 2010 the SCO had four 'observers' (India, Iran, Mongolia and Pakistan) and two 'dialogue partners' (Sri Lanka and Belarus). Current developments are reported on the SCO's official website, www.sectscp.org.

349. *Kommersant*, 9 August 2007, p. 7.

350. *Nezavisimaya gazeta*, 10 August 2007, p. 3.

351. *The Times*, 24 June 2009, p. 33.

352. *Daily Telegraph*, 17 August 2007, p. 18

353. Andrzej Walicki, *A History of Russian Thought from the Enlightenment to Marxism*, trans. Hilda Andrews-Rusiecka (Stanford, CA: Stanford University Press, 1979 and Oxford: Clarendon Press, 1980), p. 91.

354. The salience of these distinctions for Russian external relations is given particularly close attention in Iver B. Neumann, *Russia and the Idea of Europe: A Study in Identity and International Relations* (London and New York: Routledge, 1995), and the same author's *Uses of the Other: 'The East' in European Identity Formation* (Manchester: Manchester University Press and Minneapolis: University of Minnesota Press, 1999); there is a complementary Russian discussion in Ol'ga Manilova, *Rossiya i 'Zapad' v XX veke: transformatsiya diskursa o kollektivnoi identichnosti* (Moscow: Rosspen, 2009).

355. Zimmerman, 'Slavophiles and Westernizers redux', p. 184.

356. 'Strategiya natsional'noi bezopasnosti Rossiiskoi Federatsii do 2020 goda', *passim*.

357. In what follows we shall base ourselves on the threefold classification – 'Liberal Westernisers', 'Pragmatic Nationalists' and 'Fundamentalist Nationalists' – first suggested in Margot Light, 'Foreign policy thinking'. A wide variety of other terms has been proposed in the scholarly literature; for a recent inventory see Mankoff, *Russian Foreign Policy*, pp. 88–90.

358. *Diplomaticheskii vestnik*, no. 13–14, 1994, p. 30.

359. Stephen White, 'Elite opinion and foreign policy in post-communist Russia', *Perspectives on European Politics and Society*, vol. 8, no. 2 (June 2007), pp. 147–67, at p. 149.

360. *Vedomosti*, 22 May 2006, p. A04.

361. *Ibid.*, 23 June 2006, p. A04.

362. *Vremya novostei*, 19 May 2006, p. 4.

363. *Vedomosti*, 20 August 2007, p. 4.

364. Timofei Bordachev, *Novyi strategicheskii soyuz. Rossiya i Yevropa pered vyzovami XXI veka: vozmozhnosti 'bol'shoi sdelki'* (Moscow: Yevropa, 2009); these 'challenges' are set out at length on pp. 127–213.

365. *Ibid.*, pp. 235 (allies), 236 (interdependence), 244 (big deal), 299 (long run). Bordachev took part in another collective study that argued for a 'military-political union of a new type' between Russia and the European Union (Karaganov and Yurgens, eds., *Rossiya vs Yevropa*, pp. 218–20).

366. For a review of these views, see, for instance, Peter J. S. Duncan, *Russian Messianism: Third Rome, Revolution, Communism and After* (London and New York: Routledge, 2000), and Marlène Laruelle, *Russian Eurasianism: An Ideology of Empire*, trans. Mischa Gabowitsch (Washington, DC: Woodrow Wilson Center Press and Baltimore, MD: Johns Hopkins University Press, 2008).

367. The Russian translation of Zbigniew Brzezinski, *The Grand Chessboard: American Primacy and its Geostrategic Imperatives* (New York: Basic Books, 1997), had a wide circulation; it was published as *Velikaya*

shakhmatnaya doska (Moscow:
Mezhdunarodnye otnosheniya, 1999).

368. There is a substantial literature on Dugin and
his views: see, for instance, Andreas Umland,
ed., 'Issues in the study of the Russian
extreme right', a special issue of *Russian
Politics and Law*, vol. 47, no. 1 (January–
February 2009).

369. *Izvestiya*, 22 April 2005, p. 5. Dugin's views
were set out at much greater length in his
various books: see, for instance, *Osnovy
geopolitiki: geopoliticheskoe budushchee
Rossii – myslit' prostranstvom*, 4th edn
(Moscow: Arktogeiya-tsentr, 2000);
Yevraziiskii put' kak natsional'naya ideya
(Moscow: Arktogeiya-tsentr, 2002);
*Chetvertaya politicheskaya teoriya: Rossiya i
politicheskie idei XXI veka* (St Petersburg:
Amfora, 2009).

370. *Rossiiskaya gazeta*, 22 February 2005, p. 1.

371. *Izvestiya*, 13 April 2005, p. 7.

372. *Rossiiskaya gazeta*, 26 January 2005, at
www.rg.ru/2005/01/26/yushenko-
geopolitika.html, last accessed 2 April 2010
(not included in the printed edition).

373. *Ibid.*, 21 January 2005, p. 4.

374. *Kommersant*, 7 February 2008, p. 1.

375. *Izvestiya*, 3 February 2006, p. 5.

376. *Rossiiskaya gazeta*, 5 May 2006, p. 9.

377. *Izvestiya*, 15 February 2006, p. 6.
Narochnitskaya's key text is *Rossiya i
russkie v mirovoi istorii* (Moscow:
Izdatel'stvo A. V. Solov'eva /
Mezhdunarodnye otnosheniya, 2003); I rely
also on interview evidence.

378. *Sovetskaya Rossiya*, 8 June 2006, p. 1.

379. *Ibid.*, 22 April 2006, p. 3.

380. *Ibid.*, 29 March 2005, p. 2, and 19 April 2005,
p. 2.

381. 'Demokratiya i novyi peredel mira',
Svobodnaya mysl', nos. 7–8, 2006,
pp. 46–56, at pp. 50–2.

382. Glaz'ev in *Zavtra*, no. 7, 15 February 2006,
p. 3; Delyagin in *ibid.*, no. 21, 24 May 2006,
p. 2.

383. See Mikhail Delyagin, *Rossiya dlya rossiyan*
(Moscow: Algoritm, 2009), and with
Vyacheslav Sheyanov, *Mir naiznanku: chem
zakonchitsya ekonomicheskii krizis dlya
Rossii?* (Moscow: Kommersant/Eksmo,
2009). The whole range of interpretations of
the 'crisis' is examined in Valentina
Feklyunina and Stephen White, 'Reading the
krizis in Russia', *Journal of Communist
Studies and Transition Politics*, forthcoming.

384. Yuri Luzhkov, 'My i zapad', *Rossiiskaya
gazeta*, 15 June 2006, pp. 1, 11.

385. See Margot Light and Stephen White, 'Russia
and President Putin: wild theories', *The
World Today*, vol. 57, no. 7 (July 2001),
pp. 10–12, which is based on discussions
with presidential staffers. Putin himself, in
the extended interviews that were released
before his original election, spoke openly
about these alarming tendencies and warned
that the advance of Islamic fundamentalism
in particular could lead to the
'Yugoslaviaisation' of Russia via Chechnya
and the predominantly Muslim states of the
Volga basin and then the break-up of the rest
of Europe. *Ot pervogo litsa: razgovory s
Vladimirom Putinym* (Moscow: Vagrius,
2000), pp. 135–6.

386. *Komsomol'skaya pravda*, 29 September
2004, p. 4.

387. *Rossiiskaya gazeta*, 27 April 2007, p. 3.

388. 'Kontseptsiya vneshnei politiki Rossiiskoi
Federatsii', pp. 212–13.

389. For a detailed study by the Public Opinion
Foundation, see T. Vorontsova and
A. Danilova, eds., *Amerika – vzglyad iz
Rossii: do i posle 11 sentyabrya* (Moscow:
FOM, 2001).

390. See, for instance, Gennadii Zyuganov, *Na
perelome* (Moscow: Molodaya gvardiya,
2009); Nikolai Starikov, *Krizis: kak eto
delaetsya* (St Petersburg: Piter, 2010).

391. *Ibid.*, pp. 213–28.

392. *Ibid.*, pp. 229–32.

393. *Ibid.*, pp. 233–7.

394. *Rossiiskaya gazeta*, 1 September 2008, p. 1.

395. See particularly the essays by Alfred
Rieber that are listed in the Further reading
section.

8   What kind of system?

1. *Izvestiya*, 23 August 1991, p. 1.

2. Boris Yel'tsin, *Zapiski Prezidenta* (Moscow:
Ogonek, 1994), p. 67; the apparent reference to
Eric Hobsbawm's *Age of Extremes: The Short
Twentieth Century 1914–1991* (London:
Michael Joseph and New York: Viking
Penguin, 1994) was presumably unconscious.

3. Yegor Gaidar, *Dni porazhenii i pobed* (Moscow:
Vagrius, 1996), p. 8.

4. *Izvestiya*, 22 August 1991, p. 1. This was not, in
fact, the ending to the play that Pushkin had
originally intended, but the words on which the
censor had insisted: see John Bayley, *Pushkin:
A Comparative Commentary* (Cambridge and

New York: Cambridge University Press, 1971), pp. 176–7.

5. As he explained in a speech on 9 September 1991, the August events had confirmed the 'irrevocable character of the changes to which democratisation and *glasnost*' had led' (M. S. Gorbachev, *Gody trudnykh reshenii* (Moscow: Al'fa-print, 1993), p. 282).

6. An extract from Francis Fukuyama's controversial article with the same title was published in *Voprosy filosofii*, no. 3, 1990, pp. 134–48, with a critical rejoinder, pp. 148–55.

7. *Izvestiya*, 1 June 1994, pp. 1, 7.

8. Quoted in R. V. Ryvkina, 'Sotsial'nye korni kriminalizatsii rossiiskogo obshchestva', *Sotsiologicheskie issledovaniya*, no. 4, 1997, pp. 73–83, at p. 73.

9. A. N. Medushevsky, 'Rossiiskaya konstitutsiya v mirovom politicheskom protsesse: k desyatiletiyu Konstitutsii RF 1993 g.', *Mir Rossii*, no. 3, 2003, pp. 62–103, at pp. 74, 83.

10. Thomas Carothers, 'The end of the transition paradigm', *Journal of Democracy*, vol. 13, no. 1 (January 2002), pp. 5–21.

11. Steven Levitsky and Lucan A. Way, 'The rise of competitive authoritarianism', *Journal of Democracy*, vol. 13, no. 2 (April 2002), pp. 51–65. Regimes of this kind have been defined by the same authors as 'civilian regimes in which formal democratic institutions exist and are widely viewed as the primary means of gaining power, but in which incumbents' abuse of the state places them at a significant advantage vis-à-vis their opponents'; Russia was a 'stable' version of this kind of regime between 1990 and 2008, as well as Armenia, Malaysia and some African countries (*Competitive Authoritarianism: Hybrid Regimes after the Cold War* (Cambridge and New York: Cambridge University Press, 2010), pp. 5, 21).

12. See Marina Ottaway, *Democracy Challenged: The Rise of Semi-Authoritarianism* (Washington, DC: Carnegie Endowment for International Peace, 2003).

13. See, for instance, Jason Brownlee, *Authoritarianism in an Age of Democratization* (Cambridge and New York: Cambridge University Press, 2007); Paul Brooker, *Non-Democratic Regimes*, 2nd edn (Basingstoke and New York: Palgrave Macmillan, 2009).

14. *Nations in Transit 2009*, at www. freedomhouse.org/template.cfm?page=485, last accessed 20 September 2010 (in 2008 Russia had been seen as no more than 'semi-consolidated authoritarianism').

15. Roger Markwick, 'What kind of state is the Russian state – if there is one?', *Journal of Communist Studies and Transition Politics*, vol. 15, no. 4 (December 1999), pp. 111–30, at p. 127. The Communist leader Gennadii Zyuganov also spoke of a 'Bonapartist regime' (*Na perelome* (Moscow: Molodaya gvardiya, 2009), p. 60).

16. See Vladimir Shlapentokh, 'Early feudalism: the best parallel for contemporary Russia', *Europe-Asia Studies*, vol. 48, no. 3 (May 1996), pp. 393–411, at pp. 393–4, and more fully in his *Contemporary Russia as a Feudal Society: A New Perspective on the Post-Soviet Era* (New York: Palgrave Macmillan, 2007). For another example of this approach, see Richard E. Ericson, 'Does Russia have a "market economy"?', *East European Politics and Societies*, vol. 15, no. 2 (March 2001), pp. 291–319, especially pp. 298–301 and 315–19.

17. *Rossiiskaya gazeta*, 31 December 1999, p. 5.

18. On the notion of 'managed democracy', see, for instance, Kremlin spokesman Vladimir Peshkov as quoted in http://news.bbc.co.uk/1/hi/programmes/this_world/4756959.stm, last accessed 20 September 2010. Putin himself does not appear to have used the term 'managed democracy', although it was frequently attributed to him; in an interview in Poland in early 2002, he claimed not to remember when he might have used it and added that he would 'now find it difficult to define such a term' (*Gazeta wyborcza*, 16 January 2002, p. 4). Speaking some years later to German television, Putin described managed democracy as a 'democracy that is managed from outside', as in some of the post-Soviet republics, and promised that there would be nothing of the kind in Russia ('Interv'yu telekanalu TsDF', 13 July 2006, www.kremlin.ru/text/appears/2006/07/108559.shtml, last accessed 20 September 2010). The discussion in Sheldon S. Wolin, *Democracy Incorporated: Managed Democracy and the Specter of Inverted Totalitarianism* (Princeton, NJ, and Oxford: Princeton University Press, 2008), touches on Russia only in passing; Timothy J. Colton and Michael McFaul, *Popular Choice and Managed Democracy: The Russian Elections of 1999 and 2000* (Washington, DC: Brookings Institution, 2003), touch only in passing on the concept.

19. *Rossiiskaya gazeta*, 26 April 2005, p. 3.

20. *Ibid.*, 27 May 2004, p. 3.

21. See, for instance, Giulietto Chiesa, *Transition to Democracy in the USSR: Ending the*

Monopoly of Power and the Evolution of New Political Forces (Washington, DC: Kennan Institute for Advanced Russian Studies, Occasional Paper No. 237, 1990); Klaus von Beyme, *Transition to Democracy in Eastern Europe* (Basingstoke: Macmillan / New York: St Martin's in association with the International Political Science Association, 1996); G. D. G. Murrell, *Russia's Transition to Democracy: An Internal Political History, 1989–1996* (Brighton and Portland, OR: Sussex Academic Press, 1997); and Barbara Wejnert, *Transition to Democracy in Eastern Europe and Russia: Impact on Politics, Economy, and Culture* (Westport, CT: Praeger, 2002).

22. Samuel P. Huntington, *The Third Wave: Democratization in the Late Twentieth Century* (Norman and London: University of Oklahoma Press, 1991), pp. 21–6, 283–4.

23. Michael McFaul, 'The fourth wave of democracy and dictatorship: noncompetitive transitions in the postcommunist world', *World Politics*, vol. 54, no. 2 (January 2002), pp. 212–44, at pp. 213–14; see also Archie Brown, *Seven Years that Changed the World: Perestroika in Perspective* (Oxford and New York: Oxford University Press, 2007), pp. 217–23. The earliest use of the term appears to be in von Beyme, *Transition to Democracy*, pp. 3–5.

24. Claus Offe, 'Capitalism by democratic design? Democratic theory facing the triple transition in East Central Europe', *Social Research*, vol. 58, no. 4 (Winter 1991), pp. 865–92, at pp. 868–9; also in Offe, *Varieties of Transition: The East European and East German Experience* (Cambridge: Polity, 1996 and Cambridge, MA: MIT Press, 1997).

25. See http://newamericancentury.org/statementofprinciples.htm, last accessed 20 September 2010.

26. This more pessimistic mood was reflected in a number of popular works, such as Humphrey Hawksley, *Democracy Kills: What's So Good About the Vote?* (London: Macmillan, 2009), which concluded that 'poverty, ethnic and religious differences, corruption, land disputes, history and venal leaders [made] full electoral democracy a very risky system for some societies' (p. 379), and John Kampfner, *Freedom for Sale: How We Made Money and Lost Our Liberty* (London: Simon & Schuster and New York: Basic Books, 2010). Within a primarily African context, it appeared that electoral competition, 'far from disciplining a government into good policies, [drove] it into worse ones' (Paul Collier, *Wars, Guns and*

Votes: Democracy in Dangerous Places (London: Bodley Head and New York: Harper, 2009), p. 40). The 'old euphoria about democratic ideals and institutions began to fade' during the first decade of the new century, as John Keane notes in his *The Life and Death of Democracy* (London and New York: Simon & Schuster, 2009), p. 748.

27. Huntington, *Third Wave*, p. 25.

28. Larry Diamond, *The Spirit of Democracy: The Struggle to Build Free Societies throughout the World* (New York: Times Books and Henry Holt and Company, 2008), pp. 63–4; the term 'rollback' is from his 'The democratic rollback: the resurgence of the predatory state', *Foreign Affairs*, vol. 87, no. 2 (March–April 2008), pp. 36–48.

29. Jason Brownlee, *Authoritarianism in an Age of Democratization* (Cambridge and New York: Cambridge University Press, 2007), p. 2.

30. Steven L. Solnick, 'Russia's "transition": is democracy delayed democracy denied?', *Social Research*, vol. 66, no. 3 (Fall 1999), pp. 789–824.

31. Michael McFaul, 'The perils of a protracted transition', *Journal of Democracy*, vol. 10, no. 2 (April 1999), pp. 4–18.

32. The earliest use of this metaphor appears to be in Boris Kagarlitsky, *Square Wheels: How Russian Democracy Got Derailed*, trans. Leslie A. Auerbach (New York: Monthly Review Press, 1994); see also M. Steven Fish, *Democracy Derailed in Russia: The Failure of Open Politics* (Cambridge and New York: Cambridge University Press, 2005).

33. See Harry Eckstein, Frederic J. Fleron, Jr, Erik P. Hoffmann and William M. Reisinger, *Can Democracy Take Root in Post-Soviet Russia? Explorations in State–Society Relations* (Lanham, MD, and Oxford: Rowman & Littlefield, 1998). Two of the more reflective studies on the nature of political change that appeared during these years were Robert D. Grey, ed., *Democratic Theory and Post-Communist Change* (Upper Saddle River, NJ: Prentice Hall, 1997), and Richard D. Anderson, M. Steven Fish, Stephen E. Hanson and Philip D. Roeder, *Postcommunism and the Theory of Democracy* (Princeton, NJ, and Oxford: Princeton University Press, 2001).

34. Editorial, *Journal of Democracy*, vol. 10, no. 2 (April 1999), p. 3.

35. On use of the media in particular, see Stephen White, Sarah Oates and Ian McAllister, 'Media effects and Russian elections, 1999–2000', *British Journal of Political Science*, vol. 35, no. 2 (April 2005), pp. 191–208.

36. Vyacheslav Kostikov, *Roman s prezidentom* (Moscow: Vagrius, 1997), p. 347.

37. David Remnick, 'The war for the Kremlin', *New Yorker*, 22 July 1996, p. 47.

38. Interview on Radio Liberty 'Face to Face', 23 June 1996.

39. Remnick, 'The war for the Kremlin', p. 47.

40. Huntington, *Third Wave*, p. 21. Others suggested a 'one-turnover test', but others still found all these tests 'too unidimensional and too vague' (Fritz Plasser, Peter A. Ulram and Harald Waldrauch, *Democratic Consolidation in East-Central Europe* (London: Macmillan and New York: St Martin's, 1998), p. 21).

41. *Rossiiskaya gazeta*, 27 August 1991, p. 3, and *Izvestiya*, 30 August 1991, p. 2.

42. *Komsomol'skaya pravda*, 12 April 1994, p. 3.

43. Postanovlenie Gosudarstvennoi Dumy Federal'nogo Sobraniya Rossiiskoi Federatsii, 'Ob ob"yavlenii politicheskoi i ekonomicheskoi amnestii', *Vedomosti Federal'nogo Sobraniya Rossiiskoi Federatsii*, no. 2, item 137, 23 February 1994, pp. 168–9, at p. 168.

44. The latest version of this conspiracy theory appeared in a story by Scott Anderson that appeared in *GQ* magazine in September 2009, reported in *Kommersant*, 7 September 2009, p. 4 (it did not appear in the magazine's Russian edition). For an earlier version see Alexander Litvinenko and Yuri Fel'shtinsky, *FSB vzrvaet Rossiyu* (New York: Liberty Publishing House, 2002), available in English as *Blowing Up Russia: The Secret Plot to Bring Back KGB Terror*, trans. Geoffrey Andrews and Co. (New York: Encounter Books and London: Gibson Square, 2007).

45. *The Times*, 4 June 2007, p. 6; similarly in the *Wall Street Journal*, 4 June 2007, pp. A1, A11. A full Russian transcript may be consulted at http://archive.kremlin.ru/appears/2007/06/04/0727_type63379_132615.shtml, last accessed 20 September 2010.

46. Pierre Hassner, 'Russia's transition to autocracy', *Journal of Democracy*, vol. 19, no. 2 (April 2008), pp. 5–15.

47. I take this term from Marie Mendras, *Russie, l'envers du pouvoir* (Paris: Odile Jacob, 2008).

48. For the original formulation see Adam Przeworski, *Democracy and the Market: Political and Economic Reforms in Eastern Europe and Latin America* (Cambridge and New York: Cambridge University Press, 1991), p. 10.

49. Ol'ga Kryshtanovskaya and Stephen White, 'The Sovietization of Russian politics', *Post-Soviet Affairs*, vol. 25, no. 4 (October–December 2009), pp. 283–309, at p. 301. For an earlier formulation see Ol'ga Kryshtanovskaya and Stephen White, 'Putin's militocracy', *ibid.*, vol. 19, no. 4 (October–December 2003), pp. 289–306.

50. *Argumenty i fakty*, no. 4, 2007, p. 4; Andrei Soldatov, 'Re-agent', *Novaya gazeta*, 11 October 2007, p. 10. The head of the Presidential Administration, Sergei Naryshkin, was another who had gaps in his official biography and had formerly served at the Soviet embassy in Belgium; he combined his duties in the Presidential Administration with a seat on the Security Council. See K. A. Shchegolev, ed., *Kto est' kto v Rossii: spolnitel'naya vlast'. Kto pravit sovremennoi Rossiei*, 2nd edn (Moscow: AST/Astrel', 2009), pp. 354–5. The leading *silovik* was usually taken to be Igor Sechin, formerly deputy head of the Presidential Administration and then (from 2008) a deputy prime minister, whose duties as an 'interpreter' in Mozambique and Angola during the 1980s were understood to be a euphemism for intelligence activities. Another Leningrader, he was the 'only colleague that Putin [took] with him immediately to all his various positions' (*ibid.*, p. 461).

51. There has been a vigorous discussion of the 'militocracy thesis'; see particularly Sharon Werning Rivera and David W. Rivera, 'The Russian elite under Putin: militocratic or bourgeois?', *Post-Soviet Affairs*, vol. 22, no. 2 (April–June 2006), pp. 125–44; Bettina Renz, 'An alternative interpretation of *siloviki* in contemporary Russian politics', *Europe-Asia Studies*, vol. 58, no. 6 (September 2006), pp. 903–24; Daniel Treisman, 'Putin's silovarchs', *Orbis*, vol. 51, no. 1 (Winter 2007), pp. 141–53; Eberhard Schneider, 'The Russian Federal Security Service under President Putin', in Stephen White, ed., *Politics and the Ruling Group in Putin's Russia* (Basingstoke and New York: Palgrave Macmillan, 2008), pp. 42–62; Andrei Illarionov, 'The *siloviki* in charge', *Journal of Democracy*, vol. 20, no. 2 (April 2009), pp. 69–72; and Sh. Rivera and D. Rivera, 'K bolee tochnym otsenkam transformatsii v rossiiskoi elite', *Polis*, no. 5, 2009, pp. 149–57. The German scholar Michael Stuermer has called the *siloviki* a 'new ruling class' (*Putin and the Rise of Russia* (London: Weidenfeld & Nicolson, 2008 and New York: Pegasus, 2009), pp. 76–8); for Andrei Soldatov and Irina Borogan, they were a 'new nobility' (*The New Nobility: The Restoration of Russia's Security State and the*

Enduring Legacy of the KGB (New York: PublicAffairs, 2010)).

52. Leonard Schapiro, *Rationalism and Nationalism in Russian Nineteenth-Century Political Thought* (New Haven, CT, and London: Yale University Press, 1967), pp. 8–9. On the question of recurrent 'reforms from above', see Theodore Taranovski, ed., *Reform in Modern Russian History: Progress or Cycle?* (Washington, DC: Woodrow Wilson Center Press and Cambridge: Cambridge University Press, 1995).

53. See Stephen White, *Political Culture and Soviet Politics* (London: Macmillan and New York: St Martin's, 1979), pp. 36–7.

54. O. I. Chistyakov, ed., *Rossiiskoe zakonodatel'stvo X–XX vekov*, vol. IX (Moscow: Yuridicheskaya literatura, 1994), pp. 207, 224.

55. Albert Resis, '*Das Kapital* comes to Russia', *Slavic Review*, vol. 29, no. 2 (June 1970), pp. 219–37, at p. 221.

56. Hugh Seton-Watson, *The Russian Empire 1801–1917* (Oxford: Clarendon Press, 1967), p. 629.

57. 'O pechati i drugikh sredstvakh massovoi informatsii', *Vedomosti S"ezda narodnykh deputatov SSSR i Verkhovnogo Soveta SSSR*, no. 26, 1990, art. 492, 12 June 1990.

58. 'O sobstvennosti v SSSR', *ibid.*, no. 11, 1990, art. 164, 6 March 1990; 'Ob osnovnykh nachalakh razgosudarstvleniya i privatizatsii predpriyatii', *ibid.*, no. 32, 1991, art. 904, 1 July 1991.

59. By early 1991 about 20 parties had come into existence at the national level, and about 500 in the republics (see respectively *Glasnost'*, no. 12, 1991, p. 2, and *Pravda*, 28 February 1991, p. 2). For the new law see 'Ob obshchestvennykh ob"edineniyakh', *Vedomosti S"ezda narodnykh deputatov SSSR i Verkhovnogo Soveta SSSR*, no. 42, 1990, art. 839, 9 October 1990.

60. *Vedomosti S"ezda narodnykh deputatov SSSR i Verkhovnogo Soveta SSSR*, no. 37, 1991, art. 1083, 5 September 1991, and *Vedomosti S"ezda narodnykh deputatov RSFSR i Verkhovnogo Soveta RSFSR*, no. 52, 1991, art. 1865, 22 November 1991.

61. These events are reported in John Sweeney, *The Life and Evil Times of Nicolae Ceausescu* (London: Hutchinson, 1991), and Mark Almond, *The Rise and Fall of Nicolae and Elena Ceausescu* (London: Chapmans, 1992); Peter Siani-Davies, *The Romanian Revolution of December 1989* (Ithaca, NY, and London: Cornell University Press, 2005), makes full use of the sources that are now available, and there is a lively account in Stephen Kotkin with Jan T. Gross, *Uncivil Society. 1989 and the Implosion of the Communist Establishment* (New York: Modern Library, 2009), pp. 69–96. One of the executioners, with a conscience that still troubled him, was interviewed in *The Times*, 24 December 2009, pp. 6–7.

62. 'K godovshchine avgustovskogo putcha 1991 goda', 17 August 2010, at www.levada.ru, last accessed 12 September 2010. Some 30 per cent thought the country had gone in the 'right direction' thereafter, 37 per cent disagreed.

63. *Argumenty i fakty*, no. 34, 1997, p. 1.

64. See pp. 289–91.

65. As Stephen Cohen has pointed out, the Ukrainian vote was not necessarily to be understood as a vote to leave the USSR; other republics had declared 'independence' without doing so (*Soviet Fates and Lost Alternatives: From Stalinism to the New Cold War* (New York and Chichester: Columbia University Press, 2009), pp. 121–2).

66. See 'Rossiyane o raspade SSSR i budushchem SNG', 21 December 2009, at www.levada.ru, last accessed 20 September 2010. The wider issue of communist nostalgia is considered in Stephen White, 'Communist nostalgia and its consequences in Russia, Belarus and Ukraine', in David Lane, ed., *The Transformation of State Socialism: System Change, Capitalism or Something Else?* (London and New York: Palgrave, 2007), pp. 35–56, and 'Soviet nostalgia and Russian politics', *Journal of Eurasian Studies*, vol. 1, no. 1 (January 2010), pp. 1–9.

67. For the Duma's two resolutions of March 1996, see note 178, pp. 379–80.

68. *Ot pervogo litsa: Razgovory s Vladimirom Putinym* (Moscow: Vagrius, 2000), p. 86.

69. See Olga Kryshtanovskaya and Stephen White, 'From Soviet *nomenklatura* to Russian elite', *Europe-Asia Studies*, vol. 48, no. 5 (July 1996), pp. 711–33, at pp. 727–9. According to *Rossiiskaya gazeta*, up to 80 per cent of local functionaries were the same as in the Soviet period (4 March 1992, p. 2); studies in Voronezh and Belgorod reached similar conclusions (*Dialog*, no. 8, 1996, p. 10).

70. See, for instance, Jadwiga Staniszkis, *The Dynamics of the Breakthrough in Eastern Europe: The Polish Case* (Berkeley and Oxford: University of California Press, 1991), ch. 2. For a trenchant analysis along similar lines, see David M. Kotz and Fred Weir,

Revolution from Above: The Demise of the Soviet System (London and New York: Routledge, 1997); a new edition appeared as *Russia's Path from Gorbachev to Putin: The Demise of the Soviet System and the New Russia* (London and New York: Routledge, 2007). The entire process was neatly described as 'swapping *Capital* for capital' by Russian journalist Leonid Radzikhovsky ('Nomenklatura obmenyala *Kapital* na kapital', *Izvestiya*, 7 March 1995, p. 3).

71. L. D. Trotsky, *Predannaya revolyutsiya* (Moscow: NII Kul'tury, 1991), p. 210.

72. John B. Dunlop, *The Rise of Russia and the Fall of the Soviet Empire* (Princeton, NJ: Princeton University Press, 1993), p. 223; contemporaries recorded a wide range of estimates, from 'scores of Muscovites' (the official news agency Interfax) to 'many thousands' (*Pravda*) or even 'more than one million' (Budapest Radio) (all in *Foreign Broadcast Information Service*, SOV 91-162, 21 August 1991, pp. 23, 67, 68). A Lithuanian radio journalist suggested a total of between 100,000 and 150,000 (*BBC Summary of World Broadcasts: Soviet Union*, SU/1156 i, 21 August 1991. Later recollections were reported in *Izvestiya*, 17 August 1992, p. 3.

73. Christopher J. Walker, *Armenia: The Survival of a Nation*, 2nd edn (London: Routledge and New York: St Martin's, 1990), p. 400.

74. *The Times*, 25 August 1989, p. 8.

75. Bernard Wheaton and Zdeněk Kavan, *The Velvet Revolution: Czechoslovakia, 1988–1991* (Oxford and Boulder, CO: Westview, 1992), p. 95.

76. Charles S. Maier, *Dissolution: The Crisis of Communism and the End of East Germany* (Princeton, NJ: Princeton University Press, 1997), p. 143, reports demonstrations as large as 300,000.

77. Of those elected, 86.3 per cent were Communist Party members or candidates: *Pervyi s"ezd narodnykh deputatov RSFSR 16 maya – 22 iyunya 1990 goda: stenograficheskii otchet*, 6 vols. (Moscow: Respublika, 1992–3), vol. I, p. 5. This was 10 per cent more than the highest proportion of party membership ever previously recorded: *Itogi vyborov i sostav deputatov verkhovnykh sovetov soyuznykh i avtonomnykh respublik (statisticheskii sbornik)* (Moscow: Izvestiya, 1985), pp. 90–1.

78. 'O referendume RSFSR', *Vedomosti Soveta narodnykh deputatov RSFSR i Verkhovnogo Soveta RSFSR*, no. 21, item 230, 16 October 1990.

79. 'Uroki oktyabrya-93', *Konstitutsionnyi vestnik*, no. 1 (17), 1994, pp. 7–19, at p. 17. On the circumstances of its adoption, see, for instance, the Moscow University constitutional lawyer S. A. Avak'yan, 'K istorii sozdaniya novoi Konstitutsii Rossiiskoi Federatsii: sub"ektivnye zametki', in O. G. Rumyantsev, ed., *Iz istorii sozdaniya Konstitutsii Rossiiskoi Federatsii*, vol. VI (Moscow: Fond konstitutsionnykh reform, 2010), pp. 706–14, at p. 707.

80. To adapt the title of M. A. Krasnov and I. G. Shablinsky, *Rossiiskaya sistema vlasti: treugol'nik s odnim uglom* (Moscow: Institut prava i publichnoi politiki, 2008).

81. See, for instance, Stephen Holmes, 'Superpresidentialism and its problems', *East European Constitutional Review*, vol. 2, no. 4 / vol. 3, no. 1 (Fall 1993 / Winter 1994), pp. 123–6; Timothy J. Colton, 'Superpresidentialism and Russia's backward state', *Post-Soviet Affairs*, vol. 11, no. 2 (April–June 1995), pp. 144–8; and for a particularly uncompromising formulation, Fish, *Democracy Derailed*, pp. 193–245. The reference to a 'hyper-presidency' is from Lilia Shevtsova, *Russia – Lost in Transition: The Yeltsin and Putin Legacies*, trans. Arch Tait (Washington, DC: Carnegie Endowment, 2007), p. 25 and elsewhere.

82. Juan J. Linz, 'The perils of presidentialism', *Journal of Democracy*, vol. 1, no. 1 (Winter 1990), pp. 51–69.

83. *Izvestiya*, 2 June 2008, p. 2.

84. *Ibid.*, 12 December 2007, p. 3.

85. *Versiya*, 25 February 2008, p. 12 (see also p. 110).

86. *Ryazanskie vedomosti*, 26 January 2008, p. 1.

87. *Argumenty i fakty*, no. 18, 2008, p. 2.

88. 'O kontrol'nykh polnomochiyakh Gosudarstvennoi Dumy v otnoshenii Pravitel'stva Rosssiiskoi Federatsii', *Sobranie zadonodatel'stva Rossiiskoi Federatsii* [hereafter *SZ*], no. 1, 2009, item 2, 30 December 2008.

89. 'O vnesenii izmenenii v otdel'nye zakonodatel'nye akty Rossiiskoi Federatsii v svyazi s povysheniem predstavitel'stva izbiratelei v Gosudarstvennoi Dume Federal'nogo Sobraniya Rossiiskoi Federatsii', *ibid.*, no. 20, item 2391, 12 May 2009.

90. 'O garantiyakh ravenstva parlamentskikh partii pri osveshchenii ikh deyatel'nosti gosudarstvennymi obshchedostupnymi telekanalami i radiokanalami', *ibid.*, item 2392, 12 May 2009.

91. 'Ob izmenenii sroka polnomochii Prezidenta Rossiiskoi Federatsii i Gosudarstvennoi Dumy', *ibid.*, no.1, 2009, item 1, 30 December 2008.
92. There are at least two English-language studies of the Public Chamber: Alfred B. Evans, Jr, 'The first steps of Russia's Public Chamber: representation or coordination?', *Demokratizatsiya*, vol. 16, no. 4 (Fall 2008), pp. 345–62, and James Richter, 'Putin and the Public Chamber', *Post-Soviet Affairs*, vol. 25, no. 1 (January–March 2009), pp. 39–65, to both of which this discussion is indebted.
93. *Rossiiskaya gazeta*, 14 September 2004, pp. 1, 3, at p. 3.
94. *Novye izvestiya*, 23 December 2005, p. 2.
95. 'Ob Obshchestvennoi palate Rossiiskoi Federatsii', *SZ*, no. 15, item 1277, 4 April 2005. The powers of the Chamber were somewhat expanded in subsequent amendments: see particularly *ibid.*, no. 24, item 2791, 10 June 2008, and no. 52, item 6238, 25 December 2008.
96. *Rossiiskaya gazeta*, 23 January 2006, pp. 1–2, at p. 1.
97. *Kommersant*, 23 January 2006, p. 2.
98. Evans, 'First steps', p. 348.
99. *Vremya novostei*, 23 January 2006, pp. 1–2. Members of the Chamber had pushed for the legislation to be deferred, and they appeared to have persuaded the Russian President to moderate some of its more far-reaching provisions before they passed into law: *Vremya novostei*, 12 December 2005, p. 1.
100. *Izvestiya*, 3 February 2006, p. 3. Sychev had been beaten so badly on New Year's Eve in 2005 that his legs and genitals had to be amputated; an army sergeant was sentenced to four years in jail for the offence the following September.
101. *Kommersant*, 10 June 2006, p. 4.
102. *Novye izvestiya*, 14 September 2006, p. 2. Two Russians had been killed and several others injured in a fight with ethnic Chechens that had broken out on the evening of 29 August 2006; there were further disturbances over the following days. See Maksim Grigor'ev, *Kondopoga: chto eto bylo* (Moscow: Yevropa, 2007).
103. See the Chamber's website, www.oprf.ru/rus/about, last accessed 20 September 2010.
104. Over 2008–9, for instance, there were meetings on 19 March 2008, 19 September 2008 and 17 June 2009 (*ibid.*).
105. James Richter, 'The Ministry of Civil Society? The Public Chambers in the regions',

Problems of Post-Communism, vol. 56, no. 6 (November–December 2009), pp. 7–20, at p. 7.
106. *Kommersant*, 24 January 2006, p. 3.
107. Richter, 'Putin and the Public Chamber', p. 55.
108. *Ibid.*, pp. 43, 62.
109. 'O vnesenii izmenenii v nekotorye zakonodatel'nye akty Rossiiskoi Federatsii', *SZ*, no. 3, item 282, art. 3, 10 January 2006. On the association with the 'coloured revolutions', see p. 280.
110. 'O referendume Rossiiskoi Federatsii', *SZ*, no. 27, item 2710, 28 June 2004.
111. *Ibid.*, no. 17, item 1754, 24 April 2008.
112. 'O protivodeistvii ekstremistskoi deyatel'nosti', *ibid.*, no. 20, item 3031, 25 July 2002; for the extension see *ibid.*, no. 31, item 4008, art. 8, 24 July 2007. During 2008, for instance, proceedings were opened against the editor of an independent Dagestan weekly paper on the grounds that it had published articles that 'called for extremist activities' and 'incited hatred or enmity on the basis of ethnicity'; their real offence had evidently been to report widespread corruption in the republic's Ministry of Internal Affairs. During 2009 the Ministry of Justice published a list of 'extremist' publications that included a 'picture of Winnie the Pooh wearing a swastika and a popular informational website that had half a million subscribers. See US Department of State, *2009 Human Rights Report: Russia*, 11 March 2010, at pp. 18–19, www.state.gov/g/drl/rls/hrrpt/2009/index.htm, last accessed 20 September 2010. The following year the works of Scientology founder L. Ron Hubbard were added to the list of extremist publications for 'undermining the traditional spiritual values of the citizens of the Russian Federation' (*Moscow Times*, 22 April 2010, p. 3, quoting the Prosecutor General).
113. 'O vnesenii izmenenii v Federal'nyi zakon "Ob obshchikh printsipakh zakonodatel'nykh (predstavitel'nykh) i ispolnitel'nykh organov gosudarstvennoi vlasti sub"ektov Rossiiskoi Federatsii" i v Federal'nyi zakon "Ob osnovnykh garantiyakh izbiratel'nykh prav i prava na referendum grazhdan Rossiiskoi Federatsii"', *SZ*, no. 50, item 4950, art. 1, 11 December 2004.
114. See, for instance, Sarah Ashwin and Simon Clarke, *Russian Trade Unions and Industrial Relations in Transition* (Basingstoke and New York: Palgrave Macmillan, 2003); and

for the earlier postcommunist period, Walter D. Connor, *Tattered Banners: Labor, Conflict, and Corporatism in Postcommunist Russia* (Oxford and Boulder, CO: Westview, 1996). Levels of membership, in our 2010 survey, were about 10 per cent of the adult population; in the communist period membership had been all but universal.

115. See *2009 Human Rights Report: Russia*, at p. 16.

116. Sarah Oates, 'A neo-Soviet model of the media', *Europe–Asia Studies*, vol. 59, no. 8 (December 2007), pp. 1279–97, at pp. 1293–7 (the 'neo-Soviet' attitudes of the mass audience were also important). There is an abundant literature on all of these issues: see, for instance, David MacFadyen, *Russian Television Today: Primetime Drama and Comedy* (London and New York: Routledge, 2008); Birgit Beumers, Stephen Hutchings and Natalia Rulyova, eds., *The Post-Soviet Russian Media: Conflicting Signals* (London and New York: Routledge, 2008); Stephen Hutchings and Natalia Rulyova, eds., *Television and Culture in Putin's Russia: Remote Control* (London and New York: Routledge, 2009); and Anna Arutunyan, *The Media in Russia* (Maidenhead and New York: Open University Press, 2009). On the political aspects of television, see especially Sarah Oates, *Television, Democracy, and Elections in Russia* (Abingdon and New York: Routledge, 2006), and Ellen Mickiewicz, *Television, Power, and the Public in Russia* (Cambridge and New York: Cambridge University Press, 2008).

117. United Nations Development Programme, *Human Development Report 2007/8* (Basingstoke and New York: Palgrave Macmillan, 2007), pp. 273–6.

118. See US Department of State, *2008 Human Rights Report: Russia*, 25 February 2009, at p. 26, www.state.gov/g/drl/rls/hrrpt/2008/index.htm, last accessed 20 September 2010.

119. Freedom House, *Freedom on the Net: A Global Assessment of Internet and Digital Media* (2009), at p. 2, www.freedomhouse.org, last accessed 10 April 2010.

120. Ya. A. Zasursky, ed., *Sredstva massovoi informatsii Rossii: uchebnoe posobie dlya studentov vuzov* (Moscow: Aspekt Press, 2006), pp. 37–9. The first internet journal of this kind was Gazeta.ru, which began to appear in 1999 (*ibid.*, p. 343). A regular report on 'Freedom on the Net' in Russia and selected other countries is maintained by Freedom House at www.freedomhouse.org.

121. *Guardian*, 18 November 2008, p. 19 (he survived but lost a leg).

122. *Ibid.*, 10 March 2007, p. 19.

123. *Ibid.*, 1 July 2009, p. 17 (the authorities also suggested a stairwell accident).

124. *Ibid.*, 2 December 2009, p. 15 (Kaliningrad); *ibid.*, 22 January 2010, p. 23 (Tomsk).

125. See respectively www.memo98.cjes.ru/?p=3&sm2=on&reports=200711 and on the presidential election www.memo98.cjes.ru/?p=3&sm2=on&reports=200803, last accessed 20 September 2010; the results reported were for coverage between 2 and 25 February 2008. There were several other quantitative studies of election coverage on the main television channels: Medialogiya, for instance, examined news and analytical programmes on five television channels during the period before the 2007 Duma election and found that United Russia had two or three times as much coverage as its closest competitor, the Communist Party, over the periods 19–25 and 26–27 November (*Nezavisimaya gazeta*, 29 November 2007, p. 3).

126. See Freedom House, *Freedom of the Press 2009: Russia*, at pp. 1–2, www.freedomhouse.org/template.cfm?page=251&country=7689&year=2009, last accessed 20 September 2010.

127. Reporters without Borders, *Annual Report 2010: Russia*, 6 January 2010, at www.rsf.org/spip.php?page=impression&id_article=35872, last accessed 7 April 2010.

128. See www.rsf.org/spip.php?page=impression&id_article=33220, last accessed 10 April 2010. The analogy with Novocherkassk was suggested by Yevgenii Gontmakher in 'Stsenarii: Novocherkassk-2009', *Vedomosti*, 6 November 2008, p. A04; it led to a warning letter from the Prosecutor's Office (*2009 Human Rights Reports*, p. 21). The article about the funding of United Russia appeared as '"Chernaya kassa" Kremlya', *New Times*, no. 44 (10 December 2007), pp. 18–22.

129. In the case of Freedom House, for instance, its findings were produced by a 'multilayered process of analysis and evaluation by a team of regional experts and scholars', in which there was unavoidably an 'element of subjectivity'. See www.freedomhouse.org/uploads/fop/2009/FreedomofthePress2009_Methodology.pdf, last accessed 20 September 2010. Reporters without Borders consulted its fifteen partners and a network of 130 correspondents around the world as

well as journalists, researchers, lawyers and human rights activists; a scale developed by the organisation was then used to give a country score to each questionnaire. See www.rsf.org/IMG/pdf/note_methodo_en.pdf, last accessed 20 September 2010.

130. See www.freedomhouse.org/uploads/fop/2009/FreedomofthePress2009_tables.pdf, last accessed 20 September 2010.

131. For the full list see 'Press Freedom Index 2009', www.rsf.org, last accessed 14 April 2010.

132. See www.irex.org/programs/MSI_EUR/2010/2010msiee_score_compilatio.xls, last accessed 7 April 2010 (Russia had been scored 2.0 in 2001, the first year in which the exercise had been conducted).

133. The fullest study is Alexei Trochev, *Judging Russia: Constitutional Court in Russian Politics, 1990–2006* (Cambridge and New York: Cambridge University Press, 2008). A comprehensive account of all aspects of Russian law is available in William E. Butler, *Russian Law*, 3rd edn (Oxford and New York: Oxford University Press, 2009).

134. *2009 Human Rights Report: Russia*, at p. 8.

135. See www.assembly.coe.int/Documents/WorkingDocs/Doc09/EDOC11993.pdf, last accessed 20 September 2010. On 'telephone justice' in particular, see Alena Ledeneva, 'Telephone justice in Russia', *Post-Soviet Affairs*, vol. 24, no. 4 (October–December 2008), pp. 324–50.

136. 'O vnesenii izmenenii v Federal'nyi konstitutsionnyi zakon "O Konstitutsionnom Sude Rossiiskoi Federatsii"', *SZ*, no. 23, item 2784, 2 June 2009.

137. *Kommersant*, 2 December 2009, pp. 1, 4.

138. *Moscow Times*, 3 October 2008, pp. 1–2.

139. *Guardian*, 19 November 2009, p. 27.

140. *Sunday Telegraph*, 22 November 2009, p. 27.

141. The accident was reported in the *Moscow Times*, 24 May 2005, p. 3.

142. *Ibid.*, 5 March 2010, pp. 1–2, at p. 2.

143. 'Rossiyane ne doveryayut pravookhranitel'nym organam', 16 February 2010, at www.levada.ru/press/2010021605.html, last accessed 20 September 2010. There was equally little confidence that the reforms of the Ministry of Internal Affairs that had been announced by President Medvedev in 2010, including the dismissal of some of its most senior officials, would lead to a significant improvement: just a quarter (26 per cent) saw them as the beginning of a

'radical reform' and a cynical 11 per cent saw them as no more than 'echoes of a struggle for power in the higher reaches of the Russian leadership'. See 'Reformy prezidenta Medvedeva i vzaimootnosheniya obshchestva i vlasti', 5 March 2010, at www.levada.ru/press/2010030502.html, last accessed 12 March 2010.

144. 'Predstavleniya rossiyan o demokratii', 15 October 2009, at www.levada.ru/press/2009101501.html, last accessed 20 September 2010.

145. 'Ob Upolnomochennom po pravam Rossiiskoi Federatsii', *SZ*, no 9, item 1011, 26 February 1997. The office of ombudsman had originally been established by the declaration on human and civil rights that had been adopted by the Russian parliament at the end of the Soviet period, in November 1991. The prominent human rights activist Sergei Kovalev held the position between January 1994 and March 1995, although a law that defined the office had not yet been adopted. On his activities see Emma Gilligan, *Defending Human Rights in Russia: Sergei Kovalyov, Dissident and Human Rights Commissioner, 1969–2003* (London and New York: RoutledgeCurzon, 2004).

146. *Rossiiskaya gazeta*, 17 April 2009, p. 1; the full report is on pp. 10–15.

147. *Ibid.*, p. 15.

148. S. I. Glushkova, *Prava cheloveka v Rossii* (Moscow: Yurist, 2005), pp. 320–2.

149. Glushkova, *Prava cheloveka*, p. 323.

150. *Rossiiskaya gazeta*, 17 April 2009, p. 15.

151. *2009 Human Rights Report: Russia*, p. 36.

152. *Rossiiskaya gazeta*, 17 April 2009, p. 12.

153. *2009 Human Rights Report: Russia*, p. 37.

154. 'O ratifikatsii Konventsii o zashchite prav cheloveka i osnovnykh svobod i Protokolov k nei', *SZ*, no. 14, item 1514, 30 March 1998. The Convention had originally been adopted in 1950.

155. *2009 Human Rights Report: Russia*, pp. 36–7. A full collection of documentation and statistics on the work of the Court is available at its website, www.echr.coe.int.

156. Alexei Trochev, 'All appeals lead to Strasbourg? Unpacking the impact of the European Court of Human Rights on Russia', *Demokratizatsiya*, vol. 17, no. 2 (Spring 2009), pp. 145–78, at pp. 149–50.

157. *Ibid.*, p. 146.

158. *'Who Will Tell Me What Happened to My Son?' Russia's Implementation of European Court of Human Rights Judgements on*

Chechnya (New York: Human Rights Watch, September 2009), pp. 1–2.

159. Amnesty's statute and other documentation may be consulted at its website, www. amnesty.org.uk. Its origins and development are examined in Jonathan Power, *Like Water on Stone: The Story of Amnesty International* (London: Allen Lane and Boston, MA: Northeastern University Press, 2001). There are more comprehensive treatments of Russian human rights performance in Glushkova, *Prava cheloveka v Rossii*, and Jonathan Weiler, *Human Rights in Russia: A Darker Side of Reform* (Boulder, CO, and London: Lynne Rienner, 2004).

160. *Amnesty International Report 2008: The State of the World's Human Rights* (London: Amnesty International, 2008), pp. 313–16.

161. *Ibid.*, pp. 317–21.

162. For a full and discriminating account of the human rights aspects of the conflict, see Emma Gilligan, *Terror in Chechnya: Russia and the Tragedy of Civilians in War* (Princeton, NJ, and Oxford: Princeton University Press, 2010). Amnesty produced a detailed report of its own (*The Russian Federation: Denial of Justice* (London: Amnesty International, 2002)) as well as periodic statements.

163. *Amnesty International Report 2007: The State of the World's Human Rights* (London: Amnesty International, 2007), pp. 217–18.

164. *Amnesty International Report 2008*, pp. 249–50.

165. See *Amnesty International Report 2009: The State of the World's Human Rights*, various pages, at www.thereport.amnesty.org, last consulted 20 September 2010.

166. *Amnesty International Report 2007*, p. 217.

167. *Amnesty International Report 2008*, p. 248. A more comprehensive analysis was published as *Freedom Limited: The Right to Freedom of Expression in the Russian Federation* (London: Amnesty International, 2008), available online at www.amnesty.org/en/library/info/EUR46/008/2008/en, last consulted 20 September 2010.

168. *Amnesty International Report 2009*, 'Russia'.

169. *Ibid.*, 'Georgia'.

170. On this last point see *Amnesty International Report 2008*, p. 251.

171. *Amnesty International Report 2009*, various pages. There is a compelling account of the (alarming) state of the Russian prison system in Laura Piacentini, *Surviving Russian Prisons: Punishment, Economy and Politics in Transition* (Cullompton, Devon: Willan,

2004); see also Weiler, *Human Rights in Russia*, pp. 29–53.

172. See Human Rights Watch's 'Mission Statement' at www.hrw.org/en/about, last accessed 18 April 2010.

173. *Human Rights Watch World Report 2009* (New York: Human Rights Watch, 2009), pp. 393, 396.

174. *Human Rights Watch World Report 2007* (New York: Human Rights Watch, 2007), pp. 405–6.

175. *Human Rights Watch World Report 2009*, p. 398.

176. *Human Rights Watch World Report 2008* (New York: Human Rights Report, 2008), pp. 413–14.

177. *Human Rights Watch World Report 2010* (New York: Human Rights Watch, 2010), various pages. For the amendments in the form in which they were finally approved, see 'O vnesenii izmenenii v Federal'nyi zakon "O nekommercheskikh organizatsiyakh"', *SZ*, no. 29, item 3607, 17 July 2009. Opposition deputies had complained that President Medvedev was simply seeking to ingratiate himself with the new US president in advance of their first meeting (*Kommersant*, 29 June 2009, p. 2).

178. *Human Rights Watch World Report 2007*, pp. 407–8.

179. *Human Rights Watch World Report 2009*, p. 399.

180. The measurement of democracy and human rights remains a controversial issue: see, for instance, David Beetham, ed., *Defining and Measuring Democracy* (London and Thousand Oaks, CA: Sage, 1994), and the discussion of 'standards-based measures' in Todd Landman and Edzia Carvalho, *Measuring Human Rights* (Abingdon and New York: Routledge, 2010), pp. 64–90.

181. See 'Freedom in the World' at www.freedomhouse.org. Although formally independent, Freedom House is substantially funded by the US government and critics have accused it of a 'neoconservative bias'. See Diego Giannone, 'Political and ideological aspects in the measurement of democracy: the Freedom House case', *Democratization*, vol. 17, no. 1 (February 2010), pp. 68–97, at p. 69.

182. *Freedom Review*, January–February 1991, p. 8.

183. See 'Freedom in the World 2008: Country Reports: Russia', at www.freedomhouse.org/template.cfm?page=15, last accessed 20 September 2010.

184. 'Freedom in the World 2009: Russia, *ibid.*; 'Freedom of the Press 2009: Russia', *ibid.*

185. See Samuel P. Huntington, 'The clash of civilisations', *Foreign Affairs*, vol. 72, no. 3 (Summer 1993), pp. 22–49, and more fully in Huntington, *The Clash of Civilizations and the Remaking of World Order* (London and New York: Simon & Schuster, 1996). Orthodox civilisation, for Huntington, was based on a close association between church and state, and reflected long periods of foreign domination. The result was a society that was very different from those in Western Europe, and one that was 'much less likely to develop stable democratic political systems' ('The clash', pp. 30–1).

186. *Rossiiskaya gazeta*, 31 December 1999, p. 5.

187. *Ot pervogo litsa*, pp. 168–9.

188. *Rossiiskaya gazeta*, 31 December 1999, p. 4.

189. *Ibid.*, 26 April 2005, pp. 3–4.

190. *Nezavisimaya gazeta*, 25 February 2005, p. 1.

191. According, at least, to what was in effect a programmatic statement by a leading member of this group and close Putin associate, Viktor Cherkesov, who had at one time been head of the KGB in his native Leningrad and was later head of the federal narcotics agency. See his 'Moda na KGB?', *Komsomol'skaya pravda*, 29 December 2004, pp. 10–11.

192. *Rossiiskaya gazeta*, 31 December 1999, p. 4.

193. *Ibid.*, 26 April 2005, p. 3.

194. *Nezavisimaya gazeta*, 25 February 2005, p. 1.

195. Putin had already attacked foreign and domestic NGOs in his 2004 address to the Russian parliament, claiming that 'far from all of them [were] oriented towards defending people's real interests' and that the priority for 'some of them' was to obtain 'funding from influential foreign foundations' (*Rossiiskaya gazeta*, 27 May 2004, p. 4). Speaking after the legislation had been approved by the Duma on a first reading, he described externally funded NGOs as 'in essence, [the] foreign policy instruments [of] other states' and insisted that they 'must be on the state's radar screen' (*Moscow Times*, 25 November 2005, p. 1).

196. *Komsomol'skaya pravda*, 29 September 2004, p. 4. For a comprehensive collection of texts and commentaries, see L. V. Polyakov, ed., *Pro suverennuyu demokratiyu* (Moscow: Yevropa, 2007). Surkov's own writings are collected in Vladislav Surkov, *Teksty 97–07* (Moscow: Yevropa, 2008), and are available in translation with other contributions to the discussion in a special issue of *Russian Politics and Law* edited by Richard Sakwa (vol. 46, no. 5, 2008). There is a full and well-judged discussion of the development of the new doctrine in Alfred B. Evans, Jr, *Power and Ideology: Vladimir Putin and the Russian Political System* (The Carl Beck Papers in Russian and East European Studies of the University of Pitttsburgh, no. 1902, 2008).

197. Vitalii Ivanov, *Partiya Putina: istoriya 'Yedinoi Rossii'* (Moscow: Olma, 2008), p. 236.

198. Vladislav Surkov, 'Suverenitet – eto politicheskii sinonim konkurentosposobnosti', in Polyakov, ed., *Pro suverennuyu demokratiyu*, pp. 33–61, at p. 58.

199. Vladislav Surkov, 'Natsionalizatsiya budushchego', *Ekspert*, no. 43, 20 November 2006, pp. 102–8, at pp. 102–4. Extracts also appeared in *Rossiiskaya gazeta*, 21 November 2006, p. 3, and in *Izvestiya*, 22 November 2006, p. 4.

200. *Izvestiya*, 14 July 2006, p. 4.

201. Vyacheslav Nikonov, 'Suverennaya demokratiya', in *Suverennaya demokratiya: ot idei – k doktrine* (Moscow: Yevropa, 2006), pp. 21–5, at p. 23.

202. *Profil'*, no. 27, 2006, p. 14.

203. *Nezavisimaya gazeta*, 24 August 2007, p. 8.

204. Dmitrii Furman, 'Prezident Putin kak russkii Gamlet', *Nezavisimaya gazeta*, 30 August 2006, p. 8.

205. Sergei Glaz'ev, 'Privatizatsiya nastoyashchego', *Ekspert*, no. 3, 22 January 2007, pp. 56–9.

206. Dmitrii Medvedev, 'Dlya protsvetaniya vsekh nado uchityvat' interesy kazhdogo', *ibid.*, no. 28, 24 July 2006, pp. 58–65, at p. 59.

207. *Izvestiya*, 31 August 2006, p. 1.

208. *Ibid.*, 13 September 2006, p. 2.

209. Ivanov, *Partiya Putina*, p. 251.

210. 'Rossiya, kotoruyu my vybiraem', Programmatic Declaration adopted at the 7th Congress of United Russia, 17 December 2006, at www.edinros.ru/rubr.shtml?110100, last accessed 20 September 2010. An earlier and all but identical draft appeared in *Moskovskie novosti*, no. 38 (6 October 2006), p. 16.

211. *Rossiiskaya gazeta*, 9 November 2007, p. 14.

212. 'Vystuplenie na Vsemirnom ekonomicheskom forume v Davose', 27 January 2007, in Dmitrii Medvedev, *Natsional'nye proekty: stat'i i vystupleniya* (Moscow: Yevropa, 2008), pp. 107–17, at pp. 116–17.

213. Dmitrii Medvedev, 'O demokratii', 31 January 2007, in Polyakov, ed., *Pro suverennuyu demokratiyu*, pp. 501–2.
214. *Izvestiya*, 13 September 2006, p. 2.
215. *Kommersant*, 11 September 2006, p. 1.
216. *Argumenty i fakty*, no. 39, 2007, p. 2.
217. 'Rossiya: sokhranim i priumnozhim', adopted at the 11th Congress of United Russia, 29 November 2009, at http://edinros.er.ru/er/text.shtml?10/9535,110738, last accessed 6 May 2010.
218. 2010 Russia survey.
219. The fourth wave of the World Values Survey in 2005–6, for instance, found that a 'strong leader' was supported by 32 per cent in the United States but opposed by 65 per cent; 26 and 21 per cent respectively in the UK and Japan were supportive, but 66 and 67 per cent opposed. The comparable Russian figures were 47 per cent as compared with 36 per cent (variable 148, www.worldvaluessurvey.org, last accessed 14 September 2010).
220. V. V. Bakerkina and L. L. Shestakova, eds., *Kratkii slovar' politicheskogo yazyka* (Moscow: Astrel'/Russkie slovari, 2002), p. 77.
221. A. Ya. Sukharev, ed., *Bol'shoi yuridicheskii slovar'*, 3rd edn (Moscow: Infra-M, 2010), p. 166.
222. Irina Busygina and Andrei Zakharov, *Sum ergo cogito: politicheskii mini-leksikon* (Moscow: Moskovskaya shkola politicheskikh issledovanii, 2006), p. 23 (literally 'content' (*napolnenie*)).
223. *Ekonomicheskie i sotsial'nye peremeny: monitoring obshchestvennogo mneniya*, no. 1, 1995, p. 12, showing results for 1989 and 1994 (26 per cent in 1994, for instance, thought drug addicts and bikers should simply be 'liquidated', 22 per cent that homosexuals should suffer the same fate). These and comparable figures for 2001 are shown in Stephen White, Margot Light and Ian McAllister, 'Russia and the West: is there a values gap?', *International Politics*, vol. 42, no. 3 (September 2005), pp. 314–33, at p. 327.
224. Their 'main concerns', according to the survey evidence, are set out above, pp. 224–5.
225. 'Otnosheniya obshchestva i gosudarstva v glazakh rossiyan', 16 March 2010, at www.levada.ru/press/2010031602.print.html, last accessed 20 September 2010.
226. 'Reformy prezidenta Medvedeva i vzaimootnosheniya obshchestva i vlasti', 5 March 2010, at www.levada.ru/press/2010030502.print.html, last accessed 20 September 2010.
227. See, for instance, Pippa Norris, ed., *Critical Citizens: Global Support for Democratic Government* (Oxford and New York: Oxford University Press, 1999); Susan Pharr and Robert D. Putnam, eds., *Disaffected Democracies: What's Troubling the Trilateral Countries?* (Princeton, NJ: Princeton University Press, 2000); and Russell J. Dalton, *Citizen Politics: Public Opinion and Political Parties in Advanced Industrial Democracies*, 5th edn (Washington, DC: CQ Press, 2008), ch. 12.
228. *Rossiiskaya gazeta*, 11 September 2009, pp. 1, 3; his address to the Federal Assembly is in *ibid.*, 13 November 2009, pp. 3–5. United Russia's programmatic document of November 2009 is cited above, note 217.
229. *Rossiiskaya gazeta*, 14 November 2007, p. 1.

A note on surveys

Russia 1993

Conducted by Russian Public Opinion and Market Research (ROMIR) for William L. Miller and others, with the assistance of the ESRC.

Fieldwork was conducted between 25 November and 9 December 1993 (n=1095), and between 12 December 2003 and 13 January 1994 (n=1046).

A datafile and other documentation may be consulted at the UK Data Archive, reference SN 4129.

Russia 2000

Conducted by the All-Russian Centre for the Study of Public Opinion (VTsIOM) in association with the New Russian Barometer 8 sponsored by Richard Rose and others at the University of Strathclyde, with the assistance of the ESRC.

Fieldwork was conducted between 19 and 29 January 2000, n=1940.

A datafile and other documentation may be consulted at the UK Data Archive, reference SN 4550.

Russia 2001

Conducted by Russian Research for Sarah Oates and Stephen White, with the assistance of the ESRC.

Fieldwork was conducted between 10 and 26 April 2001, n=2000.

A datafile and other documentation may be consulted at the UK Data Archive, reference SN 4464.

Russia 2004

Conducted by Russian Research for Stephen White with the assistance of the ESRC.

Fieldwork took place between 21 December 1993 and 16 January 2004, n=2000.

A datafile and other documentation may be consulted at the UK Data Archive, reference SN 5671.

Russia 2005

Conducted by Russian Research for Stephen White with the assistance of the ESRC.

Fieldwork took place between 25 March and 24 May 2005, n=2000.

A datafile and other documentation may be consulted at the UK Data Archive, reference SN 5671.

Russia 2008

Conducted by Russian Research for Stephen White and Ian McAllister, with the assistance of the ESRC and the Australian Research Council.

Fieldwork took place between 30 January and 27 February 2008, n=2000.

A datafile and other documentation will be available for consultation at the UK Data Archive.

Russia 2010

Conducted by Russian Research for Stephen White and Ian McAllister, with the assistance of the ESRC and the Australian Research Council.

Fieldwork took place between 12 February and 1 March 2010, n=2000.

A datafile and other documentation will be available for consultation at the UK Data Archive.

Index